Communications
in Computer and Information Science 241

W0044154

Pit Pichappan   Hojat Ahmadi
Ezendu Ariwa (Eds.)

Innovative
Computing Technology

First International Conference, INCT 2011
Tehran, Iran, December 13-15, 2011
Proceedings

 Springer

Volume Editors

Pit Pichappan
Al Imam University
Riyadh, Saudi Arabia
E-mail: pichappan@dirf.org

Hojat Ahmadi
University of Tehran
Tehran, Iran
E-mail: hahmadi878@yahoo.com

Ezendu Ariwa
London Metropolitan University
London, UK
E-mail: e.ariwa@londonmet.ac.uk

ISSN 1865-0929   e-ISSN 1865-0937
ISBN 978-3-642-27336-0   ISBN 978-3-642-27337-7 (eBook)
DOI 10.1007/978-3-642-27337-7
Springer Heidelberg Dordrecht London New York

Library of Congress Control Number: 2011943892

CR Subject Classification (1998): H.4, H.3, I.2, D.2, C.2, I.4, H.5

Typesetting: Camera-ready by author, data conversion by Scientific Publishing Services, Chennai, India

Printed on acid-free paper

Springer is part of Springer Science+Business Media (www.springer.com)

Preface

We are pleased to publish the significant papers accepted in the First International Conference on Innovative Computing Technology (INCT 2011).

The production and the use of newer computing devices and platforms has led to a better understanding of the emerging computing paradigms. For many decades, computing systems have been based on several different models, but only the innovative models have proven to withstand this era of high obsolescence.

New models are evolving and driving the need for more powerful systems where innovative computing is required.

Realizing this significance, we decided to introduce a platform where innovating computing models could be discussed. The result is the organization of the First International Conference on Innovative Computing Technology.

The INCT consists of invited talks, papers, and presentations. The Program Committee of INCT 2011 accepted 40 papers out of a total of 121 submissions. We hope that the participants at INCT 2011 found the research presentations interesting and the discussions stimulating.

We are grateful to Tehran University for hosting this conference. We would like to take this opportunity to express our thanks to the Technical Committee and to all the external reviewers. We are grateful to Springer for publishing the proceedings. Finally, we would like to thank all the authors and the local organization.

October 2011
Hojat Ahmadi
Pit Pichappan
Ezendu Ariwa

Organization

General Chair

Hojjat Ahmadi   University of Tehran, Iran

Program Chairs

Daisy Jacobs   University of Zululand, South Africa
Ezendu Ariwa   London Metropolitan University, UK

Program Co-chairs

Simon Fong   University of Macau, China
Vladimir Fomichov   State University, Russia

Scientific and Organizing Committee

Hojjat Ahmadi	University of Tehran, Iran
Seyed Saeie Mohtasebi	University of Tehran, Iran
Ali Jafari	University of Tehran, Iran
Mehdi Behzad	Sharif University, Iran
Shahin Rafiee	University of Tehran, Iran
Mohammad Reza Shahnazari	University of K.N. Toosi, Iran
Aliraza Masoudi	University of Tehran, Iran
Arash Malekian	University of Tehran, Iran
Amir Houshang Ehsani	University of Tehran, Iran
Mahmod Omid	University of Tehran, Iran
Alireza Keyhani	University of Tehran, Iran
Hoseyni	Industrial Section, University of Tehran, Iran
Din Mohhamad Emani	Industrial Section, University of Tehran, Iran

International Program Committee

Adnan Qureshi	University of Jinan, Shandong, P.R. China
AmirHosein Keyhanipour	University of Tehran, Iran
Antonia M. Reina-Quintero	University of Seville, Spain
Arshin Rezazadeh	Applied Science University in Ahvaz, Iran
Bela Genge	"Petru Maior" University of Targu Mures, Romania

Boumedyen Shannaq   Nizwa University, Oman
Chiw Yi Lee   University Putra Malaysia, Malaysia
Chun-Wei Lin   National University of Kaohsiung, Taiwan
Cyril de Runz   Université de Reims, France
Dennis Lupiana   Dublin Institute of Technology, Ireland
George Rinard   Frostburg University, USA
Gevorg Margarov   State Engineering University of Armenia,
                               Armenia
Hrvoje Belani   University of Zagreb, Croatia
Malay Bhattacharyya   Indian Statistical Institute, India
Mohd Helmy Abd Wahab   Universiti Tun Hussein Onn Malaysia, Malaysia
Mothanna Alkubeily   Tishreen University, Syria
Mourad Amad   Université de Bejaia, Algeria
Nisheeth Gupta   Verizon, USA
Ozgur Koray Sahingoz   Turkish Air Force Academy, Turkey
Pasquale De Meo   University of Messina, Italy
Prabhat Mahanti   University of New Brunswick, Canada
Radek Koci   Brno University of Technology, Czech Republic
Reinhard Klette   The University of Auckland, New Zealand
Roma Chauhan   Institute of Management Education, India
Sabin Buraga   Alexandru Ioan Cuza University of Iasi,
                               Romania
Saqib Saeed   University of Siegen, Germany
Tzung-Pei Hong   National University of Kaohsiung, Taiwan
Victoria Repka   The People's Open Access Education Initiative,
                               Australia
Weimin He   University of Wisconsin-Stevens Point, USA
Wojciech Zabierowski   Technical University of Lodz, Poland
Xiafeng Li   TAMU, USA
Zeeshan Ahmed   University of Wuerzburg, Germany

Reviewers

Tzung-Pei Hong   National University of Kaohsiung, Taiwan
Victoria Repka   The People's Open Access Education Initiative
                               (Peoples-University), Australia
Amir Hosein Keyhanipour   University of Tehran, Iran
Radek Koci   Brno University of Technology, Czech Republic
Sabin Buraga   Alexandru Ioan Cuza University of Iasi,
                               Romania
Cyril de Runz   Université de Reims, France
Prabhat Mahanti   University of New Brunswick, Canada
Xiafeng Li   Texas A & M University, USA
Mohd Helmy Abd Wahab   Universiti Tun Hussein Onn Malaysia, Malaysia
Pit Pichappan   AISB University, Saudi Arabia
Reinhard Klette   The University of Auckland, New Zealand

Table of Contents

Data Modeling

Multimedia and Image Segmentation

Natural Language Processing

Networks

Cluster Computing

Discrete Systems

Analysis of Quality Driven Software Architecture

Ehsan Ataie, Marzieh Babaeian Jelodar, and Fatemeh Aghaei

University of Mazandaran, Babolsar, Iran
{ataie,m.babaeian,f.aghaei}@umz.ac.ir

Abstract. This paper presents an analysis on quality driven approaches which embodies non-functional requirements into software architecture design. The analysis characterizes vocabularies and concepts of the area, with exhibiting a comparison of the two main techniques. In the first technique, architectural tactics are represented and their semantics is clearly defined as a UML-based pattern specification notation called RBML. Given a set of non-functional requirements, architectural tactics are selected and composed into an initial architecture for the application. The second technique designates some attribute primitives which are similar to architectural patterns. It then introduces a method called Attribute Driven Design, to involve attribute primitives for satisfying a set of general scenarios In this analysis, we intend to give a brief description of the both approaches.

Keywords: Software, Quality, Architecture, Functional Requirement, Non-functional Requirement.

1 Introduction

The Software Architecture of a system is the set of structures needed to reason about the system, which comprise software elements, relations among them, and properties of both. Software development requires an approach to come up with an architecture when all you're given is a set of requirements. In creating Architectures, we have to build a structure that supports the functionality or services required of the system (functional requirements) with respect to the system qualities (non-functional requirements). In general, functional requirements (FRs) define what a system is supposed to do whereas non-functional requirements (NFRs) define how a system is supposed to be. The non-functional requirements are crucial factors in the system development, but unfortunately they have been neglected by the researchers and are less well understood than other factors [1].

The International Organization for Standardization (ISO) defines quality as a characteristic that a product or service must have [2]. Dropping quality requirements out of the software architecture design process may mean that a large amount of resources has been considered to build a system which does not meet its quality requirements [3]. This can result into, a poor quality-based architecture with a lot of wasted time and money.

The FRs and NFRs have effects on each other throughout the system development process. Therefore, they both have to be considered in a parallel way, throughout the process, But NFRs are often postponed to the late phase, which can make the satisfaction

P. Pichappan, H. Ahmadi, and E. Ariwa (Eds.): INCT 2011, CCIS 241, pp. 1–14, 2011.
© Springer-Verlag Berlin Heidelberg 2011

of NFRs very challenging [4-6]. Consequently, Many works have been done to address NFRs at the architectural level [7-14].

This research is based on the analysis of two main approaches that describes quality driven software architecture and discusses the differences and similarities of them. We compare these approaches together and we use the advantages of the two given ones to boost our new method.

The remainder of this paper is organized as follows: Section 2 gives an analysis of the first technique. Section 3 presents an analysis of the second technique. In section 4 the approaches are compared and their advantages and disadvantages are described. Finally, in section 5 we discuss about our current and future works.

2   Analysis of First Approach

2.1   Background

This approach presents a quality-driven mechanism that embodies non-functional requirements (NFRs) into software architecture with the employment of architectural tactics [15].

2.2   Specifying the Concepts of Architecture

Quality attributes are non-functional requirements used to evaluate the performance of a system. An architectural tactic is described as a Fine-grained reusable architectural building block provisioning an architectural solution to achieve a quality attribute [15]. Various quality attributes, such as availability, performance, security, modifiability, usability and testability are achieved by many architectural tactics [16-18]. For every individual quality attribute a set of tactics can be defined. The relationship between quality attributes and the tactics can be shown in feature models [19]. The tactics are designed in a hierarchy form. The coarse grained tactics can break into small grained ones. A specific notation for modeling tactics is introduced as the Role Based Meta modeling Language (RBML) [20-21] which is a UML-based pattern specification language. The works in [16-18], [22-23], illustrates the development of the feature models and RBML specifications. Every tactic is introduced in RBML with two parts, known as the Structural Pattern Specification (SPS) and Interaction Pattern Specification (IPS). The SPS characterizes the structural aspects of an architectural tactic in a class diagram view while the IPS defines the interaction view of the tactics. In the following, we explain some of the tactics which are introduced in this approach.

Availability Tactics. The level to which an application is available with the required functionality is called availability [15]. The tactics for availability can be categorized into: *Fault Detection, Recovery Reintroduction, Recovery-Preparation and Repair* [17], [24]. The *Fault Detection* tactic detects a fault and notifies the fault to a monitoring component or the system administrator. The *Recovery Reintroduction* tactic restores the state of a failed component. The *Recovery Preparation and Repair* tactic recovers and repairs a component from a failure. These tactics are refined into subtactics. *Ping/Echo, Heartbeat* and *Exception* are distilled from the Fault detection tactic.

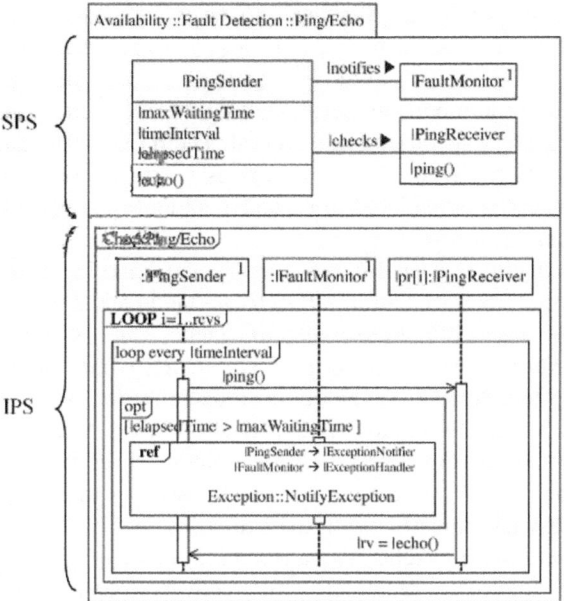

Fig. 1. (a) The *Ping/Echo* tactic

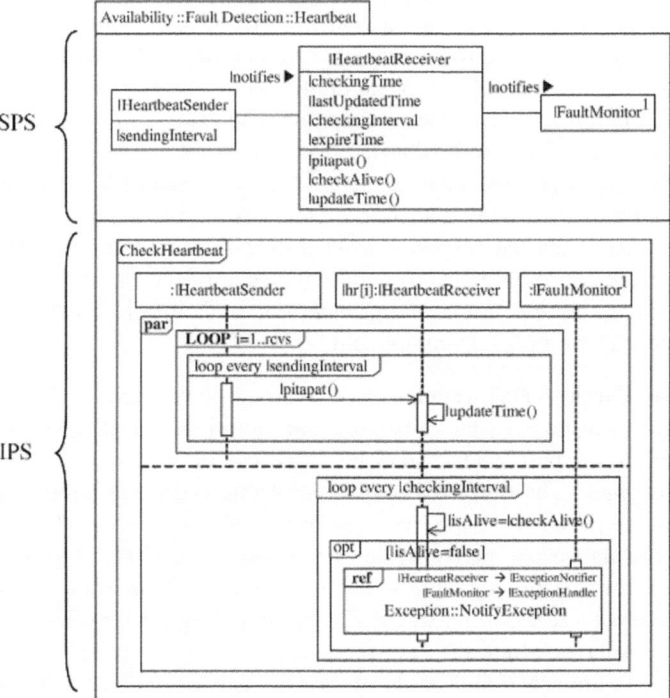

Fig. 1. (b) The *Heartbeat* tactic

The *Ping/Echo* tactic sends ping messages to receivers regularly to detect the fault. The receiver can be considered failed, if it does not respond to the sender within a certain time period. The *Heartbeat* tactic detects a fault by listening to heartbeat messages from monitored components periodically. A sender sends a heartbeat message to all the receivers every specified time interval. The receivers update the current time when the message is received. If the message is not received within a set time, the monitored component is considered to be unavailable. Fig. 1 shows the SPS and IPS of the *Ping/Echo* and *Heartbeat* tactics.

The *Exception* tactic is used for recognizing and handling faults. The *Exception* tactic is usually used together with the *Ping/Echo* tactic and *Heartbeat* tactic for handling faults. The *Recovery Reintroduction* tactic can be refined into: *Checkpoint/Rollback, State Resynchronization*. The *Checkpoint* tactic keeps track of the state of the system either periodically or in response to a specific event. The time when the system's state is updated is called checkpoint. When a failure occurs in the system, the system is restored to the state at the most recent checkpoint before the system failed. The *State Resynchronization* tactic restores the state of a source component through resynchronization with the state of a backup component. The *Recovery Preparation and Repair* tactic can be refined into: *Voting, State Redundancy*. The *Voting* tactic uses algorithm redundancy for recovery preparation. In the tactic, the same algorithm is run on redundant components, and the voter monitors the behavior of the components. When a component behaves differently from others, the voter fails the component. Although one component failed, the system itself still runs normal with other components. The *State Redundancy* tactic uses redundant state data on multiple components for recovery preparation. The *State Redundancy* tactic can be used in two ways, which are *Active Redundancy* tactic and *Passive Redundancy* tactic. The *Active Redundancy* tactic selects only one response from the responses that are received concurrently from redundant components for a service request. If a redundant component is failed, the tactic recovers the component by re-synchronizing the state of the failed component with one of the other alive component. The *Passive Redundancy* tactic uses the response from a specific component (primary) and informs other (backup) components to update the state of the backup components with that of the primary component. If the primary component fails, its state is resynchronized with the state of a backup component.

Performance Tactics. Performance is concerned with various aspects including processing time, response time, resource consumption, throughput and efficiency [15]. The tactics for performance can be classified into: *Resource Arbitration, Resource Management*. The *Resource Arbitration* tactic is used to improve performance by scheduling requests for expensive resources. The *Resource Management* tactic improves performance by managing the resources that effect response time. These two tactics are refined into subtactics. The *Resource Arbitration* tactic can be refined into: *FIFO, Priority Scheduling*. In the *FIFO* tactic, request for resources are treated equally in the order in which they are received. In the *Priority Scheduling* tactic, the resource requests are scheduled based on priority (for example, a lower priority may be given to resources that have myriad requests.). The *Priority Scheduling* tactic is captured in the *Fixed Priority Scheduling* and the *Dynamic Priority Scheduling* tactics. In the *Fixed Priority Scheduling* the scheduler assigns a fixed priority to the client based on a specific strategy (e.g., semantic importance, deadline monotonic) and In the *Dynamic Priority Scheduling* tactic, priorities are determined at runtime based on execution parameters such as upcoming deadlines or other runtime conditions. The *Resource Management* tactic can be refined into: *Introduce Concurrency*, *Maintain Multiple Copies*. The *Introduce Concurrency* tactic allocates threads or processes to resources for concurrent execution. In this way, waiting time in response can be significantly reduced. The *Maintain Multiple Copies* tactic keeps replicas of resources on separate repositories, so that contention for resources can be reduced.

Security Tactics. Security is concerned with preventing unauthorized usage of the system while providing its services to legitimate users [15]. The Tactics for Security can be classified into: *Resisting Attacks, Recovery from Attacks*. The *Resisting Attacks* tactic provides several ways of protecting the system from attacks while the *Recovery from Attacks* tactic helps to restore a system in a security regard. The *Resisting Attacks* tactic can be refined into: *Authenticate Users* tactic, *Authorize Users* tactic, *Maintain Data Confidentiality* tactic. The *Authenticate User* tactic checks the authentication of the user using the user's credentials (i.e., user IDs, passwords). The *Authorize Users* tactic restricts user access to data and services. This tactic describes that an access request is intercepted by the reference monitor to check permission and if a permission is found, the request is allowed, otherwise it is denied. The *Maintain Data Confidentiality* tactic protects data from unauthorized modifications using encryption and decryption. The *Authenticate Users* tactic can break into: *ID/Password, Onetime Password*. In the *ID/Password* tactic user credentials can be set by the user and in the *Onetime Password* tactic user credentials are generated by the system every time the user uses the system. The *Recovery from Attacks* tactic can be refined into: *Restoration* tactic. The *Restoration* tactic maintains administrative data, which is critical for security. In this way, administrative data can be better protected, and so is the system.

2.3   Building a Stock Trading System

The first approach, explains as a case study an online stock trading system (STS) that provides real-time services for checking the current price of stocks, placing buy or sell orders and reviewing traded stock volume. It sends orders to the stock exchange system (SES) for trading and receives the settlement information from the SES. This section demonstrates how the availability, performance and security tactics can be used to embody NFRs of a Stock Trading System (STS) into its architecture [15]. First, the STS non-functional requirements are defined. There are four kinds of NFRs in this case. NFR1 is related to the availability of STS during trading time. NFR2 places a lower bound on the number of transaction processed per second and per day, in order to gain performance. NFR3 is concerned with the performance of the STS's database which may be decreased by the intensive updates from the SES. NFR4 emphasizes on security and indicates that only authenticated users can access the system and their credentials should remain confidential. After introducing NFRs, the authors, described how each of the NFRs can be embodied into architecture using architectural tactic. Each NFR of the system is related to one quality attribute, and a set of tactics have to be included to obtain the quality attribute. Some of the NFRs like NFR2 and NFR3 are related to one quality attribute, but they should be gained with different tactics. The selected architectural tactics are composed to produce a composed tactic that exhibits the solutions of the selected tactics. Two kinds of rules have been introduced to compose the tactics: Binding rules and Composition rules. Binding rules define the corresponding roles in the two tactics, while composition rules define changes to be made during composition [16]. For example, in NFR1, two tactics that authors used are the Ping/Echo and Heartbeat. The Ping/Echo tactic sends a ping message regularly and checks the echo back. In some cases, the ping sender may receive an echo even if the STS is failed. To prevent this, authors compose a Heartbeat tactic with the Ping/Echo tactic. In this case, even if an echo is received from the STS, the STS is considered to be failed if there is no heartbeat message coming from the STS.

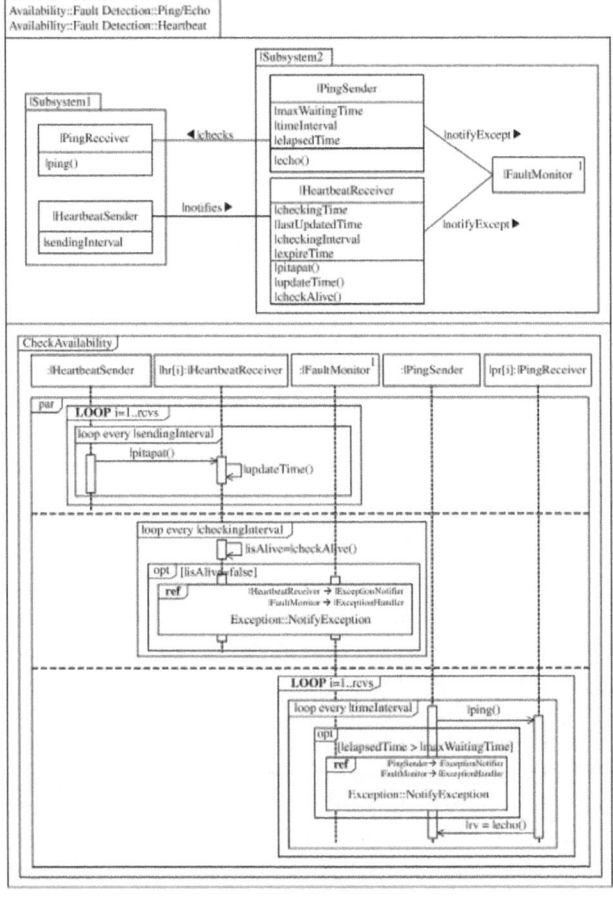

Fig. 2. The composition of the *Ping/Echo* and *Heartbeat* tactics

Other kinds of tactics can be composed in similar way. Fig. 2 shows the composition of *Ping/Echo* and *Heartbeat* tactics. The composed tactic is then consolidated to create an initial architecture of the application (stock trading system). Different instantiation of proposed generic initial architecture can be built.

There is always the possibility that the different types of quality attributes may hinder each other (e.g. security and performance may have conflicts). This approach doesn't introduce an obvious way to solve the conflict problem between quality attributes but a trade-off analysis of the two is proposed to minimize the conflicts. Finally, an architecture has been built, based on the desirable NFRs, but to add the functional requirements (FRs), we may need to make some changes in the architecture; for instance, by adding new classes, new methods and new relations between the classes.

2.4   Tool Support

This approach demonstrates tool support for automatic instantiation of architectural tactics [15]. The RBML Pattern Instantiator (RBML-PI) which is developed as an add-in component to IBM Rational Rose [25] is the main tool we use in this approach.

3   Analysis of Second Approach

3.1   Background

This approach presents a method that characterizes quality attributes and captures architectural patterns which are used to achieve these attributes. For each pattern, it's important not only how the pattern achieves a quality attribute goal but also what impact the pattern has on other attributes [26].

3.2   The Concepts

In this approach, the concept of general scenario and attribute primitive is introduced and a method is described to utilize these concepts for designing a software architecture. The mentioned concepts are described throughout this subsection. A general scenario consists of: The stimuli that requires the architecture to respond, the source of the stimuli, the context within which the stimuli occurs, the type of system elements involved in the response, possible responses and the measures used to characterize the architecture's response [26]. For each quality attribute one or more general scenario is introduced. An attribute primitive is a collection of components and connectors that 1) collaborate to achieve some quality attribute goal (expressed as general scenario), 2) is minimal with respect to the achievement of those goals [27]. A data router is an example of an attribute primitive. The data router protects producers from changes to the consumers and vice versa by limiting the knowledge that producers and consumers have of each other. This contributes to modifiability. The Attribute Driven Design (ADD) method is a recursive decomposition process where, at each stage in the decomposition, attribute primitives are chosen to satisfy a set of quality scenarios and then functionality is allocated to instantiate the component and connector types provided by the primitives [26].

3.3   The Roadmap

ADD in Life Cycle. ADD's place in the life cycle is after the requirement analysis phase. The ADD method consists of ADD input, ADD output and Beginning ADD. The ADD input is a set of requirements. The ADD output is a conceptual architecture [28]. The conceptual architecture is the first articulation of architecture during the design process therefore it is coarse grained. The conceptual architecture can be presented as a blueprint for a concrete architecture. In Beginning ADD, there are some issues that should not be dismissed. When all of the architectural drivers of the system are understood the beginning of ADD is prepared. Architectural drivers are defined as non-functional and functional requirements that are architecturally significant to the system.

Steps of ADD. The first step is to choose the first design element. Then step 2 to step 5 should be repeated for every design element that needs further decomposition. In the Following, we explain each step.

Step 1: Choose Design Element. In this step, we choose the design element to decompose. The design elements can be: The whole system, conceptual subsystem, or conceptual component. The decomposition usually starts with "the system" element, and is then decomposed into "conceptual subsystems" and those themselves get decomposed into "conceptual components". The decomposition results in a tree of parents and children.

Step 2: Choose the Architectural Drivers. This step determines what is important for this decomposition. The architectural drivers are usually in conflict with each other, therefore there should be a small number of architectural drivers. The quality architectural drivers determine the style of the architecture while the functional architectural drivers determine the instances of the element types defined by that style. For example we may have chosen the attribute primitive *"Data Router"* to support modifiability. This attribute primitive defines element types of "producer", "consumer" and the *"data Router"* itself. By looking at the functional drivers we may define a sensor application that produces data value, and a guidance as well as diagnosis application consuming the data value. Therefore, the functional drivers instantiate the element type "producer" into a sensor element and the element type "consumer" into a "guidance" and "diagnosis" element. The "data router" element type might be instantiated into a blackboard element [26]. Fig. 3 shows an instantiation of an attribute primitive.

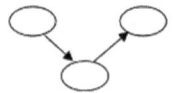

Fig. 3. (a) Attribute primitive, *Data Router*

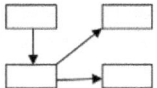

Fig. 3. (b) Instantiation of "*Data Router*" attribute primitive

Key:

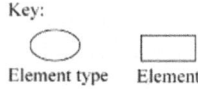

Element type   Element

Fig. 3. (c) Element and element type

Step 3: Choose the Attribute Primitives. This step, chooses the Attribute primitives and children design element types to satisfy the architectural drivers. This step is designed to satisfy the quality requirements. The selection of attribute primitives is based on two factors. The first factor is the drivers themselves and the second one is the side effects that an attribute primitive has on other qualities. Consider the situation where both modifiability and performance are architectural drivers. One attribute primitive for modifiability is *Virtual Machine* and one attribute primitive for performance is *Cyclic Executive Scheduling*. A *Virtual Machine* introduces additional checks at the interface of the virtual machine that is an obstacle for achieving performance and on the other hand, a *Cyclic Executive* delivers real-time performance. This is a barrier for achieving modifiability because functions have to run in a specific sequence. So clearly, the two attribute primitives cannot be used together without any restrictions because they neutralize each other. The approach attempts to solve this problem by dividing the system into two parts. The performance critical (assuming performance is more important) part and the rest. So the *Cyclic Executive Scheduler* would be used for the critical part and the *Virtual Machine* is used for the uncritical part.

Step 4: Instantiate Design Elements and Allocate Functionality Using Multiple Views. In this step functional requirements are satisfied. As an example in last section, we explained that the system has to be divided into two parts and the virtual machine is used for the performance irrelevant portion. In practice, most concrete systems have more than one application; One application for each *group* of functionality.

Applying functional architectural drivers, we may find that we have two different performance critical parts, such as reading and computing sensor input and keeping a radar display current. It may also be discovered that on the performance irrelevant side there should be several separate applications like diagnosis, administration and help system.

After grouping, following steps can assure us that the system can deliver the desired functionality: A) Assigning the functional requirements of the parent element to its children by defining responsibilities of the children elements, B) The discovery of necessary information exchange that creates a producer/consumer relationship between those elements. C) Finding the interactions between the element types of the primitives that make specific patterns that can mean things like: "calls", "subscribes to", "notifies", etc. [26].

Since software architecture cannot be described in a simple one-dimensional fashion, authors used some architectural views that help focus on different aspects of the conceptual architecture. They suggested using the following views: 1) The module view, shows the structural elements and their relations. 2) The concurrency view, shows the concurrency in the system. 3) The deployment view, shows the deployment of functionality onto the execution hardware.

The last part of this step indicates that analyzing and documenting the decomposition in terms of structure (module view), dynamism (concurrency view), and run-time (deployment view) uncovered those aspects for the children design elements, which should be documented in their interface. An interface of a design element shows the services and properties provided and required. It documents what others can use and on what they can depend.

Step 5: Validate and Refine Use Cases and Quality Scenarios as Constraints to Children Design Elements. The verification of the decomposition is performed by ensuring that none of the constraints, functional requirements or quality requirements can no longer be satisfied because of the design. Once the decomposition has been verified, the constraints and requirements must be themselves decomposed so that they apply to the children design elements. This step verifies that nothing important was forgotten and prepares the children design elements for further decomposition or implementation.

4   Comparison of First and Second Approaches

In this section, we describe the similarities and the differences between the first and second approaches.

4.1   Similarities

There could be a conflict between quality requirements in both approaches (e.g. performance & security). It is possible to solve the conflict between quality requirements in both methods. When a conflict occurs, both of them present a prioritization system of the quality requirements.

In both approaches, quality requirements are coarse grained and can be broken into smaller grains (hierarchy structure). Functional requirements can be added to the architecture, in both techniques.

4.2   Differences

In the first approach, a quality attribute decomposes into high level tactics; then these tactics decomposes into lower level tactics; this decomposition can be continued; but in the second approach, a quality attribute decomposes into scenarios. Scenarios can then decompose into attribute primitives and the decomposition is finished at this step.

The structure and behavior of the tactics is exactly specified using RBML in the first method, whereas the structure of the attribute primitives is defined abstractly and generally in the second one. The second approach just consists of the components and connectors, not the classes and methods.

In the first approach, there is no emphasis on functional requirements and only non-functional requirements are satisfied, but in the second approach, functional requirements are satisfied as well as non-functional requirements.

In the first approach, the requirements are assumed to be in the same level, but the second approach, pays more attention to essential requirements called architectural drivers.

Whereas the second mechanism also takes constraints into account, the first one only embodies quality attributes.

In spite of the second approach, the first approach is tool supported.

The first approach, consists of modeling notations for quality requirements (i.e. feature models and RBML), whereas the second one does not support such concepts.

As mentioned in the Similarities part, FRs can be added to the architecture in both approaches; but in spite of the first method, the second one uses a systematic way to inject functional requirements.

In the second approach, the functional requirements can be broken and there can be relations between the broken parts; but the first one does not elaborate this decomposition.

In the Similarities part, we have said that the conflict problem is solved by giving priority to the quality requirements; but the solutions to the problem are different. In the first approach, if some security tactics have conflict with the performance quality attribute (e.g. confidentiality tactic which involves encryption & decryption overhead), and the performance has more priority than security, confidentiality tactics should be discarded. In the same situation in the second approach, the ADD method divides the system into different components. Some of them are performance critical, in which security patterns should be ignored. Others are performance irrelevant, in which security attribute primitives can be applied. Table 1 summarizes the comparison between the first and second approaches.

Table 1. Comparison between first and second approaches

Specification	First Approach	Second Approach
Conflicts between NFRs	Yes	Yes
NFR modeling notation	Yes	No
Solving the NFRs conflict	Yes	Yes
Tool support	Yes	No
NFRs hierarchy structure	Yes	Yes
Unlimited NFR decomposition	Yes	No
Adding FRs	Yes	Yes
Systematic approach for adding FRs	No	Yes
Breaking FRs and interactions between them	No	Yes
Satisfying the constraints	No	Yes
Emphasis on more important requirements	No	Yes
Detailed specification of patterns	Yes	No

5   Discussion and Future Work

From the quality driven software architecture point of view, software architectures mainly depend on quality requirements. This means that quality attributes determine architectural elements. The functional requirements determine the responsibilities of architecture elements and their interfaces. Therefore, it is important to focus on quality attributes when searching for a good architecture. [29-34].

In this paper we have reviewed and analyzed two important approaches that embody NFRs into Software Architecture. This research presents a vision of the approaches and details the comparison between them. Both techniques have advantages and disadvantages.

In order to lessen the drawbacks and to use the advantages of both approaches, we intend to establish a new approach based on *pattern*. By *pattern*, we mean a general concept that can encompass both tactics and attribute primitives. This new approach could employ feature model form first approach to show the relationship between quality attributes and patterns. This model enables us to unlimitedly decompose coarse-grained patterns into more fine-grained ones. The use of RBML notation allows us to precisely describe the structure and behavior of each pattern. With the use of a compatible version of ADD method from the second technique, the new approach provides a systematic mechanism for injecting FRs, authorizes the FR break downs and the relationship between the broken parts, handles constraints, and prioritizes substantial requirements.

Our next plan is to detail a more useable and comprehensive approach based on the analyzed techniques of this paper to achieve quality driven software architecture.

References

1. Mylopoulos, J., Chung, L., Nixon, B.: Representing and Using Non-functional Requirements: A Process-Oriented Approach. Journal of IEEE Transactions on Software Engineering 18(6), 483–497 (1992)
2. Praxiom Research Group ISO 9000 Definitions, http://www.praxiom.com
3. Bosch, J.: Design and Use of Software Architectures: Adopting and Evolving a Product Line Approach. Addison Wesley, Boston (2000)
4. Cysneiros, L., Yu, E., Leite, J.: Cataloguing Non-functional Requirements as Softgoal Networks. In: Workshop on Requirements Engineering for Adaptable Architectures at Intl. RE Conference, Monterey, Bay, pp. 13–20 (2003)
5. Zou, X., Huang, J.C., Settimi, R., Solc, P.: Automated Classification of Non-functional Requirements. Journal of Requirements Engineering 12(2), 103–120 (2007)
6. Xu, L., Ziv, H., Richardson, D., Liu, Z.: Towards Modeling Non-functional Requirements in Software Architecture. In: Early Aspects 2005, Aspect-Oriented Requirement Engineering and Architecture Design Workshop, Chicago (2005)
7. Khan, K., Eenoo, C., Hylooz, S.: Addressing Non-functional Properties in Software Architecture Using ADL. In: 6th Australasian Workshop on Software and System Architectures, Brisbane, pp. 6–12 (2005)

8. Chung, L., Nixon, B., Yu, E., Mylopoulos, J.: Non-functional Requirements in Software Engineering. International Series in Software Engineering, vol. 5, p. 476. Springer, Heidelberg (1999)

9. Cysneiros, L., Leite, J.: Non-functional Requirements: From Elicitation to Conceptual Models. Journal of IEEE Transaction on Software Engineering 30(5), 328–350 (2004)

10. Franch, X., Botella, P.: Putting Non-functional Requirements into Software Architecture. In: 9th IEEE International Workshop on Software Specification and Design, pp. 60–67 (1998)

11. Metha, N., Medvidovic, N.: Distilling Software Architecture Primitives form Architectural Styles. Technical report, University of Southern California, Los Angeles (2002)

12. Rosa, N.S., Justo, G.R.R., Cunha, P.R.F.: Incorporating Non-Functional Requirements into Software Architectures. In: Rolim, J.D.P. (ed.) IPDPS-WS 2000. LNCS, vol. 1800, pp. 1009–1018. Springer, Heidelberg (2000)

13. Xu, L., Ziv, H., Alspaugh, T., Richardson, D.: An Architectural Pattern for Non-functional Dependability Requirements. Journal of Systems and Software 79(10), 1370–1378 (2006)

14. Zarate, G., Botella, P.: Use of UML for Modeling Non-functional Aspects. In: 13th International Conference on Software and System Engineering and their Application (ICSSEA 2000). CNAM, Paris (2000)

15. Kim, S.: Quality-Driven Architecture Development Using Architectural Tactics. Journal of Systems and Software 82(8), 1211–1231 (2009)

16. Bachmann, F., Bass, L., Klein, M.: Illuminating the Fundamental Contributors to Software Architecture Quality. Technical report, Software Engineering Institute, Carnegie Mellon University, Pittsburgh (2002)

17. Bass, L., Clements, P., Kazman, R.: Software Architecture in Practice. Addison Wesley, Boston (2003)

18. Ramachandran, J.: Designing Security Architecture Solutions. John Wiley, New York (2002)

19. Czarnecki, K., Eisenecker, U.: Generative Programming: Methods, Tools, and Applications. Addison Wesley, Boston (2000)

20. France, R., Kim, D., Ghosh, S., Song, E.: A UML-Based Pattern Specification Technique. Journal of IEEE Transaction on Software Engineering 30(3), 193–206 (2004)

21. Kim, D.: The Role-Based Metamodeling Language for Specifying Design Patterns. In: Taibi, T. (ed.) Design Pattern Formalization Techniques, pp. 183–205. Idea Group Inc. (2007)

22. Cole, E., Krutz, R., Conley, J.: Network Security Bible. John Wiley, Indianapolis (2005)

23. Silberschatz, A., Galvin, P., Gagne, G.: Operating System Principles. Addison Wesley, Boston (2005)

24. Schmidt, K.: High Availability and Disaster Recovery: Concepts, Design, Implementation. Springer, New York (2006)

25. Kim, D., White, J.: Generating UML Models from Pattern Specifications. In: 3th ACIS International Conference on Software Engineering Research, Management and Applications (SERA 2005), Mt. Pleasant, pp. 166–173 (2005)

26. Bass, L., Klein, M., Bachmann, F.: Quality Attribute Design Primitives. Technical report, Software Engineering Institute, Carnegie Mellon University, Pittsburgh (2000)

27. Booch, G.: Object Solutions: Managing the Object-Oriented Project. Addison Wesley, Boston (1996)

28. Hofmeister, C., Nord, R., Soni, D.: Applied Software Architecture. Addison Wesley, Boston (2000)

29. Allahawiah, S., Altarawneh, H., Tarawneh, M.M.I.: A Proposed Theoretical Framework for Software Project Success. International Journal of Web Applications 2(4), 250–260 (2010)
30. Foping, F.S., Dokas, I.M., Feehan, J., Imran, S.: An Improved Schema-Sharing Technique for a Software as a Service Application to Enhance Drinking Water Safety. Journal of Information Security Research 1(1), 1–10 (2010)
31. Bajnaid, N., Benlamri, R., Cogan, B.: Ontology-Based E-Learning System for SQA Compliant Software Development. International Journal of Web Applications 2(3), 175–181 (2010)
32. Sheta, A.F., Al-Afeef, A.: Software Effort Estimation for NASA Projects Using Genetic Programming. Journal of Intelligent Computing 1(3), 146–156 (2010)
33. Deraman, A., Yahaya, J.H.: The Architecture of an Integrated Support Tool for Software Product Certification Process. Journal of E-Technology 1(2), 98–108 (2010)
34. Thompson, S., Torabi, T.: An Observational Approach to Practical Process Non-Conformance Detection. Journal of Information Technology Review 1(2), 62–73 (2010)

Using Power Spectral Density for Fault Diagnosis of Belt Conveyor Electromotor

Hojjat Ahmadi and Zeinab Khaksar

Department of Agricultural Machinery Engineering, University of Tehran, Karaj, Iran
{hjahmadi,z_khaksar}@ut.ac.ir

Abstract. This paper focuses on vibration-based condition monitoring and fault diagnosis of a belt conveyor electromotor by using Power spectral density (PSD). The objective of this research was to investigate the correlation between vibration analysis, PSD and fault diagnosis. Vibration data had regularly collected. We calculated G_{rms}(Root-Mean-Square Acceleration)and PSD of Driven End (DE) and None Driven End (NDE) of an electromotor in healthy and unhealthy situations. The results showed that different situations showed different PSD vs. frequency. The results showed that with calculating PSD we could find some fault and diagnosis of belt conveyor electromotor as soon as possible. Vibration analysis and Power Spectral Density could provide quick and reliable information on the condition of the belt conveyor electromotor on different situations. Integration of vibration condition monitoring technique with Power Spectral Density analyze could indicate more understanding about diagnosis of the electromotor.

Keywords: Power Spectral Density, PSD, Belt Conveyor Electromotor, Condition Monitoring.

1 Introduction

Vibration sources in machines are events that generate forces and motion during machine operation [1]. Vibration signals carry information about exciting forces and the structural path through which they propagate to vibration transducers (Williams, 1994) [2]. Vibration based condition monitoring refers to the use of non-destructive sensing and analysis of system characteristics for the purpose of detecting changes, which may indicate damage or degradation [3].By analyzing the frequency spectra, and using signal processing techniques, both the defect and natural frequencies of the various structural components can be identified (Barron, 1996; Eisenmann, 1998)[4, 5].Commonly used technique is to examine the individual frequencies present in the signal. These frequencies correspond to certain mechanical component or certain malfunction. By examining these frequencies and their harmonics, the analyst can identify the location, type of problem and the root cause as well (Cempel, 1988).The vibration signal analysis was often based on the Fast Fourier Transform (FFT) [6, 7, 8].In order to overcome performance limitations of FFT such as disability of describing non-stationeries vibration signal that introduced by faults, Power spectral density is reported in several research works (Gibson, 1972; Norton and Karczub, 2003)

P. Pichappan, H. Ahmadi, and E. Ariwa (Eds.): INCT 2011, CCIS 241, pp. 15–20, 2011.

[9, 10].This paper focuses on vibration-based condition monitoring and fault diagnosis of a belt conveyor electromotor by using Power spectral density (PSD). Vibration data was regularly collected. We were calculated G_{rms}(Root-Mean-Square Acceleration)and PSD of a belt conveyor electromotor before and after repair (unhealthy and healthy situations). The results of this study have given more understanding on the dependent roles of vibration analysis in predicting and diagnosing machine faults.

2   Materials and Method

The test rig used for the experimentation was a belt conveyor electromotor. Details of the belt conveyor electromotor were given in table 1.The electromotor was running under healthy and unhealthy situations. The Vibration data were collected on a regular basis after the run in period. The experimental procedure for the vibration analysis consisted of taking vibration readings at None Driven End (NDE) and Driven End (DE) of the electromotor. There were taken on input shaft casing of electromotor. Vibration measurements were taken on the input shaft casing of electromotor using an Easy-Viber (VMI was the manufacturer). Spectra Pro4 software was used for acquisition the vibration spectrum based on the Fast Fourier Transform (FFT) at frequency domain between 0 to 850 Hz.

Table 1. Detail of the belt conveyor electromotor

Electromotor	Description
Type of motor	M2BA 315SMA 4
Power (kW)	110
Motor driving speed (rpm)	1500
Voltage(V)	400

After acquisition the vibration spectrum, Power Spectral Density (PSD) of spectrums for the higher Grms values in the range of 0-200 Hz was calculated. Power spectral density (PSD) function shows the strength of the variations (energy) as a function of frequency. In other words, it shows at which frequencies variations are strong and at which frequencies variations are weak (Irvine, 1998) [11].

Most random vibration testing is conducted using Gaussian random suppositions for both measurement and specification purposes. With Gaussian assumptions, there is no definable maximum amplitude, and the amplitude levels are measured in RMS (root-mean-squared) values [12, 13]. Random vibration can be thought of as containing excitation at all frequencies within the specified frequency band but no excitation at any specific single frequency [14, 15].An acceleration spectrum is normally specified in terms of its' acceleration density using the units of g^2 per Hz. Acceleration density is defined as (1) [13, 14]:

$$g_d = \lim {a^2}/{\Delta f} \quad , \qquad \Delta f \geq 0 \tag{1}$$

Where: g_d=acceleration density, a = rms acceleration, Δf =bandwidth

3   Results and Discussion

The experimental results of the overall vibratory velocity level of DE and NDE of the belt conveyor electromotor have shown in fig.1 and 2. The warning and critical values of DE of the electromotor are 3.08 and 4.62 mm/s, respectively (ISO TC108, 1963). The critical value of NDE of the electromotor is 5.79 mm/s. The results showed that the RMS value was on critical status in eighth measurement.

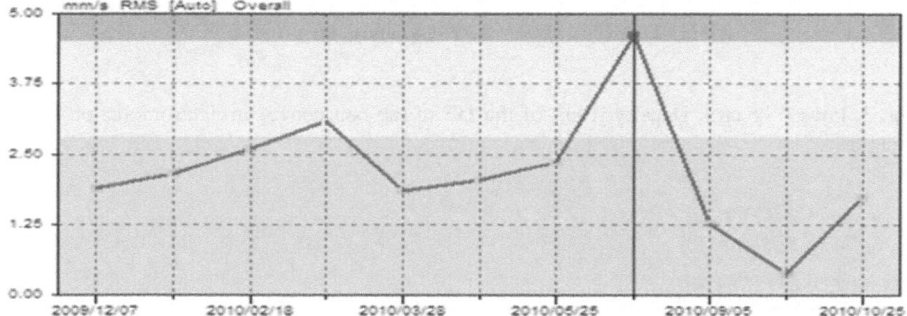

Fig. 1. Overall vibrations of DE of the belt conveyor electromotor

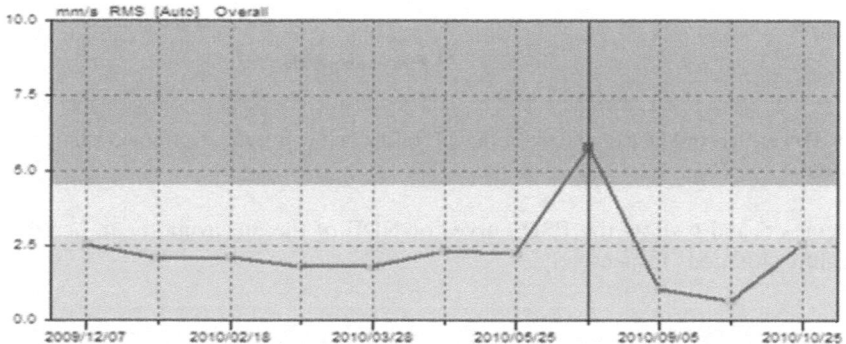

Fig. 2. Overall vibrations of NDE of the belt conveyor electromotor

We measured frequency spectrum of electromotor but it is obviously difficult to diagnose faults by using spectrum of vibration signals alone. By using of frequency spectrum result, we calculate PSD of electromotor in different situation. Figures 3 and 4 show the PSD curves of DE of the electromotor in healthy and unhealthy situations respectively.

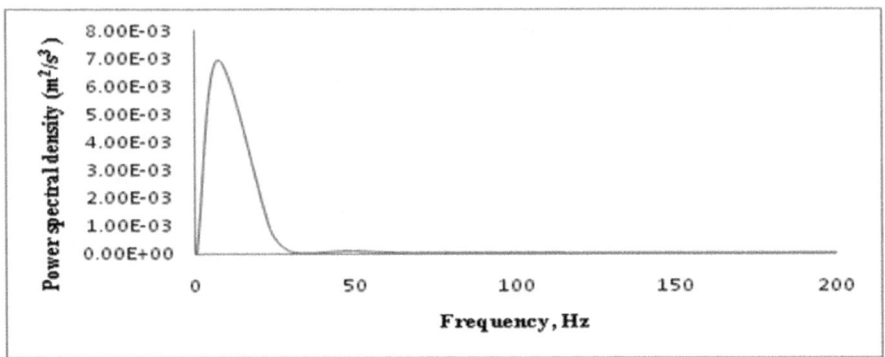

Fig. 3. Power Spectral Density result of the DE of the belt conveyor electromotor on healthy situation

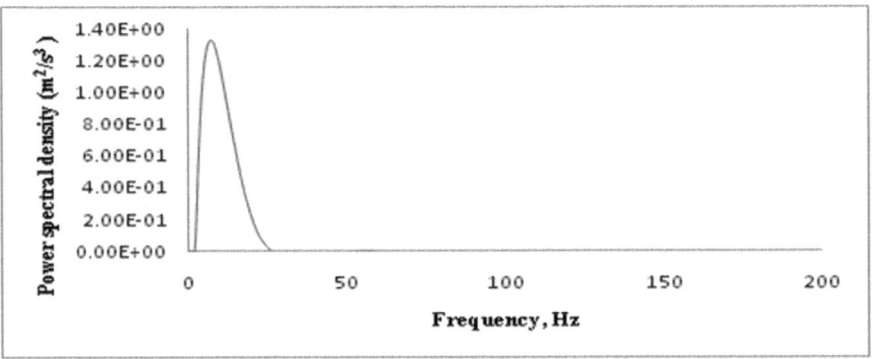

Fig. 4. Power Spectral Density result of the DE of the belt conveyor electromotor on unhealthy situation

Figures 5 and 6 show the PSD curves of NDE of the electromotor in healthy and unhealthy situations respectively.

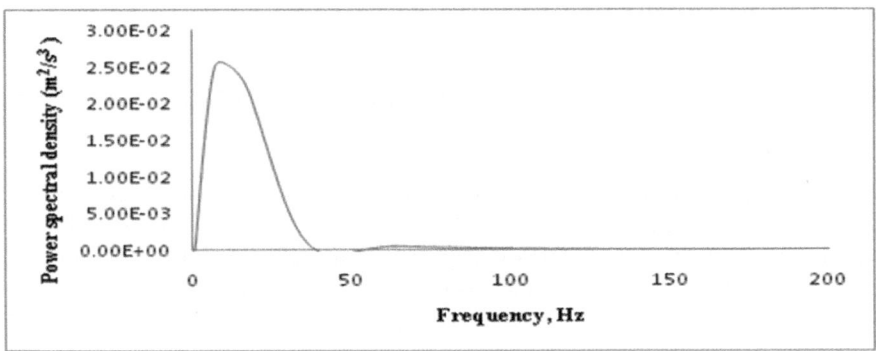

Fig. 5. Power Spectral Density result of the NDE of the belt conveyor electromotor on healthy situation

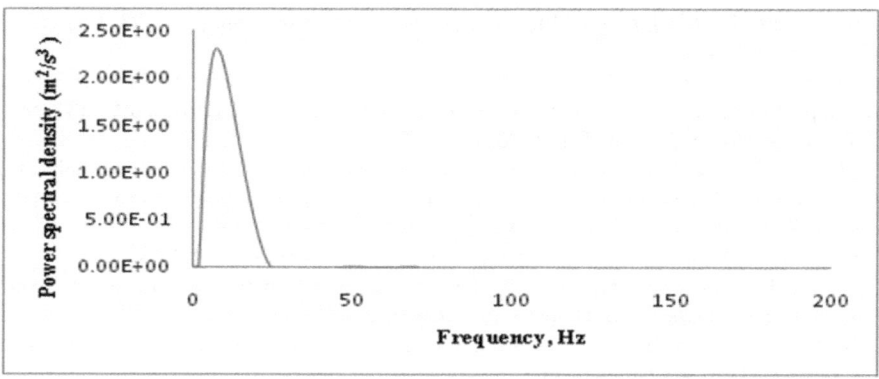

Fig. 6. Power Spectral Density result of the NDE of the belt conveyor electromotor on unhealthy situation

The results showed that area under PSD carves were indicated a problem. The more area below PSD curve showed the faults were deeper. Just as we can understand this from comprising of healthy and unhealthy figures of DE and NDE of the electromotor. The results showed that with calculating PSD we could find some fault and diagnosis of electromotor as soon as possible. Results showed that when we had deeper faults such as looseness the area under PSD carves was grown.

4   Conclusions

The work conducted, proposing the method of the belt conveyor electromotor fault identification based on power spectral density technique. Results showed that vibration condition monitoring and Power Spectral Density technique could detect fault diagnosis of the belt conveyor electromotor. Vibration analysis and Power Spectral Density could provide quick and reliable information on the condition of the electromotor on different situations. Integration of vibration condition monitoring technique with Power Spectral Density analyze could indicate more understanding about diagnosis of electromotor.

References

1. Popescu, T.: Blind separation of vibration signals and source change detection – Application to machine monitoring. Applied Mathematical Modelling 34, 3408–3421 (2010)
2. Williams, J.: Condition-based maintenance and machine diagnostics, pp. 51–57. Chapman & Hall (1994)
3. Carden, E., Fanning, P.: Vibration Based Condition Monitoring: A Review. Structural Health Monitoring 3, 355–377 (2004)
4. Barron, T.: Engineering condition monitoring, pp. 5–113. Addison Wesley Longman Publishers (1996)

5. Eisenmann, R.: Machinery malfunction diagnosis and correction, pp. 3–23. Prentice Hall Publishers (1998)
6. Ahmadi, H., Mollazade, K.: Journal-bearing fault diagnosis of an external gear hydraulic pump using power spectral density. In: ECOTRIB 2009 - 2nd European Conference on Tribology, Pisa, Italy, June 7-10 (2009)
7. Mathew, J., Stecki, J.: Comparison of vibration and direct reading Ferro graphic techniques in application to high-speed gears operating under steady and varying load conditions. Soc. Tribol. Lubr. Eng. 43, 646–653 (1987)
8. Brigham, E.: Fast fourier transform and its applications. Prentice Hall Press (1988)
9. Gibson, R.: Power spectral density: a fast, simple method with low core storage requirement. M.I.T. Charles Stark Draper Laboratory Press (1972)
10. Norton, M., Karczub, D.: Fundamentals of noise and vibration analysis for engineers. Cambridge University Press (2003)
11. Irvine, T.: An introduction to spectral functions. Vibration Data Press (1998)
12. http://analyst.gsfc.nasa.gov/FEMCI/random/randomgrms.html
13. http://www.labworksinc.com/enginfo/random_vib_test.html
14. Mathew, J., Stecki, J.: Comparison of vibration and direct reading Ferro graphic techniques in application to high-speed gears operating under steady and varying load conditions. Soc. Tribol. Lubr. Eng. 43, 646–653 (1987)

Assessment of Watermelon Quality Using Vibration Spectra

R. Abbaszadeh[1], A. Rajabipour[1], H. Ahmadi[1], M. Delshad[2], and M. Mahjoob[3]

[1] Faculty of Agricultural Engineering and Technology, Tehran University, Karaj, Iran
{Abaszadeh,arajabi,hjahmadi,delshad,mmahjoob}@ut.ac.ir
[2] Faculty of Agricultural Sciences and Engineering, Tehran University, Karaj, Iran
[3] Faculty of Mechanical Engineering, Tehran University, Tehran, Iran
{Abaszadeh,arajabi,hjahmadi,delshad,mmahjoob}@ut.ac.ir

Abstract. Judging watermelon quality based on its apparent properties such as size or skin color is difficult. Traditional methods have various problems and limitations. In this paper a nondestructive method for quality watermelon test using laser Doppler vibrometery technology (LDV) have been presented which hasn't some limitations. At first the sample was excited by a vibration generator in a frequency range. Applied vibration was measured using accelerometer attached in resting place of fruit. Synchronically vibrational response of fruit upside was detected by LDV. By means of a fast Fourier transform algorithm and considering response signal to excitation signal ratio, vibration spectra of fruit are analyzed and the first and second resonances were extracted. After nondestructive tests, watermelons were sensory evaluated. So the samples were graded in a range of ripeness by panel members in terms of overall acceptability (total desired traits consumers). Using two mentioned resonances as well as watermelon weight, a multivariate linear regression model to determine watermelon quality scores obtained. Correlation coefficient for calibration model was 0.82. For validation of model leave one out cross validation method was applied and r= 0.78 was achieved. Stepwise discriminant analysis was also used to classify ripe and unripe watermelons. The results showed 87.5% classification accuracy for original and cross validation cases. This study appeared utilization of this technique for watermelons sorting based on their costumer acceptability.

Keywords: watermelon, Doppler vibrometery, vibration spectra, costumer acceptability, regression model, discriminant analysis.

1   Introduction

According to statistics published by FAO (2008), Iran ranked third among watermelon producing countries. Watermelon quality during consumption mainly depends on the ripeness of the fruit. Typically optimum quality watermelon fruits for eating feature an appropriate balance among sugar, flavour, colour and texture (Stone et al., 1996).

P. Pichappan, H. Ahmadi, and E. Ariwa (Eds.): INCT 2011, CCIS 241, pp. 21–29, 2011.
© Springer-Verlag Berlin Heidelberg 2011

Watermelons are usually harvested from the farm only one or two times according to their weight at harvest. Decreasing labor costs and increasing harvesting speed are the two main reasons that explain this harvesting strategy. This may result in watermelons with varying degrees of ripeness reaching the market. Many consumers dispose of the watermelons that are immature, of poor-quality or spoiled. However, if it was possible to identify those lower quality watermelons and remove them from the distribution system, this could result into increased consumer satisfaction.

The determination of watermelon ripeness on the basis of its apparent properties such as size or skin colour is very difficult. The most common way by which people traditionally determine watermelon ripeness includes knocking on the fruits and to assess the ripeness using the reflected sound. This method is prone to human factor errors as only well-experienced individuals can use it in a reliable way (Stone et al., 1996). The limitations of this method have led researchers to study acoustic methods to determine the watermelon ripeness (Armstrong et al., 1997; Diezma-Iglesias et al., 2004; Farabee et al., 1991; Stone et al., 1996; Xiuqin et al., 2006; Yamamoto et al., 1980). Most of the researchers who have studied the acoustic method were not satisfied with the results of their reports. Acoustic methods present many limitations and problems for watermelon grading at an industrial scale. For example, the location and number of excitations, microphone distance, angle of hitting, and hitter device material can all affect the test results. (Diezma-Iglesias et al., 2004; Taniwaki and Sakurai, 2010).

Another potential method for the assessment of watermelon ripeness is the use of vibration impulses. Impulses are applied to samples and the generated vibrations are measured by accelerometers. However, one important limitation of this method is the need to paste accelerometers on the watermelon surface, which can be impractical in the grading and sorting industry. The mass of the accelerometers can also be the source of errors (Muramatsu et al., 1997; Nourain et al., 2004). In addition, the use of hitting devices results in the excitation energy being focused within narrow specific frequency and time bands. This particular issue results into limitations for the determination of the exact value of the parameters (Taniwaki et al., 2009).

In recent years researchers have been studying a new non-destructive vibration technique using Laser Doppler Vibrometry (LDV) technology to test the quality of some fruits. Muramatsu et al. (1997) have evaluated the texture and ripeness of some varieties of kiwi, peach and pears. They excited samples at different stages of ripeness by means of a 5 to 2000 Hz sine wave. The vibration response at the top of the fruit samples was measured by LDV. Then the phase shift between the input and output signals was compared with the data obtained from the method of force - displacement. A significant relationship between these two methods was found for the 1200 and 1600 Hz excitation frequencies. The ability of the LDV technique for detection of internal defects of some citrus varieties was deemed appropriate (Muramatsu et al., 1999). These authors compared the use of accelerometers and of the LDV system to measure the firmness of some varieties of apple, pear, kiwi, and citrus. They found that the LDV measurements were more accurate than those obtained by means of the accelerometers. Muramatsu et al. (1997) also used the LDV method to determine fruit texture changes during the ripening process. This technique was used for persimmon, apple, and kiwi. For a certain range of frequencies, phase shift as a function of fruit ripeness significantly changed. They also determined that resonance frequencies for all fruits under test were a function of their ripeness (Muramatsu et al., 2000).

Terasaki et al. (2001) used LDV to assess the properties of kiwi fruit at different stages of ripeness. Two following factors were considered by them

$$S = (f_n)^2 m^{2/3} \qquad (1)$$

$$\eta = \frac{f_2 - f_1}{f_n} \qquad (2)$$

Where fn is second peak resonance frequency, m is mass of a fruit and f2 and f1 are frequencies determined at 3 dB below peak resonance. The relationship between S and the firmness of kiwi fruit was significantly high. η also showed a good correlation with soluble solids content. (Terasaki et al., 2001). Sakura et al. (2005) conducted some experiments to assess persimmon tissue. They found that the data obtained by the LDV method were significantly correlated with the three variables softness, firmness, and brittleness for persimmon kept in 60% and 100% relative humidity storage. These three variables were evaluated by sensory method (Sakurai et al., 2005). Murayama et al. (2006) conducted research on pear ripeness by means of the LDV method in which the fruits harvested at different times and under different periods of storage were tested. Their results showed that the correlation coefficients between firmness and elasticity index were significantly high and were dependent on storage duration and harvest time, except for pears that were kept for 4 months in storage temperature of 1°C (Murayama et al., 2006). Taniwaki et al. (2009) also conducted a separate investigation to review change trends in elasticity index (EI) for melon, persimmon, and pear after harvest. They determined elasticity index from the formula

$$EI = f_n{}^2 m^{2/3} \qquad (3)$$

Where f_n is the second resonance frequency of sample was obtained using LDV and m is mass of the fruit. The fruit samples were separately assessed for features such as appearance, sweetness, and firmness using professional people for sensory evaluation. Also the overall fruits acceptability was evaluated. High correlation between the elasticity index and the above mentioned properties was observed. So, the researchers could determine the optimum fruit ripeness time, which is the most appropriate time for eating, according to their elasticity index (Taniwaki et al., 2009). The main objective of present study is establishing a relation among parameters measured by LDV and watermelon consumers' opinion using multiple linear regression models.

2   Materials and Methods

In this study forthy watermelons were selected for the experiments. The variety of watermelons was Crimson Sweet which is one of the varieties for export from the Iran. It is nearly round with bright green and medium dark stripes.

The experimental setup has been presented in Figures1and 2. A fruit sample was placed on a shaker, and excited with random wave signals (frequencies, 0–1000Hz) generated and amplified using a computer and amplifier respectively. While the excitation signal was detected by accelerometer (Model Endevco 4397) installed on vibrational plate, the response of the fruit was optically sensed using a Laser Doppler Vibrometer (Model Ometron VH1000-D, Denmark).

Briefly laser beam from the LDV is directed to the upper surface of sample and the vibrations are measured from the Doppler shift of the reflected beam frequency due to the motion of the surface. Considering the response signals, the excitation signals and using FFT, the frequency resonances were extracted from entire frequency range. Using frequency response curves from the accelerometer and LDV system, the resonance frequencies of the first two vibrational modes were determined.

Fig. 1. Excitation signal was measured as input signal by accelerometer installed on shaker

After determining the vibration response of the samples and measuring their weight, they were cut at the midpoint. Then watermelons were sensory evaluated. Panelists graded the fruits in a range of ripeness in terms of overall acceptability (total desired traits consumers). The fruit ripeness indices were scored on a scale of 1–5 (1: unripe, 3: ripe, and 5: overripe).

Finally the correlation between LDV-test results and the consumer opinions was determined. The frequency resonances and mass were used for making prediction model. This step was carried out using MATLAB (7.6.0 R2008a, The Math- Works Inc., USA)

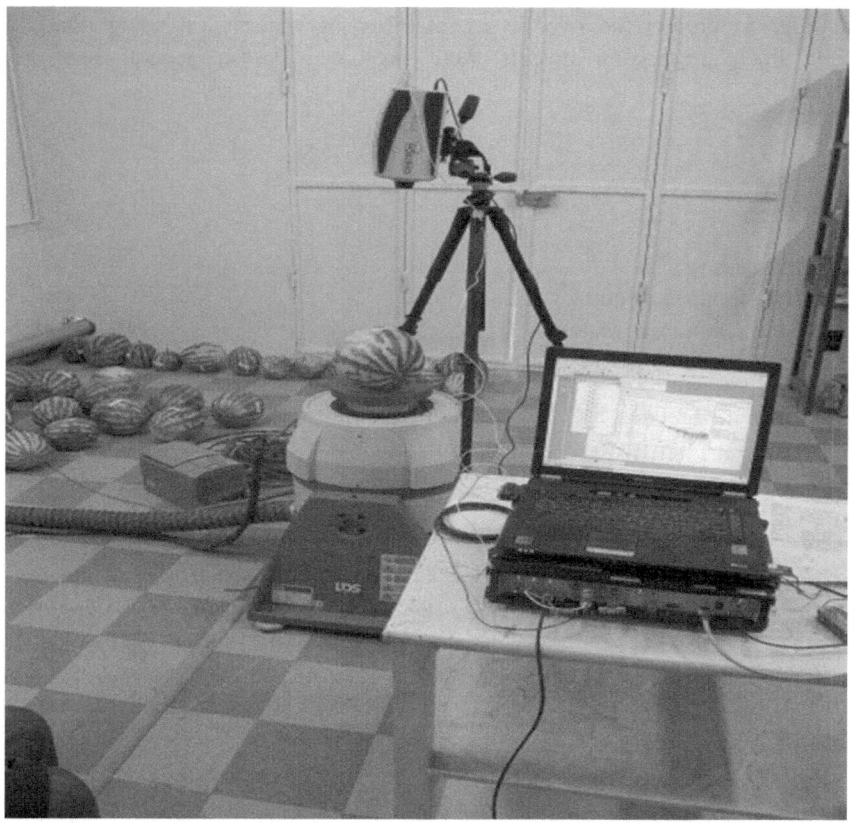

Fig. 2. LDV sensed response of the fruit in upper surface as output signal

To quantify the predictive ability of the models, the calibration coefficient (r) and root mean squared error (RMSE) were obtained. Leave-one-out cross validation was applied for validating models. This technique separates a single observation case from all cases as the validation data, and the remaining cases use for deriving predictive function. This procedure is repeated such that each observation in the sample is used once as the validation data. Discriminate analysis was used to build predictive model of group membership based on observed characteristics of each case. The procedure generates a discriminate function for two groups (ripe and unripe) based on linear combinations of the predictor variables that provide the best discrimination between the groups.

3   Results

By investigating the whole spectrum the first and second peaks were considered as resonances.

In order to predict the overall acceptability of watermelon using phase shift, multiple linear regression models were presented whose general form is the following:

$$y = a_0 + \sum_{i=1}^{3} a_i x_i \qquad (1)$$

Where

x$_1$: Fruit mass (g)
x$_2$: First resonance frequency (Hz)
x$_3$: second resonance frequency (Hz)
y: overall acceptability (1: unripe to 5: overripe).

The coefficients of models for calculation of overall acceptability are showed in table 1.

Table 1. Numerical values of the regression model coefficients

Coefficient	Unit	overall acceptability
a_0	-	4.729051
a_1	1/g	0.000203
a_2	s	-0.15079
a_3	s	0.01294

Table2 shows performance of MLR models in prediction in terms of correlation coefficient and RMSE.

Table 2. MLR models for predicting overall acceptability of watermelon

Acceptability	Calibration		Validation	
	r	RMSE	r	RMSE
	0.82	0.5725	0.78	0.6392

Actual and predicted values of consumer opinions were plotted in figures 3 to visually evaluate the performance of the models.

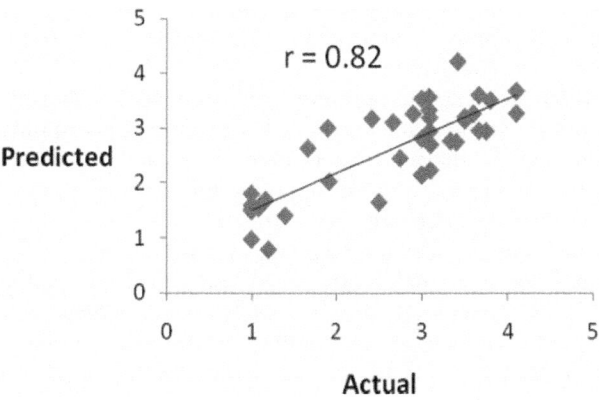

Fig. 3. Actual and predicted values for overall quality

The results of stepwise discriminant analysis for classifying ripe and unripe watermelons were showed in table 3. 87.5% of original grouped cases and 87.5% of cross-validated grouped cases correctly classified.

Table 3. Classification results

| | | | Predicted group membership | | |
			ripe	unripe	Total
Orginal	count	ripe	23	2	25
		unripe	3	12	15
	%	ripe	92	8	100
		unripe	20	80	100
Cross-validated	count	ripe	23	2	25
		unripe	3	12	15
	%	ripe	92	8	100
		unripe	20	80	100

4   Discussion

Vibration response was obtained ratio of imposed and perceived signals. It seems variations of total solvable solids, pigmentation in the cells and internal restructuring of watermelon during ripeness cause changes of modal properties derived vibration response such as resonance frequency Because of this phenomenon the first and second resonance frequencies can be used as variables in the watermelon ripeness modeling. Former studies with LDV which applied vibration response for other fruit considered only second resonance.

It is suggested to study utilization of damping ratio as well as variations of phase difference between imposed and perceived signals on certain frequencies for developing predictive models.

Employing the panel test, the optimum quality range of watermelons depended on consumers' opinion can be achieved in terms of vibration response. Therefore after vibrations tests and predicting watermelon acceptability, distributors enable to separate fruits whose score are not in the optimum range of overall acceptability. In general the optimum range depends on customers' taste.

Using LDV technology vibration response of watermelon is sensed without contact and in real-time that is a major advantage for industrial grading and sorting of watermelons. It is concluded present study demonstrates feasibility of laser vibrometry for predicting overall acceptability of fruit as an online contactless sensing method. There is also capability to investigate and develop nondestructive vibration – based methods for simultaneous analysis of other internal properties of watermelon like total soluble solid (TSS). It is obvious that buying a poor-quality watermelon, in comparison with other fruits includes more financial loss. Diagnosing those watermelons in a bottleneck (like the main fruit and vegetable farms, ports and other terminals) and separate them, this could increase the consumer satisfaction, and providing a plan for using those products is conceivable. The results of this research can be used for developing a rapid sorting system for watermelon.

Acknowledgments. The study was supported by a grant from council of research (7109012/1/04) of Tehran University. The researchers would like to thank Iran Test & Research Auto Company for its collaboration.

References

1. Armstrong, P.R., Stone, M.L., Brusewitz, G.H.: Nondestructive acoustic and compression measurements of watermelon for internal damage detection. Appl. Eng. Agric. 13(5), 641–645 (1997)
2. Diezma-Iglesias, B., Ruiz-Altisent, M., Barreiro, P.: Detection of internal quality in seedless watermelon by acoustic impulse response. Biosyst. Eng. 88(2), 221–230 (2004)
3. Ebrahimi, E., Mollazade, K.: Integrating fuzzy data mining and impulse acoustic techniques for almond nuts sorting. Aust. J. Crop. Sci. 4(5), 353–358 (2010)
4. Farabee, M.: Stone ML Determination of watermelon maturity with sonic impulse testing. ASAE Paper No. 91-3013. ASAE, St. Joseph, Mich. The American Society of Agricultural Engineers, USA (1991)
5. Food and Agriculture Organization (FAO) (2008), http://www.fao.org (November 10, 2010)
6. Muramatsu, N., Sakurai, N., Wada, N., Yamamoto, R., Tanaka, K., Asakura, T., Ishikawa-Takano, Y., Nevins, D.J.: Critical comparison of an accelerometer and a laser Doppler vibrometer for measuring fruit firmness. Horttechnology 7, 434–438 (1997b)
7. Muramatsu, N.L., Sakurai, N., Wada, N., Yamamoto, R., Takahara, T., Ogata, T., Tanaka, K., Asakura, T., Ishikawa-Takano, Y., Nevins, D.J.: Evaluation of fruit tissue texture and internal disorders by laser doppler detection. Postharvest. Biol. Tec. 15(1), 83–88 (1999)

8. Muramatsu, N., Sakurai, N., Wada, N., Yamamoto, R., Tanaka, K., Asakura, T., Ishikawa-Takano, Y., Nevins, D.J.: Remote sensing of fruit textural changes with a laser Doppler vibrometer. J. Am. Soc. Hortic. Sci. 125(1), 120–127 (2000)
9. Murayama, H., Konno, I., Terasaki, S., Yamamoto, R., Sakurai, N.: Nondestructive method for measuring fruit ripening of 'La France' pears using a laser Doppler vibrometer. J. Jpn. Soc. Hortic. Sci. 75, 79–84 (2006)
10. Nourain, J., Ying, Y., Wang, J., Rao, X.: Determination of acoustic vibration in watermelon by finite element modeling. In: Proceedings of SPIE, The International Society for Optical Engineering, vol. 5587(24), pp. 213–223 (2004)
11. Sakurai, N., Iwatani, S., Terasaki, S., Yamamoto, R.: Evaluation of 'Fuyu' persimmon texture by a new parameter "Sharpness index". J. Jpn. Soc. Hortic. Sci. 74, 150–158 (2005)
12. Stone, M.L., Armstrong, P.R., Zhang, X., Brusewitz, G.H., Chen, D.D.: Watermelon maturity determination in the field using acoustic impulse impedance techniques. T. Asae. 39, 2325–2330 (1996)
13. Taniwaki, M., Hanada, T., Sakurai, N.: Postharvest quality evaluation of "Fuyu" and "Taishuu" persimmons using a nondestructive vibrational method and an acoustic vibration technique. Postharvest. Biol. Tec. 51(1), 80–85 (2009)
14. Taniwaki, M., Hanada, T., Tohro, M., Sakurai, N.: Non-destructive determination of the optimum eating ripeness of pears and their texture measurements using acoustical vibration techniques. Postharvest. Biol. Tec. 51(3), 305–310 (2009)
15. Taniwaki, M., Sakurai, N.: Evaluation of the internal quality of agricultural products using acoustic vibration techniques. J. Jpn. Soc. Hortic. Sci. 79(2), 113–128 (2010)
16. Taniwaki, M., Takahashi, M., Sakurai, N.: Determination of optimum ripeness for edibility of postharvest melons using nondestructive vibration. Food Res. Int. 42(1), 137–141 (2009)
17. Terasaki, S., Wada, N., Sakurai, N., Muramatsu, N., Yamamoto, R., Nevins, D.J.: Nondestructive measurement of kiwifruit ripeness using a laser Doppler vibrometer. T. Asae. 44, 81–87 (2001)
18. Xiuqin, R., Yibin, Y.: Inspection of watermelon maturity by testing transmitting velocity of acoustic wave. Ama 37(4), 41–45 (2006)
19. Yamamoto, H., Iwamoto, M., Haginuma, S.: Acoustic impulse response method for measuring natural frequency of intact fruits and preliminary application s to internal quality evaluation of apples and watermelon. J. Texture Stud. 11, 117–136 (1980)

Fault Diagnosis of Journal-Bearing of Generator Using Power Spectral Density and Fault Probability Distribution Function

Hojjat Ahmadi and Ashkan Moosavian

University of Tehran
{hjahmadi,a.moosavian}@ut.ac.ir

Abstract. Developing a special method for maintenance of equipments of industrial company is necessary for improving maintenance quality and reducing operating costs. Because of many vibration environments are not related to a specific driving frequency and may have input from multiple sources which may not be harmonically related, for more accurate and interest to analyze and test using random vibration. In this paper, for fault detection of generator journal-bearing using two technique of vibration analysis, namely, Power Spectral Density (PSD) and Fault Probability Distribution Function(PDF). For this we were calculated G_{rms}, PDS and PDF of generator journal-bearing in healthy and unhealthy situation. The results showed that with calculating PSD and PDF we could find some fault of engine and diagnosis them possiblity.

Keywords: Fault diagnosis, Maintenance, generator journal-bearing, PDS, PDF, G_{rms}.

1   Introduction

Machine condition monitoring has long been accepted as one of the most effective and cost-efficient approaches to avoid catastrophic failures of machines. It has been known for many years that the mechanical integrity of a machine can be evaluated by detailed analysis of the vibratory motion [1].

Most of machinery used in the modern world operates by means of motors and rotary parts which can develop faults. The monitoring of the operative conditions of a rotary machine provides a great economic improvement by reducing the operational and maintenance costs, as well as improving the safety level. As a part of the machine maintenance task, it is necessary to analyze the external relevant information in order to evaluate the internal components state which, generally, are inaccessible without dismantle the machine [2].

Condition monitoring of machines is gaining importance in industry because of the need to increase reliability and to decrease possible loss of production due to machine breakdown. The use of vibration and acoustic emission (AE) signals is quite common in the field of condition monitoring of rotating machinery. By comparing the signals

P. Pichappan, H. Ahmadi, and E. Ariwa (Eds.): INCT 2011, CCIS 241, pp. 30–36, 2011.
© Springer-Verlag Berlin Heidelberg 2011

of a machine running in normal and faulty conditions, detection of faults like mass unbalance, rotor rub, shaft misalignment, gear failures and bearing defects is possible. These signals can also be used to detect the incipient failures of the machine components, through the on-line monitoring system, reducing the possibility of catastrophic damage and the machine down time [3].

Because of whirl and friction between components and producing heat, in any rotary machine the journal-bearing is used. Journal-bearing prevent damage to components like burn them. Actually failure journal-bearing can damage to rotary machines. So condition monitoring of journal-bearing is important issue.

2   Materials and Methods

The procedure of doing experiment is given the vibration data from generator in health y and unhealthy situation of journal-bearing. The vibration data consist of velocity and frequency of generator are collected in different times. For this work, the accelerometer sensor (ap3419) is used that is placed on crankshaft case of generator. Spectra Pro4 software is used based on Fast Fourier at frequency domain between 0 to 850Hz .

2.1   Grms

The metric of G_{rms} is typically used to specify and compare the energy in repetitive shock vibration systems. The root mean square (rms) value of each signal can be calculated by squaring the magnitude of the signal at every point, finding the average (mean) value of the squared magnitude, then taking the square root of the average value. The resulting number is the G_{rms} metric.

G_{rms} is typically thought of as a frequency domain measurement taken from the Power Spectrum, or Power Spectral Density, curve. A brief review of the basics of Fourier theory will make this method of determining G_{rms} clearer.

When G_{rms} is calculated using Power Spectrum information it is often thought of as the area under the curve of the Power Spectrum display. More accurately, it is the square root of the integral of the Power Spectrum [4].

Parseval's Theorem states that the energy of a signal is the same whether calculated in the time domain or the frequency domain [5]. Since the Power Spectrum display is in units of G^2, the integral of the Power Spectrum, or the area under the curve, satisfies the right side of Parseval's Theorem, while the summation of the squared values of the digitally sampled time domain signal satisfy the left side of the equation. Taking the square root of each side results in equivalent G_{rms} calculations. Parseval's Theorem, is

$$\int_{-\infty}^{+\infty} h^2(t)dt = \int_{-\infty}^{+\infty} |H(f)|^2 df \qquad (1)$$

When you look at the Power Spectrum of a typical vibration signal in Figure 1, one thing that can be confusing is the units of the Y axis. For a Power Spectrum, the units are shown as G^2/Hz, or often G_{rms}^2/Hz. It is an indication of the measurement used for the sinusoidal components represented in the Fourier Transform.

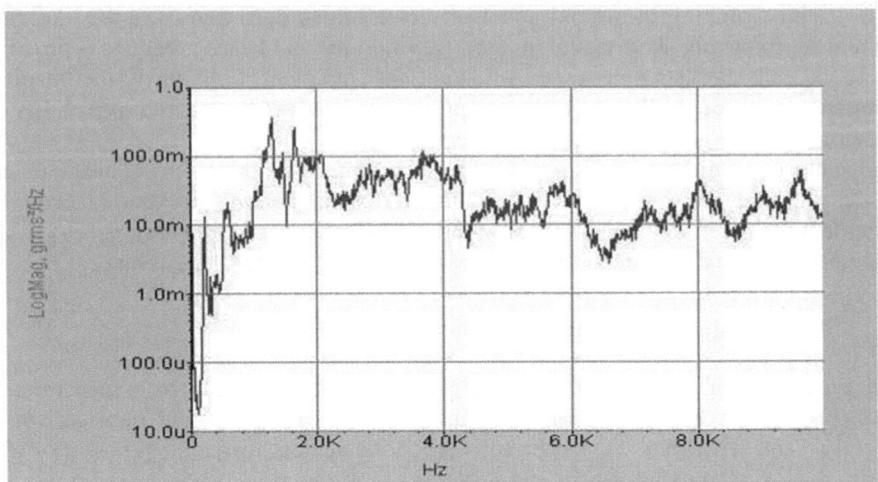

Fig. 1. Power Spectrum of a repetitive shock vibration system

The Fourier Transform of a signal shows the frequency and amplitude of the sine waves that, when summed, would form the time domain signal. If the amplitude of these sine waves is measured as an rms value,then the resultant Y axis units for the Power Spectrum in the frequency domain is G_{rms}^2/Hz. Indeed, the definition of the Power Spectrum requires that the units be in this form. While some spectrum analyzers will allow choices of Y axis units that include G_{rms}^2/Hz, G_{peak}^2/Hz, etc., the only units that result in a Power Spectrum (and hence that can be used to directly calculate G_{rms} as described above) are G_{rms}^2/Hz [4].

2.2   Power Spectral Density (PSD)

Power spectral density function (PSD) shows the strength of the variations (energy) as a function of frequency. In other words, it shows at which frequencies variations are strong and at which frequencies variations are weak. The unit of PSD is energy per frequency (width) and you can obtain energy within a specific frequency range by integrating PSD within that frequency range. Computation of PSD is done directly by the method called FFT or computing autocorrelation function and then transforming it.

PSD is a very useful tool if you want to identify oscillatory signals in your time series data and want to know their amplitude. For example let assume you are operating a factory with many machines and some of them have motors inside. You detect unwanted vibrations from somewhere. You might be able to get a clue to locate offending machines by looking at PSD which would give you frequencies of vibrations. PSD is still useful even if data do not contain any purely oscillatory signals. We quite often compute and plot PSD to get a "feel" of data at an early stage of time series analysis. Looking at PSD is like looking at simple time series plot except that we look at time series as a function of frequency instead of time. Here, we could say that frequency is a transformation of time and looking at variations in frequency domain is just another way to look at variations of time series data. PSD tells us at which frequency ranges variations are strong and that might be quite useful for further analysis [7].

The RMS value of a signal is equal to the standard deviation, assuming a zero mean. The standard deviation is usually represented by sigma σ.

A pure sinusoidal function has the following relationship:

$$peak = \sqrt{2}RMS \tag{2}$$

Random vibration, however, is very complicated. Random vibration has no simple relationship between its peak and RMS values. The peak value of a random time history is typically 3 or 4 times the RMS value.

A power spectral density can be calculated for any type of vibration signal, but it is particularly appropriate for random vibration [6]. There are several equivalent methods for calculating a power spectral density function, as explained in below.

In an analogy to the energy signals, define a function that would give us some indication of the relative power contributions at various frequencies, as $S_f(\omega)$. This function has units of power per Hz and its integral yields the power in f(t) and is known as power spectral density function. Mathematically,

$$p = \frac{1}{2\pi} \int_{-\infty}^{+\infty} S_F(\omega)d\omega \tag{3}$$

Assume that we are given a signal f(t) and we truncate it over the interval (-T/2,T/2). This truncated version is f(t)Π(t/T). If f(t) is finite over the interval (-T/2,T/2) then the truncated function f(t)Π(t/T) has finite energy and its Fourier transform $F_T(\omega)$ is

$$F_T(\omega) = \Gamma\{f(t)\Pi(t/T)\} \tag{4}$$

Parseval's theorem of the truncated version is

$$\int_{-T/2}^{+T/2}|f(t)|^2 dt = \frac{1}{2\pi} \int_{-\infty}^{+\infty}|F_T(\omega)|^2 d\omega \tag{5}$$

Therefore, the average power P across a one-ohm resistor is given by

$$p = \lim_{T\to\infty}\frac{1}{T}\int_{-T/2}^{+T/2}|f(t)|^2 dt = \lim_{T\to\infty}\frac{1}{T}\frac{1}{2\pi}\int_{-\infty}^{+\infty}|F_T(\omega)|^2 d\omega \tag{6}$$

2.3   Probability Distribution Function (PDF)

Dealing with basic probability as a discrete counting process is satisfactory if you have reasonably small numbers, like throwing dice or picking cards. But if the number of events is very large, as in the distribution of energy among the molecules of a gas, then the probability can be approximated by a continuous variable so that the methods of calculus can be used.

Using the variable x to represent a possible outcome or event, then in the discrete case the basic framework could be summarized. If you allow the outcome x to take a continuous range of values, then the probability P(x) takes a different character, since to get a finite result for probability, you must sum the probability over a finite range of x. Since x is a continuous variable, this sum takes the form of an integral. A common practice to define a distribution function as a derivative of the probability,

$$f(x) = \frac{dp(x)}{dx} \tag{7}$$

The probability of finding outcomes between x=a and x=b can then be expressed as

$$\int_a^b f(x)dx = \int_a^b \frac{dp(x)}{dx}dx = \text{probability of finding x between a and b} \tag{8}$$

and the normalization condition is then

$$\int_{x=0}^{\infty} f(x)dx = 1 \tag{9}$$

For application of probability to physical processes, the use of the distribution function is a very useful strategy.

3   Result and Discussion

Schematic of overall vibrations of generator at different dates is given in Figure 2. According to ISO TC108, 1963 standard, the warning and critical reference value of overall vibration velocity level is 7.31 mm/s and 13.33 mm/s respectively. By attention to figure 2, it's seen that vibratory velocity level of generator is in warning status at the sixth and eighth measurement.

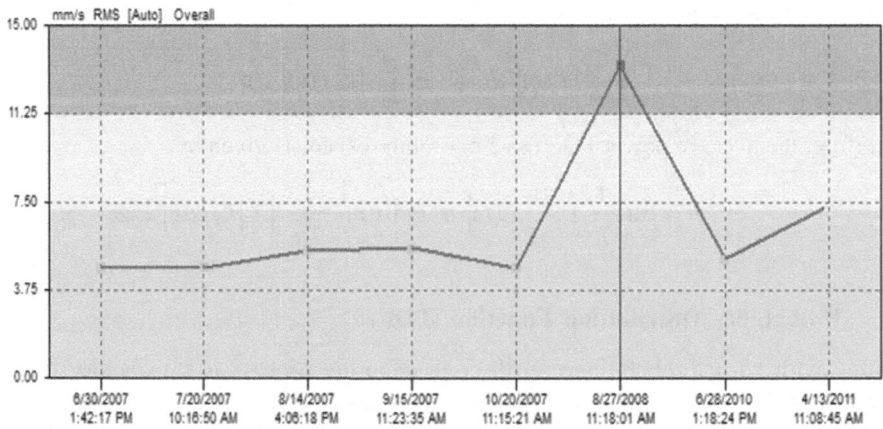

Fig. 2. Overall vibrations of generator

Figure 3 and 4 show frequency spectrum results of generator   in healthy and unhealthy situation, respectively.

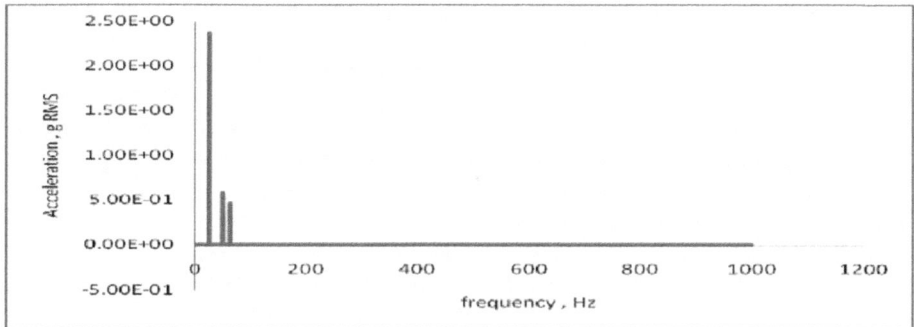

Fig. 3. Frequency spectrom results of generator in healthy situation

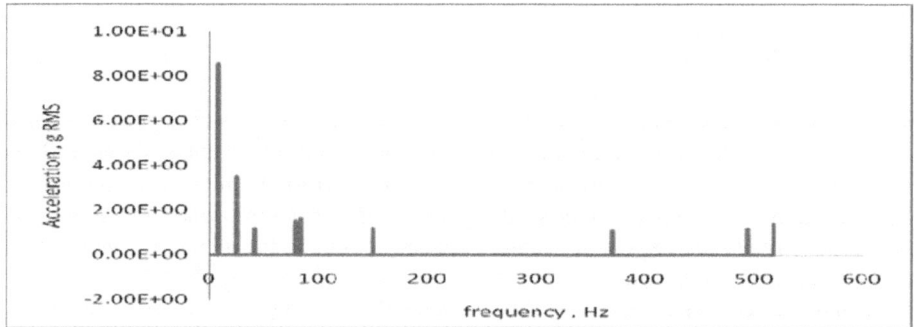

Fig. 4. Frequency spectrom results of generator in unhealthy situation

Figure 5 show the power spectral density of generator   in healthy and unhealthy situation. It's seen that difference between two situations is very big in special range of frequency.

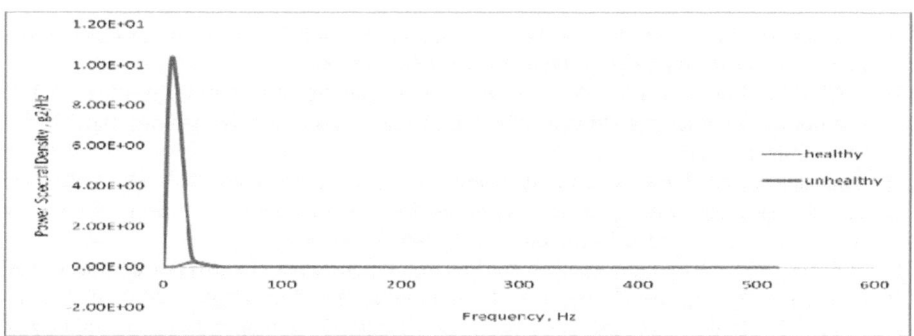

Fig. 5. Power Spectral Density of generator in healthy and unhealthy situation

Figure 6 show the Probability of generator fault in unhealthy situation. Compare to the results of this function about healthy generator, the results show that we had higher probability of faults in this situation. Results are given in Figure 6.

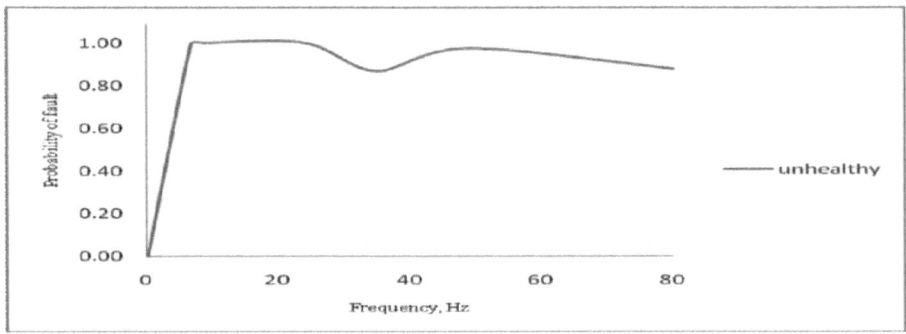

Fig. 6. Probability of generator fault in unhealthy situation

4   Conclusions

Results showed that vibration condition monitoring and Power Spectral Density technique could detect fault diagnosis of generator. Vibration analysis and Power Spectral Density could provide quick and reliable information on the condition of the generator on different faults. Integration of vibration condition monitoring technique with Power Spectral Density analyze could indicate more understanding about diagnosis of generator.

Results showed that we were able to find fault range by Fault Probability Distribution Function technique and also became apparent that in rotary speed of generator we have 100 percent probability of fault. It was first time that we used this function to show that the generator faults.

References

[1] Ahmadi, H.: Power Spectral Density Technique for Fault Diagnosis of an Electromotor. In: International Conference on Electrical Machines (2008)
[2] Patel, P.M., Prajapati, J.M.: A review on artificial intelligent system for bearing condition monitoring. International Journal of Engineering Science and Technology (IJEST) 3(2), 1520–1525 (2011)
[3] Samanta, B., Al-Balushi, K.R., Al-Araimi, S.A.: Artificial neural networks and support vector machines with genetic algorithm for bearing fault detection. Engineering Applications of Artificial Intelligence 16, 657–665 (2003)
[4] Steinberg, D.S.: Vibration Analysis for Electronic Equipment. John Wiley & Sons (1988)
[5] Brighan, E.O.: The Fast Fourier Transform. Prentice Hall, Inc., Englewood Cliffs (1974)
[6] Irvine, T.: Power Spectral Density Units: [G^2/Hz], Vibrationdata.com Publications (1998)
[7] http://www.cygres.com

Design an Adaptive Competency-Based Learning Web Service According to IMS-LD Standard

Nour-eddine El Faddouli, Brahim El Falaki, Mohammed Khalidi Idrissi,
and Samir Bennani

Computer Science Department, Mohammadia Engineering School, Mohammed Vth
University Agdal, BP 765, Agdal Avenue Ibnsina Rabat, Morocco
{faddouli,elfalaki,khalidi,sbennani}@emi.ac.ma

Abstract. Equal opportunities and the democratization of education, promoted by
the establishment of the same content for all learners, can stigmatize and widen
the differences and inequalities. Thus, the learner's heterogeneity is inevitable and
often regarded as unmanageable. Thus, customizing the environment to learners
improve the learning process quality. There are several adaptation approaches of
e-learning environment, such as; adaptive hypermedia system, semantic web, etc.
In our proposed service, we adopt the competency based approach (CBA), and we
consider that the adaptation relevance depends on the adequacy of the information
collected through a personal diagnosis. This diagnostic takes place via an adaptive
test using the Item Response Theory (IRT) in a formative perspective without trying to situate the learner in relation to others. This intelligent test, administered
items in an appropriate order in a short time and produces relevant results. Thus
learning system can lead the learner to gradually acquire a competency taking into
account its needs and predispositions. The system will be implemented as an activity in a pedagogical scenario defined responding to the learner's needs, while
aligning with the norms and standards. Thus, some technical choices are required
as far as standards and norms are concerned

Keywords: E-learning, adaptive learning system, Service Oriented Architecture, item response theory, learner model IMS-LIP, IMS-LD, IMS-QTI,
IMS-RDCEO, LOM.

1   Introduction and Context

In Traditional mode, equal opportunities and the democratization of education, promoted by the establishment of the same content for all learners, can stigmatize and
widen the differences and inequalities. Thus, the heterogeneity of learners is inevitable and often regarded as unmanageable. Concretely, learners have different
objectives and predispositions. Thus, an optimal learning path for one learner is not
necessarily the same for the other [1]. Consequently, Adapting learning path is crucial
to manage learner differences. However, to achieve this adaptation, many approaches
can be considered. Our approach [2] proposes the implementation of adaptive test in
formative perspective as a means to adaptive learning system. The proposed system
relies mainly on assessment and the Competency-based learning [3].

P. Pichappan, H. Ahmadi, and E. Ariwa (Eds.): INCT 2011, CCIS 241, pp. 37–47, 2011.
© Springer-Verlag Berlin Heidelberg 2011

The purpose is to individualize the learning path through a personalized diagnosis of learner. To design the proposed service, first, we modelled competency. Then, we modelled learner according to competency based approach (CBA) [4]. Then, we design a bank of items (questions) calibrated on a common scale by using the TRI [5]. This will provide a series of consecutively selected items. The answer to an item determines the selection of the next one taking into account the previous responses and performances recorded in the learner model. To achieve this goal, we implement adaptive test using the Item Response Theory (IRT). Then, we consider assessment as an activity to incorporate into a learning unit in a platform. To enable reuse and operability, the environment will be designed according to standards, such as IMS-LD [6], IMS-QTI [7] and IMS-LIP [8] that we will discuss to justify our choice.

The next section deals with the individualization in learning and tackles the adaptive learning system. The ensuing section concern the proposed service that will regulate learning process using the enhanced formative assessment cycle and IRT to administrate the optimal item and estimate skill level. Standards adopted to interact with our proposed web service will be presented and justified in section 3, and we terminate with a conclusion and perspectives

2   Individualization of Learning

The individualization concept in learning involves a set of procedures and educational theories to organize training. In this organization, first, we must build a learning path taking into account an individual request, expressed or implied. Then precede this path via planned and regulatory activities to achieve purpose or skill expected. The regulatory activities will take into account the learner level, his experiences and expectations.

The individualization goal is to adjust the learning path focusing on the design of learning sequences. Its implementation, in an educational adaptive system, is the same for all learners who are not doing necessarily the same thing, but they use the same standard tools.

The learning adaptation is implemented through the adaptive learning systems; its purpose is to provide each learner with the feeling that the training is designed specifically to meet their expectations taking into account their capacities. These systems implement methods and techniques to provide activities and educational content customized. The mechanisms vary from system to another and can be summarized mainly in adaptive hypermedia systems, semantic web or theories from the education field. However, most research work focuses on the production of educational resources and referrals without giving importance to their operation.

In our proposal, the adaptation is based on the learner identification, his ability, prior knowledge and current performance for the acquisition of competency. Thus, we stipulate that two ingredients are essential, namely learner modelling and a relevant diagnosis vis-à-vis the current activity. In this perspective, we modelled [9] formative assessment to offer to the learning system a relevant diagnosis to regulate the learning process to each learner.

In this paper, it would be prominent to justify our technical choices that will support the operationalization of educational theory implemented in the proposed service.

These theories are essentially; the CBA and formative adaptive assessment by proposing adaptive test administrating optimal items in a sequence taking into account the characteristics and progression of learner.

3   Proposed Service

The implemented system comprises, besides the three processes of formative assessment [10], a step that we found necessary to insert between the interpretation and regulation processes: Service Pre-Regulation [11].

3.1   The Observation Process

To reorient the learning process for a learner, we must have an idea about their effective level of competence. In this stage (Fig.1), we calculate the actual level of competence (current) noted θ_{eff} of the learner and identifies the level required θ_s to deduce the competency gap noted E_c: $E_c = \theta_s - \theta_{eff}$

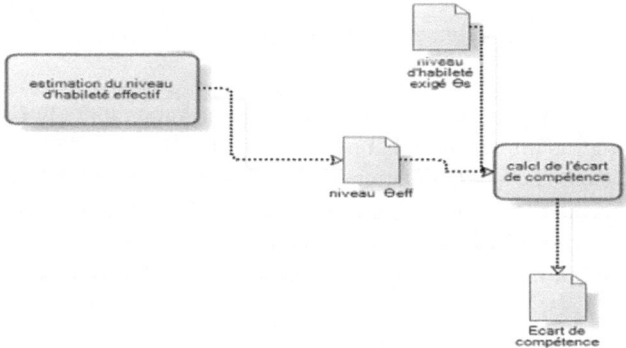

Fig. 1. Internal logic of the observation service

3.2   Intervention Process

The interpretation process (Fig.2) starts with catching the result of the previous step: the competency gap E_c and the effective competency level θ_{eff}. Then, if the gap is not tolerated, the actual level of competence θ_{eff} is transmitted to the pre-regulation service. Finally, if the difference is tolerated for the third iteration, the learner model is updated by the competency level θ_{eff} instead of the level recorded θ_s, and regulation process will take the hand to determine the regulatory activity

3.3   Pre- regulation Process

The learning environment implement, in most cases, conventional tests in which the questions presented to learners and their sequence are the same. In this step, a relevant diagnosis must be established through an adaptive testing. In an adaptive test, the order of questions administered to the learner is not predefined. It varies the items

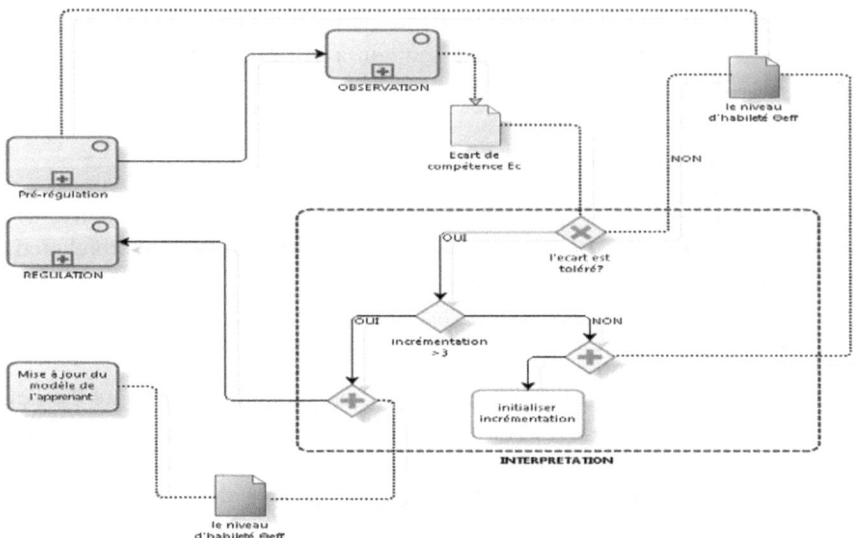

Fig. 2. Internal logic of the observation service

presented to the learner based on their responses on items already passed. Each answer of the learner is information that refines the estimate of his level of competence.

In our proposal, the pre-regulation process implements an adaptive test, which takes place according to the item response theory (IRT) [4]. Is to design the path (trajectory) for optimum evaluation from all items meeting the IMS QTI specifications and calibrated to an assumption by the adaptive tests. This process has two components [4].

1) a component for selecting the optimal item
2) a component for estimating the skill level of the learner.

4   Models to Implement the Web Service in the Platform

The emergence of distance learning platforms invites stakeholders to seek ways to integrate technology learning objects and control their use. In our work, the service implementation in a platform requires its integration in an educational scenario. Several standards exist, so we have to choose one that responds efficiently to our context. Therefore, a comparative study of LOM, SCORM and IMS LD is needed.

4.1   SCORM

Created as part of the Advanced Distributed Learning (ADL) [12], SCORM is a standard for course design in learning management systems. It is a reference model that allows e-learning systems to find, import, share, reuse and export learning content.

SCORM format is independent of context and execution environment. The model includes three major elements:

1) SCORM Content Aggregation Model:
Its purpose is to structure content using three classes: the aggregation of content (Content Aggregation), the basic unit of SCO (Sharable Content Object) and the resource asset. Thus, this element defines a representation structure that breaks the course content into pieces (Fig.3), with the highest level course (organization), composed of blocks, which are themselves composed of sub-blocks (SCO). The SCO is the most basic level of content that can be reused. It is independent of any educational context, and the execution of other SCO. It consists of Assets, ie digital resources such as text, images, etc. Finally, each level (asset, SCO, item, organization) has a set of descriptive metadata. This metadata, in earlier versions, are from the IMS Learning Resource Meta-data Information Model, based on the LOM [13]. Currently in its latest specification 1.2 published on 1 October 2001, has defined its own SCORM Content Packaging Information Model, which extend IMS Content Packaging Information Model [14] with more factors specific to SCORM.

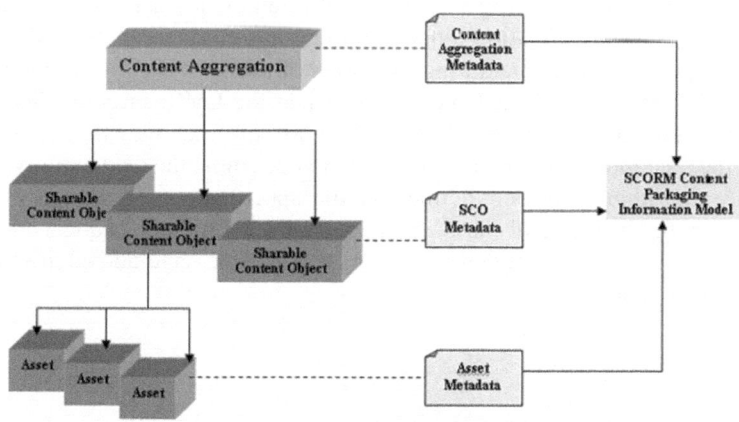

Fig. 3. Aggregation Model in SCORM standard

2) Run Time Environment for content management in the platform through the definition of the execution environment and API for communication;

3) Sequencing and Navigation Model:
When a student leaves a SCO, the sequencing process is responsible for determining what happens next. It orchestrates the flow and status of the course as a whole. In SCORM 2004, the sequencing and navigation specification are derived from the standard IMS Simple Sequencing (IMS SS) specification. In sequencing, aggregations and SCO are designated by the generic term "activity". Thus, every element is an activity. Sequencing activities correspond to the elements in the manifest of the

course. They are embedded within the father-son relationships and organized in a tree of activities.

Each activity has two sets of data associated with it: (1) monitoring data "tracking data" representing the current state of activity (status, score, etc.). And (2) data to define the sequence "sequencing definition". This data is managed through the two following models:

a) The tracking model "Tracking Model":
The pattern of activity followed by capture data representing the current state of the activity, the state of completion, the state of satisfaction, the score and data on the progress of each learner. It also monitors some data specifically related to the sequence as the number of attempts on the activity.

b) The model definition sequencing "Sequencing Definition Model"
The model definition defines the rules for sequencing path and sequence and how this activity should be sequenced and is specified in the manifest of the course. Thus, it describes how SCORM content can be organized according to events navigation initiated by the learner or by the system.

The sequencing process (Fig.4) is activated when the learner starts a course, even a SCO or expresses a navigation request through an interface of the LMS. When the sequencer is invoked the data during execution of the SCO are transferred to the business model followed by "Tracking Model." Then the LMS starts the "loop sequencing." Loop sequencing is a set of defined algorithms and rules that apply to all the sequencing data monitoring being conducted to determine the next activity.

These algorithms are well defined in the specification of sequencing a set of pseudo-code the behavior of the LMS should reflect. The loop sequence leads to: (1) the choice of an activity, (2) leaves the course, (3) a message delivered to the learner or (4) an error condition.

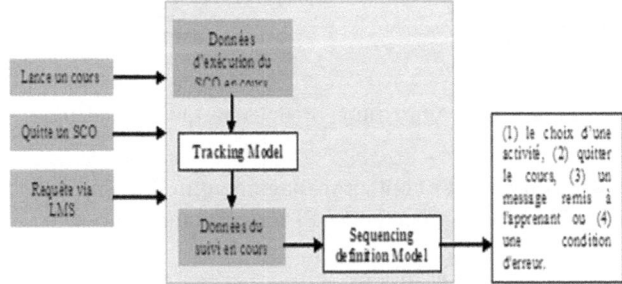

Fig. 4. Sequencing and navigation in the SCORM standard

Content authors are able to specify sequencing rules via an XML document in the manifesto of the course. Each activity has a definition of complete sequence associated with it (Fig.5).

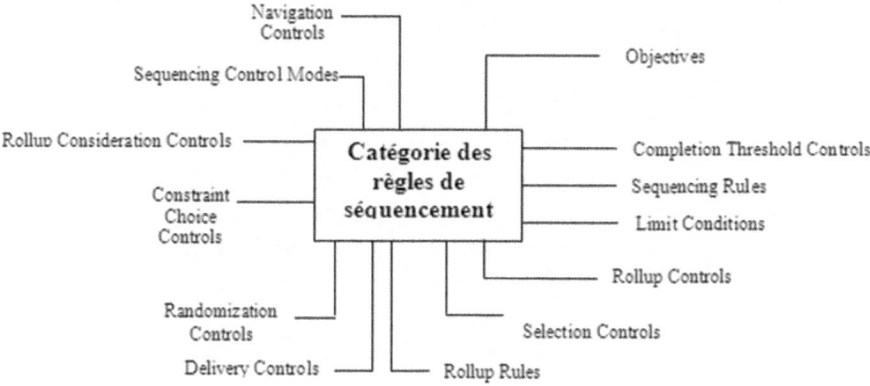

Fig. 5. Some categories of sequencing rules

4.2 IMS LD

The IMS-LD specification [15] is based on a meta-model (Fig.. 6) that uses the theatrical metaphor to define the structure of a unit of learning (learning design) as a set of acts, each consisting of partitions combining activities (activities) and roles [17].

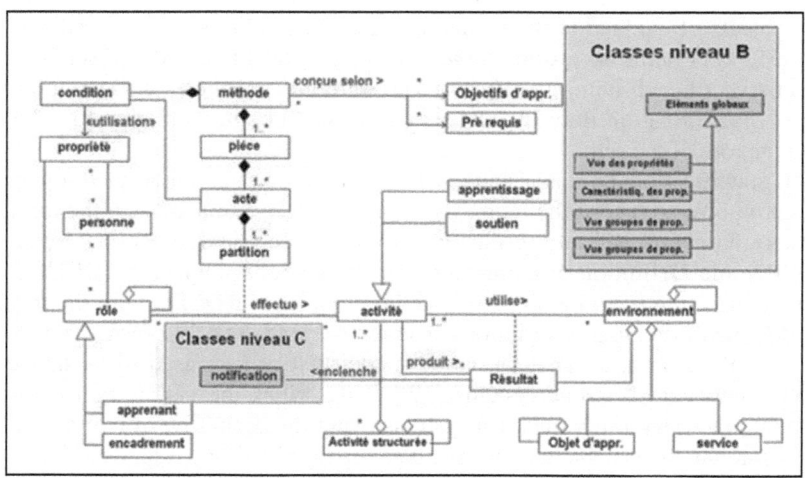

Fig. 6. The activity according to IMS-LD specifications [16]

The involvement of different actors in a learning unit is described and organized according to a scenario, using an environment.

IMS LD is the result of work-OUNL EML and also incorporates other existing specifications.

• IMS Content Packaging: IMS Learning Design describes "learning units" according to a standardized "IMS Content Package" (Fig.7).

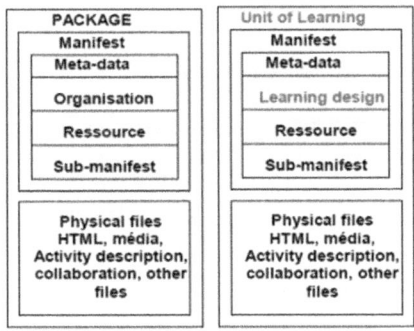

Fig. 7. IMS Content Packaging and learning unit [15]

• IMS Simple Sequencing: This specification is used for scheduling of learning objects and "services" in an "environment" (an "environment" is part of "Learning Design"). This promotes the reuse of "environment" other "units of learning".
• IMS / LOM Meta-Data: The LOM is used for defining metadata.
• IMS Question and Test Interoperability: we plan to expand to allow the calibration of item objects of evaluation in an adaptive test. This calibration is intended to rehabilitate IMS-QTI items according to participate in an adaptive test by establishing the characteristics of each item, namely, (a) The setting of difficulty of the item, (b) The setting of discrimination Item (c) The setting of the guessing and item (d) The maximum asymptote of the item.

In this specification, an item includes the information that is presented to a meeting and those on how to record the item. The scoring will take place when the candidate's responses are transformed into results through the processing rules for answers.
• IMS Reusable Definition of Competency or Educational Objective (RDCEO) [18]: We can describe the learning objectives and prerequisites RDCEO with the format, as can be done with free text descriptions. The format IMS-RDCEO formalizes the definition of skills. It defines an information model that can be used to exchange these definitions between different systems [19]. It describes the skills regardless of the context and interoperability between systems using the definition of competence. The specification has the competence in five categories: identifier, title, description, definition and metadata.
• IMS Learner Information Package. IMS LIP can be used as a model for the properties of the LD (learning model). IMS LIP model defines a structure of user data into eleven categories [table] are: Identification, Accessibility, QCL, Activity, Goal, Competency, Interest, Transcript, Affiliation, SecurityKey, and Relationship.

After analyzing the three models (LOM, SCORM and IMS LD), three main approaches emerged successively: data indexing languages, models of IT implementation and finally the educational modeling languages [17]. Our synthesis (Fig.8) extends this analysis by including: (1) the notion of activity, structure and sequencing and (2) the ability to develop theories and approaches

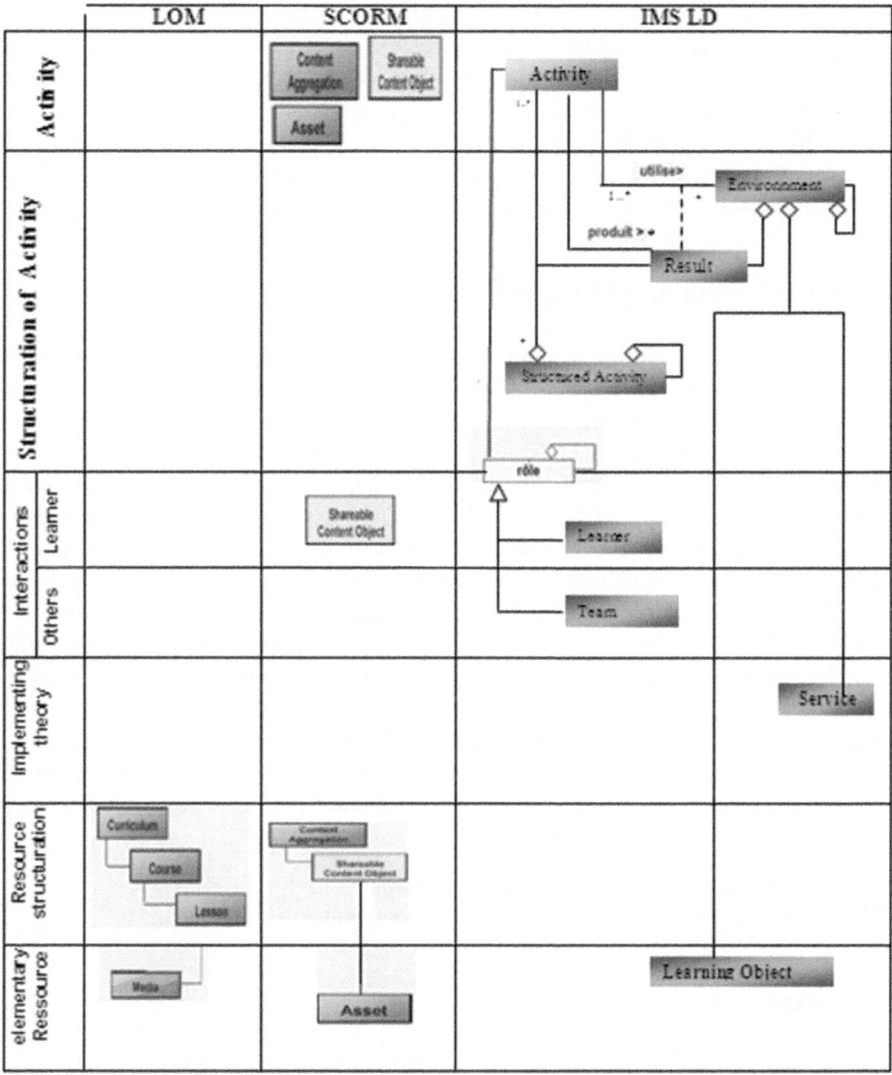

Fig. 8. Comparative study of standards

The study that we conducted, we find that the LOM model is designed to return the production of learning objects; it promotes a type of learning-centered content. on the SCORM, which is an application profile of LOM, it appeared to facilitate the technical operation of the objects on the Internet with the advent of platforms of open and distance learning. Finally, IMS LD as a modeling language teaching pedagogy that places the center of the process by providing methods and modeling tools of learning situations

IMS LD does not impose any pedagogical models, it is a pedagogical metamodel. In our proposal, the adoption of IMS LD is justified by its ability to integrate the notion of activity and the ability to support the development of theories and pedagogical approaches (table). Also, it integrates IMS RDCEO (objectives and prerequisites), IMS LIP (Learner), IMS Simple Sequencing (reusability of the environment)

The choice of IMS LD is motivated by references and recent efforts for implementations in many engineering educational system and development of several tools for modeling and execution of pedagogical scenarios (Reload, CopperCore,..).

5   Conclusion and Perspectives

To provide an interactive environnment tailored to the learner's needs is one of the most important goals of e-learning environments. Interactivity and adaptation do not rely solely on technical artefacts, but are the result of a combination involving educational theory, and technological advances in the field of ICT

Several studies have addressed the individualization from different angles. Ours is different, both in the approach and tools; it offers a system that individualizes the evaluation process offering a personalized diagnosis to decide upon the remediation activity. In the implementation of the proposed system, interoperability and reuse justify the choice of components and the environment interacting with the system. As far as the technical architecture is concerned, we adhere to our research team's global vision. In this vision, the e-learning platform should be composed of a set of reusable, interoperable and interacting services

The proposed service is the composition of the four services. This service will be implemented as an activity in a learning unit. In this scenarization several standards are possible. In our proposal, we opted for the standard IMS LD. Several perspectives are considered, and can be summarized in:

1) The deployment and testing in a learning unit.
2) The collecting and analysis of formative assessment activity traces.

References

1. Perrenoud, P.: Construire des compétences dès l'école. ESF, Paris (2000)
2. El Falaki, B., Khalidi Idrissi, M., Bennani, S.: Formative assessment in e-learning: an approach to personnalize diagnosis and adapt learning path. In: IADIS e-Society 2010 (ES 2010), à Porto, Portugal, pp. 391–395 (2010) ISBN: 978-972-8939-07-6
3. El Faddouli, N., El Falaki, B., Khalidi Idrissi, M., Bennani, S.: Towards an Adaptive competency-based learning System using assessment. International Journal of Computer Science Issues 8(1) (January 2011) ISSN (Online): 1694-0814
4. El Faddouli, N., El Falaki, B., Khalidi Idrissi, M., Bennani, S.: Formative adaptive testing service web to individualize elearning process. International Journal of Engineering Science and Technology (IJEST) 3(6) (June 2011) ISSN : 0975-5462
5. El Faddouli, N., El Falaki, B., Khalidi Idrissi, M., Bennani, S.: Adaptive assessment in learning system. In: Proceedings of IADIS International Conference E-Learning 2011, Rome, Italy, July 20-23, vol. II, p. 306 (2011) ISBN: 978-972-8939-38-0

6. IMS LD IMS. IMS Learning Design Information Model, IMS Global Learning Consortium, `http://imsglobal.org/learningdesign/`
7. IMS Question and Test Interoperability, Version 2.1 public draft (revision 2) specification (2006), `http://www.imsglobal.org/question/`
8. IMS Learning Design Information Model, Version 1.0 Final Specification, `http://www.imsglobal.org/learningdesign/ldv1p0/imsld_infov1p0.html#1529256`
9. Khalidi Idrissi, M., El Falaki, B., Bennani, S.: Implementing the formative assessment within competency-based-approach applied in e-learning. In: 3rd International Conference on SIIE, Sousse, Tunisia, 18-20, pp. 362–368. IHE edn. (2010) ISBN: 978-9973-868-24-4
10. Allal, L., Mottier Lopez, L.: Régulation des apprentissages en situation scolaire et en formation. De Boeck, Bruxelles (2007)
11. El Falaki, B., Khalidi Idrissi, M., Bennani, S.: A Formative Assessment Model within competency-based-approach for an Individualized E-learning Path. World Academy of Science, Engineering and Technology (64), 208–212 (2010) ISSN 1307-6892
12. ADL SCORM, Advanced Distributed Learning, `http://www.adlnet.org/`
13. Advanced Distributed Learning (ADL), Sharable Content Object Reference Model (SCORM) — Content Aggregation Model (CAM) Version 1.3
14. IMS Global Learning Consortium, Inc., IMS Content Packaging Specification V1.1.2, `http://www.imsproject.org/content/packaging/index.html`
15. IMS, `http://www.imsglobal.org/`
16. IMS Global Learning Consortium, Inc., IMS Learning Design Information Model (2006a)
17. Pernin, J.P., Lejeune, A.: Dispositifs d'Apprentissage Instrumentés par les Technologies: vers une ingénierie centrée sur les scénarios. In: actes du colloque, TICE 2004, Compiègne, pp. 407–414 (October 2004)
18. IMS GLC (2002), `http://www.imsglobal.org/specificationdownload.cfm`
19. CEN/ISSS cwa 15455, A European Model for Learner Competencies", ICS 03.180; 35.240.99 (November 2005)

Resolving Impassiveness in Service Oriented Architecture

Masoud Arabfard and Seyed Morteza Babamir

Department of Computer Engineering, University of Kashan, Kashan, Iran
Arabfard@grad.kashanu.ac.ir,
Babamir@kashanu.ac.ir

Abstract. In a Service Oriented Architecture, service registry called UDDI (Universal Description Discovery & Integration) is used as a database that includes description of published services. UDDI has an important defect called impassiveness that means the lack of consumer interaction with UDDI after he/she found some desired service. This means that consumers are not notified when some deletion or change of a service happens in UDDI. This paper aims to deal with resolving the problem of UDDI impassiveness by means of techniques of active database rules. To this end, we present new architecture for UDDI. In addition, the proposed architecture puts Web service invocation with toleration and includes the consumer classification.

Keywords: Service Oriented Architecture, Web service, UDDI, Active Database.

1 Introduction

Service Oriented Architecture called SOA [1] provides a suitable infrastructure for collaboration and integration of application programs. SOA is an enterprise-scale IT architecture for connecting resources on appeal. These resources are represented as services which can participate and be constituted in an enterprise, or line of business to accomplish business needs. A service is a software resource which has a service description for describing an operation. The service description is available for searching, binding and invocation by a consumer. The service description implementation is accomplished through a service provider who delivers quality of service requirements for the consumer [2]. Enterprise applications are being architected in an SOA style progressively, in which components to complete the business logic are constituted. The properties of such applications are improved as a way for an active business to adapt its processes to an ever changing landscape of opportunities, priorities, partners and competitors quickly [3]. In SOA, as we have shown in Figure 1, service information is exchanged between service repository called UDDI and service consumers and service producers [4]. UDDI is a platform-independent framework for describing services, discovering businesses, and integrating business services. UDDI uses WSDL to describe interfaces to Web services. In other words:

- UDDI is an acronym for Universal Description, Discovery and Integration
- UDDI is a directory for storing information of Web services

P. Pichappan, H. Ahmadi, and E. Ariwa (Eds.): INCT 2011, CCIS 241, pp. 48–60, 2011.

- UDDI is a directory of Web service interfaces described by WSDL
- UDDI communicates via SOAP

UDDI undertakes task of registering Web services provided by the producers and task of discovering Web services request by consumers [5]. In SOA, services are distributed components published on the Web [6]. UDDI [7] is a database consisting of published services description (Figure 2). This description describes specific information about services providers such that any service provider can include one or more Web services. Web services include one or more templates called BINDING. Any template is related to a specific operation of service. Each service includes an access point through which the desired service can be invoked. It should be noted that any template of TMODEL adhere to a TMODEL feature that defines the services means that what this Web service supports operations [6].

UDDI renders a directory for the publication, discovery and retention of categorized Web services. A UDDI directory is implemented by an application termed UDDI registry, which is comprised of several data-holding entities called the UDDI nodes. Service registries play an important role in SOA. Most today service registries comply with UDDI specifications, whose initial focus was geared to working as UBR (Universal Business Registry), a master directory for all public Web services. UDDI Information is stored as tables within a database. But this database has the passive form, that is, after a consumer finds one's desired service he has no interaction with this database. However, this work may get into trouble the consumer. Once the Web services addresses change or the desired Web service is removed, the consumer will not be notified that may result in error when it reuses Web services. To gain new Web service address it has to query the UDDI database.

This paper aims to present an idea to resolve the impassiveness of this database to solve the problem of being passive UDDI and adds some capabilities to the database. The general problems of UDDI are introduced in Section 2. The main basics of active database are presented in Section 3 and in Section 4 a proposed model for repository monitoring is provided. In Section 5 the proposed model is compared with some other models and finally the results achieved by comparison are shown in the form of a table in Section 6 .The future work is also provided in the last Section.

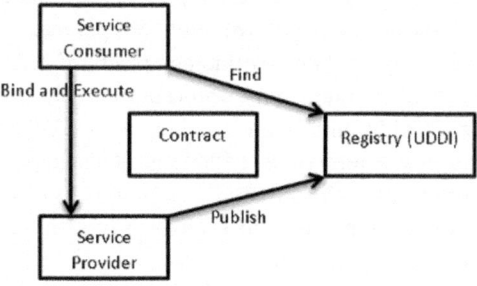

Fig. 1. SOA Architecture

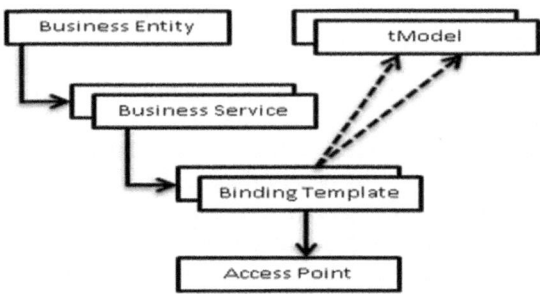

Fig. 2. UDDI Structure

2   UDDI Fundamental Problems

An UDDI is to hold information about Web services created by providers and acts as an interface for introducing Web service to the consumer. Several disadvantages are discussed for UDDI [6]:

- In the terms of structure: This is related to the implementation of Web services.
- In terms of lack of sufficient Meta: It is used to describe the operation of Web services.
- The long process: To discover and to select services (these are not reviewed in this paper).

These are many problems for UDDI. These disadvantages include broken and invalid links or irrelevant entries. To inhibit these problems, there is a need of having a general mechanism for removing outdated entries from the UDDI. Also, a mechanism for validating entries must be in place. In other words, the integrity of the data in the UDDI registry must be respected. But UDDI major disadvantage is that it is related to being passive of UDDI, meaning that if any service is removed or access point changes, consumer will not be aware of it unless he/she would visit the repository again and recover information again. Passive repository can block the operation to be done. For example as shown in paper [8] only 34 percent of total Web services addresses are valid and many of them are facing structural error and an also a lot of them have been edited after publishing information. These are the reasons for occurrence of an error. In addition to mentioned cases, a UDDI repository is a simple repository that only registers and finds addresses. This paper aims to resolve the impassiveness of repository as well as to add capabilities to this repository to develop its effectiveness from simple repository to a modern repository. We consider adding the following capabilities for this repository:

- Fault tolerance for invoking Web services.
- Classification of consumers according to defined categories.
- Introducing new Web services to related consumers.

- Ability to get statistics by the repository and the centralized management.
- Interoperability consumers through the repository.

As noted UDDI repository is passive because UDDI is a database that we can support the mentioned capabilities through activation of this database in the form of active database.

3   Active Database

First of all, it is necessary to understand the concept of active systems. According to [9], an active database management system (Figure 3) is a system that react the events appropriately without intervention of user to resolve the impassiveness of systems. According to [10], there are two methods of implementation. The first method is that any application that manipulates the database verifies necessary condition; of course this method is poor method in software engineering.

The second method is to write an application that verifies the necessary condition cyclically. But in our active system the system's responsibility is to monitor itself, that is, it is not required to monitor conditions by the application and when conditions are appropriate, the systems will perform appropriate actions dynamically [11]. For example, we can express safety sensitive systems that in certain conditions it must do the appropriate reaction. In active systems events use active rules to verify specific conditions and these rules are described in the form of <E,C,A>,E stands for event and C stands for Condition and A stands for Action and it is called ECA rules. Parts of an ECA are defined as follows: An event happens inside or outside of the system at a time instant and the system detects it. A condition is a predicate that allows/disallows firing the rule. When this predicate is set to true, the action is carried out. The action is an operation that must be carried out to answer the event. The ECA rules are implemented in database by means of triggers. Triggers are mechanisms for implementation of ECA rules in relational database systems. A trigger is a stored procedure that is invoked in response to a certain and specific change in database by the system itself. An active rule is described in the form of relation (1) [12].

$$\text{ON EVENT IF CONDITION THEN ACTION   (1)}$$

An active system has the following advantages:

- Certainty of High operation
- Increasing Performance
- Reducing volume of applications
- Rapid detection of abnormal events and Notification users
- Centralized control of monitoring services

This paper aims to resolve the impassiveness of UDDI repository according to advantages of active databases.

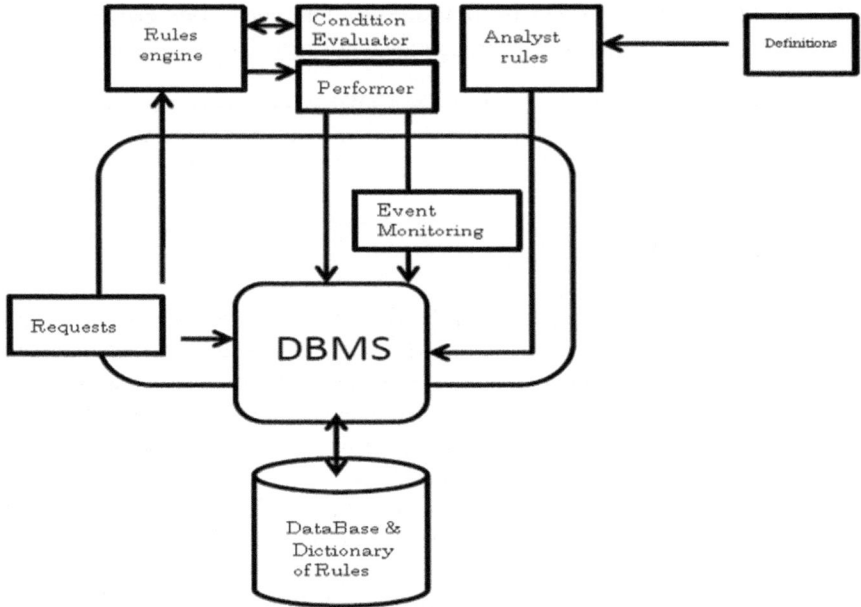

Fig. 3. Active database architecture

4   Proposing Model for Monitoring UDDI

In SOA, UDDI repository as a simple repository is used only to search and register a service, but we want to solve the problem of being passive regarding a change in structure of UDDI database into active database and since active database contain some advantages we add capabilities to UDDI according to these advantages.

Our proposed model (Figure 4) as original SOA model contains three components but the difference is that the other repository is not an ordinary repository. However this repository is an active repository that includes a series of trigger to inform the consumers.

These triggers are written on service table and when adding a new service or editing or deletion of other services is occurred, these triggers do necessary notification to consumers and also when the address of a service or an operation of service will be edited, the new address or new capabilities of service should be notified to the consumers. Meanwhile all of these works can be implemented by Triggers.

Figure 5 shows the state diagram. As an example, when a new service is added to the services table (the INSERT event is occurred in the database), consumers would be automatically notified with this new event in order to update their information on new service inclusion.

Trigger 1 is applied to achieve this goal. In addition to new service inclusion, the alteration trigger may use when Web service attributes are altered (e.g. changing Web service address) which is appeared in the Trigger 2. Similarly deletion trigger is enabled whenever a service is removed from service repository (e.g. the service is no longer supported by the service provider), shown as Trigger 3.

The activation process is unfolded by these triggers and ECA rules formulated for them. Besides the monitor, there is also an extra component called Observer which is responsible for frequently retrieving service list from repository. Then, it checks availability of each service in time intervals and if there is an unavailable service, observer informs the monitor. Consequently, the monitor will broadcast service unavailability to all service consumers. Interactions between repository and extra components are shown in Figure 6.

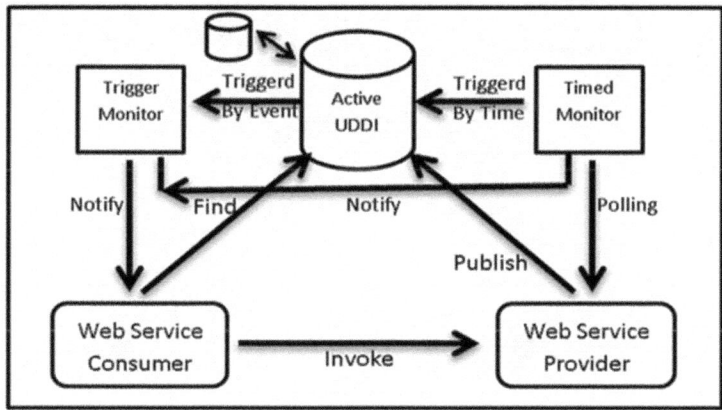

Fig. 4. The Proposed Model

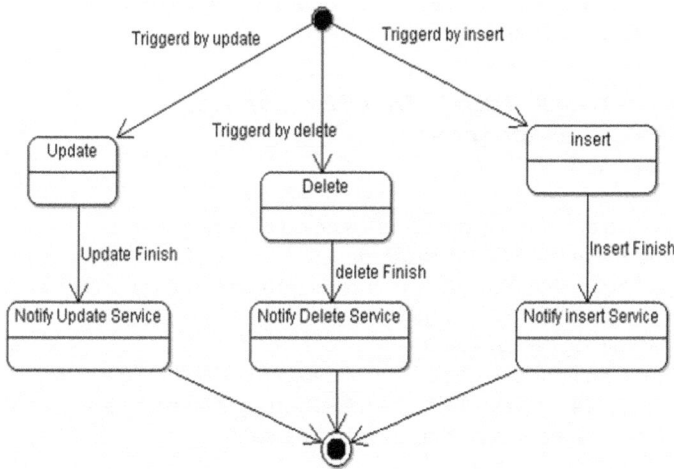

Fig. 5. State diagram for monitor

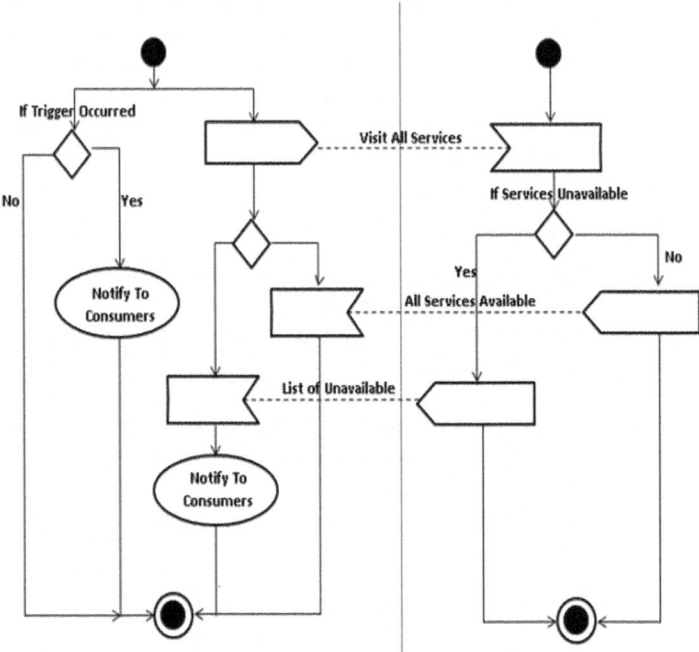

Fig. 6. State diagram for monitor

In this interaction if the trigger occurs, monitor will immediately notify relevant consumers. Even if observer realizes unavailability of a service during observation, it informs all service consumers; otherwise it would not do anything at all.

The trigger structure is as follows:

```
1. ALTER TRIGGER [dbo].[notify_insert]
   ON [dbo].[endpoints]
   AFTER insert AS
   BEGIN
        declare @endpoint nvarchar(max)
        declare @cmd sysname
        select @endpoint=access_point from inserted
        declare @type_inst nvarchar(1)
        set @type_inst=0
        set @cmd='h:\Notifier.exe '+CAST (@endpoint as
        nvarchar(max))+' '+CAST(@type_inst as nvarchar(1))
        exec test..xp_cmdshell @cmd

   END
```

```
2.  ALTER TRIGGER [dbo].[notify_update]
    ON  [dbo].[endpoints]
    AFTER update AS
    BEGIN
        declare @endpoint nvarchar(max)
        declare @cmd sysname
        select @endpoint=access_point from inserted
        declare @type_inst nvarchar(1)
        set @type_inst=2
        set @cmd='h:\ Notifier.exe '+CAST(@endpoint as
        nvarchar(max))+' '+CAST(@type_inst as nvarchar(1))
        exec test..xp_cmdshell @cmd
    END

3.  ALTER TRIGGER [dbo].[notify_delete]
    ON  [dbo].[endpoints]
    AFTER delete AS
    BEGIN
        declare @endpoint nvarchar(max)
        declare @cmd sysname
        declare @type_inst nvarchar(1)
        set @type_inst=1
        select @endpoint=access_point from deleted
        set @cmd='h:\ Notifier.exe '+CAST(@endpoint as
        nvarchar(max))+' '+CAST(@type_inst as nvarchar(1))
        exec test..xp_cmdshell @cmd
    END
```

Table 1. Strenghs and Weaknesses of the proposed model

Weaknesses	Strengths
1. To hold additional information about consumers. 2. To overhead time for notification of consumers.	1. Prevent errors in invoking Web services. 2. Central management of consumers and ability of consumer's census while using Web services. 3. Introducing new Web service with new capabilities. 4. Interaction between the consumers to cooperate with each other. 5. Ability of consumer's category on the base of various Web services.

It is clear that we need keep consumers information to notify them and this information includes the access point to consumers. This why that we add a small database to keep users information along with UDDI database which this additional database gives us other capabilities such as the ability for category of consumers.

This database includes tables for storing the address of consumer with an address of service which is used and also includes table to store information about active service and passive service and includes other table related to capabilities that were stated in Section 2. As seen in Figure 4 first of all producers register his Web service in active repository and then the consumer can find this service and then invoke it meanwhile the repository introduce a new Web service to other consumers related to this category of service.

This work is done by insert trigger. If you pay attention to Figure 4, in addition to 3 main components, there is an extra module consists of an observer and a monitor. This component polls to repository in the terms of time, and when the Web service is not available, this component notifies it to its consumers.

These two components enable UDDI repository and act as a trigger monitor so that aware for happening trigger. The monitor retrieves the relevant information from the additional database to notify to consumers from the event. The additional task of serving to monitor that our monitor according to the time take information services on the UDDI repository and poll the service. If the service is not available, it notify to trigger monitor and also trigger monitor inform unavailability of the service to the relevant consumers.

But adding these two components to the original model has strengths and weakness. Table 1 shows strengths and weaknesses of the proposed model. This proposed model is relevant to resolving impassiveness of UDDI repository.

5   Related Works

Resolving the impassiveness of UDDI repository is one on of the research topics that little focus has been done on it and the most of researches is based on activation by a broker. In [13, 14], we introduced broker structures for activating qualities and security of Web services. By activating UDDI, [15] implemented a distributed active service repository for monitoring services. By monitoring all service operations, it considers a monitor to service status that triggers in terms of time. However, the monitoring technique described in the distributed form has some difficulties. One of them is that reaction of monitoring is based on the time. This leads to a series of problems occurred for the consumers including invoking an invalid service when monitor is activated through the time. In [16] impassiveness is resolved by the RSS in which there are a series of information collectors and RSS collects services information and it notifies consumers by means of this the information.

In [17], the main focus is allocated to keep fault tolerance and dynamic invoking of Web services. In this paper there is an active Web service that keeps a list of both active services and inactive ones. In this paper active service is able to send a series of orders to rest of services and when the message of service unavailability is received, active service changes information related to active Web service in its list. It notifies this information through a SOAP message to consumers and it also detects availability of Web services again and invokes them dynamically. The main problem of this research in active service is known as a bottleneck.

In [6] the focus is on discovering and invoking Web services dynamically in which a model is discussed. In this model there are two queues which keep a list of active services and inactive ones. In this model, there is a listener which copes with the management of repository through periodical polling and it polls services and it puts pooled services at the end of relevant queue so as to keep services' priority and it puts inactive services that are activated in queue of active services.

In [4], based on broker some architecture for Web service monitoring is described in which a monitor is put for each Web service and it controls all cases of Web services and reports this case to the broker. This model is established to control quality of Web services.

In [19], architecture is expressed as a specific service quality monitoring that adds a component called the broker and it contains five main components and it copes with monitoring of Web services. The main feature of this architecture is to make relationships between brokers.

6   Empirical Results

To show the proposed model works correctly, we applied our model on workstations that equipped with quad-core CPU 2.83 GHz, RAM 8 GB, and OS 64bit. We implemented an HIS (Hospital Information System) as a service-oriented system in a local network consisting of 15 individual systems where 6 systems play the role of service provider. HIS is an appropriate case study to be deployed in service oriented architecture. The following states basic services of the system we implemented.

- Admission Service
- Outpatient Service
- Hospital Ward Service
- Pharmacy Service
- Laboratories Service
- Radiology Service
- Operating Room Service
- Medical Document Service
- Discharge Service

The above-mentioned services are used in hospital and they are integrated with each other to form the whole of HIS. The organization chart shown in Figure 7, demonstrating required interactions among HIS subsystems.

Our experiment is based on publishing services in stations with different operating systems in a local network and then consuming them. Our model was evaluated in a variety of situations that shows a proper UDDI activation as well as extended framework.

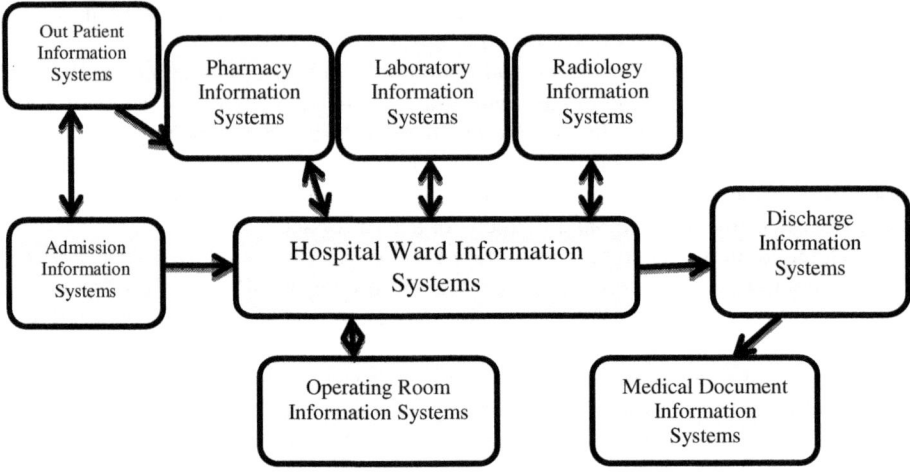

Fig. 7. Organization chart in HIS system

Implementing the proposed model, if some event happens in the repository, relevant consumers are notified. Our proposed model uses a program server to inform online consumers (Figure 8) and also the consumers use the client program to communicate with the server (Figure 9).All events that occur in the repository are informed to consumers by the program server. The implementation code of the model is available in http://ce.kashanu.ac.ir/babamir/auddi .

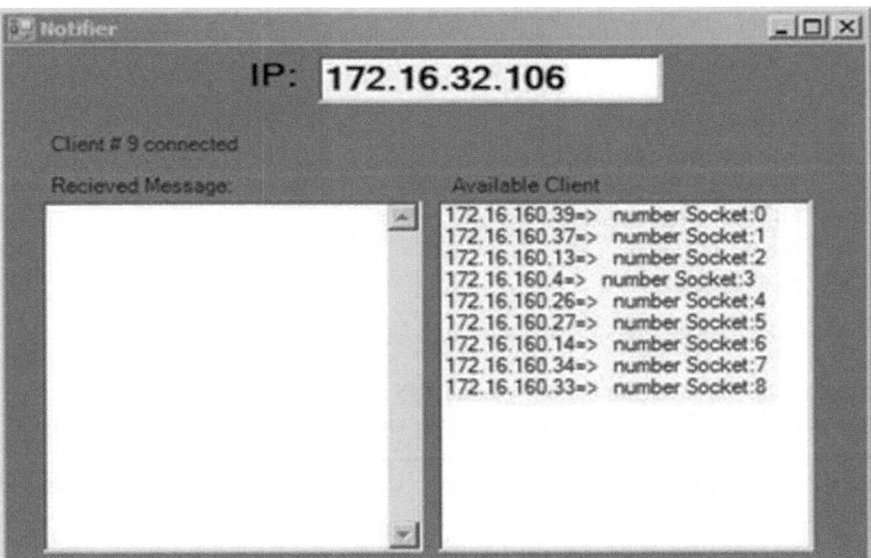

Fig. 8. Server Program

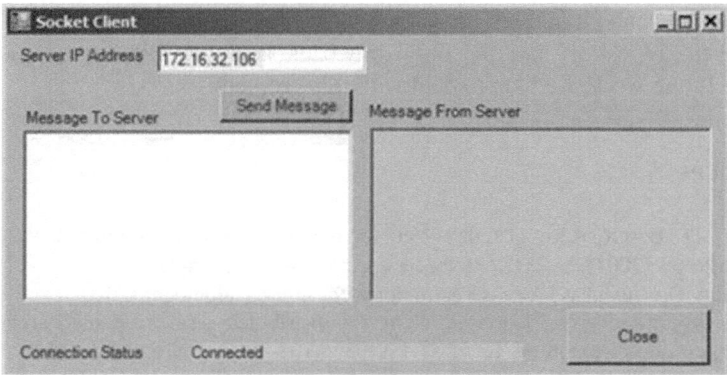

Fig. 9. Client Program

7   Conclusion and Future Work

In this paper we have tried to remove passiveness of repository through activation. To achieve this goal we try to make UDDI database active:

It is inferred the following results through the comparison of our proposed model with studied models in Table 2:

1. To prevent errors in invoking Web service that our proposed model prevents invoking unavailable Web service with the notification of consumers through repository.
2. The ability of censusing through which it can evaluate the performance of active systems and it measures parameters in system.
3. The ability to classification of services based on operations or even classification based on categories defined for the system.
4. Centralize control on services through the repository and not through applications.
5. Interaction between consumers to builds combined services or making relationship between consumers in specific circumstances.
6. Layered architecture for implementing system as a set of layers that each layer performs a specific task.
7. Searching Web service automatically in which consumer is not involved in selecting the service and broker would be responsible for the selection of a service.
8. The distribution capabilities that enables distribution of resources and repositories.

Table 2. Comparison of our model with other models

Model Name	1	2	3	4	5	6	7	8
The Proposed Model	√	√	√	√	√	×	×	×
[14]	√	×	√	√	×	√	×	√
[16]	√	×	√	×	×	×	×	×
[6]	√	×	√	√	×	×	√	×
[18]	×	√	√	√	×	×	√	×

According to Table 2 it can be shown that the proposed model is suitable for activating the repository but the only drawback is the problem of single point of failure. In future work, we plan to deal with this problem.

References

1. Austin, D., Barbir, A., et al (eds.) Web service architecture requirements, W3C Working Group Notes (2004), http://www.w3.org/TR/wsa-reqs
2. Draheim, D.: Business Process Technology. Springer, Heidelberg (2010)
3. Li, G., Muthusamy, V., Jacobsen, H.-A.: A distributed service oriented architecture for business process execution. In: ACM TWEB (2010)
4. Alonso, G., et al.: Web services: Concepts, Architectures and Applications. Springer, Germany (2004)
5. Du, Z., Huai, J., Liu, Y., Hu, C., Lei, L.: IPR: Automated Interaction Process Reconciliation. In: Proceedings of the International Conference on Web Intelligence, WI 2005 (2005)
6. Yu, J., Zhou, G.: Web Service Discovery and Dynamic Invocation Based on UDDI/OWL-S. In: Bussler, C.J., Haller, A. (eds.) BPM 2005. LNCS, vol. 3812, pp. 47–55. Springer, Heidelberg (2006)
7. Clement, L., Hately, A., Riegen, C., Rogers, T.: Universal Description Discovery & Integration (UDDI) 3.0.2 (2004), http://uddi.org/pubs/uddi_v3.htm
8. Kim, S.M., Rosu, M.C.: A Survey of Public Web services. In: Proceedings of the 13th International Conference on the World Wide Web, WWW 2004 (2004)
9. Surhone, L.M., Tennoe, M.T., Henssonow, S.F.: Active Database. VDM Verlag Dr. Mueller AG & Co. Kg (2010)
10. Hoffer, J.A., Venkataraman, R., Topi, H.: Modern Database Management. Pearson Education, Canada (2010)
11. Ramez, E., Sham, N.: Fundamentals of database systems. Pearson/Addison Wesley (2007)
12. Governatori, G., Hall, J., Paschke, A. (eds.): RuleML 2009. LNCS, vol. 5858. Springer, Heidelberg (2009)
13. Babamir, S.M., Babamir, F.S., Karimi, S.: Design and Evaluation of a Broker for Secure Web service Composition. In: International Symposium on Computer Networks and Distributed Systems. IEEE Press (2011)
14. Babamir, S.M., Karimi, S., Shishehchei, M.R.: A Broker-Based Architecture for Quality-Driven Web services Composition. In: International Conference on Computational Intelligence and Software Engineering. IEEE Press (2010)
15. Du, Z., Huai, J.-P., Liu, Y.: Ad-UDDI: An Active and Distributed Service Registry. In: Bussler, C.J., Shan, M.-C. (eds.) TES 2005. LNCS, vol. 3811, pp. 58–71. Springer, Heidelberg (2006)
16. Treiber, M., Dustdar, S.: Active Web service Registries. IEEE Internet Computing 11(5), 66–71 (2007)
17. Jeckle, M., Zengler, B.: Active UDDI -An Extension to UDDI for Dynamic and Fault-Tolerant Service Invocation. In: Web and Database-Related Workshops on Web, Web-Services and Database Systems, pp. 91–99. Springer, Heidelberg (2003)
18. Guimarães Garcia, D.Z., de Toledo, M.B.F.: A UDDI Extension for Business Process Management Systems (2007)
19. Ye, G., Wu, C., Yue, J., Cheng, S., Wu, C.: A QoS-aware Model or Web services Discovery. In: The First International Workshop on Education Technology and Computer Science (2009)

A Neuro-IFS Intelligent System
for Marketing Strategy Selection

Vahid Khatibi, Hossein Iranmanesh*, and Abbas Keramati

Industrial Engineering Department, Faculty of Engineering,
University of Tehran, Tehran, Iran
{vahid.khatibi,hiranmanesh,keramati}@ut.ac.ir

Abstract. The business intelligence (BI) provides businesses with the computational and quantitative support for decision making using artificial intelligence
and data mining techniques. In this paper, we propose a neuro-IFS inference
system for marketing strategy selection. For this purpose, first we develop an
IFS inference system which operates on rules whose antecedents, including
industry attractiveness and enterprise strength, have membership and
non-membership functions. Then, we use a radial basis function (RBF) neural
network on rules to enhance the proposed system with learning from the
previous experiences. After 350 epochs, the 3-layer RBF neural network could
distinguish the appropriate strategy with 95% accuracy rate.

Keywords: Business Intelligence, Fuzzy Inference System, Intuitionistic Fuzzy
Sets, Radial Basis Function Neural Network, Marketing Strategy.

1 Introduction

The rate of growth in the amount of information available nowadays within a corpo-
rate environment poses major difficulties as well as challenges in decision making.
Business intelligence (BI) consists of a collection of techniques and tools, aiming at
providing businesses with the necessary support for decision making. Examples of
simple BI services that already exist are various search and filtering services, as well
as various content providers and aggregators that deliver semi-custom information
bundles to particular users [1].

In the contemporary business environment, customers are considered to be the central element of all marketing actions, and customer relationship management (CRM)
has become a priority for companies [2]. This is highlighted by the claim of academ-
ics and practitioners that a customer orientation strategy is necessary for companies to
survive and be successful in saturated markets [3]. Business firms, regardless of the
size of their organization, as a whole, are spending billions of dollars each year on
customer relationship management [4].

---

* Corresponding author.

P. Pichappan, H. Ahmadi, and E. Ariwa (Eds.): INCT 2011, CCIS 241, pp. 61–70, 2011.

On the other hand, the purpose of strategic planning is to guide an organization to achieve its desired goals of the long-term development under the variation of environment [5]. Therefore, the future events play a key role in business strategic planning and managers need a mental model of the future to make better decisions. There are some differences among uncertainties pertaining to future occurrence probability. When there is the low level of uncertainties in environment, quantitative approaches such as probability distribution and forecasting techniques are very useful for managing the existing risk and uncertainty. In the high level of uncertainty, qualitative approaches such as scenario planning may be useful to employ [6].

Fuzzy set (FS), proposed by Zadeh [7], as a framework to encounter uncertainty, vagueness and partial truth, represents a degree of membership for a member of the universe of discourse to a subset of it. Therefore, we could have a spectrum of truth values. Intuitionistic fuzzy set (IFS), proposed by Atanassov [8], by adding the degree of non-membership to FS, looks more accurately to uncertainty quantification and provides the opportunity to model the problem precisely based on the existing knowledge and observations [9]. Both of these frameworks are considered as soft methods which in turn, lead to soft computing [10] and approximate reasoning.

Also, an extremely powerful neural network type is the radial basis function (RBF) neural network, which differs strongly from the multilayer perceptron (MLP) network both in the activation functions and in how it is used [11]. Generally, an RBF network can be regarded as a feed-forward network composed of three layers of neurons with different roles. The first layer is the input layer, and this feeds the input data to each of the nodes in the second or hidden layer. The nodes of second layer differ greatly from other neural networks in that each node has a Gaussian function as the nonlinearity processing element. The third and final layer is linear, supplying each network response as a linear combination of the hidden responses. It acts to sum the outputs of the second layer of nodes to yield the decision value [12].

In this paper, we proposed a neuro-IFS system for marketing strategy selection to encounter and model the uncertainties of the factors influencing the marketing strategy. For this purpose, first an IFS inference system is developed which operates on rules whose antecedents, including industry attractiveness and enterprise strength, have membership and non-membership functions. Then, we used a radial basis function (RBF) neural network on rules to enhance the proposed system with learning from the previous experiences.

This paper is organized as follows. After representing the preliminaries of the fuzzy systems, intuitionistic fuzzy sets and radial basis neural networks in Section 2, the proposed system is represented and then examined in Section 3.

2   Preliminaries

In this section, the preliminaries needed to understand the proposed system are represented. For this purpose, the fundamentals of the fuzzy systems, intuitionistic fuzzy sets and radial basis function neural networks are described in following.

2.1 Fuzzy Systems

A fuzzy system maps an input fuzzy set into an output fuzzy set. The characteristics of this mapping are governed by fuzzy rules in the fuzzy system. One of the important design issues of fuzzy systems is how to construct a set of appropriate fuzzy rules [13]. There have been thus far two major approaches: manual rule generation and automatic rule generation.

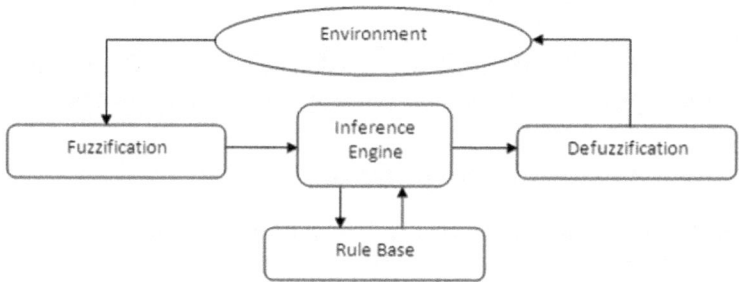

Fig. 1. A General Schema of a Fuzzy System [13]

As shown in Fig. 1, a fuzzy system is a class of expert systems that make decisions using built-in fuzzy rules. Fuzzification and defuzzification are the essential interfaces from a fuzzy system to an environment. The fuzzy system maps an input fuzzy set X into an output fuzzy set Y:

$$Y = X \circ R \tag{1}$$

where $\circ$ denotes the compositional rule of inference. The fuzzy rule base denoted by a fuzzy relation R governs the characteristics of the mapping given in Eq. 1. One way to look at automatic rule generation is to find a proper fuzzy relation from a set of numerical data. Fuzzy associative memory (FAM) developed by Kosko [14] provides a natural structure to store a fuzzy relation and to process fuzzy inference in parallel. Learning an FAM involves clustering of a set of given numerical data in the product space. Using the centers of the resultant clusters the weight matrix of the FAM which is equivalent to the elements of the fuzzy relation in Eq. 1 is computed as:

$$\mu_R(x, y) = \overset{m}{\underset{i=1}{T^*}} \left\{ T(\mu_{X_i}(x), \mu_{Y_i}(y)) \right\} \tag{2}$$

where m is the number of clusters, X_i is the centre of the ith cluster, and Y_i is its corresponding output. T and T* are the t-norm and t-conorm, respectively.

2.2 Intuitionistic Fuzzy Sets

In fuzzy set theory, the membership of an element to a fuzzy set is a single value between zero and one. But in reality, it may not always be certain that the degree of non-membership of an element in a fuzzy set is just equal to 1 minus the degree of membership, i.e., there may be some hesitation degree. So, as a generalization of fuzzy sets, the concept of intuitionistic fuzzy sets was introduced by Atanassov in 1983, which contains a non-membership degree besides membership degree [15]. Both degrees of membership and non-membership belong to the interval [0,1], and their sum should not exceed 1. Formally, an IFS A in a universe of discourse X was defined as an object of the form:

$$A = \left\{ (x, \mu_A(x), v_A(x)) | x \in X \right\}$$
(3)

where $\mu_A(x)$ is called "the degree of membership of x in A", and $v_A(x)$ "the degree of non-membership of x in A". Also, $\pi_A(x)$ is called "the hesitation degree of the element x to A", so as:

$$\pi_A(x) = 1 - \mu_A(x) - v_A(x)$$
(4)

Bustince and Burillo showed that this notion coincides with the notion of vague sets (VSs) proposed by Gau and Buehere in 1994. But in [16], differences between vague sets and intuitionistic fuzzy sets have been shown. As important contents in fuzzy mathematics, similarity and distance measures between IFSs have attracted many researchers, which can be used as tools in pattern recognition. Li and Cheng proposed similarity measures of IFSs and applied these measures to pattern recognition [17]. But Liang and Shi [18], Mitchell [19] pointed out that Li and Cheng's measures are not always effective in some cases, and made some modifications respectively. Also, Szmidt and Kacprzyk proposed four distance measures between IFSs which were in some extent based on the geometric interpretation of intuitionistic fuzzy sets, and have some good geometric properties [20]. With this point of view, researches of pattern recognition in IFS can be classified into three groups:

- Using the distance concept and assigning each case to the nearest pattern [20];
- Using the similarity concept, introduced as duality of distance measure [15, 21];
- Using cross-entropy concept [22].

Many researches are focused on the distance measures between intuitionistic fuzzy sets in recent years. Let $A = \left\{ (x, \mu_A(x), v_A(x)) | x \in X \right\}$ and $B = \left\{ (x, \mu_B(x), v_B(x)) | x \in X \right\}$ be two IFSs in $X = \{x_1, x_2, \ldots, x_n\}$. Based on the geometric interpretation of IFS, Szmidt and Kacprzyk [23] proposed the following four distance measures between A and B:

- Hamming distance:

$$d^1_{IFS}(A, B) = \frac{1}{2} \sum_{i=1}^{n} \left(|\mu_A(x_i) - \mu_B(x_i)| + |v_A(x_i) - v_B(x_i)| + |\pi_A(x_i) - \pi_B(x_i)| \right)$$
(5)

- Euclidean distance:

$$e^1_{IFS}(A,B) = \sqrt{\frac{1}{2}\sum_{i=1}^{n}(\mu_A(x_i)-\mu_B(x_i))^2 + (v_A(x_i)-v_B(x_i))^2 + (\pi_A(x_i)-\pi_B(x_i))^2} \tag{6}$$

- Normalized Hamming distance:

$$l^1_{IFS}(A,B) = \frac{1}{2n}\sum_{i=1}^{n}(|\mu_A(x_i)-\mu_B(x_i)|+|v_A(x_i)-v_B(x_i)|+|\pi_A(x_i)-\pi_B(x_i)|) \tag{7}$$

- Normalized Euclidean distance:

$$q^1_{IFS}(A,B) = \sqrt{\frac{1}{2n}\sum_{i=1}^{n}(\mu_A(x_i)-\mu_B(x_i))^2 + (v_A(x_i)-v_B(x_i))^2 + (\pi_A(x_i)-\pi_B(x_i))^2} \tag{8}$$

Obviously, these distance measures satisfy the conditions of the metric and the normalized Euclidean distance has some good geometric properties. But in reality it may not fit so well [15].

2.3 Radial Basis Function Neural Network

A radial basis function (RBF) neural network consists of an input layer, hidden layer and output layer with the activation function of the hidden units being radial basis functions (Fig. 2). Normally, an RBF consists of one hidden layer, and a linear output layer. One of the most common kinds of radial basis function is the Gaussian bell-shaped distribution [13, 24].

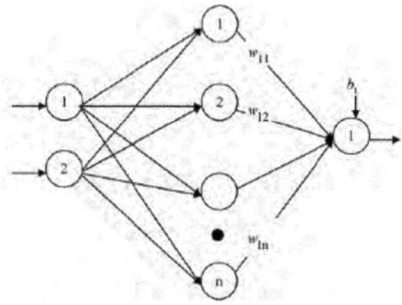

Fig. 2. The Structure of the RBF Network [13]

The response of the hidden layer unit is dependent on the distance an input is from the centre represented by the radial basis function (Euclidean Distance). Each radial function has two parameters: a centre and a width. The width of the basis function determines the spread of the function and how quickly the activation of the hidden node decreases with the input being an increased distance from the centre [25]. The output layer neurons are weighted linear combination of the RBF in the hidden layer. An RBF network can be modeled by the following equations:

$$y_j(x) = \sum_{i=1}^{n} w_{ji} \psi_i(x) + b_j \tag{9}$$

where $y_j(x)$ is the output at the jth node in the output layer, n is the number of hidden nodes, w_{ji} is the weight factor from the ith hidden node to the jth output node, $\Psi_i(x)$ is the radial basis activation function of the hidden layer and b_j is the bias parameter of the jth output node. Some of the common types of RBF are linear function, Duchon radial cubic, radial quadratic plus cubic and Gaussian activation function [24]. The last function has the form:

$$\psi_i(x) = \exp\left(\frac{-||X - u_i||^2}{2\sigma_i^2}\right) \tag{10}$$

where X is the input vector, u_i is the center vector of ith hidden node and σ is the width of the basis function. There are two distinct types of Gaussian RBF architectures. The first type uses the exponential activation function, so the activation of the unit is a Gaussian bump as a function of the inputs. The second type of Gaussian RBF architecture uses the softmax activation function, so the activations of all the hidden units are normalized to sum to one. This type of network is often called a "normalized RBF" or NRBF network. An NRBF network with unequal widths and equal heights can be written in the following form:

$$\psi_i(x)(\text{softmax}) = \frac{\exp(h_i)}{\sum_{i=1}^{n} \exp(h_i)} \tag{11}$$

$$h_i = \left(-\sum_{l=1}^{2} \frac{(X_l - u_{il})^2}{2\sigma_i^2}\right) \tag{12}$$

Again, X is the input vector, u_{il} is the centre of the ith hidden node that is associated with the lth input vector, σ_i is a common width of the ith hidden node in the layer and softmax (h_i) is the output vector of the ith hidden node. The radial basis activation function used in this study is the softmax activation function [26]. At first, the input data is used to determine the centers and the widths of the basis functions for each hidden node. The second step includes the procedure, which is used to find the output layer weights that minimize the quadratic error between the predicted values and the target values. Mean square error (the average sum of squares error) is defined as:

$$\text{MSE} = \frac{1}{N}\sum_{k=1}^{N}\left((\text{TE})_k^{\text{exp}} - (\text{TE})_k^{\text{cal}}\right)^2 \tag{13}$$

3   A Neuro-IFS System for Marketing Strategy

In this section, a neuro-IFS system is proposed for marketing strategic planning. For this purpose, a hypothetical problem is assumed in which we want to determine the appropriate strategy for a enterprise based on two vague and uncertain variables including industry attractiveness (X1) and the enterprise strength (X2). The connections between these variables and the strategic choices are determined by the fields' experts, as shown in Table 1. For instance, if the variable X1 has high value (comprising high membership and low non-membership values), and variable X2 has weak value (comprising low membership and high non-membership values), then the strategy 1 is recommended which is vertical integration by acquisition or establishment of supplier and distribution units. In this problem, the objective function is determination of the most appropriate strategy based on the uncertain input variables. The other recommended strategies mentioned in Table 1 are as follows: Strategy 2) Market development, Strategy 3) Market penetration, Strategy 4) Retrenchment, Strategy 5) Diversification, Strategy 6) Geographic expansion, Strategy 7) Divestiture, Strategy 8) Joint venture and Strategy 9) Product development.

Table 1. The Connections between Uncertain Input Variables and the Strategic Choices

Market attractiveness (X1)	Enterprise strength (X2)	Strategic choice
	Weak	Strategy 1
High	Moderate	Strategy 2
	Strong	Strategy 3
	Weak	Strategy 4
Moderate	Moderate	Strategy 5
	Strong	Strategy 6
	Weak	Strategy 7
Low	Moderate	Strategy 8
	Strong	Strategy 9

Based on these extracted rules, we constructed our IFS rules for the inference system. In this system, the most appropriate rule would be selected according to the input variables. Then, the consequent of the rule would be assigned to the output variable. In this phase, we augment the proposed system with learning from previous

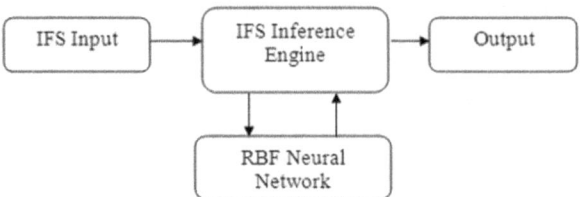

Fig. 3. The Architecture of the Proposed Neuro-IFS System

experiences. For this purpose, we designed an RBF neural network to learn various situations of industry attractiveness and market strength variables, and their appropriate strategy. In this way, the proposed network has three layers with two input variables of industry attractiveness and market strength, and one output variable of the strategic choice. Therefore, the architecture of the proposed system includes a neuro-IFS system comprising of IFS input, inference engine and crisp output which is enhanced with the RBF-based learning in the rule base, as shown in Fig. 3.

In following, the training and test data were determined, so as 60% of the data was used for the learning, and the remained 40% of the data was used for checking. Also, because the neural network's input variables should be numerals, the quantitative values of the experts' opinions were converted to numerical equivalents of membership and non-membership values, as shown in Table 2.

Table 2. Some of the Training and Testing Data and Their Appropriate Strategic Choices

No.	Market attractiveness (X1)	Enterprise strength (X2)	Strategic choice
Training data			
	0.6/0.3	0.2/0.9	Strategy 9
	0.9/0.1	0.8/0.1	Strategy 1
	0.65/0.32	0.42/0.4	Strategy 8
Testing data			
	0.8/0.25	0.5/0.4	Strategy 4
	0.5/0.2	0.2/0.8	Strategy 9
	0.75/0.2	0.7/0.2	Strategy 4

Also, the learning rate and acceptance error of the proposed network were determined 0.02 and 0.005, respectively. At the end of 350 training epochs, the network error convergence curve can be derived as shown in Fig. 4. Also, the proposed network was checked by the testing data, so as it could distinguish the appropriate strategy with 95% accuracy rate. Also, some of the proposed system outcomes are represented in Table 3.

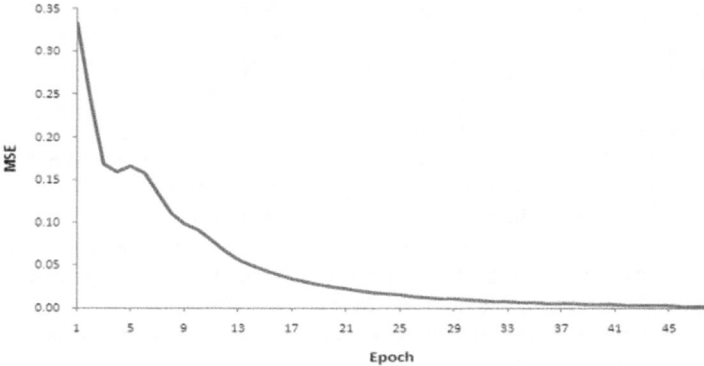

Fig. 4. The Curve of the Network Error Convergence

Table 3. Some of The Proposed System Outcomes

No.	Market attractiveness (X1)	Enterprise strength (X2)	Strategic choice
1	0.6/0.1	0.2/0.5	Strategy 8
2	0.8/0.2	0.2/0.7	Strategy 5
3	0.5/0.2	0.1/0.8	Strategy 9
4	0.8/0.2	0.7/0.2	Strategy 1
5	0.6/0.3	0.3/0.35	Strategy 8
6	0.7/0.2	0.4/0.6	Strategy 4

4   Conclusions

In this paper, we proposed a neuro-IFS system for marketing strategy selection, so as considering the uncertain variables of industry attractiveness and enterprise strength, the appropriate strategic choices were determined in an IFS inference system based on IFS rules. Also, an RBF neural network was used for learning from previous experiences in the rule base. After training and testing of the designed neural network, it could distinguish the appropriate strategy with 95% accuracy rate.

References

1. Mikroyannidis, A., Theodoulidis, B.: Ontology management and evolution for business intelligence. International Journal of Information Management 30, 559–566 (2010)
2. Karakostas, B., Kardaras, D., Papathanassiou, E.: The state of CRM adoption by the financial services in the UK: An empirical investigation. Information & Management 42, 853–863 (2005)
3. Heinrich, B.: Transforming strategic goals of CRM into process goals and activities. Business Process Management Journal 11(6), 709–723 (2005)

4. Keramati, A., Mehrabi, H., Mojir, N.: A process-oriented perspective on customer relationship management and organizational performance: An empirical investigation. Industrial Marketing Management 39, 1170–1185 (2010)
5. Wang, H.-F.: A fuzzy approach to scenario analysis in strategic planning. In: IEEE International Fuzzy Systems Conference (1999)
6. Alessandri, T.M.D., et al.: Managing risk and uncertainty in complex capital projects. The Quarterly Review of Economics and Finance 44, 751–767 (2004)
7. Zadeh, L.A.: Fuzzy Sets. Information Control 8, 338–353 (1965)
8. Atanassov, K.: Intuitionistic fuzzy sets. Fuzzy Sets and Systems 20(1), 87–96 (1986)
9. Vlachos, I., Sergiadis, G.D.: Intuitionistic fuzzy information: Applications to pattern recognition. Pattern Recognition Letters 28, 197–206 (2007)
10. Zadeh, L.A.: Fuzzy Logic, neural networks, and soft computing. Communications of ACM 37, 77–84 (1994)
11. Kennedy, M.P., Chua, L.O.: Neural networks for nonlinear programming. IEEE Transactions on Circuits and Systems 35(3), 554–562 (1988)
12. Broomhead, D.S., Lowe, D.: Multivariable functional interpolation and adaptive networks. Complex Systems 2, 321–355 (1988)
13. Cho, K.B., Wang, B.H.: Radial basis function based adaptive fuzzy systems and their applications to system identification and prediction. Fuzzy Sets and Systems 83, 325–339 (1996)
14. Kosko, B.: Fuzzy associative memories. In: Kandel, A. (ed.) Fuzzy Expert Systems (1987)
15. Wang, W., Xin, X.: Distance measure between intuitionistic fuzzy sets. Pattern Recognition Letters 26, 2063–2069 (2005)
16. Li, Y., Olson, D.L., Qin, Z.: Similarity measures between intuitionistic fuzzy (vague) sets: A comparative analysis. Pattern Recognition Letters 28, 278–285 (2007)
17. Dengfeng, L., Chantian, C.: New similarity measures of intuitionistic fuzzy sets and applications to pattern recognitions. Pattern Recognition Letters 23, 221–225 (2002)
18. Liang, Z., Shi, P.: Similarity measures on intuitionistic fuzzy sets. Pattern Recognition Letters 24, 2687–2693 (2003)
19. Mitchell, H.B.: On the Dengfeng-Chuitian similarity measure and its application to pattern recognition. Pattern Recognition Letters 24, 3101–3104 (2003)
20. Szmidt, E., Kacprzyk, J.: Distances between intuitionistic fuzzy sets. Fuzzy Sets and Systems 114, 505–518 (2000)
21. Hung, W.-L., Yang, M.-S.: Similarity measures of intuitionistic fuzzy sets based on Hausdorff distance. Pattern Recognition Letters 25, 1603–1611 (2004)
22. Vlachos, I.K., Sergiadis, G.D.: Intuitionistic fuzzy information: Applications to pattern recognition. Pattern Recognition Letters 28, 197–206 (2007)
23. Szmidt, E., Kacprzyk, J.: Distances between intuitionistic fuzzy sets. Fuzzy Sets and Systems 114(3), 505–518 (2000)
24. Aminian, A.: Prediction of temperature elevation for seawater in multi-stage flash. Chemical Engineering Journal 162, 552–556 (2010)
25. Bishop, C.M.: Neural Networks for Pattern Recognition. Oxford University Press Inc., New York (1995)
26. Haykin, S.: Neural Networks: A Comprehensive Foundation. Prentice-Hall, Upper Saddle River (1999)

Prediction of Moisture Content of Bergamot Fruit during Thin-Layer Drying Using Artificial Neural Networks

Mohammad Sharifi[*], Shahin Rafiee, Hojjat Ahmadi, and Masoud Rezaee

Department of Agricultural Machinery Engineering, Faculty of Agricultural Engineering
and Technology, University of Tehran, Karaj, 31587-77871, Iran
shahinrafiee@ut.ac.ir, m.sharifi@ut.ac.ir

Abstract. In this study thin-layer drying of bergamot was modelled using artificial neural network. An experimental dryer was used. Thin-layer of bergamot slices at five air temperatures (40, 50, 60, 70 & 80 ºC), one thickness (6 mm) and three air velocities (0.5, 1 & 2 m/s) were artificially dried. Initial moisture content (M.C.) during all experiments was between 5.2 to 5.8 (g.g) (d.b.). Mass of samples were recorded and saved every 5 sec. using a digital balance connected to a PC. MLP with momentum and levenberg-marquardt (LM) were used to train the ANNs. In order to develop ANN's models, temperatures, air velocity and time are used as input vectors and moisture ration as the output. Results showed a 3-8-1 topology for thickness of 6 mm, with LM algorithm and TANSIG activation function was able to predict moisture ratio with R^2 of 0.99936. The corresponding MSE for this topology was 0.00006.

Keywords: bergamot, thin-layer, artificial neural network, levenberg-marquardt, momentum.

1 Introduction

Citrus are of great important among agricultural products in the world. Iran produces 3.5 million tonnes of citrus and is ranked 22nd in the world (Anonymous, 2010). Bergamot is an evergreen and a small tree from Rue family (Fig. 1). Its fruit is pear like and bergamot oil is extracted from the skin which is used as an ingredient in perfume industries. The fruit skin with bitter and fragrant taste is used in jam production and also in pharmaceutical and medical applications. The name of the tree

Fig. 1. Bergamot Fruit

---

[*] Corresponding author.

P. Pichappan, H. Ahmadi, and E. Ariwa (Eds.): INCT 2011, CCIS 241, pp. 71–80, 2011.
© Springer-Verlag Berlin Heidelberg 2011

is citrus bergamia and belongs to bergamot family. Another citrus fruit from Rue family is citron which is called cedrate. The tree is called citrus medica and the fruit is used in jam production as well (shry and Reiley, 2010).

Bergamot fruit consists of flevedo, albedo and an oval shape meat. The flevedo is initially green and as the fruit ripens, becomes yellow. The albedo is white in both green and yellow stages of the flevedo and its thickness is manifold than that of the flevedo. The meat is edible and very sour and can be used in place of lemon juice or in making various pickles.

Bergamot is usually grown in south Iran like Jahrom (in Fars province). Before the yellow stage, the crop is harvested and the skin is dried. Dried skins are used in jam production in seasons that fresh fruit is not available. In addition, bergamot as dried fruit is exported to many countries (Mojtahedi, 2006).

Drying is defined as a process of moisture removal due to simultaneous heat and mass transfer (Hernandez, 2009). It is also a classical method of food preservation, which provides longer shelf-life, lighter weight for transportation and smaller space for storage. Natural sun drying is practiced widely in the world and also in Iran, but has some problems related to the contamination by dirt and dust and infestation by insects, rodents and other animals. Therefore, the drying process should be undertaken in closed equipments, to improve the quality of the final product.

Artificial neural networks in reality are the simplified model of man mind which is one of the tools for predicting physical phenomena, and were considered as an application on 50s of 20th century for the first time, when Frank Rosenblatt introduced Perceptron network in 1958 (Menhaj, 2001).

The smallest unit of artificial neural network is Neuron. Every network consists of one input, one output and one or several middle layers. Each layer's neurons are connected to next layer neurons by some neurons. In the network training process, these weights and the permanent amounts are added to them and named Bias idiomatically, changes continuously until the sum of the squares of error gets minimum. Weights and biases changes are on the base of learning law. For transferring every layer outcome to next layers, actuator functions are used. Sigmoid, linear, and preliminary functions can be mentioned from famous actuator functions. To build artificial neural network, data are divided to two series of instruction data and examination data. About eighty percent of data are applied to instruction and the remaining is used for examination and evaluation. In the duration of learning process, network learning level is being measured continuously by some error indices and finally, the network is being selected which has minimum error (Kishan et al., 1996).

One of the important usages of artificial neural network is training and predicting outcome with new data. In FFBP[1] network, with BP[2] learning algorithm, at first, outcome layer weights are compared with optimum values. If error is excessive, outcome layers weights will be modified on the basis of updating rules and if training error is less than predefined error, learning process will finish. Also, CFBP[3] network uses BP algorithm for weight correction like FFBP network. But the main property of that network is every layer's neurons are connected to all of the neurons of previous

---

[1] Feed-Forward Back Propagation.
[2] Error Back Propagation.
[3] Cascade-Forward Back Propagation.

layers (Khanna, 1990). Used training algorithms for updating applied network weights are: Momentum algorithm and Levenberg-Marquardt (LM) algorithm. Whereas for instructing neural network on the base of LM algorithm, computations are done in parallel mode, that is known for one of the fastest methods for instructing back propagation neural network with less than one hundred weight connection. LM algorithm mainly is on the base of Hessian Matrix that is used for nonlinear optimization on the base of minimum squares (Hernandez, 2009).

Many researchers have used artificial neural networks for predicting desirable parameters in dryers. Omid et al., (2009) used a multilayer feed-forward neural network (MFNN) for drying kinetics of pistachio nuts (Akbari v.). Experiments were performed at five drying air temperatures (ranging from 40 to 80 ºC) and four input air flow velocities (ranging from 0.5 to 2 m/s) with three replicates in a thin-layer dryer. The (3-8-5-1)-MLP is the best-suited model estimating the moisture content of the pistachio nuts at all drying runs. For this topology, R^2 and MSE values were 0.9989 and 4.20E-06, respectively.

Erenturk and Erenturk (2006) compared the use of genetic algorithm and ANN approaches to study the drying of carrots. They demonstrated that the proposed neural network model not only minimized the R^2 of the predicted results but also removed the predictive dependency on the mathematical models (Newton, Page, modified Page, Henderson-Pabis). They also suggested that the application of the artificial neural networks could be used for the on-line state estimation and control of the drying process.

Erenturk et al. (2004) did a research about comparison of dynamic drying estimation of plant Acenasea Angostifulia (a plant with more medical usage) by regression analysis and neural network. In this research, thin layer dynamic drying of this plant and its comparison in a regression analysis and neural network. Experiments was done in three thermal levels 15, 30 and 45 degrees of centigrade and air velocity in three levels 0.3, 0.7 and 1.1 meters per second and sample length in three measures less than 3 millimeters, 3 up to 6 millimeters and more than 6 millimeters. 150 grams of samples was put under mentioned cures in dryer after exit of refrigerator. Regression analysis was done with four models of Newton, Henderson and Pubis, page, and modified page and in the same time, analysis was done in neural network and two-layer optimized network with one hidden layer and 30 neurons was resulted. Gotten results indicate neural network model estimated moisture capacity with 0.1 percent better precision than modified page model.

Islam et al. (2003) did a research about predicting drying velocity by neural network. This research was done on the layers of tomato. Cures included air velocity in range of 0.5 up to 2 meters per second, dryer air temperature in the range of 40 up to 55 degrees of centigrade, air relative moisture in the range of 5 up to 50 percent, and sample plates thickness in the range of 3 up to 10 millimeter. In this research, page drying model was used thus this model analyzed in neural network.

Chen et al. (2001) used multilayer ANN models with three inputs (concentration of osmotic solution, temperature, and contact time) to predict five outputs (drying time, color, texture, rehydration ratio, and hardness) during osmo-convective drying of blueberries. The optimal configuration of the neural network consisted of one hidden layer with 10 neurons. The predictability of the ANN models was compared with that of multiple regression models.

The results confirmed that ANN models had much better performance than the conventional empirical or semiempirical mathematical models. The effects of different drying conditions (temperature, air velocity, drying time, and sample thickness) and different osmotic treatments (use of sorbitol, glucose, and sucrose solutions) on the drying time and quality of osmotically dried pumpkins through the application of ANNs and image analysis was predicted (Nazghelichi et al., 2011). Optimum artificial neural network (ANN) models were developed based on one to two hidden layers and 10-20 neurons per hidden layer (Movagharnejad and Nikzad, 2007). Lertworasirikul (2008) presented a comparative study among mechanistic and empirical models to estimate dynamic drying behavior of semifinished cassava crackers using a hot air dryer. The prediction performance of different approaches such as the diffusion model, Newton model, Page model, modified Page model, Henderson and Pabis model, ANN model, and Adaptive-Network-Based Fuzzy Inference System (ANFIS) in modeling the drying processes of semifinished cassava crackers under different drying air temperatures was investigated. Overall, the ANN model performed superior to the diffusion model but was marginally better than ANFIS and modified Page models.

2   Material and Methods

2.1   Thin-Layer Drying Equipment

Figure 2 shows a schematic diagram of a dryer used for experimental work. It consists of a fan, heaters, drying chamber and instruments for measurement. The airflow rate was adjusted by the fan speed control. The heating system consisted of an electric 2000 W heater placed inside the duct. The drying chamber temperature was adjusted by the heater power control. Two drying trays were placed inside the drying chamber. In the measurements of temperatures, thermocouples were used with a digital thermometer (LM35), with reading accuracy of 0.1°C. A thermo hygrometer

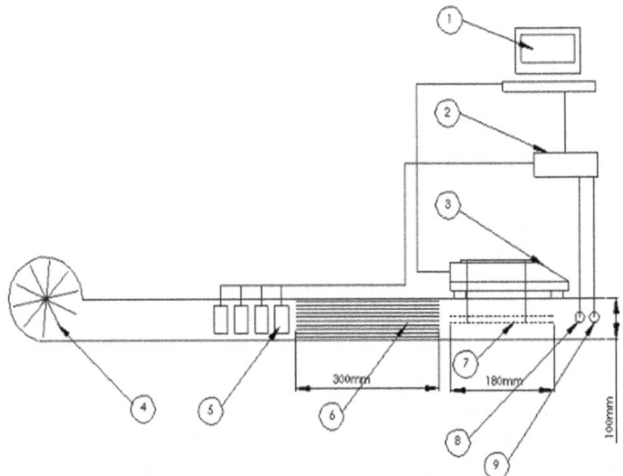

Fig. 2. Schematic of thin-layer drying equipment used in this work
1. computer 2.microcontroler 3.digital balance 4.fan 5.heaters 6.straightener 7.tray
8.temperature sensor 9.humidity sensor

(capacitive, Philippine made) was used to measure humidity levels at various locations of the system. The velocity of air passing through the system was measured by a hot wire (Testo, 405 V1, Germany) with 0.01 meters per second sensitivity was used and a digital scale with 0.01 gram sensitivity and capacity of 3100 grams.

To do the algorithm of controlling and monitoring information, an application has designed in visual basic 6 environment that demonstrates information related to temperature and moisture sensors and also being on or off of every heaters every time (Yadollahinia, 2006).

Drying mechanism is in this way that circulated air in channel by blower, passes heater and after getting warm, leads to bergamot slices by channel. Airflow absorbs bergamot moisture when it passes slices and makes it getting warm. So temperature increase speeds up water exit from sample tissue and resulted product dryness. 165 grams of bergamot thin layer was flatten on two grid square aluminium dishes with 25 centimeters side length in a way that on every dish one layer of product was put.

2.2   Sample Preparation Method

After washing bergamot surface, bergamot layers with thickness 6 millimetres prepared by cutter device. Drying experiments in five temperature levels 40, 50, 60, 70 and 80 degrees of centigrade and input air flow velocity in three levels 0.5, 1 and 2 meters per second in three repetitions was done. While drying, layers weights were being recorded by a digital scale connected to computer and dryer air temperature and moisture was being measured and registered every 5 seconds. Drying continued up to the time that bergamot thin layer weights, approximately would not change (sample weight changes approximately reached zero). Then samples were put on oven with temperature 105°C and after getting dried during 24 hours, samples dry weights were gained (ASABE, 2006).

2.3   Designing Artificial Neural Network

By imaging three input factors applied in all of thin layer drying experiments, the moisture ratio of bergamot slices was gained in one thickness. Artificial neural network with three neurons input layer (drying time, dryer temperature and velocity) and one neuron output layer (moisture ratio) was designed (Fig. 3). The software Neurosolutions version 5 was used in this study. To achieve proper answer, Feed-Forward Back Propagation network was used. Training process by mentioned network is a repetitive process includes weights changes between different layers and gets gradually to stability of these weights during training, as the error between desired amounts and predicted amounts gets minimum.

The used activation function to find out optimized condition is: (Khanna, 1990). (1). hyperbolic tangent function[4]

$$Y_j = \frac{2}{(1+\exp(-2X_j))} - 1 \tag{1}$$

---

[4] TANSIG.

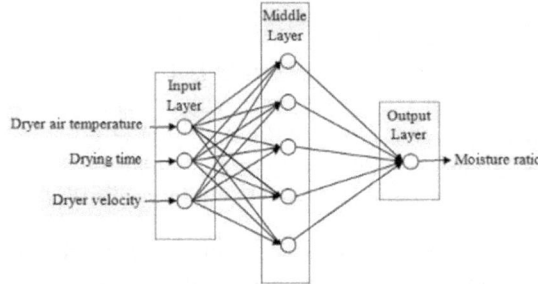

Fig. 3. A schematic of designed artificial neural network

where X_j is the sum of with weight inputs of every neurons of layer j and is calculated by below equation:

$$X_j = \sum_{i=1}^{m} W_{ij} \times Y_i + b_j \tag{2}$$

where m is the number of output layer neurons, W_{ij} is the weight between layer i and layer j, Y_i is neuron i output and b_j is the bias amount of layer j neuron.

About %60 of data for training, %15 for validity evaluation and %25 randomly for evaluating trained network were used. For finding a network with proper topology by training algorithms, mean square error criterion has been used while the purpose is to get minimized mentioned error and is defined by equation (3): (Kishan et al., 1996; Khanna, 1990)

$$MSE = \frac{\sum_{p=1}^{M} \sum_{i=1}^{N} \left(S_{ip} - T_{ip}\right)^2}{NP} \tag{3}$$

where *MSE* is mean square error in training step, S_{ip} is network output in neuron i and pattern p, T_{ip} is desirable output in neuron i and pattern p, N is number of output neurons and M is number of training patterns.

3   Result and Discussion

Table 1 present error amount simulated by artificial neural network method, with number of neurons and different hidden layers in thickness 6 mm of bergamot thin layer. According to tables 1, when Levenberg-Marquardt algorithm has been used, in thickness 6 mm when 1 hidden layer with 8 neurons, the best answer has been presented.

Figure 4 demonstrates modeling error reduction procedure of thin layer bergamot drying with thickness 6 mm in velocities and temperature of dryer, by epoch increase.

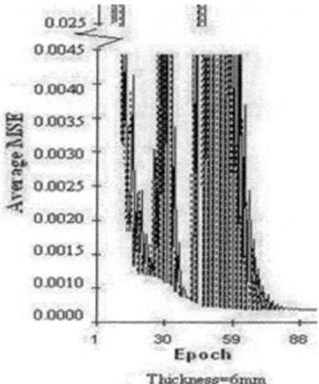

Fig. 4. Modeling error reduction procedure of bergamot thin layer drying by epoch increase

According to equation (2), weight matrixes for input layer to hidden layer for optimized topology in thickness 6 mm of bergamot is:

$$\begin{bmatrix} -0.89 & 2.66 & 0.15 \\ 9.79 & 4.67 & 1.29 \\ 2.58 & -0.12 & -0.14 \\ -7.49 & 1.68 & -0.04 \\ 0.06 & 0.03 & 0.06 \end{bmatrix}$$

Weight matrixes for hidden layer to output layer for optimized topology in thickness 6 mm of bergamot is:

$\begin{bmatrix} -4.78 & 0.05 & 3.60 & 0.75 & -0.55 \end{bmatrix}$ Bias matrixes for input layer to hidden layer for optimized topology in thickness 6 mm of bergamot is:

$$\begin{bmatrix} -0.76 \\ 2.81 \\ -0.23 \\ 9.54 \\ 4.99 \end{bmatrix}$$

Bias matrixes for hidden layer to output layer for optimized topology in thickness 6 mm of bergamot is: $\begin{bmatrix} 4.49 \end{bmatrix}$.

In figure 5 as a sample, a comparison between experimental moisture ratio and modeling on the base of artificial neural network method in air velocity 1 meter per second and thickness 6 mm of bergamot layer has been made.

Table 1. Comparison of the effect of hidden layers number and number of neurons of every hidden layer, on prediction precision in dryer air temperatures and velocities with 6 mm thickness of bergamot

Algorithm	Number of neurons of hidden layer			MSE	R^2
	One	Two	Three		
Levenberg-Marquardt	2	---	---	0.00112	0.99876
	3	---	---	0.00053	0.99234
	4	---	---	0.00042	0.99654
	5	---	---	0.00032	0.99864
	6	---	---	0.00028	0.99888
	7	---	---	0.00017	0.99801
	8	**---**	**---**	**0.00006**	**0.99936**
	2	1	---	0.00129	0.99653
	2	2	---	0.00356	0.97366
	1	1	1	0.00068	0.99773
	2	1	1	0.00088	0.99831
	2	2	1	0.00040	0.99582
	3	1	1	0.00041	0.99668
	3	2	1	0.00018	0.99898
	3	3	1	0.00056	0.99780
Momentum	1	---	---	0.00563	0.96961
	2	---	---	0.00279	0.98789
	3	---	---	0.00344	0.98672
	4	---	---	0.00384	0.98954
	6	---	---	0.00162	0.97707
	7	---	---	0.00344	0.98440
	2	1	---	0.00025	0.98274
	2	2	---	0.00480	0.96833
	1	1	1	0.00671	0.96950
	2	1	1	0.03369	0.74482
	2	2	1	0.05789	0.58965
	3	3	1	0.08176	0.90048

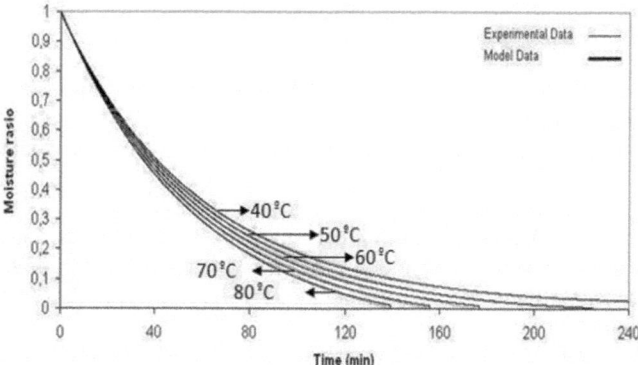

Fig. 5. A comparison between experimental moisture ratio and modeling on the base of ANN method in velocity 1 m/s and thickness 6 mm

4   Conclusions

Results of this research show that:

1-   Artificial neural network predicts moisture ratio of bergamot thin layers by three input parameters time, drying air velocities and dryer temperatures. The best neural network for instructing data is Feed-Forward Back Propagation network with Levenberg-Marquardt training algorithm and TANSIG activation function for layers with topology 3-8-1 and coefficients of determination 0.99936 for thickness 6 mm of bergamot layers in different situations of thin layer drying.

2-   Finally it can be concluded that artificial neural network is a much proper tool to predict moisture ratio in the field of thin layer drying of agricultural products.

NOMENCLATURE

X_j sum of with weight inputs of every neurons of layer j
m number of output layer neurons
W_{ij} weight between layer i and layer j
Y_i neuron i output
b_j bias amount of layer j neuron
MSE   is mean square error in training step
S_{ip} network output in neuron i and pattern p
T_{ip} desirable output in neuron i and pattern p
N   number of output neurons
M   number of training patterns.

Acknowledgements. This study was partly supported by Faculty of Agricultural Engineering and Technology, University of Tehran, Karaj, Iran.

References

1. Anonymous, Annual agricultural statistics. Ministry of Jihad-e-Agriculture of Iran (2010), http://www.maj.ir
2. Shry, C., Reiley, E.: Introductory Horticulture. Delmar Cengage Learning Press, India (2010)
3. Mojtahedi, M.: Horticulture. Behnashr publication, Tehran (2006)
4. Hernández, J.A.: Optimum operating conditions for heat and mass transfer in foodstuffs drying by means of neural network inverse. Food Control 20(4), 435–438 (2009)
5. Menhaj, M.B.: Artificial Neural Networks Principles. Amirkabir University of Technology Press, Tehran (2001)
6. Kishan, M., Chilukuri, K., Ranka, M.: Elements of Artificial Neural Networks (1996)
7. Khanna, T.: Foundations of Neural Networks. Addison-Wesley Publishing Company, USA (1990)
8. Omid, M., Baharlooei, A., Ahmadi, H.: Modeling Drying Kinetics of Pistachio Nuts with Multilayer Feed-Forward Neural Network. Drying Technology 27, 1069–1077 (2009)
9. Erenturk, S., Erenturk, K.: Comparison of genetic algorithm and neural network approaches for the drying process of carrot. Journal of Food Engineering 78, 905–912 (2006)
10. Erenturk, K., Erenturk, S., Lope, G.: Comparative study for the estimation of dynamical drying behavior of Echinacea angustifolia: regression analysis and neural network. Computers and Electronics in Agriculture 45(3), 71–90 (2004)
11. Islam, M.R., Sablani, S.S., Mujumdar, A.S.: An artificial neural network model for prediction of drying rates. Drying Technology 21(9), 1867–1884 (2003)
12. Chen, C.R., Ramaswamy, H.S., Alli, I.: Predicting quality changes during osmo-convective drying of blueberries for process optimization. Drying Technology 19, 507–523 (2001)
13. Nazghelichi, T., Aghbashlo, M., Kianmehr, M.H.: Optimization of an artificial neural network topology using coupled response surface methodology and genetic algorithm for fluidized bed drying. Computers and Electronics in Agriculture 75(1), 84–91 (2011)
14. Movagharnejad, K., Nikzad, M.: Modeling of tomato drying using artificial neural network. Computers and Electronics in Agriculture 59, 78–85 (2007)
15. Lertworasirikul, S.: Drying kinetics of semi-finished cassava crackers: A comparative study. Lebensmittel-Wissenschaft und-Technologie 41, 1360–1371 (2008)
16. Yadollahinia, A.: A Thin Layer Drying Model for Paddy Dryer. Master's thesis. University of Tehran, Iran (2006)
17. Asabe. Moisture measurement: grain and seeds. ASABE Standard S352.2. FEB03. American Society of Agricultural and Biological Engineers, St Joseph, MI 49085, USA (2006)

An Expert System for Construction Sites Best Management Practices

Leila Ooshaksaraie[1,*], Alireza Mardookhpour[2], Noor Ezlin Ahmad Basri[3],
and Azam Aghaee[4]

[1] Department of Environmental Studies, Faculty of Natural Resources, Lahijan Branch,
Islamic Azad University, Lahijan, Iran
[2] Department of Civil and Water Engineering, Lahijan Branch,
Islamic Azad University, Lahijan, Iran
[3] Department of Civil and Structural Engineering, Faculty of Engineering and Built
Environment, Universiti Kebangsaan Malaysia, 43600 Bangi, Selangor Darul Ehsan, Malaysia
[4] Lahijan Branch, Islamic Azad University, Lahijan, Iran
{l.ooshaksaraie,Alireza.mardookhpour,lahijanpajohesh}@yahoo.com,
ezlin@eng.ukm.my

Abstract. The construction industry has the potential to significantly impact our environment. Using Best Management Practices (BMPs) at construction sites is the most effective way to protect our environment and prevent pollution. In recent years, intelligent systems have been used extensively in different applications areas including environmental studies. As an aid to reduce environmental pollution originating from construction activities, expert system software - CSBMP- developed by using Microsoft Visual Basic. CSBMP to be used for BMPs at construction sites was designed based on the legal process. CSBMP primarily aims to provide educational and support system for environmental engineers and decision-makers during construction activities. It displays system recommendations in report form. When the use of CSBMP in construction sites BMPs becomes widespread, it is highly possible that it will be benefited in terms of having more accurate and objective decisions on construction projects which are mainly focused on reducing the environmental pollution.

Keywords: Expert system, construction site, pollution mitigation measures, Best Management Practices (BMPs), Microsoft Visual Basic, Geographic Information System (GIS).

1   Introduction

Rapid urbanization is one of the emerging problems of our time. In urban development, construction activities play major role that is one of the major contributors to the environmental pollution [1]. Most of the resources consumed in construction sites are non-renewable and some may even create adverse environmental effects during their manufacture [1], [2]. Environmental issues in construction typically include water

---

* Corresponding author.

P. Pichappan, H. Ahmadi, and E. Ariwa (Eds.): INCT 2011, CCIS 241, pp. 81–93, 2011.
© Springer-Verlag Berlin Heidelberg 2011

pollution, soil and ground contamination, soil erosion and sedimentation, construction and demolition waste, vibration and noise, dust, hazards emissions and odours, and natural features demolition [3], [4].

Environmental problems due to construction sector in developing countries are at different levels. There is often weak management at construction sites [5]. The major type of construction stormwater violations is related to the lack of Best Management Practices (BMPs) [6]. Construction sites lack of proper BMPs is a result of lack of knowledge about the fundamental scientific data [6], [7]. Environmental Protection Agency enforced the Clean Water Act rather than negotiate compliance [6], [8]. It is through enforcement that communities receive incentives to comply with the law [6], [9]. Enforcement of environmental regulations can increase compliance by conducting more inspections [6], [10].

Numerous studies have been performed by other researchers worldwide to define guidelines for minimizing environmental pollution on construction sites within various countries. However, expert system for environmental pollution prevention plan during construction activities is not being done presently. Therefore, this study develops a system for assessing construction sites to recommend BMPs during construction activities.

Assessing and preparing the environmental management plan are the most important and time-consuming task that relates to various data, information, domain law, expert experience and knowledge in terms of construction activities and environmental protection. Therefore, there needs to be a support system for collecting, analyzing and reporting information [11], [12]. Expert system is a computer based system utilizes data and model to support decision maker for solving unstructured problems [13]. It is a promising technology that manages information and data and provides the required expertise [11], [14]. It thus seem well suited to many of tasks associated with environmental management plan.

In this study, an expert system called the Construction Sites Best Management Practices (CSBMP) was developed with a particular emphasis on new development projects. CSBMP has two subsystem; Best Management Practices (BMP), and Construction Site Inspection (CSI). The CSBMP described in this paper has the capacity to advise the end-users regarding Best Management Practices Plan for construction industry, especially related to new development projects.

2   Methodology

CSBMP was developed according to standard expert system development methods. The expert system design and development process is guided by a five-step process: problem assessment, knowledge acquisition, task analysis, system design, system testing and evaluation.

2.1   Problem Assessment

The foremost step for problem assessment is to ensure that the domain under consideration is suited to the application of expert system technology. The domain of construction sites BMPs plan is characterized by many features that make it appropriate and relevant for this purpose. BMPs plan is for detection the problem and guide the user that a system needs to develop through the diagnostic and advisory process. Development of a system for diagnostic tasks usually needs explanation facilities that enable the system to justify their solutions to the user. Such facilities are an essential component of expert system [15]. The important characteristic of expert system is that it should have a clearly defined scope. For construction sites BMPs in this study, it is limited only to the temporary BMPs during construction activities and preliminary design, within which the conceptual nature of the problem and recommendations are identified.

2.2 Data and Knowledge Acquisition

The Best Management Practices (BMPs) identified in this study were drawn from multiple sources of expertise in the field of construction industry in order to control erosion and the discharge of sediment and other pollutants into our environment. Pre-requisite basic knowledge was acquired from textbooks, manuals and guidelines that served as the basis for the development of the initial prototype modules [16]. Expertise drawn from research publications in journals and conference proceedings were used as recent and more specialized data sources within the domain. Current research publications facilitated a more practical approach to various environmental concerns, including legislative enforcement, technological considerations, and finances aspects [16].

Experts in the field were contacted directly to obtain additional information and experience. Yialouris illustrated [17] that two meetings were organized with three experts to elicit opinions about developing an integrated expert geographical information system for soil suitability and soil evaluation. To this end for this study, three meeting were organized with five experts each with experience in practical (from industry), theoretical (from university) or a combination of both circumstances. Experts were specialist in the field of construction management, BMPs for construction sites and environmental impact assessment. After the third meeting, the experts were asked to provide their recommendations on the following topics:

- The properties of construction sites that are most important for BMPs selection,
- BMPs that should be considered for contractor activities, and
- BMPs that should be considered for erosion and sedimentation control.

Expert responses to these questions are summarized in Table 1, 2, and 3.

Table 1. BMPs for construction sites

BMPs for contractor activities	Construction practices
	Material management
	Waste management
	Vehicle and equipment management
	Non-storm water management
	Contractor training
BMPs for erosion and sedimentation control	Site planning consideration
	Soil stabilisation
	Tracking control
	Diversion of runoff
	Velocity reduction
	Sediment trapping

Table 2. BMPs for contractor activities

Construction practices	Paving operation
	Structure construction and painting
Material management	Material delivery and storage
	Material use
	Spill prevention and control
Waste management	Solid waste management
	Hazardous waste management
	Contaminated soil management
	Concrete waste management
	Sanitary/ septic waste management
Vehicle and equipment management	Vehicle and equipment cleaning
	Vehicle and equipment fueling
	Vehicle and equipment maintenance
Non-storm water management	Water conservation practices
	Dewatering operation
	Clear water diversion
	Pile driving operations
	Structure demolition
Contractor training	Employee/ subcontractor training

Table 3. BMPs for erosion and sedimentation control

Site planning consideration	Scheduling
	Preservation of existing vegetation
	Location of potential sources of sediment
Soil stabilisation	Seeding and planting
	Mulching
	Geotextiles and mats
	Streambank stabilisation
	Protection of stockpile
	Dust control
Tracking control	Temporary stream crossing
	Construction road stabilisation
	Stabilised construction entrance
Diversion of runoff	Earth dike
	Temporary drain
	Slope drain
Velocity reduction	Outlet protection
	Check dam
	Slope roughening/ terracing
Sediment trapping	Street sweeping and vacuuming
	Silt fence
	Sand bag barrier
	Storm drain inlet protection
	Sediment trap
	Sediment basin

The primary goal of this stage was to acquire expert experience and knowledge based on information obtained during the previous stage. Five distinct sets of questionnaires were designed in order for the experts to share answers or other information. Knowledge acquired from experts generally includes some conflicting information. Conflicts were resolved by applying Certainty Factors (CF), which quantify the confidence of an expert's belief. The minimum value for the certainty factor was -1.0 (definitely false) and the maximum was +1.0 (definitely true). A negative value represents a degree of disbelief, and a positive a degree of belief. Other CF values are interpreted as "Definitely not" (-1.0), "Almost certainly not" (-0.8), "Probably not" (-0.6), "Maybe not" (-0.4), "Unknown" (-0.2-0.2), "Maybe" (+0.4), "Probably" (+0.6), "Almost certainly" (+0.8), and "Definitely" (+1.0). In expert system, the knowledge base consists of a set of rules that have a common syntax of disjunctive and conjunctive rules. Disjunctive rules are written as follows: IF <evidence E1> OR <evidence E2> ... OR <evidence En> THEN <hypothesis> {cf}. The certainty of hypothesis H is established by Equation 1 [15]. Conjunctive forms are written as follows: IF <evidence E1> AND <evidence E2> ... AND <evidence En> THEN <hypothesis> {cf}. The net certainty of hypothesis H is established as shown in Equation 2 [15].

$$cf\,(H, E1 \cup E2 \cup \ldots \cup En) = \max\,[cf\,(E1), cf\,(E2), \ldots, cf\,(En)] \times cf \qquad (1)$$

$$cf\,(H, E1 \cap E2 \cap \ldots \cap En) = \min\,[cf\,(E1), cf\,(E2), \ldots, cf\,(En)] \times cf \qquad (2)$$

To cope with some conditions that have various alternatives, Expert Choice 11 software was applied on decision making. It was applied as a multi-criteria decision support tool [18], where the research problems were classified into three-level of hierarchy: objective, criteria, and alternative (Fig. 1). Determining the criteria was based on the evaluation obtained from experts. The criteria which were suggested by experts could be availability of technical expertise, efficiency, durability, and cost. For integrating the opinions of multiple experts, number of experts, goal, alternatives, and criteria were modeled by Expert Choice 11 software. The ultimate goal of evaluating the ideal model can be achieved, followed by evaluation alternatives and finally the criteria [19]. After the knowledge engineer has formulated specialized rules for particular problems, the rules are revised to be as general as possible without destroying their ability to contribute to a solution to the original problems.

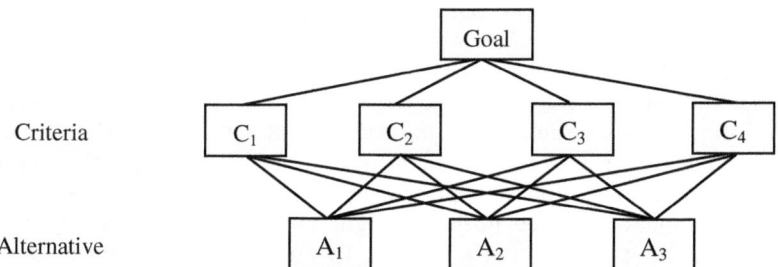

Fig. 1. Goal evaluation by criterion and alternative

2.3   Development of a Prototype System

BMPs for new development projects incorporate many distinct tasks in diverse subject areas. Each of these tasks defined a knowledge base module that contributed to the system. The tasks used to organize BMPs are as follows:

Task 1: Construction practices
Task 2: Material management
Task 3: Waste management
Task 4: Vehicle and equipment management
Task 5: Contractor training
Task 6: Site planning consideration
Task 7: Vegetative stabilisation
Task 8: Physical stabilisation
Task 9: Diversion of runoff
Task 10: Velocity reduction
Task 11: Sediment trapping

Microsoft Visual Basic 6 software (VB) was applied to develop the CSBMP by using a rule-based technique to represent knowledge. The CSBMP reasoning process was controlled by a forward-chaining strategy which represented collections of facts. In this control strategy, rules are formatted to read "IF 'condition is true', THEN 'perform action' ". If the conditions are true within the context of the available knowledge base, the newly generated fact will be stored in the working memory of the knowledge base to perform procedure [20].

A prototype system was built to validate the project and to provide the guidance for future work. Initially, it was used to solve domain tasks in order to explore and test the concepts of problem definition, scoping and domain representation.

2.4   Development of Complete System

The system was further refined to meet the project objectives. Additional data and expert knowledge were acquired and codified in the form of production rules. The overall CSBMP system consists of the data input, BMPs module, and accessories. The data input object represents the facility for data entry that is required before commencing the CSBMP process, while the accessories object and the BMPs module provide support features for the system.

The user interface development began with CSBMP prototype development. A standard Microsoft Windows interface was used so that the users familiar with similar programs could easily adapt to the interface [21]. VB provides a Session Window in which the system developer can create images that allow the user to interact with the knowledge base. It also permits user interaction through forms. The Windows dialogue box guides the user through system operation [20], by presenting the user with a series of questions. The answers provided by the user are used to determine the element or factor. Questions used in this dialogue are described in the dependency diagram. System development was guided by information obtained through knowledge elicitation sessions and tests.

The basic organizational structure of the computer-assisted CSBMP expert system is given in Fig. 2.

2.5   Evaluation and Revision of the System

One construction site was used as a case study for testing and validating modules of the CSBMP. The objective of the case study was to evaluate the performance of the

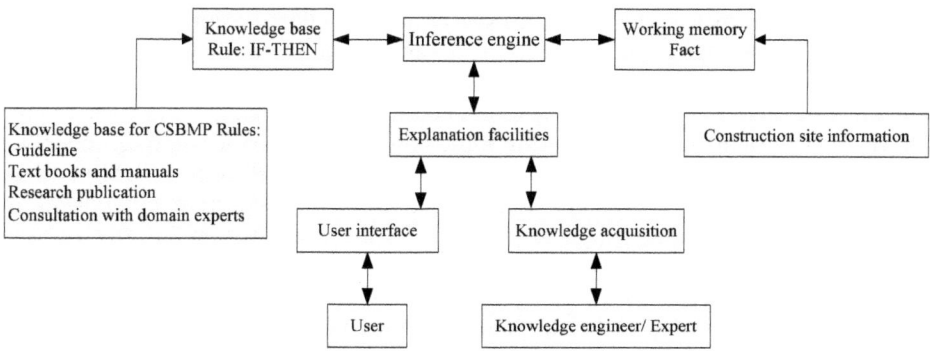

Fig. 2. Basic organizational structure of a computer-assisted CSBMP expert system

CSBMP consultation process when it was applied to a construction site. To do this, a typical questionnaire was designed and given to three domain experts and two software development specialists. The most important issues were considered in evaluating the degree of user acceptance include ease of use, nature of questions, nature of explanations, presentation of results, system utilities, and general considerations [22]. In this study, evaluation was conducted by collecting responses from domain experts and software development specialists who were asked to use the CSBMP and provide comments. Experts approved the system recommendations based on the real practices that through their feedback the CSBMP performed as well as the human experts.

Finally, the user-friendliness of the user interface was evaluated. The main screen of the CSBMP consists of several buttons with test images similar to most other software applications. It contains a selection of commands in each window for the user to select with a mouse. Therefore, the user is only required to perform a minimum amount of work with the keyboard, and very few computer commands and syntax are involved [21]. The CSBMP also provides a teaching feature that is designed to aid inexperienced engineers by guiding them through the process of selecting BMPs, preliminary design steps, and explaining maintenance and inspection requirement associated with BMPs. These features are available to the user through the *General Information* and *User Guide* menus. Furthermore, the users are able to access the *help* features if they are having difficulty at any stage during the consultation process.

3   The CSBMP System

Expert system simulates the learning, reasoning and action processes of a human expert in a given area of science. In this way, it gives a consultant that can substitute the human expert systems with reasonable guaranties of success. These characteristics allow expert system to store data and knowledge, learn from experience and existing data, draw logical conclusions, make decisions, communicate with other experts, explain why decision have been made and take actions as a consequence of all the above [23]. The expert system has been successfully applied in various domains, such as agricultural management, engineering, urban design, water quality management, environmental protection, waste management, and wastewater treatment [24]. Therefore, it seem well suited to environmental management study. GIS (Geographic Information System) tool is one of the most powerful devices for storing, modeling and analysis of geographic data [25]. For this reason, the interface of CSBMP utilizes Geographic Information System (GIS) functions as a supportive component to display spatial maps for visualization of BMPs location. It is more effective and efficient that is able to fulfill the need for mapping and planning [26].

CSBMP is designed in such a way that a series of general and specific questions can be answered by a proposed conceptual structure of the relational database such as:

- What is the probable source of pollutant from the site?
- How can pollution be reduced at its source onsite?
- Which type of BMPs can be recommended for contractor activities?
- Which type of BMPs can be suggested for erosion and sedimentation control?

System enables to compare the site inspection information with recommended BMPs. Therefore, CSBMP can check three hypotheses:

- Hypothesis 1: The uninstalled BMPs would indicate the pollutants discharged into environment if BMPs are not compliance with system recommendation.
- Hypothesis 2: The unmaintained BMPs would indicate the pollutants discharged into environment if BMPs are not compliance with system recommendation.
- Hypothesis 3: BMPs are compliance with system recommendation.

The goal is to identify, the most probable construction activities as environmental friendly and to give proposal on the implementation of BMPs in order to minimize environmental pollution.

4   Results and Discussion

The content of the program consists of BMPs plan for construction sites. The working system of the program is given in Fig. 3. The database, including information about construction stage, site characteristic, and adverse impact of pollutants on environment has been prepared.

The program primarily aims to inform the project owners, engineers, consultants and decision-makers on the following themes:

- Probable effects of pollutants on environment: The program presents adverse impacts of pollutants on environment.
- Pollution source from construction site: Pollution source that indicated to the construction site is informed to the user.
- General information about BMPs plan- The program presents the user various information related to BMPs plan on construction sites:
- Information about BMPs location onsite,

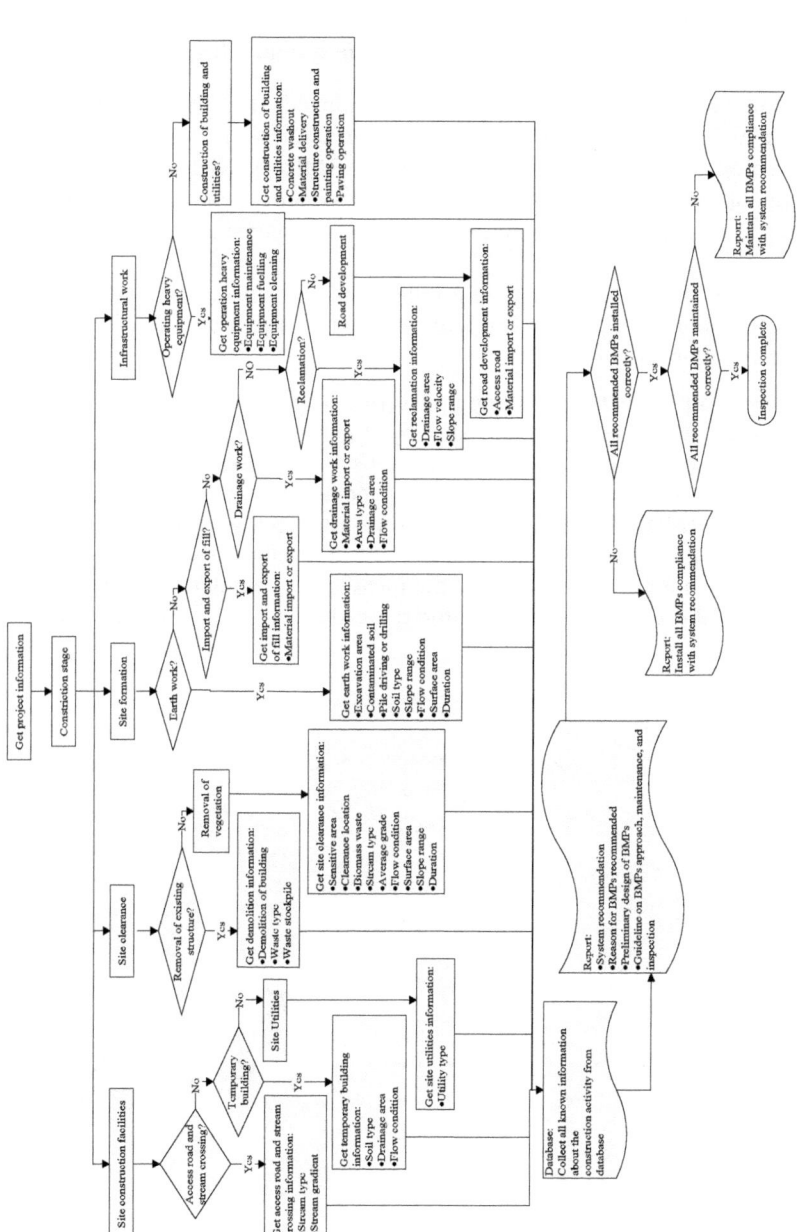

Fig. 3. General structure of CSBMP

BMPs checklist for site inspection,

- Explanation about inspection location,
- General information about the inspection frequency during periods when rainfall results in any discharge from the site and there is no rainfall,
- Example report form about the site inspection, and
- Locations for BMPs in a Geographical Information System (GIS) map.

- Pollution mitigation measures: Finally it recommends the user on pollution prevention plan by referring to the BMPs on construction site.
- System also presents all information and result about BMPs plan in a report form.
- Comparison of site inspection information with system recommendation: The comparison of inspection information with system recommendation in different legal regulations is done.
- Present situation of the site: The uninstalled and unmaintained BMPs would indicate the pollutants discharged into environment if BMPs are not compliance with system recommendation.

The user is advised on project steps through a series of choices from CSBMP. An example was made for a construction site by running the software. At each consultation step, the set of requested data from the user are shown in Fig 4. As a first step, after entering the information of the project's location, the construction site can be seen on screen. CSBMP delivers immediate results after receiving data as shown in Fig 4. The system then presents all results and a preliminary design of the recommended BMPs in a report form. After the queries are completed, related result map is linked from the database and monitored on the screen to view the BMPs locations (Fig 5).

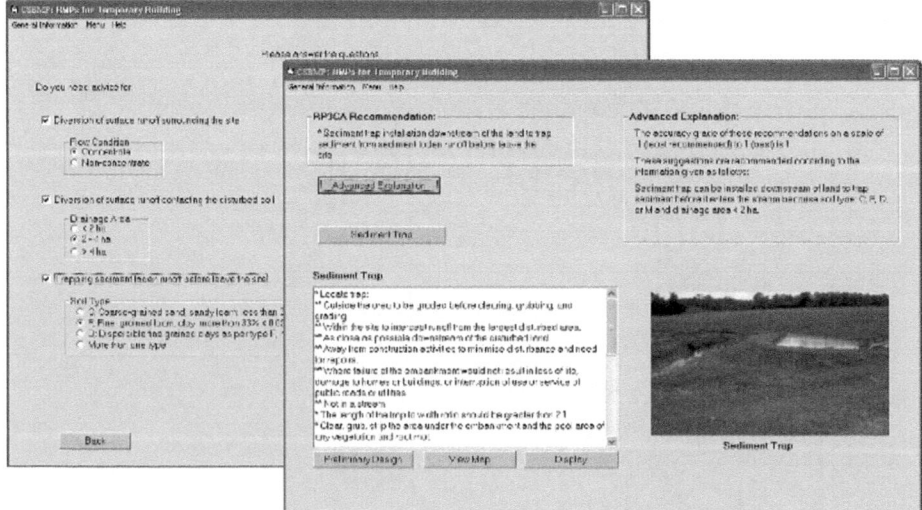

Fig. 4. The system requested data and recommended BMPs

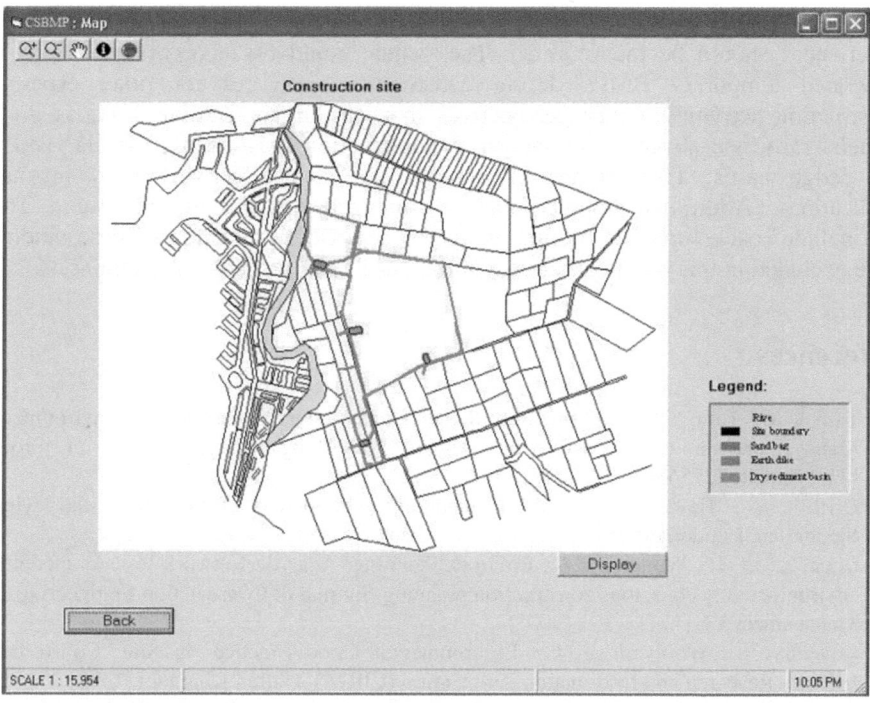

Fig. 5. BMPs locations in a Geographical Information System (GIS) map

5   Summary

This research has briefly defined expert system with respect to its use in selecting temporary BMPs plan; it also developed an expert system as a BMPs advisor for users to apply at new development projects. VB is used to develop the user interface and knowledge base to provide system suggestion. The study employs questionnaire to acquire experts knowledge, uses certainty factor for measuring the expert belief and disbelief of system rules, applies Expert Choice 11 software for integrating multiple experts opinion where various alternatives are available by considering cost, durability, efficiency and availability of technical expertise as criteria, transforms experts experience into rules, stores rules in knowledge base, uses a forward-chaining mechanism to build the inference engine, develops an explanation facility to retrieve advice details, and provides recommendations and results. To carry out the development of CSBMP, it is found that the knowledge acquisition and establishment of knowledge base are the most difficult and important task. Although knowledge sources in this study include books, guidelines, research publication, and expertise about BMPs for construction sites. Knowledge base in CSBMP that is generated by using questionnaire depends on the knowledge gained from experts who were interviewed. This required the development of an in-depth comprehension of knowledge modeling in particular and of the applicable domain in general. The knowledge base in an expert system is a continuously changing entity, which required continuous improvement and expansion, hence, the latest findings in literature or experiences should be incorporated. The system could be incorporated as part of integrated temporary BMPs during construction activities for other types of construction activities. Other perspectives in terms of applications such as dams, tunnels, railways, airports and industrial construction may need particular special knowledge bases. These types of systems are also effectively used in other applications. [Additional module could be combined with the present system. They can include cost estimation, design, and permanent BMPs technique. These modules were excluded in this research because of time and other resources limitations.

References

1. Tam, C.M., Tam, V.W.Y., Tsui, W.S.: Green Construction Assessment for Environmental Management in the Construction Industry of Hong Kong. Journal of Project Management 22, 563–571 (2004)
2. Griffith, A.: Environmental management in construction (Building & Surveying). Macmillan, London (1995)
3. Chen, Z., Li, H., Wong, C.T.C.: EnvironalPlanning: Analytic Network Process model for environmentally conscious construction planning. Journal of Construction Engineering and Management 131(1), 92–101 (2005)
4. Coventry, S., Woolveridge, C.: Environmental Good Practice on Site. Construction Industry Research and Information Association (CIRIA), United Kingdom (1999)
5. Baris, D.P., Erik, J.: Construction and Environment-Improving Energy Efficiency. Journal of Building Issues 10(2), 3–21 (2000)
6. Alsharif, K.: Construction and Stormwater Pollution: Policy, Violations, and Penalties. Journal of Land Use Policy 27, 612–616 (2010)
7. Kaufman, M.M.: Erosion Control at Construction Sites: the Science–policy Gap. Environmental Management 26, 89–97 (2000)
8. Hunter, S., Waterman, R.W.: Determining an Agency's Regulatory Style: How Does the EPA Water Office Enforce the Law? The Western Political Quarterly 45, 403–417 (1992)
9. Houck, O.: The Clean Water Act TMDL Program: Law, Policy, and Implementation. Environmental Law Institute, Washington, DC (2002)
10. Winter, S., May, P.J.: Regulatory Enforcement and Compliance: Examining Agro-environmental Policy. Journal of Policy Analysis and Management 18, 625–651 (1999)
11. Say, N.P., Yucela, M., Yılmazerb, M.: A Computer-based System for Environmental Impact Assessment (EIA) Applications to Eenergy Power Stations in Turkey: C- EDINFO. Journal of Energy Policy 35, 6395–6401 (2007)
12. Muthusamy, N., Ramalingam, M.: Environmental Impact Assessment for Urban planning and Development Using GIS. In: Third International Conference on Environment and Health, India, Chennai (2003)
13. Hartati, S., Sitanggang, I.S.M.: A Fuzzy Based Decision Support System for Evaluating Land Suitability and Selecting Crops. Journal of Computer Science 6, 417–424 (2010)
14. Lohani, B.N., Evans, J.W., Everitt, R.R., Ludwig, H., Carpenter, R.A., Liang Tu, S.: Environmental Impact Assessment for Developing Countries in Asia. Overview Asian Development Bank, vol. 1 (1997)
15. Negnevitsky, M.: Artificial Intelligence: A Guide to Intelligent System, 2nd edn. Addison-Wesley, England (2005)

16. Ahmad Basri, N.E.: An Expert System for the Design of Composting Facilities in Developing Countries, PhD thesis, School of Civil Engineering, University of Leeds (1999)
17. Yialouris, C.P., Kollias, V., Lorentzos, N.A., Kalivas, D., Sideridis, A.B.: An Integrated Expert Geographical Information System for Soil Suitability and Soil Evaluation. J. Geographic Information and Decision Analysis 1(2), 89–99 (1997)
18. Adamović, P., Časlav Dunović, C., Nahod, M.M.: Expert choice model for choosing appropriate trenchless method for pipe laying (June 20, 2010),
    https://www.crosbi.znanstvenici.hr/.../348146.Adamovic_Dunovic_Nahod_Prag_09_2007.pdf
19. Nikmardan, A.: Expert system Choice 11. Jihad Amirkabir University, Iran (2007)
20. Pauziah, H.G., Mohd, K.Y., Latifah, M., Mohamed, D.: Knowledge-Based System for River Water Quality Management. J. Scientific Research 33(1), 153–162 (2009)
21. Islam, M.D.N.: Development of an Expert System for Making High Performance Concrete Using Hybrid Knowledge Representation System. PhD thesis, Universiti Kebangsaan Malaysia (2004)
22. Durkin, J.: Expert systems: design and development. Macmillan Publishing Company, United State of America (1994)
23. Deprizon, S., Amiruddin, D., Atiq, R.: Development of knowledge-based expert system for flexible pavement design. J. Applied Sci. 9, 2372–2380 (2009)
24. Liao, S.H.: Expert system methodologies and applications-a decade review from 1995-004. J. Expert Syst. Appl. 28, 93–103 (2005)
25. Khojastehfar, E., Daryan, A.S., Assareh, M.A.: Probabilistic Empirical Green's Function Method in Ground Motion Simulation. American Journal of Engineering and Applied Sciences 2, 160–164 (2009)
26. Hasmadi, H., Pakhriazad, Z., Mohamad, F.S.: Geographic Information System-Allocation Model for Forest Path: A Case Study in Ayer Hitam Forest Reserve. American Journal of Applied Sciences 7, 376–380 (2010), doi:10.3844/ajassp.2010.376.380.
27. Pushpa, S., Elias, S., Easwarakumar, K.S., MaamarI, Z.: Indexing Scholarly Publications using Telescopic Vector Trees to Discover Authors with Multiple Expertise. International Journal of Information Studies 2(3), 166–173 (2010)
28. Liu, C., Jiang, Z., Chen, B., Huang, Y., Lu, D., Ma, Y.: An Expert acquiring method of Diagnosis and Senario based on maximum knowledge entropy. International Journal of Web Applications 1(2), 90–101 (2009)

Target Tracking on Re-entry Based on an IWO Enhanced Particle Filter

Mohamadreza Ahmadi, Mehrnoosh Shafati, and Hamed Mojallali

Electrical Engineering Department, Faculty of Engineering,
University of Guilan, Rasht, Iran
mrezaahmadi@aol.com, mehrnoosh.sh@gmail.com,
mojallali@guilan.ac.ir

Abstract. Tracking a ballistic object on re-entry from radar observations is an extremely complex and intriguing problem among aerospace and signal processing experts. Since mathematical models for ballistic targets and sensors are subject to nonlinearity and uncertainty, conventional estimation methodologies cannot be utilized. In this study, a new meta-heuristic particle filtering (PF) strategy established upon the nature-inspired invasive weed optimization (IWO) is applied to the challenging re-entry target tracking problem. Firstly, the sampling step of PF is translated into a non-concave maximum likelihood optimization problem, and then the IWO algorithm is integrated. Subsequently, the PFIWO algorithm is applied to a benchmark re-entry target tracking problem. Results are given which demonstrate the proposed scheme has superior tracking performance in comparison with other nonlinear estimation techniques.

Keywords: Particle Filter, Nonlinear Filtering, Re-entry Target Tracking, Invasive Weed Optimization.

1 Introduction

Tracking ballistic objects is one of the most cumbersome and interesting problems in aerospace and signal processing communities. The ultimate goal of this research is to track, intercept, and destroy a ballistic target before it collides and causes damages. The interest in the target tracking topic stems from the fact that the global proliferation of ballistic missiles has augmented the need for developing highly reliable tracking algorithms. However, since the mathematical models for ballistic targets and sensors (e.g. radar) are subject to severe nonlinearity and uncertainty, traditional estimation strategies are not functional. Hence, optimal solutions [1,2] to the filtering problem within a Bayesian estimation framework cannot be achieved. Analytic approximations like extended Kalman filter (EKF), unscented Kalman filter (UKF), and sampling approaches like PF can lead to sub-optimal solutions, despite the presence of nonlinearities and measurement noises [3]. Literature asserts that the tracking algorithms established upon the PF method outperform other estimation algorithms [3, 4].

In a seminal paper [4], Gordon et al. proposed the particle filter which could handle nonlinear/non-Gaussian estimation problems. Unlike the previously suggested sub-optimal

P. Pichappan, H. Ahmadi, and E. Ariwa (Eds.): INCT 2011, CCIS 241, pp. 94–107, 2011.
© Springer-Verlag Berlin Heidelberg 2011

approaches which were mostly based on local linearization, the PF algorithm utilizes a set of N random samples (or particles) to approximate the posterior distribution via the importance sampling or more generally Monte Carlo techniques. In fact, the continual evolution of the particles is determined by a group of importance sampling and re-sampling steps. Briefly, the re-sampling step performs the task of adaptively clustering the particles in the regions of high posterior probability. This is usually done by statistically multiplying and/or discarding particles at each time step [5].

Recently, the interest in the subject of integrating meta-heuristic algorithms in PF has increased. In [6], Tong *et al.* proposed an optimized PF based on particle swarm optimization (PSO) algorithm which exposed improved estimation accuracy. Many subsequent studies also followed the same trend using the PSO method; e.g., refer to [7]. Notably, Akhtar *et al.* [8] suggested a PSO accelerated immune particle filter by incorporating meta-heuristic computational methods such as immune algorithm (IA) and, of course, the PSO. However, the integration of other meta-heuristic algorithms in PF has not yet been addressed to the authors' knowledge.

The PF approach used in the present paper is optimized based on the IWO algorithm. Since sampling in PF is performed in a sub-optimal manner, it can bring about some performance defects such as "sample impoverishment" [3]. Using an appropriate fitness function for particles, such problems are circumvented and an enhanced PF algorithm is achieved thanks to the IWO approach. It is worth noting that the aforementioned fitness function is equivalent to a non-concave maximum likelihood optimization problem, in which the particles represent the variables. Throughout this paper the modified method is referred as PFIWO. The usefulness of the combined method becomes clear as it is evaluated against a benchmark re-entry target tracking problem. In addition, the results based on other estimation methods are given and compared which again demonstrates the PFIWO algorithm's capabilities.

The framework of this paper is described next. Section 2 includes a concise description of the recursive Bayesian estimation and the particle filtering algorithm. The IWO algorithm is discussed in section 3. The proposed PFIWO method is outlined in section 4. The mathematical formulations for the re-entry target tracking problem are presented in section 5. Target tracking results based on the PFIWO algorithm are addressed in section 6. Concluding remarks are given in section 7.

2   The Particle Filter

2.1   The Recursive Bayesian Estimation Method

Suppose a nonlinear/non-Gaussian system with a state-space model as described below

$$x_t = f(x_{t-1}) + v_{t-1}, \qquad x_t \sim p(x_t | x_{t-1}) \tag{1.a}$$

$$y_t = g(x_t) + w_t, \qquad y_t \sim p(y_t | x_t) \tag{1.b}$$

where x_t is the unobserved n-dimensional state vector at time t with probability distribution $p(x_t | x_{t-1})$. y_t is the noise corrupted m-dimensional observation vector at time t with likelihood $p(y_t | x_t)$. v and w represent the independent additive process and measurement noises, respectively. $f(.)$ the system model and $g(.)$ the observation model are generally nonlinear functions. Fig. 1 illustrates this special system framework.

Filtering is the task of sequentially estimating the states (parameters or hidden variables) of a system as a set of observations become available on-line [1,3]. In other words, filtering is aimed at estimating the posterior distribution $p(x_t|y_t)$ as a set of observations $Y_t = (y_1, y_2, ..., y_t)^T$ becomes available. The Bayesian solution to the filtering problem consists of two stages [1]:

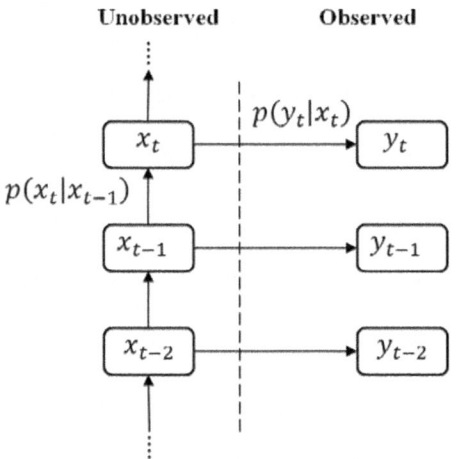

Fig. 1. A graphical representation of the state-space model described by Eq. (1)

1) Prediction: using the prior density function and the Chapman-Kolomogrov equation we derive

$$p(x_t|y_{t-1}) = \int p(x_t|x_{t-1})p(x_{t-1}|y_{t-1})dx_{t-1} , \qquad (2)$$

2) Update: based on the Bayes' formula

$$p(x_t|y_t) = \frac{p(y_t|x_t)p(x_t|y_{t-1})}{p(y_t|y_{t-1})} , \qquad (3)$$

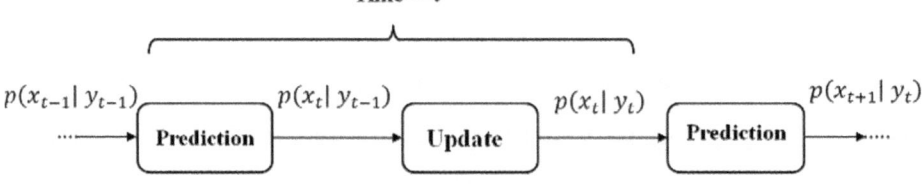

Fig. 2. The Bayesian approach to filtering problem

The algorithm is initialized with $p(x_0|y_0) = p(x_0)$ and $p(x_1|y_0) = p(x_1)$. One step operation of the Bayesian filtering is portrayed in Fig. 2. However, it is apparent that achieving a closed form analytical solution to the untraceable integral in Eq. (2) and therefore the solution to Eq. (3) is very difficult, not to mention the severity caused when the state dimensions increase.

So, an optimal solution cannot be attained except under very limited conditions (linear transition functions and Gaussian noise) using the well-known Kalman filter (KF). The interested readers are referred to a good expository overview of optimal approaches found in [1].

Sub-optimal solutions exist for rather general models with nonlinear evolution functions and non-Gaussian noises [3]. Nevertheless, due to the nature of these methods (EKF and UKF) which are based on local linearization, the estimation performance is, more or less, limited. Estimation techniques established upon sequential Monte Carlo methods, namely the PF, are a promising alternative to local linearization algorithms.

2.2   The Generic Particle Filter

PF is a sequential Monte Carlo (SMC) method within Bayesian models which approximates the state of a system using sample points (particles). Specifically, it utilizes a number of samples (particles) to deal with the untraceable integrals given by (2) and (3). In other words, the recursive Bayesian estimation algorithm (discussed in the previous section) is implemented via the Monte Carlo sampling rather than solving equations (2) and (3) directly. A graphical representation of the SMC method is provided in Fig.3. The flow of the PF algorithm is as described next. Let $\tilde{x}^i$, $i = 1, 2, ..., N$ be the drawn samples from the posterior distribution $p(x_t|y_t)$. The filter is initialized as [3, 4, 9]:

$$\tilde{x}_0^i \sim p(x_0), \qquad i = 1, 2, ..., N \tag{4}$$

For $t = 1, 2, ...$, in the first step, the posterior distribution is estimated based on the Monte Carlo method as

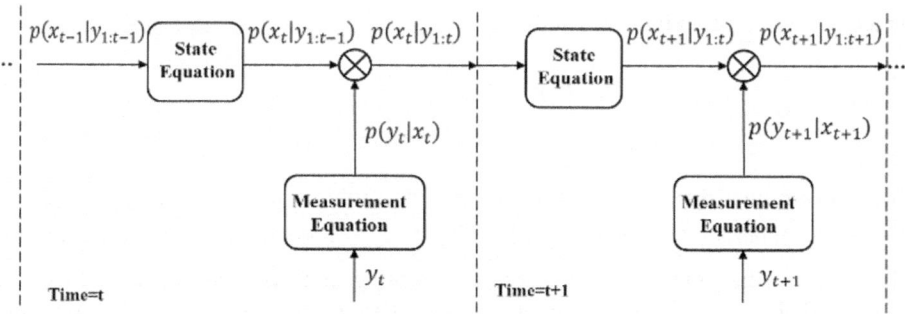

Fig. 3. Illustration of the SMC method

$$p(x_t \mid y_t) = \sum_{i=1}^{N} w_i^t \delta(x - \tilde{x}_t^i), \quad s.t. \quad \sum_{i=1}^{N} w_i^t = 1 \tag{5}$$

Then, for $i = 1, 2, ..., N$ sample from the proposal distribution $q(x_t \mid x_{t-1})$ as

$$\tilde{x}_t^i \sim q(x_t \mid \tilde{x}_{t-1}^i) , \tag{6}$$

Subsequently, update the importance weights

$$w_i^t = w_i^{t-1} \frac{p(y_t \mid \tilde{x}_{t-1}^i) p(\tilde{x}_t^i \mid \tilde{x}_{t-1}^i)}{q(\tilde{x}_t^i \mid \tilde{x}_{t-1}^i)} , \tag{7}$$

Note that if $p(x_t \mid x_{t-1}) = q(x_t \mid x_{t-1})$, equations (6) and (7) converts to

$$\tilde{x}_t^i \sim p(x_t \mid \tilde{x}_{t-1}^i) , \tag{8.a}$$

$$w_i^t = w_i^{t-1} p(y_t \mid \tilde{x}_{t-1}^i) , \tag{8.b}$$

Afterwards, for $i = 1, 2, ..., N$ the weights are normalized

$$w_i^t = \frac{w_i^t}{\sum_{j=1}^{N} w_j^t} , \tag{9}$$

A prevalent problem with PF is the degeneracy phenomenon where after a few iterations, the weights of most samples become trivial whereas those of a few samples become dominant. This is a commonplace phenomenon when the system or measurement noise is small. In extreme cases when there is no noise, the approximated posterior distribution could be limited to a peak, and no further measurements can affect the posterior distribution. As a consequence, most samples cannot contribute to the posterior estimation, and the distributions are determined by a few dominant samples. This phenomenon wastes the computational resources on samples with negligible importance weights, and may abate the applicability of the Monte Carlo technique. A measure of degeneracy is the effective sample size N_{eff} which can be empirically evaluated as

$$\hat{N}_{eff} = \frac{1}{\sum_{i=1}^{N} (w_i^t)^2} , \tag{10}$$

The conventional approach to solve around the problem of sample degeneracy is to define a degeneracy threshold N_{th}. If $\hat{N}_{eff} < N_{th}$, "re-sampling" should be initiated [5]. It should be noted that excessive re-sampling can also lead to an unfavorable outcome known as sample impoverishment wherein samples with high probability distribution are over-sampled. This can be avoided by choosing a suitable $\hat{N}_{eff}$, and by increasing the number of particles. The pseudo-code of the basic particle filter with the assumption that the proposal distribution is equal to the prior distribution is shown in Fig.4.

1. *Initialization*

- $t = 0$. For $i = 1, ..., N$, Sample $x_0^{(i)}$ From an initial distribution and set $t = 1$

2. *Prediction*

- For $i = 1, ..., N$, Sample $\tilde{x}_t^{(i)} \sim p(x_t | x_{t-1}^{(i)})$

- For $i = 1, ..., N$, evaluate the importance weights $\tilde{w}_t^{(i)} \sim p(y_t | x_t^{(i)})$

- Normalize the weights

3. *Resampling*

- Resample N new particles $\left\{ x_t^{(i)}, \text{For } i = 1, ..., N \right\}$ with replacement from the set $\left\{ \tilde{x}_t^{(i)}, \text{For } i = 1, ..., N \right\}$ according to the importance weights.

- Set $t = t + 1$ and go to step 2.

Fig. 4. The pseudo-code of the generic PF

3   Invasive Weed Optimization

The bio-inspired IWO algorithm was introduced by Mehrabian and Lucas [10] which imitates the colonial behavior of invasive weeds in nature. The IWO algorithm has shown to be successful in converging to optimal solution by incorporating some basic characteristics of weed colonization in nature, e.g. seeding, growth and competition. The process flow of the IWO algorithm is outlined below:

1) Initially, disperse the seeds $S_i = (s_1, s_2, ..., s_n)^T$, where n is the number of selected variables, over the search space randomly such that each seed contains random values for each variable in the $n - D$ solution space.

2) The fitness of each individual seed is calculated according to the optimization problem, and the seeds grow to weeds able to produce new units.

3) Each individual is ranked based on its fitness with respect to other weeds. Subsequently, each weed produces new seeds depending on its rank in the population. The number of seeds to be created by each weed alters linearly from N_{min} to N_{max} which can be computed using the equation given below

$$\text{Number of seeds} = \frac{F_i - F_{worst}}{F_{best} - F_{worst}} (N_{max} - N_{min}) + N_{min} , \tag{11}$$

in which, F_i is the fitness of i'th weed. F_{worst}, and F_{best} denote the respective best and the worst fitness in the weed population. This step ensures that each weed take part in the reproduction process.

4) The generated seeds are normally distributed over the field with zero mean and a varying standard deviation of σ_{iter} described by

$$\sigma_{iter} = (\frac{iter_{max} - iter}{iter_{max}})^n (\sigma_f - \sigma_0) + \sigma_f \,, \tag{12}$$

where, $iter_{max}$ and $iter$ are the maximum number of iteration cycles assigned by the user, and the current iteration number respectively. σ_0 and σ_f represent the pre-defined initial and final standard deviations. n is called the nonlinear modulation index. In order to obtain a full and swift scan of possible values of standard deviation, it has been examined that the most appropriate value for nonlinear modulation index is 3 [11]. The fitness of each seed is calculated along with their parents and the whole population is ranked. Those weeds with less fitness are eliminated through competition and only a number of weeds remain which are equal to *Maximum Weed Population*.

5) The procedure is repeated at step 2 until the maximum number of iterations allowed by the user is reached.

4   The Proposed PFIWO Method

The sampling step of the basic PF is not performed in an optimal manner, and can result in tracking errors. Thus, the IWO is exploited as a means to enhance the sampling step. We make a remark that the objective of the IWO algorithm in the sampling step is to locate the particles which contribute to greater weights. In other words, the PFIWO algorithm can bring about better estimation performance with less number of particles; because, the particles in PFIWO correspond to greater weights.

The fitness of the i'th particle can be computed conveniently as

$$F_i = \frac{p(y_t|\tilde{x}_{t-1}^i) p(\tilde{x}_t^i|\tilde{x}_{t-1}^i)}{q(y_t|\tilde{x}_{t-1}^i)} \,, \tag{13}$$

which in case of $p(x_t|x_{t-1}) = q(x_t|x_{t-1})$ reduces to

$$F_i = p(y_t|\tilde{x}_{t-1}^i) \,, \tag{14}$$

From the above formulation, the task of the IWO algorithm would be to maximize the fitness function given by equations (13) or (14). Correspondingly, the sampling step is modified as follows:

1. After the fitness of each particle is computed and evaluated, the particles are ranked based on their fitness in the population; i.e., those particles with greater weights correspond to higher ranks.

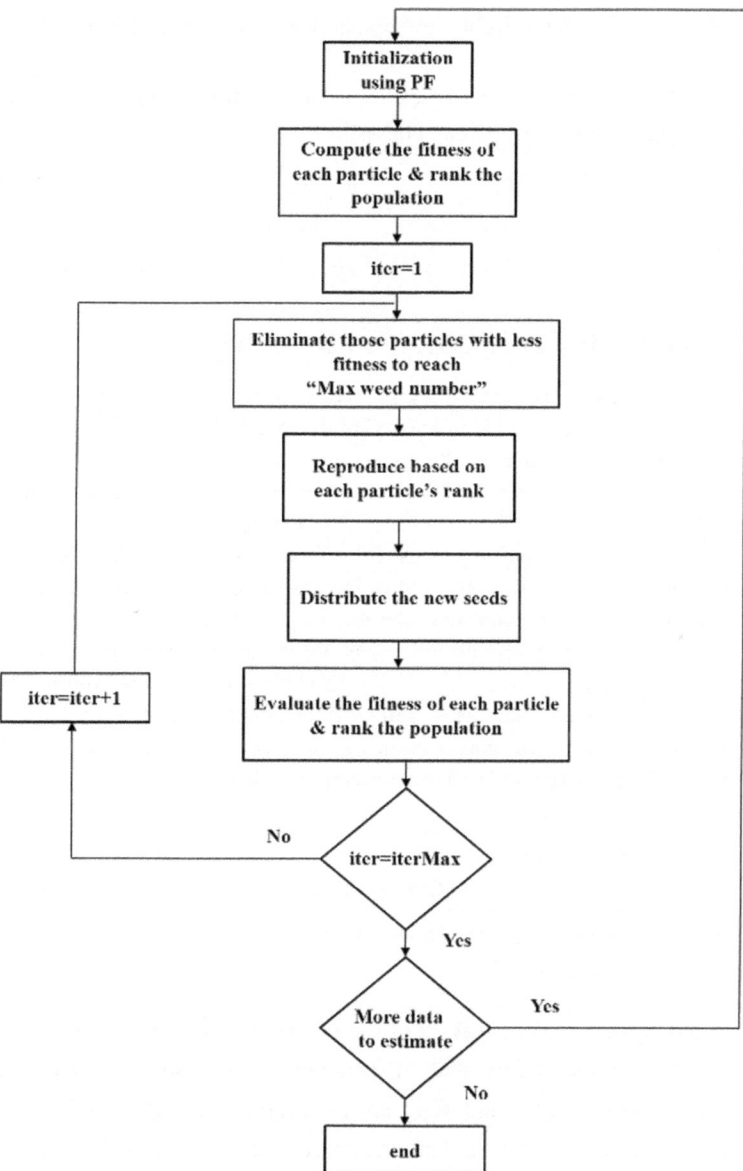

Fig. 5. The flowchart of the proposed PFIWO algorithm

2. Perform steps 3, 4, and 5 of the IWO algorithm as discussed in section III until a preset maximum number of iteration cycles is attained. It is worth noting that since the basic PF is considerably time-consuming the maximum number of iteration cycles should be chosen as a compromise between estimation accuracy and algorithm run-time.

3. Subsequently, the weights are updated and normalized using equations (7) and (9).
4. In order reproduce and pick out the particles with larger weights a resampling step is followed. That is,

$$\left\{ \tilde{x}_t^i, w_i^t \right\}_{i=1}^N = \left\{ \tilde{x}_t^i, \frac{1}{N} \right\}_{i=1}^N , \tag{15}$$

A simple flowchart of the proposed PFIWO algorithm is given in Fig. 5.

5   Tracking a Ballistic Object on Re-entry

This section considers the re-entry tracking problem, where a ballistic object enters the atmosphere at high altitude and at a very high speed. The position of the object is tracked by radar which measures the range and the bearing. This problem has been addressed in a number of papers [12-14] on nonlinear filtering, since the forces which affect the object possess strong nonlinearities and are a challenge to any filtering method. There are three major forces in effect. The chief force in operation is aerodynamic drag, which is a function of object speed and has a considerable nonlinear variation in altitude. The second one is the gravity, which accelerates the object toward the center of the earth. The remaining forces are random buffeting terms [12]. Under such forces, the trajectory of the object is almost ballistic at the beginning. But, as the density of the atmosphere increases, drag effects become important and the object decelerates rapidly until its motion becomes almost vertical. The state-space model for the system described above can be characterized as follows [13]:

$$\dot{x}_1(t) = x_3(t) , \tag{16.a}$$

$$\dot{x}_2(t) = x_4(t) , \tag{16.b}$$

$$\dot{x}_3(t) = D(t)x_3(t) + G(t)x_1(t) + \omega_1(t) , \tag{16.c}$$

$$\dot{x}_4(t) = D(t)x_4(t) + G(t)x_2(t) + \omega_2(t) , \tag{16.d}$$

$$\dot{x}_5(t) = \omega_3(t) , \tag{16.e}$$

wherein x_1 and x_2 denote the position of the object in two dimensional space, x_3 and x_4 are the velocity components, and x_5 is a parameter associated with the object's aerodynamic properties. $D(t)$ and $G(t)$ are the drag-related and gravity-related force terms, respectively. $\omega_i(t)$, $i = 1, 2, 3$ are the process noise vectors. The force terms can be calculated as

$$D(t) = \beta(t) \exp\left(\frac{R_0 - R(t)}{H_0} \right) V(t) , \tag{17.a}$$

$$G(t) = -\frac{G_{m_0}}{R^3(t)} , \tag{17.b}$$

$$\beta(t) = \beta_0 \exp\left(x_5(t) \right) , \tag{17.c}$$

where $R(t) = \sqrt{x_1^2(t) + x_2^2(t)}$ is the distance from the center of the earth and $V(t) = \sqrt{x_3^2(t) + x_4^2(t)}$ is the object speed. The radar (which is located at $(R_0, 0)$) is able to measure r (range) and θ (bearing) at a frequency of 10Hz as follows

$$r = \sqrt{(x_1(t) - R_0)^2 + x_2(t)^2} + \xi_1(t) , \tag{18.a}$$

$$\theta = \arctan(\frac{x_2(t)}{x_1(t) - R_0}) + \xi_2(t) , \tag{18.b}$$

where $\xi_1(t)$ and $\xi_2(t)$ are zero-mean uncorrelated noise processes with variances of $1\,m$ and $17\,mrads$ [12,13].

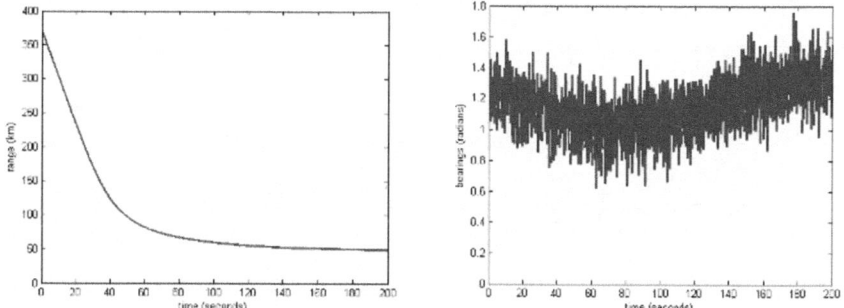

Fig. 6. The measured range (left) and bearing (right) of the simulated ballistic target

6   Simulation Results

In this section, the estimation performance of the proposed PFIWO method is examined and compared with the conventional PF. Let the simulated discrete process covariance be [14]

$$Q(k) = \begin{bmatrix} 2.4064 \times 10^{-5} & 0 & 0 \\ 0 & 2.4064 \times 10^{-5} & 0 \\ 0 & 0 & 10^{-6} \end{bmatrix} , \tag{19}$$

The values for different constants are set as [13]

$$\beta_0 = -0.59783 ,$$

$$H_0 = 13.406 ,$$

$$G_{m_0} = 3.9860 \times 10^5 ,$$

$$R_0 = 6374 , \tag{20}$$

The stochastic differential equations (16) was simulated using 2000 steps of the Euler-Maruyama method with $\Delta t = 0.1s$. The measured range and bearing are portrayed in Fig.6.

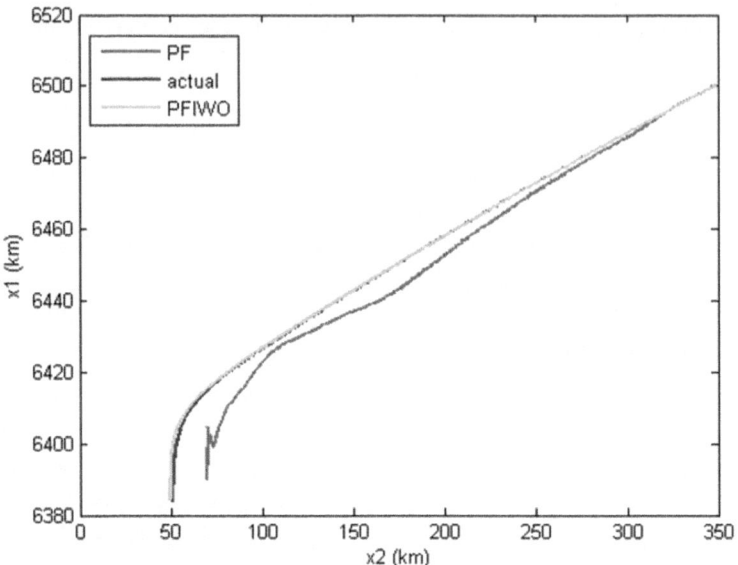

Fig. 7. Re-entry target tracking results obtained from PF and PFIWO

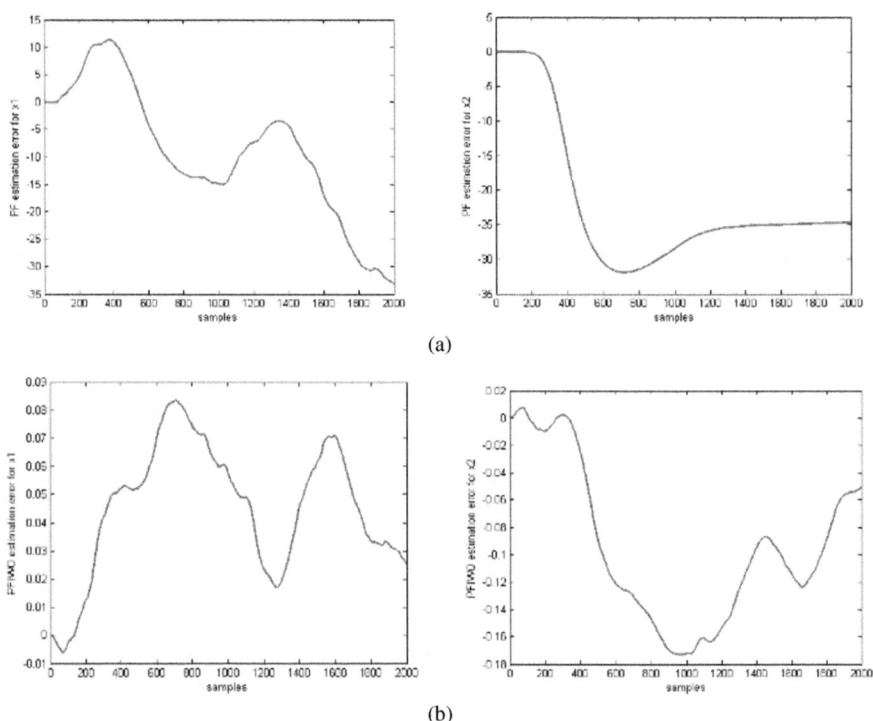

Fig. 8. The target tracking errors for (a) PF and (b) PFIWO

Table 1. Parameters used in PFIWO algorithm

$iter_{max}$	σ_0	σ_f	N_{max}	N_{min}	Max. Weed Number
15	0.1	0.00001	3	1	1500

The number of particles was set to 1500 which is relatively low for a target tracking problem. The main reason for this choice is to demonstrate the ability of the PFIWO method to estimate the states of the ballistic object with less number of particles where PF cannot reach an acceptable result. The degeneracy threshold N_{th} was selected as 1200, and a systematic re-sampling scheme [5] has been chosen for the PF method. The parameters of the PFIWO algorithm are given in Table 1. Note that the "Max. Weed Number" should be equal to the number of particles. The target tracking results obtained using the PF and PFIWO methodologies are depicted in Fig.7. The corresponding estimation errors are also provided in Fig.8. As it is observed from the figures, when the PFIWO scheme is used, the tracking errors are in the satisfactory range and PFIWO is capable of tracking the object's trajectory. On the other hand, large state estimation errors result as the traditional PF algorithm is utilized. It is obvious that the deteriorated estimation accuracy of PF is a consequence of the number of particles, whereas the proposed PFIWO method has preserved its approximation performance with the same number of particles.

For the sake of comparison, we have implemented other estimation techniques such as EKF, and UKF. For a comprehensive description of the EKF and UKF algorithms, the readers are referred to [3]. The parameters of the UKF are set as selected in [14]. The number of particles was set to 2500 in order to arrive at a logical assessment. The threshold was preset to 2000. The parameters of the PFIWO algorithm are given in Table 2. The estimation errors are portrayed in Fig.9. The aforementioned figures include root mean square error (RMSE) and standard deviation of error (STDE). It should be noted that the left figures are the results for x_1 and the right figures illustrate the results for x_2. It is apparent from the figures that the PFIWO algorithm yields better estimation performance compared with EKF, UKF, and PF.

Table 2. Parameters used in PFIWO algorithm

$iter_{max}$	σ_0	σ_f	N_{max}	N_{min}	Max.Weed Number
20	0.1	0.00001	4	2	2500

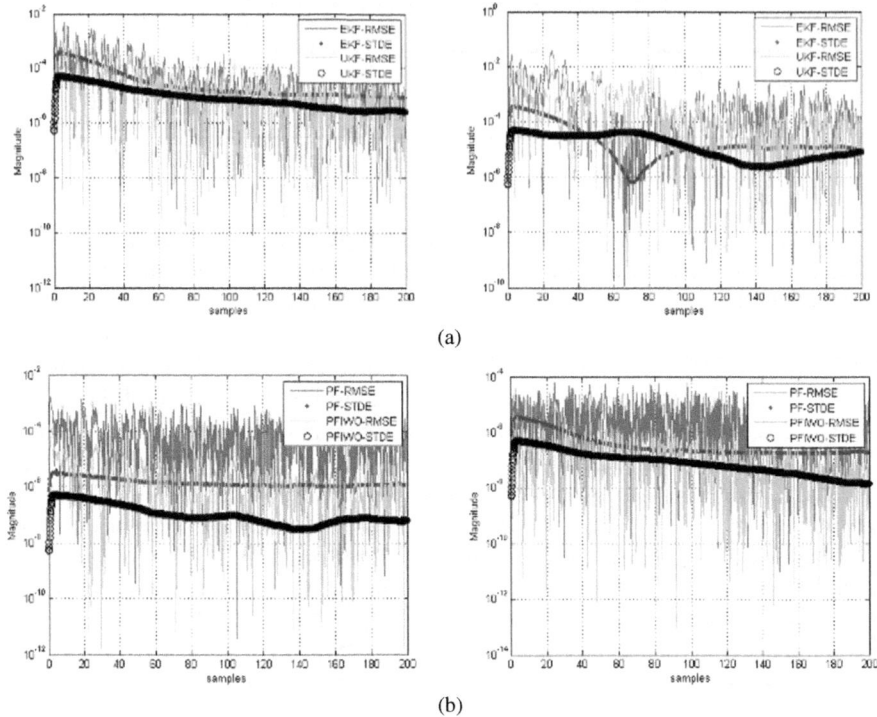

(a)

(b)

Fig. 9. The estimation results for the re-entry tracking problem (a) PF and (b) PFIWO

7   Conclusions

An enhanced PF algorithm established upon the IWO scheme is applied to the re-entry target tracking problem. Firstly, the sampling step is transformed into an optimization problem by defining an apt fitness function. Then, the IWO algorithm is adopted to deal with the optimization challenge efficiently. The simulation results on a benchmark re-entry vehicle tracking problem based on the proposed methodology and other previously proposed estimation methods are included which verifies the algorithm's accuracy. A suggested subject for future research could be to integrate other meta-heuristic algorithms as a means to optimize the PF. Another interesting topic could be to investigate the performance of the PFIWO method when applied to other problems in nonlinear estimation such as state estimation of extremely nonlinear chemical plants.

References

[1]   Kailath, T., Sayed, A., Hasibi, B.: Linear estimation. Prentice Hall (2000)
[2]   Kalman, R.E., Bucy, R.S.: New results in linear filtering and prediction theory. Trans. ASME, J. Basic Eng. 83, 95–108 (1961)

[3] Ristic, B., Arulampalam, M., Gordon, A.: Beyond Kalman Filters: Particle filters for tracking applications. Artech House (2004)

[4] Gordon, N., Salmond, D., Smith, A.F.: A Novel Approach to Nonlinear/non-Gaussian Bayesian Estimation. IEEE Proc. F, Radar Signal Process. 140, 107–113 (1993)

[5] Douc, R., Cappe, O., Moulines, E.: Comparison of Resampling Schemes for Particle Filtering. In: 4th International Symposium on Image and Signal Process. and Analysis (ISPA), Zagreb, Croatia (September 2005)

[6] Tong, G., Fang, Z., Xu, X.: A Particle Swarm Optimized Particle Filter for Nonlinear System State Estimation. In: IEEE Congress on Evolutionary Computing (CEC 2006), pp. 438–442 (2006)

[7] Zhao, J., Li, Z.: Particle Filter Based on Partilce Swarm Optimization Resampling for Vision Tracking. Expert Systems with Applications 37, 8910–8914 (2010)

[8] Akhtar, S., Ahmad, A.R., Abdel-Rahman, E.M., Naqvi, T.: A PSO Accelerated Immune Particle Filter for Dynamic State Estimation. In: 2011 Canadian Conf. Computer and Robot Vision (CRV), pp. 72–79 (2011)

[9] Kunsch, H.R.: Recursive Monte Carlo Filters: Algorithms and Theoretical Analysis. Ann. Statist. 33(5), 1983–2021 (2005)

[10] Mehrabian, A.R., Lucas, C.: A Novel Numerical Optimization Algorithm Inspired from Weed Colonization. Ecological Informatics 1, 355–366 (2006)

[11] Karimkashi, S., Kishk, A.A.: Invasive Weed Optimization and Its Features in Electromagnetics. IEEE Trans. on Antennas and Propagation 58(4), 1269–1278 (2010)

[12] Julier, S.J., Uhlmann, J.K.: Corrections to Unscented Filtering and Nonlinear Estimation. Proc. IEEE 92, 1958–1958 (2004)

[13] Costa, P.J.: Adaptive Model Architecture and Extended Kalman–Bucy Filters. IEEE Trans. Aerosp. Electron. Syst. 30, 525–533 (1994)

[14] Sarkka, S.: On Unscented Kalman Filtering for State Estimation of Continuous-Time Nonlinear Systems. IEEE Trans. Automatic Control 52(9), 1631–1640 (2007)

Knowledge Discovery in Discrete Event Simulation Output Analysis

Safiye Ghasemi[1,*], Mania Ghasemi, and Mehrta Ghasemi

[1] Department of Computer, Sepidan Branch, Islamic Azad University, Sepidan, Iran
ghasemi.ss@gmail.com

Abstract. Simulation is a popular methodology for analyzing complex manufacturing environments. According to the large number of output of simulations, interpreting them seems impossible. In this paper we use an innovative methodology that combines simulation and data mining techniques to discover knowledge that can be derived from results of simulations. Data used in simulation process, are independent and identically distributed with a normal distribution, but the output data from simulations are often not i.i.d. normal. Therefore by finding associations between output data mining techniques can operate well. Analyzers change the sequences and values of input data according to the importance they have. These operations optimize the simulation output analysis. The methods presented here will of most interest to those analysts wishing to extract much information from their simulation models. The proposed approach has been implemented and run on a supply chain system simulation. The results show optimizations on analysis of simulation output of the mentioned system. Simulation results show high improvement in proposed approach.

Keywords: Discrete Event Simulation, Data Mining Techniques, and Output Analysis.

1 Introduction

The simulation modeling methodology has several stages that begin with defining the objective of the study, model abstraction, model verification, and model validation. At the end of model validation, you finally have a working model.

Many simulations include randomness, which can arise in a variety of ways. For example, in a simulation of a manufacturing system, the processing times required at a station may follow a given probability distribution or the arrival times of new jobs may be stochastic. Because of the randomness in the components driving a simulation, its output is also random, so statistical techniques must be used to analyze the results.

The most useful and general advice one can give with respect to measurement and estimation would be to only use simulation for direct comparison of alternative forms

---

* Corresponding author.

P. Pichappan, H. Ahmadi, and E. Ariwa (Eds.): INCT 2011, CCIS 241, pp. 108–120, 2011.

of the simulated system. In other hand the output data these simulations produce are huge and analysts are aware of the vast amount of data that can flood their information systems. Many organizations use data mining techniques to extract knowledge in order to improve their understanding of complex systems.

A simulation study consists of several steps such as data collection, coding and verification, model validation, experimental design, output data analysis, and implementation. The methods presented here will of most interest to those analysts wishing to extract more information from their simulation models.

The paper is organized as follows. In Section 2 we briefly describe the background that is existed about optimization of simulation. In the next section, we discuss about simulation concept and process. The forth section that follows describes the data mining methodology. Our approach to the optimization of simulation models can be found in section 5 in details. The final section presents our concluding remarks and avenues for future research.

2   Related Work

Simulation and improvement needed in the field is recently noted in researches. Optimization modules are added to many simulation tools. [15] describes the role of ontologies in facilitating simulation modeling. It outlines the technical challenges in distributed simulation modeling and describes how ontology-based methods may be applied to address these challenges. The paper concludes by describing an ontology-based solution framework for simulation modeling and analysis and outlining the benefits of this solution approach.

In [7], the authors introduce an integration study that combines data mining and agent based modeling and simulation. This study, as a new paradigm is concerned with two approaches: (i) applying data mining techniques in agent based modeling and simulation investigation, and inversely (ii) utilizing the results in data mining research. The former phase is to provide solutions to the *open problem* in agent based modeling and simulation investigation, based on data mining techniques; and the later has the objective to surpass the *data limitation* of data mining research, based on the simulation results of agent based modeling and simulation. Mimosa is an extensible modeling and simulation platform used to investigate the challenges as well as knowledge representation.

Some researches can be used to provide significantly improved or better to say semantic search and browsing, integration of heterogeneous information sources, and improved analytics and knowledge discovery capabilities. In [9], the design and development of draft ontology for Modeling and Simulation called the Discrete-event Modeling Ontology (DeMO) are discussed, which can form a basis for achieving a broader community agreement and adoption. Relevant taxonomies and formal frameworks are reviewed and the design choices for the DeMO ontology are made explicit. Prototype applications that demonstrate various use and benefits from such ontologies for the Modeling and Simulation community are also presented.

3   Simulation

Discrete event simulation is an approach that meets the requirements of high fidelity and high flexibility. Simulation is a powerful manufacturing systems analysis tool that can capture complicated interactions and uncertainties in the system. Performance of some complex systems is typically difficult to understand. In other words, the performance of these systems, even in a specific area, is usually affected by system dynamics as bottlenecks move regularly in these systems.

Simulation is the imitation of the operation of a real-world process or system over time. Simulation involves the generation of an artificial history of the system, and the observation of that artificial history to draw inferences concerning the operating characteristics of the real system that is represented. A model is a representation of a real system. An event is an occurrence that changes the state of the system. The system state variables are the collection of all information needed to define what is happening within the system to a sufficient level (i.e., to attain the desired output) at a given point in time. A discrete-event simulation model is defined as one in which the state variables change only at those discrete points in time at which events occur.

Simulation is the imitation of the operation of a real-world process or system over time. Simulation involves the generation of an artificial history of the system, and the observation of that artificial history to draw inferences concerning the operating characteristics of the real system that is represented. A model is a representation of a real system. An event is an occurrence that changes the state of the system. The system state variables are the collection of all information needed to define what is happening within the system to a sufficient level (i.e., to attain the desired output) at a given point in time. A discrete-event simulation model is defined as one in which the state variables change only at those discrete points in time at which events occur.

3.1   Modeling Concepts

There are several concepts underlying simulation. These include system and model, events, system state variables, entities and attributes, list processing, activities and delays, and finally the definition of discrete-event simulation.

A model is a representation of an actual system. Immediately, there is a concern about the limits or boundaries of the model that supposedly represent the system. The model should be complex enough to answer the questions raised, but not too complex. Consider an event as an occurrence that changes the state of the system.

There are both internal and external events, also called endogenous and exogenous events, respectively. For example, an endogenous event in the example is the beginning of service of the customer since that is within the system being simulated. An exogenous event is the arrival of a customer for service since that occurrence is outside of the system. However, the arrival of a customer for service impinges on the system, and must be taken into consideration. This encyclopedia entry is concerned with discrete-event simulation models. These are contrasted with other types of models such as mathematical models, descriptive models, statistical models, and input-output models. A discrete-event model attempts to represent the components of a system and their interactions to such an extent that the objectives of the study are met. Most mathematical, statistical, and input-output models represent a system's inputs and outputs explicitly, but represent the internals of the model with mathematical or statistical relationships.

Discrete-event simulation models include a detailed representation of the actual internals. Discrete-event models are dynamic, i.e., the passage of time plays a crucial role. Most mathematical and statistical models are static in that they represent a system at a fixed point in time. Consider the annual budget of a firm. This budget resides in a spreadsheet. Changes can be made in the budget and the spreadsheet can be recalculated, but the passage of time is usually not a critical issue. Further comments will be made about discrete-event models after several additional concepts are presented. The system state variables are the collection of all information needed to define what is happening within the system to a sufficient level (i.e., to attain the desired output) at a given point in time. The determination of system state variables is a function of the purposes of the investigation, so what may be the system state variables in one case may not be the same in another case even though the physical system is the same. Determining the system state variables is as much an art as a science.

An entity represents an object that requires explicit definition. An entity can be dynamic in that it "moves" through the system, or it can be static in that it serves other entities. In the example, the customer is a dynamic entity, whereas the bank teller is a static entity. An entity may have attributes that pertain to that entity alone. Thus, attributes should be considered as local values. However, if the time in the system for all parts is of concern, the attribute of color may not be of importance.

3.2   Steps in a Simulation

Here a set of steps to guide a model builder in a simulation study has been written.

1. Problem formulation: Every simulation study begins with a statement of the problem.

2. Setting of objectives and overall project plan: The objectives indicate the questions that are to be answered by the simulation study. The project plan should include a statement of the various scenarios that will be investigated. The plans for the study should be indicated in terms of time that will be required, personnel that will be used, and hardware and software requirements if the client wants to run the model and conduct the analysis, stages in the investigation, output at each stage, cost of the study and billing procedures, if any.

3. Model conceptualization: The real-world system under investigation is abstracted by a conceptual model, a series of mathematical and logical relationships concerning the components and the structure of the system. It is recommended that modeling begin simply and that the model grow until a model of appropriate complexity has been developed.

4. Data collection: Shortly after the proposal is "accepted" a schedule of data requirements should be submitted to the client. In the best of circumstances, the client

has been collecting the kind of data needed in the format required, and can submit these data to the simulation analyst in electronic format.

5. Model translation: The conceptual model constructed in Step 3 is coded into a computer recognizable form, an operational model.

6. Verified: Verification concerns the operational model. Is it performing properly? Even with small textbook sized models, it is quite possible that they have verification difficulties.

7. Validated: Validation is the determination that the conceptual model is an accurate representation of the real system. Can the model be substituted for the real system for the purposes of experimentation?

8. Experimental design: For each scenario that is to be simulated, decisions need to be made concerning the length of the simulation run, the number of runs (also called replications), and the manner of initialization, as required.

4   Data Mining

Data mining refers to the analysis of the large quantities of data that are stored in computers. Data mining has been called exploratory data analysis, among other things. Masses of data generated from cash registers, from scanning, from topic specific databases throughout the company, are explored, analyzed, reduced, and reused. Searches are performed across different models proposed for predicting sales, marketing response, and profit. Classical statistical approaches are fundamental to data mining. Automated AI methods are also used. However, systematic exploration through classical statistical methods is still the basis of data mining.

Data mining requires identification of a problem, along with collection of data that can lead to better understanding and computer models to provide statistical or other means of analysis. This may be supported by visualization tools, that display data, or through fundamental statistical analysis, such as correlation analysis.

Data mining can be achieved by Association, Classification, Clustering, Predictions, Sequential Patterns, and Similar Time Sequences. In Association, the relationship of a particular item in a data transaction on other items in the same transaction is used to predict patterns.

In Classification, the methods are intended for learning different functions that map each item of the selected data into one of a predefined set of classes. Given the set of predefined classes, a number of attributes, and a "learning (or training) set," the classification methods can automatically predict the class of other unclassified data of the learning set. Two key research problems related to classification results are the evaluation of misclassification and prediction power. Decision Trees are considered to be one of the most popular approaches for representing classifiers.

Cluster analysis takes ungrouped data and uses automatic techniques to put this data into groups. Clustering is unsupervised, and does not require a learning set. It shares a common methodological ground with Classification. In other words, most of the mathematical models mentioned earlier in regards to Classification can be applied to Cluster Analysis as well.

Prediction analysis is related to regression techniques. The key idea of prediction analysis is to discover the relationship between the dependent and independent variables, the relationship between the independent variables (one versus another, one versus the rest, and so on).

Sequential Pattern analysis seeks to find similar patterns in data transaction over a business period. These patterns can be used by business analysts to identify relationships among data. As an extension of Sequential Patterns, Similar Time Sequences are applied to discover sequences similar to a known sequence over both past and current business periods. In the data mining stage, several similar sequences can be studied to identify future trends in transaction development. This approach is useful in dealing with databases that have time-series characteristics.

Association rules are basic data mining tools for initial data exploration usually applied to large data sets, seeking to identify the most common groups of items occurring together. An association rule is an expression of $X \rightarrow Y$, where X is a set of items, and Y is a single item. Association rule methods are an initial data exploration approach that is often applied to extremely large data set. Association rules mining provide valuable information in assessing significant correlations. They have been applied to a variety of fields, to include medicine and medical insurance fraud detection.

5 Proposed Approach

5.1 The Problem

Typically, the output of a large number of simulations is reduced to one or two summary statistics, such as sample moments. While such summarization is useful, it overlooks a vast amount of additional information that might be revealed by examining patterns of behavior that emerge at lower levels. In this paper, we propose an approach to interpreting simulation results that involves the use of so-called data mining techniques to identify the ontology hidden in results.

In order to provide the purpose of simulation, we assumed that all the steps of simulation process have been run properly. This assumption assures that the output data which is the resource of the data mining process is valid without any doubt about incorrectness of data. Thus, there has been significant effort in developing sophisticated output analysis procedures.

The ability of a data mining technique to extract repeating functional structures and data flows is the first essential step to reduce exploration, save development time, and re-use simulation software components. Such a tool must reveal the relationships and hierarchies of data that allow event-based simulations to interact. Knowledge discovery is useful across the simulation modeling and analysis lifecycle, particularly in the problem analysis and conceptual model design phases.

Care is taken that the data are independent and identically distributed (i.i.d.) with a normal distribution, but the output data from simulations are often not i.i.d. normal. Simulation models are built with the intent of studying the behavior of the real system represented by the model. However, a simulation model generates random outputs;

thus, the data generated by it can only be used to estimate the true measure of performance. Researchers need to find the right combination of the input parameters.

In the proposed approach introduced later, we have tried to use output data directly in data mining process. But the input data has sufficient influence on quality of analysis results.

5.2   Proposed Approach Details

In our proposed approach a main phase has been assumed. The phase adds data mining techniques to the data retrieved from simulation model after enough executions. Care is taken that the data are prepared before data mining techniques operated on them and the techniques are used according to the relations found in data preparation. The remainder of this section describes about the mentioned phase in details.

As mentioned before in simulation section of this paper, although input data is i.i.d but output data is not. In fact output data is dependant to each other. As an example, consider waiting time of each customer in a queue system[1]. When waiting time of a customer increases then the waiting time of next one will be increased too undoubtedly.

In other hand the input parameters are completely independent to each other. For an instance enter arrival times of customers are identity independent. This means that when a customer enters the system, his or her arrival to the system does not depend on the previous customer. In other words there are some relations between output parameters and between outputs and input ones.

In a queue system the time each customer starts his or her service can be get as follows, the time which previous customer finished the service is compared to the time which current customer entered to the system, then the greater one is assigned to the time of starting service for current customer. It is clear that such relations can be easily found for every variable in simulation output. Some of these variables and their relations with each other and with input parameters are depicted in table 1.

Analyzer firstly finds all of such relations. These relations can be discovered by studying more and more the system according to what has be done on the first, second and third steps of the simulation process. These steps help analyzer to understand the system and its objectives well. Then data mining techniques are ran on output simulation. The first stage of the data mining process is to select the related data from many available outputs to correctly describe a given problem. There are at least three issues to be considered in the data selection. The first issue is to set up a concise and clear description of the problem. The second issue would be to identify the relevant data for the problem description. The third issue is that selected variables for the relevant data should be independent of each other.

In a discrete event simulation result generally just quantitative data appears. Quantitative data can be readily represented by some kind of probability distribution. A probability distribution describes how the data is dispersed and shaped.

---

[1] Additional information on these topics is available from [2].

Data processing is the first step which consists of several sub steps. The purpose of data preprocessing is to clean selected data for better quality. One of the advantages of using output simulation is that selected data has the same format. Redundant data are the same information recorded in several different ways. By aggregating data, data dimensions are reduced to obtain aggregated information. An aggregated data set has a small volume while the information is not disappeared. Another technique useful here is transforming. This technique groups the data and assigns the appropriate category in terms of a string, such as a flag type for income (low, middle, high).

According to the problem definition, important variables are determined among output simulation variables.

Then cluster analysis of the data is usually applied. If the task is to group data, and the groups are given, discriminant analysis might be appropriate. If the purpose is estimation, regression is appropriate if the data is continuous (and logistic regression if not). Care is taken that clustering is done in a way that each cluster has the most similarities between its members and the least similarities between other cluster members. The mentioned similarities are determined according to the properties of the problem and objectives of simulation. The next step is to classify. The classification methods which can automatically predict the class of other unclassified data of the learning set. Two key research problems related to classification results are the evaluation of misclassification and prediction power. Both of these fields are useful in simulation results analysis.

The next section describes the proposed approach implementation on a supply chain system. This simulation introduced optimal decision into performance measurement of supply chain, and evaluated ordering policy with the performance measurement simulation model.

6   Experiments

6.1   Supply Chain Concepts

A supply chain is a network of facilities and distribution options that performs the following functions; the procurement of materials, transformation of these materials into intermediate and finished products; distribution of these finished products to customers. Supply chain management is a strategy through which the integration of these different functions can be achieved [4].

In recent years, multi-site production planning has emerged as one of the most challenging problems in industry. As a consequence, the focus in production planning and scheduling is shifting from the management of plant specific operations to a holistic view of the various logistics and production stages, i.e. an approach in which suppliers, production plants, and customers are considered as constituents of an integrated network. A supply chain consists of all parties involved, directly or indirectly, in fulfilling a customer request. The supply chain not only includes the manufacturer and the suppliers, but also transporters, warehouses, retailers, and customers themselves. Within each organization, such as a manufacturer, the supply chain includes all functions involved in receiving and filling a customer request.

Thus, supply chain management can be regarded as the process of managing transactions and orders between the various stages involved.

Performance measurements supposed to be considered in simulation can act as a support for supply chain decision making (strategic, tactical and operational): rapid responses, collaborative planning, aggregated planning, forecasting demand, subcontracting third parties, etc.

6.2   Supply Chain Simulation

There are several reasons to simulate the supply chain. It could prove impossible or costly to observe certain processes in a real supply chain, for instance, sales in forthcoming years, etc. A supply chain can be too complex to describe it as mathematical equations. Even if a mathematical model was formulated, it could be too complex to obtain a solution by means of analytical techniques. It is feasible to study changes in a supply chain in a model and/or to verify analytical solutions. Supply chain simulation can provide a valuable idea about the most important variables and how they interact. It can also be used to experiment with new situations about which little or no information is available, and to check new policies and decision rules before risking experiments with the real supply chain.

Simulation is widely used in practice, as it does not require sophisticated mathematics. Simulation may offer an idea about the causes and effects of supply chain performance. What inputs significantly affect what outputs? Simulation can help understand causality, and it is a methodology that might not treat a supply chain as a black box.

Below there is a list of the different objectives indicated for simulation run here:

- Generating supply chain knowledge.
- Reproducing and testing different decision-based alternatives. Determining a policy for ordering without interrupting the real supply chain. The ordering strategy has to be done according to the costumers' requirements.

The remainder of this paper defines supply chain simulation procedures and results. Consider the scenario of supply chain industry discussed here as follows: "A retailer who has to sell the products to the customers and buy the needed products from distributers, is the central part of studied supply chain. The goal here is to minimize retailer's loss. The loss can be known as the value of products requested by customers but the retailer's warehouse is lack of the product. To do this analyzer had better focus on ordering planning.

The first procedure to be carried out refers to understanding mentioned industry's characteristics, as well as the supply chain's business and planning processes. There are 20 products in the retailer's industry. The rate of customers' requests of each product is one of the following distributions: N (μ, σ), UNIF (α, β). The values of parameters of distributions are selected randomly as follows, μ is between 1.5 and 2.5, σ is between 0.3 and 1.3, α is 0.1 to 7 and β is selected from 11 to 35. The unit of time for these distributions is minute. The rate of retailer's orders for each product is one of the POIS (μ) or UNIF (α, β). Here μ is between 30 and 45, α is 5 to 15 and β is selected from 20 to 50. The unit of time for these distributions is day that means the time interval between two orders. Each product has a rank that shows its value for retailer. The more profit he gains by selling product the greater rank that product be gotten. This concept will be used in performance measurement of industry. The amount of orders is determined according to the maximum size of the warehouse. The retailer first checks the inventory and then orders number of products that fills the warehouse.

We assumed that order delivery is zero that means that retailer receives orders immediately after his ordering. Furthermore the logistic costs are ignored. These assumptions are considered to simplify the simulation. Simulation is run for two months.

Table 1 presents the simulation results of mentioned scenario of retailer. The output is summarized for four products. The initialization of simulation is as follows, the warehouse is full and no order has been produced. Some requests are generated every day according to the given distributions.

The inventory of the warehouse decreases while responding to customers' requests. The column named days to deliver orders represents the days remained to orders received by the retailer. Each day a unit is decreased from this column until it is zero, and then the inventory of that product gets full. Care is taken that requests enter at the beginning of the day and the orders enter at the end of the day. The average loss of the system is 18.75.

Table 1. Some parts of simulation output of supply chain

Days to get orders				Customer's Request				Inventory				Day
EC-M092	CB-2903	CA-5965	BL-2036	EC-M092	CB-2903	CA-5965	BL-2036	EC-M092	CB-2903	CA-5965	BL-2036	Product ID
22	9	12	10	25	9	13	18	106	113	163	109	1
21	8	11	9	21	21	19	21	81	104	150	91	2
20	7	10	8	22	27	12	10	60	83	131	70	3
19	6	9	7	19	8	25	26	38	56	119	60	4
18	5	8	6	22	27	17	17	19	48	94	34	5
17	4	7	5	11	16	21	9	0	21	77	17	6
16	3	6	4	27	8	24	12	0	5	56	8	7
15	2	5	3	11	10	18	9	0	0	32	0	8
14	1	4	2	22	23	14	12	0	0	14	0	9
13	0	3	1	27	15	24	15	0	0	0	0	10
12	7	2	0	26	23	14	15	0	113	0	0	11
11	6	1	8	14	12	27	20	0	90	0	109	12
10	5	0	7	19	25	8	27	0	78	0	89	13
9	4	3	6	17	9	25	8	0	53	163	62	14
8	3	2	5	10	23	23	13	0	44	138	54	15

6.3   Proposed Approach Implemented on Supply Chain

The last phase of this simulation is assigned to data mining techniques. In this step we have used dependency rules to make the classification more productive. In fact the retailer wants to predicate how many of each product will be requested in future, then before any loss he will order enough number of products which may surely be demanded in future. Therefore some much information about the customers is needed to discover their buying pattern. Furthermore some dependencies exist between products which indicate that requesting some products is followed by some other ones. To gain these dependencies binary activation matrix is used as shown in table 2.

Table 2. Some parts of simulation output of supply chain

	BL-2036	CA-5965	CA-6738	CA-7457	CB-2903	CN-6137	CR-7833	CR-9981	CS-2812	DC-8732	DC-9824	DT-2377	EC-M92	EC-R098	EC-T209	FE-3760	FE-3737	FH-2981	FW-1000	BA-8327
1st Obs.	1	0	0	0	0	0	0	0	0	0	0	0	1	1	1	0	0	0	1	0	1
2nd Obs.	1	0	1	0	0	1	1	0	1	1	1	0	0	1	0	1	0	1	0	1	1	0
3rd Obs.	0	1	1	1	0	1	1	0	0	0	1	0	1	0	1	0	0	0	0	0	1	0
...																				

After discovering these rules, the decision tree can be produced. Decision tree must be produced for all products of the retailer. Then retailer decides precisely about the customers' requests. Totally he can change the rate of ordering each product according to his prediction about future requests. Table 3 shows the simulation output of retailer's industry by changing the ordering rate of products. The output is summarized for four products.

Table 3. Some parts of simulation output of supply chain

Loss				Inventory of end				Days to get orders				Customer's Request				Inventory of beginning				Day
EC-M092	CB-2903	CA-5965	BL-2036	EC-M092	CB-2903	CA-5965	BL-2036	EC-M092	CB-2903	CA-5965	BL-2036	EC-M092	CB-2903	CA-5965	BL-2036	EC-M092	CB-2903	CA-5965	BL-2036	
0	0	0	0	81	104	150	91	8	4	9	7	25	9	13	18	106	113	163	109	1
0	0	0	0	60	83	131	70	7	3	8	6	21	21	19	21	81	104	150	91	2
0	0	0	0	38	56	119	60	6	2	7	5	22	27	12	10	60	83	131	70	3
0	0	0	0	19	48	94	34	5	1	6	4	19	8	25	26	38	56	119	60	4
3	0	0	0	0	134	77	17	4	0	5	3	22	27	17	17	19	48	94	34	5
14	0	0	0	0	118	56	8	3	11	4	2	11	16	21	9	0	134	77	17	6
41	3	0	4	0	110	32	0	2	10	3	1	27	8	24	12	0	118	56	8	7
52	13	0	13	0	0	14	109	1	9	2	0	11	10	18	9	0	110	32	0	8
74	36	0	13	106	0	0	97	0	8	1	5	22	23	14	12	0	0	14	109	9
74	51	24	13	79	113	163	82	13	7	0	4	27	15	24	15	106	0	0	97	10
74	51	24	13	53	90	149	67	12	6	8	3	26	23	14	15	79	113	163	82	11
74	51	24	13	39	78	131	47	11	5	7	2	14	12	27	20	53	90	149	67	12
74	51	24	13	20	53	163	20	10	4	6	1	19	25	8	27	39	78	131	47	13
74	51	24	13	3	44	138	121	9	3	5	0	17	9	25	8	20	53	163	20	14
81	51	24	13	0	21	115	118	8	2	4	8	10	23	23	13	3	44	138	121	15

The average loss of system is equal to 13.23 in this simulation run after applying second phase of the proposed approach. Such loss will improve the performance of the supply chain.

7   Conclusion

Thousands of simulation models create large amount of data as output. Analyzer is supposed to describe the behavior of the system. Understanding the correlation between the simulation input and output parameters is critical to analyzing simulated system behavior. We have described some techniques for intelligent analyzing the output from a simulation. In the proposed approach firstly we find the relations between input parameters and output ones. Therefore in this phase the correlation between them and the output data should be determined. Some additional information is added to output. Finally the data mining techniques are added to output data. The dependency rules are discovered. Output data is classified according to information gotten from previous step which qualifies the simulation process well. The classification is appeared by decision tree.

The approach is implemented on a supply chain system by using Arena and SQL Analysis Service. The results show improvements on profit of the supply chain that dictates the proposed approach.

References

1. Smith, T.F., Waterman, M.S.: Identification of Common Molecular Subsequences. J. Mol. Biol. 147, 195–197 (1981)
2. May, P., Ehrlich, H.C., Steinke, T.: ZIB Structure Prediction Pipeline: Composing a Complex Biological Workflow through Web Services. In: Nagel, W.E., Walter, W.V., Lehner, W. (eds.) Euro-Par 2006. LNCS, vol. 4128, pp. 1148–1158. Springer, Heidelberg (2006)
3. Olson, D.L., Delen, D.: Advanced Data Mining Techniques. Springer, Heidelberg (2008)
4. Banks, J., Carson, J., Nelson, B.: Discrete-Event Systems Simulation, 2nd edn. Prentice-Hall, Upper Saddle River (1996)
5. Rozinat A., van der Aalst, W.M.P.: Workflow simulation for operational decision support. Data & Knowledge Engineering Elsevier Journal (2009)
6. Campuzano, F., Mula, J.: Supply Chain Simulation. Springer, Heidelberg (2011)
7. Painter, M.K., Beachkofski, B.: Using simulation, data mining, and knowledge discovery techniques for optimized. In: Proceedings of the 2006 Winter Simulation Conference (2006)
8. Young, M.: Data mining techniques for analysing complex simulation models. In: SCRI (2009)
9. Remondino, M., Correndo, G.: Data mining applied to agent based simulation. In: Proceedings 19th European Conference on Modelling and Simulation (2005)
10. Wong, Y., Hwang, S., Yi-Bing, L.: A parallelism analyzer for conservative parallel simulation. IEEE Transactions on Distributed Systems (1995)
11. Huyet, A.L.: Optimization and analysis aid via data mining for simulated production systems. Elsevier (2004)

12. Steiger, N., Wilson, J.: Experimental Performance Evaluation of Batch Means Procedures for Simulation Output Analysis. In: Winter Simulation Conference. IEEE (2000)
13. Remondino, M., Correndo, G.: Data Mining Applied to Agent Based Simulation. In: ECMS (2005)
14. Fayyad, U., Stolorz, P.: Data mining and KDD: Promise and challenges. FGCS (1997)
15. Morbitzer, M., et al.: Application of Data mining Techniques for Building Simulation Performance Prediction Analysis. In: 8th International IBPSA Conference (2003)
16. Petrova M., Riihij J., Labella S.: Performance Study of IEEE 802.15.4 Using Measurements and Simulations. IEEE (2006)
17. Benjamin P., Patki M., Mayer R.: Using Ontologies for Simulation Modeling. In: Winter Simulation Conference. IEEE (2006)
18. Zhao, W., Wang, D.: Performance Measurement of Supply Chain Based on Computer Simulation. In: IEEE ICCDA 2010 (2010)
19. Better M., Glover F., Laguna M.: Advances in analytics: Integrating dynamic data mining with simulation optimization. In: International Business Machines Corporation (2007)

From UML State Machines
to Verifiable Lotos Specifications

Reza Babaee and Seyed Morteza Babamir

University of Kashan, Ravand Blvd., Kashan, Iran
rbabaeecar@grad.kashanu.ac.ir,
babamir@kashanu.ac.ir

Abstract. The theoretical prospect of Formal specification languages
has been improved during last years. The pragmatic aspects of the formal
methods has been scrutinized especially in the safety-critical systems.
However there still remains a constant fear among industry practitioners
to work with purely theoretical specification methods even though their
software system operates in highly safety-critical applications.

We propose a hands-on approach in order to gradually transform popular UML 2.0 State Machines (SM) to verifiable Lotos specifications. In
this algorithm the partial logical view of the system ,represented by the
UML 2.0 SM, would be converted to verifiable Basic Lotos specification,
it then may be developed as an executable program to mechanize the
transformation.

1 Introduction

Formal methods have been proved to be an essential technique for specifying
safety-critical systems in which desired properties have to be satisfied by the
software. Formal specification languages provide the capability of constraints
proof by means of mathematical foundations. However from the practical point
of view, developing mathematical models is supposedly an onerous task disregard
of considerable overall benefits obtained by using these models.

On the other hand, Unified Modeling Language (UML) semi-formal diagrams
[1], support practitioners by means of visual conceptual illustrations while they
usually suffer from lack of formality required for specifying sufficiently reliable
systems. Several attempts have been succeeded in bringing formality to the UML
models, like OCL [2], however their widespread formal adoption in the industry
is still arguable. Besides, the verifiability of UML equipped by such methods,
particularly in ultra-reliable systems, yet has to be corroborated.

Conversely we strongly believe that instead of making UML strictly formal
by introducing new tools, exploiting current conventional formal methods is
rather more acceptable in many industrial situations. However the conceptual
visuality earned by UML diagrams should also be taken into account in the
software development processes which are more actively engaged by human.
The solution to this problem is trivial: depute automatic programs to work
with formal methods while human-centric approaches (such as UML) provide

P. Pichappan, H. Ahmadi, and E. Ariwa (Eds.): INCT 2011, CCIS 241, pp. 121–129, 2011.
© Springer-Verlag Berlin Heidelberg 2011

inputs for these programs. In fact we need to develop specific programs that receives visual models as inputs and produce corresponding formal specification as output.

Achieving this goal requires specific algorithms to translate prevalent UML illustrations, into desired formal specification languages regarding system application domains. In this paper we have chosen *Lotos* formal specification language as one of the predominant formal methods in order to specify Open Systems Interconnection (OSI) architecture [3]. On the other side, we use UML 2.0 State Machines (SM) [4] as the modeling charts to specify a system behavior, and then translate them into a *Basic* form of Lotos specification language in a relatively straightforward manner.

In the next Section we briefly introduce the Basic Lotos specification language, then we proceed with presenting the core elements of SM that is important for a Lotos specification in the Section 3. In the Section 4 we provide our main approach to transform SMs into Basic Lotos specifications. Needed refinements on SM to generate a better Lotos specification is presented in the Section 5 following by our conclusion and future works in the Section 6.

2   Basic Lotos

Lotos (Language Of Temporal Ordering Specification) is mainly developed within International Standards Organization (ISO) for specifying Open Systems Interconnection or OSI computer network architecture [3]. Its main features have been inspired by *process algebra* [5] in which the process synchronized communications are described in terms of Calculus of Communicating Systems (CCS) [6]. Lotos has two basic components: one for control aspects of the system which is based on CCS, and one for data structures description which is based on abstract data type technique ACT-ONE [7]. In this paper we focus on the control aspect of the system, which is also called *Basic Lotos*, and leave the abstract data type description for future researches.

The constitute element of a Basic Lotos specification is *process*. A process itself might involve other processes called subprocess; thus a Lotos specification describes a system by means of hierarchy of process descriptions [3]. Considerable strength of Lotos stems from its outstanding process *parallelization* features as well as process *synchronization* [8]. The elementary atomic parts in Lotos Specifications are events, or generally *actions*. Actions are the elements by which processes can be synchronized with each other. In the case that the data is not exchanged between processes (our focus), the actions and the *gates* (process input parameteres) are identical. All possible actions in a system specification shape the *action alphabet* of that specification.

A combination of actions assembled by Lotos operators builds *behavior expressions*. Processes are described in terms of behavior expressions which represent states of processes. A behavior expression might be combined with other behavior expressions and/or actions by Lotos operators to form larger behavior expressions. To be fitted into the convention standards applied in Lotos context, the actions are given lower-case names while behavior expressions are appeared in upper-case names. For the space sake we are not going to explain each operator individually, but we will clearly explicate them when we want to describe the mapping function between them and the corresponding SM notations.

3   UML 2.0 State Machines

We use behavior state machines as our modeling language since it has wider basic elements to describe the behavior of a system. Thankfully SM possesses extremely advantageous properties and features that make it an eminently rational modeling language choice for Lotos specifications:

- As we mentioned in the Section 2, Lotos describes processes in terms of their states (i.e. behavior expressions) thus we need to a specific modeling language to show states of processes precisely.
- The main power of Lotos arises from process parallelization and synchronization, therefore its correspondent modeling language requires appropriate instruments for representing parallelization and synchronization. The former is satisfied in UML 2.0 SM by using *composite states* which allows to define several parallel state machines, and the latter is represented by special *choice* or *signal* pseudostates (See Section 4).

There are also various practical options within a state so that one can define internal behaviors when system gets into a state (by *Entry* option), remains in a state (by *Do* option) or leaves a state (by *Exit* option).

4   SM-to-Lotos Transformation

There are several significant steps towards transforming a system model represented by SM into the Lotos specification. In this Section we demonstrate how to translate each element of a SM into the corresponding Basic Lotos elements. For understandability we illustratively present our approach step-by-step on a well-known simple network example.

Assume a system including two processes, *Sender* which is aimed to send messages away to a remote system via an unreliable network channel, and *Receiver* that receives messages which have been already sent by Sender and reply to it by an *acknowledge* message. Both Sender and Receiver are vulnerable and work in parallel although synchronously. In other words if Sender does not receive any acknowledge message from receiver at fixed interval time, it will send the message again and both Sender and Receiver might crash within any given time of system execution. An equivalent SM for the Sender is depicted in Figure 1. The Receiver is not represented here due to the limited space but it is basically analogs to the shown Sender diagram except that states *Sending* and *Waiting* are substituted by *Receiving* and *Acknowledging* states.

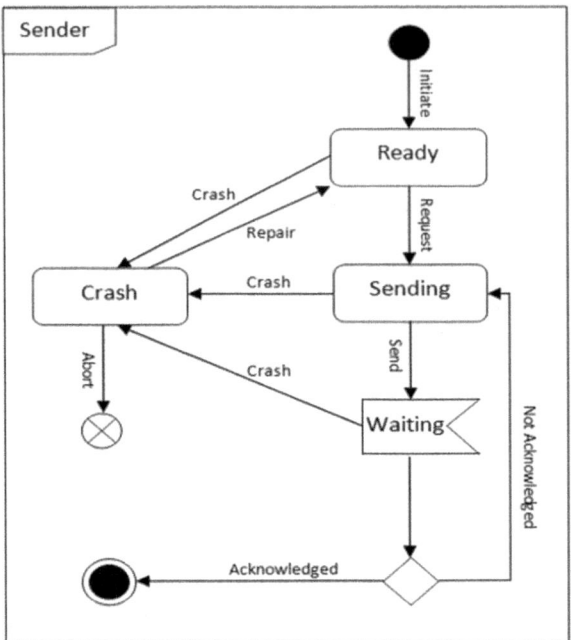

Fig. 1. Network Sender State Machine

4.1   Process Extraction

As the first step it is vital to extract all possible modeled processes from SM.
There may exist broad indications in the SM that point to process entities in the
system. Generally a set of states, which might form a composite state, represents
the condition of a *process* at a certain time. Hence, this can be a tangible sign
so as to extract processes.

In our example shown in Figure 1, obviously there are two main processes:
Sender and *Receiver* (Receiver is not shown). This indicates that the Lotos
specification must have two processes which have to be synchronized with each
other.

4.2   Individual Process Description

Before we proceed with the whole system specification, we take a divide-and-
conquer approach. In fact we do not concern about processes composition but
rather we initially offer an individual description for each process. We try to
create a fairly comprehensive description for each extracted process using SM
models. In the following we first present SM equivalents of the main elements
of process description to build process descriptions, i.e. actions and behavior
expressions. Then the operators that are applicable to combine the actions and
behavior expressions would be provided to form a single process description.

Actions and Behavior Expressions. Generally the states within a behavior state machine represent an activity or *behavior* of a process [9]. This properly signifies that a state in SM is simply mapped to a behavior expression in Lotos descriptions. Additionally the transition between two states is taken place when the specified written *event* on the transition occurs and that means the events on transitions are equivalent to actions in Lotos specifications. Consequently the composite states which includes other behavior expressions or actions are transformed into appropriate behavior expressions. If a state is a simple state, i.e. it is undividable to other expressions or actions, then a simple action with similar name is added to the actions alphabet. For example in Figure 1 *Ready,* *Sending* or *Waiting* simple states are behaviors of the Sender process and the *initiate, request* and *send* are corresponding events or actions. Please note that there might be also some internal behaviors for a single state. In this case a sub-process would be created to represent the internal behaviors of equivalent state; thus the remaining portion of *process extraction* step may be followed when the system becomes more expanded.

The Action Prefix Operator. The action prefix operator shown as ';' in Lotos, expresses the sequential combination of actions before a behavior expression. This operator is represented in SM by the sequential transitions (actions) before states (behavior expressions). In Figure 1 the *initiate* event is before *Sending* state so a possible behavior expression which shows *initiate* prefixes *READY* state is: `initiate;READY`

Choice Operator. One of the principal features of Basic Lotos is the choice operator shown as '[]' which indicates a non-deterministic selection between its two operands. Two leaving transitions with the same source state as well as identical *guards* or conditions on the transitions, can be transformed into a choice operator in Lotos with two target states as two choice operands. For instance two outgoing transitions *request* and *crash* leaving the *Ready* state and get into *Sending* and *Crashed* states respectively, are translated into Lotos as follows:

```
initiate;READY;SENDING
[]
initiate;READY;CRASHED
```

4.3   Process Termination

There are two pseudostate symbols within a state machine indicating a termination: *Final* pseudostate and *Abort* pseudostate. Thankfully Lotos supports two kinds of process termination as well: `exit` and `stop`; the former implies a successful process termination and the latter denotes an unsuccessful or a *deadlock* termination. In our sample Sender can whether receives an acknowledgment and successfully terminates (shown as a filled circle with a ring around) or it can stop working if an unrepairable crash occurs (shown as a circle with cross-lines in the middle). We can simply translate SM into the correspondent Lotos expression as below:

```
initiate;ready;crash;abort;stop
[]
initiate;ready;request;sending;send;exit
```

4.4   Process Composition

After finding how to describe an individual process, we should compose these processes (or behavior expressions) to form larger process specifications. There are principal operators in Lotos for process composition.

Enabling Composition. The *enable operator*, displayed by '>>' in Lotos has fairly the same semantic as prefix operator (Section 4.2); except that it is applied to illustrate two behavior expressions (or processes) sequential composition. For example Receiver can be enabled by process Sender; thus we have in Lotos: SENDER >> RECEIVER

Disabling Composition. Lotos has a special operator to specify how one behavior interrupts another behavior which is called *Disable* operator and shown as '[>'. To find the comparable notations in the SM, we should semantically find a situation in which a state machine might be interrupted by another process. If for every state of a state machine (process) there is an outgoing transition to a single state (whether simple or composite), it can be mentioned that the process is interrupted by that state showing the behavior of an intervening process. In Figure 1 *crash* state is the state whose incoming transitions are originated from all other states; therefore the corresponding Lotos expression might be as:

```
initiate;ready;request;sending;send;exit
[>
crash;stop
```

Interleaving Operator. The interleaving operator displayed by '|||' allows the first operand to alternate its actions or behavior expressions with the second one. SM composite states provide a matching visual concept with interleaving operator: the *substate* machines within a composite state in several different *regions* can be executed simultaneously and independently. In other words states within various regions can be *interleaved* while the composite state machine is executing. This approach can be followed for two or more different processes, as well. In our example assuming the Receiver as a separate process with an identical SM as the Sender, the interleaved execution of them leads to the following Lotos program:

```
request;SENDING ||| receive;RECEIVING
```

Synchronization. There is not only the process parallelism of importance but it is also crucial to synchronize processes with shared events or actions. Synchronization operator displayed by '||' synchronizes its two operands with the action appeared between two vertical lines. In other words two operand processes are interleaved but the process which has reached to the synchronized action earlier than the other process, has to wait until the second process reach to the synchronization state. If there is no any actions between two synchronization symbol lines it means that all events occurred in two behavior expression operands have to be synchronized, otherwise they have to be synchronized with only determined actions (In this case the synchronization operator is shown as '|[...]|' within the shared actions between two brackets).

SM synchronization equivalent is relatively more complex than aforementioned operators. A synchronization between two processes is appeared in the SM when there is firstly at least one (or more) shared event(s) between two processes and secondly a transition in one process may not be enabled unless the same event in the other process has occurred. This situation is modeled in SM by a combination of notations. There are two pseudostates in SM demonstrating signal exchanges between processes: *send* and *receive* signal pseudostates. They are often followed by conditional transitions that are regularly represented by *choice* pseudostates (not to be mistaken by *choice* operand in Lotos -See Section 4.2). For instance in the Figure 1, the Sender has to be synchronized with the Receiver in the *acknowledge* event. A receive pseudostate followed by the choice pseudostate represents this synchronization. The equivalent Lotos expression is as follows:

```
initiate;ready;sending;acknowledge;exit
|[acknowledge]|
initiate;ready;receiving;acknowledge;exit
```

Sometimes a synchronization is modeled with a conditional transition as well as a *waiting* state; although the waiting state can be eliminated.

Full Lotos specification of the Sender process is as follows:

```
Process Sender : exit :=
initiate;READY;SENDING;WAITING;exit
[> (
crashed; (
recover;READY
[]
abort;stop
))
endproc
```

5   State Machine Refinement

Lotos specifications have very distinctive features which specify the process interactions by means of parallelism and synchronization. Consequently there may not be possible to transform any UML 2.0 State Machines into a Lotos specification, we still require some particular refinements in order to make SMs directly interpretable in terms of Lotos. According to above transformation algorithm we strongly recommend to undergo the following refinements on SM to have a much more validated specification:

1. Try to create a separate SM for each process within your system.
2. Find specific events within your system that are the share points of your processes, i.e. they synchronize with each other on that events. Represent these points in every involved state machine with send/receive signal notations and identical names as well as a choice pseudostate. A *waiting* state is an alternative notation for signal pseudostates.
3. Specify successful/unsuccessful points of processes termination. Use final and abort pseudostate notations respectively to model them.
4. Determine the prohibitive behaviors for each process and model them by inserting an outgoing transition for every state of the process to a single destination state.

6   Conclusion and Future Works

A quite straightforward algorithm is proposed in this paper so that the system specification is translated from UML 2.0 State Machines into Basic Lotos formal specifications. Lotos specification then can be comprehensively verified, validated and evaluated using favored toolboxes like CADP[1].

The idea of transforming SM into Lotos is relatively new but not original as within [10] authors present a model transformation applied in the automotive industries. Lotos is used in [11] to give a semantic model for compositional UML state charts. Compare to our work, in some aspects it seems more inclusive, because we try to cover the essential elements of Lotos specification like process compositions (i.e. enabling, disabling, interleaving and synchronization operators- see Section 4.4). Moreover our presented algorithm is elaborately designed in such a way that could be straightforwardly developed as a program in order to mechanize transforming SM to Lotos specifications. We hope to experiment the transformation algorithm with a practical real-world problem called Flight Computer Warning (FCW) whose corresponding Lotos specification has been already produced in [12]. This allows us to compare our generated Lotos specification with the original one; but before, we have to seek for a broadly similar approach to embed the data abstract specification into modeling language. Therefore it might be essential to deliberate on other UML 2.0 commercially desired diagrams in order to support the state machine models.

References

1. Booch, G., Rumbaugh, J., Jacobson, I.: Unified Modeling Language User Guide. The (Addison-Wesley Object Technology Series). Addison-Wesley Professional (2005)

---

[1] http://www.inrialpes.fr/vasy/cadp/

2. O.M.G.A. Object constraint language (specification) (2007)
3. Bolognesi, T., Brinksma, E.: Introduction to the iso specification language lotos. Computer Networks and ISDN systems 14, 25–59 (1987)
4. (OMG), Object Management Group: Unified modeling language: Superstructure (2005)
5. Baeten, J.: A brief history of process algebra. Theoretical Computer Science 335, 131–146 (2005)
6. Milner, R. (ed.): A Calculus of Communication Systems. LNCS, vol. 92. Springer, Heidelberg (1980)
7. Ehrig, H., Fey, W., Hansen, H.: Act one an algebraic specification language with two levels of semantics (1983)
8. Logrippo, L., Faci, M., Haj-Hussein, M.: An introduction to lotos: learning by examples. Computer Networks and ISDN systems 23, 325–342 (1992)
9. Miles, R., Hamilton, K.: Learning UML 2.0. O'Reilly Media, Inc. (2006)
10. Chimisliu, V., Schwarzl, C., Peischl, B.: From uml statecharts to lotos: A semantics preserving model transformation (2009)
11. Mrowka, R., Szmuc, T.: Uml statecharts compositional semantics in lotos. In: ISPDC 2008, pp. 459–463 (2008)
12. Garavel, H., Hautbois, R.: An experiment with the lotos formal description technique on the ight warning computer of airbus 330/340 aircrafts. In: First AMAST International Workshop on Real-Time Systems, Iowa City, Iowa, USA, p. 20 (1993)

A Model Driven Approach for Personalizing Data Source Selection in Mediation Systems

Imane Zaoui, Faouzia Wadjinny, Dalila Chiadmi, and Laila Benhlima

Computer Sciences Department, Mohammadia Engineering School, BP 765
Rabat Agdal, Morocco
{zaoui,wadjinny,chiadmi,benhlima}@emi.ac.ma

Abstract. Nowadays, there is a real trend to personalize mediation systems to improve user satisfaction. The mediator answers should be adapted to the user needs and preferences. In this paper, we propose a solution for this problem. Our solution is based on models for users and data sources. These models are used to perform a content matching and a quality matching between user profile and data sources profiles. The objective of matching is to rank sources according to user preferences and needs, and to select the most relevant ones. Our solution for personalizing data source selection provides the mediator with a set of relevant data sources. These are then involved in the rewriting process to give more satisfying response. By reducing the number of integrated data sources, the mediator performances are also optimized.

Keywords: Personalization, User profile, Mediation systems, Source selection.

1 Introduction

With the phenomenal increase of available data, their disparity, and their heterogeneity, mediation systems [1] are emerging as a solution to provide an efficient and uniform access to multiple autonomous and heterogeneous data sources. Unfortunately, with a huge number of heterogeneous data sources, especially in the context of the Web, a user query addressed to the mediator, takes a lot of time to be executed. Moreover, the mediator responses lead to an informational overload. So, the user spends significant time to distinguish between relevant information from secondary one or even from noise. Another limitation is the inability of the system to distinguish between users having different preferences and needs and to deliver relevant results according to user profiles. Thus, a fundamental aspect of user interaction in mediation systems is user satisfaction. This is clearly mentioned by industry reports who stress that although data integration initiatives succeed in achieving a common technology platform, they are rejected by the user communities due to the information overload or the presence of poor data quality [2]. To insure user satisfaction, mediation systems should give personalized responses that meet the user needs and respect his quality requirements. In this paper, we present our solution for increasing user satisfaction in mediation systems. It's a personalization process based on user modeling, data source modeling and data source selection. User

P. Pichappan, H. Ahmadi, and E. Ariwa (Eds.): INCT 2011, CCIS 241, pp. 130–145, 2011.
© Springer-Verlag Berlin Heidelberg 2011

modeling gives to the system a structured knowledge about the user interests and preferences. Data source modeling provides a common description of candidate data sources. Finally, data source selection returns the most relevant data sources that respect both user interests and quality preferences.

The reminder of this paper is structured as follows. In section 2, we present how we model users through a user profile. Section 3 gives our source profile. Section 4 explains how we rank and select relevant sources according to user interests and quality preferences. In section 5, we present some related works. We conclude in section 6.

2   User Modeling

Providing personalized responses to users requires accurate modeling of their interests, goals and preferences. User modeling is thus a key issue in personalizing mediation systems. A user model, also called user profile is a knowledge source which contains explicit assumptions on all aspects of the user that may be relevant for the dialogue behavior of the system [3]. Several approaches for user modeling exist depending on the nature of the application and the system goals [4][5]. We propose a generic and multi-dimensional profile that could be used in a large variety of domains and applications. Furthermore, the genericity of our model ensure cross domain mediation of user profiles [6]. In the following we present the organization of our user profile. We focus on two elements, which are user interests and user quality preferences. User interests help in content source selection. In the other hand, user quality preferences are used to perform a quality aware source selection and ranking. For more details about the proposed user profile, refer to [7].

2.1   User Profile Organization

We organize the user profile in two entities: the *persistent profile* and the *session profile*.

Persistent profile contains general characteristics of a user which don't change for a long period. It includes five dimensions: the *personal identity* (name, age, address, etc); the *domains of interest* which group all attributes and preferences related to the general information needs of a given user; the *general expected quality*; the *security data* and the *interaction history*. This persistent profile is used in constructing user communities which is a key issue for mediation systems providing recommendation and collaborative filtering services [8].

Session profile is a short term profile describing the user during one session. It represents a particular instance of the persistent profile. The session profile contains four dimensions: the *user context* which informs about the location, time, used devices, etc; the *user goals* which relates to the specific user domains of interest during a particular session; the *user quality preferences* that covers required quality parameters and values in the current session. The session profile helps to catch the evolution of user characteristics and needs through multiple sessions. This is necessary in updating the knowledge about the user and adapting the system behavior.

To build our user profile, we adopt an explicit approach where users describe their goals, preferences, security parameters and quality requirements through an interactive interface. Then, we update the profile through learning techniques. In the literature, there are three approaches of profile learning methods which are the Bayesian Networks [9], the Case Base Reasoning (CBR) [10] and data mining techniques such as Clustering [11]. We will not discuss these update mechanisms since it is not the scope of this paper. In addition, in the reminder of this paper, we consider only the session profile.

2.2   User Goals Representation

During an interaction session, user queries revolve around a single objective, for example organizing a holiday in Morocco. This objective is declined into multiple goals. Each goal represents a domain of interest related to that objective such as transport, dinning, entertainment, cultural activities, monuments etc. It is obvious that users may have different preferences concerning the importance of goals. For example, User A is more interested on entertainments than cultural activities; he also does not care about monuments. We represent these preferences through weights which are numerical values entered directly by the user.

To formalize the user goals dimension, several approaches have been proposed in the literature, in particular ontologies and vectors. Ontologies depend on the application domain [12]. Furthermore, in the context of mediation, integrated sources may have different ontologies. To take advantage from this semantic representation, user goals ontology and all sources ontologies requires alignment. This is a hard task especially in the context of the web. Since we propose a user model that could be used in a large variety of domains, it is clear that the model of the ontology does not meet our expectations. We adopt the vector model [13]. So the user goals dimension is a weighted vector of key words, where key words are user goals (domains of interests during the session), and weights reflects user preferences. For convenience to theoretical studies, we consider for the weights, a range of [0,1]. In reality, user preferences are normalized according to a given scale so that the user preferences are values into [0,1]. For example, the user could choose his preferences via a slider into the user interface. The slide position is then transformed to the corresponding value.

The *user goals* dimension is given by definition 1.

Definition 1. The *user goals* of a user U_i is a weighted vector of key words given by: $UG(U_i)=(tu_{i1},wu_{i1};\ tu_{i2},wu_{i2};....tu_{in},wu_{in});$ where tu_{ij} are key words and wu_{ij} their respective weights.

Using this formalism, let's give bellow the user goals vectors $UG(Ui)$ of two different user profiles. User 1(U_1) is participating to a conference hold in Morocco and User 2(U_2) is a student invited by a friend. The objective of both users is the same: *Preparing a holiday in Morocco*, but their needs, their interests and preferences are different:

-$UG(U_1)$ (transport, 0.9; accommodation, 0.6; restaurants, 0.7; conference, 0.8)
-$UG(U_2)$ (transport , 0.7; entertainment , 0.9; monuments , 0.5; conference , 0.3)

2.3   User Quality Preferences

In mediation systems, user satisfaction depends on the quality of returned responses. Since mediation systems combine responses from different integrated data sources, the quality of the final response relies on the quality of the involved sources. Consequently, we believe that indicating the user quality preferences among data sources in the user profile makes the personalization process more accurate. The *user quality preferences* dimension is the aggregation of multiple quality criteria, such as accuracy, popularity, completeness, freshness, etc. [14]. For more details about these criteria, refer to section 3. To build this dimension, we propose a model where the user chooses his desired quality criteria from a global list in each session. Then, he gives a ranking of these criteria from the most important one to the less important using weights. Weighting quality criteria helps the system to emphasize the priority of the quality criterion to satisfy. After, he states his desired values for each criterion. Usually, user preferences values are expressed with a numerical score in an appropriate scale, a percentage, words like "good", "bad", etc. or even a predicate (e.g., He prefer sources having recent documents than those published before 2004). In this case, the user expresses his preference about the freshness of the source. To simplify our model, we suppose that the user states required preferences either by putting a score directly or by a slider on an appropriate scale. The position of the slide gives the corresponding score.

The *user quality preferences* dimension is formalized by definition 2.

Definition 2. The *user quality preferences* of a user U_i is a vector given by: $UQP(U_i)=(qu_{i1},wu_{i1},\ vu_{i1};\ qu_{i2},wu_{i2},vu_{i2};....qu_{in},wu_{in},\ vu_{in});$ where qu_{ij} are quality criteria, wu_{ij} their respective weights and vu_{ij} their desired values.

An example of user quality preferences is given in section 4.

3   Source Modeling

Data sources in mediation systems are heterogeneous, distributed and autonomous. To describe them, local schemas and ontologies are generally used. But these descriptions are not sufficient to give details about the content and the quality criteria of the integrated data sources. For this reason, we refine the sources description by building a source profile. The source profile contains a variety of information including source location, identity, owner, content, quality criteria and so on, which helps in the source selection process. In the following, we present our source profile and we focus on the dimensions describing the content and the quality of the source.

3.1   Source Profile Organization

The source profile we propose is generic and multidimensional. It can be used in a variety of application domains. We adopt the same multidimensional representation used for the user profile. Our objective by doing so is to perform the matching between the source profile and the user profile. A brief description of our source profile dimensions is given bellow.

Source identity describes the source identity with the following attributes: Id, name, URL, port, owner, size, principal languages and principle types of content.

Source content represents the most important topics treated by the sources. This information is available in the form of key words or concepts.

Source ontology represents the concepts used in the data source and describes the semantic relationship between them. This dimension is used by the mediator to insure the semantic interoperability during the rewriting processing [15].

Source quality describes the main quality characteristics of the source in terms of quality criteria such as freshness, popularity, response time, etc.

In the following we give our formalism for *source content* dimension and more details about the *source quality* characteristics. We present some quality criteria and define metrics to measure their values.

3.2   Source Content Dimension

To represent the *source content* dimension, we use the same formalism than the *user goals* of the user profile. This is necessary to perform content matching between the *source profile* and the *user profile*. So, the *source content* dimension of the source profile is represented by a weighted vector of key words or concepts. The concepts are extracted from the source ontology if it exists or through an indexing method. The weights of the terms (key words or concepts) are calculated using the well known *Tf*IDf* schema explained in the vector model of Salton [13]. *Tf* is the term frequency which represents the occurrence of the term in a given document; *IDf* is the inverse document frequency which represents the relative frequency of occurrence of the term in a corpus of documents. For example, consider a source containing 100 documents, 20 of them contains the concept *trip*. To calculate the weight of the concept *trip*, we suppose that all documents containing that term compose one big document. With this assumption, we are able to calculate *Tf* among this big document and *IDf* among the other documents in the source. The weight of the concept *trip* is the product *Tf*IDf*. This statistical measure characterizes the importance of the concept in the data source. It is widely used in information retrieval and text mining domains. Using this formalism, we give in definition 3 the *source content* dimension of the source profile.

Definition 3. The *source content* $SC(S_i)$ of the source S_i is a weighted vector of concepts given by: $SC(S_i)=(cs_{i1},ws_{i1};\ cs_{i2},ws_{i2};\ldots.cs_{in},ws_{in})$, where cs_{ij} represents the concepts and ws_{ij} their respective weights.

3.3   Source Quality Dimension

We define the source quality dimension as the main quality criteria that make a significant difference between data sources. In the next, we focus on four information quality metrics which are reputation, freshness, completeness and time of response.

Reputation
Reputation, also called popularity, means the degree to which a source is in high standing [16]. Reputation of a source is related to several factors depending on the

user context: (i) the quality and quantity of information and documents in the source; (ii) the authority and credibility of the source owner (e.g., an official data source has a higher reputation than a wiki web site); (iii) the quality of service including time of response, cost and security parameters. Indeed, a source having a good response time and a lower cost is more appreciated by the users.

Source reputation depends on the user judgment according to his context. It's a highly subjective criterion. For this reason, we consider that the reputation of a source S expressed by a user U is measured by a score from 1(bad reputation) to 5 (very high reputation). In the following, we denote this score by *Reputation_Score(U,S)*.

We need now to measure the reputation of a source S. For this purpose, we define a metric called *Global_Reputation_Score* which is the average of all *Reputation_Scores* expressed by a set of users $U=\{U_1, U_2...U_n\}$. The *Global_Reputation_Score* is computed using formula 1.

$$\text{Global\_Reputation\_Score(S)} = E[\textstyle\sum_{i=1}^{n} \text{Reputation\_Score}(U_i, S)/n] + 1 \qquad (1)$$

Freshness

There are various definitions of source freshness in the literature, as well as different metrics to measure it. Peralta [17] Gives a state of the art of these definitions and presents taxonomy of metrics to measure it depending on the application domain. For example, in data warehouse systems, one of the metrics used to measure source freshness is currency [18]. Currency reflects the degree of change between data extracted and returned to the user and data stored in the source. In our model, we consider that freshness refers to the age of information in the source and the update of its content. To measure this factor, we use the *timeliness* factor [14], which expresses how old is data in the source since its creation or update. This factor is bounded with the update frequency of the source. We define a metric called *Timeliness_Score* which measures the time elapsed since data was updated. For example, a "*Timeliness_Score=2 years*" means that the source contains documents updated 2 years ago. We also suppose that sources give the *Timeliness_Score* as a meta-data in their descriptions.

Completeness

Completeness is the extent to which data is not missing and are of sufficient breadth, depth, and scope for the task at hand [16]. In other words, it expresses the degree to which all documents relevant to a domain have been recorded in the source. Completeness of a source is also called in the literature: coverage, scope, granularity, comprehensiveness and density. For example, a specialized web site is more complete than a non specialized one. We measure completeness using sampling queries which estimate the coverage of a source regarding some specific topic. We define a metric called *Completeness_Score* which represents the percentage of relevant documents returned by the source S out of the size of this source. *Completeness_Score* is given by formula 2, Where *Size(S)* is the number of documents stored in S and *Size(D)* is the number of documents that answer the sample queries.

$$\text{Completeness\_Score(S)} = \left(\frac{\text{Size(D)}}{\text{Size(S)}}\right) * 100 \qquad (2)$$

Time of response

Time of response is the time that a source takes to answer a given query. It is calculated in seconds. Time of response could be very high if the source is saturated or doesn't have the capability to answer the query [19]. In this paper, we suppose that all sources could answer all queries so that the problem of source capabilities is resolved. Consequently, the time of response depends only on the communication process with the source. We use sample queries to determine this factor. Let SQ= {SQ_1, SQ_2,...,SQ_k} be the set of sample queries. For each sample query SQ_i, we measure the time of response denoted *Query_Time_of_Response*. The Time of Response of the source S is then computed as the maximum of all *Query_Time_of_Responses* using formula 3.

$$\text{Time\_of\_Response}(S) = \max_{i=1}^{k}(\text{Query\_Time\_of\_Response}(SQ_i)) \tag{3}$$

More quality factors exist in the literature [20]. For example, understandability, credibility, precision, correctness, etc. All these factors could be added in our model easily. The user then chooses those meeting his quality requirements. In this step of work, we think that the defined quality factors are sufficient for a mediator to make a quality aware source selection and ranking.

To illustrate our formalism, we give in table 1 the formal description of the dimensions *identity, content,* and *quality* for two data sources. Source 1 is the portal of the tourism ministry; source 2 is the portal of a tourism agency. Note that values are purely illustrative.

Table 1. Formal description of the dimensions Identity, Content and Quality for two data sources

	Source 1	Source 2
Identity	Id=1, Name , TOURISM Portal URL:www.tourisme.gov.ma Owner : Moroccan Tourism Ministry	Id=2, Name: Tourism Agency URL:http://TAgency.com Owner: BestTrip Agency
Content	(Holidays , 0,7; Restaurants , 0.8; Transport , 0.5; Monuments , 0.4, Tourists guides, 0.3)	(Cities , 0.9; Monuments , O.8; Transport , 0.6; Entertainments , 0.4)
Quality	Reputation= 5, Freshness= 1 year, Completeness= 70% Time of response= 1s	Reputation= 2, Freshness= 5 years, Completeness= 20% Time of response= 3s

4   Source Selection

Let's remind that in most mediation systems, source selection is done during the rewriting process. Once the user submit a query, formulated in terms of mediated schema (global schema), the mediator analyses it syntactically and semantically and then decomposes it into a set of sub-queries targeted to the appropriate sources. This method gives the same results for the same queries and does not respect user preferences. Furthermore, the increasing number of integrated data sources penalizes the system performances [19]. Personalizing source selection makes it possible to get more accurate responses by integrating only the most relevant sources. To personalize the mediator answers, we propose an approach where we select the most relevant sources according to the user profile before the rewriting process. Our source selection process is based on matching the user profile and the sources profiles. This profile matching is done at two levels: (1) A content matching, which finds out the relevant sources according to the user needs. It is based on calculating a similarity measure between the *user goals* dimension and the *source content* dimension; (2) A quality matching, which returns the relevant sources according to the user quality preferences. It is based on a multi-attribute decision making method. To sum up, our approach has two strengths. It helps personalizing the mediator answer, and reduces the number of integrated sources by selecting only the most relevant ones. This is an important factor to improve the mediator performances [19].

4.1   Content Profile Matching

In this step, we are interested in the *user goals* $UG(U_i)$ and the *source content* $SC(S_j)$ dimensions. To perform a content matching, we face two major problems. First, UG and SC vectors have different cardinalities and contain different terms. So, they could not be compared since they are not homogenous. Second, we have to rank the sources from the most to the less relevant ones according to the user goals and preferences. The ranking is given by a similarity score which measures the degree of content matching between user profile and source profile.

4.1.1 Homogenizing Vectors

To overcome the problem of vector homogeneity, we propose to take into account the common terms with their relative weights and add absent concepts in each source content vector with a weight of zero. To illustrate this method, let's consider UG of User 1 presented in Section 2, and the SC vectors of Source 1 and Source 2 presented in Section 3. Table 2 contains the homogenized vectors.

Table 2. Homogenizing SC vectors according to UI vector for user 1

	Transport	Accommodation	Restaurant	Conference
User 1	0.9	0.8	0.7	0.6
Source 1	0.5	0	0.8	0
Source 2	0.6	0	0	0

4.1.2 Measuring Similarities

Once the *source content* and the *user goals* vectors are homogenized, we are able to calculate the similarity scores. Similarities between two homogenous vectors could be calculated in different manners: using distances like the Euclidian distance, Manhattan distance, Hamming distance etc.[21], or using similarity measures based on the inner product of the vectors. The most popular ones are the Cosine angle,

Jaccard coefficient, and Dice Coefficient [22]. Distances and similarity measures are equivalent. Indeed, the more the vectors are similar, the less is the distance between them. For next, we focus on similarity measures instead of distances. The Cosine angle is the most simple and widely used similarity measure. The main advantage is its sensitivity to the relative importance of terms in each vector. Jaccard and Dice measures were initially defined for binary vectors, thus, measuring the similarity as a proportion of common terms (having a weight of 1) and non common ones (having a weight of 0). These measures have been extended to support weighted vectors. Similarities between *SC* and *UG* depend on the number of common terms and also on their weights. Furthermore, we need to emphasize the importance to the common terms instead of terms that are not shared. For these reasons, we propose in definition 3 to calculate the similarity score as the average of the Cosine, Jaccard and Dice coefficients.

Definition 3. Given $UG(U_i)=(tu_{i1},wu_{i1}; tu_{i2},wu_{i2};....tu_{in},wu_{in})$ and $SC(S_j)=(cs_{j1},ws_{j1}; cs_{j2},ws_{j2};....cs_{jn},ws_{jn})$, the homogenized vector representing the *source content* dimension of source S_j. We note $sim(U_i,S_j)$ the similarity score between $UG(U_i)$ and $SC(S_j)$. It is given by formula 4:

$$sim(U_i,S_j)= \frac{a}{3}(\frac{1}{\sqrt{bc}} + \frac{1}{b+c-a} + \frac{2}{b+c}) \qquad (4)$$

where $a=\sum_{k=1}^{n} wu_{ik}^2 \cdot ws_{jk}^2$; $b=\sum_{k=1}^{n} wu_{ik}^2$ and $c=\sum_{k=1}^{n} ws_{jk}^2$

4.1.3 Ranking and Selecting Relevant Sources

The similarity score measures how closest are the *user goals* and the *source content* vectors.   By definition, $sim(U_i,S_j)$ is based on the Cosine, Dice and Jaccard coefficients. Egghe prove in [22], that all these coefficients respect the properties of OS-Similarity measures. That means that they allow ordering sets of comparable items, which is the purpose of assumption 1. It is easy to verify that *Sim* score, based on the average of the cosine, Dice and Jaccard coefficients, is an OS-similarity. Consequently, the higher the score is, the higher the vectors are close. Also we can consider that a source is relevant if the *source content* and the *user goals* vectors are close. This proves assumption1 which allows ranking the sources from the most relevant to the less relevant according to their similarity scores.

Assumption 1. Given a user U_i and two sources S_j and S_k., S_j is more relevant than S_k if $sim(U_i,S_j) \geq sim(U_i,S_k)$. We note: $S_j> S_k$.

But this relevancy ranking is not sufficient to select only the most relevant sources. According to Pareto principle [23], we can say that 80% of user satisfaction comes only from 20% of available sources. That means we can considerably reduce the amount of integrated sources with a satisfying result. As we mentioned before, reducing the number of integrated sources improves considerably the mediator performances. To attempt this goal, user defines a relevancy threshold *(Rt)*. For example, *Rt*= 60% means that the sources having a similarity score less than 0.60 are considered irrelevant. This relevancy threshold depends on user preferences. To select only the most relevant sources, called *m-relevant*, we use definition 4.

Definition 4. *Given a user threshold Rt and a similarity score $sim(U_i,S_j)$, S_j is m-relevant if $sim(U_i,S_j)*100 \geq Rt$.*

To illustrate our approach for content matching and content source selection, consider 10 sources $\{S_1, S_2,..S_{10}\}$. We seek to select the m-relevant ones according to $UG(U_1)$ defined previously. The relevancy threshold is (Rt= 50%). Table 3 gives the homogenized vectors, the similarity measures and the corresponding sources ranking.

Table 3. Measuring similarity scores and ranking sources according to User1 goals

	Transport	Accommodation	Restaurant	Conference	Sim	Rank
User 1	0.9	0.8	0.7	0.6		
S1	0.5	0	0.8	0	0.596	4
S2	0.6	0	0	0	0.433	6
S3	0.2	0.6	0.4	0	0.650	2
S4	0	0.7	0	0.1	0.430	7
S5	0	0.3	0	0	0.276	8
S6	0.8	0	0.2	0.1	0.593	5
S7	0	0	0	0.6	0.270	9
S8	0.2	0.4	0.3	0.1	0.643	3
S9	0.7	0.6	0.5	0.3	0.933	1
S10	0	0	0	0	0	10

Table 3 shows that for *Rt=50%*, the ordered set of selected sources is $\{S9>S3>S8>S1>S6\}$. This example explains our content source selection procedure. In the case of low relevancy threshold, or if the majority of sources are m-relevant, also if the amount of selected sources is still high, the user prefers to select only the sources respecting his quality requirements and preferences. This is the issue of quality profile matching presented in next session.

4.2 Quality Profile Matching

In the previous section, we explain how we select sources according to *user goals*. The selected sources may have different quality characteristics, and respect more or less the user quality preferences. To perform an accurate source selection, it is important to refine the content selection by a selection based on quality criteria. This is ensured through the quality profile matching. Since the source quality is measured with several criteria, the quality profile matching could be studied as a multi-attribute decision making problem (MDMP). In the literature, several methods have been developed to resolve this problem such as SAW, TOPSIS and AHP [24]. We choose to apply SAW (Simple Additive Weighting) [25], because it is one of the most simple but nevertheless a good decision making procedure. SAW results are also usually close to more sophisticated methods [24]. The basic idea of SAW is to calculate a quality score for each source using a decision matrix and a vector of preference weights. Although SAW solves the problem of the heterogeneity of quality criteria by scaling their values, this method ranks sources considering only the user quality preferences weights. This ranking is based on the priority and importance of quality criterion but does not consider the preferences values. Consequently, we could not select the best sources unless the user defines a limit of the acceptable scores or a number of desired sources. To overcome these limitations, we develop a selection and ranking algorithm that respect both the user quality preferences weights and values. The values defined by the user correspond to the criteria thresholds. Our algorithm is performed in two stages: source selection and source ranking using SAW method. It is described in the following.

Input:
$S=\{S_1,S_2,..,S_n\}$: Set of candidate sources
$Q=\{Q_1,Q_2,..,Q_m\}$: set of sources quality metrics.
$M=[v_{ij}]_{(n*m)}$: the decision matrix, where v_{ij} is the value of Q_j measured on source S_i
$W=[w_i]_m$: the vector of user quality preference weights
$Qt(Q_i)$: Quality threshold defined by user for each Q_i
Output:
$S'=\{S'_1,S'_2,..,S'_k\}$: Set of selected and ranked sources
Begin
// Stage 1: Source Selection
1.   for all Q_i select the one having the highest weight and call it Q_{max}
2.   from S, select S_i having Q_{max} value $\geq Qt(Q_{max})$
// Stage 2: Sources Ranking using SAW Algorithm
3.   Scale v_{ij} to make them comparable using some transformation function. With this scaling all source's quality values are in [0, 1]. We obtain a scaled decision matrix $M'=[v'_{ij}]_{(n*m)}$ where:

$$v'_{ij} = \frac{v_{ij} - \min_i(v_{ij})}{\max_i(v_i) - \min_i(v_i)}$$

4.   Apply W to M'
5.   Calculate sources scores; the score of source S_i is given by:

$$Score\ (S_i) = \sum_{j=1}^{m} (v'_{ij} \cdot w_j)$$

6.   Rank sources according to the sources scores obtained in step3.
    End
    To illustrate our algorithm, let's perform the quality matching of the five sources selected in the previous section. These sources have different values of quality parameters summarized in table 4.
    We suppose that users set their preference priorities based on the following scale: {0.4: mandatory, 0.3: desirable, 0.2: not desirable, 0.1: indifferent}. Suppose also that User 1 requires that the selected sources must have a *Global_Reputation_Score>3*. So, this criterion is mandatory. He also prefers sources with a *Completeness_Score>30%*. This criterion is desirable and he is indifferent among the other quality factors.

Table 4. Sources quality parameters

	Global_Reputation_Score	Timeliness_Score	Completeness_Score	Time_of_Response
S_1	5	20	50	1
S_3	5	30	80	1
S_6	3	2	60	0.5
S_8	4	5	10	2
S_9	1	10	20	1

The corresponding user quality preferences of User 1 are given in table 5.

Table 5. User quality preferences (weights and values) (Ø means no preferred value for the criterion)

	Global_Reputation_ Score	Timeliness_Score (years)	Completeness_Score (%)	Time_of_Response (s)
Weight	0.4	0.1	0.3	0.1
Value	>3	Ø	>30%	Ø

Remind that our main objective is to identify sources that best fit with the user quality preferences. For this purpose, we apply our source selection and ranking algorithm.

Stage 1: We select only sources having a *Global_Reputation_Score>3*. The remaining sources are: S_3, S_1, and S_6. Then we select only sources having a *Completeness_Score>30%*. S_3, S_1, and S_6 verify this criterion. Note that although S_9 is the best relevant source for the content matching, it is not selected in the quality matching because its quality characteristics don't meet the user quality preferences.

Stage 2: We apply SAW to the selected sources S_3, S_1 and S_6. We scale the decision matrix to make the quality values comparable. Then, we apply the vector of user weights W. The scaled decision matrix, the vector of user weights and the sources scores are presented in table 6.

Table 6. Calculating sources scores using SAW

	Global_Reputation_ Score	Timeliness_Score (years)	Completeness_Score (%)	Time_of_Response (s)	Source Score
S_1	1	0.642	0	1	0.5642
S_3	1	1	1	1	0.9
S_6	0	0	0.333	0	0.0999
W	0.4	0.1	0.3	0.1	

Sources scores give the following ranking: S_3 is more appreciated than S_1 and finally S_6. As shown in this example, our source selection and ranking algorithm returns to the user a set of relevant sources that satisfies his quality preferences both in terms of quality weights and quality values.

5   Related Works

Several systems have been developed to integrate disparate and heterogeneous data sources, but few of them address the source selection problem. To select the relevant sources, two approaches exist [26]. The first one considers each candidate source as a big document constructed via document concatenation, so the source selection becomes a problem of document retrieval. The most used source selection algorithms CORI [27], GIOSS [28] and K-L divergence based algorithms [29] are based on this assumption. The second approach considers the candidate source as a repository of documents. So the selected sources are those who are the most likely to return the maximum of relevant documents. ReDDE [30] algorithm and the DTF (decision theoretic framework) [31] give a source ranking by estimating the number of relevant documents for each query. The estimation is based on calculating a cost function which includes quality and time factors. Both approaches require a source representation in their selection and ranking process. The source characteristics used are either given by the source, for example the protocol STARTS [32] requires sources to provide an accurate description of their content and quality, or discovered automatically through sampling queries [30]. Our source selection and ranking process combines both methods for sources representation. Indeed, the source gives its content and quality dimensions in the source profile when it is possible. If not, the source profile could be filled using sampling queries especially for quality characteristics. The source profile is then used to perform a personalized source selection based on content matching and quality matching. The main contribution is that the source selection and ranking is not based on user queries but on user profiles. Consequently, the selected set of candidate sources meets the user goals and also his quality requirements. In addition, the source selection process belongs to an interaction session which is usually composed of many user queries. This allows us to reduce the system treatments and improve the mediator performances. The selected sources are used later in the rewriting process to give a personalized response.

6   Conclusion

In this paper, we aim to improve user satisfaction in the context of mediation systems by selecting the most relevant sources according to user needs and preferences. We give an approach to personalize source selection so the mediator responses are more accurate and the amount of integrated data sources is reduced. The main challenge we face is representing the user profile regardless of the application domain. We propose a generic and multidimensional model divided in two parts, which are the persistent profile and the session profile. The persistent profile contains the long term information about the user whereas the session profile is related to a unique interaction session. Both persistent and user profiles are composed of several dimensions. We focus in this work on the user goals and the user quality preferences related to the session profile. The second challenge is sources representation. We describe the available sources through a multidimensional source profile constructed directly if the information is given by the sources, or through sampling queries. We focus on two dimensions which are the source content and the source quality characteristics. The user profile and the sources profiles are then compared through a content matching and a quality matching. The content matching gives relevant sources for the user goals, and the quality matching helps to select only those who respect the user quality requirements. The selected sources are then involved in the rewriting process to return an integrated response. In future works, we plan to extend our personalizing process in three directions. First, we will develop a learning mechanism to update and enrich user preferences by analyzing his interaction history. Second, we will build user communities by regrouping similar profiles and exploit neighbors interaction to offer a collaborative source selection. Finally, our model could be easily implemented in any mediation system because the proposed profiles are generic and independent from application domains. In particular, we integrate our solution into WASSIT [19] which is a mediation framework developed by our laboratory. We develop 2P-Med [33], a personalization platform for mediation systems that we plug into WASSIT. This platform concretizes our model driven approach for personalizing mediation systems.

References

1. Wiederhold, G.: Mediators in the Architecture of Future Information Systems. In: IEEE Computer Conference, vol. 25(3), pp. 38–49 (1992)
2. Peralta, V.: Data Quality Evaluation in Data Integration Systems. Ph.D. dissertation, Versaille University (2006)
3. Kobsa, A., Wahlster, W.: User Models in Dialog Systems. Springer, Heidelberg (1989)
4. Gowan, J.P.: A multiple model approach to personalized information access, Thesis of Master in computer science. Faculty of science, University College Dublin (Februrary 2003)
5. Amato, G., Straccia, U.: User Profile Modeling and Applications to Digital Libraries. In: Abiteboul, S., Vercoustre, A.-M. (eds.) ECDL 1999. LNCS, vol. 1696, pp. 184–187. Springer, Heidelberg (1999)
6. Berkovsky, S., Kuflik, T., Ricci, F.: Mediation of user models for enhanced personalization in recommender systems. User Model. User-Adapt. Interact. 18(3), 245–286 (2008)
7. Zaoui, I., Wadjinny, F., Chiadmi, D., Benhlima, L.: Construction d'un profil utilisateur pour un médiateur de bibliothèques électroniques. In: Proceedings of WOTIC, Agadir, Morocco (2009)
8. Nguyen, A.T.: COCoFil2 : Un nouveau système de filtrage collaboratif basé sur le modèle des espaces de communautés. Joseph-Fournier University, Grenoble I (2006)
9. Fink, J., Kobsa, A.: A Review and Analysis of Commercial User Modeling Servers for Personalization on the World Wide Web. User Modeling and User-Adapted Interaction 10, 209–249 (2000)
10. Mobasher, B., Dai, H., Luo, T., Nakagawa, M.: Discovery and Evaluation of Aggregate Usage Profiles for Web Personalization. Data Mining and Knowledge Discovery 6(1), 61–82 (2002)

11. Bradley, K., Rafter, R., Smyth, B.: Case-Based User Profiling for Content Personalization. In: Brusilovsky, P., Stock, O., Strapparava, C. (eds.) AH 2000. LNCS, vol. 1892, pp. 62–72. Springer, Heidelberg (2000)

12. Tanudjaja, F., Mui, L.: Persona: A contextualized and personalized web search. In: Proc. 35th Hawaii International Conference on System Sciences, Big Island, Hawaii, p. 53 (January 2002)

13. Salton, G., Wong, A., Yang, C.: A vector space model for automatic indexing. Communications of the ACM 18, 613–620 (1975)

14. Wang, R., Strong, D.: Beyond accuracy: what data quality means to data consumers. Journal on Management of Information Systems 12(4), 5–34 (1996)

15. Wadjinny, F., Chiadmi, D., Benhlima, L., Moujane, A.: Query processing in the WASSIT mediation framework. Proceedings of the seventh ACS/IEEE International Conference on Computer Systems and Applications (AICCSA 2009), Rabat, Morocco (May 2009)

16. Naumann, F., Leser, U., Freytag, J.C.: Quality–driven integration of heterogenous information systems. In: Proceedings of the 25th International Conference on Very large Data Bases (VLDB 1999), pp. 447–458 (1999)

17. Bouzeghoub, M., Peralta, V.: A Framework for Analysis of Data Freshness. In: International Workshop on Information Quality in Information Systems (IQIQ 2004), co-located with SIGMOD Conference, Paris (2004)

18. Segev, A., Weiping, F.: Currency-Based Updates to Distributed Materialized Views. In: Proceedings of the 6th International Conference on Data Engineering (ICDE 1990), Los Angeles, USA (1990)

19. Wadjinny, F.: Adaptation des requetes aux capacites de sources dans un système de mediation. Ph.D. dissertation, Computer Sciences Department, Mohammadia Engineering School, Rabat, Morocco (2010)

20. Burgess, M., Alex Gray, W., Fiddian, N.: Establishing Taxonomy of Quality for Use in Information Filtering. In: Eaglestone, B., North, S.C., Poulovassilis, A. (eds.) BNCOD 2002. LNCS, vol. 2405, pp. 103–113. Springer, Heidelberg (2002)

21. Walters-Williams, J., Li, Y.: Comparative Study of Distance Functions for Nearest Neighbors. In: Advanced Techniques in Computing Sciences and Software Engineering, pp. 79–84 (2010), doi:10.1007/978-90-481-3660-5_14

22. Egghe, L.: Good properties of similarity measures and their complementarity. JASIST 61(10), 2151–2160 (2010)

23. Hardy, M.: Pareto's Law. The Mathematical Intelligencer 32(3), 38–43 (2010), doi:10.1007/s00283-010-9159-2

24. Naumann, F.: Data fusion and data quality. In: Proceedings of the New Techniques and Technologies for Statistics (1998)

25. Hwang, C.L., Yoon, K.: Multiple Attribute Decision Making: Methods and Applications. Springer, Heidelberg (1981)

26. Paltoglou, G.: Algorithms and strategies for source selection and results merging (Collection fusion algorithms) in distributed information retrieval systems. PhD thesis, Department of Applied Informatics, University of Macedonia (2009)

27. Callan, J.: Distributed information retrieval. In: Croft, W.B. (ed.) Advances in Information Retrieval, ch. 5, pp. 127–150. Kluwer Academic Publishers (2000)

28. Gravano, L., Garcia-Molina, H.: Generalizing GlOss to vector-space databases and brocker hierarchies. In: Proc. of 21st International Conference on Very Large Data Bases (VLDB 1995), pp. 78–89 (1995)

29. Xu, J., Croft, W.B.: Cluster-based language models for distributed retrieval. In: Proc. of the 22nd Annual International ACM SIGIR Conference on Research and Development in Information Retrieval (1999)
30. Si, L., Callan, J.: Relevant document distribution estimation method for resource selection. In: Proc. of the 26th Annual International ACM SIGIR Conference on Research and Development in Information Retrieval (2003)
31. Nottelmann, H., Fuhr, N.: Evaluation different methods of estimating retrieval quality for resource selection. In: Proc. of the 26th Annual International ACM SIGIR Conference on Research and Development in Information Retrieval (2003)
32. Gravano, L., Chang, C., Garcia-Molina, H., Paepcke, A.: STARTS: Stanford proposal for internet meta-searching. In: Proc. of the ACM-SIGMOD International Conference on Management of Data (1997)
33. Zaoui, I., Chiadmi, D., Benhlima, L.: Building 2P-Med: A personalization platform for mediation. IJEST (International Journal of Engineering Science and Technologies) 3(5) (May 2011) ISSN: 0975-5462

Towards a Framework for Conceptual Modeling of ETL Processes

Ahmed Kabiri, Faouzia Wadjinny, and Dalila Chiadmi

Computer Sciences Department, Mohammadia Engineering School,
Mohammed Vth University-Agdal, Ibn Sina Avenue, BP765, Agdal, Rabat, Morocco
{akabiri,wadjinny,chiadmi}@emi.ac.ma

Abstract. Data warehousing involves many moves of data from several sources into a central repository. Extraction-Transformations-Loading (ETL) processes are responsible for the extraction of data, their cleaning, conforming and loading into the target. It is widely recognized that building ETL processes, in a data warehouse project, are expensive regarding time and money. During the building phase, the most important and complex task is to achieve conceptual modeling of ETL processes. Several solutions have been proposed for this issue. In this paper, we present our approach, which is based on a framework for modeling ETL processes. Comparing with existent solutions, our approach has numerous strengths. Besides extensibility and reusability, it offers support and guideline to the designer. It has also the advantage to use a shorten notation, to design an ETL, consisting mainly on three components.

Keywords: Data warehouse, Extract-Transform-Load (ETL), Conceptual modeling of ETL.

1 Introduction

In order to develop a successful strategy, managers need constantly to know the situation of their business. For this reason, they have to analyze their own data[1]. Business Intelligence (BI) projects are launched to meet this need. BI is the process of turning data into information then into knowledge [16]. It aims to improve decision process. In BI system, data warehouse (DW) constitutes the central element. In this environment, shown in figure 1, Extraction Transformations Loading (ETL[2]) tools pull data from several sources (databases tables, flat files, internet, and so on), apply complex transformation to them and then move them to the target (DW).

Furthermore, it is widely recognized that building DW refreshment processes, during BI project, are expensive regarding time and money. ETL consume up to 70% of resources [3], [5], [4], [2]. Interestingly [2] reports and analyses a set of studies showing this fact of life. It is well known too, that the accuracy and correctness of data are key factors of the success or failure of BI projects.

---

[1] Enterprise data collected from operational applications.

[2] Has several appellations: DW backroom [3], DW backstage [6], DW refreshment processes or DW population processes [2].

P. Pichappan, H. Ahmadi, and E. Ariwa (Eds.): INCT 2011, CCIS 241, pp. 146–160, 2011.
© Springer-Verlag Berlin Heidelberg 2011

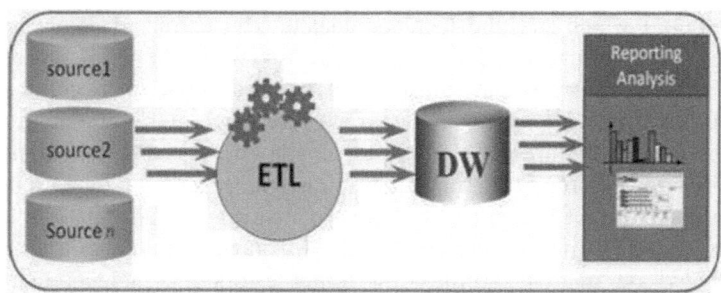

Fig. 1. Classical BI System

ETL is a critical component in BI system. Specifically, the transform task is the complex one. Gathering data from many datasets and loading it into the target, are the basic missions of ETL. While these two steps are necessary, they are not enough. Indeed, the transformation step is the main phase, where ETL adds value [3]. During this step, challenges of data cleaning and conforming arise. A detailed study of these issues is available in [1]. These issues   can be classified in three classes of conflicts and problems: schema problems, record problems and value problems [22].

At the conceptual level, the designer solves these problems by identifying necessary transformations. More specifically, he defines how to map sources attributes to the target ones. Depending on the quality of data sources, he has to specify how to clean and how to conform data. For example, removing duplicates and standardizing attributes values. Conceptual modeling of ETL processes is an active topic. Several proposals have been suggested. To fix the drawbacks of these proposals, we intend to enrich the field of conceptual modeling of ETL processes by proposing a helpful platform for defining and maintaining ETL systems. Namely, we suggest an approach which is framework-based aiming at:

- Designing ETL process;
- Providing support and guidelines for designing ETL system;
- Decreasing time and cost of ETL project;
- Enhancing communication and understandability between designer and developer;
- Easing maintenance and optimization of the ETL system.

The remainder of this paper is organized as follows. While section 3 presents related works, section 2 gives information and overview of ETL processes. Section 4 is reserved to our proposal. It outlines the architecture of our framework and our notation for designing ETL processes. Besides, it offers a motivating example, over which our discussion will be based. We conclude and present our future works in section 5.

2   Background

An ETL process (also known as job) integrates heterogeneous sources to a data warehouse. To this end, an ETL extracts data from multiple sources (flat files, databases, etc.) which may be local or distant. The extracted data pass through a sequence of transformations. This is the critical phase in the whole process for three reasons. Firstly, it carries out the logic of business process. Secondly, it lasts in running time. Thirdly, it consumes disk resources since multiple temporary files and directories are made during this step, especially for sort and join transformations. Transformation is a broad term meaning all the data processing operations performed from sources to target (mapping attributes). However, not all data will arrive at the destination, since it may be incorrect. Indeed, sources may contain erroneous data, which should be treated carefully by fixing errors and defects that it contain. Otherwise, this kind of data has to be filtered and rerouted to reject file. Another important aspect of ETL is the management of job crash, because ETL processes take a lot of time. Consequently, it is a good practice to create checkpoints, which consist on storing physically the outcome of a complex transformation. Hence, when the job fails, especially when the volume of treated data is important, it is possible to go back to the last checkpoint and to continue the processing. However, one will lose in performance and overhead running time, when there is no crash and checkpoints are activated. At the end of the way, processed data are loaded into the data warehouse.

Since ETL is the provider of DW, the success of DW is mainly dependent on ETL project success. To meet this need, it is desirable to understand the lifecycle of building ETL processes and to identify the participants to this project.

2.1   Key Participants

Understanding and constantly examining business need (what end-users want as information), is a core activity of an ETL team [3]. In addition, design and implementation are typical steps in every software life cycle [5]. Consequently, the main contributors to ETL project are end-users, the designer and the developer (cf. figure 2). Each one has its core activity. On the one hand, end-users specify what they want to get. They are characterized by changing their requirements. On the other hand, designer and developer, who are corner pillars in ETL project, turn up the business need into running processes. Often, they co-work in close locations and cooperate as a team. But recently, with the growing of offshore[3] style, both parts are geographically distant. This new situation noises to the communication and cooperation between the two sides.

In the sequel, we omit end-user and focus more on developer and designer participants. The reason is that the design modeling and implementation are the main phases in ETL project, which cost heavily as said before.

Key to achieving successfully an ETL project is to understanding how the ETL stakeholder work and how they collaborate. In other words, we need to know how the developer and the designer perform their tasks. In the following, we don't discriminate between the designer and the conceptual modeler.

---

[3] The load of developing and maintaining applications is assumed by external sides. Activities are outsourced to countries where the cost is lower. However, there is an obstacle of language.

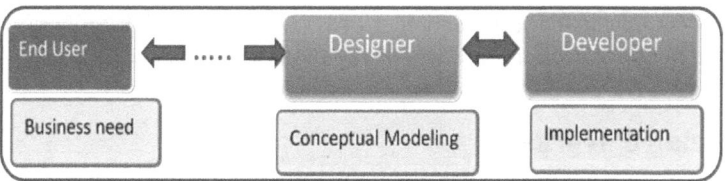

Fig. 2. Main participants of an ETL project

2.2   Developer versus Designer Toolboxes

At the beginning of an ETL project, a decisive decision should be making about the architecture of the ETL system. Two choices are possible: (a) either to buy an ETL tool or (b) to build ETL processes from scratch. There is no consensus about this decision. A survey presented in [7] shows this disparity. Each policy has it pros and cons. While option (a) saves time, option (b) saves money. The intermediate option and solution will be open source tools like [17], [18]. Nevertheless, designing ETL processes by the intermediate of an ETL tool or programming language is a technical task. It is the matter of being familiar with processing or scripting paradigms. In other words, the technology is enough strong to handle any data processing (in the scope of structured data). Therefore, ETL developers are well armed with tools, languages and frameworks to perform their tasks.

The mission of the designer is to produce two fundamental outputs which are mapping rules and data flow. In that sense, a set of solutions have been proposed, as we will see in related work section. Moreover, in real project, he uses text editor (like Ms Word) or spreadsheets (like Ms Excel. Thus, without a helpful tool dedicated to checking and supplying support in expressing specifications during design exercise, the designer makes mistakes such as:

- Including inexistent fields in a business rule (BR);
- Miss-ordering BRs;
- Missing/Mistyping the key of joint;
- Calculating the same fields twice in the same flow.

2.3   Developer and Designer Relationship

ETL designer deals with specifying moves and transforms of data. His job includes defining formatting fields, transforming schemas, joining and filtering records (at conceptual level). Given that, designer output (delivery) will be used by developer as an exercise book. All errors and imprecision, made by the conceptual modeler, will make specifications incompressible and fuzzy. Then, developer should email or have direct conversation with designer for fixing problems and making things clean and unambiguous. Often, designer justifies his defects by the fact that he develops over text editor. Unlike developers, he cannot neither compile nor check the correctness of his deliverable. The impact is delay in delivery, which noises to the project plan and image of ETL team. Stated differently, extra time is needed to accomplish the mission. This means that time and cost of ETL project, which are very expensive as mentioned in above sections, are increasing more and more.

3   Related Works

A plethora of commercial ETL tools [19], [20] as well as a set of open sources [17], [18] exist. Both of them offer graphical interface to build ETL system. However, they do not supply deep support to conceive ETL processes. They focus on technical and running aspects more than designing ones.

On the other side, research community enriches the field of conceptual modeling of ETL system with several approaches. The story starts with [21] where authors suggest to model ETL processes as a workflow application. The model proposed by [8], present a notation associated with constructs for modeling ETL activities. The model proposed is governed by a meta-model. It is customizable and supplies a subset of frequently used ETL activities. Additionally, authors complete their model, through an extended version [9], with a methodology for the conceptual modeling. Thus, they define a set of steps to get the specification of mapping rules and data flow. In [10] proposal, Simitis reinforces the model by suggesting a mapping from conceptual design to logical one. He defines a correspondence between two models, and then he provides a semi automatic method leading to an execution order of activities in logical model. This effort concludes by listing a sequence of steps that guarantee the transition from conceptual to logical model.

There are also approaches based on semantic web technologies. Thus, authors present in [11] an ontology-based model. They construct ontology via OWL (web ontology language) for describing application domain. Data sources and target semantics are expressed via the constructed ontology. These formal descriptions constitute inputs for matching between sources and target, leading so to the mapping rules and necessary transformations to perform. Same authors enhance their model in [12] proposal by expanding the scope of data stores to both structured and semi-structured data whereas it was restricted to relational sources in previous work. The construction of the ontology and annotation of data stores is enhanced too. Another approach [13] presents a conceptual language for modeling ETL processes based on the Business Process Modeling Notation (BPMN). The model provides an extensible palette of functionalities needed in conceptual design. A transition from BPMN (conceptual model) to executable specifications using Business Process Execution Language (BPEL) was shown too.

On the other hand, there exist UML-based approaches. Many propositions enrich the literature [14], [15], [16]. For example, an MDA-oriented framework is introduced for the development of ETL processes built through a set of reusable and parameterized modeling elements [14]. This proposal is based on a meta-model developed via primitive UML modeling elements. The main objective of this proposal is to reduce ETL cost by defining mechanism to automatically generating code for specific platform. More specifically, the core reference of this framework is the proposal described by [15], in which the modeling through UML class diagrams is presented. The model presents a set of operators needed in conceptual task.

These approaches, above mentioned, are precious and interesting. However, they suffer from at least one of the following limitations:

1)   They do not get profit from data profiling tools, which examine data sources.
2)   Designer cannot check automatically what he is doing.
3)   Is not easy to apply such solutions to real project and maintain[4] them. In landscape of practice, ETL project contains complex jobs that involve several sources and hundreds of fields.

The model presented in this paper proposes a framework to overcome the gaps mentioned above. It constitutes a middle position between easiness and completeness. In this sense, our approach is orthogonal to the aforementioned models.

4   Our Framework for Modeling ETL Processes

KANTARA (A framework for designing Extraction Transformation Load Process) is our framework for modeling ETL processes. Our proposal will help designer in defining ETL specifications, which focuses both on human readable and machine processable representation of ETL design.

Actually KANTARA adopts components architecture as shown in figure 3. We distinguish three levels: (1) the source level, including the data sources and their metadata, (2) the designing level, containing few sub-components, (3) and finally the user level containing the user interface.

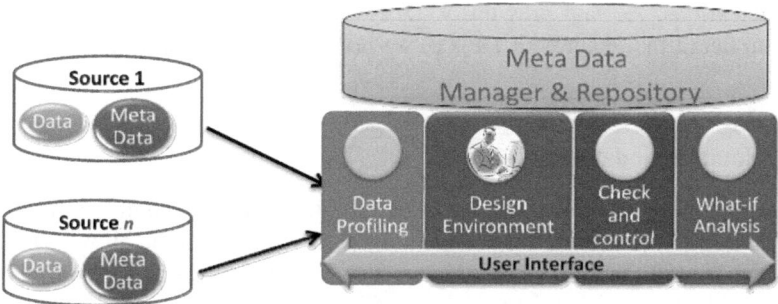

Fig. 3. KANTARA Architecture

KANTARA is composed of five modules:

*   ***Data Profiling (DP):*** This module examines a set of candidate sources to populate the DW. It output is metadata about data, which states about the

---

[4] Often functional specifications and running jobs are asynchronous. To accomplish new needs, without a risk to alter an existent treatment, demands an effective approach to detect the impact and how to satisfy the new requirements. This is where the seniority of participants adds value. But the stuff and the outsider are changing.

accuracy of data. The delivery of this module is useful for designer, since it helps him to specify necessary transformation.

- **Design Environment (DENV):** This is a working area where one can designs ETL job (at conceptual level). Having requirements and DP information (last module), designer builds conceptual modelling of ETL processes via graphical notation. The next sections give further explanations about this module.
- **Checks and Control:** This module is in charge to check and to control the model made by the designer (in design environment). Based on a meta-model, (presented in next section) besides some defined rules, this module suggests to the designer defects that it detects. Doing so, saves time and reduces cost, because designer finds out errors at early time.
- **What if Analysis:** The main mission of this module is to make easy the task of maintaining ETL processes. It intends to sustain and support designer to achieve new requirements dealing with adding or deleting even fields or business rules. This component serves managing risk by identifying the impact of changes in sources or in targets.
- **Meta data manager & repository:** This is the backbone of other modules. It manages and stores defined metadata involved in other parts. It contains information about sources, targets (schema, type of sources, etc.), mapping rules, description of each object included in design environment, etc.

In the following, we focus on design environment (DENV) component. Other modules and deep details of interaction between themes will be detailed in coming communications. As said previously, DENV allows designing ETL processes. Thus before to detail the features of DENV, we present its graphical notation and its meta-model.

4.1   Notation and Meta MODEL

Obviously, more a conceptual model provides details more it is ready for implementation. This is our thinking. Nevertheless, our solution allows making high-level overview of the ETL process, subject of modelling. The key factor of success is to find middle position between easiness and completeness.

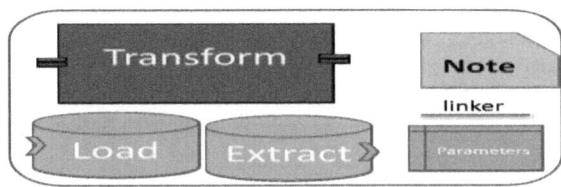

Fig. 4. Design Environment Notation

Our proposal is based on notation presented in figure 4. It involves six diagrams:

- Three core components(extract, transform and load components) that we will detail more in next sections;
- *note* area which can be placed anywhere or attached to any component:
- *linker* a simple line to link between components, it represents flow transition from one component to another;
- *Parameters* correspond to special text area, which supply general information about environment. It is helpful to insure coordination between ETL processes.

The mechanism and all features of DENV refer to entities of the meta-model illustrated in figure 5. As one can see, we conceive an ETL processes as an agglomeration of components, comments, links and parameters. While parameters and comments are optional, two components and one link are mandatory. The main element in this diagram is components class. This interface is a set of three subcomponents: extraction, transformation and load. More specifically, the transform class is the most laborious. It can be merge, join, filter, etc. Similarly, extract and load classes take into account the nature of source and target respectively. Extract class send data to other subcomponents, whereas load class receives from others. Transform class has hybrid behaviour. Actually, it sends and receives. Some functionalities and attributes have been described in the diagram. We will make theme clear later.

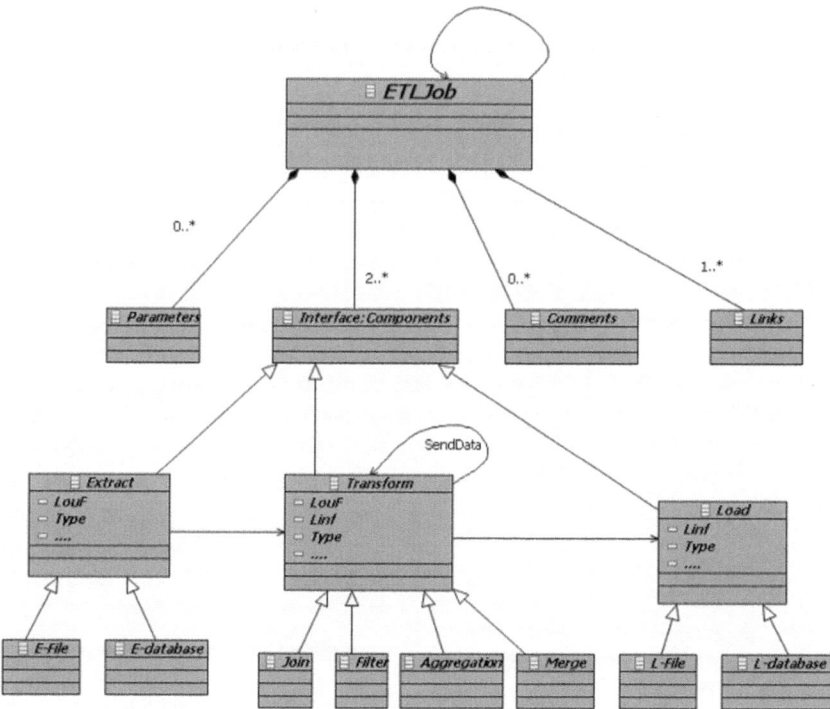

Fig. 5. Meta model of Design Environment

4.2   A Running Example

To show the artifacts of DENV, we use an example of sale activity. We start by describing the target and sources then, we will bridge between them with an ETL process.

Data warehouse or Target: Figure 6 represents a star schema. The central table is sale table (fact table) encountered with 4 dimensions tables: customer, product, promotion and Date.

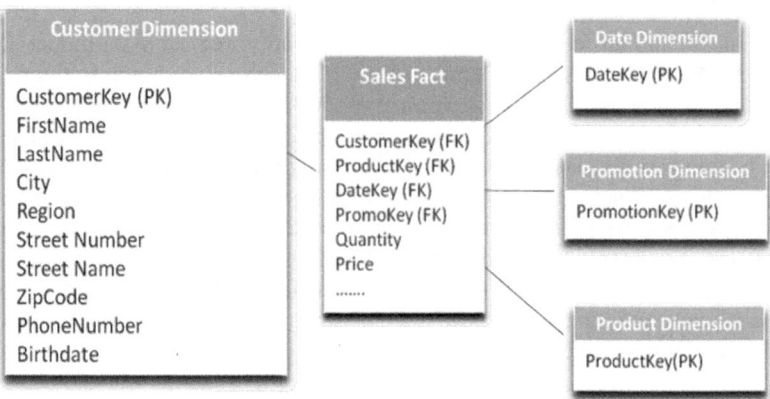

Fig. 6. Star schema for the running example

Sources: For concision, we limit our scenario to populate customer dimension. Thus figure 7 describes the customer in two source databases S1 and S2 involved in the example.

S1 Customer		
Field	Explanation	Format
CustId	Customer ID	Number
Fname	First name	string (20)
Lname	Last name	string (20)
City	city Name	string (20)
Title	Mr, Ms, Miss	string (4)
Address	home address	string (50)
ZipCode	zip code	number
Birthdate	date of birth	DD/MM/YYYY
Region	region	string (20)
PhoneId	phone number	string (20)

S2 Customer		
Field	Explanation	Format
Custcodeld	Customer ID	Number
firstname	First name	string (30)
lastname	Last name	string (30)
City	city Name	string (30)
mr-or-ms	mr, ms, mss	string (2)
Address	address mail	string (50)
ZipCode	zip code	number
Birthdate	date of birth	MM/DD/YYYY
HomeAdd :	home address	string (30)

Fig. 7. Customer description in database source S1 and S2

ETL: The plan is to load customer dimension from pertinent sources. Figure 8 shows how to meet this need using DENV notation. This diagram expresses how to standardize the two flows before merging them. The flow is then cleaned by eliminating redundant records. Finally, the diagram specifies conforming data before loading them.

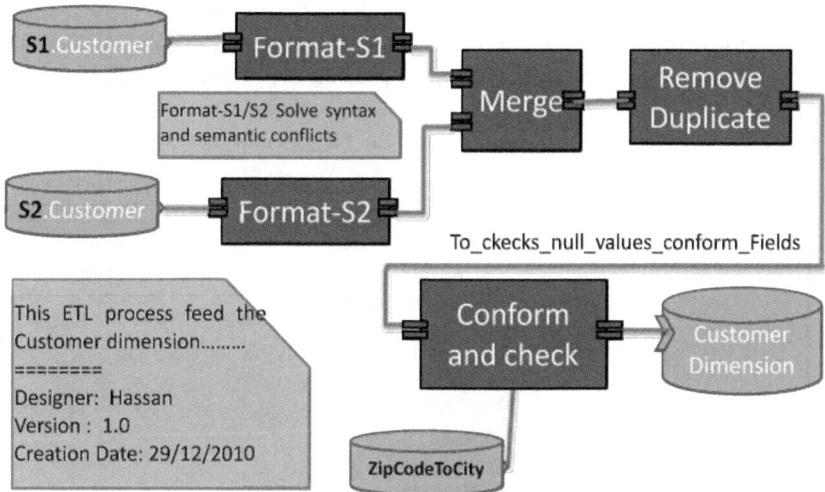

Fig. 8. ETL process feeding Customer Dimension

The way to the target is not straight. It involves many steps. The data-flow depicted in figure 8 illustrates this fact. Each step defines attributes mapping between input and output flows. Therefore, it can be rewriting as below.

Step 1.1: select and extract pertinent data from S1;
Step 1.2: select and extract pertinent data from S2;
Step 2.1, 2.2 (respectively Format-S1 and Format-S2): We have to solve syntaxic and semantic conflicts. As one can see in figure 7, attributes S1.address and S2.address have same syntax but different meanings. Contrarily, same concepts first/last name are represented differently in S1 and S2. Furthermore, we have to homogenize the size of these fields.

Cleaning and conforming are necessary steps in ETL process. Then, in reference to figure 7 the field title (mr_or_ms) which takes values (Mr, Ms Mis) in S1 and values (mr,mrs,mss) in S2 should be consolidated. Through transformation rules, the target field has to take unified values like (Mr, Mrs, Miss). Also conversion format of the field date-of-birth is required while we need to split address attribute to fill street number and street name in the target. Figure 9 describes how the component format-S1 handles these transformations.

Step 3.1(Merge): We combine the two flows after having standardized them.
Step 4.1 (Remove Duplicate): It is a good practice to filter records at the top of the treatment. The benefit will be in the performance. In other side de-duplicating the

flow; especially when joining several sources; is a vital step. Thus the dimension customer mustn't contain more than one record per customer. Otherwise, all analysis made over customers may be erroneous.

Step 5.1 (Conform and checks): ETL enhances data by completing missing data and removing mistakes. In particular, nulls values should be substituted by default values defined by the administrator or to derive new values. According to our example, the city of the customer is important. Thus it shouldn't be null neither inconsistent to zip code. Therefore via en external source, we can retrieve city values by associating zip-code keys. Then we can check if the selected value is in harmony with the one filled in customer city.

Step 6.1 (Customer dimension): load data to the target customer dimension.

	Liste of Input fields	Transformations	Liste of Output fields
S1	CustId	S1.CustId	CustomerKey
	Fname	UPCASE(S1.Fname)	FirstName
	Lname	LowerCASE(S1.Lname)	LastName
	City	S1.City	City
	Title	Split(S1.Address) Then Return 4 part	Region
	Address	Split(S1.Address) Then Return first part	Street Number
	ZipCode	Split(S1.Address) Then Return 2 part	Street Name
	Birthdate	if null or empty set to '00000' else copy S1.ZipCode	ZipCode
	Region	S1.PhoneId	PhoneNumber
	PhoneId	format (S1.Birthdate) to YYYY/MM/DD	Birthdate
	Country		

Fig. 9. Mapping associated with Component format-S1

The following sections, explains the three core components presented in figure 8: Extraction, Transformation and Loading components.

4.3   Extraction

Extraction component (EC) symbolizes the extraction step. Conceptually EC should allow representing all information connected with extraction operation. For instance, we need to know where to get data, and which relevant data to select.

Below, we define some proprieties of EC which are handled graphically by KANTARA. Those metadata are either supplied by the designer or automatically recuperated from DP module.

1) *Name* or label property serves as a logic name and differentiator of each EC. Implicitly, each EC represents a unique source: S1.customer, for example in figure 8.
2) *Path* means logical name or even physical path of data store.
3) *Louf* stands for list of output fields which determine the selected fields. The reason is that we do not need all the source attributes. They are the input fields of component format-S1 presented in figure 9.

4) *Type* describes the type of data source either a flat file or database where in that case further sub-proprieties are defined.
5) *Description* is free text zone for writing comments and notes about data store.

Graphically, each EC has an output port corresponding to the gateway where data transit.

4.4   Loading

Loading component (LC) deals with loading step. EC and LC are similar but act in opposite direction. Indeed, LC has the following proprieties: *Name* (1), *Path* (2), *Type* (4) and *Description* (5).

While we do read operations in extraction component, we do write operations in LC. Thus, the specific option and differentiator characteristic of LC is *Linf*, which stands for list of input fields. Often, when the target is a database, *Linf* represents even the schema of target table or a part of its structure, depending on type of operation, insertion or update respectively.

Graphically, each LC has an input port corresponding to the gateway where data arrives. Like EC, all these properties are managed by KANTARA.

4.5   Transformation

As the transform step is the most important and complex one in ETL process, the Transform Component (TC) is the most laborious component. Thus, TC should represent any data processing like filtering, switching, assigning key. So, in order to distinguish between these transformations, TC has *type* propriety. Furthermore, sub-properties are associated to each specific transformation. For instance, join operation requires a set of fields called keys to match and group flows, whereas in filtering operation we need an expression to discriminate between records. Such expression involves input fields and may be simple like (age > 20) or complex including regular expression[5].

TC reads data via input port and writes data through output port. Thus TC has two important proprieties Linf (List of input fields) and Louf (List of output fields). Often Linf is different from Louf. Sometimes, we add new fields to store new information (outcome of aggregation functions for example) and sometimes we delete unuseful fields to improve performance. However, it is possible that TC acts without altering the structure of input flow (Linf = Louf). For example, sort or repartition operations deals with the order and partition of records and do not modify the scheme of the flow. Additionally, as Extract Component and Load component, TC has two other proprieties: (1) *name* and (5) *description*.

---

[5] Sometime abbreviated to regex is, a sophisticated way to express how a string should look like for or how to match a token in text. For example to check if the attribute CalledNumber contains only digits and respect the format +00_212_([0-9][0-9][0-9]){3}).

It is difficult even impossible to expect all transformations that a designer will need to specify. Therefore, regarding KANTARA, we have limited the list of available transformations to the most frequently used like Join, Filter, Merge, and Aggregate. However KANTARA is extensible to overcome the gap of completeness and offers a feature for that purpose.

Graphically, TC has two types of ports: input port where data arrives, and output port where data leaves.

All these information are metadata of TC component. They are managed by KANTARA.

4.6   Describing Data

ETL processes involve many moves of data that comes from many sources under various formats. From the first treatment to the last one, the structure of processed data is changing. Furthermore, data may be loaded to several targets having different structures. Hence, the description of data and control of its structure during the whole process is fundamental.

In the scope of structured data, a data source is a set of records, which consist on an arrangement of fields. The field also known as attribute, is the atomic element of data. So describing data is describing fields. We distinguish two modes of describing data, which we call light mode and detailed mode.

Light mode: in this mode, fields are described only by their names. However we believe that this manner of acting is not safe and leads to rework requests. Hiding details about fields and trying to define mapping rules is an indication of code, load and explode symptom.

Detailed mode: this mode extends light mode by catching more information than field name: size of fields for instance. For example when mapping *S1.city to Out.City* it's helpful to know whether both sides has same size. Otherwise, a business rule should be defined, telling how to solve the conflict.

Our framework operates in detailed mode. Thus a field has three following properties:

- *field-name* represents the attribute.
- *Type* specifies the category of data to handle. It includes values like decimal, date, date-time, etc.
- *Length* precise the measurement of fields.

These properties are quite technical. Besides it takes time to build them. But, we cannot skip them as mentioned before: this is where DP module takes value. The above proprieties are metadata automatically generated by DP. Therefore, by the mechanism of propagation, we can easily transfer them from component to component.

5   Conclusion

ETL mission is to feed targets like data warehouse. Once data are extracted from sources, they pass through a set of transformations. At the end of the way, the processed data are loaded to the target. ETL processes are famous with two tags: complexity and cost. So, in order to overcome this situation and simplify maintenance task, the modeling of these processes becomes a necessity.

In this paper, we have seen, at organizational level, different participants that an ETL project involves; particularly designer and developer. Moreover we had sketched their interaction and conclude that designer need helpful tool, which will make easy the design and maintenance of ETL processes.

This paper introduces KANTARA, our framework for modeling ETL processes. We have outlined its architecture based on five modules. Namely, Data Profiling, Design Environment, Checks and Control, What-if Analysis and Metadata Manager. The Design-environment module is the heart of KANTARA. It includes new graphical metamodel-based notation. It consists mainly on three core components which are extract, transform and load components. Others modules serve the central one.

Our framework offers support and guidelines to designer for defining ETL specifications. In addition, it has the advantage of providing short notation to carry out ETL activities. Therefore, it is appropriate as a platform for collaboration between the key participants to ETL project.

KANTARA constitutes a middle position between easiness and completeness. On the one hand, it offers graphical working area and encapsulates technical complexity of data. Designer deals with data by light description. On the other hand, in background, it takes into account deep information about data, besides saving time by reusing details of data instead of building them from scratch.

At high level, the main goal is to achieve all components and validate our methodology of designing ETL processes with KANTARA artifacts. However, the great challenge that we face is the management of involved metadata either passive or active. Therefore, we intend to adapt and extend an open source tool, dedicated to manage metadata. Another way to advance this work is to elaborate more the header of our model. We focus on and we intend to define an SLA (Service Line Agreement) between DP and DENV modules.

References

1. Erhard, R., Hong Hai, D.: Data Cleaning: Problems and Current Approaches. Bulletin of the Technical Committee on Data Engineering (2000)
2. Simitisis, A., Vassiliadis, P., Skiadopoulos, S., Sellis, T.: Datawarehouse Refreshment, Data Warehouses and OLAP: Concepts, Architectures and Solutions. IRM Press (2007)
3. Kimball, R., Caserta, J.: The Data Warehouse ETL Toolkit: Practical Techniques for Extracting, Cleaning, Conforming, and Delivering Data. Wiley Publishing, Inc. (2004)
4. Inmon, W., Strauss, D., Neushloss, G.: DW 2.0 The Architecture for the next generation of data warehousing. Morgan Kaufman (2007)

5. Golfarelli, M.: Datawarehouse life-cycle and design. In: Liu, L., Özsuzsu, T. (eds.) Encyclopedia of Database Systems. LNCS, vol. 4128, pp. 1148–1158. Springer, Heidelberg (2009)
6. Adzic, J., Fiore, V., Sisto, L.: Extraction,Transformation,and Loading Processes, Data Warehouses and OLAP: Concepts, Architectures and Solutions. IRM Press (2007)
7. Eckerson, W., White, C. : Evaluating ETL and Data Integration Platforms. TDWI Report Series, 101communications LLC (2003)
8. Vassiliadis, P., Simitsis, A., Skiadopoulos, S.: Conceptual modeling for ETL processes. In: Proc. of the 5th ACM Int Workshop on Data Warehousing and OLAP (2002)
9. Simitsis, A., Vassiliadis, P.: Methodology for the conceptual modeling of ETL processes. In: Eder, J., Mittermeir, R., Pernici, B. (eds.) CAiSE Workshops. CEUR Workshop Proceedings, vol. 75. CEUR-WS.org (2003)
10. Simitsis, A.: Mapping conceptual to logical models for ETL processes. In: Proc. of the 8th ACM Int. Workshop on Data Warehousing and OLAP (2005)
11. Skoutas, D., Simitsis, A.: Designing ETL processes using semantic web technologies. In: Proc. of the 9th ACM Int. Workshop on Data Warehousing and OLAP (2006)
12. Skoutas, D., Simitsis, A.: Ontology-based conceptual design of ETL processes for both structured and semi-structured data. J. on Semantic Web and Information Systems 3(4), 1–24 (2007)
13. ElAkkaoui, Z., Zimányi, E.: Defining ETL Workflows using BPMN and BPEL. In: Proc. of the 12th ACM Int. Workshop on Data Warehousing and OLAP (2009)
14. Muñoz, L., Mazón, J., Trujillo, J.: Automatic Generation of ETL processes from Conceptual Models. In: Proc. of the 12 th ACM Int. Workshop on Data Warehousing and OLAP (2009)
15. Trujillo, J., Luján-Mora, S.: A UML Based Approach for Modeling ETL Processes in Data Warehouses. In: Song, I.-Y., Liddle, S.W., Ling, T.-W., Scheuermann, P. (eds.) ER 2003. LNCS, vol. 2813, pp. 307–320. Springer, Heidelberg (2003)
16. Golfarelli, M.: New Trends in Business Intelligence. In: Proc 1st International Symposium on Business Intelligent Systems (BIS 2005), Opatija, Croatia, pp. 15–26 (2005) (invited paper)
17. Talend Open Studio, http://www.talend.com
18. Vanilla Open source, http://www.bpm-conseil.com
19. IBM InfoSphere DataStage, http://www-01.ibm.com/software/data/infosphere/datastage/
20. Informatica, http://www.informatica.com/FR/Pages/index.aspx
21. Bouzeghoub, M., Fabret, F., Matulovic-Broqué, M.: Modeling Data Warehouse Refreshment Process as a Workflow Application. In: Proc of the Int. Workshop on Design and Management of Datawarehouse (DMDW 1999), Heidelberg, Germany (1999)
22. Vassiliadis, P., Simitsis, A.: Extraction, Transformation, and Loading, http://www.cs.uoi.gr/~pvassil/publications/2009_DB_encyclopedia/Extract-Transform-Load.pdf

Dynamics Invariant Extension of Arrays in Daikon Like Tools

Hani Fouladgar, Hamid Parvin[*], Hosein Alizadeh, and Behrouz Minaei

Nourabad Mamasani Branch, Islamic Azad University, Nourabad Mamasani, Iran
hamidparvin@mamasaniiau.ac.ir,
{fouladgar,halizadeh,b_minaei}@iust.ac.ir

Abstract. Software engineering comprises some processes such as designing, implementing and modifying of code. These processes are done to generate software fast and have a high quality, efficient and maintainable software. In order to perform these processes, invariants can useful and help programmers and testers. Arrays and pointers are frequent data types and are used in program code repeatedly. Because of this conventional use, these two data types can be the reason of fault in some program codes. First and last elements of arrays can confront to fault because of carelessness in using index in loops. Also arrays with the same type mostly have some relations which can be probably faulty. Therefore invariants which can report array and pointer properties are functional. This paper presented some constructive extension to Daikon like tools so that can produce more relevant invariants in the case of array.

Keywords: dynamic invariant detection, software testing, array property, array's first and last elements, mutual element between arrays.

1   Introduction

Invariant are program valuable properties and relations which are true in all executions. For example in a sort function such as bobble sort, while leaving the function, all the elements of the array are sorted so invariant (array **a** sorted >=) is reported. Such properties might be used in *formal specification* or *assert statement*. Invariant is introduced in [1]. Since invariants repeat the properties and relations of program variables, invariants can express the behavior of a program. Therefore after an updating to the code, invariants can determine which properties of the code remain unchanged and which properties are changed. Invariants are kind of *documentation* and *specification*. Since specification and documentation are essentials in software engineering, Invariants can be used in all processes of software engineering from design to maintenance [2]. There are two different approaches to detent invariants, *static* and *dynamic*.

In the static approach the syntactic structure and runtime behavior of program are checked without actually running of code [3]. Data-flow is a kind of invariant which

---

[*] Corresponding author.

P. Pichappan, H. Ahmadi, and E. Ariwa (Eds.): INCT 2011, CCIS 241, pp. 161–171, 2011.
© Springer-Verlag Berlin Heidelberg 2011

is traditionally used in compilers for optimizing of codes. Data-flow analysis can determine the properties of program points. *Abstract interpretation* is a theoretical framework for static analysis [4]. The most precise imaginable abstract interpretation is called the *static semantics* or *accumulating semantics*.

In contrast to static analysis, dynamic invariant detection tools elicit invariants by actually executing of the code with different test suits and inputs. Properties and relations are extracted through the execution of the code. Dynamic invariant detection emerged to software engineering realm during recent ten years by *Daikon* [2]. By using different test suits in different executions, in each program point, variable properties and relationships are extracted. These Program points are usually the points of entry and exist of program functions. Extracted properties and relations are invariants. These invariants are not certainly true but indeed they are true in all executions in test suit. One of the most important advantages of this approach is that what invariant reports not only shows the properties and relations of variables via execution but also utters the inputs properties and relations. This advantage of dynamic invariants doubles its usage.

This paper focuses on dynamic invariant detection. We plan to introduce two ideas in the case of array which can improve the relevance of invariants in a Daikon like tools. We intend to add our idea to Daikon, as a robust dynamic invariant detection tool. In the following, we discuss related work in section 2 and express our contribution in section 3. In section 4, we propose some simple examples to clarify the idea. One actual example is brought in section 5 and then we discuss how our idea improves the invariant power. We evaluate our idea in section 6. Finally, we talk about conclusion and future work (section 7).

2   Related Work

In this section, we discuss some implementations of dynamic invariant detection. We mention some implementations which are more relevant to our job but it is worth to mention there are many valuable efforts in this topic.

Dynamic invariant detection is first time introduced by *Daikon* [3] - a full-featured and robust implementation of dynamic invariant detection. Daikon is the most prospering tool for detecting dynamic invariant and until now, comparing with other dynamic invariant detection methods [3]. Most of other tools and method are inspired by Daikon. Though Daikon is potent, one of the greatest problems of this tool is being time-consuming.

DySy [8] is a dynamic inference tool which uses dynamic symbolic execution to expand the quality of inferred invariants. In the other words, besides executing test cases, DySy contemporarily perform a symbolic execution. These symbolic executions cause to produce program path condition. Then DySy combines the path conditions and build the final result. The result includes invariants which are expressed according to the program path condition.

Agitator [9] is a commercial testing tool and is inspired by Daikon. Software agitation was introduced by Agitar. Software agitation joins the results of research in test-input generation and dynamic invariant detection. The results are called observations. Code developer checks these observations to find out if there is any fault in the code. If there is any fault programmer or tester remove it and so on. Agitar won the Wall street Journal's 2005 Software Technology Innovation Award.

The DIDUCE is a dynamic invariant inference tool which extracts not only program invariants but also helps programmer to detecting errors and to determine the root causes [10]. Besides detecting dynamic invariant, DIDUCE checks program behavior against extracted invariants up to each program points and reports all detected violations. DIDUCE checks simple invariants and does not need up-front instrument.

3   Paper Contributions

One of the most time consuming parts of software engineering is testing because regarding to different inputs, different paths in execution happen. However tester tries to test all different paths by different inputs, unchecked paths can be faulty. In this situation, because of their structure, *arrays* and *pointers* are more probable to be faulty. By means of invariants, programmer or tester can recognize the behavior of program. Invariants detection tools report the properties and relations among variables. These properties and relations can be use in code testing after each up-date. Therefore if any improvement is achieved for the reporting some relevant invariant about arrays can help tester to find out program fault.

The first and the last elements of an array possess very crucial properties because these elements are impacted by the carelessness in using the indexes. By involving some array elements in invariant detection, a dramatic improvement in fault detection might happen. The number of these elements can be the least size of an array or they can be optional. This contribution exposes inattention in using index which mostly happens with the first and the last indexes and corresponding to the first and last elements of an array.

Besides employing array elements, enlisting the number of mutual elements of same type arrays for each program point is useful in detecting faults. In other words, for each program point, the number of elements' values which are shared in two different same type arrays is employed in invariants detection. It helps the programmer to evaluate his program in the cases that an array is gained from changes in another array. The mutual elements show the correct elements which should be unchanged through the process. We discuss more about this contribution in the next sections and clarify the number of mutual elements of same type arrays for each program point.

Overall our contributions comprise the following:

- Using the some of first and last elements of an array as new variables for invariant detection.
- Using the number of mutual elements of same type arrays for each program point.

4   Clarifying of Contributions

To simplify and clearing up the contributions we talk over before, in this section, we illustrate our idea by some pieces of program code and their post-condition invariant. We state the *Exit* program point invariants which represent post-condition properties for a program point because post-condition properties can determine both the pre-condition and post-condition values of variables.

4.1   First and Last Elements of Array

Now we introduce first paper contribution. In order to determine probable faults in arrays we employ some of first and last elements of array to invariant detection. The number of these elements can be the least size of the array or can be optional. This contribution exposes carelessness in using index which mostly happens to first and last indexes.

To clarify our contribution consider Fig. 1. This figure shows a faulty version of bubbleSort(). It accepts 2 values as input. One of which is the array and another is the length of the array. The output is the sorted array. This version of bubbleSort has a fault. The index *j* starts at 1 instead of 0 so the first element of array is not considered in the sorting. By using of the first and last elements of the array in invariants detection, some useful invariants are produced which help us to detect the fault.

```
int *bubbleSort(int *digits,int length)
{
  int *numbers;
  number <- digits;
  for(i=1;i<length;i++)
    for(j=1;j<length-i;j++)
      if(numbers[j]>numbers[j+1])
      {
        int temp=numbers[j];
        nembers[j]=numbers[j+1];
        numbers[j+1]=temp;
      }
  return numbers;
}
```

Fig. 1. Program A: Inattention in using index

By employing the first and the last elements of array in invariant detection, related invariants in the *Exit* point of the bubbleSort() of Fig.1 is shown in Fig.2. The presented invariants in Fig.2 are in the form of Daikon output. For array x, $x[-1]$ is the last element of x, $x[-2]$ the element before the last one and so forth. In Fig.2, line 14 expresses that the first element of the input array always equals to the first element of the return value. Lines 15 to 20 express that the rest of the elements are sorted. Therefore obviously only the first element is never involved in sorting. This helps the programmer to detect the fault.

```
 1 digits[] >= return[] (lexically)
 2 digits[] == orig(digits[])
 3 orig(length) == size(return[])
 4 return != null
 5 return[] elements <= return[-1]
 6 digits[] elements <= return[-1]
 7 return[1] in digits[]
 8 return[2] in digits[]
 9 return[3] in digits[]
10 return[-1] in digits[]
11 return[-2] in digits[]
12 return[-3] in digits[]
13 return[-4] in digits[]
14 return[0] == digits[0]
15 return[1] < return[2]
16 return[2] < return[3]
17 return[3] < return[-4]
18 return[-4] < return[-3]
19 return[-3] < return[-2]
20 return[-2] < return[-1]
21 length != return[0]
```

Fig. 2. Related invariants to the code of Fig 1

4.2   Number of Mutual Elements between two Arrays

Another contribute we discuss in this paper is the number of mutual elements of same type arrays for each program point. It helps programmer to test the code in situations that an array is generated as a result of performing some activities on another array. To illustrate the idea you may consider function in Fig.3. This function accepts 4 parameters as inputs. The first parameter is a sorted array and others are respectively array length, the value of element which must be replaced, and the new value, respectively. This function replaces m's value with n's value as a new value.

```
void replace(int *d,int l,int m,int n)
{
   int i;
   for(i=0;i<l;i++)
    if(d[i]==m)
    {
      d[i]=n;
      break;
    }
}
```

Fig. 3. Program B: An example of "replace code"

Exit point invariants of replace() is shown in the Fig.4. In this figure, invariants in lines 6 and 7 express the number of mutual elements between d (the first parameter of the function) and the return value. The number of mutual elements between d and *return* value must be equals to the number of mutual elements between *orig(d)* and the *return* value (line 6). Also, the number of mutual elements between *d* and the *return* value equals to the size of *d* minus 1. However, besides this invariant, other invariants quote that the *return* value is not sorted despite *d* is sorted and this might be a fault in the program.

```
1  d[] == orig(d[])
2  orig(1) == size(return[])
3  d[] sorted by <
4  return != null
5  orig(m) in d[]
6  Mutual(d[] , return[]) == Mutual(orig(d[]), return[])
7  Mutual(d[] , return[]) == size(d[])-1
8  d[] elements <= d[-1]
9  orig(n) in return[]
10 orig(1) < d[-1]
11 orig(1) < return[-1]
12 orig(m) != size(d[])-1
13 orig(m) < d[-1]
14 orig(m) != return[-1]
15 orig(n) != d[-1]
16 d[-1] >= return[-1]
```

Fig. 4. Related invariants to the replace code of Fig 3

5   Actual Example and Justification

Now, we plan to illustrate our ideas in some actual examples. We intend to know how our idea can practically help programmer to detect faults and their line of code. To do this, we study some rather small and simple subprograms which are caused "gold standard" invariants [9]. Our reasonable assumption is that every program, either big or small, can be divided in small parts and might be raised in small subprograms. In other words, in all programs, when working with arrays the programmer uses iteration expressions such as the *"for"* block and carelessness can result independently of whether the program is big or small. The presented code does not assume the use of any specific programming language.

5.1   Try-Catch and Effectiveness of the Ideas

Try-Catch statements, which prevent program from facing to a halt, can be a point of fault. Function AVG(), which is shown in Fig.5, contains a *Try-Catch* statement. It accepts an array (a[]) and the length (l) and sums all the elements in sum, then divides each array element by n/5 and finally returns the sorted array. Although the programmer has considered that if n is zero a division-by-zero happens and prevented it from happening by introducing an if-condition statement, the code has a fault. "temp" been declared as an integer and for $0<n<5$, n/5 is zero subsequently the variable temp can become 0 as well, and therefore division-by-zero happens. In these situations a division-by-zero exception is thrown and the return array has all its elements equal to 0 instead of being the sorted input array.

```
1  int* AVG(int* a,int l,long* sum,int n)
2  {
3    int i,j,*numbers,temp;
4    numbers=malloc(sizeof(int[l]));
5    numbers[]<-0;
6    Try
7    {
8      *sum=0;
9      for(i=0;i<l;i++)
10     {
11       *sum=a[i]+*sum;
12       if(n!=0)
13       {
14           temp=n/5;
15           a[i]/=temp;
16       }
17     }
18     numbers=Sort(a,l);
19   }
20   Catch(e)
21   {
22     *sum=0;
23   }
24   return numbers;
25 }
```

Fig. 5. Program C: First example for the justification of the proposed algorithm

In Fig.6, the related invariants in the *Exit* program point of the function are shown. As before, invariants are in the form of Daikon output but here we add also our proposed part. AVG() does sort the input array and return a sorted array as we see in the line 9 of Fig. 6. This invariant merely express that the program seems to work properly. However, by considering lines 10 to 16 and specially lines 17 and 34, it is obvious that in some situations the sorting of the array is not reached. Lines 10 to 16 show that in some cases all the return values are equal to 0. Line 17 express that mutual elements between a[] and the return values can be zero. In line 34 we observe that the mutual elements between a[] and the return values can be less than l whereas it is expected to be equal to l. consequently, we find out that the program does not work properly and in some cases we do not have sorted elements of a[] in the return array.

5.2   A Comparison with Original Daikon

Now in this subsection, we compare our result with result of original Daikon. We plan to do comparison in the function Fig. 1. In Fig.1 we presented a faulty version of "bubble sort". In Fig. 2 we showed our the related invariants generated by a modified version of Daikon (a version of daikon which we add our idea to it). Now in Fig.7, the original Daikon invariants of this subprogram are presented.

```
 1 a[] > return[] (lexically)
 2 a[] >= return[] (lexically)
 3 a[] == orig(a[])
 4 sum > return[] (lexically)
 5 sum >= return[] (lexically)
 6 orig(l) == size(return[])
 7 return != null
 8 return[] elements >= 0
 9 return[] sorted by <=
10 return[0] >= 0
11 return[1] >= 0
12 return[2] >= 0
13 return[3] >= 0
14 return[-2] >= 0
15 return[-3] >= 0
16 return[-4] >= 0
17 Mutual(a[],return[]) >= 0
18 a[] elements >= return[0]
19 a[] elements >= orig(n)
20 sum > Mutual(a[],return[])
21 sum > orig(l)
22 sum > orig(n)
23 sum > a[-1]
24 sum > return[orig(n)]
25 return[] elements >= return[0]
26 return[] elements <= return[-1]
27 return[0] <= return[1]
28 return[1] <= return[2]
29 return[2] <= return[3]
30 return[3] <= return[-4]
31 return[-4] <= return[-3]
32 return[-3] <= return[-2]
33 return[-2] <= return[-1]
34 Mutual(a[],return[]) <= orig(l)
35 orig(l) < a[-1]
```

Fig. 6. Related invariants for the code of Fig 5

As we see in Fig.7, original Daikon invariant do not help us to determine the fault. Despite the reality, line 6 and 9 express that the program works properly and returns the sorted array.

```
 1 ..bubbleSort():::EXIT
 2 digits[] >= return[] (lexically)
 3 digits[] == orig(digits[])
 4 orig(length) == size(return[])
 5 return != null
 6 digits[] elements <= return[orig(length)-1]
 7 return[orig(length)-1] in digits[]
 8 digits[orig(length)-1] in return[]
 9 return[] elements <= return[orig(length)-1]
10 orig(length) < digits[orig(length)-1]
11 orig(length) < return[orig(length)-1]
12 digits[orig(length)-1] <= return[orig(length)-1]
```

Fig. 7. Related invariants to the bubblesort code of Fig 1 using original Daikon

6   Evaluation

In this section, we plan to evaluate our proposed idea. In order to reach this goal, we intend to come up with two kind of comparison between modified Daikon and Original one. At first we evaluate the running time and time order of both version of Daikon. Then we measure the quality of produced invariants by using of *relevance* [8].

The running times of the proposed modified Daikon and the original one in terms of millisecond is shown in the Fig.8. As seen, the time-order of both modified and original versions of Daikon are linear. In other words, by adding our idea to the original Daikon the time order remains linear. However as there are more variable to check, modified Daikon has the higher slope of time order.

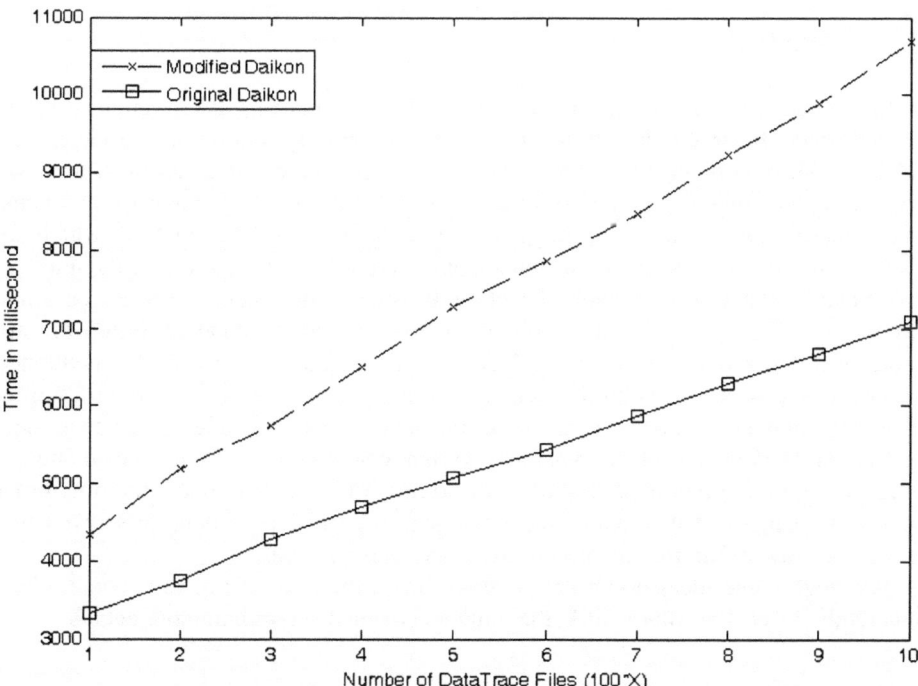

Fig. 8. Time order of code of Fig 1 using different numbers of Data-trace files

From another perspective, the relevance of the modified Daikon over some typical programs is summarized in Table.1. We study some rather simple and small pieces of program. Our reason is that every program, either big or small, has small parts and might be raised in small subprograms. These subprograms include arrays as their variables and effectively present the effect of the ideas.

Now, consider Table.1. Rows are some different rather simple programs which we discussed some them in previous sections. Columns are representative of quality of invariants. As expected, all the inferred invariants are not proper. In table.1 we

Table 1. Relevance of modified Daikon in some case studies

	# of detected invariants	# of implied invariants	# of irrelevant invariants	# of proper invariants
Delete one element of array	50	5	4	41
AVG	67	14	7	46
Replace	48	2	2	44
Mix	230	48	12	170

proposed the number of implied and irrelevant invariant. For example if two invariants "$x \,!= 0$" and "$x \ in \ [7..13]$" are determined to be true, there is no sense to report both because the latter implies the former.

7   Conclusion

In this paper, we discussed invariant as a significant entity in software engineering in recent years. Invariant detection tools report properties of program variables and relations between them. Since useful properties lead to more relevant invariants, we try to introduce two new properties of arrays which can cause new kinds of invariants. We focused on arrays because arrays are very conventional data structures which are used in all programs. As most of faults happen in the first and last elements of arrays we enhance the effect of fault detecting by employing these elements as some properties of the array. Another property which prepares a good condition to gain more useful invariants is the mutual element for same type arrays. As mentioned earlier, this property is helpful when in a program point an array is returned after changing elements in another array. After introducing these two ideas, we added them to Daikon. Daikon is a robust dynamic invariant detection tool. Then we evaluate our idea by comparing modified Daikon with original one. As mentioned, the time order does not change and it remains linear but with higher slope. Then we showed that more than 76% of inferred invariants are proper and relevant.

Although some ideas about arrays are valid in the case of pointers, some others inherently differ. For future work, the pointers can be dealt with in more details.

References

1. Floyd, R.W.: Assigning meanings to programs. In: Symposium on Applied Mathematics, pp. 19–32. American Mathematical Society (1967)
2. Ernst, M.D., Cockrell, J., Griswold, W.G., Notkin, D.: Dynamically discovering likely program invariants to support program evolution. IEEE TSE 27(2), 99–123 (2007)
3. Weiß, B.: Inferring invariants by static analysis in KeY. Diplomarbeit, University of Karlsruhe (March 2007)
4. Jones, N.D., Nielson, F.: Abstract interpretation: A semanticsbased tool for program analysis. In: Abramsky, S., Gabbay, D.M., Maibaum, T.S.E. (eds.) Handbook of Logic in Computer Science, vol. 4, pp. 527–636. Oxford University Press (1995)

5. Boshernitsan, M., Doong, R., Savoia, A.: From Daikon to Agitator: Lessons and challenges in building a commercial tool for developer testing. In: ISSTA, pp. 169–179 (2006)
6. Hangal, S., Lam, M.S.: Tracking down software bugs using automatic anomaly detection. In: ICSE, pp. 291–301 (2002)
7. Csallner, C., et al.: DySy: Dynamic symbolic execution for invariant inference. In: Proc. of ICSE (2008)
8. Ernst, M.D., Czeisler, A., Griswold, W.G., Notkin, D.: Quickly detecting relevant program invariants. In: ICSE, Limerick, Ireland, June 7-9 (2000)
9. Ernst, M.D., Griswold, W.G., Kataoka, Y., Notkin, D.: Dynamically Discovering Program Invariants Involving Collections, Technical Report, University of Washington (2000)

Theoretical Feasibility of Conditional Invariant Detection

Mohammad Hani Fouladgar, Hamid Parvin[*], and Behrouz Minaei,

Nourabad Mamasani Branch, Islamic Azad University, Nourabad Mamasani, Iran
hamidparvin@mamasaniiau.ac.ir,
{fouladgar,b_minaei}@iust.ac.ir

Abstract. All software engineering process, which includes designing, implementing and modifying of software, are done to develop a software as fast as possible and also to reach a high quality, efficient and maintainable software. Invariants, as rather always true properties of program context, can help developers to do some aspect of software engineering more easily; therefore any improvement in extracting of more relevant invariant can help software engineering process. Conditional invariant is a novel kind of invariant which is turned in when some conditions are provided in program execution. Conditional invariant can exhibit program behavior much better. In order to extract this kind of invariants, it might be used some technique of data mining such as association rule mining or using decision tree to obtain rules. This paper spans feasibility of conditional invariant and advantageous of this kind of invariant compared to ordinary invariant.

Keywords: Daikon, Invariant, Association Rules, Variable Relations, Decision tree, Program point, Data mining, Software engineering, Predicate, Verification.

1   Introduction

In last decade, program invariants have had significant effect on software engineering and especially in software testing and verification. Invariants are variables properties in and relationships between these variables in a specific line of code which is called program point. For example assume a subprogram that its task is to sort array of integers. In the post-condition of the mentioned subprogram, invariant (array **a** sorted >=) exists. This invariant means all element of array **a** is sorted by descending order. Extraction of invariants is a significant key in program verification. In all executions, these properties and relationships among the program variables or constants are always true; thus invariants help programmer or tester to be able to determine the behavior of program in different program points. Software behavioral model [1] uses invariant also is used in generating hence this can be mentioned as another usage of invariant in software engineering. Software behavioral model is used to perform design, validation, verification, and

---

[*] Corresponding author.

P. Pichappan, H. Ahmadi, and E. Ariwa (Eds.): INCT 2011, CCIS 241, pp. 172–185, 2011.
© Springer-Verlag Berlin Heidelberg 2011

maintenance. One of the most prominent contributions of invariants is in code modifying that properties help programmer to verify the code. Software testing takes a considerable time in software development life cycle. Although software testing is done automatically in present day, but traditionally the onus of software testing was human's obligation [2]. Invariants might be used in automatically software testing. Invariants are detected and extracted by different methods which are divided into two major approaches, static and dynamic [4].

Static approach analyzes syntactic structures and runtime behavior of program without actual running of code [5]. Static analysis is a thoroughly automatic process. Compilers traditionally analyze Data-flows as a static analysis to collect necessary information for code optimization. Data-flows analysis extracts some needful invariants in each program point and uses these invariants to assess the program behavior. This kind of behavior is used in compilers for optimization. *Abstract interpretation* is a theoretical framework for static analysis [6]. The most precise imaginable abstract interpretation is called the *static semantics* or *accumulating semantics*.

On the other hand, Dynamic approaches elicit program properties and relationships by the help of actual executing of the program code [7]. In these approaches, program is executed with different inputs and test suits and variable properties and relations are detected according to variables value during execution time. Dynamic invariant detection first appeared in Daikon [4]. By using different test suits in different executions, in each program point, variable properties and relationships are extracted. These Program points are usually the points of entry and exist of program functions. Extracted properties and relations are invariants. These invariants are not certainly true but indeed they are true in all executions in test suit. One of important advantages of dynamic invariant detection is the inferred invariants not only show the properties and relations of variables via execution but also utter the inputs properties and relations. This is because invariants are extracted from some real inputs in actual executions. This attitude of dynamically detected invariants causes double usage of it.

In this paper we introduce dynamic inference of conditional invariant. Conditional invariant is a new sort of invariant which are revealed in specific situation and not in all runs of program. These invariants are extracted through a fully automatic process. This kind of invariant is more relevant and helps programmer or tester to have better view about program behavior. In order to extract invariants, we encounter with two significant issues [2]: we would be able to determine the beneficial invariants; and then to exert inference on program context. In this paper we solve these two issues and declare two models to elicit the conditional invariants. In the following we discuss about some related work (section 2) and some frequently used definitions (section 3). Then we introduce what exactly conditional invariant is (section 4). Section 5 proposes two different models to extract conditional invariant then it continues with predominance of conditional in section 6. Finally, we talk about conclusion and future work.

2   Related Work

In this section, we discuss some implementations of dynamic invariant detection. We mention some implementations which are more relevant to our job but it is worth to mention there are many valuable efforts in this topic.

Dynamic invariant detection is first time introduced by *Daikon* [3] - a full-featured and robust implementation of dynamic invariant detection. Daikon is the most prospering tool for detecting dynamic invariant and until now, comparing with other dynamic invariant detection methods [3]. Most of other tools and method are inspired by Daikon. Though Daikon is potent, one of the greatest problems of this tool is being time-consuming.

DySy [8] is a dynamic inference tool which uses dynamic symbolic execution to expand the quality of inferred invariants. In the other words, besides executing test cases, DySy contemporarily perform a symbolic execution. These symbolic executions cause to produce program path condition. Then DySy combines the path conditions and build the final result. The result includes invariants which are expressed according to the program path condition.

Agitator [9] is a commercial testing tool and is inspired by Daikon. Software agitation was introduced by Agitar. Software agitation joins the results of research in test-input generation and dynamic invariant detection. The results are called observations. Code developer checks these observations to find out if there is any fault in the code. If there is any fault programmer or tester remove it and so on. Agitar won the Wall street Journal's 2005 Software Technology Innovation Award.

The DIDUCE is a dynamic invariant inference tool which extracts not only program invariants but also helps programmer to detecting errors and to determine the root causes [10]. Besides detecting dynamic invariant, DIDUCE checks program behavior against extracted invariants up to each program points and reports all detected violations. DIDUCE checks simple invariants and does not need up-front instrument.

Despite the large number of related work in the dynamic invariant detection, there is lack of any prominent related work. Therefore we try to consider to dynamic invariant detection more and introduce some now aspect to this concept. We study the feasibility of a new type of invariant called conditional invariant.

3   Terminology

To better understanding of following contents we define some repeatedly used concept. Our purpose is to help readers to have a better perception of the pater.

Definition 1. *Invariants* are some properties of different program points which are true in all executions of the program. These properties can be seen in formal specification or assert statement. Invariants are relations among variables values that is unchanged in all different execution of the code.

Definition 2. *Program points* are specific points in a program, such as the *Enter* or *Exit* point of a function, which are apt place to check the properties and values of variables to extract the invariants. These points are the report points for variable relations and invariants. Most common program points are Enter point and Exit point of functions and sub-programs as well as loops.

Definition 3. *Pre-conditions* of a program point are invariants, properties and relations which exist immediately before entering the program point. For instance Pre-conditions of a function as a program point are variables' value and properties exactly before entering the function. In this paper *Pre-condition* and *Enter* point are used interchangeably.

Definition 4. *Post-conditions* of a program point are invariants, properties and relations which exist immediately after exiting the program point. For instance post-conditions of a function as a program point are variables' value and properties exactly after exiting the function. In this paper *Post-condition* and *Exit* point are used interchangeably. Typically, post-condition contains relations between the original values of a variable and their modified one (before and after that program point). In other words, invariants in post-conditions contain relations between variables in pre-condition and post-condition.

4   Paper Contributions

Invariant inference systems focus on definite invariant and mostly they do not extract invariants which exist in some special situations. In the other word, we want to have a kind of invariants which are not always true but they are true in a specific condition. To clarify the matter, consider Fig. 1. (This example is artificial and illustrates several points we are going to discuss.) In this Figure x and y are global invariants and procedure *compute()* swaps x values and y value only if x<y. An appropriate unit test for this function might be x<y and its complement. In an ordinary invariant extraction system the *post-condition* invariant which could be detected for this procedure is:

- x>y

This invariant shows after leaving compute() the x values are always are greater than y values. This invariant is completely true and comes up with an adequate behavior but it does not present a complete behavior of this procedure. This means this mere invariant can not be useful neither in *formal specification* nor *assert statement*.

```
void compute()
{
    if (x < y)
    {
        int temp = x;
        x = y;
        y = temp;
    }

}
```

Fig. 1. Example method whose invariant we want to infer

This flaw in expressing of procedure behavior makes us think to have a set of invariants which can appropriately show the program behavior. In the other words we need a set of invariants which express compute() behavior properly. The final outcome of post-condition of compute() invariants (or compute():::Exit in our method) in a conditional invariant inference system are shown in Fig.2:

```
1 orig(x)>orig(y)  -> x=orig(x)
2 orig(x)>orig(y)  -> y=orig(y)
3 orig(x)<orig(y)  -> x=orig(y)
4 orig(x)<orig(y)  -> y=orig(x)
```

Fig. 2. Related invariants in our method

In upon invariants, *orig(var)* shows *var* value just before entrance of compute(). This approach removes the weakness of previous dynamic invariant inference. As seen, Fig. 2 completely describes the function behavior.

Over all our work contains following parts:

- We introduce the idea of using data mining methods, such as association rule mining, for conditional invariant inference. We believe our method makes up the next generation of dynamic invariant inference tools. We believe our approach opens a new ways to perform dynamic invariant inference in not far future.
- We describe our approach by flowcharts.
- We compare the probability of existence of ordinary invariants with probability of existence of conditional invariants.

5   Conditional Invariant Detection Framework

In this section, we plan to propose a framework for conditional invariant detection. Vital entity should be provided is *predicates*. Predicate is a Boolean expression which is representative of a program property in a program point. If the property exists, the value of predicate is true otherwise it is false. In order to extract the conditional invariant, first we should provided any possible predicate in each program point. Then we can extract rules from these predicates. Extracted rules show behavior of program point in conditional form.

To provide predicates in pre-conditions all values of global variables and parameters participate are meddled in and in post-conditions all values of global variables and parameters as well as their prior values participate are used. With having more variety of invaluable predicates, more beneficial invariants are produced. In following we define the classes of predicates and clarify all predicates then in Fig. 3 we show the algorithm flowchart which illustrates our process tendency step by step. Datatrace files in Fig. 3 contains possible predicate in a program point.

5.1   Classes of Predicate

First step of extracting conditional invariant is to extract predicates in all program points. In following we introduce a terse set of classes of predicates which should be checked for all variables in each program point. The following presents classes of predicates which are used in our approach, where x and y are variables:

- Predicates over any numeric variable:

  — IsNonZero: when the variable is never set to 0
  — IsOne: when the variable is always equal to 0
  — IsMinesOne: when the variable is always equal to -1
  — IsEven: when the variable is always even
  — IsPowerOfTwo: when the variable is always power of two

- Predicates over any string variable:

  — IsNull: when the variable is always null
  — IsEmpty: when the variable contains no characters

- Predicates over two numeric variable:

  — Ordering comparison: $x < y$, $x \le y$, $x > y$, $x \ge y$, $x = y$, $x \ne y$
  — functions: $y = fn(x)$ or $x = fn(y)$, for fn a built-in unary function (absolute value, negation, bitwise complement)

- Predicate over two string variable:

  — Equality: $x = y$ when two strings are equal
  — Substring: $y=sub(x)$ when y is substring of x
  — Reversal: $y=rev(x)$ or $y=rev(x)$ when x is the reverse of y

- Predicates over a array:

  — Element relationship: when the array elements are equal or sorted by $(=>,>,<,<=)$
  — IsNonZero: when none of array elements are equal to 0

- Predicate over an array and a numerical variable:

  — Membership: $x \in y$ (x and y are common type arrays)

- Predicate over two arrays:

  — comparison: $x < y$, $x \le y$, $x > y$, $x \ge y$, $x = y$, $x \ne y$
  — Sub-array : $y=sub(x)$ when y is sub-array of x
  — Reversal: $y=rev(x)$ or $y=rev(x)$ when x is the reverse of y

In each program point these classes of predicates are produced. As we mentioned before, predicates have Boolean values. In order to extract rules (conditional invariants) from these predicates, association rule mining might be used. To support our aim, in following we discuss about association rule mining Model and its possibility.

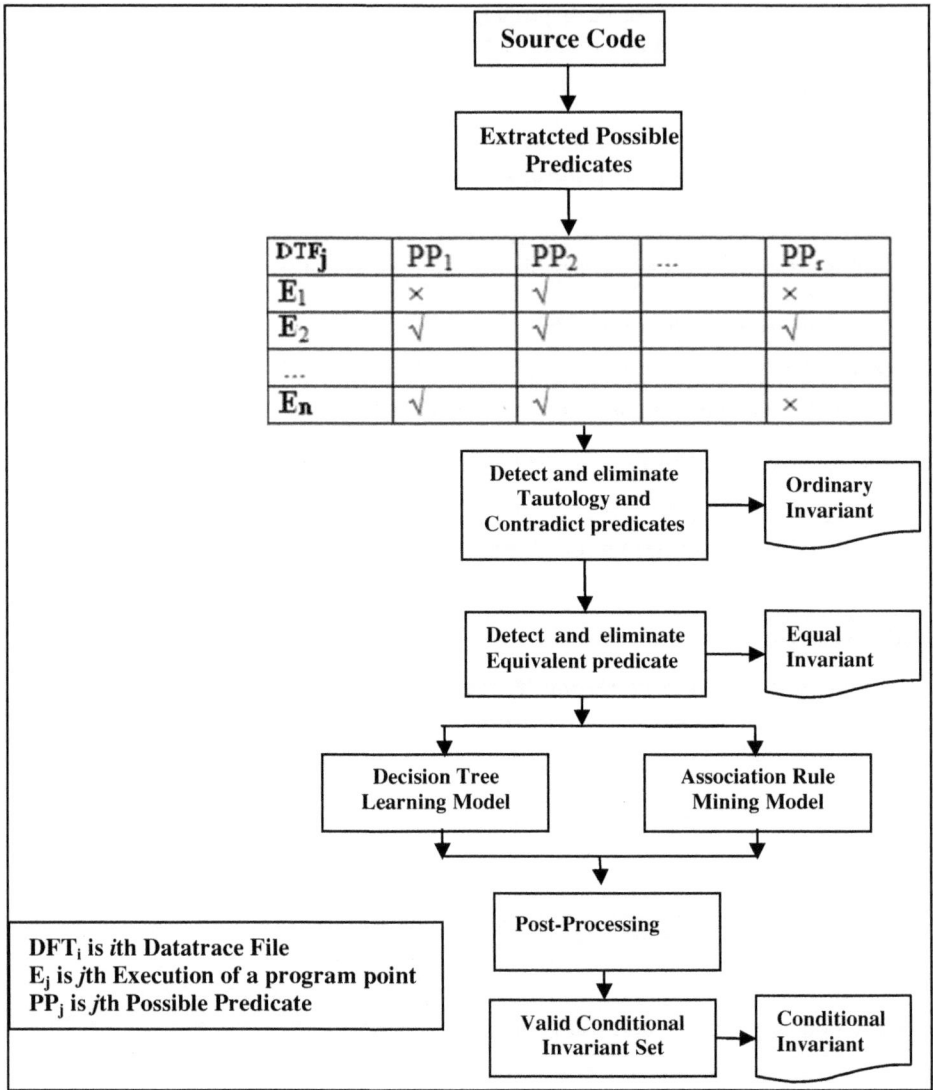

Fig. 3. Algorithm flowchart of employing association rule mining in extracting conditional invariants

5.2   Association Rule Mining Model

Now we introduce all classes of predicates. All of these predicates are Boolean value therefore we are able to extract some association rules from these predicates. These rules are actually conditional invariants. To have association rules we check if each predicate as consequence has relation with other predicates. Consider we have predicates $P_1, P_2, P_3, \ldots, P_q$. We start with P_q we check all predicates if they result P_q. It means we check if P_1 as the antecedent can result P_q otherwise we conjunct P_1 and P_2 and check if now they result P_q and so forth. Then we will perform these steps for P_{q-1}. To better understanding of this process, a flowchart for this algorithm is presented in Fig. 5.

To clarify whole process which is presented in Fig. 3, consider presented procedure in Fig. 1. We intend to extract conditional invariants in post-condition of procedure compute() in Fig. 1. First of all as seen in Fig. 3, we should extract possible predicates in this program point. The result is put in a table such as Fig. 4.

Transaction	orig(x)>orig(y)	orig(x)<orig(y)	x=orig(x)	y=orig(x)	x=orig(y)	y=orig(y)
T_1	true	false	true	false	false	true
T_2	false	true	false	true	true	false
T_3	false	true	false	true	true	false
T_4	true	false	true	false	false	true
T_5	true	false	true	false	false	true
T_6	false	true	false	true	true	false

Fig. 4. Related transaction for Fig. 1

Fig. 4 shows neither all transaction nor all predicates but it presents just some of them to manifest the method. The minimum support and minimum confidence respectively are 50% and 100%. Two large itemsets which are inferred from Fig. 4 is:

- orig(x)>orig(y), x=orig(x),y=orig(y)
- orig(x)<orig(y), y=orig(x), x=orig(y)

And following rules are archived:

- orig(x)>orig(y)$\Rightarrow$ x=orig(x)
- orig(x)>orig(y)$\Rightarrow$y=orig(y)
- orig(x)<orig(y)$\Rightarrow$y=orig(x)
- orig(x)<orig(y)$\Rightarrow$x=orig(y)
- x=orig(x)$\Rightarrow$orig(x)>orig(y)
- x=orig(x)$\Rightarrow$y=orig(y)
- y=orig(y)$\Rightarrow$orig(x)>orig(y)
- y=orig(y)$\Rightarrow$x=orig(x)
- y=orig(x)$\Rightarrow$orig(x)<orig(y)
- y=orig(x)$\Rightarrow$x=orig(y)
- y=orig(y)$\Rightarrow$ orig(x)<orig(y)
- y=orig(y)$\Rightarrow$ y=orig(x)

As seen, rules Consequence part contains only one predication. It is worth noting our method does not extract compound consequences. All presented rules are true and obey minimum support and minimum confidence but only four first one are tangible and others must be filtered. The four first rules are the same as rules we represent in

Fig. 2. In this subsection we discuss about *Association Rule Mining Model*. This Model is an alternative to extract the rules and is shown as a box in Fig.3. In following, we propose another model to extract the association rules whose name is Decision Tree Learning Model. But before discussing about Decision Tree Learning Model we assess time order of Association Rule Mining Model.

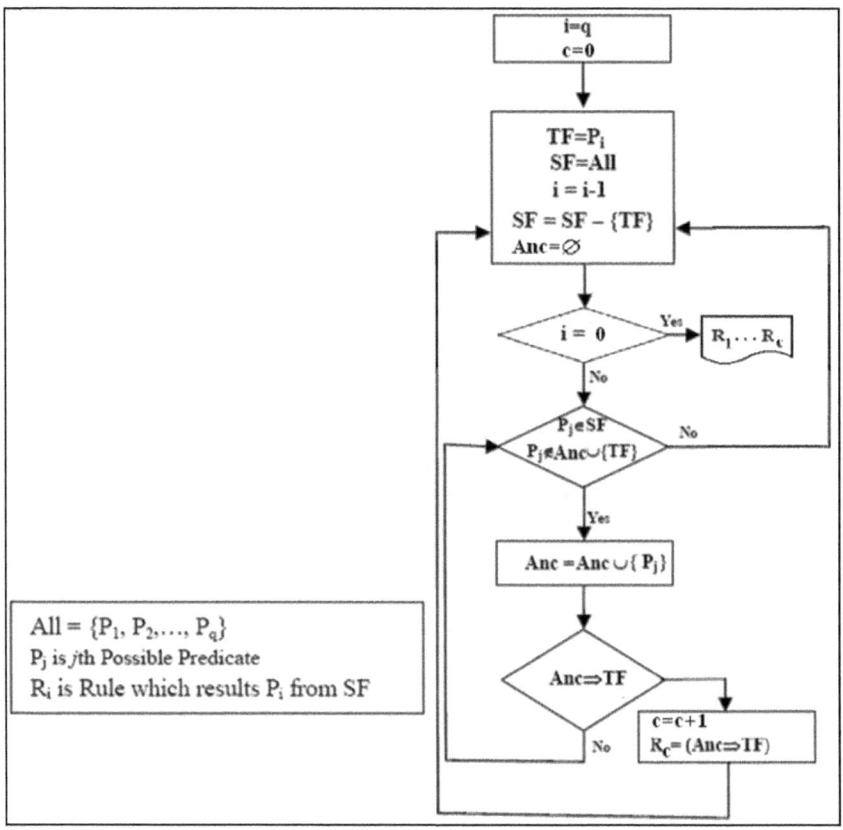

Fig. 5. Association Rule Mining Model

5.3   Time Order

In subsection we check our time order of Association Rule Mining Model. We check the time order to see if it is affordable. Assume we have m variables in a program point. However it is not exactly true but we assume each two variables make a predicate so overall we have q predicates. q is obtained via equation (1):

$$\binom{m}{2} = q \tag{1}$$

The predicates are $P_1, P_2, P_3, \ldots, P_q$. We plan to extract a rule which results P_q. Association Rule Mining Model must check if each of $P_1, P_2, P_3, \ldots, P_{q-1}$ has relationship with P_q then it has to check if two of $P_1, P_2, P_3, \ldots, P_{q-1}$ have relationship and so forth. Therefore to have a rule with P_q as its consequence, our tool has to handle (2) number of checks:

$$\binom{q-1}{1} * 2 + \binom{q-1}{2} * 2^2 + \cdots + \binom{q-1}{q-1} * 2^{q-1} \tag{2}$$

Totally, the association rule mining tool must handle (3) number of checks:

$$\sum_{i=1}^{q-1} \sum_{j=1}^{i} \binom{i}{j} * 2^j \tag{3}$$

This time order (3) is exponential and is not acceptable at all. For example for 7 variables in a specific program point, there are 7 variables, total numbers of checks might be 2097152 and if we have 10 variables, total numbers of checks is 3518437208832. Something is worth to mention is that all these checks are not handled because if for example P_1 has relationship with P_q other sets of predicates which contains P_1 will not be checked anymore and will not be interfered but it does not affect the time order so much and overall time order is exponential.

5.4   Decision Tree Learning Model

In this subsection we intend to use Decision Tree for our aim. In decision tree, one attribute, which is called *goal* or *class*, is obtained by other attributes. In the other words it is possible to predict goal value by means of other attributes value. Decision tree has two properties which are really advantageous for our aim. These properties are:

- Approximately lowest number of antecedents
- Feasible highest confidence of the rule

These two properties are helpful because it helps us to have rules with lowest number of antecedents with high confidence. Now we try to use decision tree for extracting rules. In order to reach this aim, we should consider each predicate as the *goal* and try to capture the predicates which result our goal. Consider we have predicates $P_1, P_2, P_3, \ldots, P_q$. We start with a predicate such as P_1 as our goal or class. We make the decision tree for P_1 and then we try to figure out other predicates which defined P_1's result. If we go upward from leaves to root in obtained tree, they can be rules which show when P_1 is true and when it is false. Then we obtain the P_2's tree and so forth. Fig. 6 demonstrates process of *Decision Tree Learning Model* box in the Fig. 3.

Since decision tree splits the attributes into some smaller attributes and then classify them, using decision tree is not time-consuming. By using decision tree for extracting rules all the predicates are not checked but they are split into smaller subset and each subset is checked. Therefore Using Decision Tree Learning Model is faster than using Association Rule Mining Model.

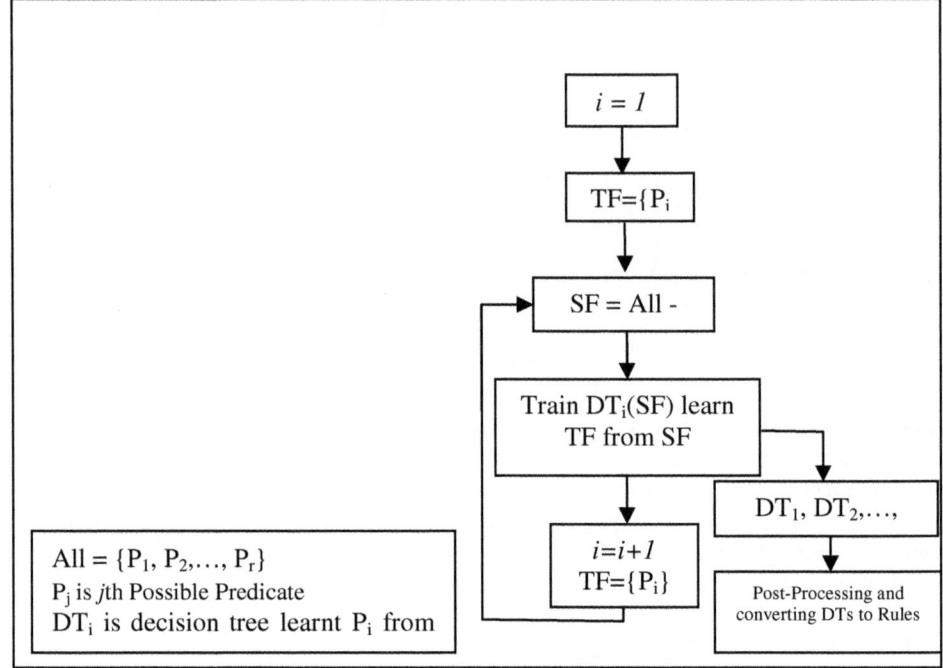

All = {P_1, P_2,..., P_r}
P_j is jth Possible Predicate
DT_i is decision tree learnt P_i from

Fig. 6. Decision Tree Learning Model

6   Importance of Conditional Invariants

In this section, we plan to check if conditional invariants are really express some more relevant invariants. In order to clarify this, consider Fig. 7 which is a truth table. This truth table shows the predicates in a given program point. Each column of the table is a predicate and each row of the table is a execution of code in the program point. In this table, T means the checked predicate satisfies and F means the predicate does not satisfy.

	C_1	C_2	...	C_{r-1}	Cr
1	T	T		F	F
2	T	F		T	F
.	.				
.	.				
.	.				
N	F	F		T	F

Fig. 7. Predicates' condition in a program point in different execution

Now we plan to study the probability of existing of at least on ordinary invariant and probability of at least on conditional invariant. With this method, we manage to show that conditional invariant is more frequent than ordinary one. First, we start with ordinary invariant. To have an ordinary invariant, one column of table in Fig. 7 should be T or F. Probability of being T or F in all rows of one given column is $\frac{2}{2^n}$. Therefore To assess the probability of existing of an ordinary invariant is shown in equation (4):

$$P(OI) = 1 - (1 - \frac{2}{2^n})^r \tag{4}$$

Now we try to demonstrate the probability of conditional invariant. First we try to calculate the probability of existing of rule $C_1 \rightarrow C_2$. To reach to this goal we suppose to only in one row of table rule $C_1 \rightarrow C_2$ exists. The probability of existing of this rule in one row is shown in equation (5):

$$\binom{n}{1} \times \frac{2}{2^n} \times \frac{2}{2^1} - \binom{n}{1} \times \frac{2}{2^n} \times \frac{2}{2^1} \times \frac{1}{2^{n-1}} = \binom{n}{1} \times \frac{2}{2^n} \times \frac{2}{2^1} \times (1 - \frac{1}{2^{n-1}}) \tag{5}$$

The probability of existing of this rule in one row is shown in equation (6):

$$\binom{N}{2} \times \frac{2}{2^n} \times \frac{2}{2^2} - \binom{n}{2} \times \frac{2}{2^n} \times \frac{2}{2^2} \times \frac{1}{2^{n-2}} = \binom{n}{2} \times \frac{2}{2^n} \times \frac{2}{2^2} \times (1 - \frac{1}{2^{n-2}}) \tag{6}$$

Now we calculate the probability of $C_1 \rightarrow C_2$. Equation (8) is this goal:

$$f(i) = \binom{n}{i} \times \frac{2}{2^n} \times \frac{2}{2^i} \tag{7}$$

$$g(n) = \sum_{i=1}^{n-1} (f(i) - f(i) \times \frac{1}{2^{n-i}}) \tag{8}$$

Totally, probability of existence of at least one conditional invariant is shown in equation (9):

$$P(CI) = 1 - (1 - g(n))^{r(r-1)} \tag{9}$$

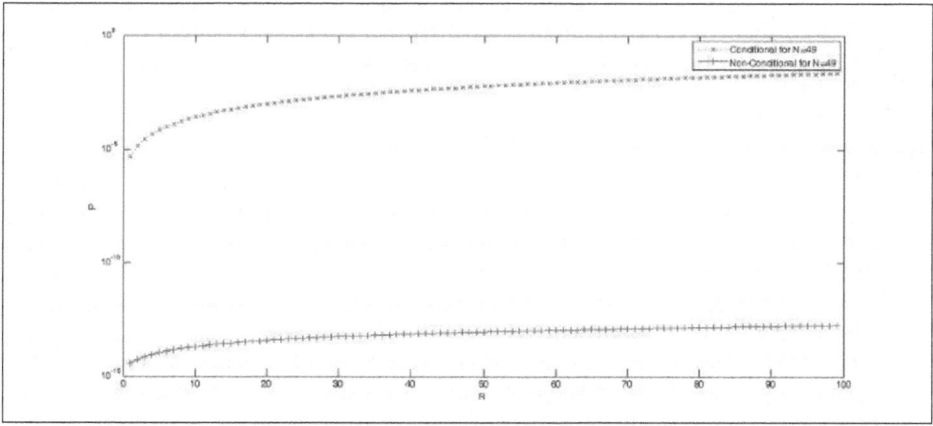

Fig. 8. Comparison of probabilities

Now we reach to *P(OI)* as the probability of existence of at least one ordinary invariant and *P(CI)* as the probability of existence of at least one conditional invariant, we plan to compare these to probability to consider which probability is higher. For comparison the probabilities, consider Fig. 8 which shows the probability of existence of ordinary and conditional invariant. These probabilities are achieved via 50 times executions for different number of predicates. X-axis shows the number of predicates and Y-axis demonstrates the probabilities. Diagram with star is the probability of existence of conditional invariant and the other diagram is the probability of existence of ordinary invariant. As seen, probability of existence of conditional invariant is higher than probability of existence of ordinary invariant.

7   Conclusion and Future Work

Invariants are different properties of variables and relations between them in each program point in all executions. Invariants usually illustrate the program behavior. Invariant is an always true concept so they are not able to express program behavior which is true with assuming of a condition. In this paper we introduced a new sort of invariant named conditional invariant. Since this newly introduced type is able to be extract when a particular condition happens, conditional invariant can express program behavior better. In order to extract conditional invariant, we introduce some classes of predicate which show valuable properties and relations in each execution. These predicates are expression with Boolean values. Then, we try to extract association rules from predicates. These association rules are in fact conditional invariants. In this paper we introduce two models to have these association rules. The first model, Association Rule Mining Model, extracts rule by the means of myriad of checks. Time order in this model is exponential and is not acceptable. Another model, Decision Tree Learning Model, uses decision trees to extract rules. This model is more reasonable. We consider each predicate as a goal and try to find related predicates which result the goal.

In the future, we plan to use Bayesian Network to extract the rules and conditional invariants. Bayesian Network is another data mining technique which can predict the goal by the means of other input attributes. Bayesian Network is more useful in the cases that input attributes (predicates in our work) do not have correlation.

References

1. Krkay, I., Brunx, Y., Popescuy, D., Garciay, J., Medvidovic, N.: Using dynamic execution traces and program invariants to enhance behavioral model inference. In: ICSE NIER (2010)
2. Vanmali, M., Last, M., Kandel, A.: Using a neural network in the software testing process. International Journal of Intelligent Systems 17(1), 45–62 (2002)
3. Ernst, M.D., Cockrell, J., Griswold, W.G., Notkin, D.: Dynamically discovering likely program invariants to support program evolution. IEEE TSE 27(2), 99–123 (2007)
4. Ernst, M.D., et al.: Dynamically discovering likely program invariants to support program evolution. In: Proc. ICSE 1999, pp. 213–224. ACM (1999)

5. Weiß, B.: Inferring invariants by static analysis in KeY. Diplomarbeit, University of Karlsruhe (March 2007)
6. Jones, N.D., Nielson, F.: Abstract interpretation: A semanticsbased tool for program analysis. In: Abramsky, S., Gabbay, D.M., Maibaum, T.S.E. (eds.) Handbook of Logic in Computer Science, vol. 4, pp. 527–636. Oxford University Press (1995)
7. Ernst, M.D., Perkins, J.H., Guo, P.J., McCamant, S., Pacheco, C., Tschantz, M.S., Xiao, C.: The Daikon System for Dynamic Detection of Likely Invariants. Science of Computer Programming (2006)
8. Csallner, C., et al.: DySy: Dynamic symbolic execution for invariant inference. In: Proc. of ICSE (2008)
9. Boshernitsan, M., Doong, R., Savoia, A.: From Daikon to Agitator: Lessons and challenges in building a commercial tool for developer testing. In: ISSTA, pp. 169–179 (2006)
10. Hangal, S., Lam, M.S.: Tracking down software bugs using automatic anomaly detection. In: ICSE, pp. 291–301 (2002)

Managing Network Dynamicity in a Vector Space Model for Semantic P2P Data Integration

Ahmed Moujane, Dalila Chiadmi, Laila Benhlima, and Faouzia Wadjinny

Laboratoire SIR
Ecole Mohammadia d'Ingénieurs
Avenue Ibn-Sina B.P. 765 Agdal
Rabat Morocco
{Moujane,Chiadmi,Benhlima,Wadjinny}@emi.ac.ma

Abstract. P2P data integration is one of the prominent studies in recent years. It relies on two principal axes, including data integration and P2P computing. It aims to combine the advantages of data integration and P2P technologies to overcome centralized solutions shortcomings. However, dynamicity and large scale are the most difficult challenges faced for efficient solutions. In this paper, we investigate P2P computing and data integration fundamentals and detail the challenges that face the P2P data integration process. In addition, we present a vector space model based approach our P2P semantic data integration framework. In a first stage, we detail the various modules of our framework and specify the functions of each one. Then, we present our vector space model to represent semantic knowledge. We present also the knowledge base components that hold semantic. Finally, we explain how we deal with network dynamicity and how semantic should be adjusted accordingly.

Keywords: Semantic Integration, P2P, Ontology, Vector Space, OWL, semantic clustering.

1   Introduction

With the great growth of online sources, thanks to the Web and Network infrastructures advances, it is uncomplicated that the user could be flooded by the amount of distributed information and systems that can access during information search. Unfortunately, this easy access is not transparent and consequently does not satisfy end users ambitions. This is due to the heterogeneity issues. That is why integrating heterogeneous data is an omnipresent problem [1] for nowadays researches. Effectively, several data integration works are proposed, but most of them are mediator-based and do not really cope with distribution. Indeed, they suffer from static matching in mediator architecture, which is client/server-like architecture. Consequently, they lack of scalability and flexibility. The birth of the P2P computing was seen as a magic ring to resolve most centralized solutions shortcomings. Thus, new distributed architectures taking advantage of P2P infrastructure to support data integration were proposed.

P. Pichappan, H. Ahmadi, and E. Ariwa (Eds.): INCT 2011, CCIS 241, pp. 186–200, 2011.

Recently, computer systems tendency has moved toward the use of classical P2P infra-structure and architecture for integrating distributed data sources. In this case, peer-to-peer systems consist of a set of completely autonomous peers in the definition of their data and knowledge. There is no global schema or any kind of centralized services which could cause a bottleneck or a single point of failure. Thus, models of P2P architectures are privileged, in decentralized data integration and management, for their extensibility and flexibility where a peer is both a client and a server, and can cooperate with other peers in a transparent way depending on the capabilities previously concluded.

However, this combination of data integration and P2P computing is not challenges-free. Indeed, most proposed works do not cope with semantic data integration.

In this paper, we study the problem of data integration in the P2P setting: How can P2P techniques help data integration in distributed environment? What new issues and challenges should be surmounted? Then, we present our solution for P2P semantic data integration for which we will detail the architecture, the vector space model for formalizing the data model. Then, we present our approach for network dynamicity management.

2   Data Integration

Data Integration aims to query heterogeneous, autonomous and distributed data sources. Different kinds of heterogeneities are identified. According to this, we distinguish three levels of data integration.

-        Syntactic integration intends to overcome heterogeneities that come from the use of different data types and models to structure the same information (Relation in relational databases, classes in OO databases, XML tags, etc.).

-        Structural integration has for task to resolve heterogeneities that rise from using different schemas to represent the same data. They are closely related to the choices of conception. For example, the name of a person can be represented by only one field "name" or by two fields "fisrt_name" and "last_name".

-        Semantic integration is by far the most complicated task. It aims to resolve heterogeneities that outcomes from the differences of significance, interpretation or use of the same data. For instance, (1) Words that have similar meaning but have different forms (e.g. Book and manuscript) will not match each other; (2) Words having multiple meaning (e.g. java) will make confusion and brings noisy responses.

To defeat these heterogeneities and provide access to heterogeneous and distributed data sources, several works and studies from the early 80's have been proposed. In this context, solutions using conceptual models, such as relational models, XML and ontologies were adopted. For example, we mention systems like Information Manifold [2], TSIMMIS [6], WASSIT ([3], [4], [5]). These classical centralized approaches are based on the supposition that it is possible to define a virtual global schema using approaches like GAV [6] and LAV [2, 27]. These approaches serve to establish mappings between the global schema and the local schemas. User's queries are then posed on the global schema to be translated, rewritten and optimized in further stages. However, most of these solutions suffer from client-server drawbacks. For this reason, we should take advantages from the P2P computing techniques.

3   P2P Computing

"Peer to peer" is a set of techniques permitting to build a data sharing system among several users. As pointed out by Shirky [7], peer-to-peer can be defined as "A class of applications that take advantage of resources-storage, CPU cycles, content, human presence- available at the edges of the Internet". The birth of P2P networks is one of the events that have marked the Internet growth in the current decade. The P2P flux percentage, in relation to the Internet communication traffic, has been estimated, by the Cache Logic P2P technology company, to be between 64% and 84% for the year 2005. No statistics can ever be entirely truthful on the internet traffic but this is a really good estimation. Classical P2P networks have become recently a great infrastructure. Systems like Napster, Gnutella, Kazaa have showed their exploits for file sharing. Indeed, file sharing was the main incentive for several of these successful platforms. However, most of them focus on handling semantic-free items and support only key-based and in some cases keyword-based search. Doing so restricts classical P2P networks convenience and limits the techniques that can be employed for distributed data.

With the growth of P2P as an alternative for Client/Server systems, several works and architectures have been presented about different aspects of P2P computing. Any P2P computing application relays on a logical network, called overlay network, composed of a set of nodes and links between them that form logical connections. This overlay network is virtual and has its architecture based on a physical IP network. We can classify this P2P architecture depending on two criteria: decentralization and structure. We present these two points in the next sections.

3.1   Decentralization

Theoretically, overlay networks are supposed to be purely decentralized. However, this is not always true in practice and different degrees of decentralization are met. Generally, we can distinguish three architectures of decentralization: pure, hybrid and super peer or partial architecture. In the totally distributed architecture, all nodes are equivalents and play the same role. There is no central control or coordination of their tasks. Each node acts as both a client and a server. There are no relaying services and the whole communication exchange process is accomplished directly between nodes. In the hybrid centralized architecture, there is at least one central point of control. All peers store their indices in the central server or cluster of servers. Peer localization and reference are done by the global control servers. The data transfer is accomplished in an end-to-end way directly between peers. This architecture has client-server-like drawbacks. Finally, in the partially centralized architecture, some nodes called super peershave roles that are more important. Each super peer contains indexes of files contained in the subscribed peers. The super peers and the nodes that it subscribes constitute a cluster. From the outside of a cluster, the communication with each node within this cluster must be initiated through its super node. The way the super node is designed by the network varies between systems. We must note that the set of super nodes would not be a point of failure because the designation is dynamic. In case of failure, a new super peer is designed for the cluster concerned. Thus, super peer architecture offers more advantages than the other ones for P2P data integration.

3.2   Structure

Network structure refers to where and how nodes and data are added to the system. In-deed, the overlay network can be created in an undetermined way (ad hoc) as nodes and content are added, or whether based on specific policies. We classify peer-to-peer structure in two classes, which are structured and unstructured. The two classes are described below.

1. Structured

Structured P2P networks are characterized by the use of identifiers assigned to data items. The overlay network organizes its nodes into a graph that maps each data identifier to a peer offering a highly controlled logical topology. This mapping between content and location is accomplished through a form of distributed routing table permitting queries to be efficiently routed to the peer with the desired data. In this way, structured overlay networks can partially resolve scalability issues encountered in P2P environment and rare items are easily located. However, it is hard to maintain the network structure for efficient routing process due to the volatile nature of P2P systems. Representative systems of Structured P2P overlay networks include Content Addressable Network (CAN) [8], Tapestry [9], Chord [10], Pastry [11] and Kademlia [12].

2. Unstructured

In unstructured networks, peers join the system without any prior knowledge of the network topology. Consequently, data files are located independently from the overlay topology. The location of files is not restricted or founded on any network knowledge. This makes data locating a hard task in systems that offer query functionalities. Search mechanisms are based on a large spectrum of techniques varying from basic methods such as flooding the network by propagating the queries, to more sophisticated techniques that uses routing indexes and random walks. Flooding-based techniques are useful for locating highly replicated items and are flexible for peer joining and leaving but they are less adequate for locating rare data objects. Obviously, those techniques make unstructured systems faced to scalability and availability issues because peers are quickly overloaded as the systems size and the number of queries increase. On the other hand, unstructured networks are accommodated for highly volatile node populations where nodes are joining and leaving at high rate. Among unstructured networks, we find Napster, Kazaa, Gnutella and Edutella.

4   P2P Data Integration Issues

As introduced in section 2, data Integration issues were widely investigated in the literature [13], [14]. Several centralized solutions based on the assumption that it's possible to define a virtual global schema using approaches like GAV and LAV were proposed.

However, in the P2P context, this assumption does not hold anymore due to the highly distributed and dynamic nature of the P2P infrastructure. Each peer has a limited view on the system, and cannot give complete answers. Therefore, data integration brings and raises new challenges in the P2P environment. Many P2P solutions have been proposed to resolve some of these issues using different techniques and concepts. We can distinguish two main categories, PDMS (peer data management system) and OPDMS (ontology-based PDMS). The first family is characterized by the combination of schema-based integration techniques and P2P infrastructure. Among solutions that we classify in this family, we find LRM Model [15], PIAZZA [16]. The second category arises by combining PDMS techniques and the use of ontologies that has been acknowledged to be an efficient approach to advance interoperation of distributed data sources at a semantic level [17], [14]. Among solutions that belong to this second family, we can mention SWAP architecture and those founded on it like the Bibster system [18]. P2P ontology mappings and query processing are two main issues in an OPDMS. Ontologies are used in local peers as a conceptual schema of the underlying information. Nevertheless, the use of ontologies in a P2P setting creates new issues because we have to deal with more than one ontology. In fact, ontologies have been lately introduced for knowledge representation in information systems. Indeed, resources are generally described by XML schemas, relational schemas, etc. Even in the case where they are described by ontologies, their representation doesn't adopt the same standards and do not use the same languages (OWL, DAML+OIL, RDFS, etc.) [4]. In most cases, the answering Peer does not know all the terms used in the query expressed according to the local ontology of the requesting peer. Thus, to solve this problem, a mapping between both requesting and answering peer local ontologies must be accomplished. Due to these mapping challenges and incomplete knowledge, it is unfeasible to assure efficient query processing without exhaustive research, which is inconceivable in large-scaled P2P systems. So, query routing, processing and optimization techniques should be considered.

However, Query processing and routing in a PDMS is different from querying in flat P2P system. In fact, in PDMS, indexes take the form of schemas and we do not have hash functions or global indexes that could permit to find the requested data because of the presence of heterogeneous schemas at the peers. In contrast, the originality of PDMS lies in its ability to exploit the transitive relationships among such schemas. Thus, efficient query processing should generate distributed query plans according to the information returned by the routing process. The query plans are calculated according to the cost of alternative operator order (e.g., join/ aggregation reordering) and execution strategies (e.g., data or query shipping) for these plans. The query plans are then executed by the selected peers according to their capabilities.

PDMS policies to deal with query processing are diversified but most of them are inspired from the classical P2P world. Edutella [19] uses routing indices [20] for their super-peers providing RDFS schemas and RDF metadata of their description. Queries are based on a Datalog-based query exchange language called RDF-QEL to serve as a common query interchange format. Systems like PeerDB [21] uses flooding and information retrieval (IR) approaches to decide, at the query run-time, the mappings between two peer schemas. In PeerDB, no predefined mapping tables are established, only descriptive metadata are associated to schema attributes. Query routing is accomplished through flooding neighbor's peers which uses IR techniques to decide if matching attributes for the query exist in the local schema. Then, the user based on the returned suggestions, must choose which queries are relevant and which ones can be executed. The system use caching mechanisms for the user selected preferences to route future similar queries. Piazza [16] utilizes a declarative XQuery-based mapping language to define the mappings established between peers of individual peer schemas. Based on the chains of mappings between peers of nodes, a reformulation algorithm produces query expressions equivalent to a given query; that can be routed and distributed across the Piazza network. Like Piazza, Hyperion [22] uses mapping tables and mapping expressions (mapping tables permitting variables) to define correspondences between local schemas in peers. Based on the mapping tables and mapping expressions, a query manager rewrites queries posed in terms of the local schema, in order to be processed by the acquainted peers.

5   Our Solution

Racall that, in the light of having investigated the mechanisms for data integration and techniques for P2P computing, we have explored issues for P2P data integration and querying in peer-to-peer data management systems. Based on this exploration, we now focus on presenting our solution for semantic P2P data integration framework that is based on our platform WASSIT (*frameWork d'intégrAtion de reSSources de données fondée sur la médIaTion*) for central data integration. In this paper, we present our architecture and detail each of its components. Then, we give an overview for our knowledge representation. Afterward, we present our approach to manager network dynamicity and volatility.

Our work is motivated by the need to integrate several heterogeneous data sources and systems that belongs to different governmental institutions. Each system can be seen as an autonomous system managed independently and no global schema can be conceived. These systems hold semantically equivalent our related information of different domains.Due to the large scale of the systems and data, and financial constraints, centralized solutions like WASSIT or TSIMMIS [6]wouldn't do the job. Consequently, the recourse to both P2P and data integration technologies seems to be promising for an efficient solution. For feasibility raisons, we will implement our solution for institutional digital libraries as a case study.

5.1   Architecture

We have adopted, for our framework, an unstructured super peer architecture where each node can be a peer or a super peer (Fig.1). A super peer and the peers that are connected to it constitute a cluster. The super peer is responsible for lookup with the network for its cluster. Each node should contact its super peer to submit user queries out of the cluster. Each peer that hopes to join the P2P network should have an entry point. Through its entry point, a new peer should provide descriptions about the information resources that it manages. Then, based on these descriptions, each peer is registered by a super peer.

For us, each node represents an autonomous information system, and data integration is accomplished by establishing mappings among the various peers.

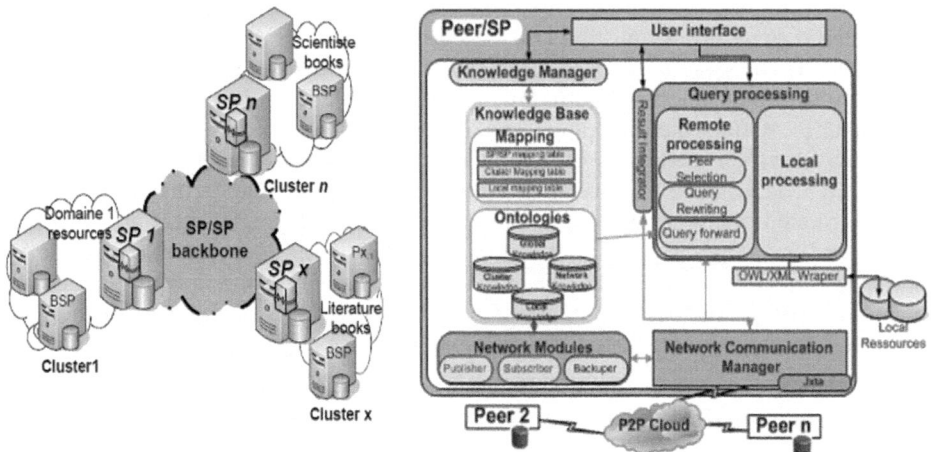

Fig. 1. Our P2P network scenario   **Fig. 2.** Our functionalarchitecture

We introduce a new concept that we called Backup Super Peer ($\mathcal{BSP}$) whose role is to ensure a passive backup for the super peer. The $\mathcal{BSP}$ is different from the k-redundant super peer that ensures an active backup or load balancing. The $\mathcal{BSP}$ is elected among peers that have enough hardware and network resources and it contains an image of the super peer knowledge.

In a first stage, our solution will be adopted for digital libraries context. However, it is in-tended to be a general framework. The architecture of our solution is presented in the figure 2 and contains the modules described below.

Query processing: it is a coordinating module managing the process of query resolution. It receives queries from the user interface or from remote peers. Either way, it undertakes to answer the query locally and/or forward it to remote peers depending on the query specifications. The routing decision to which peers a query should be forwarded is based on the knowledge about other peers. This module is composed of two sub-modules. The first one is dedicated for local processing and interacts directly with the wrappers of local resources as it is detailed in the [23] for the WASSIT platform. The second sub-module accomplishes remote query processing. It has for mission peer selection, query rewriting and query distribution for remote processing.

The network module: it has for task to manage peer joining to the network by choosing the pertinent cluster. The joining process is based on the available knowledge at the peer and on the network. Each peer that wants to join the P2P network should submit through its entry point a TTL-query containing description of its local knowledge using a summary of the most heavy-weighted concepts $\mathcal{M}_c$ and a threshold $\mathcal{S}_s$ for semantic similarity to satisfy by the available super peers. This mechanism is used to avoid network congestion and resources waste. Each super peer $\mathcal{SP}_x$ that receives the subscribing query of the new peer $\mathcal{P}_{new}$, calculates the semantic similarity $Sim(\mathcal{O}_{Cl\text{-}SPx}, \mathcal{O}_{Ls\text{-}Pnew})$ between its cluster knowledge and the asking peer description. If the semantic similarity is over the specified threshold $\mathcal{S}s$ than the super peer sends an acceptation response containing the calculated similarity value to the asking peer $\mathcal{P}new$. Among the returned values, the query initiating peer chooses the better cluster to join. The decision is taken by the initiating peer to avoid inter-super peer conflict and inter-blockage.

The network modules have also for task to accomplish another role of backuping in the case of the $\mathcal{BSP}$ nodes. The backup consists of backuping the super peer knowledge, providing a proactive rescue and preventing reactive election in the case of super peer failure.

The knowledge component differs depending on the nature of the node. In the case of the peer nodes, the knowledge component contains local expertise and information about cluster knowledge. However, for the $\mathcal{SP}$ and $\mathcal{BSP}$ the knowledge component contains also the network expertise. The knowledge contained in this component is represented by ontologies and mapping tables that we describe in section 5.3.

User interface allows users to formulate and submit queries. It is also used by the peer's administrators to manage resources and to define constraints and mapping.

Network communication manager is a component that is responsible for network communication between peers. It provides transport mechanisms to hide low-level communication details for the other components of the system, while sending and forwarding queries. In a first stage, we have opted to use the JXTA system as the communication platform for the implementation of our framework. Thus, the peers will be identified by the JXTA ID URN in the underlying P2P infrastructure.

5.2   Architecture Formalization

Formally, we present our PDM as acouple (G, M) where

G= {(SPU P),(Eg$_{SP\text{-}SP}$U Eg$_{SP\text{-}P}$)} is a labeled non-directed graph where:

SP= {SP$_1$, SP$_2$, ..., SP$_n$} is a set of super-peers, each one with its ontology and expertise

P= {(P$_1$, P$_2$, ..., P$_m$)} is a set of peers each one with its own ontology and expertise

Eg$_{SP\text{-}SP}$= {(SP$_i$, SP$_j$) | SP$_i$, SP$_j$∈SP$_2$} is a set of semantic links between Super-peers inside the backbone network.

EgSP-P = { (SP$_i$, P$_j$) | SP$_i$∈SP, P$_j$∈P } is a set of semantic links between peers and super peer inside each cluster.

M = {M$^{ij}_{SP\text{-}SP}$} U {M$^{kl}_{SP\text{-}P}$ } is a set of correspondence or alignment matrix, each one is associated with a semantic link Ls$_{i,j}$∈Eg$_{SP\text{-}SP}$, Ls$_{l,k}$∈Eg$_{SP\text{-}P}$ containing alignment information between the peers ontologies and those of the superpeers of a cluster for the M^{ij}_{SP-P} matrix and the semantic alignment between superpeers representing different clustersfor the M^{ij}_{SP-SP} matrix.

5.3   Knowledge Representation

One of the major challenges in P2P data integration is the definition of the knowledge and semantic to share across the network. Once this semantic is specified, we should define the format of its representation, the way of semantic construction (manual, automatic or semi-automatic), the semantic that could be shared between peers and between superpeers and how it is distributed across the whole system.

Data Model

In each node, sources are indexed using a semantic vector that describes the weight of concepts calculated using TF-IDF or similar schemes. These weighted indexes and schemas are used to construct local ontologies. The construction of the ontology is not our principal goal in this works. We suppose that local ontologies are already established.

For simplicity raisons, we define a space model for ontologies, we denote Ω this ontology space. Each ontology $O \in \Omega$ is defined as a four-tuple $<\mathcal{C}, \mathcal{R}, \mathcal{AC}, \mathcal{AR}>$ where $\mathcal{C}$ is a set of unary predicates called concepts, $\mathcal{R} \subseteq \mathcal{C} \times \mathcal{C}$ is a set of binary relations called properties and $\mathcal{AC}$ are $\mathcal{AR}$ are axioms for concepts and relations respectively. The definition of an otology space is dictated by necessity to use computational operations for ontology comparison, mapping, alignment and merging or for similarity measurement.

To be simpler, the ontology space is projected on a Vector Space Model (VSM), in which each ontology, is represented by a vector $\mathcal{V}_O$ in this space where the concepts are the dimensions. In the same manner, a user query is represented as a query vector $\mathcal{V}_Q$ and the similarity between the user query and the target peer ontology is estimated by the distance between $\mathcal{V}_O$ and $\mathcal{V}_Q$. In this way, we merge the problem of semantic-based search with query routing in our overlay network.

Data Model Pivot Language

As presented in our framework for centralized data integration, WASSIT we have chosen to use OWL ontologies to represent the semantic knowledge. The benefits of using OWL ontology are not to be demonstrated in this context. Indeed, in [4] we have presented how to build semantic knowledge using semi-automatic mapping from XML-documents to owl ontologies. We have also developed and tested a Wrapper from relational to XML documents in order to map theme into OWL ontologies[24].

XQuery [25] is the query language we adopt in our platform since it is the W3C standard for querying XML documents. In order to achieve efficient query processing, we represent the queries according to an algebraic model.

As our P2P integration uses semantic clustering based on peer's content, we have introduced the notion of expertise for each peer.This notion is used during the stage of peer's clustering. Each node that hops to get into the network should publish a summary called also expertise of its data sources and capabilities. The expertise notion is used to optimize the clustering process by preventing heavy computations of calculating similarity measuresbetween the holes ontologies. In this way, the peer expertise is used as a light weighted ontology containing the potentially most important concepts and relations.

For freshness reasons, we introduce in our data model a freshness parameter which will be incremented after update of the ontology published by each node. The idea of introducing freshness is to keep cluster and network ontologies up to date regarding to the peer knowledge. This parameter permits to elaborate an infrastructure permitting to manage knowledge freshness depending on the network dynamicity. To this end, we use *owl:priorVersion* and *owl:versionInfo* constructs to implement the freshness parameter.

Ontology Concepts and Properties

In our OWL ontology, we consider all concepts and relation between themes. For the relations, we distinguish two types of relations between nodes:

- The first one are Relations defined by the users or administrators using *OWL:objetProperty* construct. For instance, the "Is_the_author_of" relation in the example below:

    <owl:ObjectPropertyrdf:ID="Is_the_author_of">
    <rdfs:domainrdf:resource="#Author"/>
    <rdfs:rangerdf:resource="#Book"/>
    </owl:ObjectProperty>

- The second one is are OWL natives semantic and hierarchical implicit relations such as equivalence (*owl:equivalentClass, owl:equivalentProperty*), specialization and generalization (*rdfs:subClassOf, rdfs:subPropertyOf*), etc. For simplicity raisons, in a fist stage, *owl:DataTyeProperty* are not taken into account.

To represent the knowledge in our approach, we have taken into account two types of components: ontologies and mapping tables.

Ontologies: As presented before, our ontologies are assumed to be described in a language like OWL-DL for raisons of decidability and reasoning. We distinguish four types of ontologies, the local ontology O_{Ls} that represents the knowledge of local resources of each node. The second one represents the ontology contained in a cluster $O_{Cl\text{-}SPx}$ and is shared between peers of the cluster. The network ontology $O_{Net\text{-}SPx}$ is hosted by each super peer and describes the knowledge out of the local cluster as seen by the super peer SP_x. These three ontologies will be merged to obtain the global ontology $O_{g\text{-}SPx}$ of the super peer SP_x.

*Mapping tables:*We distinguish three types of mapping tables. The basic one MT_{Ls} is used locally in each peer to assure it as an autonomous information system. The second mapping table $MT_{Cl\text{-}SPx}$ is between peers and their super peer. The third one $MT_{Net\text{-}SPx}$ is between Super peers of different clusters.

Mapping tables are presented as matrix of semantic vectors $\mathcal{SV}$ where lines represent concepts and columns represent peers for the $\mathcal{MT}_{\text{Cl-SPx}}$ and clusters for the $\mathcal{MT}_{\text{Net- SPx}}$.

Vector Space Model

Graph Ontology

Before analyzing any relation type, we should present our owl ontology as a semantic graph where the nodes are concepts and the edges are the semantic relations between the concepts to be taken in semantic analysis. As defined in [26], we define an ontology graph as below.

Definition: Given an ontology O, the ontology graph $G_o = (V, E, l_V, l_E)$ of O is a directed labeled graph. V is a set of nodes representing all concepts in O. E is a set of directed edges representing all relations in O. l_V and l_E are labeling functions on V and E, respectively. $e_{s,t}$ is the edge connecting ontology nodes s and t, where edge e belongs to edges set E, node s and t belong to nodes set V, we denote by $e \in E$, $s,t \in V$.

As we are interested in the semantic of the two types of relations detailed before, our ontology graph will be represented in a vector space model with a matrix $n \times n \times k$, where n is the number of concepts V and k is the number of types of relations E. So, our graph ontology can be represented as bellow

$$
M = \begin{pmatrix} \left(d_1, d_2, ...d_k\right)_{11} & \left(d_1, d_2, ...d_k\right)_{12} & \left(d_1, d_2, ...d_k\right)_{1n} \\ \left(d_1, d_2, ...d_k\right)_{21} & \left(d_1, d_2, ...d_k\right)_{22} & \left(d_1, d_2, ...d_k\right)_{2n} \\ \left(d_1, d_2, ...d_k\right)_{n1} & \left(d_1, d_2, ...d_k\right)_{n2} & \left(d_1, d_2, ...d_k\right)_{nn} \end{pmatrix}
$$

Where $m_{c,i} = (d_1, d_2, .. , d_k)_{c,i}$ represents the relationship between the concepts C and I based on the K dimensions we take into account. It defines also similarity correlation between concept C and I.

The Concept C is represented by the vector of vectors: $V_c = (m_{c,1}, m_{c,2}, ..., m_{c,n})$

The Similarity between two concepts X and Y is equal to the similarity between their vectors in our vector space model. It is calculated by the scalar product between the two vectors V_x and V_y which we denote X and Y:

$$
S'_{X,Y} = X \times Y = \sum_{i=1}^{k} \sum_{j=1}^{n} X_{ij} \times Y_{ij}
$$

As we defined the similarity function in the interval [0..1], the similarity is normalized by the equation bellow:

$$
S_{X,Y} = \frac{S'_{X,Y}}{\| \sum_{X \in O} \sum_{Y \in O} X \times Y \|}
$$

5.4   Network Dynamicity Management

To offer more flexibility to our solution, we have adopted an enhanced super peer model for which we describe the dynamic behavior under normal conditions. This model should cope with the situations of node joining, peer leaving, peer update, super peer leaving, $\mathcal{BSP}$ and $\mathcal{SP}$ election. In this section, we present how the semantic knowledge of each node is adjusted according to the network dynamicity.

1.   Node joining

To join the network, a new node $\mathcal{P}$new should have an entry point $\mathcal{P}_{ent}$ that could be a peer or a super peer. If $\mathcal{P}$new has a predefined mapping $\mathcal{M}ap(O_{\mathcal{P}new}, O_{\mathcal{P}nent})$ to its entry point $\mathcal{P}_{ent}$, which means that it has pre-defined idea on the network knowledge, then, $\mathcal{P}$new joins the cluster of its entry point and the mapping between its resources and the hosting super peer is accomplished using mapping composition $\mathcal{M}ap(O_{\mathcal{P}new}, O_{Cl\text{-}\mathcal{SP}x}) = \mathcal{M}ap(O_{\mathcal{P}new}, O_{\mathcal{P}ent}) \otimes \mathcal{M}ap(O_{\mathcal{P}ent}, O_{Cl\text{-}\mathcal{SP}x})$. Otherwise, $\mathcal{P}$new sends a join request using TTL of $\mathcal{T}$ for the super peer of its entry point. This join request contains expertise metadata about $\mathcal{P}$new contents and computing resources, and is forwarded to super peer neighbors in the backbone network of $\mathcal{T}$-hops. Every super peer that receives the join query will estimate if the querying node could semantically be hosted in its cluster or not, by calculating semantic similarities, based on the expertise received, $\mathcal{S}im(O_{Cl\text{-}SPx}, O_{Ls\text{-}Pnew})$ about the context. In the affirmative case, the super peer compares its computing resources to those of the asking node. If the new node has greater computing power, it is prompted to be a new super peer for the cluster. But for more stability and to reduce computation and topology changes, we limit the clustering changes to only new peers that offer more significant power than the current super peer. A function for computing resources comparison should be defined based on the cluster size and the computing resources.

A new node that joins the network and has enough computing resources could build a new cluster if no super peer validates its join query. This case could happen if all clusters have reached the maximum size or if the new peer concerns a new topic.

Once a new peer $\mathcal{P}_{new}$ joins a cluster $\mathcal{X}$, a mapping between its knowledge and these of the hosting $\mathcal{SP}_x$ is calculated in an ascendant approach.

2.   Peer leaving

When a peer $\mathcal{P}_L$ fails or simply leaves the network, its super peer would update its cluster knowledge accordingly. The changes are notified across the backbone network for neighbor's super peers. Peer could fail for many raisons such as network bottlenecks or maintenance problems. Peer failure is detected using keep-alive massages or when it does not re-play to queries. However, the procedure of leaving is initiated on demand by the asking peer using a disconnect request.

Once the peer departure is confirmed, the super peer adjusts the cluster knowledge $O_{Cl\text{-}\mathcal{SP}x}$ accordingly to obtain $O'_{Cl\text{-}\mathcal{SP}x}$. Our process for peer leaving follows a descendant approach and works as follows. For each concept $\mathcal{C}$ in the $O_{Cl\text{-}\mathcal{SP}x}$ ontology that refer to $\mathcal{P}_L$ in the mapping table $\mathcal{MT}_{Cl\text{-}SPx}$, if this concept refers to another peer $\mathcal{P}_{I\neq L}$ then keep $\mathcal{C}$ else mark it for later deletion. A new mapping $\mathcal{M}(O'_{Cl\text{-}\mathcal{SP}x}, O_{Cl\text{-}\mathcal{SP}x})$ between $O'_{Cl\text{-}\mathcal{SP}x}$ and the $O_{Cl\text{-}\mathcal{SP}x}$. The new mapping is transmitted to the peers of the cluster to update their knowledge through mapping composition $\mathcal{M}(O'_{Cl\text{-}\mathcal{SP}x}, O_{Ls\text{-}\mathcal{P}}) = \mathcal{M}ap(O'_{Cl\text{-}\mathcal{SP}x}, O_{Cl\text{-}\mathcal{SP}x}) \otimes \mathcal{M}ap(O_{Cl\text{-}\mathcal{SP}x}, O_{Ls\text{-}\mathcal{P}})$. These changes are then forwarded out of the cluster $\mathcal{X}$ to update the Backbone overlay network.

3.   Super peer leaving

As mentioned before, the super peer constitutes as single point of failure in super peer architectures. The super peer of a cluster could become unreachable due to failure or by simply leaving the network. In this case, the $\mathcal{BSP}$ proposed in our enhanced model will take the relief and prevents communication breakdown. No changes should be accomplished. Then, the $\mathcal{BSP}$ is converted to be the effective super peer and the cluster knowledge is updated accordingly. Afterward, the IP address and computing resources of the new super peer is communicated to the peers of the cluster and to the other super peers of the backbone network. Thus, super peer failure becomes as simple as any other node of the cluster.

4.   The Backup Super Peer election

As mentioned, the $\mathcal{BSP}$ has for task to ensure fault tolerance in our enhanced super peer model. It is elected among cluster peer's that have enough hardware resources and offers more stability by being alive for long periods. This is accomplished throw historical activities. The election procedure is done in proactive way under normal conditions. The $\mathcal{BSP}$ continue polling periodically the $\mathcal{SP}$ to ensure the stability of the cluster. Moreover, a peer that could not communicate with its $\mathcal{SP}$ could query the $\mathcal{BSP}$ about the $\mathcal{SP}$ availability. Synchronization between the $\mathcal{SP}$ and $\mathcal{BSP}$ knowledge bases is accomplished periodically to ensure fault tolerance and self-organizing functionalities. The $\mathcal{BSP}$ knowledge is seen and processed as those of the other peers. Once the $\mathcal{BSP}$ is active, the knowledge of the old $\mathcal{SP}$ must be removed as explained for the peer leaving procedure. Then, the process of electing a new $\mathcal{BSP}$ is triggered.

5.   Node update

It presents the most delicate procedure that can happen in P2P data integration systems. This is due to the fact that download information by a peer should be shared in running time even before download accomplishment. However, fort simplicity raisons, we limit our approach to only totally downloaded documents. Thus, upon peer's knowledge changes, the cluster and network knowledge will be updated. To take into account these changes, two principal ideas can be adopted. The first and easiest one treats the peer as new one and deletes its old knowledge, and then uses the approach proposed in the node joining section. This idea do not reuse calculated mapping even more it should delete the old knowledge and re-compute the new knowledge and consequently, it is time and resources consuming. The second idea calculates a new mapping $\mathcal{M}(\mathcal{O}'_{Ls\text{-}\mathcal{P}m}, \mathcal{O}_{Ls\text{-}\mathcal{P}m})$ between the old local ontology $\mathcal{O}_{Ls\text{-}\mathcal{P}m}$ of the updated peer $\mathcal{P}_m$ and its update local otology $\mathcal{O}'_{Ls\text{-}\mathcal{P}m}$. The new mapping is communicated to the super peer for composition of mapping to update cluster and global knowledge of the super peer $\mathcal{SP}_x$. This second idea is better than the first one because it permits knowledge and mapping reuse.

6   Conclusion and Perspectives

Through the present paper, we have presented different P2P network features and capabilities. The set of smart features of Peer-to-Peer architectures including decentralization, self-organization, scalability and fault tolerance offers significant advantages that can help semantic P2P data integration. Besides, we have showed that combining data integration techniques in a P2P context generates a multitude of challenges. Indeed, a peer has very little knowledge of its network and this information becomes obsolete very quickly. In addition, before worrying about how to process a query, a peer has to select which neighbor nodes should be queried. This decision is based on the knowledge that a peer has or shares across the system. As presented, knowledge representation and routing techniques are applied to deal with peer's selection.

Based on this study, we have developed our framework for semantic P2P data integration for which we have detailed the architecture and argued the conceptual choices. Besides, we have proposed a vector space model to represent the semantic knowledge. In addition we have presented an approach for managing network dynamicity for our solution based on the WASSIT mediation framework.

We assume that our P2P framework has a plenty opportunities to support P2P semantic data integration and has the advantage to shun the scalability problem of most existing systems that uses centralized indexing, index flooding, or query flooding. To be competitive on a large number of PDMS, we must meet some other important challenges for optimization and efficiency. We are currently studying solutions for some of these P2P challenges and issues. Especially, we will focus in further works, on semantic query routing and processing. In parallel, we are working on implementing (similarity function, alignment process and knowledge construction) our approach. To show the performance of our framework, experimental and simulation results will be published in future works.

References

1. Moujane, A., Chiadmi, D., Benhlima, L.: Semantic Mediation: An Ontology-Based Architecture Using Metadata. In: CSIT 2006, Amman, Jordan, pp. 317–326 (2006)
2. Levy, A.Y., Rajaraman, A., Ordille, J.J.: Query-Answering Algorithms for Information Agents. In: AAAI 1996, Portland, Oregon (1996)
3. Benhlima, L., Chiadmi, D., Moujane, A., Gounbarek, L.: Construction de la base de connaissances pour WASSIT. Journal Marocain d'automatique, d'informatique et de traitement de Signal 3(3) (Mai 2007)
4. Moujane, A., Chiadmi, D., Benhlima, L.: An approach for knowledge base construction. In: ICSSEA 2007, Paris (2007)
5. Wadjinny, F., Chiadmi, D., et al.: Capacités de sources et optimisation de requêtes dans WASSIT. In: MCSEAI 2008, Oran, Algeria (2008)
6. Chawathe, S.H., Garcia-Molina, J., Hammer, K., Ireland, Y., Papakonstantinou, J., Ullman, D., Widom, J.: The TSIMMIS project: Integration of heterogeneous information sources. Journal of Intelligent Information System 8(2), 117–132 (1997)
7. Shirky, C.: What is p2p... and what isn't. Network. O'Reilly (2000),
   http://www.oreillynet.com/pub/a/p2p/2000/11/24/
   shirky1-whatisp2p.html
8. Ratnasamy, S., Francis, P., Handley, M., Karp, R.: A scalable content-addressable network. In: Proceedings of SIGCOMM (2001)
9. Zhao, B., Kubiatowicz, J., Joseph, A.: Tapestry: An infrastructure for fault-tolerant wide-area location and routing. Tech. Rep. UCB/CSD-01-1141, Computer Science Division, University of California, Berkeley, 94720 (2001)

10. Stoica, I., Morris, R., Karger, D., Kaashoek, M., Balakrishnan, H.: Chord: A scalable peer-to-peer lookup service for internet applications. In: Proceedings of SIGCOMM (2001)

11. Rowstron, A., Druschel, P.: Pastry: Scalable, Distributed Object Location and Routing for Large-Scale Peer-to-Peer Systems. In: Liu, H. (ed.) Middleware 2001. LNCS, vol. 2218, pp. 329–350. Springer, Heidelberg (2001)

12. Maymounkov, P., Mazières, D.: Kademlia: A Peer-to-Peer Information System Based on the XOR Metric. In: Druschel, P., Kaashoek, M.F., Rowstron, A. (eds.) IPTPS 2002. LNCS, vol. 2429, pp. 53–65. Springer, Heidelberg (2002)

13. Lenzerini M.: Data integration: A theoretical perspective. In: Proc. of the 21st ACM SIGACT SIGMOD SIGART Symp. PODS 2002, pp. 233–246 (2002)

14. Fridman, N.N.: Semantic Integration: A Survey Of Ontology-Based Approaches. SIGMOD Record 33(4), 65–70 (2004)

15. Bernstein, P., Giunchiglia, F., Kementsietsidis, A., Mylopoulos, J., Serafini, L., Zaihrayeu, I.: Data management for peer-to-peer computing: A vision. In: Proc. of WebDB 2002 (2002)

16. Halevy, A., Ives, Z., Mork, P., Tatarinov, I.: Piazza: Data management infra-structure for semantic web applications. In: Proc. of the 12th International Conference on World Wide Web, Hungary, pp. 556–567 (2003)

17. Kalfoglou, Y., Schorlemmer, M.: Ontology Mapping: the State of the Art. The Knowledge Engineering Review 18(1), 1–31 (2003)

18. Haase, P., Broekstra, J., Ehrig, M., Menken, M., Mika, P., Olko, M., Plechawski, M., Pyszlak, P., Schnizler, B., Siebes, R., Staab, S., Tempich, C.: Bibster A Semantics-Based Bibliographic Peer-to-Peer System. In: McIlraith, S.A., Plexousakis, D., van Harmelen, F. (eds.) ISWC 2004. LNCS, vol. 3298, pp. 122–136. Springer, Heidelberg (2004)

19. Nejdl, W., Wolf, B., Qu, C., Decker, S., Sintek, M., Naeve, A., Nilsson, M., Palmer, M., Risch, T.: Edutella: A p2p networking infrastructure based on rdf. In: Proceedings of the 12th International Conference on World Wide Web, Budapest, Hungary (2003)

20. Crespo, A., Garcia-Molina, H.: Routing indices for peer-to-peer systems. In: Proceedings International Conference on Distributed Computing Systems (ICDCS), pp. 23–34 (July 2002)

21. Ng, W.S., Ooi, B.C., Tan, K.-L., Zhou, A.: Peerdb: A p2p-based system for distributed data sharing. In Intl. Conf. on Data Engineering (ICDE) (2003)

22. Arenas, M., Kantere, V., Kementsietsidis, A., Kiringa, I., Miller, R.J., Mylopoulos, J.: The Hyperion Project: From Data Integration to Data Coordination. SIGMOD Record 32(3), 38–53 (2003)

23. Wadjinny, F., Gounbark, L., Benhlima, L., Chiadmi, D., Moujane, A.: Query pro-cessing in the WASSIT mediation framework. In: The Seventh ACS/IEEE International Conference on Computer Systems and Applications (AICCSA 2009), Rabat, Morocco, May 10-13 (2009)

24. El Marrakchi, M.: Mise en place d'un adaptateur XQuery/SOAP pour l'interrogation des Web services à partir d'un système de médiation. M.S Thesis, Computer Sciences Department, Mohammadia Engineering School, Rabat, Morocco (2009)

25. Fernández, M., Malhotra, A., Marsh, J., Nagy, M., Norman, W.: XQuery 1.0 and XPath 2.0 Data Model (XDM) W3C Recommendation (January 23, 2007), http://www.w3.org/TR/xpath-datamodel/

26. Wu, G., Li, J., Feng, L., Wang, K.-H.: Identifying Potentially Important Concepts and Relations in an Ontology. In: Sheth, A.P., Staab, S., Dean, M., Paolucci, M., Maynard, D., Finin, T., Thirunarayan, K. (eds.) ISWC 2008. LNCS, vol. 5318, pp. 33–49. Springer, Heidelberg (2008)

27. Levy, A.Y., Rajaraman, A., Ordille, J.J.: Querying heterogeneous information sources using source descriptions. In: Proceedings of the 22nd International Conference on Very Large Data Bases (VLDB 1996), Mumbai (Bombay), India, pp. 251–262 (1996)

Affinity and Coherency Aware Multi-core Scheduling

Hamid Reza Khaleghzadeh and Hossein Deldari

Department of Computer Science, Young Researchers Club, Mashhad Branch,
Islamic Azad University, Mashhad, Iran
khaleghzadeh@mshdiau.ac.ir, hdeldari@yahoo.com

Abstract. Reducing the cost of program memory access can improve program performance. In this paper, a scheduling approach based on coherency and thread affinity has been introduced which is able to estimate scheduling cost according to the number of common data blocks and their coherency cost. The estimated results are used to find the appropriate thread mapping to cores so that the number of common data blocks between cores and their coherence cost are reduced. In the proposed model, the effect of shared cache size on affinity and coherency is considered. Since the shared cache behavior on different architectures is not the same and changes according to the cache size, stack distance analysis is used to estimate the behavior of shared cache on different architectures. Finally, the model is evaluated by a synthetic application and SPLASH-2 benchmark.

Keywords: multi-core, thread scheduling, thread affinity, coherency, effective access graph.

1 Introduction

The multi-core processors have been studied in different aspects for a few years. Placing several cores with hierarchical shared caches on one chip distinguishes these processors from multi-processor and distributed shared memory systems.

Since program memory access allocates a part of the application execution cost, reduction of this cost can increase the user program performance. In the parallel applications, there are data blocks that are accessed in common by application threads. One of the solutions that can improve application performance and its execution time is reduction of the access cost to common blocks between threads of an application by increasing thread affinity. Thread affinity refers to placing threads with common data on a shared memory module. This increases overlapping of memory footprint between threads.

The goal of this paper is to search a thread schedule for multi-threaded application that improves data reuse inside cores and shared caches of multi-core memory hierarchy, and to reduce affinity strength between cores and non-shared caches, and to decrease coherence cost of common blocks. We know that threads of a parallel application can be mapped onto a parallel machine in various forms. This paper offers an analytical model to estimate cost of running an affinity- and coherency-based thread schedule on multi-core systems. This model is used to find an appropriate

P. Pichappan, H. Ahmadi, and E. Ariwa (Eds.): INCT 2011, CCIS 241, pp. 201–215, 2011.
© Springer-Verlag Berlin Heidelberg 2011

thread scheduling on the considered multi-core machine where memory access cost of program is reduced. The obtained scheduling will be used for mapping threads to cores in next runs of the application.

Coherence of the common blocks is one of the effective metrics on the memory access cost. The authors intend to reduce block coherency cost by thread affinity. Therefore, the proposed method considers the number of common blocks between threads and type of access to common blocks for estimating memory access cost.

The shared caches are one of the main resources of multi-core processors that have a significant role in thread affinity and scheduling cost. For this reason, effect of hierarchical shared caches on the proposed scheduling method is studied in the second half of paper. For this purpose, the number of common blocks on each cache level which access to them leads to hit is estimated, and then the obtained information is used to improve the estimate of memory access cost.

The proposed method in [1] has used the number of common data items between application threads in order to find optimal scheduling. The introduced solution in the present paper is the same as the proposed method in [1], except that authors have extended cost estimation model by considering coherency cost of common blocks and shared cache size.

Finally, the model is evaluated by synthetic application and SPLASH-2 benchmark.

The rest of the paper is organized as follows: In section two, the related works is described. Section three proposes methodology. In this section we have explained our thread scheduling method based on affinity and coherency. Section four introduces simulation environment, and presents simulation results, and section five summarizes the results and contributions of our work.

2   Related Works

Thread affinity has been studied in shared memory systems with various views. Solaris and Linux operating systems introduce pset_bind [2] and sched_setaffinity [3] system calls, respectively, for binding threads to determined core(s). Sun [4] and Intel [5] compilers allow programmer to control thread binding by using environment variables.

C.P. Ribeiro et al. [6] developed a solution independent from architecture and compiler which is called Minas. They assured memory affinity in ccNUMA machines by reducing number of remote access or memory contention. Minas consists of three modules: Memory Affinity interface (MAi) is an API that called by application source code to deal with data allocation and placement. Memory Affinity preprocessor (MApp) performs automatic optimizations in the application source code, and NUMA Architecture Module (numarch) provides the machine information for helping to placing the data.

[7] binds threads to cores manually instead of binding by Linux Kernel, and gains a better performance because there are thread switching in Linux.

F. Song et al. [1] proposed an analytical model to estimate cost of thread scheduling on multi-core systems. This model consists of three sub models. Memory affinity in the user program is described by affinity graph that determines number of accessed data items in common by each two threads of program. Memory hierarchy sub-model characterizes memory hierarchy of considered multi-core system. Cost sub-model is used in order to characterize thread scheduling cost. They have divided the affinity graph of program to find optimal thread schedule. The goal is to minimize the sharing between processors in the order of level 0 (last level memory) to level h − 1 (the nearest memory to core) in a top-down fashion.

[8] works on heterogeneous multi-cores that the cores are connected by a mesh network. It attempts to assign a thread to previous core which was run on it, and if previous core is not available, it schedules the thread on the nearest cores in order to minimize the communication time.

3   Methodology

Song et al. [1] have proposed an analytical model to find an optimal thread schedule to improve the memory effectiveness on all levels in the multi-level memory hierarchy of multi-core systems. The model consists of three sub-models: Affinity graph sub-model, memory hierarchy sub-model, and cost sub-model that characterize number of common data items between application's threads, memory hierarchy of the considered machine and execution cost, or in other words thread scheduling cost, by considering number of common data items between application's threads, respectively. In this model, Affinity graph is a weighted undirected graph where its vertexes show application's threads and the weight for edge e_{ij} denotes the total number of distinct addresses accessed in common by threads i and j. The proposed approach in this model, that we call it AFF-Model (affinity-model), does following operations in order to find an optimal schedule: obtaining and analyzing the memory trace of each thread and determining number of distinct common data items between application's threads for creating affinity graph, partitioning the affinity graph to some sub-graphs by considering memory hierarchy sub-model (one sub-graph per processor), finding an optimized schedule for each processor, and finally saving the obtained thread scheduling into a file as a feedback for next runs of the application.

Definition 1. Sharing(T_x , T_y): The number of distinct data items that are accessed in common by threads (or set of threads) T_x and T_y. Value of the parameter is extractable from affinity graph.

Definition 2. NearestShareCache(P_x , P_y): Level of the nearest shared cache between processors P_x and P_y. This information is extractable from memory hierarchy sub-model.

Definition 3. Lat(P , L): Latency of accessing processor P to a cache that is in level L.

Definition 4. Proc(T): The processor that thread T is mapped on it.
The proposed analytical method in AFF-Model has used the following relation to estimate execution cost for each pair of threads:

$$Cost(T_x , T_y) = \text{Sharing}(T_x , T_y) * \\ \text{Lat}(Proc(T_x , \text{NearestShareCache}(Proc(T_x), Proc(T_y))))$$

(1)

In relation 1, cost(T_x , T_y) is the estimated cost of execution of threads T_x and T_y when they are mapped on Proc(T_x) and Proc(T_y) and the nearest cache between them is located in level NearestShareCache (Proc(T_x) , Proc(T_y)).

Song et al. demonstrated by cost sub-model that in order to reduce program memory access cost to common data, threads with more affinity strength must be mapped on the cores that the shared cache between them is located in the lower level (nearest to processor) in memory hierarchy.

Therefore, in order to find optimal scheduling, AFF-Model proposes a hierarchical partitioning algorithm to divide the affinity graph for minimizing the sharing between partitions in the order of level 0 to level h − 1 in a top-down fashion.

Relation 2 shows affinity strength of two disjoint partitions T_x and T_y.

$$Sharing(T_x , T_y) = \sum_{\forall u \in T_x, \forall v \in T_y} w(u, v), \tag{2}$$

where w(u,v) is affinity strength between threads u and v.

It's clear that AFF-Model estimates execution cost of thread scheduling in terms of thread affinity, and doesn't consider first access to data and missed accesses. The only considered parameter in this relation is data reuse in threads that helps to reduce memory access cost.

The proposed method in this paper is based on AFF-Model. We intend to extend AFF-Model which considers more details of architecture and application behavior to estimate execution cost of affinity- and coherency-based thread scheduling, and finally find appropriate thread scheduling. So, this paper, in addition to using the number of distinct common data items, which used in [1], estimates cost of thread scheduling by considering coherence cost of common blocks between threads and shared cache size in memory hierarchy of multi-core processors.

In the following, the proposed method is described in more detail.

3.1   Coherency

Data coherency in multi-core machines is essential due to shared cache. One of the weaknesses of the proposed model in AFF-Model is that it doesn't pay attention to the coherency cost of common blocks, and it only considers number of data items that are accessed in common by threads of application. In addition to the number of common distinct data blocks between threads, type and number of access to these blocks affect the thread scheduling cost because of the need to provide coherent common data. In order to clarify the discussion, suppose that the data block X is common between threads T_x and T_y. We consider two cases: (i) block X is read only. In this case, cost of access to this block equals with Lat(Proc(T_x) , NearestShareCache(Proc(T_x), Proc(T_y)). In case (i) if block X is read several times by T_x and T_y, There is not any cost in terms of coherency, and the block can be read from the closer caches to processor (if the block exists in the cache) without accessing to NearestShareCache (Proc(T_x) , Proc(T_y)). (ii) in this case if block X is write-read, this block is read each time, if the block is modified by another thread, access cost to this block will be Lat(Proc(T_x) , NearestShareCache(Proc(T_x) , Proc(T_y)).

According to the recent explanation, coherency cost of common blocks should be considered to estimate affinity strength of threads. For this purpose, in this paper, affinity graph is created by considering type and number of access to common blocks. Finite state machine (FSM) in fig. 1 shows that how to estimate the affinity strength between the two threads T_x and T_y.

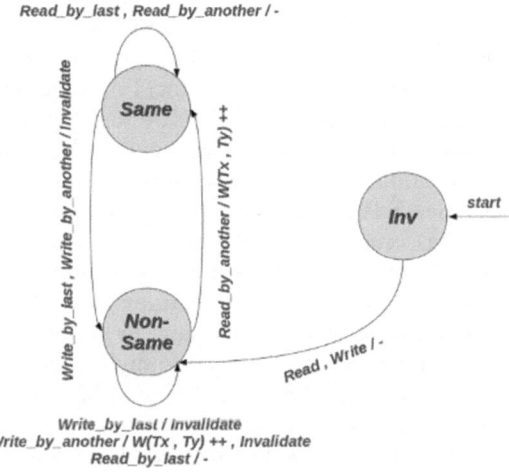

Fig. 1. Affinity strength estimator FSM

The FSM consists of three states Same, non-Same, and Inv. Suppose that threads T_x and T_y have separate copies of common data block X. If these replicas are coherent, X is Same. If these two replicas aren't coherent and this incoherency is because of modifying block X by T_x or T_y, the block is non-same, and if other thread as T_z modifies block X, then this block is Inv from view of T_x and T_y.

The transitions between states in the FSM are defined as follow:

- Read_by_last: if block X is accessed by T_x and then is read by this thread, this access to X is Read-by_last.
- Read_by_another: if block X is accessed by T_x and now this block is read by T_y, this access is Read_by_another.
- Write_by_last: if block X is accessed by T_x and then is written by this thread, this access to X is Write-by_last.
- Wrte_by_another: if block X is accessed by T_x and now this block is written by T_y, this access is Read_by_another.

As shown in fig. 1, an action is done along with each transition, where:

- $W(T_x , T_y)$ ++: affinity strength of threads T_x and T_y increases one unit.
- Invalidate: if block X is written by threads T_x or T_y, state of X in all threads that have accessed to X is changed to Inv state.

By using the proposed FSM, affinity strength of every program thread pairs can be estimated, and weight of each edge of affinity graph is determined by type and number of access to common blocks.

3.2   Cache Size

AFF-Model has not considered shared cache size, and supposed that common data items are stored in shared cache completely. In this section, we intend to study impact of cache size on cost of running an affinity- and coherency-based thread schedule, and to extend AFF-Model which considers cache size to estimate execution cost.

Suppose that threads T_x and T_y access to block X in common. First, T_x accesses to X and then the block is read by T_y. If access of T_y to X in cache level NearestShareCache(Proc(T_x) , Proc(T_y)) is hit, cost of access to X will be Lat(Proc(T_x) , NearestShareCache(Proc(T_x) , Proc(T_y))), otherwise, block X is not in cache level NearestShareCache(Proc(T_x) , Proc(T_y)) and lower level caches. So, the block should be read from upper level memories that it will increase access cost to the block. Our goal is estimation of thread scheduling cost and, as described at last section, this parameter depends on type and number of access to common data on each level of shared caches. But we know that hitting or missing an access to a block depends on cache size. Therefore, to find a thread schedule to reduce access cost to common data, in addition to type and number of access to common blocks, the shared cache size (In order to estimate number of access to common blocks between two threads that the access is done without the need to higher cache levels and via cache level NearestShareCache(Proc(T_x) , Proc(T_y))) should be considered. We call these kinds of accesses effective accesses.

The number of effective accesses is architectural-dependent and change by cache size. On the other hand, multi-core machines consist of hierarchical caches where the cache size of each level varies with other levels. Therefore, number of effective access should be estimated for different architectures. We have used stack distance analysis to estimate effective accesses. Mattson et al. defined the stack distance as the number of distinct data elements accessed between two consecutive references to the same element [9].

According to the above explanation, we intend to develop the proposed method to estimate affinity strength by considering shared cache size, type, and number of access to common blocks. So, number of effective accesses should be estimated.

Presented FSM in fig. 2 is similar with first one, except that this finite state machine records stack distance of access to common blocks between threads T_x and T_y. In this FSM, StackDist$_{xy}$ is a one-dimensional array that StackDistxy[i] determines the number of common accesses of threads T_x and T_y with stack distance i.

Now, we obtain number of effective accesses, the number of common accesses that hit on the considered architecture, by using of the created StackDist array for each pair of thread by relation 3. This relation, which we have evaluated in [10], estimates probability of eviction a block (p(R)) with stack distance R on an N-line and S-way cache. Suppose that cache replacement policy in the relation 3 is LRU.

$$p(R) = 1 - \sum_{i=0}^{S-1} \binom{R}{i} * \left(\frac{S}{N}\right)^i * \left(\frac{N-S}{N}\right)^{R-i} \tag{3}$$

The introduced code in fig. 3 calculates number of effective accesses for threads T_x and T_y.

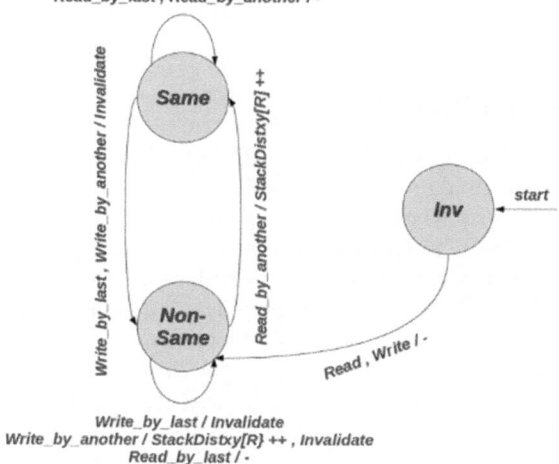

Fig. 2. Stack reuse distance FSM

```
TotalMiss = 0;
TotalCommonAccess  = 0;
For all non-zero elements in StackDistxy with index i
{
        TotalMiss += StackDist[i] * p(i);
        TotalCommonAccess  += StackDistxy[i];
}
effectiveAccess = TotalCommonAccess - TotalMiss;
```

Fig. 3. Estimating effective access count

The created affinity graph by the proposed method is similar with AFF-Model one, except that weight of each edge (affinity strength) equals with the number of effective accesses that estimated by the introduced pseudo code in fig. 3. We called this affinity graph effective access graph. It's clear that there is one affinity graph per cache size that is defined by memory hierarchy sub-model which determines affinity strength of application's threads by considering cache size.

3.3   Find Appropriate Thread Scheduling

In this paper, finding appropriate thread schedule refers to mapping of application's threads to the considered multi-core architecture, so that effective access strength (number of effective access) between cores and non-shared caches are minimized for each cache level in memory hierarchy. Therefore, similar to the introduced method in [1], hierarchical graph partitioning is used to find appropriate thread schedule, except that in AFF-Model, affinity strength between two partitions for each level of the memory hierarchy sub-model was estimated by using of number of words that accessed in common, but proposed method uses effective access graph to extract the number of effective access between the threads for each cache level.

We have called the proposed model ACS-Model (Affinity-Coherency-cache Size-Model).

4   Experimental Results

In this paper, all simulations are done by SIMICS [11] and GEMS [12]. SIMICS is a functional full system simulator. We use SIMICS to simulate a Solaris-Sparc system (We have installed Solaris 10 on SIMICS). GEMS is an extension of SIMICS, which works together with SIMICS. GEMS can support chip multiprocessor simulations. It has two modules, which are all built on top of SIMICS. One is called Ruby and the other is Opal. The Ruby module implements a detailed memory system. In our work, we use Ruby module to simulate the memory hierarchy.

Simulated architecture is an 8 cores processor that consists of 4 packages. Each package contains two cores with private DL1 and IL1 cache and shared L2 cache. Packages are connected by a peer-to-peer network to each other. Packages are grouped in two categories. Each category contains two packages of the simulated machine. L2 cache size of one category is larger than the other one. The authors have modified GEMS which can support this architecture.

Execution time is used as a metric for evaluating the proposed scheduling approach. It is the milliseconds that application runs in parallel, and doesn't include preparation time.

We selected 4 benchmark applications from the SPLASH-2 [13] suite and one parallel application to use in the simulation.

4.1   Comparing ACS with Solaris Thread Scheduling

In this section, we intend to compare the proposed thread schedule with Solaris one. For obtaining performance of original schedule, we have executed each application without any direct thread to core binding. Then, for each application, an appropriate schedule is obtained by ACS approach. We have exclusively bound each thread of application to the simulated cores by pset-bind() system call. In this experiment, L2 cache size for each category is determined 2MB and 4MB, respectively. Fig. 4 shows that use of proposed thread schedule reduces execution time up to 32%.

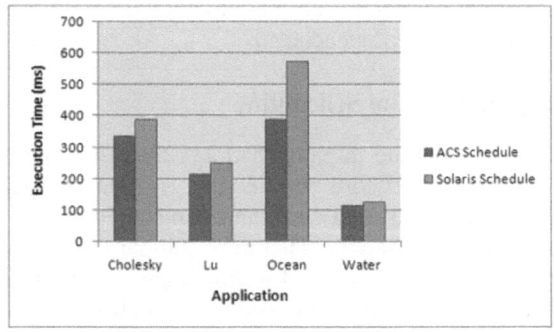

Fig. 4. Comparing proposed thread scheduling with Solaris scheduling

4.2   Impact of Cache Size on Thread Affinity

As described in section 3, size of shared caches affects effective access strength and accordingly on thread scheduling cost. We have studied this issue by using Cholesky, Lu, Ocean, and Water 8-threaded applications from SPLASH-2. The applications can be scheduled on the simulated machine in 630 ways ($\frac{8!}{2!^6}$). Fig. 5, 7, 9, and 11 show execution time of the best and the worst thread schedule based on L2 cache size. In these figures, horizontal axis shows L2 cache size of the two categories in the simulated architecture. If the mapped threads on each package are considered as a partition, inter-package effective access strength can be calculated by relation 2. Fig. 6, 8, 10, and 12 show inter-package effective access strength for each application based on the considered L2 cache sizes. Effective access strength of two threads is extracted from application effective access graph by considering the shared cache size that the two threads are mapped on it. By comparing execution time and inter-package effective access strength diagrams of every application, it can be understood that if difference of inter-package effective access count between the best and the worst schedule is increased, impact of affinity on execution time is increased, too. But this deduction is not valid for Cholesky (first experiment).

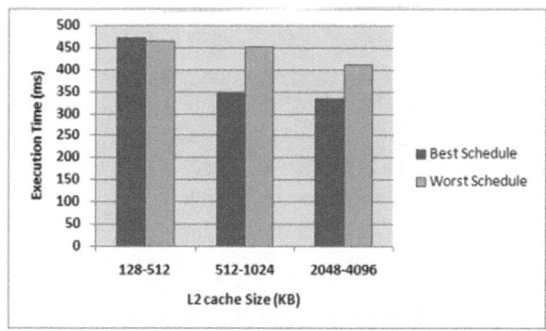

Fig. 5. Cholesky execution time for three possible thread schedule

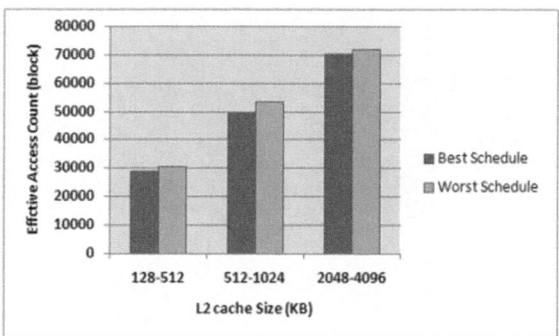

Fig. 6. Cholesky inter-package effective access count

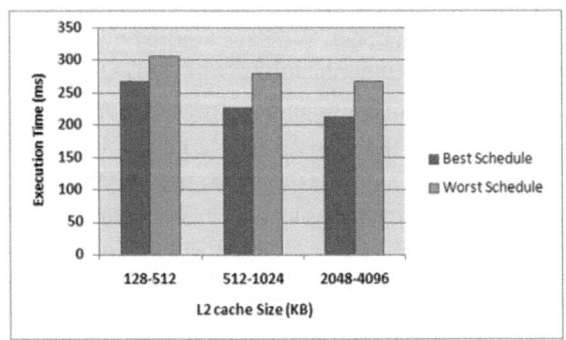

Fig. 7. Lu execution time for three possible thread schedule

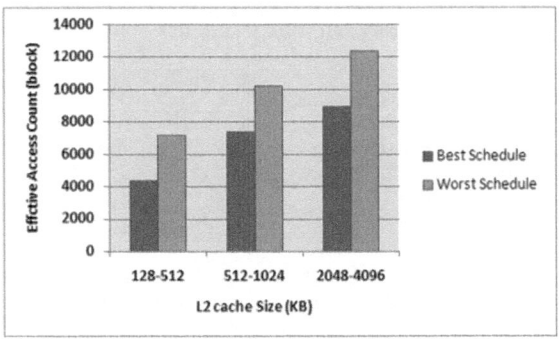

Fig. 8. Lu inter-package effective access count

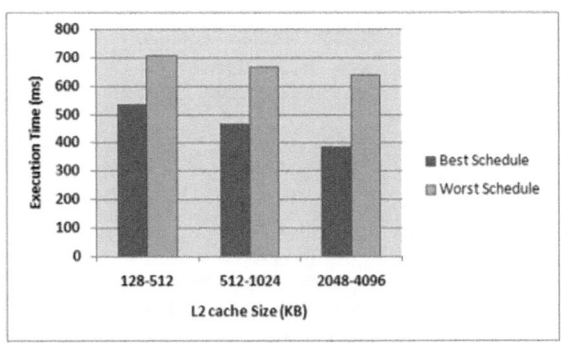

Fig. 9. Ocean execution time for three possible thread schedule

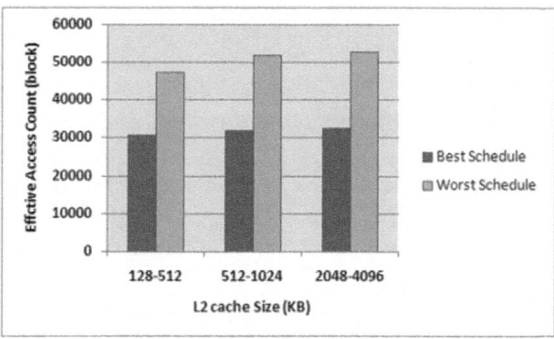

Fig. 10. Ocean inter-package effective access count

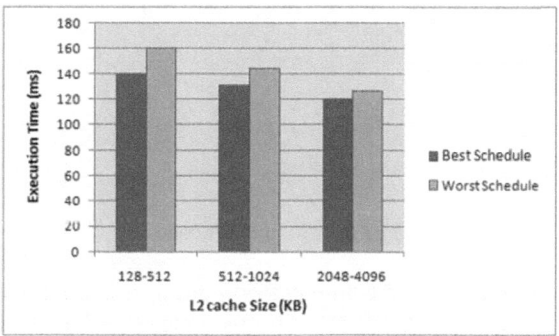

Fig. 11. Water execution time for three possible thread schedule

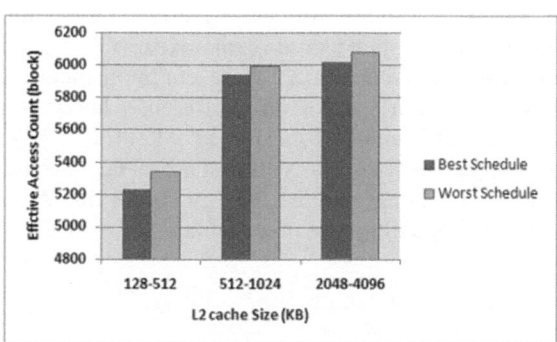

Fig. 12. Water inter-package effective access count

We can see that the best schedule is 4% to 40% faster than the worst one.

4.3   AFF-Model vs. ACS-Model

We have evaluated performance of AFF-model and ACS-Model by using ComputePi multi-threaded application and four other applications from SPLASH-2.

```
void compute_pi (void *value)
{
  int i, *hit_pointer;
  double rand_no_x, rand_no_y;
  hit_pointer = (int *) value;
  for (i = 0; i < sample_points_per_thread; i++)
  {
      rand_no_x =(double) (rand_r(&seed))/((2<<14)-1);
      rand_no_y =(double) (rand_r(&seed))/((2<<14)-1);
      if (((rand_no_x - 0.5) * (rand_no_x - 0.5) +
        (rand_no_y - 0.5) * (rand_no_y - 0.5)) < 0.25)
          (*hit_pointer) ++;      // modifying hitx, x=0, 1, 2, 3.
      seed *= i;
  }
}


int main ()
{
  int hits0;
  // Insert padding
  int hits1 , hits2;
  // Insert padding
  int hits3
  creatre_thread (ComputePi , &hits0);//T0
  creatre_thread (ComputePi , &hits1);//T1
  creatre_thread (ComputePi , &hits2);//T2
  creatre_thread (ComputePi , &hits3);//T3
}
```

Fig. 13. ComputePi code

Fig. 13 shows pseudo code of ComputePi program. It is a pthread application that consists of four worker threads T0- T3. In this code, variables hits0 and hit3 are in different blocks but hits1 and hit2 are in same block.

In terms of AFF-Model, affinity strength between threads T0 and T3 equals with threads T1 and T2. But ACS_Model estimates effective access strength of T1 and T2 more than other thread pairs. It is because of the existence of false sharing between T1 and T2 that increases coherence cost of the common block between these two threads. So, AFF-Model doesn't make any difference between these two thread mapping: (T0 , T1) - (T2 , T3) and (T0 , T3) - (T1 , T2) ((Tx , Ty) means that thread Tx and thread Ty mapped on two cores that share a L2 cache). But ACS-Model prefers co-scheduling of T1 along with T2. Fig. 14 shows that ACS-Model estimates thread schedule cost of ComputePi more precise than AFF-Model.

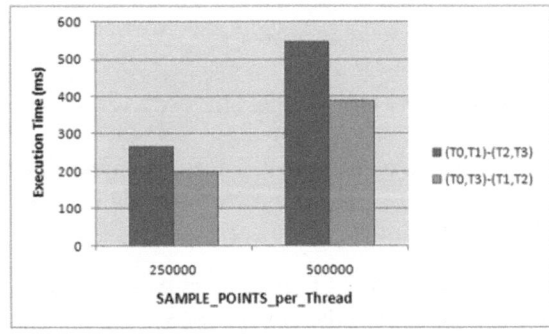

Fig. 14. ComputePi execution time for two thread schedules

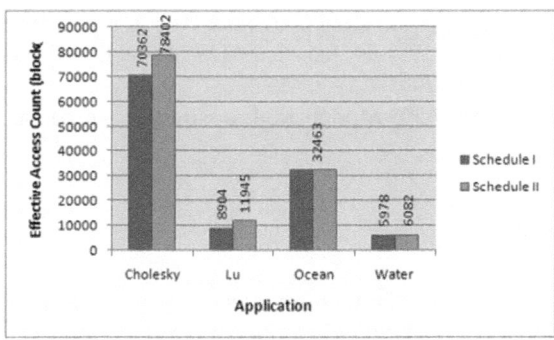

Fig. 15. Inter-package effective access strength estimated by ACS-Model

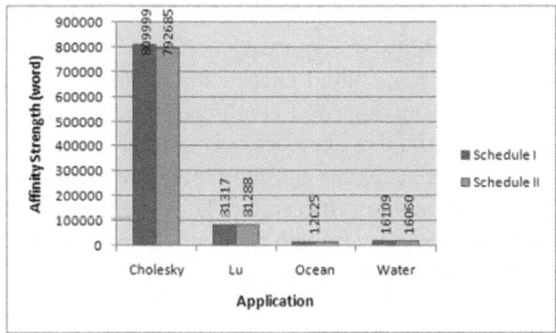

Fig. 16. Inter-package affinity strength estimated by AFF-Model

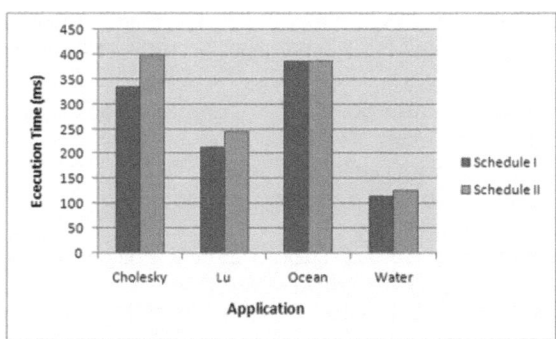

Fig. 17. Execution time of SPLASH-2 benchmark for three possible thread schedule

Finally, we have compared performance of ACS-Model thread schedule with AFF-Model one by Cholesky, Lu, Ocean, and Water applications from SPLASH-2 benchmark. Each application consists of 8 threads. If the mapped threads on each package are considered as a partition, inter-package effective access count can be calculated by relation 2. Fig. 15 and 16 show inter-package effective access strength and inter-package affinity strength (number of common words) for each application, respectively. ACS-Model selects schedule I for Cholesky, Lu and water. But AFF-Model considers schedule II for these thread applications. According to execution time of each program that is shown in fig. 17, it is clear that ACS-Model thread schedule is better than AFF-Model for these application.

Both ACS-Model and AFF-Model find a similar thread schedule for Ocean application.

5   Conclusion

The placement of threads onto the memory hierarchy often has an impact on program performance if they have overlapping memory footprints. Also, the coherence cost of common data can be reduced by enhancing affinity strength of threads.

The goal of proposed analytical approach is finding an appropriate thread schedule for a multi-threaded application, so that block reuse is enhanced inside cores and shared caches, and also affinity strength and coherence cost of shared blocks are reduced between cores and non-shared caches for all levels of multi-core memory hierarchy. In order to find an appropriate thread schedule for an multi-threaded application, the number of effective accesses between the two threads is estimated by using type and the number of access to common blocks, and an effective access graph is created per cache size of memory hierarchy. Then, application threads are divided into partitions that effective access strength between them is minimized in the order of level 0 to level h − 1 in a top-down fashion.

References

1. Song, F., Moore, S., Dongarra, J.: Analytical Modeling and Optimization for Affinity Based Thread Scheduling on Multicore Systems. In: IEEE CLUSTER 2009, New Orleans, LA (2009)
2. http://developers.sun.com/solaris/articles/solaris_processor.html
3. http://linux.die.net/man/2/sched_setaffinity
4. http://www.oracle.com/technetwork/indexes/documentation/index.html
5. http://www.fkf.mpg.de/edv/docs/intel_composer/Documentation/en_US/compiler_f/main_for/index.htm
6. Ribeiro, C.P., Méhaut, J., Carissimi, A.: Memory affinity management for numerical scientific applications over Multi-core Multiprocessors with Hierarchical Memory. In: IPDPS Workshop, pp. 1–4 (2010)
7. Rapan, A., Nita, I., Lazarescu, V., Seceleanu, T.: Efficient threads mapping on multicore architecture. In: Proceedings 8th International Conference on Communications Bucharest, pp. 53–57. IEEE Conference number 16421 (June 2010)
8. Sibai, F.N.: Nearest Neighbor Affinity Scheduling in Heterogeneous Multi-Core Architectures. Journal of Computer Science & Technology (Magazine/Journal), 144–150 (2008)
9. Mattson, R.L., Gecsei, J., Slutz, D., Traiger, I.L.: Evaluation techniques for storage hierarchies. IBM System Journal 9(2), 78–117 (1970)

10. Khaleghzadeh, H.R., Deldari, H.: A program phase detection method based on architectural signature for multicore processors. In: International Symposium on Performance Evaluation of Computer & Telecommunication Systems (SPECTS), pp. 46–53 (2011)
11. Magnusson, P.S., Christensson, M., Eskilson, J., Forsgren, D., Hallberg, G., Hogberg, J., Larsson, F., Moestedt, A., Werner, B., Werner, B.: Simics: A full system simulation platform. Computer 35(2), 50–58 (2002)
12. Martin, M.M.K., Sorin, D.J., Beckmann, B.M., Marty, M.R., Xu, M., Alameldeen, A.R., Moore, K.E., Hill, M.D., Wood, D.A.: Multifacet's general execution-driven multiprocessor simulator (gems) toolset. SIGARCH Comput. Archit. News 33(4), 92–99 (2005)
13. Woo, S.C., Ohara, M., Torrie, E., Singh, J.P., Gupta, A.: The SPLASH-2 Programs: Characterization and Methodological Considerations. In: Proc. 1995 International Symposium on Computer Architecture, pp. 24–36. ACM, Italy (1995)

A New Clustering Ensemble Framework

Hosein Alizadeh, Hamid Parvin[*], Mohsen Moshki, and Behrouz Minaei

Nourabad Mamasani Branch, Islamic Azad University, Nourabad Mamasani, Iran
hamidparvin@mamasaniiau.ac.ir,
{halizadeh,moshki,b_minaei}@iust.ac.ir

Abstract. In this paper a new criterion for clusters validation is proposed. This new cluster validation criterion is used to approximate the goodness of a cluster. The clusters which satisfy a threshold of the proposed measure are selected to participate in clustering ensemble. To combine the chosen clusters, some methods are employed as aggregators. Employing this new cluster validation criterion, the obtained ensemble is evaluated on some well-known and standard datasets. The empirical studies show promising results for the ensemble obtained using the proposed criterion comparing with the ensemble obtained using the standard clusters validation criterion. Besides to reach the best results, the method gives an algorithm based on which one can find how to select the best subset of clusters from a pool of clusters.

Keywords: Clustering Ensemble, Stability Measure, Cluster Evaluation.

1   Introduction

Data clustering or unsupervised learning is an important and very difficult problem. The objective of clustering is to partition a set of unlabeled objects into homogeneous groups or clusters [3]. There are many applications which use clustering techniques for discovering structure in data, such as data mining [10], information retrieval [2], image segmentation [9], linkage learning [16] and machine learning. In real-world problems, clusters can appear with different shapes, sizes, data sparseness, and degrees of separation. Clustering techniques require the definition of a similarity measure between patterns. Since there is no prior knowledge about cluster shapes, choosing a specific clustering method is not easy [14]. Studies in the last few years have tended to combinational methods. Cluster ensemble methods attempt to find better and more robust clustering solutions by fusing information from several primary data partitionings [8].

We propose a new criterion for clusters validation. Then we employ this criterion to select the more robust clusters in the final ensemble. We also propose a new method named Extended Evidence Accumulation Clustering, EEAC, to construct the matrix of similarity from these selected clusters. Finally, we apply a hierarchical method over the obtained matrix to extract the final partition.

Fern and Lin [4] have suggested a clustering ensemble approach which selects a subset of solutions to form a smaller but better-performing cluster ensemble than using

---

[*] Corresponding author.

P. Pichappan, H. Ahmadi, and E. Ariwa (Eds.): INCT 2011, CCIS 241, pp. 216–224, 2011.

all primary solutions. The ensemble selection method is designed based on quality and diversity, the two factors that have been shown to influence cluster ensemble performance. This method attempts to select a subset of primary partitions which simultaneously has both the highest quality and diversity. The Sum of Normalized Mutual Information, SNMI [15], [5] and [6], is used to measure the quality of an individual partition with respect to other partitions. Also, the Normalized Mutual Information, NMI, is employed for measuring the diversity among partitions. Although the ensemble size in this method is relatively small, this method achieves significant performance improvement over full ensembles. Law et al. proposed a multi objective data clustering method based on the selection of individual clusters produced by several clustering algorithms through an optimization procedure [12]. This technique chooses the best set of objective functions for different parts of the feature space from the results of base clustering algorithms. Fred and Jain [7] have offered a new clustering ensemble method which learns the pairwise similarity between points in order to facilitate a proper partitioning of the data without the a priori knowledge of the number of clusters and of the shape of these clusters. This method which is based on cluster stability evaluates the primary clustering results instead of final clustering.

Rest of this paper is organized as follows. In section 2, we explain the proposed method. Section 3 demonstrates results of our proposed method against traditional comparatively. Finally, we conclude in section 4.

2   Proposed Method

In this section, first our proposed clustering ensemble method is briefly outlined, and then its phases are described in detail.

The main idea of our proposed clustering ensemble framework is utilizing a subset of best performing primary clusters in the ensemble, rather than using all of clusters. Only the clusters which satisfy a stability criterion can participate in the combination. The cluster stability is defined according to Normalized Mutual Information, NMI. Figure 1 depicts the proposed clustering ensemble procedure.

The manner of computing stability is described in the following sections in detail. After, a subset of the most stable clusters is selected for combination. This is simply done by applying a stability-threshold to each cluster. In the next step, the selected clusters are used to construct the co-association matrix. Several methods have been proposed for combination of the primary results [1] and [15]. In our work, some clusters in the primary partitions may be absent (having been eliminated by the stability criterion). Since the original EAC method [5] cannot truly identify the pairwise similarity while there is only a subset of clusters, we present a new method for constructing the co-association matrix. We call this method: Extended Evidence Accumulation Clustering method, EEAC. Finally, we use the hierarchical average-link clustering to extract the final clusters from this matrix.

2.1   Cluster Evaluation

Since goodness of a cluster is determined by all the data points, the goodness function $g_j(C_i, D)$ depends on both the cluster C_i and the entire dataset D, instead of C_i alone. The stability as measure of cluster goodness is used in [11]. Cluster stability reflects the variation in the clustering results under perturbation of the data by resampling.

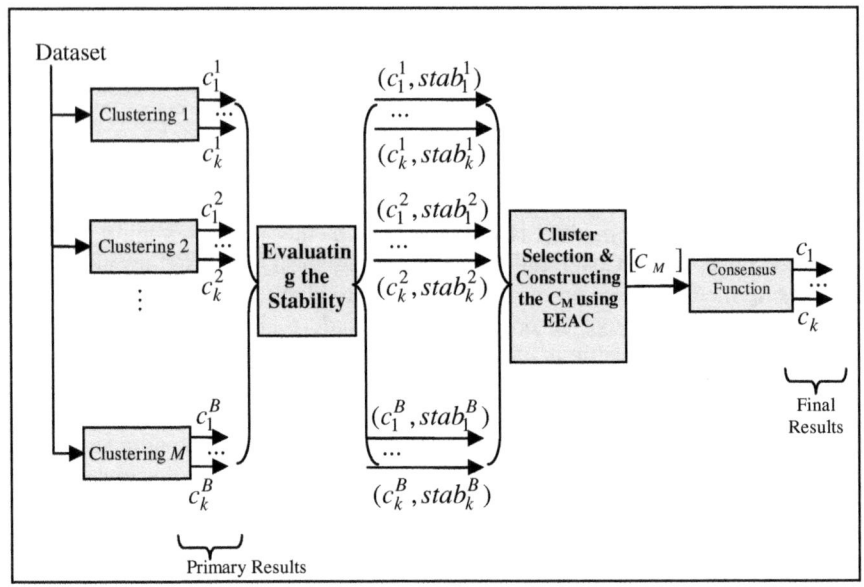

Fig. 1. Training phase of the Bagging method

A stable cluster is one that has a high likelihood of recurrence across multiple applications of the clustering method. Stable clusters are usually preferable, since they are robust with respect to minor changes in the dataset [12].

Now assume that we want to compute the stability of cluster C_i. In this method first a set of partitionings over resampled datasets is provided which is called the reference set. In this notation D is resampled data and $P(D)$ is a partitioning over D. Now, the problem is: "How many times is the cluster C_i repeated in the reference partitions?" Denote by NMI($C_i,P(D)$), the Normalized Mutual Information between the cluster C_i and a reference partition $P(D)$. Most previous works only compare a *partition with another partition* [15]. However, the stability used in [12] evaluates the similarity between a *cluster and a partition* by transforming the cluster C_i to a partition and employing common partition to partition methods. To illustrate this method let $P_1 = P^a = \{C_i, D/C_i\}$ be a partition with two clusters, where D/C_i denotes the set of data points in D that are not in C_i.

Then we may compute a second partition $P_2 = P^b = \{C^*, D/C^*\}$, where C^* denotes the union of all "positive" clusters in $P(D)$ and others are in D/C^*. A cluster C_j in $P(D)$ is positive if more than half of its data points are in C_i. Now, define NMI($C_i,P(D)$) by NMI(P^a,P^b) which is calculated as [6]:

$$NMI(P^a, P^b) = \frac{-2\sum_{i=1}^{k_a}\sum_{j=1}^{k_b} n_{ij}^{ab} \log\left(\frac{n_{ij}^{ab}.n}{n_i^a.n_j^b}\right)}{\sum_{i=1}^{k_a} n_i^a \log\left(\frac{n_i^a}{n}\right) + \sum_{j=1}^{k_b} n_j^b \log\left(\frac{n_j^b}{n}\right)} \tag{1}$$

where n is the total number of samples and n_{ij}^{ab} denotes the number of shared patterns between clusters $C_i^a \in P^a$ and $C_j^b \in P^b$; n_i^a is the number of patterns in the cluster i of partition a; also n_j^b are the number of patterns in the cluster j of partition b.

This computation is done between the cluster C_i and all partitions available in the reference set. Fig. 2 shows this method.

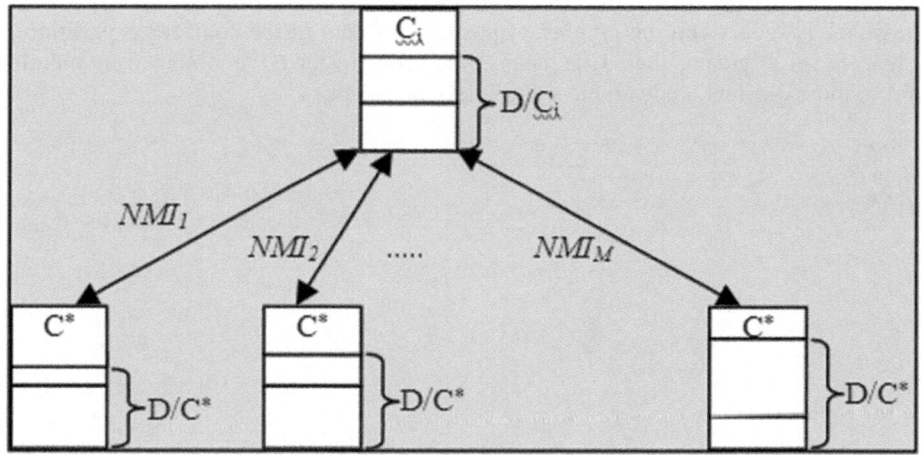

Fig. 2. Computing the Stability of Cluster C_i

NMI_i in Fig. 2 shows the stability of cluster C_i with respect to the i-th partition in reference set. The total stability of cluster C_i is defined as:

$$Stability(C_i) = \frac{1}{M}\sum_{i=1}^{M} NMI_i \qquad (2)$$

where M is the number of partitions available in reference set. This procedure is applied for each cluster of every primary partition.

2.2   Cluster Validation Criterion

In this section a drawback of computing stability is introduced and an alternative approach is suggested which is named Max method. Fig. 3 shows two primary partitions for which the stability of each cluster is evaluated. In this example K-means is applied as the base clustering algorithm with K=3. For this example the number of all partitions in the reference set is 40. In 36 partitions the result is relatively similar to Fig 3a, but there are four partitions in which the top left cluster is divided into two clusters, as shown in Fig 3b. Fig 3a shows a true clustering. Since the well separated cluster in the top left corner is repeated several times (90% repetition) in partitionings of the reference set, it has to acquire a great stability value (but not equal to 1), however it acquires the stability value of 1. Because the two clusters in right hand of Fig 3a are relatively joined and sometimes they are not recognized in the reference set as well, they have less stability value. Fig. 3.b shows a spurious clustering which the two right clusters are incorrectly merged. Since a fixed number of clusters is forced in the base algorithm, the top left cluster is divided into two clusters. Here the drawback of the stability measure is apparent rarely. Although it is obvious that this partition and the corresponding large cluster on the right reference set (10% repetition), the stability of this cluster is evaluated equal to 1. Since the NMI is a symmetric equation, the stability of the top left cluster in fig 3.a is exactly equal to the large right cluster in fig 3.b; however they are repeated 90% and 10%, respectively. In other words, when two clusters are complements of each other, their stabilities are always equal. This drawback is seen when the number of positive clusters in the considered partition of reference set is greater than 1. It means when the cluster $C*$ is obtained by merging two or more clusters, undesirable stability effects occur.

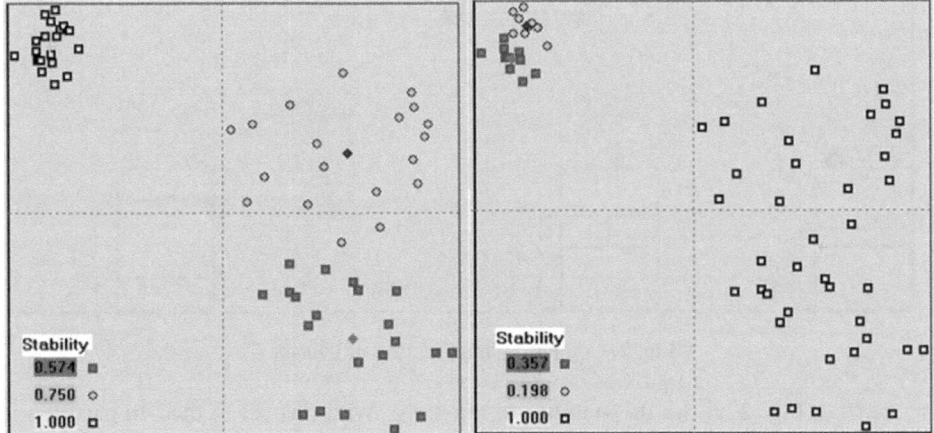

Fig. 3. Two primary partitions with k=3. (a) True clustering. (b) Spurious clustering.

To solve this problem we allow only one cluster in reference set to be considered as the $C*$ (i.e. only the most similar cluster) and all others are considered as $D/C*$. In this method the problem is solved by eliminating the merged clusters.

2.3   Consensus Function

In this step, the selected clusters are used to construct the co-association matrix. In the EAC method the m primary results from resampled data are accumulated in an $n \times n$ co-association matrix. Each entry in this matrix is computed from this equation:

$$C(i, j) = \frac{n_{i,j}}{m_{i,j}} \qquad (3)$$

where n_{ij} counts the number of clusters shared by objects with indices i and j in the partitions over the primary B clusterings. Also m_{ij} is the number of partitions where this pair of objects is simultaneously present. There are only a fraction of all primary clusters available, after thresholding. So, the common EAC method cannot truly recognize the pairwise similarity for computing the co-association matrix. In our novel method (Extended Evidence Accumulation Clustering, or EEAC) each entry of the co-association matrix is computed by:

$$C(i, j) = \frac{n_{i,j}}{\max(n_i, n_j)} \tag{4}$$

where n_i and n_j are the number present in remaining (after stability thresholding) clusters for the i-th and j-th data points, respectively. Also, n_{ij} counts the number of remaining clusters which are shared by both data points indexed by i and j, respectively.

3   Experimental Results

This section reports and discusses the empirical studies. The proposed method is examined over 5 different standard datasets. It is tried for datasets to be diverse in their number of true classes, features and samples. A large variety in used datasets can more validate the obtained results. Brief information about the used datasets is available in Table 1. More information is available in [13].

Table 1. Brief information about the used datasets

	Class	Features	Samples
Glass	6	9	214
Breast-C	2	9	683
Wine	3	13	178
Bupa	2	6	345
Yeast	10	8	1484

All experiments are done over the normalized features. It means each feature is normalized with mean of 0 and variance of 1, N(0, 1). All of them are reported over means of 10 independent runs of algorithm. The final performance of the clustering algorithms is evaluated by re-labeling between obtained clusters and the ground truth labels and then counting the percentage of the true classified samples. Table 2 shows the performance of the proposed method comparing with most common base and ensemble methods.

Table 2. Experimental results

Dataset	Simple Methods (%)				Ensemble Methods (%)			
	Single Linkage	Average Linkage	Complete Linkage	Kmeans	Kmeans Ensemble	Full Ensemble	Cluster Selection by NMI Method	Cluster Selection by max Method
Breast-C	65.15	70.13	94.73	95.37	95.46	95.10	95.75	**96.49**
Wine	37.64	38.76	83.71	96.63	96.63	97.08	**97.75**	97.44
Yeast	34.38	35.11	38.91	40.20	45.46	47.17	47.17	**51.27**
Glass	36.45	37.85	40.65	45.28	47.01	47.83	**48.13**	47.35
Bupa	57.68	57.10	55.94	54.64	54.49	55.83	58.09	**58.40**

The four first columns of Table 2 are the results of some base clustering algorithms. The results show that although each of these algorithms can obtain a good result over a specific dataset, it does not perform well over other datasets. For example, according to Table 2 the K-means algorithm has a good clustering result over Wine dataset in comparison with linkage methods. But, it has lower performance in comparison to linkage methods in the case of Bupa dataset. Also, the complete linkage has a good performance in Breast-Cancer dataset in comparison with others; however it is not in the case of all datasets. The four last columns show the performance of some ensemble methods in comparison with the proposed one. Taking a glance at the last four columns in comparison with the first four columns shows that the ensemble methods do better than the simple based algorithms in the case of performance and robustness along with different datasets. The first column of the ensemble methods is the results of an ensemble of 100 K-means which is fused by EAC method. The 90% sampling from dataset is used for creating diversity in primary results. The sub-sampling (without replacement) is used as the sampling method. Also the random initialization of the seed points of K-means algorithm helps them to be more diverse. The average linkage algorithm is applied as consensus function for deriving the final clusters from co-association matrix. The second column from ensemble methods is the full ensemble which uses several clustering algorithms for generating the primary results. Here, 70 K-means with the above mentioned parameters in addition to 30 linkage methods provide the primary results. The third column of the ensemble methods is consensus partitioning using EEAC algorithm of top 33% stable clusters, employing NMI method as measure of stability. The fourth column of the ensemble methods is Also consensus partitioning using EEAC algorithm of top 33% stable clusters, employing max method as measure of stability.

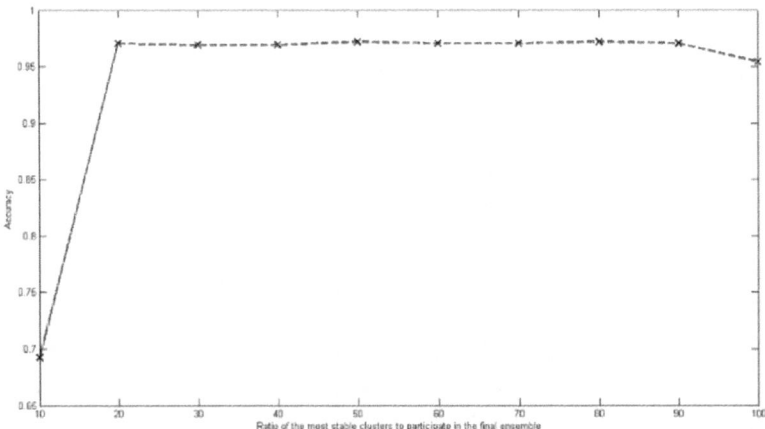

Fig. 4. Two primary partitions with k=3. (a) True clustering. (b) Spurious clustering.

To better understand the effect of proposed clustering ensemble framework, consider Fig. 4 which is different accuracies of the consensus partitions obtained out of different ratios of the most stable clusters in Breast-C dataset. In Fig. 4, the different size of the most stable clusters in terms of max metric are selected to participate in final ensemble. The accuracy of consensus partition extracted out of the selected clusters is presented in vertical axis. As it is obvious participating 20~30% of total clusters in the final ensemble is a very promising option. Also participation all clusters is not a good option.

4   Conclusion and Future Works

In this paper a new clustering ensemble framework is proposed which is based on a subset of total primary spurious clusters. Also a new alternative method for common NMI is suggested. Since the quality of the primary clusters are not equal and presence of some of them can even yield to lower performance, here a method to select a subset of more effective clusters is proposed. A common cluster validity criterion which is needed to derive this subset is based on normalized mutual information. In this paper some drawbacks of this criterion is discussed and an method is suggested which is called max mehod. The experiments show that the proposed framework commonly outperforms in comparison with the full ensemble; however it uses just 50% of primary clusters. Another innovation of this chapter is a method for constructing the co-association matrix where some of clusters and respectively some of samples do not exist in partitions. This new method is called Extended Evidence Accumulation Clustering, EEAC.

References

1. Ayad, H., Kamel, M.S.: Cumulative Voting Consensus Method for Partitions with a Variable Number of Clusters. IEEE Trans. on Pattern Analysis and Machine Intelligence 30(1), 160–173 (2008)
2. Bhatia, S.K., Deogun, J.S.: Conceptual Clustering in Information Retrieval. IEEE Trans. Systems, Man, and Cybernetics 28(3), 427–536 (1998)
3. Faceli, K., Marcilio, C.P., Souto, D.: Multi-objective Clustering Ensemble. In: Proceedings of the Sixth International Conference on Hybrid Intelligent Systems (HIS 2006) (2006)
4. Fern, X.Z., Lin, W.: Cluster Ensemble Selection. In: SIAM International Conference on Data Mining (SDM 2008) (2008)
5. Fred, A., Jain, A.K.: Data Clustering Using Evidence Accumulation. In: Proc. of the 16th Intl. Conf. on Pattern Recognition, ICPR 2002, Quebec City, pp. 276–280 (2002)
6. Fred, A., Jain, A.K.: Combining Multiple Clusterings Using Evidence Accumulation. IEEE Trans. on Pattern Analysis and Machine Intelligence 27(6), 835–850 (2005)
7. Fred, A., Jain, A.K.: Learning Pairwise Similarity for Data Clustering. In: Proc. of the 18th Int. Conf. on Pattern Recognition (ICPR 2006) (2006)
8. Fred, A., Lourenco, A.: Cluster Ensemble Methods: from Single Clusterings to Combined Solutions. SCI, vol. 126, pp. 3–30 (2008)
9. Frigui, H., Krishnapuram, R.: A Robust Competitive Clustering Algorithm with Applications in Computer Vision. IEEE Trans. Pattern Analysis and Machine Intelligence 21(5), 450–466 (1999)
10. Judd, D., Mckinley, P., Jain, A.K.: Large-Scale Parallel Data Clustering. IEEE Trans. Pattern Analysis and Machine Intelligence 19(2), 153–158 (1997)

11. Lange, T., Braun, M.L., Roth, V., Buhmann, J.M.: Stability-based model selection. In: Advances in Neural Information Processing Systems, vol. 15. MIT Press (2003)
12. Law, M.H.C., Topchy, A.P., Jain, A.K.: Multiobjective data clustering. In: Proc. of IEEE Conference on Computer Vision and Pattern Recognition, vol. 2, pp. 424–430 (2004)
13. Newman, C.B.D.J., Hettich, S., Merz, C.: UCI repository of machine learning databases (1998), http://www.ics.uci.edu/~mlearn/MLSummary.html
14. Roth, V., Lange, T., Braun, M., Buhmann, J.: A Resampling Approach to Cluster Validation. In: Intl. Conf. on Computational Statistics, COMPSTAT (2002)
15. Strehl, A., Ghosh, J.: Cluster ensembles - a knowledge reuse framework for combining multiple partitions. Journal of Machine Learning Research 3, 583–617 (2002)
16. Parvin, H., Helmi, H., Minaei-Bidgoli, B., Alinejad, H., Shirgahi, H.: Linkage Learning Based on Differences in Local Optimums of Building Blocks with One Optima. International Journal of the Physical Sciences, IJPS, 3419–3425 (2011)

3D Machine Vision Employing
Optical Phase Shift Moiré

Fatemeh Mohammadi[1], Amir Hossein Rezaie[1], and Khosro Madanipour[2]

[1] Automation and Intelligent Monitoring Systems Research lab, Electrical Department,
Amirkabir University of Technology, Hafez Street, Tehran, Iran
`f_mohammadi_e@yahoo.com, rezaie@aut.ac.ir`
[2] Optical Measurement Lab & Optics Research Group, Amirkabir University of Technology,
Hafez Street, Tehran, Iran
`madanipour@aut.ac.ir`

Abstract. The aim of this paper is 3D machine vision of surface based on optical phase shift Moiré. In measurement process we generate Moiré contours on a surface by using shadow moiré technique. The current work use phase shift analysis in order to increase the accuracy of measurement and extract the 3D profile of surface. In comparison with recent methods this technique is simple and easy to implement. In order to show validity and feasibility of this method, we apply it on a human face. The feedbacks indicate that this technique is low cost, simple and powerful method in 3D reconstruction of every surface without any disturbance.

Keywords: 3D machine vision, 3D reconstruction of human face, shadow Moiré, phase shift analysis, 2D phase unwrapping.

1 Introduction

3D model of a surface can be captured using different methods including: Coordinate Measuring Machine (CMM), laser scanning, stereo vision, lines projection etc. Each method has its own advantages and disadvantages.

For example CMM has good accuracy but it is so expensive. Moreover it needs to contact with object that it is not good for fragile surface like historical objects or human face. Besides it measures the height point by point, so it is time consuming.

3D laser scanner is an active scanner that uses laser light to probe the subject. This technique is valid and reliable, but also more expensive and slower to use. Moreover, we have to use low power lasers in order to reduce its disturbing influence on surfaces like human face.

Another method is stereo vision, which utilizes two cameras. This method is based on camera calibration, establishing point correspondences between pairs of points from the left and the right image and reconstruction of the 3D coordinates of the points in the scene. The main drawback of this technique is that it has complicated computation in order to find the corresponding pairs and it needs two cameras.

Lines projection is another method that needs a video projector in order to cast lines pattern on the surface. In comparison with Moiré, it is unable to show the

P. Pichappan, H. Ahmadi, and E. Ariwa (Eds.): INCT 2011, CCIS 241, pp. 225–234, 2011.
© Springer-Verlag Berlin Heidelberg 2011

topography of surface without processing of patterns. While by using Moiré technique we could see the topography of surface directly by viewing the patterns.

Moiré effect is one of powerful technique in displaying and measuring the form of the object in three dimensions. Moiré topography allows the shape of objects and deformations to be measured without contact. Moreover its measurement is whole field that has advantage over point to point methods. Besides, data acquisition and processing is relatively fast, so it can be done in real time and automated process. In addition in comparison with other methods, this technique is so simple and fast to operate in retrieving the 3D profile of surface [1].

In this study we use shadow Moiré technique in order to generate Moiré contours on the test surface. After generating Moiré fringe on surface we captured the contours with a digital camera. In order to retrieve information of surface's heights, we need to extract the phase map from captured images. The methods to retrieve phase map generally divided into two categories: Fourier transform and phase shift analysis [2].

Fourier transform method usually used for open fringe pattern like structured light or lines projection pattern [3]. This method caused phase jump when it used for closed fringe, so it needs another frame with phase shift to correct this ambiguity [4].

The simplest method to extract phase map from closed fringe is phase shift analysis. In this method three or more phase stepped images are needed [5].The main advantage of the phase-shifting technique is its high spatial resolution, accuracy and dynamic range but the main drawbacks are the sensitivity to noise and the degrading effect of higher frequency components. Moreover because of using at least three frames from object, the implementation of phase shift technique is impossible for dynamic objects.

Digital phase shift Moiré instead of optical phase shift Moiré is a good solution for this problem [6]. Based on digital phase shift technique we omit any physical translation. In addition we could apply phase shift technique in every moving object.

In order to generating Moiré contour on object based on digital phase shift technique, at first we project line pattern on the test surface. Then in computer we generate a virtual lines pattern that has the same pitch as the reference lines pattern used in experimental setup. Finally superimposition of virtual line pattern with captured image generates Moiré pattern on the object. By shifting the virtual pattern up and down on the captured image the phase shift will be achieved numerically.

So this technique could reconstruct 3D profilometry of dynamic objects based on phase shift technique just by a frame [7].

In Phase Shifting method, some modified images of the same surface are used. The question returns to the method of generation of that phase shifting. Based on optical phase shift Moiré, the phase shift image is generated by physical displacement of grid. So by approaching or receding of grid to the test surface we could generate phase shift in every frame optically [8]. Finally the phase map which consist height information of surface is extracted based on phase shift technique.

Because of arc tan function has a range between π and $-\pi$, phase shift method gives the phase wrapped in this range. Eventually by applying efficient 2D phase unwrapping algorithms, the 3D profile of the test surface can be reconstructed.

In phase unwrapping procedure we could remove the discontinuity of wrapped phase and obtain a continuous phase map. The 2D phase unwrapping algorithms divided into two categories: local and global algorithms. In current work we use weighted least square phase unwrapping algorithm which is belong to global algorithms and well discussed in [9].

The paper is organized as follow. In section 2.1 the principle of shadow Moiré is described in details. In Section 2.2 we review phase shift analysis for extraction of wrapped phase map. In Section 3, we implement the proposed method on a complex object like human face.

2   Methodology

2.1   Principle of Shadow Moiré

The Moiré effect is a fascinating visual display that often occurs when two periodic patterns are overlaid [10]. The image of Moiré fringe on the object can be used directly to check for surface features and three dimensional plot of the object. The ways of generating Moiré patterns on the test surface can be divided into two main categories: projection Moiré and shadow Moiré [1].

In projection Moiré a pair of line gratings is used; one is called the projection grating which is in front of light source and the other is viewing grating which is in front of digital camera. The line pattern of the projection grating is cast on the object and its deformed lines pattern is imaged back on the viewing grating. The superimposition of deformed line pattern and viewing grating, generate Moiré pattern on the test object. In comparison with shadow Moiré the projection Moiré could be applied on large objects. Fig.1 demonstrates the optical configuration of implementing projection Moiré [11].

In shadow Moiré technique, only one linear amplitude grating is placed just in front of the object under study and is obliquely illuminated. The shadow, in the form of grid, cast on the object is viewed through the grid itself. Beating will occur between the special frequency of the shadow grid and the grid itself, resulting in the formation of Moiré fringe. Fig.2 shows the optical setup of shadow Moiré. In this figure α, β are light incidence and light reflection angel, P is grating pitch and W is distance between grid and surface.

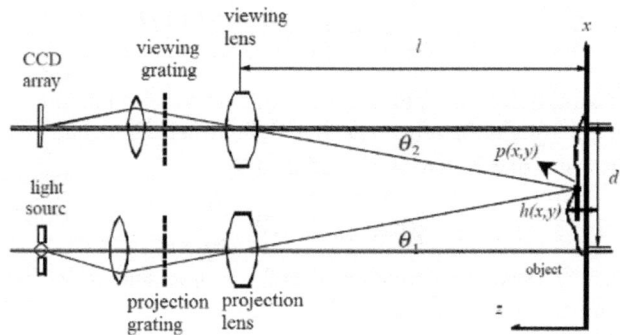

Fig. 1. Optical setup for projection Moiré

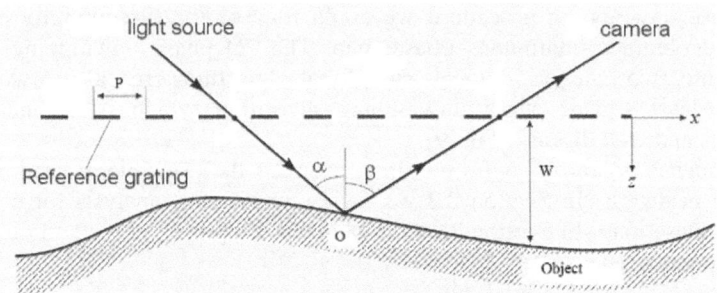

Fig. 2. Optical setup for shadow Moiré

The main advantage of shadow Moiré over projection Moiré is its simplicity and easy to implement. So in this paper we use shadow moiré in order to retrieve the 3D profilometry of complex object like human face.

2.2   Optical Phase Shift Technique

After capturing Moiré fringe on the surface, we could use different image processing techniques for reconstruction of 3D profile of surface. In order to reconstruct 3D profile of the object, we need to extract phase information from captured image. Phase shifting and Fourier transform are two commonly used techniques for retrieving phase. Fourier Transform analysis is the most famous technique which in close pattern, it caused phase jump and needs additional frame to correct [4]. Among different techniques in fringe analysis we use phase shift analysis which is able to analysis both open and close fringe without any phase jump.

The fringes intensity on the test surface is given by Equation (1):

$$I(x, y) = A(x, y) \times \{1 + V(x, y)\cos[\varphi(x, y)]\} \tag{1}$$

Where the phase $\varphi(x, y)$ contains the desired information of surface, $A(x,y)$ and $V(x,y)$ represent background illumination and visibility of fringe pattern.

Based on geometrical analysis and optical setup in Fig.2, the phase of surface $\varphi(x, y)$ is:

$$\varphi(x, y) = 2\pi W \frac{\tan \hat{\alpha} + \tan \hat{\beta}}{P} \tag{2}$$

For the sake of simplicity, we put the camera's axis perpendicular to master grid which is shown in Fig. 3. In this way, the light reflection angle in the observer's direction becomes zero and Equation (2) reduced to:

$$\varphi(x, y) = 2\pi W \frac{b}{Ph} \tag{3}$$

Where b is distance between camera and light source and h is distance between camera and grating.

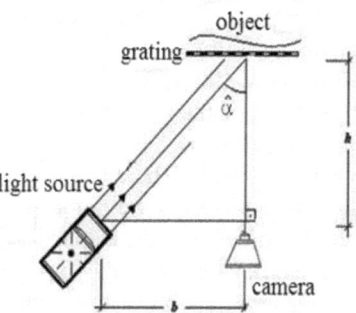

Fig. 3. Experimental arrangement in shadow Moiré

In phase shifting method, three or more phase stepped images are needed [12]. For capturing each frame we should shift the Moiré contours on the object. There are different ways to shift the phase but only by Equation (4) the phase shift is same in all points of the surface [8].

$$\delta\varphi(x, y) = 2\pi \frac{b}{Ph} \delta W \tag{4}$$

Equation (4) indicates that to generate phase shift on each frame, we should change the distance of object with grating. The principle of phase shifting method based on three frames is as follow [13]:

$$I_1(x, y) = a(x, y) + b(x, y)\cos(\varphi(x, y)) \tag{5}$$

$$I_2(x, y) = a(x, y) + b(x, y)\cos(\delta\varphi_{12} + \varphi(x, y)) \tag{6}$$

$$I_3(x, y) = a(x, y) + b(x, y)\cos(\delta\varphi_{13} + \varphi(x, y)) \tag{7}$$

I_1, I_2 and I_3 are intensity distribution of three frame with phase shift. Based on these three frames, phase map could be extracted according to Equation (8):

$$\varphi(x, y) = Tan^{-1}\frac{(I_3 - I_2) - (I_1 - I_2)\cos\delta\varphi_{13} + (I_1 - I_3)\cos\delta\varphi_{12}}{(I_1 - I_2)\sin\delta\varphi_{13} - (I_1 - I_3)\sin\delta\varphi_{12}} \tag{8}$$

Because of arc tan function has a range between π and -π, the result phase is discontinued in this range. Therefore unwrapping phase procedure is inevitable. By applying efficient 2D phase unwrapping algorithms, 3D profile of the test surface can be reconstructed.

The 2D phase unwrapping algorithm is generally divided into two categories: local and global phase unwrapping techniques. Local algorithms unwrap the phase, pixel by pixel based on guidance path [14-16] while global algorithms, unwrap all pixels simultaneously by using cosine transform. The main disadvantages of local methods are error propagation along the guidance path so the unwrapped phase varies in different paths.

In this paper we use global phase unwrapping algorithms due to its high speed and minimum propagation of error. Least square phase unwrapping, established by

Ghiglia and Romero, is one of the most robust technique to solve the two dimensional phase unwrapping problem. This algorithm is well discussed in [9]. The procedure is to minimize the least squared distance (the squared difference) between the estimated phase gradient and the true gradient of the unknown unwrapped phase. In this way, we could achieve a smooth unwrapped phase.

When the wrapped phase is too noisy, it is better to use weighted least square phase unwrapping. In this algorithm we multiply a weighted matrix to the wrapped phase and then use iterative methods to extract unwrapped phase. There are different methods to calculate the weighted matrix but the best one is derivative variance correlation map [17]. Preventing propagation of error through the whole phase and rectification of phase in noisy area are two important characteristic of weighted least square phase unwrapping algorithm.

3   Experimental Results

The exprimental demonstration includes the 3D recounstruction of human face based on optical Moiré technique. Fig. 4 demonstrates the optical configuration of implementing shadow Moiré. In this study we use shadow Moiré technique in order to generate Moiré contours on the test surface. Our setup consists of a linear grid, two light sources and digital camera. Superimposition of grid itself with its shadow on the surface generate Moiré fringe on the surface.

In this method, measuring resolution can be readily adjusted to suit the measurement precision by varying the line pitch of the gratings and geometry of optical system.

In this setup a line grating with the pitch of 2milimeter is placed in front of mannequin face. Fig. 5 shows the Moiré countors based on one and two light sources. By using two light sources arranged symmetrically about camera, shadow free illumination is possible [18].

Moiré fringes are contours with equal heights on the surface. These contours are generated based on superimposition of shadow of grating on the object and grating itself. In this setup we use halogen lamp 50W. The distance between camera and light source is b=50cm and the distance between camera and grating is h=100cm. In order to generate phase shift on each farme, we use a XYZ positioner for changing distance between grating and surface.

Fig. 4. Experimental arrangement in shadow Moiré technique

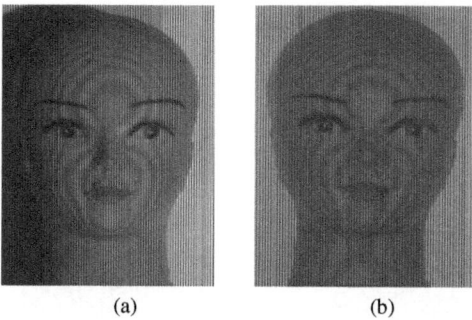

(a)   (b)

Fig. 5. Moiré pattern on human face based on (a) one light source. (b) Two light sources arranged symmetrically.

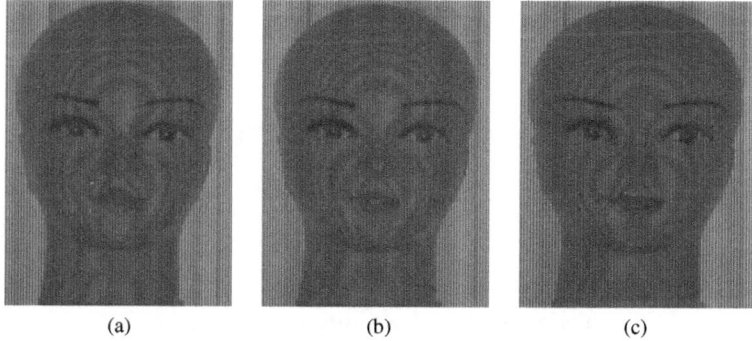

(a)   (b)   (c)

Fig. 6. Phase shift images (a) $\delta\varphi = 0$, (b) $\delta\varphi_{12} = {}^{2\pi}\!/_3$, (c) $\delta\varphi_{13} = {}^{4\pi}\!/_3$

To produce the favorite phase shift ($\delta\varphi(x, y)$), we can calculate the amount of translation of grid from human face (δW) based on Equation. 4. Fig. 6 shows three images with $2\pi/3$ phase shift in each frame. We can see the phase shift in each frame by concentrating in forehead and chin.

In order to remove grating line and extracting Moiré contours we have to remove inevitable noise in preprocessing stage. This procedure could be done by a 2D low pass filter.

After capturing all three farmes with phase shift, we could extract wrapped phase map based on Equation. 8. Fig. 7 demonstrates wrapped phase map which extracted based on three phase shift technique. As shown in Fig. 7(a) the extracted phase is discontinuous between π and $-\pi$, hence implementing 2D phase unwrapping algorithm is necessary.

Because the extracted wrapped phase is too noisy, using weighted matrix is absolutely essential to underestimate true phase in noisy area. Eventually by applying weighted least square phase unwrapping algorithm we could achieve the continuous phase map . However, the success of such a method relies on choosing the weights, which puts a huge load on the performance of this algorithm. In this paper, the

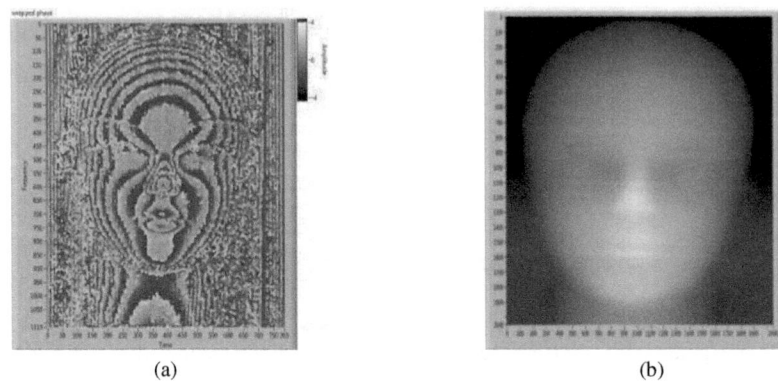

(a)   (b)

Fig. 7. (a) Wrapped phase map (b) Unwrapped phase map

Fig. 8. 3D view of reconstructed human face

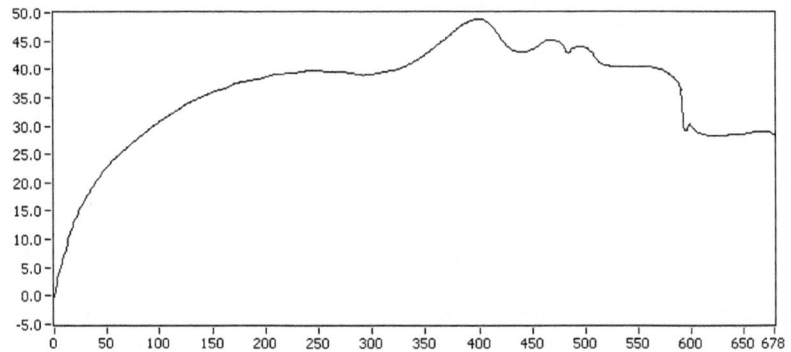

Fig. 9. A cross section of reconstructed 3D profile of human face

weighting coefficient is derived from a derivative variance correlation map. Fig. 7(b) represent unwrapped phase map. The 3D reconstruction of human face in different view is represented in Fig. 8. Finally the cross section of 3D reconstruction of human face is shown in Fig. 9.

4   Conclusion

In this research a powerful optical technique based on phase shift Moiré was developed for 3D machine vision. The principle of this technique was described and implemented on a complex object like human face. The results is carried out to validity of propose method.

3D machine visions based on recent methods has lots of problem and disturb the surface, while a Moiré vision system would solve many of these problems. The main advantage of this method is simplicity and low cost, so it could be applied easily in every surface.

This technique could provide a feasible possibility in providing 3D machine vision for diversity task such as role to role inspection in industry, intelligent robot and pattern recognition.

References

1. Patorski, K., Kujawinska, M.: Handbook of the Moiré Fringe Technique. Elsevier (1993)
2. Hu, Q., Harding, K.G.: Science, Conversion from phase map to coordinate: Comparison among spatial carrier, Fourier transform, and phase shifting methods. Optics and Lasers in Engineering 45(2), 342–348 (2007)
3. Mohammadi, F., Madanipour, K., Rezaie, A.H.: Three dimensional surface topography based on digital fringe projection. In: Optical Metrology in Videometrics, Range Imaging, and Applications section of SPIE, vol. 8085, 80850W, pp. 80850W-1–80850W-8
4. Kreis, T.: Digital holographic interference-phase measurement using the Fourier-transform method. J. Optical Society of America 3(6) (June 1986)
5. Tay, C.J., Quan, C., Chen, L.: Phase retrieval with a three-frame phase-shifting algorithm with an unknown phase shift. Applied Optics 44(8), 1401–1409 (2005)
6. Mohammadi, F., Madanipour, K., Rezaie, A.H.: Application of digital phase shift Moiré to reconstruction of human face. In: UKSim 4th European Modeling Symposium on Mathematical Modeling and Computer Simulation, pp. 306–309 (2010)
7. Zhang, S.: Recent progresses on real-time 3D shape measurement using digital fringe projection techniques. Optics and Lasers in Engineering 40, 149–158 (2010)
8. Neto, P.S., Coelho, G.C.: The Shadow Moiré method using the phase shifting technique and digital image processing: computational implementation and application to the 3D-reconstruction of a buckled plate. J. Braz. Soc. Mech. Sci. 22(3) (2000)
9. Ghiglia, D.C., Romero, L.A.: Robust two-dimensional weighted and unweighted phase unwrapping that uses fast transforms and iterative methods. J. Opt. Soc. Am. 11(1), 107–117 (1994)
10. Creath, K., Wyant, J.C.: Moiré and Fringe Projection Techniques. John Wiley & Sons, Inc. (1992)
11. Oh, J.-T., Lee, S.-Y., Kim, S.-W.: Scanning Projection Grating Moiré Topography (2008)
12. Magalhaes Jr., P.A.A., Neto, P.S., De Barcellos, C.S.: Phase shifting technique using generalization of carre algorithm with many image. Optical Review 16(4), 432–441 (2009)
13. Hu, Y., Xi, J., Chichar, J., Yang, Z.: Improved three-step phase shifting profilometry using digital fringe pattern. In: International Conference on Computer Graphics, Imaging and Visualization (CGIV 2006). IEEE (2006)

14. Su, X., Chen, W.: Reliability-guided phase unwrapping algorithm: a review. Optics and Lasers in Engineering 42(3), 245–261 (2004)
15. Asundi, A., Wensen, Z.: Fast phase-unwrapping algorithm based on a gray-scale mask and flood fill. Applied Optics 37(23), 5416–5420 (1998)
16. Lo, C.F., Peng, X., Cai, L.: Surface normal guided method for two-dimensional phase unwrapping. International Journal for Light and Electron Optics, Optik 113(10), 439–447 (2002)
17. Lu, Y., Wang, X., Zhang, X.: Weighted least squares phase unwrapping algorithm based on derivative variance correlation map. Optik, 62–66 (2007)
18. Takasaki, H.: Moiré Topography. Appl. Opt. 9(6), 1467–1472 (1970)

Farsi Font Recognition Using Holes of Letters and Horizontal Projection Profile

Yaghoub Pourasad[1], Houshang Hassibi[1], and Azam Ghorbani[2]

[1] Department of electrical and computer engineering,
K.N. Toosi University of Technology, Tehran, Iran
{dpoorasad,Hassibi}@eetd.kntu.ac.ir
[2] Department of engineering, Islamic Azad University, Saveh branch, Saveh, Iran
a.ghorbani@iau-saveh.ac.ir

Abstract. In spite of important role of font recognition in document image analysis, only a few researchers have addressed the issue. This work presents a new approach for font recognition of Farsi document images. In this approach using two types of features, font and font size of Farsi document images are recognized. The first feature is related to holes of letters of text of document image. The second feature is related to horizontal projection profile of text lines of document image. This approach has been applied on 7 widely used Farsi fonts and 7 font sizes. A dataset of 10*49 images and another dataset of 110 images were used for testing and recognition rate more than 93.7% obtained. Images have been made using paint software and are noiseless and without skew. This approach is fast and is applicable for other languages that are similar to Farsi, such as Arabic language.

Keywords: Farsi Font Recognition, Document Image, Horizontal Projection Profile, Holes of Letters.

1 Introduction

There are many text documents which have been scanned and stored electronically in digital libraries. These imaged documents are simply presented as raw bit maps and this leads to some difficulties in document retrieval. One way to overcome this problem is OCR (Optical character Recognition). An OCR system consists of several modules that one of them is character recognition. There are many researches on Farsi OCR such as [1]. It is clear that understanding the font and font size of text of document image, can help us to have better results in character recognition and retrieval systems. Although there has been a great attempt in producing Omni-font OCR systems for Farsi/Arabic language [2, 3], the overall performance of such systems are far from perfect. The field of text font recognition in document images especially in Farsi language is new and needs more attention. There are two common approaches in font recognition field: first is based on typographical features and second is based on textural features. In the first approach, features like character weights, space width and various projections are used. Whereas in second approach textural features are extracted using wavelet transform, Gabor filter or other

P. Pichappan, H. Ahmadi, and E. Ariwa (Eds.): INCT 2011, CCIS 241, pp. 235–243, 2011.
© Springer-Verlag Berlin Heidelberg 2011

techniques. In [4] an approach for the recognition of Farsi fonts is proposed. In this paper font recognition is performed in line level using a feature based on Sobel and Roberts gradients in 16 directions, called SRF. SRF is extracted as texture features for the recognition. This feature requires much less computation rather than other textural features and therefore can be extracted very faster than common textural features like Gabor filter, wavelet transform or momentum features. The reported recognition rate is about 94.2% using 5000 samples of 10 popular Farsi fonts. In [5] an approach for Arabic font recognition is presented. Their proposal is to use a fixed length sliding window for the feature extraction and to model feature distributions with Gaussian Mixture Models (GMMs). The main advantage of this approach is that a priori segmentation into characters is not necessary and the authors reports performances above 99% on a set of 9 different fonts and 10 different sizes. In [6] the use of global texture analysis for Farsi font recognition in machine-printed document images is examined. They consider document images as textures and use Gabor filter responses for identifying the fonts. Two different classifiers including Weighted Euclidean Distance (WED) and Support Vector Machine (SVM) is used for classification. Authors reported average accuracy of 85% with WED and 82% with SVM classifier on 7 different face types and 4 font styles.

All above references that are about font recognition [4, 5, 6], are font size independent and don't give information about font size of document. Although methods based on typographical features and approaches based on textural features are common methods, but there are a few other works that are different of these approaches. In [7] first, dots of document are extracted and size of dots is estimated using weighted sum variance. Then pen width is supposed to be nearly square of dot size. But for font size estimation as writers have noticed, there isn't fixed relation between pen width and font size; therefore they assumed an approximate relation between font size and pen width. This approach is fast but only estimates an approximate value for font size and doesn't recognize the font of text of document. In [8] first, second and third order moments of the input image are used as features and correlation coefficients are used to recognize Farsi fonts. As mentioned, one important part of any OCR system is recognition part, and one of tasks that is done in recognition module, is pen width calculation. The field of pen width calculation is near to the field of font size recognition and some approaches that are used in pen width calculation can be used in font size recognition. But it should be noted that with knowing the pen width, we only have an approximate value for font size. Because there isn't fixed relation between pen width and font size. So, many approaches directly find pen width and use it in recognition part, and then if it was required, can give an approximate value for font size. The most common method for finding pen width, is using horizontal or (and) vertical projection profile [9, 10] and obtaining base line or height of each line [8]. Anyway, these methods only calculate pen width and can give an approximate value for font size but don't recognize font of document.

In this work we don't calculate pen width to estimate font size. Our method directly calculates the font size and recognizes the font of Farsi document. In fact we use horizontal projection profile and size of bounding box of holes of words to recognize font and font size of Farsi document images.

In Farsi, there are more than 500 different fonts. Developing a system that considers all these fonts is difficult and useless. Therefore we concentrate on 7 widely used fonts and 7 different font sizes. 'Lotus', 'Nazanin',' Mitra','Yaghut',' Zar',' Koodak',' Homa' , are some of the most popular fonts in Farsi that we focused on them. The font sizes that we considered in this paper are, 8,10,12,14,16,18,20.

This paper is organized as follows. In section 2 dataset description, in section 3 feature extraction and in section 4 experimental results are presented and finally section 5 is conclusion.

2   Dataset Description

In this paper we constructed three sets of text document images. In first set we constructed 5 images for every state (one font of 7 fonts and one font size of 7 font sizes). We used this set to extract robust features for every state. In second set we constructed 10 images for every state. Second set is used for testing the system. In construction of both sets we tried to have images with different issues and different sizes (8, 10, 12, 14, 16, 18, and 20). For example we made images that their issues were about electronics, chemistry, sports, etc. In these images there are documents that have only a few lines and documents with more than 10 lines. For second set that is used for test, we constructed documents that were written in one state of 49 predefined states. In third set we constructed 110 images of fonts that aren't in one of predefined 49 states. In order to construct all three sets, first, we prepared a text in Microsoft word software. Then using print screen key of keyboard, a picture of that text was provided. After that, using paint software, we did necessary corrections and then saved it in bmp format. For all images these steps have been done.

3   Feature Extraction

A large number of Farsi alphabet letters have one or two holes. These holes have different shapes and sizes in different fonts and font sizes. Therefore with analyzing the holes of a document image we can approximately recognize the font and font size of that document image. In figure 1 some Farsi letters which have one or two holes, are showed. Another feature that can be helpful for font recognition of a text line, is horizontal projection profile of that text line. Several features can be extracted from horizontal projection profile of a text line. One of these features is the height of text line. Another feature can be the distance between top of text line and base line. Base line is part of a text line that the most letters of text line are written on it. Third feature is distance between bottom of text line and base line. We show this feature with D. Experimental results show that in Farsi documents, for every text line, third feature is more permanent and reliable than first and second features. It can be said that in absence of some especial letters such as (ح ، غ ، ق) for a text line, D is approximately half of font size of that text line. For example, for font size 8, D=4. Or for font size 10, often D=5. While extracting D features of text lines, states of existence of special letters (ح ،غ ،ق) must be considered. For example for text lines written in 'Nazanin 8' font, if there is one or more especial letters D=6 and else, D=4.

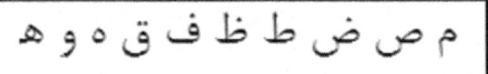

Fig. 1. Some letters that have hole

Another useful feature that can be extracted from horizontal projection profile of a text line is the location of second maximum or third maximum of projection profile related to the location of base line. In some fonts second maximum is above the base line whereas in some other fonts second maximum is under the base line. In some fonts especially in small fonts such as 8, 10, there is only one maximum in horizontal projection profile of a text line and that maximum is related to base line.

3.1   Holes of Letters Extraction

As mentioned before, we constructed 5 images for every state in set1. In order to H (holes) feature extraction of one state, all 5 images of that state, are binarized using threshold value of 1.4*K; Where K is threshold value that is obtained from Otsu global binarization method [11] and 1.4 is a selective value that has been obtained experimentally. In this method normalized histogram of an image is considered as a probability density function:

$$p(r_q) = \frac{n_q}{n} \qquad\qquad q= 0, 1, 2,\ldots, L\text{-}1$$

Where n is total number of image pixels, n_q is number of pixels having intensity level of r_q and L is number of intensity levels in an image. In order to obtain threshold value of K, it is considered that there exist two collections: collection C_0 with level values of $[0,1,2,\ldots,K\text{-}1]$ and collection C_1 with level values of $[K,K+1,\ldots,L\text{-}1]$. Value of K which for it inter class variance δ_B^2 be maximum, is answer as global thresholding value:

$$\delta_B^2 = \omega_0(\mu_0 - \mu_T)^2 + \omega_1(\mu_1 - \mu_T)^2 \tag{1}$$

$$\omega_0 = \sum_{q=0}^{K-1} p_q(r_q) \tag{2}$$

$$\mu_0 = \sum_{q=0}^{K-1} q p_q(r_q)/\omega_0 \tag{3}$$

$$\omega_1 = \sum_{q=K}^{L-1} p_q(r_q) \tag{4}$$

$$\mu_1 = \sum_{q=K}^{L-1} q p_q(r_q)/\omega_1 \tag{5}$$

$$\mu_T = \sum_{q=0}^{K-1} q p_q(r_q) \tag{6}$$

After transferring the gray scale document image to binary, holes of text of document are extracted and then connected component algorithm is applied. Then histogram of size of bounding box of holes is obtained. With analyzing all 5 histograms of one state, we can register all important sizes of holes as that state's H feature. In figure 2, a Farsi text document and its extracted holes are illustrated.

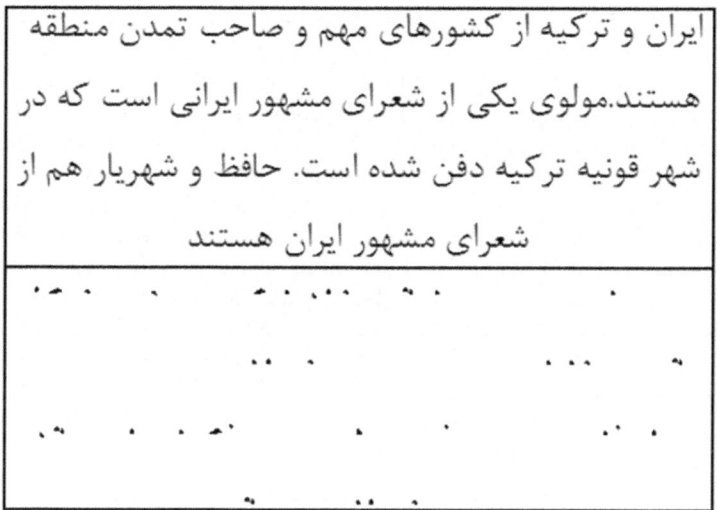

Fig. 2. A Farsi text document and its extracted holes

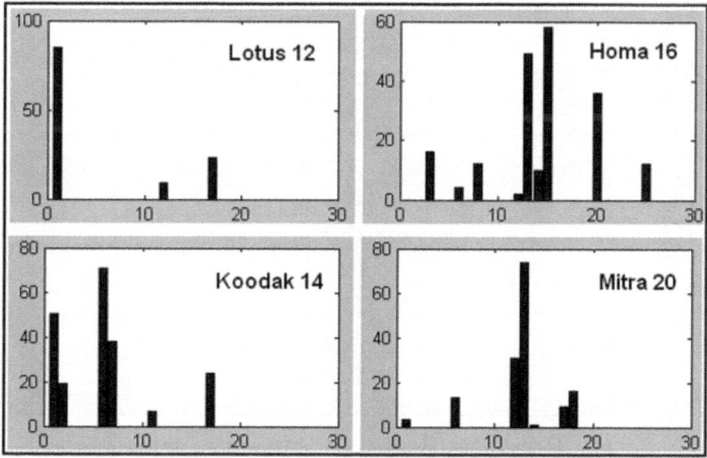

Fig. 3. Histogram of size of bounding box of 4 states

In figure 3 histogram of size of bounding box of 4 states are illustrated. As seen in the figure 3 size of bounding box of holes and consequently, histograms of them in different fonts and font sizes are different; thus we use this manner of fonts to describe them.

3.2   Projection Profile's Feature Extraction

To extract PP (projection profile) features of text lines of an image, after binarization step, horizontal projection profile of that document image is obtained. From resultant projection profile, location of text lines is determined. For all text lines of document

D is calculated. For each state of 49 states two value of D is registered; one with existence of special letters (ق ، ع ، ح) and another without existence of special letters.

Another feature that is registered for each state after horizontal projection profile is the number of maximums of projection profile and location of them rather than location of base line. Experimental results show text lines that are written in small fonts such as 8 and 10 only have one maximum in their horizontal projection profiles while larger fonts have two, three or more maximums. First order maximum (max1) projection profile corresponds to base line. Location of second order (max2) or third order maximum (max3) rather than location of base line is different in different fonts and font sizes. It means that in some fonts, max2 is above the base line but in other fonts max2 is under the base line. Same manner occurs for max3. In figure 4 horizontal projection profile (PP) of four different states is showed. In (d), PP of text lines of a document image written with font of 'Homa 14' is represented. This PP has one maximum. PP of (b) has three maximums. In (c) max2 is under the base line whereas in (a) max2 is above the base line.

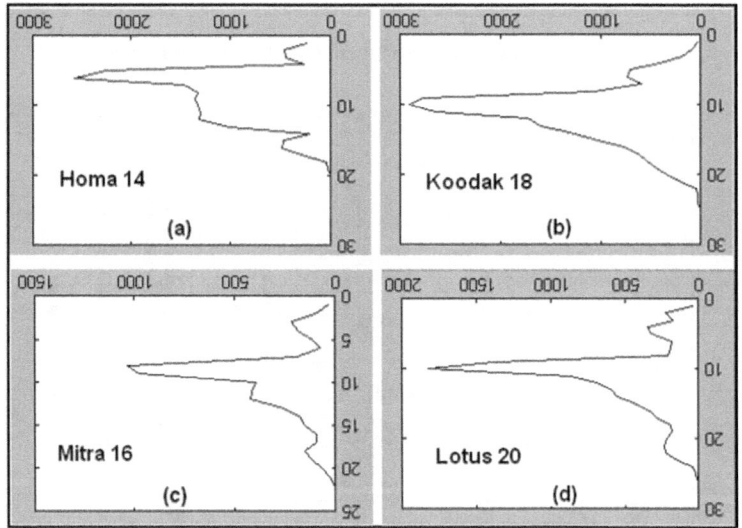

Fig. 4. Horizontal projection profile of four different states

For all 49 states that there are in set1, PP (projection profile) and H (letters' holes histogram) features extracted and registered. When a query document image is given to our font recognition system, PP and H features of it, is extracted and is compared with the features of 49 states that have been extracted and reserved before and if features of query be compatible with any of features of 49 states, font and font size of that query document image is recognized.

4   Experimental Results

In this approach all feature extraction and evaluating steps have been done using MATLAB software by a dual core 2.4 GHz Pentium PC. To test our approach, we first used set2. Testing results show that PP features for smaller fonts are more precision and reliable than larger fonts. Because in small fonts such as 8,10,existence of special letters (ق ، غ ، ح) increases only one or two pixels to D; whereas in bigger fonts such as 18 or 20, existence of those letters increases even up to 4 pixels to D. But in bigger font sizes, H feature is more helpful. Because in bigger font sizes holes won't be decomposed after binarization and almost all holes are extractable while in small font sizes such as 8 , holes are filled or broken after binarization and aren't extractable easily. In font size 8, even after holes extraction, almost all fonts present similar H features, hence only we can recognize font size but can't recognize font type. But for font sizes 12 and greater, font and font size is exactly recognizable.

While testing system, observed that fonts which substantially are thicker, such as 'Homa' and 'Koodak', present better results rather than substantially thin fonts such as 'Zar'; because in thick fonts holes of even small font sizes are easily extractable.

After testing system with set2, we used set3 for system testing. While testing, whether set2 or set3, four types of errors were observed:

Error1: Query image was from set2 but our system didn't recognize any state. Error2: Query was from set2 but system recognized an incorrect state from set2.

Error3: Query was from set2, system recognized an incorrect state in addition to correct state.

Error4: Query image was from set3, system instead of announcement of 'no font', recognized an incorrect state.

In table 1 number and percentage of each type of errors are showed. As seen in this table, our system error rate is 6.3% and recognition rate is 93.7%. Experimental results show that our approach is fast. Reason of this advantage is related to very few features that are considered for each state. For example for recognizing an A4 document which is full of text, less than 0.3 second is required. Our proposed method could recognize font face and font size of an A4 document image in about 210 ms but most of other papers aren't able to do in this time. For example if we use a 8-channel Gabor filter for font recognition, it requires 3.3s. Or in [7] required time for font estimation of an A4 document is about 1s. In [12] required time is about 0.51s. Experimental results show that our approach is fast. There are some reasons for this advantage. First reason is related to few features that are considered for each state. Because feature vector length of each state in this approach is utmost 10; whereas in [4] SRF feature length is 512 and length of textural features that are extracted with 8-channel Gabor filter are 256. Or in [13] each image is described with 644 features.

Table 1. Number and percentage of each type of errors

Error Type	Error Numbers	Error Percentage
Error 1	6/490	1.2%
Error 2	4/490	0.8%
Error 3	8/490	1.6%
Error 4	3/110	2.7%
Total Errors	21	6.3%

Another reason for high speed of this approach is that in this approach there is no need for word extraction, normalization, pen with calculation, or some time consuming operations such as convolution operations or other works that are done in textural methods. whatever the number of text lines and the words that have holes, be more, PP and H features will be more reliable and recognition rate will be better.

5   Conclusion

This paper is the first paper which recognizes font face and font size of a Farsi document image simultaneously. Most of the papers that are about font recognition are font size independent and only recognize the font but don't recognize the font size of the text of document image. Our approach recognizes both font face and font size of a document image. For this purpose we used two types of features which the first type of features are extracted with constructing and analyzing horizontal projection profile and the second type of features are related to size of bounding box of holes of document. We applied this approach on 7 widely used fonts and 7 font sizes and recognition rate of 93.7% obtained. Whatever the number of text lines and the words that have holes be more, used features will be more reliable and recognition rate will be better. This approach is fast and is applicable for other languages that are similar to Farsi, such as Arabic language.

References

1. Pourasad, Y., Hassibi, H., Banaeyan, M.: Persian Characters Recognition Based on Spatial Matching. International Review on Computers and Software (IRECOS) 6(1), 55–59 (2011)
2. Mehran, R., Pirsiavash, H., Razzazi, F.: A Font-end OCR for Omni-font Persian/Arabic Cursive Printed Documents. In: Proceedings of Digital Image Computing, Techniques and Applications (DICTA 2005), pp. 385–392 (2005)
3. Azmi, R., Kabir, E.: A New Segmentation Technique for Omni-font Farsi Text. Pattern Recognition Letters 22(2), 97–104 (2001)
4. Khosravi, H., Kabir, E.: Farsi font recognition based on sobel-roberts features. Pattern Recognition Letters 31(1), 75–82 (2010)
5. Slimane, F., Kanoun, S., Alimi, A.M., Ingold, R., Hennebert, J.: Gaussian Mixture Models for Arabic Font Recognition. In: International Conference on Pattern Recognition (2010)
6. Borji, A., Hamidi, M.: Support Vector Machine for Farsi font recognition. World Academi of Science, Engineering and Technology 28 (2007)
7. Shirali- Shahreza, M.H., Shirali-Shahreza, S.: Farsi/Arabic text font estimation using dots. In: IEEE International Symposium Signal Processing and Information Technology (2006)
8. Rashedi, E., Nezamabadi-Pour, H., Saryazdi, S.: Farsi Font Recognition Using Correlation Coefficients. In: 4th Conference on Machine Vision and Image Processing, Ferdosi Mashhad, Iran (2007) (in Farsi)
9. Omidyeganeh, M., Nayebi, K., Azmi, R., Javadtalab, A.: A New Segmentation Technique for Multi Font Farsi/Arabic Texts. In: Proceedings of IEEE International Conference on Acoustics, Speech, and Signal Processing (ICASSP 2005), vol. 2, pp. 757–760 (2005)

10. Bushofa, B.M.F., Span, M.: Segmentation of Arabic characters using their contour information. In: Proceedings of 13th International Conference on Digital Signal Processing Proceedings (DSP 1997), Greece, vol. 2, pp. 683–686 (1997)
11. Otsu, N.: A Threshold Selection Method for Gray-Level Histogram. IEEE Trans. on System Man Cybernetics SMC-9, 62–66 (1979)
12. Abuhaiba, I.S.I.: Arabic Font Recognition Using Decision Trees Built from Common Words. Journal of Computing and Information Technology 3, 211–223 (2005)
13. Zramdini, A., Ingold, R.: Optical Font Recognition Using Typographical Features. IEEE Trans. Pattern Anal. Machine Intell. 20, 877–882 (1998)

Gaze Interaction – A Challenge for Inclusive Design

Moyen Mustaquim

Department of Informatics and Media
Uppsala University
Box 513, 75120 Uppsala, Sweden
moyen.mustaquim@im.uu.se

Abstract. Gaze interaction for many people is the only means of communication because of extremely limited conditions like traumatic brain injuries, cerebral palsy to multiple sclerosis. No doubt it holds great undertake of the disable people while the 'design for all slogans' is highly supported by this feature. However, on the other hand people those who do not need such special need are intentionally excluded from using gaze technology even though a lot of promising research is being done in this field. There are several limitations and at present there is no model which can guide towards the design of sustainable, stable, eye tracking system for majority people. This paper examines such limitations of gaze interactions and proposes an accessibility passport model to overcome the challenges, thereby opening opportunity better design of gaze interaction for achieving universal and inclusive design.

Keywords: Universal Design, Inclusive Design, Gaze Interaction, Accessibility Passport.

1 Introduction

From simple day to day work like chatting or writing an email to advance work on computer, communication and interaction is the primary focus to the human understanding. To most of us entering text is as simple as typing on keyboard. To those suffering from physical disabilities, that same routine task may resent a significant challenge. Severe disabilities such as amyotrophic lateral sclerosis (ALS), cerebral palsy (CP), or locked-in syndrome (LIS) often lead to complete loss of control over voluntary muscles, except the eye muscles, rendering the individual paralyzed and mute[1]. Conventional physical interfaces, specialized switches, and voice recognition systems are not viable interaction solutions in these cases [1]. The eyes, therefore, become an important input modality to connect persons with a severe motor impairment to the digital world, and through the digital world to the friends, colleagues, and loved ones with whom they wish to communicate [1].

Nevertheless, as off today as it seems that the gaze interaction system is solely used and dedicatedly designed for the users with special needs. While one of the challenges of universal or inclusive design is to design for all or include all categories of users in a certain system design, that purpose is partially achieved so far by gaze interaction since it focuses on creating a communication means for disabled people.

P. Pichappan, H. Ahmadi, and E. Ariwa (Eds.): INCT 2011, CCIS 241, pp. 244–250, 2011.
© Springer-Verlag Berlin Heidelberg 2011

Consequently, according to the universal design or inclusive design metaphor, rest of the group of people who are not suffering from disabilities are excluded from using this technology, because of design issues, or other challenges. This paper explores such challenges which are originated from universal design principles and tries to map them in gaze interaction system design requirements for everyone, not just people with disabilities. An accessibility passport model is being proposed which can perhaps opens the door of opportunity to use gaze interaction system for people of different manner in today's society.

2   Inclusive Design

The British Standards Institute [2] defines inclusive design as "The design of mainstream products and/or services that are accessible to, and usable by, as many people as reasonably possible ... without the need for special adaptation or specialized design." By meeting the needs of those who are excluded from product use, inclusive design improves product experience across a broad range of users. Put simply, inclusive design is better design. Inclusive design should be embedded within the design and development process, resulting in better designed mainstream products that are desirable to own and satisfying to use. In Europe, the term Design for All has a similar meaning to universal design. However, the term inclusive design also includes the concept of reasonable in the definition.

2.1   Universal Design Principles

The original set of universal design principles, described below was developed by a group of U.S. designers and design educators from five organizations in 1997 [3]. The principles are copyrighted to the Center for Universal Design. The principles are used internationally, though with variations in number and specifics analogy.

- **Equitable Use:** The design does not disadvantage or stigmatize any group of users.
- **Flexibility in Use:** The design accommodates a wide range of individual preferences and abilities.
- **Simple, Intuitive Use:** Use of the design is easy to understand, regardless of the user's experience, knowledge, language skills, or current concentration level.
- **Perceptible Information:** The design communicates necessary information effectively to the user, regardless of ambient conditions or the user's sensory abilities.
- **Tolerance for Error:** The design minimizes hazards and the adverse consequences of accidental or unintended actions.
- **Low Physical Effort:** The design can be used efficiently and comfortably, and with a minimum of fatigue.
- **Size and Space for Approach & Use:** Appropriate size and space is provided for approach, reach, manipulation, and use, regardless of the user's body size, posture, or mobility.

These principals are considered as a rule of thumbs since years, for achieving universal design of a system, product or service. However, the argument in this paper is that, while gaze interaction is helping a large group of people who are suffering from disabilities, it at the same time is excluding mass population who are technologically inclined to use a cutting edge technology like gaze interaction, despite of numerous research in this field. These principals are thereby used to identify challenges to create an accessibility passport features which is the basis of the propose model in the paper.

2.2   Accessibility Passport

The Accessibility Passport is a way of creating a focused dialogue between the developers and the users of online resources. It offers developers a way of explaining how they have taken accessibility and inclusion into account in designing learning materials [4]. It also offers users and practitioners a way of giving feedback on how effective the mechanism has been. Also known as online document like a wiki, it is editable at all stages by anyone involved in the process of specifying, designing, creating or using software or learning objects[4]. It carries information about the materials to which it refers and is thus a form of metadata. Unlike much metadata it is delivered using everyday language and is accessible to a much wider range of stakeholders than conventional forms of metadata[4]. All those involved in the writing, sharing and delivering of software or learning materials have a high level of responsibility for the accessibility of their output but currently there is no standard means for them to inform others about the way they intended the materials to be used - this information is important to those who may reuse the materials.

2.3   Diversity of Users Requirements

The quality of the Design-for-all product comprises the quality of use of different users in a large variety of situations. In the three loops the feedback of user experience and user opinion is very important. It is mandatory to consider different abilities of the users as proposed in the "product design ideas browser" [http:// trace. wisc.edu/docs/browser/] [5]. Lists of criteria for different disabilities and application domains can help to get an understanding of potential problems. Experts in usability, psychology, disability might help to identify requirements, too. However, it always needs to be accompanied by interaction with the users themselves. The immediate contact of users and staff in design/ development/ marketing provides deeper insight and is much more authentic than the statements of experts[5]. The choice of environment scenarios is also a crucial task. Instead of concentrating on a fixed scenario like in a laboratory, variations of the conditions of use are required. In the end the Design-for all product or service needs to be competitive in terms of quality of the solution and the market price[5]. This consideration is taken up in the market orientation of the universal design and especially in the European "three strategies approach[5].

3   Gaze Interaction Challenges-User Satisfaction Factors

For making gaze interaction available for everyone without considering that the users are suffering from disabilities or not the challenges that at available at present are lot. However, some factors are considered here as parameters of accessibility passport creation. It is first and foremost assumed that these are the basic challenges any users will feel while using gaze interaction since it is important to find out about the user's feelings of these parameter while using gaze interaction. Also the universal design standard principal was considered for selecting these factors. The factors are classified in to three categories: how comfortable users are using gaze interaction, how easy to use the system will be and how much physical effort will be needed to accomplish a task using gaze interaction. Based on these factors some co factors are formulated and used to create the accessibility passport features described in method section.

4   Method

The accessibility passport features are being derived based on the user's satisfaction factors described in section 4.1. The co factors are written in question form and narrowed down to make the design of gaze interaction system easy and to identify the limitation or challenges of using gaze communication in general.

4.1   Accessibility Passport Features

Tait and Vessey [6] described the need to reduce the number of factors being studied: Rather than attempting to investigate all factors affecting user involvement and its impact on systems success, the model provides a structure within which to examine constructs central to influence of user involvement on system success [6, 7].

The proposed accessibility passport features are hence narrowed down with four different types of inputs.

- Factors effecting workload for accomplishing a task using gaze interaction
- Level of comfort of using the gaze technique
- Ease of use and
- Participatory experience and performance

Factors effecting workload for accomplishing a task using gaze interaction
The user of the gaze interaction system specifies what they would like to have in a system, controlled by eye in terms of accessibility and whether they are ready to use any particular technology or not. The questions from user end may be of as follows:

- For whom the gaze system is indented for?
- How much physical and mental effort is needed to use the gaze system?
- What will be the price of such gaze system?
- Does the gaze application will have specific accessibility objective? Or general accessibility objective?
- Does the gazing system lead frustration to the user as it is hard to learn or use?

- Does the application require use of special technology or device?
- Does the performance depend on any other factor?

Level of comfort of using the gaze technique
The developer provides detail information of what they are capable to provide the users and also what learning methodology or material they have used for development. They can also provide information about similar gaze interface or gaze control system designed by them earlier to help user getting an idea what the developer is ready to deliver. The questions from developers end relating comfortless may be of as follows:

- How comfortable the user will be feeling using the provided gaze interaction system in terms of eye comfort?
- What might be the difficulties of learning the system to use?
- Does the interaction system meant for a particular disability group? Or does it generalized for several groups?
- What kind of problem user might feel in their face, head and neck during eye movement while using the gaze technique? What are the alternatives to solve such problems?
- Does the program require using any special input device? If yes what type? How much the cost will be?
- What interactive or enhance function user will miss if they do not want to use special input device?

Ease of use
After the use testing of the gaze interaction system is done, the accessibility issues are being asked from both user and developers point of view. This is important before finding a good user feedback of the system, designed for them. The questions from developers and users end may be of as follows:

- How accurate the pointing was by using eye? How difficult it was to point accurately?
- Was the speed of pointing alright? How the speed of pointing did affected the overall performance of the system usage?
- How accurate was the selection by using eye movement? What are the problems faced by users for trying to achieve accurate and fast selection?
- Was the overall ease of system control matched with projected result? If not, why?

Participatory experience and performance
The accessibility passport should allow the user to give their feedback about interface they are using which in return will help the finding of functional requirements. The questions from developers end for users may be of as follows:

- How flexible the users were while using the gaze system?
- Does the user feel psychologically included in a special system controlled by gaze, for example playing games?
- Would the user recommend this product to someone with similar or such limitation of accessibility or someone without any accessibility problem? If not, why?

- Was there any other inclusion than physical limitation, also achieved by using the system designed this way for the user or not?
- How hard it was to learn controlling the movement in different way and get used to with the special designed interface?

5   Proposed Model

The accessibility passport features stated in the previous section is used to build the accessibility passport model for gaze interaction system design which is showed on Figure 1. The requirements engineering phase can be enhanced by the proper accessibility passport information which is not shown here and not the scope of this paper. The four parameters from the accessibility passport features are having direct impact on requirement engineering process. The user and developer work under one umbrella in the accessibility passport method. Right requirements finding for gaze interaction for the 'general users', not only for the disabled people is possible by following this model. As from the Figure 1 it is obvious accessibility passports features helps finding better requirements which can lead to user satisfaction. A satisfied user in general is considered to be a member of inclusively designed gaze interaction system. So user satisfaction leads towards achieving inclusiveness goal aiming for a sustainable system.

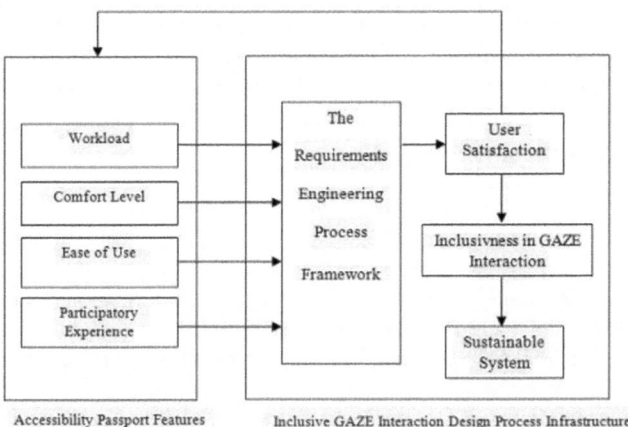

Fig. 1. The Accessibility Passport Model for Inclusive GAZE Interaction Design

6   Results and Discussion

The proposed accessibility passport model is a combination of requirements engineering process and accessibility features described in this paper. However, this kind of requirements engineering is a very complex thing to come up with. It requires a lot of time, resource and efficiency to run them successfully. Accessibility features can trigger requirements engineering in a wrong way if not picked up properly, resulting poor designed gaze control system, not serving the purpose for the user group. The model shown in Figure 1 is a continuous process. The satisfied user impacts on updating or modifying accessibility features for better enhancement of future design of gaze control system. Sustainable system in this paper's context is considered to be a system that is built upon the parameters obtained from universal design principals and used to create accessibility passport. Hence a satisfied user of gaze system can further contribute on enhancing accessibility passport features; the probability of a stable, sustainable gaze interaction system becomes higher with time.

From designer's standpoint this model is beneficial as, even without user satisfaction, good feedback from users lead towards better accessibility passport features which loops back towards a sustainable inclusive designed gaze interaction system.

7   Future Work

The planned framework can be viewed as three individual plans. It will be interesting to see the accessibility passport model at action where user and developer collaborate to find the requirements regarding accessibility for sustainable system development. Also a customized requirement engineering model is in need to integrate with the accessibility passport features which opens another new research opportunity. The result of building a system following this model will build up the accessibility passport features database. A comparison of two different types of gaze interaction design, based on two different accessibility passport features, running with the same requirements engineering model will be appealing also, to compare and finding out how it affects the user's satisfaction level. Finally, further study of the proposed model with different results, can find other parameters that may be included in the requirements engineering model.

References

1. MacKenzie, I., Ashtiani, B.: Universal Access in the Information Society 10(1), 69–80 (March 1, 2011), doi:10.1007/s10209-010-0188-6
2. British Standard 7000-6:2005. Design management systems - Managing inclusive design – Guide
3. The Principles of Universal Design: Version 2.0- 4/1/97. The Center for Universal Design, NC State University,
   http://home.earthlink.net/~jlminc/tools_principles.html
4. Ball, S., Sewell, J.: Accessibility Standards Are Not Always Enough: The Development of the Accessibility Passport. In: Miesenberger, K., Klaus, J., Zagler, W.L., Karshmer, A.I. (eds.) ICCHP 2008. LNCS, vol. 5105, pp. 264–267. Springer, Heidelberg (2008)
5. Bühler, C.: Design for All – from Idea to Practise. In: Miesenberger, K., Klaus, J., Zagler, W.L., Karshmer, A.I. (eds.) ICCHP 2008. LNCS, vol. 5105, pp. 106–113. Springer, Heidelberg (2008)
6. Tait, P., Vessey, I.: The effect of user involvement on system success. MIS Quarterly 12(1), 90–107 (1988)
7. Terry, J., Standing, C.: Inform. Science Journal 7, 31–45 (2004)

Hierarchical Key-Frame Based Video Shot Clustering Using Generalized Trace Kernel

Ali Amiri[1], Neda Abdollahi[2], Mohammad Jafari[2], and Mahmood Fathy[3]

[1] Computer Engineering Group, Zanjan University, Zanjan, Iran
a_amiri@znu.ac.ir
[2] Department of Electronic and Computer Engineering, Zanjan, Branch,
Islamic Azad University, Zanjan, Iran
{abdollahi_neda,jafari_m_2006}@yahoo.com
[3] Department of Computer Engineering, Iran University of Science and Technology,
Tehran, Iran
Mahfathy@iust.ac.ir

Abstract. In this paper, we propose a new generalized trace kernel for measuring the similarity between data points of matrices form which have the same number of rows and different number of columns. Also, we propose a hierarchical clustering algorithm based on this kernel function. The clustering algorithm has been utilized in a video indexing system to cluster video shots. The experimental results on TRECVID 2006 data set confirm the effectiveness of the proposed kernel function and clustering algorithm.

Keywords: content based video retrieval, video indexing, trace kernel, shot clustering, key frame.

1 Introduction

Hierarchical modeling of the video content plays an essential role in content based video indexing and retrieval for developing high speed search engines on large video databases.

In content based video indexing literature, many of the research efforts have been focusing on using low-level features to segment video into shots, each of which is comprised of a sequence of consecutive frames recording a video scene or event contiguous in time and space [1]-[6]. After the video is segmented into shots, a number of key frames can be extracted from each shot to represent the salient content of the shot for video analysis, indexing, and retrieval purposes [7]. In hierarchical indexing, these key frames are utilized to cluster the video shots into groups. Based on the extracted clusters and key frames from video data, video retrieval can be performed by evaluating the similarity between the query vector(s) and the feature vectors in the database [5].

In spite of recent improvements, hierarchical indexing of large video data is still a very difficult task, with many unsolved challenges. In the recent works, video shots are described by the same number of key frames. It is obvious that the number of keyframes is required for representing each shot must be relative to the shot

P. Pichappan, H. Ahmadi, and E. Ariwa (Eds.): INCT 2011, CCIS 241, pp. 251–257, 2011.

dynamicity. In [7], the authors defined some criteria for measuring dynamicity in shot, scene and video levels, and present a straightforward algorithm for determining the number of keyframes which is required each shot. These researches make some new challenging tasks. Some of these challenges are as follows:

Clustering of video shots which are represented by different number of key frames can be very essential in defining hierarchical index for video databases. However, no clustering algorithms have ever been presented for data point with various lengths and this remains to be very important.

Comparing the similarity of two shots with different number of key frames is still a critical challenge in video retrieval.

To attach to these challenges in a unified way, we develop a generalized trace kernel for rectangular matrices to evaluate the similarity of data points with different lengths. Also, we present a hierarchical clustering algorithm to cluster video shots with different number of key frames.

An overview of the proposed hierarchical indexing system is considered in Section 2. In Section 3 the generalized trace kernel is defined. Section 4 includes the proposed hierarchical video shot clustering algorithm. In Section 5, the simulation results are demonstrated. Section 6 clarifies our conclusions.

2   System Overview

Fig.1 shows the block diagram of the proposed video indexing system. We apply the algorithm presented in [1] to detect the video shot boundaries. Also, to extract the key frames from each shot relative to its dynamicity, we utilize the approach presented in [7].

Let the input video be segmented into N various shots $S_1, S_2, ..., S_N$, and n_i keyframes are extracted from each shot i, and i = 1, ..., N. In order to represent the key frames of an arbitrary shot in a compact form, we extract a feature matrix for key frames of that shot. Let $Keys_i = \{K_1^{(i)}, ..., K_{n_i}^{(i)}\}$ be the key frames of shot i. We extract an m-dimensional feature vector for each key frame $K_j^{(i)}$ such as $A_j^{(i)} = [A_{j,1}^{(i)}, ..., A_{j,m}^{(i)}]^T$ and j = 1, ..., n_i. Using $A_j^{(i)}$ as column vector j, we obtain feature matrix $A^{(i)}$ for key frames of shot i as follows:

$$A^{(i)} = \begin{bmatrix} A_{1,1}^{(i)} & A_{2,1}^{(i)} & \cdots & A_{n_i,1}^{(i)} \\ A_{1,2}^{(i)} & A_{2,2}^{(i)} & \cdots & A_{n_i,2}^{(i)} \\ \vdots & \vdots & \ddots & \vdots \\ A_{1,m}^{(i)} & A_{2,m}^{(i)} & \cdots & A_{n_i,m}^{(i)} \end{bmatrix} \tag{1}$$

In order to extract spatial features of each key frame, from a broad range of image features, we used color histograms which are essential features for signifying the overall spatial features of each key frame [1]. Specially, we created a 1728-dimensional feature vector $A_j^{(i)}$. To compute the feature vector in our system implementation, we made three-dimensional histograms in RGB color space with twelve bins for R, G and B, respectively, leading to a total of 1728 bins. These produced a 1728-dimensional feature vector for the key frame. Finally, utilizing the feature vector of frame   as the jth column, we generated the feature matrix $A^{(i)}$ for key frames of shot   in the video sequence.

Now, let $A^{(i)}, \dots, A^{(N)}$ of order $m \times n_1$, $m \times n_2, \dots, m \times n_N$ respectively, be the feature matrices of   shots of input video. It is obvious that, the number of columns of these matrices is different, and no clustering algorithms have ever been presented for clustering them. To attach this challenge, we will define the generalized trace kernel in the next section.

3   Generalized Trace Kernel

A kernel function $k: X \times X \to \mathbb{R}$ is an arbitrary symmetric and real value function which is defined on two patterns $x, x' \in X$ and can be considered as a similarity measure [8]. In machine learning area, many different kernel functions, such as trace and determinant kernels, have been used to evaluate the similarity of two data points. The main properties of these functions are that their inputs are data point of the same lengths, and no kernel functions have ever been defined to evaluate the similarity of data points of different lengths. As we mentioned in the previous section, the data points of various lengths are important and we need to define an appropriate kernel function to measure their similarities. In the following, we generalize the trace kernel definition on these data points. At first, we bring a simple example.

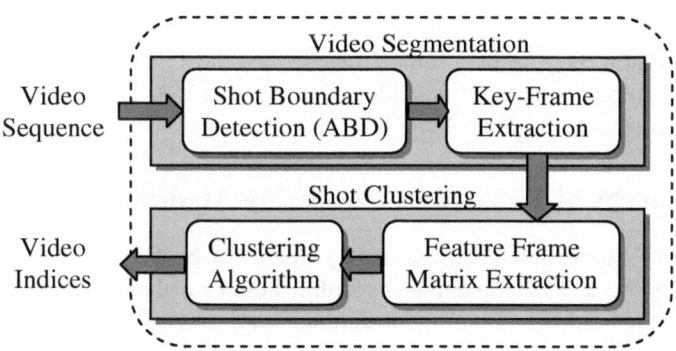

Fig. 1. Block diagram of the proposed video indexing system

Example 1. Given matrices A and B of order 4×3 and 4×5 respectively. We define the generalized trace of matrix $A^T B$ as follows:

$$A^T B = [A_1, A_2, A_3]^T . [B_1, B_2, B_3, B_4, B_5]$$

$$= \begin{bmatrix} a_{11} & a_{12} & a_{13} \\ a_{21} & a_{22} & a_{23} \\ a_{31} & a_{32} & a_{33} \\ a_{41} & a_{42} & a_{43} \end{bmatrix}^T \cdot \begin{bmatrix} b_{11} & b_{12} & b_{13} & b_{14} & b_{15} \\ b_{21} & b_{22} & b_{23} & b_{24} & b_{25} \\ b_{31} & b_{32} & b_{33} & b_{34} & b_{35} \\ b_{41} & b_{42} & b_{43} & b_{44} & b_{45} \end{bmatrix} \tag{2}$$

$$\Rightarrow A^T B \; = \begin{bmatrix} A_1B_1 & A_1B_2 & A_1B_3 & A_1B_4 & A_1B_5 \\ A_2B_1 & A_2B_2 & A_2B_3 & A_2B_4 & A_2B_5 \\ A_3B_1 & A_3B_2 & A_3B_3 & A_3B_4 & A_3B_5 \end{bmatrix}$$

$\Rightarrow \text{Trace}(A^T.B) = \max\{(A_1B_1 + A_2B_2 + A_3B_3), (A_1B_2 + A_2B_3 + A_3B_4), (A_1B_3 + A_2B_4 + A_3B_5)\}$ (3)

Also, we define the trace kernel as

$$\Phi_{\text{Trace}}(A, B) = \text{Trace}(A^T B) \tag{4}$$

Now, we bring the following definitions.

Definition 1. Let $A = [A_1, \dots, A_{n_1}]$ and $B = [B_1, \dots, B_{n_2}]$ be $m \times n_1$ and $m \times n_2$ matrices respectively, and $n_1 \leq n_2$. Then, the generalized trace of rectangular matrix $A^T B$ or order $n_1 \times n_2$ is defined as

$$\text{Trace}(A^T B) = \max_{0 \leq j \leq n_2 - n_1}\{\textstyle\sum_{i=1}^{n_1} A_i B_{i+j}\} \tag{5}$$

Definition 2. Let $A = [A_1, \dots, A_{n_1}]$ and $B = [B_1, \dots, B_{n_2}]$ be $m \times n_1$ and $m \times n_2$ matrices respectively, and $n_1 \leq n_2$. Then, the generalized trace kernel for evaluating the similarity of   and   is defined as

$$\Phi_{\text{Trace}}(A, B) = \text{Trace}(A^T B) \tag{6}$$

It is obvious that if the $A^T B$ be a square matrix, then the $\text{Trace}(A^T B)$ is the same with standard trace function. Also, It is evident that $\Phi_{\text{Trace}}(A, B)$ computes the maximum correlation between columns of A and B.

4   Hierarchical Video Shot Clustering Algorithms

Let $A^{(1)}, \dots, A^{(N)}$ be feature matrices of key frames of N shots of an arbitrary video. Here, we propose a shot clustering algorithm based on these feature matrices and generalized trace kernel. Fig.2 demonstrates the pseudo code of the proposed algorithm. In this algorithm, the number of clusters C must be determined initially. This clustering algorithm is bottom-up, and treats each feature matrix as a singleton cluster at the outset and then successively merge pairs of clusters until the number of clusters equals C. This algorithm uses a proximity matrix to compute similarity between clusters and to merge the most similar clusters. Let the number of clusters at an arbitrary iteration of the algorithm be $k < C$. Then the proximity matrix M is a matrix of order $k \times k$ which its entries are calculated as

$$M(i, j) = \max_{\forall A_k \in C_i, \forall A_h \in C_j}\{\Phi_{\text{Trace}}(A_k^T. A_h)\}, \tag{7}$$

$1 \leq i, j \leq k$

Where $\Phi_{\text{Trace}}(A_k^T. A_h)$ is the generalized trace kernel and computed according to definition 2.

5   Simulation Results

In order to evaluate the proposed video indexing system with standard data sets, we have demonstrated the outcomes of the tests using a large-scale test set provided by the TRECVID 2006 [9].

Fig. 3 illustrates the key frames of some shots of "20051101_142800_LBC_ NAHAR_ARB.mpg" file in TRECVD 2006. It is evident that the first and 9th shots, and 5th and 7th are very similar. The similarity of these shots using generalized trace kernel have been demonstrated in Table 1. These results confirm the effectiveness of the proposed generalized kernel function.

---

1.   let $A^{(1)}, ..., A^{(N)}$ be feature matrices of key frames of each shot

2.   calculate proximity matrix using each matrix $A^{(i)}$ as data points

3.   let each matrix $A^{(i)}$ be a cluster

4.   While (number of clusters > C) do

      (a). merge the two similar clusters according to proximity matrix

      (b). update proximity matrix using (3)

end

5.   select the most similar matrix to all matrix of each cluster as center of the cluster

---

Fig. 2. Proposed clustering algorithm

Table 1. Measuring The Similarities Between Shots of Fig.3

Compared shots		Φ_{Trace}
5	7	1.149
1	9	1.339
1	5	0.599
7	9	0.709

For video indexing purpose, we construct two-level indices for TRECVID 2006 data set: shot-level index, which is created by using key frames of each shot, and cluster level which is generated by utilizing shot cluster centers. Also, for video retrieval purpose, we utilize clip-based query method. In this method, the user interested to search some video shots from the video database that are similar to the input video of the user.

In the experiments, to assess the efficiency of the hierarchical indexing, we consider two cases and compute the average of responding time to 500 different queries. In the first case, we consider only shot-level indices, and in the second case we considered shot-level and cluster level indices. Fig.3 compares the average times of responding to 500 different queries in video retrieval systems that use shot level indexing or hierarchical indexing. These results confirm the effectiveness of the proposed video indexing and shot clustering algorithm.

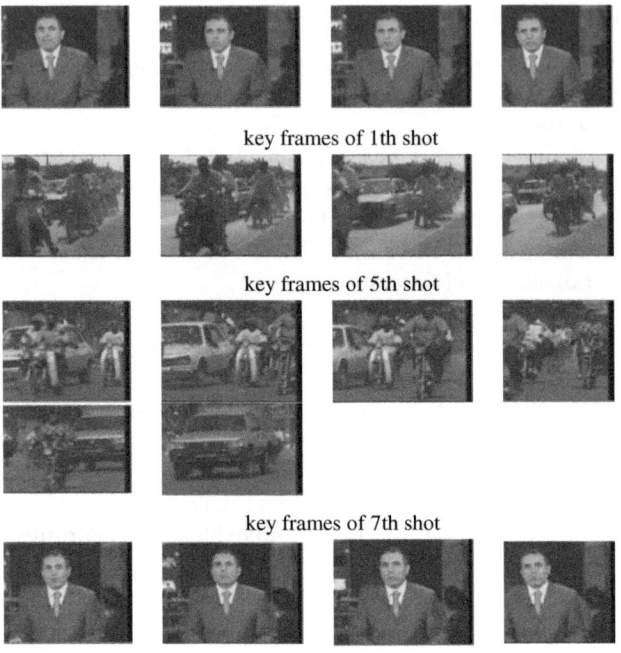

Fig. 3. Key frames of some shots of file 20051101_142800_LBC_NAHAR_ARB.mpg in TRECVID 2006

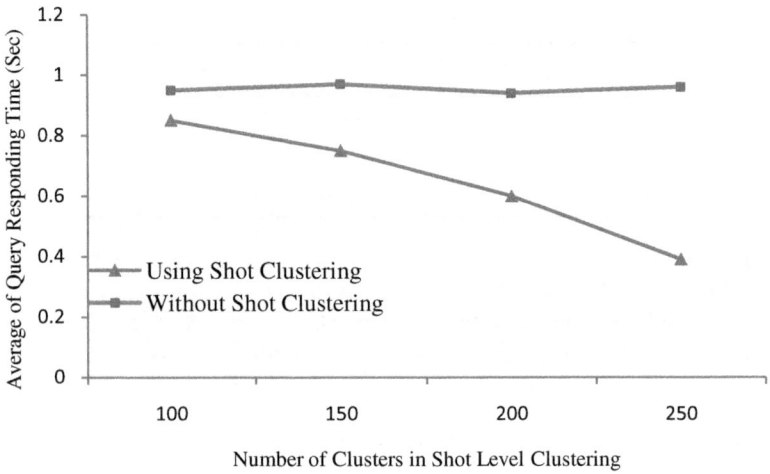

Fig. 4. Average time of responding to 500 different queries in video retrieval systems that uses proposed clustering algorithm or not

6   Conclusion

Hierarchical video indexing is one of the most important challenges in video retrieval research. In this paper, a novel video hierarchical video indexing system is developed based on video shot clustering. We derive a generalized trace kernel to measure the similarity of matrix form data points with the same number of rows and different number of columns. Also, we utilize it in developing a hierarchical clustering algorithm for that data points. The proposed system is implemented and evaluated on TRECVID benchmark platform. The experimental results confirm the effectiveness of the proposed system.

References

1. Amiri, A., Fathy, M.: Video shot boundary detection using QR-Decomposition and Gaussian transition detection. EURASIP Journal on Advances in Signal Processing, 12 pages (2009)
2. Zhou, X., Chen, L., Bouguettaya, A., Xiao, N., Taylor, J.A.: An efficient Near-Duplicate video shot detection method using shot-based interest points. IEEE Transactions on Multimedia 11(5), 879–891 (2009)
3. Chasanis, V.T., Likas, A.C., Galatsanos, N.P.: Scene detection in video using shot clustering and sequence alignment. IEEE Transactions on Multimedia 11(1), 89–100 (2009)
4. Dyana, A., Das, S.: MST-CSS (Multi-Spectro-Temporal Curvature Scale Space), a novel spatio-temporal representation for content-based video retrieval. IEEE Transactions on Circuits and Systems for Video Technology 20(8), 1080–1094 (2010)
5. Amiri, A., Fathy, M.: Video Shot Boundary Detection Using Generalized Eigenvalue Decomposition. In: Gervasi, O., Taniar, D., Murgante, B., Laganà, A., Mun, Y., Gavrilova, M.L. (eds.) ICCSA 2009. LNCS, vol. 5593, pp. 780–790. Springer, Heidelberg (2009)
6. Amiri, A., Fathy, M.: Video shot boundary detection using generalized eigenvalue decomposition and Gaussian transition detection. Journal of Computing and Informatics 30(3) (2011)
7. Amiri, A., Fathy, M.: Hierarchical key-frame based video summarization using QR-Decomposition and modified k-means clustering. EURASIP Journal on Advances in Signal Processing, 16 pages (2010)
8. Hofmann, T., Scholkopf, B., Smola, A.J.: Kernel methods in machine learning. The Annals of Statictics Journal 36(3), 1171–1220 (2008)
9. NIST, homepage of Trecvid evaluation,
   http://www-nlpir.nist.gov/projects/trecvid/

Improving Face Recognition Based on Characteristic Points of Face Using Fuzzy Interface System

Mohammadreza Banan[1], Alireza Soleimany[2], Esmaeil Zeinali Kh[3], and Akbar Talash[4]

[1] Department of Computer Engineering, Master of Computer Science,
Islamic Azad University, Qazvin Branch, Qazvin, Iran
engineerbanan@gmail.com
[2] Islamic Azad University, Meshkin-shahr Branch
Alireza.soleimany@meshkin-iau.ac.ir
[3] Department of Computer Engineering, Islamic Azad University, Qazvin Branch, Qazvin, Iran
Zeinali@QIAU.AC.IR
[4] Applicate Ministry of Commerce Fars Province Center Education &
Manager Education and Research Scientific
talashuae@yahoo.com

Abstract. Three main cases that often are considered for identifying face figures are: happy, sad, and surprised. Face states are created by changes in different points. In this article, first eight characteristic points of face are considered and then five different features are extracted from them that these features form a feature vector for each of the face state. Then, we get a rules database based on these features and with fuzzy inference systems and considering the membership function, a method is presented for identifying happiness and sadness, and surprise states . Three important advantages Compared with other available methods are that it has less number of feature points and features and it has a higher accuracy than other methods.

Keywords: face states detection, face characteristic points, Fuzzy Inference System.

1 Introduction

In face recognition field, many works have been done. For example, Kobayashi and Hara presented a method with identifying 30 characteristic points of face and extract some features of these points using of neural network for detection of fear, surprise, disgust, anger, happiness and sadness states that obtained detection power approximately 78% with training by 5 faces, 83% with training by 10 faces and 88% with the training by 15 figures [2].

Yoshida and his colleagues expressed a method to detect cases of anger, happiness and sadness using of fuzzy sets and considering the 27 characteristics points of face. With testing 56 picture files, their offered system presented power detection approximately 87%.[3] Jamoto and his colleagues offered a model for face state detection using fuzzy clustering and process characteristics on some parts of the face and information. This method had 89% accuracy. [4]

P. Pichappan, H. Ahmadi, and E. Ariwa (Eds.): INCT 2011, CCIS 241, pp. 258–263, 2011.

Yekob and his colleagues, obtained, motion of active units using of optical flow in successive frames, which is represented a specific state. The frames started of the normal and ended to one of the main face state. With this method, for each of the states face a feature vector was obtained based on the motion of active units and was used for training a RBF neural network. The above system in frames classification offered detection power approximately 80% to one of six major face states. [1]

Listen Read phonetically Mirhadi Sayed Arabi and his Colleagues, presented a fuzzy inference system and a neural network to recognize happiness and sadness, and surprise states, (they used 17 characterized points of face and extracted seven features from them) that reached to 95.6% accuracy in the fuzzy inference system and to 93.4% accuracy in neural network for 15 files of the Yale A database. [5]

In this paper, five different properties were calculated using of 8-point characteristic face, and then using a fuzzy inference system, a method is presented for the diagnosis of happiness and sadness, and surprise states that has three important advantages compared with other existing methods which has the less number of face's characterized points and features and it has higher precision than other methods.

Commonly, face image uses in all identification (IDs, driver's license, passport, etc.). In particularly, to improve the social security of city life, automatic face detection and face recognition systems are needed and there is a lot of study for this purpose [7]. In [8-10] the face and image recognition features are analyzed in a multidimensional scale.

2   Characteristic Points of Face

In figure (1), 8 characteristic points of face is displayed:

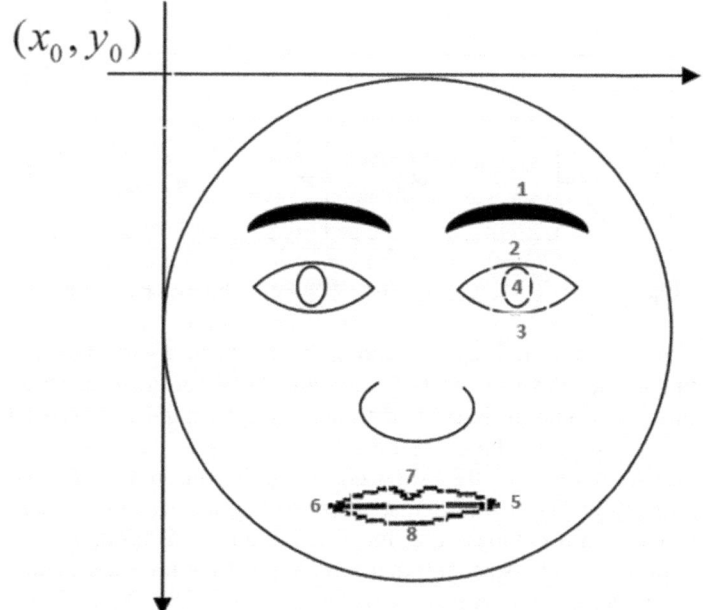

Fig. 1. Face characteristic points

3   Features Extracted Using Characteristic Points of Face

Using the coordinates of eight characteristic points of face, five features are extracted as follows:[6]

A – Openness of Eye

$$O_e = y_3 - y_2 \tag{1}$$

B – Height of Eyebrow

$$He = y_3 - y_1 \tag{2}$$

C – Weight of Mouth

$$W_m = x_5 - x_6 \tag{3}$$

D – Openness of Mouth

$$O_m = y_8 - y_7 \tag{4}$$

E- Lower Lip-Lip Corners List

$$LL = ((y_8 - y_5) + (y_8 - y_6)) / 2 \tag{5}$$

4   Face States Detection System Using of Fuzzy Inference System

In this system, according to the figure (2) five stages is performed from left to right respectively:

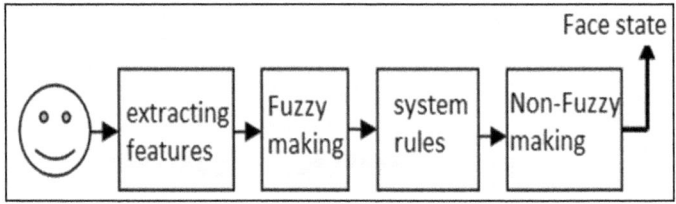

Fig. 2. State detection system based on Fuzzy Inference System [5]

In this way, extracted quintuplet features are intended as an input of fuzzy inference system and membership functions are calculated for each feature. A membership function of each feature is type of triangle and is obtained based on maximum and minimum and `average of each feature.

It is noteworthy that firstly, the proposed system is educated for the recognition of membership functions [1], it means that when testing an input face image, other features of nine faces in a database and mean maximum and minimum corresponding features, functions, membership automatically input files for each feature are determined. For example, membership functions and features Om Oe, as forms of (3) and (4) are:

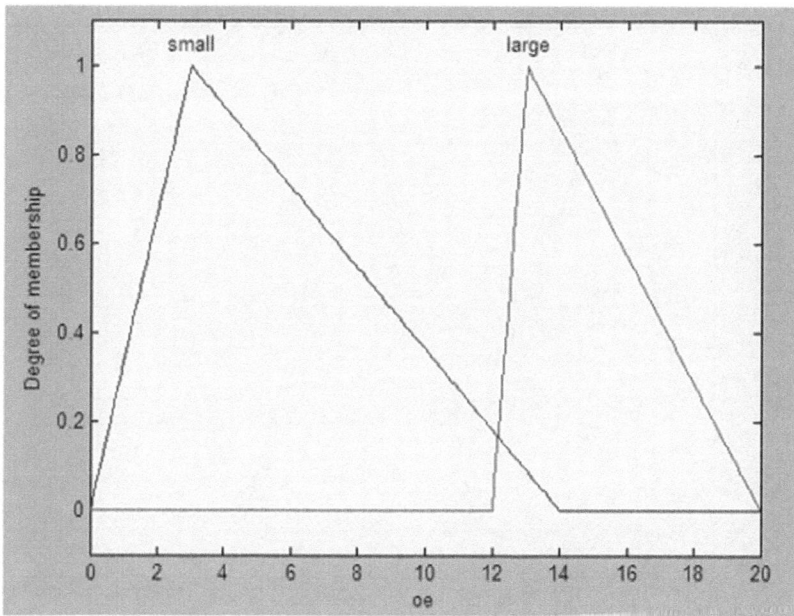

Fig. 3. Membership function for OE feature

Considering the membership functions and features extracted, like table (1), rules is considered for the fuzzy inference system:

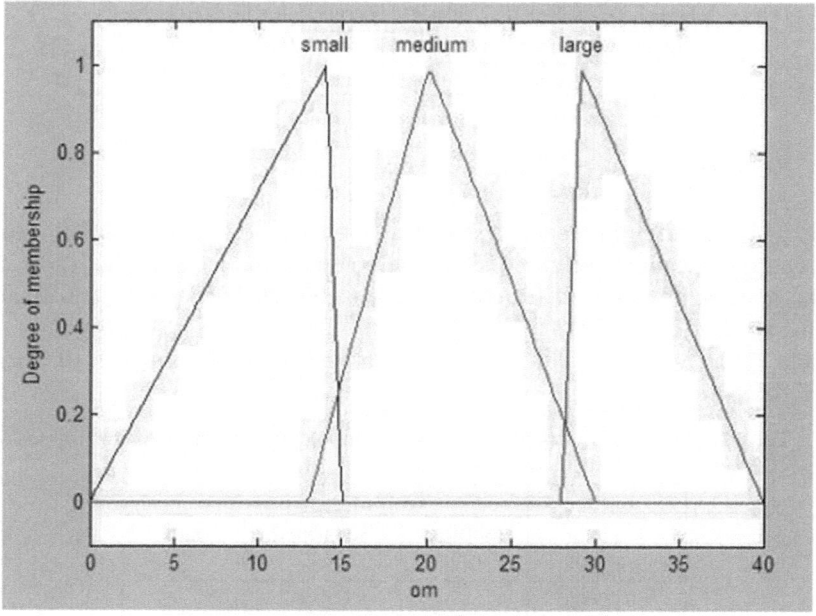

Fig. 4. Membership function for Om feature

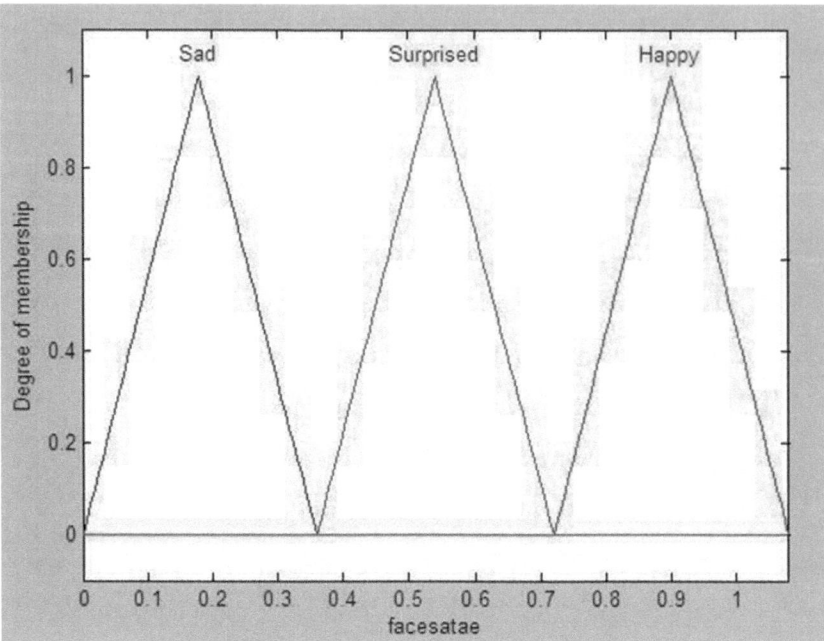

Fig. 5. Membership function for state of face in Output result

Table 1. Fuzzy System Rules in Classification States of face

	OE	HE	WM	OM	LL
Happy	Small	Small	Large	medium	Large
Surprised	Large	Large	Small	Large	Large
sad	small	small	Small	Small	Small

5   Results

In this paper, a fuzzy inference system was used for detection of face states. Most important specifications include: Using of less number of characteristic points, reducing the number of extracted features of face's characteristic points, and finally increasing accuracy.

Table (2) shows the results of applying the proposed idea for the 10 images of JAFFE database.

Table 2. Results of Fuzzy inference system in Recognition of three facial states

input	Output = face state		
	happy	Surprised	sad
happy	100%	-	-
Surprised	-	100%	-
sad	-	-	100%

6   Conclusion

The documented study can be utilized for face recognition with the application of fuzzy recognition. In the last few years the literature has many studies which address a number of efforts. They have been made on pose-invariant face recognition; however still we need more future research as the performance of current face recognition system are still not complete.

References

[1] Yann, H., Yang, J., Yang, J.: Bimode model for face recognition and face representation. Int. Journal Neurocomputing (2010)

[2] Bartlett, M.S., Movellan, J.R., Sejnowski, T.J.: Face Recognition by Independent Component Analysis. IEEE Transactions on Neural Networks 13(6) (2002)

[3] Sellahewa, H., Jassim, S.A.: Image-Quality-Based Adaptive Face Recognition. IEEE Transactions on Instrumentation and Measurement 59(4) (2010)

[4] Ahonen, T., Hadid, A., Pietikinen, M.: Face description with local binary patterns: application to face recognition. IEEE Transactions on Pattern Analysis and Machine Intelligence 28(12), 2037–2041 (2006)

[5] Ushida, H., Taking, T., Yamayuchi, T.: Recognition of Facial Expression Using Conceptual Fuzzy Sets. In: IEEE Int. Conf., on Fuzzy Systems, vol. 1 (March 1993)

[6] Black, M.J., Yacoob, Y.: Recognizing facial Expression in image sequences using local parameterized Model of image motion. Int. Journal of Computer Vision (2003)

[7] Serdar Yilma, M.A.: Gray Level Based Face Detection Using Template Face Mask and L1 norm. International Journal of Web Applications 2(4), 243–249 (2010)

[8] Sauvaget, C., Vittaut, J.-N., Suarez, J., Boyer, V., Manuel, S.: Automated Colorization of Segmented Images Based on Color Harmony. Journal of Multimedia Processing and Technologies 1, 228–244 (2010)

[9] Kosch, H., Maier, P.: Content-Based Image Retrieval Systems - Reviewing and Benchmarking. Journal of Digital Information Management 8(1), 315–331 (2010)

[10] Wali, A., Alimi, A.M.: Multimodal Approach for Video Surveillance Indexing and Retrieval. Journal of Intelligent Computing 1(4), 165–175 (2010)

Modes Detection of Color Histogram and Merging Algorithm by Mode Adjacency Graph Analysis for Color Image Segmentation

Halima Remmach[1,2], Aziza Mouradi[2], Abderrahmane Sbihi[1],
Ludovic Macaire[3], and Olivier Losson[3]

[1] Laboratoire Systèmes des Télécommunications et Ingénierie de la Décision (LASTID),
Université Ibn Tofail, Faculté des Sciences, Kénitra-Maroc
[2] Laboratoire de Biochimie, Biotechnologies et Environnement (LBBE),
Université Ibn Tofail, Faculté des Sciences, Kénitra-Maroc
[3] Laboratoire d'Automatique, Génie Informatique et Signal (LAGIS),
Université des Sciences et Technologies, Lille1-France
h.remmach@gmail.com

Abstract. In this work we present an approach for color image segmentation based on pixel classification. Such methods are based on the assumption that meaningful regions are defined by homogeneous colors and give rise to compact clusters in the color space. Each cluster defined a class of pixels which share similar color properties The construction of the pixel classes is performed by detecting the modes of the color histogram of the image. To identify these modes, mathematical morphology techniques are used. The application of watersheds on the color histogram leads to an over partitioning of the color plane, which can be processed by mode merging algorithms based on mode adjacency graph analysing. Depending the merging criterion we present in this paper two merging algorithms, the first relies on the gravity centers of the modes as a merging criterion, and in the second we introduce a new merging criterion: the spatial-color compactness degree.

Keywords: Color image, Segmentation, mode detection, Color histogram, Mathematical morphology, merging algorithms.

1 Introduction

Color image segmentation is a process of partitioning an image into several regions which are groups of connected pixels with homogeneous color properties.

Many types of color image segmentation methods have been proposed in the literature [1], [2], they can be divided into two main families, depending on the distribution of the pixel colors is analyzed either in the image plane or in a color space.

In this work we consider the second category which is the segmentation methods by pixel classification, such approaches proceed by analyzing the color distribution in a color space. The most widely used is the (R,G,B) color space, where a color point is characterized by the color component levels of the corresponding pixel. Other color

P. Pichappan, H. Ahmadi, and E. Ariwa (Eds.): INCT 2011, CCIS 241, pp. 264–273, 2011.

spaces can be used and the performance of an image segmentation procedure is known to depend on the choice of the color space [3]. Several works have tried to determine the color spaces which are the most appropriate for their specific color image segmentation problems [4]. But there does not exist a color space which provides satisfying results for the segmentation of all kinds of images.

The segmentation methods by pixel classification rely on the assumption that homogeneous regions in the image give rise to clusters of color points in the color space. Each cluster defined a class of pixels which share similar color properties. To identify the classes we proceed by analyzing the histogram of the image. We seek to identify the modes of the histogram, namely the areas of color space with a high density of probability (Fig.2). In order to detecting the modes of the histogram, we use the mathematical morphology techniques, and more precisely the watershed algorithm. This algorithm is applied to image histogram [5], [6], [7], in order to detect the modes which correspond to the pixel classes, this gives an over-partitioning of the color plane, hence the need to merge modes by analyzing the modes adjacency graph.

This paper is organized as follows. Section 2 presents the watershed algorithm is appleid to color histogram. Section 3 presents the merging algorithm by analyzing the mode adjacency graph. Then, we detail this algorithm, namely search an merging criterion respecting the distribution of colors in the color space both taking into account their spatial location in the image plane. Finally, some results and conclusion are shown in Section 4.

2   Color Plane Partition by Color Histogram Analysis

2.1   Color Histogram Modes Detection Based on Watershed Algorithm

In order to perform the color image segmentation, the classes of pixels corresponding to homogeneous regions are constructed by detecting the modes of the color histogram. For this purpose the watershed algorithm is aplied. The principle of watershed is drawn from a topographic analogy. Consider the histogram of the image as a topographic relief, where the densities of the histogram are interpreted as altitudes in the relief. There are also many different algorithms to compute watersheds, in this work we use the watershed algorithm as was introduced by Vincent and Soille[8], based on the immersion principle.

We can imagine that we have pierced holes in each regional minimum of the relief. We then immerse the relief into water. Starting from the minima of lowest altitude, the water will progressively fill up the different catchment bassins. The water coming from two different minima would merge. Finaly two or more such catchment bassins expand to a point at which they would come into contact unless the waters are separated. This is the moment that a dam is raised. At the end of this immersion procedure, each minimum is completely surrounded by dams, which delimit its associated catchment bassin. these dams correspond to the watersheds.

The watershed algorithm will apply on the additive inverse histogram [7] to identify color histogram modes. The color histogram is constructed by considering two color component levels among the three color component levels (R, G , B) To simplify the implementation and first validate the algorithm in two dimensional 2-D.

To apply the watershed algorithm on the additive inverse of 2-D color histogram, we chose to store the data histogram in an image (Fig. 3 (a)), where the coordinates of each pixel are the color component levels (R,G), (G,B) or (R,B) according to the used color plane and its gray level is the probability density of the color represented by these components.

The application of the watershed algorithm, on the inverted histogram of the color image leads to an over-partitioning of the modes (Fig.3 (c)), due to the presence of non significant local minima [9], hence the need to merge modes by a modes adjacency graph, which is analyzed in order to iteratively merge adjacent modes.

3   Modes Merging by Mode Adjacency Graph Analysis

The overpartitioned modes are merged by analyzing a mode adjacency graph. This is a data structure constituted by a set of nodes representing modes and a set of links connecting two neighboring nodes (Fig.1). The modes adjacency graph consists of associating a node at each mode and an edge at each pair of adjacent modes. This definition provides the adjacency relationships between modes.

The merging process consists of merging two adjacent nodes which verify merging criteria. According the order of scan the nodes and the merging criteria, several algorithms by analyzing the adjacency graph are proposed in the literature [10], [11], [12].

Tremeau and Colantoni [10] have developed two algorithms to perform the merging of nodes of adjacency graph, based on the same rules than the two image algorithms process, except that apply to nodes and not to pixels. The first approach is a vertices-graph growing process, and the second is a vertices-graph watershed process.

The vertices-graph growing process relies on a sequential scanning of the nodes of the adjacency graph, by considering a current node at each step of the analysis. At each current node corresponds a set which defines the set of neighbors nodes. The current node could be merged with one of its neighbors if the distance between this current node and all neighboring nodes is small enough. These criteria enable us to gather the current node to a set of nodes being processed not because only one node of this set is adjacent and sufficiently similar to current one, but above all because most of adjacent nodes already belonging to the set of nodes being processed are also similar to the current one.

In adjacency graph each node is associated with the relevant properties of the entity (mode), and each edge is weighted by a value indicating the similarity between two adjacent nodes(modes) [13], corresponding to a distance between these two adjacent nodes.

In this work we present two merging algorithms to merge the over-partitioned modes, in the first we use the gravity centers of the modes as a merging criterion, and in the second the merging criterion is the spatial-color compactness degree.

3.1   The Gravity Centers of the Modes as a Merging Criterion

To merge the over-partitioning modes of the color plane, each node is represented by the gravity center of the corresponding mode, and each edge is weighted by the distance between two gravity centers of the two adjacent modes.

Let M the set of modes of the color plane C, over-partitioning by the watershed algorithm:

$$M = \cup_i M_i \qquad (1)$$

The color plane C is defined by two color component levels C^1 and C^2 among the three color component levels C^1, C^2 and C^3 (red, green, and blue levels, in this work the (R, G, B) color space is considered).

The mode M_i is defined as:

$$M_i = \{d_1, d_2, \dots d_{N_i}\} \qquad (2)$$

Where d_j is the set of N_i color points constituting the mode M_i, and C_j^1, C_j^2 the two color component levels of the point d_j.

Each mode M_i is represented by its gravity center $G_i(g_i^1, g_i^2)$.

$$g_i^1 = \frac{\sum_j C_j^1 H(C_j^1, C_j^2)}{\sum_j H(C_j^1, C_j^2)} \qquad g_i^2 = \frac{\sum_j C_j^2 H(C_j^1, C_j^2)}{\sum_j H(C_j^1, C_j^2)} \qquad (3)$$

$H(C_j^1, C_j^2)$ is the density of the color whose components are (C_j^1, C_j^2).

Each edge connecting two adjacent modes is weighted by the euclidean distance $d^2(M_i, M_k)$ which can be used to compare the proximity of these two modes.

$$W(M_i, M_k) = d^2(G_i, G_k) \qquad (4)$$

Where $d^2(G_i, G_k)$ is the euclidean distance

In order to merge the over-partitioning modes we proceed to merge firstly two adjacent modes which a weight(distance) enough small taking into account the merging threshold S.

$$W(M_i, M_k) \text{ is enough small} \qquad \text{and} \quad d^2(G_i, G_k) < S$$

At each iteration step of the merging process the modes adjacency graph is updating by considering the new adjacencies and the new gravity centers of the new modes.

The merging process achieves a new iteration step provided there the distance between tow adjacent modes is lower than the threshold S. the results merging are represented in Fig. 3.((e), (f))

In this work our purpose is to perform the color image segmantation by pixel classification. The classes of pixels are constructed by detecting the modes of the color histogram taking into account that the regions of the image are the groups of pixels with homogeneous color properties, but two over-partitioning modes with two closed gravity centers can tend to fail in constructing pixel classes which correspond to the actual regions in the image. In order to avoid this problem we will consider a new merging criterion respecting the correspondence between modes of the histogram and significant regions of the image.

3.2   Modes Merging by Analysis the Spatial-color Compactness Degree

Most segmentation methods by pixel classification proceed by analysis the distribution of colors in the color space without taking into account their spatial location in the image plane. In order to introduce the spatial information of pixels in the image plane, Macaire and al [14] define a region as a group of connected pixels with homogeneous color properties which give rise to a compact cluster in the color space. The construction of the pixel classes is performed by considering both color distribution and spatial location. To measure such properties a new concept is introduced, this is the spatial-color compactness degree [14, 15], which takes into account both pixel connectedness in image plane and color homogeneity in color space. The spatial-color compactness degree is defined as the product of the connectedness degree and the homogeneity degrees, it is even higher that the pixels are highly connected in the image and that the color points corresponding to these pixels are concentrated in the color space.

3.2.1 Spatial-color Compactness Degree of a Color mode

Let S_1 the set of pixels in the original image I corresponding to a mode M_1 of color plane over-partitioning by watershed algorithm, and S_2 the set of pixels corresponding to a mode M_2. With M_1 and M_2 are two adjacent modes in the over-partitioning color plane.

S is the union of two sets S_1 and S_2 associated to the two adjacent modes M_1 and M_2 respectively

$$S_1 = \{P \in I / I(P) \in M_1\} \qquad S_2 = \{P \in I / I(P) \in M_2\} \qquad S = S_1 \cup S_2$$

$I(P)$ is a color point in the color space where the coordinates are the color component levels of the pixel P.

The homogeneity degree of a set of pixels S is defined as a comparison between the local dispersion $\sigma_{locale}(S)$ and the global dispersion $\sigma(S)$ of the color points $I(P)$:

$$DH(S) = 1 \; if \; \sigma(S) = 0, \qquad DH(S) = \frac{\sigma_{locale}(S)}{\sigma(S)} \; if \; \sigma(S) > 0. \qquad (5)$$

$$\sigma(S) = \frac{1}{card\{P \in S\}} \times \sum_{p \in s} \sqrt{(I(P) - M(S)^T (I(P) - M(S))}$$

And $M(S)$ is the mean color of the pixels which belong to S.

The connectedness degree is defined as the average number of neighbors of each pixel of S which also belong to S :

$$DC(S) = \sum_{p \in S} \frac{card\{Q \in N_S(P)\}}{card\{P \in S\} * 8} \qquad (6)$$

where $Ns(P)$ is the neighboring pixels of P.

Taking into account both pixel connectedness and color homogeneity give rise to the spatial-color compactness degree :

$$DCO(S) = DC(S) \times DH(S)$$

(7)

A high value of the spatial-color compactness degree indicates that the pixels in the current set are highly connected in the image (close to 1), and that the color points corresponding to these pixels are compact in the color space.

3.2.2 Merging of the Over-partitioning Modes by Analysis of the Spatial-color Compactness Degree

To merge the over-partitioning modes of the color histogram obtained from the watershed algorithm, respecting the correspondence between modes of the histogram and significant regions of the image, we will consider the spatial-color compactness degree of the pixels corresponding to two adjacent modes as a merging criterion. Two adjacent over-partitioning modes could be merged if the union of the subsets of pixels, associated to these two adjacent modes, corresponds in the image plane to a connected and homogeneous set of pixels. The consideration of the homogeneity degree as a comparison between the local dispersion and the global dispersion does not give the highest homogeneity degree for most homogeneous color subsets. So we ended to a new equation based on the only measure of the global dispersion of the color points of modes:

$$DH'(S) = 1 \ if \ \sigma(S) = 1 \qquad DH'(S) = \frac{1}{\sigma(S)} \ if \ \sigma(S) > 0$$

(8)

The consideration of the connectedness degree of the set S by taking into account the neighboring pixels belong to the union of two subsets S_1 and S_2 does not privilege the union of two most connected subsets.

We define the new connectedness degree of the set of pixels corresponding to a mode taking into account the neighboring pixels in the set of pixels corresponding to the adjacent mode.

Let P a pixel belong to the subset S_1, and $N_{S2}(P)$ the neighboring pixels of P belong to S_2 :

The connectedness degree of the set of pixels corresponding to a mode taking into account the neighboring pixels in the set of pixels corresponding to the adjacent mode is :

$$DC'(S_1, S_2) = Max\{dc'(S_1 / S_2), dc'(S_2 / S_1\}$$

(9)

$$dc'(S_1 / S_2) = \sum_{P \in S1} \frac{card\{Q \in N_{S2}(P)\}}{card\{P \in S_1\} \times 8}$$

(10)

Finally the spatial-color compactness degree of the pixels corresponding to two adjacent modes is defined as the product of the connectedness degree and the homogeneity degrees :

$$DCO'(S_1, S_2) = DC'(S_1, S_2) \times DH'(S_1 \cup S_2) \tag{11}$$

The merging of the over-partitioning modes of the color histogram using the spatial-color compactness degree as a merging criterion consist to merge firstly the two adjacent modes which are a high value of the spatial-color compactness degree.

After this step of merging, the modes adjacency graph is updating by considering the new adjacencies and the new spatial-color compactness degrees.

This analysis is repeated until to have the desired number of modes, the results merging are represented in Fig.3 ((g) ,(h)).

By examining the segmented image, we notice that we were able to identify all regions in the image plane and the coresponding modes of the color histogram.

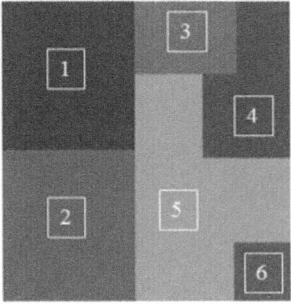   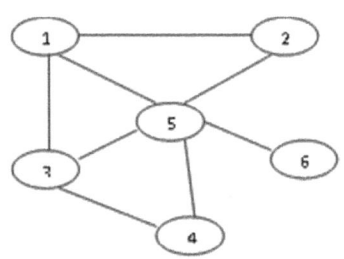

Fig. 1. (a) Partitioning modes histogram   (b) Modes adjacency graph

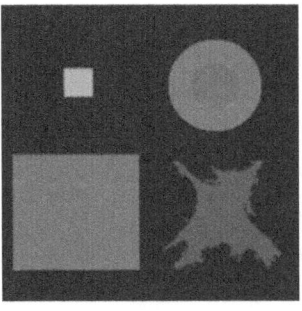   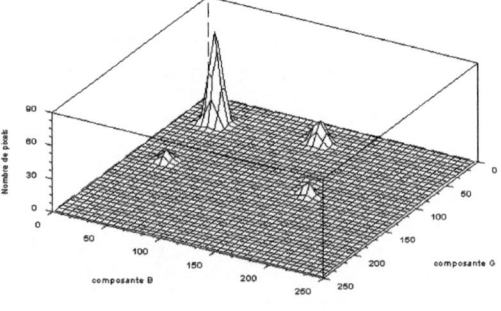

Fig. 2. (a) Synthetic Image   (b) 3-D Representation of Histogram (G, B)

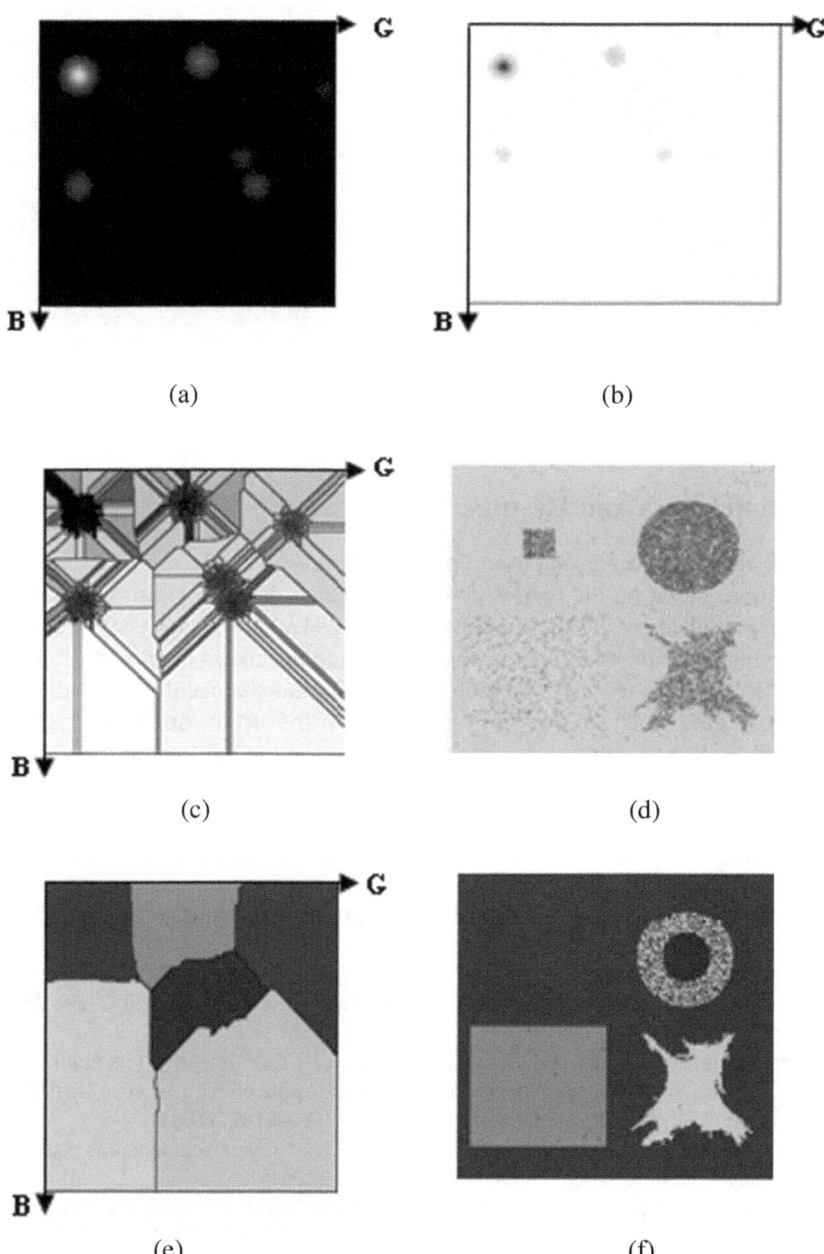

Fig. 3. (a) 2D Histogram in the (G, B) plane. (b) 2D inverted histogram in the (G, B) plane. (c) partitioning histogram by watershed. (d) segmented image. (e) histogram after merging by gravity centers. (e) segmented image using the gravity centers criterion. (g) histogram after merging by spatial-color compactness degree criterion. (h) segmented image using the spatial-color compactness degree criterion.

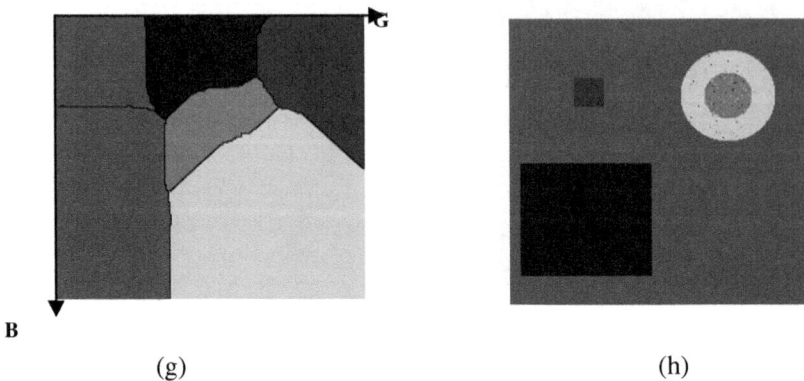

(g)   (h)

Fig. 3. (*Continued*)

4   Conclusion and Results

In this work we have presented an approach for color image segmentation by pixel classification, based on the modes detection of the color histogram by the watershed algorithm followed by the merging step of modes by mode adjacency graph using a new merging criterion which is the spatial-color compactness degree. As future work, we plan to generalize our approach from two dimensional to three dimensional histograms. And use other color spaces than the RGB space to perform the segmentation. Finaly apply our approach on the seaweed images in order to separate the different species.

References

1. Lucchese, L., Mitra, S.: Colour image segmentation: A state of the art Survey. PINSA 67(2), 207–221 (2001)
2. Deng, Y., Manjunath, B.S., Shin, H.: Color Image Segmentation. In: IEEE Computer Society Conference on Computer Vision and Pattern Recognition, vol. 2, pp. 2446–2451 (1999)
3. Vandenbroucke, N., Macaire, L., Postaire, J.-G.: Color image segmentation by pixel classification in an adapted hybrid color space: Application to soccer image analysis. Computer Vision and Image Understanding 90(2), 190–216 (2003)
4. Cheng, H.-D., Jiang, X.-H., Sun, Y., Wang, J.: Color image segmentation: advances and prospects. Pattern Recognition 34(12), 2259–2281 (2001)
5. Shafarenko, L., Petrou, M., Kittler, J.V.: Histogram based segmentation in a perceptually uniform color space. IEEE Trans. on Image Processing. 7(9), 1354–1358 (1998)
6. Géraud, T., Strub, P.-Y., Darbon, J.: Color Image Segmentation Based On Automatic Morphological Clustering. In: The Proceedings of the IEEE International Conference on Image Processing, vol. 3, pp. 70–73 (2001)
7. Dai, S., Zhang, Y-J.: Color image segmentation with watershed on color histogram and Markov random fields. In: Proceedings of the 4th International Conference on Information, Communications and Signal Processing, and the 4th Pacific-Rim Conference on Multimedia (ICICS-PCM 2003), vol. 1, pp. 527–531 (2003)

8. Vincent, L., Soille, P.: Watersheds in Digital Spaces: an Efficient Algorithm Based on Immersion Simulations. IEEE Transactions on Pattern Analysis and Machine Intelligence 13(6) (1991)
9. Shafarenko, L., Petrou, M., Kittler, J.: Automatic watershed segmentation of randomly textured color images. IEEE Transactions on Image Processing 6(11), 1530–1543 (1997)
10. Trémeau, A., Colantoni, P.: Region adjacency graph applied to color image segmentation. IEEE Transactions on Image Processing 9(4), 735–744 (2000)
11. Duarte, A., Sanchez, A., Fernandez, F., Montemayor, A.: Improving image segmentation quality through effective region merging using a hierarchical social metaheuristic. Pattern Recognition Letters 27(11), 1239–1251 (2006)
12. Lezoray, O., Elmoataz, A., Saint-Lo, F.: Graph based smoothing and segmentation of color images. In: Proceedings of Seventh International Symposium on Signal Processing and Its Applications (2003)
13. Colantoni, P.: Contribution des structures de données à la segmentation d'images couleur-Élaboration d'un outil d'infographie textile. PhD thesis, Université Jean Monnet de Saint-Etienne (1998)
14. Macaire, L., Vandenbroucke, N., Postaire, J.-G.: Segmentation d'images par classification spatio-colorimétrique des pixels. Traitement du Signal 21(5), 423–438 (2004)
15. Montagnuolo, M., Messina, A., Borgotallo, R.: Automatic Segmentation, Aggregation and Indexing of Multimodal News Information from Television and the Internet. Journal of Digital Information Management 8(6), 387–395 (2010)

Video Stabilization and Completion Using the Scale-Invariant Features and RANSAC Robust Estimator

Moones Rasti and Mohammad Taghi Sadeghi

Electrical and Computer Engineering Department, Yazd University, Yazd, Iran
mrasti64@yahoo.com,
m.sadeghi@yazduni.ac.ir

Abstract. Video stabilization is an important video enhancement process which attempts to remove unwanted vibrations from the video frames. Software solutions to this problem consist of three main stages namely "motion estimation", "motion smoothing and correction" and "frames completion". In motion estimation, a global motion model is determined by extracting a set of feature points within frames and matching them in neighboring frames. We use the Scale Invariant feature and RANSAC robust estimator for acquiring the motion parameters. The effect of high frequency components which are related to the unwanted vibrations are then removed using a spatio-temporal Gaussian lowpass filter. A modified mosaicing algorithm is finally applied in order to complete the undefined regions resulted from motion correction. In our modified mosaicing algorithm, considering the original unstabilized neighboring frames and their associated motion models, the value of an undefined pixel is determined by minimizing the distance between its nearest defined pixels and the corresponding pixels in the neighboring frames.

Keywords: Video stabilization, Scale Invariant Feature Transform (SIFT), RANSAC, Gaussian interpolation, mosaicing.

1   Introduction

A video stream is an important source of information as compared to a static image. A static image provides a snapshot of a scene, but a video stream records also scene's dynamics. The recorded motion contains information about the temporal and spatial relationship between the scene objects. This information can be used in many applications such as traffic monitoring, safety supervision and so on.

Video captured by video camera often has frame-to-frame jitter due to camera shake. The camera movement is caused because of unsteady hold or support for example where the camera is hold by hand or the recording is performed from a moving vehicle. This problem hardens automatic processing and analysis of the video frames and degrades the visual quality of the video significantly. Video stabilization is an attempt to remove the unwanted vibrations effects. Video stabilization solutions are divided into two main categories: Mechanical and Software methods. In the former, unwanted camera motions are detected using motion sensors such as accelerometers and gyroscopes. The unwanted vibrations are then removed using an

P. Pichappan, H. Ahmadi, and E. Ariwa (Eds.): INCT 2011, CCIS 241, pp. 274–281, 2011.
© Springer-Verlag Berlin Heidelberg 2011

active optical system. In the latter one, the effects of vibration are compensated by post processing of the recorded video stream.

The software solutions consist of three main stages. First, a global motion model is estimated. In feature based motion estimation, distinctive features are extracted within each frame. The feature points which are extracted from the successive frames are then matched. The motion parameters are obtained from these feature points correspondences. In [1-4], the Scale-Invariant Feature Transform, SIFT, algorithm [5] has been proposed for detecting the feature points. Scale-invariant features are invariant to image scale and rotation. They provide robust matching across a range of affine distortion, illumination changes and change in 3D viewpoint. Due to these desired properties, scale invariant features have been widely used in object recognition [5] and recently in our intended application.

In the next stage, motion smoothing process is performed using the estimated motion model. In this step, the intentional camera motion such as image zooming and translational or dolly motion with respect to the scene should be retrieved. This aspect of motion is desirable and should not be removed. Since the intentional camera movement is usually slow, we can retrieve it using a lowpass filter. In practice, there is no unified standard for evaluating the desired level of motion smoothness and the goal is usually to obtain a video which is visually pleasant. Low-pass filtering in the Fourier domain on the camera motion trajectory [6] and Gaussian lowpass filtering in the spatio-temporal domain [1,7] are among the well known proposed approaches. These solutions provide a smoothed stabilized motion and can be applied for off-line stabilization of a recorded video. However, these methods are not suitable for real-time implementation because of the large amount of memory which is needed to store several frames. In this study an offline scenario has been considered. So, we apply the spatio-temporal domain Gaussian filter. For real-time applications, a causal low-pass filter is preferred. In [4,8], it has been shown that robust solutions for on-line video stabilization can be provided by applying Kalman filtering procedures.

Based on the estimated motion parameters and the associated transform, the motion compensation process is performed using the frame warping technique. At the final stage, the value of undefined pixels which are appeared in the margins of the stabilized frames as a result of frame warping should be determined. This is performed using the value of the corresponding pixels of the neighboring frames. In a mosaicing algorithm proposed in [8], this process is performed considering the stabilized video. However, since the neighboring frames of the stabilized video contain undefined regions too, a lot of neighboring frames should be taken into account especially when the corrective displacement is large. In this study, the associated neighbors from the original unstabilized video have been used in the mosaicing process. These frames do not contain any undefined regions. Apparently, the transformation between the central stabilized frame and its unstabilized neighbors should be taken into account. Considering the potential candidates from the neighboring frames, the value of an undefined pixel is set to the value of the pixel which has the minimum R,G,B difference to the nearest defined neighboring pixels of the undefined pixel.

Nowadays, commercial software packages are available for video stabilization but they are not very accurate for complex scenarios. They usually do not include any video completion stage too. The modified frames are usually cropped in order to remove any undefined region. As the result, a set of lower resolution frames are achieved. Matlab Toolbox for video stabilization and Digistudio filter in Virtual dub are examples of these packages. In the Matlab toolbox, a pre-determined target which is almost fixed in all frames has to be existed. This is not the case in many taken videos. The Digistudio filter also does not distinguish any differences between the intentional and unwanted motions.

The rest of this paper is organized as follows. In Section 2, our adopted motion estimation and modeling process is explained. The motion smoothing approach using the Gaussian filter is discussed in Section 3. Section 4, describes the applied mosaicing method. Our experimental results are shown in Section 5.

2   Motion Estimation

As we mentioned, the SIFT descriptor gives us the key-points of each frame. The nearest neighbor algorithm is used to match the key-points of the successive frames [5]. Since the SIFT features are highly distinctive, a correct match can often be found.

2.1   Motion Model

Estimating a full 3D model of a scene under fundamental transformation including depth variations is generally a complicated problem. At least, seven point's correspondences are required to find such a transform function. Therefore, in this work, similar to most of the prior works in this field, a 2D affine model with 6 degrees of freedom describing rotation, panning, small translation of camera and small depth variations is chosen.

The affine transformation between 2 points of [x y] and [u v] can be written as:

$$\begin{bmatrix} u \\ v \end{bmatrix} = \begin{bmatrix} m1 & m2 \\ m3 & m4 \end{bmatrix} \begin{bmatrix} x \\ y \end{bmatrix} + \begin{bmatrix} t_x \\ t_y \end{bmatrix} \tag{1}$$

where t_x and t_y demonstrate the model translation and m_i s describe the affine rotation, scale and stretch. The minimum required point's correspondences in this affine estimation are three.

2.2   Model Parameters Estimation

Among the extracted feature points, there usually are a number of outliers. For example, in our problem, the key-points which are related to the moving objects act as outliers. Thus, a robust estimator should be used for estimating of the affine motion parameters. Since, the RANSAC estimator is robust against up to 50% outliers, we choose this estimator.

Unlike the common techniques that use as much of the data as possible to obtain an initial solution and then attempt to eliminate outliers, RANSAC uses the minimum number of initial data and then enlarges this set with the consistent data points [9]. The minimum number of required feature point's correspondences between two images for affine model estimation is three. For attaining affine parameters, (1) can be written as:

$$
\begin{bmatrix} x & y & 0 & 0 & 1 & 0 \\ 0 & 0 & x & y & 0 & 1 \\ & & \cdots\cdots & & & \\ & & \cdots\cdots & & & \end{bmatrix}
\begin{bmatrix} m_1 \\ m_2 \\ m_3 \\ m_4 \\ t_x \\ t_y \end{bmatrix}
=
\begin{bmatrix} u \\ v \\ \cdot \\ \cdot \\ \cdot \\ \cdot \end{bmatrix}
\tag{2}
$$

$$A\,X = b$$

As we mentioned, only 3 pairs of points are sufficient for solving this equation. The Least Square solution which minimizes the sum of the squares of distances between the model and the location of the points can be used to solve (2):

$$X = [A^T\ A]^{-1}\ A^T b \tag{3}$$

Actually, the RANSAC algorithm uses the above equation in the iterations of the model estimation process using a selected set of the data points.

3   Motion Smoothing

The motion parameters are smoothed by applying a spatio-temporal Gaussian lowpass filter. In order to prevent from accumulative error due to the cascade of original and smoothed transformation chain, the local displacement between the neighboring frames is smoothed.

Suppose I_t and $T_t^{\,j}$ respectively represent the under-processed frame and the coordinate transform from frame t to frame j found by the RANSAC robust estimator. Considering $2k$ neighboring frames, $N_t = \{\, j\,|\,t-k\leq j \leq t+k\,\}$, the smoothed transform from I_t to the compensated frame, $I_t^{'}$, is obtained by:

$$S_t = \sum_{j\in N_t} T_t^{\,j} \times G(K) \tag{4}$$

where $G(K)$ is a Gaussian kernel with $\sigma = \sqrt{K}$. The corrected frame, $I_t^{'}$, can be obtained by warping the original frame I_t using:

$$I_t^{'}(p_t^{'}) = I_t\,(S_t\ p_t) \tag{5}$$

An appropriate level of smoothness can be obtained by tuning of K. A larger value of K leads to a smoother result. We found that K equal to 6 is suitable in most of the cases. Fig. 1 contains plots of translation element of camera motion path along frames before and after motion smoothing for x and y coordinates.

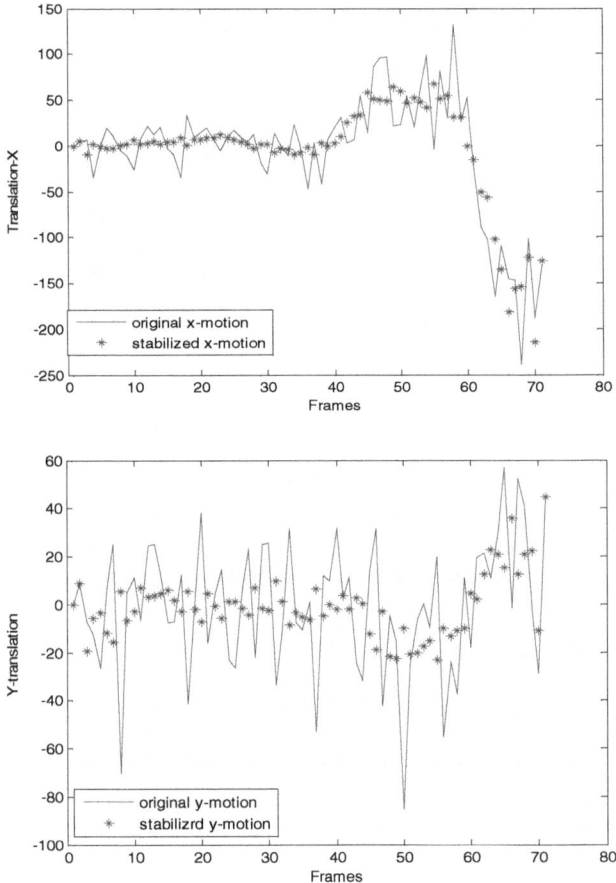

Fig. 1. The original and smoothed motion path

Although a smoother video is obtained by using a larger K, but more amount of memory is needed for saving the video frames and the process becomes slower.

4   Frame Mosaicing

After motion compensation, undefined regions are appeared around the frames. In these regions, no data is available yielding visual artifacts. We use mosaicing method for completing of these regions.

For this purpose, the registration transform between the neighboring frames and the stabilized frame that we want to complete it have to be found. Actually, the undefined pixels are filled using their corresponding values in the neighboring frames. In prior works such as [8], the completion process is performed using the stabilized neighboring frames. However, since these frames have undefined regions too, we prefer to use the original unstabilized frames in order to fill the undefined regions.

Fig. 2 contains examples of the associated results using these two methods. It can be seen that more appropriate results are obtained by using the original frames within the framework of the completion process. It should be noted that in both cases (using either the original neighboring frames or the stabilized neighbors), the spatial transformation between the frames has to be taken into account.   Thus, we find registration parameters between the central frame and its neighbors using the RANSAC estimator. Based on the mosaicing methods presented in [1] and [8], we propose a novel approach in which the undefined pixels of stabilized frame are sorted with respect to their distances from the boundary of the defined region. The filling process is started from the nearest undefined pixel to the boundary and continues towards the more far ones. Among the candidate pixels for replacing, we choose the value of the pixel that sum of its R,G,B differences with the R,G,B values of its 4-nearest defined neighbors in stabilized frame is minimum. Our experimental results show that more appropriate values are selected using the proposed method. This method prevents from misalignment of central defined pixels and the pixels defined by completion process due to some inaccurate interframe transformations.

(a)   (b)

Fig. 2. Proposed mosaicing method using (a) original video (proposed) and (b) satabilized video for neiboring frames

5   Results

The performance of our stabilization algorithm has been evaluated using several video streams. Based on our experiments, the smoothing parameter, K, is set to 6, 6 frames before and 6 frames after the central frame. In the mosaicing process also, 12 neighboring frames are considered. Fig. 3 contains the associated results using one of the video streams. The first row represents original unstabilized video frames 8, 18, 28, 48. The second row shows motion compensated frames before completion of undefined regions. The completed frames are shown in the third row.

Fig. 3. Result of video stabilization. First row: original unstabilized video frames 8, 18, 28, 48. Second row: motion compensated frames before completion of undefined regions, and third row: stabilized and completed frames.

The video streaming is empirically addressed in a few recent studies [10, 11]. Our work support the results obtained in the above studies. Further we have addressed video stabilization in an elegant way.

References

1. Hu, R., Shi, R., Shen, I., Chen, W.: Video Stabilization Using Scale-Invariant Features. In: 11th International Conference Information Visualization, IV 2007 (2007)
2. Shen, Y., Buckles, B.P.: Video Stabilization Using Principal Component Analysis and Scale Invariant Feature Transform in Particle Filter Framework. IEEE Transactions on Consumer Electronics 55(3) (2009)

3. Battiato, S., Gallo, G., Puglisi, G., Scellato, S.: SIFT Features Tracking for Video Stabilization. In: 14th International Conference on Image Analysis and Processing, ICIAP (2007)
4. Yang, J., Schonfeld, D., Chen, C., Mohamed, M.: Online video stabilization based on particle filters. In: IEEE International Conference on Image Processing, ICIP (2006)
5. Lowe, D.G.: The Physiology of the Grid: Distinctive image features from scale-invariant keypoints. International Journal of Computer Vision 60(2), 91–110 (2004)
6. Erturk, S., Dennis, T.: Image sequence stabilization based on DFT filtering. IEE Proc. on Vision Image and Signal Processing 147(2), 95–102 (2000)
7. Matsushita, Y., Ofek, E., Tang, X., Shum, H.Y.: Full-frame video stabilization. In: IEEE Computer Society Conference on Computer Vision and Pattern Recognition, vol. 1, pp. 50–57 (2005)
8. Litvin, A., Konrad, J., Karl, W.: Probabilistic video stabilization using kalman filtering and mosaicking. In: Proc. SPIE Image and Video Communications and Process., vol. 5022, pp. 663–674 (2003)
9. Hartley, R., Zisserman, A.: Multiple View Geometry in Computer Vision, 2nd edn. University Press, Cambridge (2003)
10. Ali, A., Fathy, M.: Key-Frame Based Video Summarization Using QR-Decomposition. Journal of Networking Technology 1(3), 138–147 (2010)
11. Kang, L., Lim, K.B., Yao, J.: Image Recognition of Occluded Objects Based on Improved Curve Moment Invariants. Journal of Digital Information Management 7(3), 152–158 (2009)

Improvement in Automatic Classification of Persian Documents by Means of Support Vector Machine and Representative Vector

Jafari Ashkan[1], Ezadi Hamed[2], Hossennejad Mihan[1], and Noohi Taher[3]

[1] Islamic Azad University Jolfa Branch, Jolfa, Iran
[2] Islamic Azad University Eghlid Branch, Eghlid, Iran
[3] Islamic Azad University Najafabad Branch, Najafabad, Iran
{ajafari35,hamed_ezadi,mihan.hossennejad,t.noohi}@gmail.com

Abstract. Representative Vector is a kind of Vector which includes related words and the degree of their relationships. In this paper the effect of using this kind of Vector on automatic classification of Persian documents is examined. In this method, preprocessed documents, extra words as well as word stems are at first found. Next, through one of the known ways, some features are extracted for each category. Then, the Representative Vector, which is made based on the elicited features, leads to some more detailed words which are better Representatives for each category. Findings of the experiments show that Precision and Recall can be increased significantly by extra words omission and addition of few words in the Representative Vectors as well as the use of a famous classification model like Support Vector Machine (SVM).

Keywords: Documents Classification, Representative Vector, Stemming, Support Vector Machine.

1 Introduction

As information is producing increasingly, pressing need to classify it in order to optimize information retrieval is highlighted. Finding necessary information is only possible through searching keywords by search engines. Scientists usually find their required information easily through reading valid journals related to their scientific fields. This is because most of the times a person who is searching some information doesn't know a specific definition about what he needs and can not choose a certain keyword based on which he can search. Therefore, people can better find their necessary information through paging books. When information is classified topically, every specialist can get some necessary information easily by searching information related to their fields and will not waste their time searching a lot of unrelated information and retrieved documents [1]. Here, classification of digital resources seems vital. Unless digital resources classify, because they are absent physically it looks they have lost. The text mining studies are gaining more importance recently because of the availability of the increasing number of the electronic documents from a variety of sources. The resources of unstructured and

P. Pichappan, H. Ahmadi, and E. Ariwa (Eds.): INCT 2011, CCIS 241, pp. 282–292, 2011.

semi structured information include the world wide web, govermental electronic repositories, news articles, biological database, chat rooms, digital libraries, online forums, electronic mail and blog repositories. Therefore, proper classification and knowledge discovery form these resources is an important area for research.

Natural Language Processing (NLP), data mining, and machine learning techniques work together to automatically classify and discover patterns from the electronic documents. The main goal of text mining is to enable users to extract information from textual resources and deals with the operations like, retrieval, classification (supervised, unsupervised and semi supervised) and summarization. However how these documented can be properly annotated, presented and classified. So it consists of several challenges, like proper annotation to the documents, appropriate document representation, dimensionality reduction to handle algorithmic issues [2], and an appropriate classifier function to obtain good generalization and avoid over-fitting. Extraction, integration and classification of electronic documents from different sources and knowledge discovery from these documents are important for the research communities.

Today the web is the main source for the text documents, the amount of textual data available to us is consistently increasing, and approximately 80% of the information of an organization is stored in unstructured textual format [3], in the form of reports, email, views and news etc. the [4], shows that approximately 90% of the worlds data is held in unstructured formats, so information intensive business processes demand that we transcend from simple document retrieval to knowledge discovery. The need of automatically retrieval of useful knowledge from the huge amount of textual data in order to assist the human analysis is fully apparent [5]. This paper examines automatic classification in Persian texts by means of Representative Vectors and Support Vector Machine. Finally, findings of the research on some data texts are presented.

Related Works. Market trend based on the content of the online news articles, sentiments, and events is an emerging topic for research in data mining and text mining community [6]. For these purpose state-of-the-art approaches to text classifications are presented in [7], in which three problems were discussed: documents representation, classifier construction and classifier evaluation. So constructing a data structure that can represent the documents, and constructing a classifier that can be used to predicate the class lable of a document with high accuracy, are the key points in text classification.

Text classification is an important component in many informational management tasks, however with the explosive growth of the web data, algorithms that can improve the classification efficiency while maintaining accuracy, are highly desired [8].

Based on ant colony optimization a new feature selection algorithm is presented in [9], to improve the text categorization. Also in [10] the authors introduced a new weighting method based on statistical estimation of the importance of a word categorization problem.

The authors in [11] focused on the document representation techniques and demonstrate that the choice of document representation has a profound impact on the quality of the classifier. They used the centroid-based text classifier, which is a simple and robust text classification scheme, and compare four different types of document representations: N-grams, Single terms, phrases and RDR which is a logic-based documents representation. The N-gram is a string-based representation with no linguistic processing. The Single term approach is based on words with minimum linguistic processing. The phrase approach is based on linguistically formed phrases and single words. The RDR is based on linguistic processing and representing documents as a set of logical predicates. In [12] the authors present significantly more efficient indexing and classification of large document repositories, e.g. to support information retrieval over all enterprise file servers with frequent file updates.

Document classification has many uses such as, automatic question answering systems [13], information filtering, unimportant e-mail classification and other related areas [14]. In [15], a new technique based on ontology is offered for classification. The authors in [16] propose a Poisson Naïve Bayes text classification model with weight enhancing method, and shows that the new model assumes that a document is generated by a multivariate Poisson model. They suggest per-document term frequency normalization to estimate the Poisson parameter, while the traditional multinomial classifier estimates its parameters by considering all the training documents as a unique huge training document.

In [17], some results about automatic Persian text classification by indexing 4-gram and 3-gram measures are shown. Investigation of different approaches about automatic text classification in a new environment is dealt with in [17]. In [18], Persian text classification through KNN algorithm and its phase copy is presented. In [19], age ranges in speakers can be determined by examination of the related features in their vocal cords. In order to do that and to make optimal distinction among different categories including several age ranges, SVM is used.

Innovation in This Paper. Here, Representative Vector is used to improve text classification in texts to which learning collection is possible, for example, a collection of news which is elicited from different resources automatically and is not patterned. Thus, in classification process, use of one special resource for learning step can not present all words of that category. Structure of the article is as follows:

In the next section, we will introduce the aforesaid issue and its related terms. In Section 3, we elaborate on the proposed solution. In Section 4, the relevant experiments and their results are shown. The last Section includes conclusions and further researches.

2   Statement of the Problem

The objective of document classification is to find the best category for each document. We have a good collection which is labeled by people as train set. Some words are usually selected from the train set. This process is called characteristic elicitation. Characteristic elicitation includes a selection of subordinate words which are available in the train set. This is done in such a way that only the same words are used for the classification. This has two reasons: first, the speed of training and classification is increased because of reduction in words numbers in the set. Second, noise word omission leads to Precision increase. A noise word is a kind of word that causes error increase in classification after learning process, we use the acquired knowledge in a new data collection called test set [20]. Our purpose is to expand the characteristic elicitation in order to use it in classification of new documents. The instrument that we use here to find the related words with selected characteristic and to improve classification results is named Representative Vector. Representative Vector includes all related words and the degree of their relationships [21]. In the next section, we will be familiar with this concept, its use and some ways of making it.

Support Vector Machine (SVM). Support Vector Machines (SVMs) are one of the discriminative classification methods which are commonly recognized to be more accurate. The SVM classification method is based on the Structural Risk Minimization principle from computational learning theory [22]. The idea of this principle is to find a hypothesis to guarantee the lowest true error. Besides, the SVM are well-founded that very open to theoretical understanding and analysis [23]. The SVM need both positive and negative training set which are uncommon for other classification methods. These positive and negative training set are needed for the SVM to seek for the decision surface that best separates the positive from the negative data in the n-dimensional space, so called the hyper plane. The document representatives which are closest to the decision surface are called the support vector. The performance of the SVM classification remains unchanged if documents that do not belong to the Support Vectors are removed from the set of training data [24].

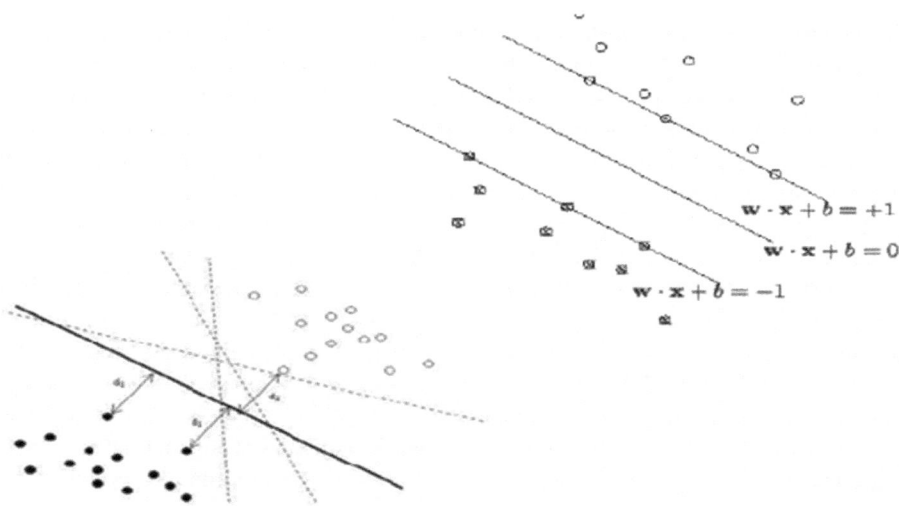

$$\mathbf{w} \cdot \mathbf{x} + b = +1$$
$$\mathbf{w} \cdot \mathbf{x} + b = 0$$
$$\mathbf{w} \cdot \mathbf{x} + b = -1$$

Fig. 1. Illustration of optimal separating hyper plane, hyper planes and Support Vectors[24]

The SVM classification method is outstanding from the others with its outstanding classification effectiveness [24] [25] [26] [27] [28] [29]. Furthermore, it can handle documents with high dimensional input space, and culls out most of the irrelevant features. However, the major drawback of the SVM is their relatively complex training and categorizing algorithms and also the high time and memory consumptions during training stage and classifying stage. Besides, confusions occur

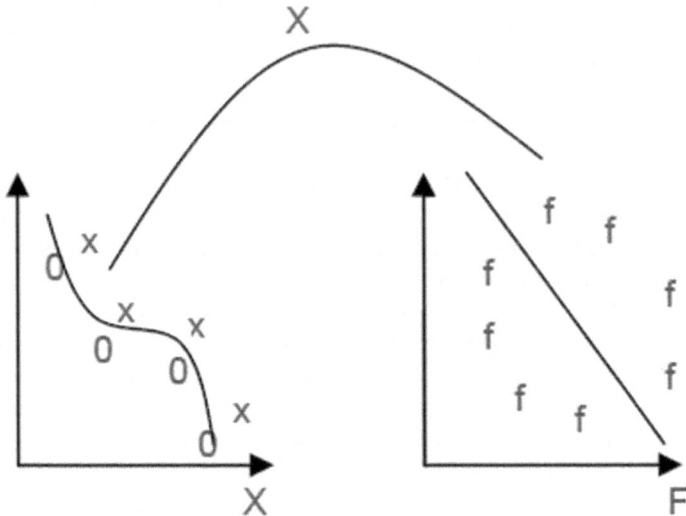

Fig. 2. Mapping non linear input space onto high dimensional space [24]

during the classification tasks due to the documents could be a notated to several categories because of the similarity is typically calculated individually for each category [24]. So SVM is supervised learning method for classification to find out the linear separating hyperplane which maximize the margin, i.e., the optimal separating hyperplane (OSH) and maximizes the margin between the two data sets. To calculate the margin, two parallel hyperplanes are constructed, one on each side of the separating hyperplane, which are "pushed up against" the two data sets. Intuitively, a good separation is achieved by the hyperplane that has the largest distance to the neighboring data points of both classes, since in general the larger the margin the lower the generalization error of the classifier. The SVM is a best technique for the documents classification [30]. The authors in [29] implemented and measured the performance of the leading supervised and unsupervised approaches for multilingual text categorization; they selected support vector machines (SVM) as representative of supervised techniques as well as latent semantic indexing (LSI) and self-organizing maps (SOM) techniques for unsupervised methods for system implementation.

3   Solution Steps

General steps in the figure 3 are shown. At first, some features are elicited for each category. The corpus includes HAMSHAHRI news in which categories have already specified. In the next step, Representative Vectors are made for the elicited features. Representative Vectors present some words for features that have semantic relationship with that feature. We use these words to improve the collection of features for each category. In next sections we will explain these steps and demonstrate the results.

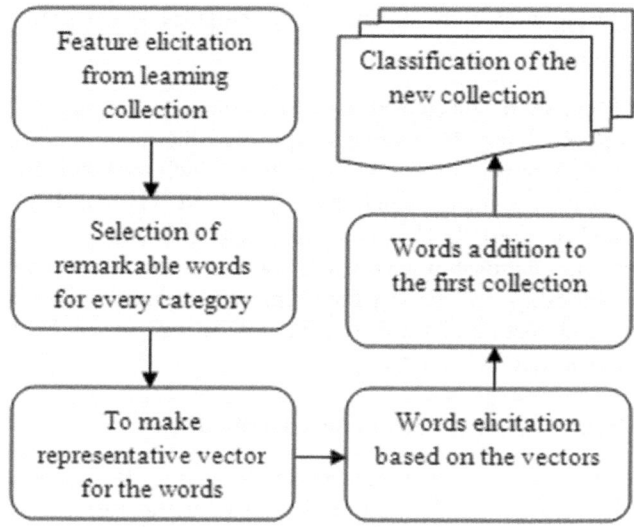

Fig. 3. General steps in the offered algorithm

3.1   Feature Elicitation

For feature elicitation in every category, we have used the method MI. By means of MI we can realize to what extent presence or absence of a word in a document may inform us about a category [20]. Based on formula 1, every word and category is given a score. Then all words in each category should be ordered based on the weight that they gain in that category and the top ones should be chosen.

$$I(U, C) = \sum_{e_t \text{ in } \{1,0\}} \sum_{e_c \text{ in } \{1,0\}} \left(P(U = e_t, C = e_c) \times \log \frac{P(U=e_t, C=e_c)}{P(U=e_t) \times P(C=e_c)'} \right) \quad (1)$$

3.2   How to Make a Representative Vector

At first, we explain how to make Representative Vector. A series of documents used to make a Representative Vector are labled C. the process starts with a word for which we want to make a Representative Vector. At first we assume that the given word is a kind of search. Then C is organized based on the search (according to one of retrieval methods like OKAPI). We select ten first documents and calculate a weight for each of the present words in these ten documents formula 2.

$$W_{d,t_i} = \frac{tf(t_{i,d}) \times (C_{doc} - df(t_i))}{\sum_i tf(t_{i,d}) \times C_{doc}} \quad (2)$$

w_{d,t_i} is the weight of t_i in document D. Next, the final weight of every word in the collection of selected words for each category is calculated by formula 3.

$$W_{t_i} = \frac{\sum_{j=1}^{NoDocs} W'_{d_j,t_i}}{NoDocs} \quad (3)$$

W'_{d_j,t_i} is the weight of t_i in document d_j. NoDocs is equal to the number of retrieved documents (i.e. 10).

Optimization Step. we have selected ten first words from among the best documents related to a word X so far. We have also specified the most important words from among all available words in these ten documents, which are labeled t_i. The acquired words by this way are those which have got high TF and IDF scores among documents related to word X. However, this high score may be because of factors other than semantic relationship between X and t_i. Thus, we add an extra phase to improve the relationship. All the steps are repeated for each t_i in this phase. If X is also present in the collection of words related to t_i, it is highly probable that there is a close relationship between X and t_i.

3.3   Use of Representative Vectors for Classification

Up to now, we elicited ten words for each category and made a Representative Vector for each of them. Now, we have ten Representative Vectors that each includes some related words with a concept. For example, in Table 1, ten elicited words form category اقتصاد ("economy") are shown in the left table by MI method. The right table demonstrates the Representative Vectors for the word بازار ("market") which are ordered based on their weights calculated in formula 3.

Table 1. The left table: elicited words from economy category, the right table Representative Vector of the word بازار ("market")

دسته اقتصاد ("economy category") English Translation		بازار ("Market") English Translation		وزن ("weight")
سال	year	نفت	petrol	0.87320001
گزارش	report	دلار	dollar	0.83331113
افزایش	increase	جهانی	universal	0.70001112
ایران	iran	قیمت	cost	0.68998710
درصد	precentage	طلا	gold	0.66663331
تولید	production	بانک	bank	0.57783333
اقتصادی	economical	فروش	sale	0.49999877
توسعه	extension	تورم	inflation	0.45321111
برنامه	program	سکه	coin	0.44398900
بازار	market	بشکه	barrel	0.41116111

4   Expriments and Results

In this project, we have used the HAMSHAHRI corpus [31], as the train and test set. This corpus contains 160000 news between 1997 and 2002 years. We have only four categories including economy, politics, science and sport for the experiments. To make Representative Vectors ISNA corpus [21], which has more than 500 mega bytes of data, is used. In many other studies [32-38], large text collections are subjected to corpus testing. Our experiment is comprised of two main phases. The steps done in the first phase are as follows:

The first step: extra words, prepositions and numbers are omitted for every category that is in the train set. Then by a simple evolution algorithm stems of the words are offered.

The second step: preprocessed documents are indexed and some features are elicited by MI. In the third step according to the elicited features and the documents to the category, word-document matrix is made. In this matrix, columns indicate features and rows demonstrate the documents including the features. Each cell in this matrix indicate the weight TF-IDF of the feature in the mentioned document. The last column shows the category of documents. In the last step, we use Support Vector Machine and the train set is made. The test set is also made in this way. For the precise evaluation, first we use the test set while the documents are not preprocessed. Table 2, shows the details of the experiment.

Table 2. Precision and Recall of SVM Classifier While the Documents are not Preprocessed

Category	Recall	Precision
Economy	0.62	0.939
Politics	0.49	0.7
Science	0.55	0.797
Sport	0.92	0.472
Average	64.5%	72.7%

In the next step, we preprocess the test set and omit extra words, prepositions and numbers and find the stems of the words. Table 3, shows the details of the experiment.

Table 3. Precision and Recall of SVM Classifier after Documents Preprocessing

Category	Recall	Precision
Economy	0.75	0.852
Politics	0.61	0.685
Science	0.84	0.808
Sport	0.82	0.689
Average	75.5%	76%

As we expect, preprocessing ways improve Precision and Recall in SVM. In the second phase of the experiments, all the steps done in the previous phase are repeated. Only with the difference that this time, we have an additional step called "how to make Representative Vector". For each elicited feature during this step, we make a Representative Vector MI, then we add a few words to the collection of available features which are better Representatives for that feature. Table 4, demonstrates the effect of Representative Vector on Precision and Recall of classification by Support Vector Machine.

Table 4. The Impact of Representative Vector on Precision and Recall of SVM Classifier

Category	Recall	Precision
Economy	0.72	0.947
Politics	0.7	0.753
Science	0.82	0.854
Sport	0.89	0.659
Average	78.3%	80.3%

5   Conclusion and Further Research

The main purpose of the paper, was to make a basis for the efficiency evaluation in Support Vector Machine. Document preprocessing plays an important role in the improvement of Precision and Recall of the model. After preprocessing these two measures increase to 3%, 11% Respectively. More over, the significant effect of the added words is that they improve the two mentioned measures remarkably as 4%, 3% Respectively. In economy and science categories, after using the representative vector recall measures have decreased. Probably this is because some words like گزارش ("report") are so common in these two categories, that their presence can not help the improvement of the measures.

Now, we conclude that words increase in the train set as well as preprocessing improve the efficiency and precision of the classification. In further research we aim at examining the efficiency and Precision of other classifiers by this way. Furthermore, we offer an eclectic method for feature selection in order to improve efficiency and Precision of Support Vector Machine and other classifiers.

References

1. Bina, B., Rahgozar, M., Dahmouyad, A.: Automatic classification of Persian texts. In: 13th National Conference Computer Forums Kish, Iran (2007)
2. Dasgupta, A.: Feature selection methods for text classification. In: Proceeding of the 13th International Conference on Knowledge Discovery and Data Mining, pp. 230–239 (2007)
3. Structure in Text Extraction and Exploitation. In: Raghavan, P., Amer-Yahia, S., Gravano, L. (eds.) Proceeding of the 7th International Workshop on the Web and Databases (WebDB), vol. 67(4), pp. 240–255. ACM Press (2004)
4. Oracle corporation (2008), http://www.oracle.com
5. Lynch, M.: e-Business Analytics. Depth Report (2000)
6. Falinouss, P.: Stock Trend Prediction using News Article's: a text mining approach. Master thesis (2007)
7. Sebastiani, F.: Machine learning in automated text categorization. ACM Computing Surveys (CSUR), 1–47 (2002)
8. Liu, H., Motoda, M.: Feature Extraction, construction and selection: A Data Mining Perpective. Kluwer Academic Publishers, Boston (2006)
9. Sccuy, P., Mineanu, G.W.: Beyoned TF-IDF weighting for text Categorization in the Vector Space Model. In: Proceeding of 2nd International Conference on Recent Advances in Natural Language Processing, pp. 241–248 (2007)

10. Forman, G., Kirshenbaum, E.: Extremely Fast Text Feature Extraction for Classification and Indexing. In: Proceeding of 3rd International Conference on Recent Machine Learning, Napa Valley California, USA, pp. 341–348 (2008)

11. Keikha, M., Khonsari, A., Oroumchian, F.: Rich document representation and classification: An analysis. In: Proceeding of 2nd International Conference on Knowledge-Based Systems, pp. 67–71 (2009)

12. Tam, V., Santoso, A., Setiono, R.: A comparative study of centroid-based neighborhood-based and statistical approaches for effective document categorization. In: Proceeding of the 16th International Conference on Pattern Recognition, pp. 235–238 (2002)

13. Moschitti, A.: Answer filtering via text categorization in question answering systems. In: Proceeding of 2nd International Conference on Recent Advances in Natural Language Processing, pp. 241–248 (2007)

14. Huang, Y.: Support vector machines for text categorization based on latent semantic indexing. Technical Report, electrical and computer engineering department. Johns Hopkins University (2006)

15. Shang, W., Huang, H., Zhu, H.: A Noval Feature Selection Algorithm for text catogorization. Science Direct Expert System with Application 1, 1–5 (2006)

16. Domingos, P., Pazzani, M.J.: On the Optimality of the Simple Bayesian Classifier under Zero-One Loss. Journal of Machine Learning 29(2-3), 103–130 (1997)

17. Esmail Pour, M.: Approaches and challenges category automatic classification of information resources in new environment. Library and Information Update 10(2) (2006)

18. Basiri, M., Neimati, S., Ghasem Aghayi, N.: Compare Persian texts classified using KNN algorithm and the F-KNN and select features based on information gain and document frequency. In: 13th National Conference Computer Forums Kish, Iran (2007)

19. Homaun Puor, M.M., Khosravi, M.H.: To help determine the age range speaker sound using support vector machines. In: 13th National Conference Computer Forums Kish, Iran (2007)

20. Christopher, D., Manning, P.: Introducion to Information Retrieval. Cambridge University Press (2008)

21. Amiri, H., AleAhmad, A.: Keyword Suggestion Using Concept Graph Construction from Wikipedia Rich Documents. In: ECIR 2008 Workshop on Exploiting Semantic Annotations for Information Retrieval, Glasgow (2008)

22. Joachims, T.: Text Categorization with Support Vector Machines: Learning with Many Relevant Features. In: Nédellec, C., Rouveirol, C. (eds.) ECML 1998. LNCS, vol. 1398, pp. 137–142. Springer, Heidelberg (1998)

23. Sahay, S.: Support Vector Machines and Document Classification, `http://www-static.cc.gatech.edu/~ssahay/sauravsahay7001-2.pdf`

24. McCallum, A., Nigam, K.: A Comparison of Event Models for Naïve Bayes Text Classification. Journal of Machine Learning Research 2(3), 1265–1287 (2003)

25. Chakrabarti, S., Roy, S., Soundalgekar, V.: Fast and Accurate Text Classification via Multiple Linear Discriminant Projection. International Journal on Very Large Data Bases (VLDB) 1(2), 170–185 (2003)

26. Lin, Y.: Support Vector Machines and the Bayes Rule in Classification. Technical Report, No.1014, Department of Statistics, University of Wisconsin, Madison (1999)

27. Sahay, S.: Support Vector Machines and Document Classification, `http://www-static.cc.gatech.edu/~ssahay/sauravsahay7001-2.pdf`

28. Yang, Y., Liu, X.: A Re-examination of Text Categorization Methods. School of Computer Science, Carnegie Mellon University (1999)

29. Lee, C.H., Yang, H.C.: Construction of supervised and unsupervised learning systems for multilingual text categorization. In: Proceeding of Expert Systems with Applications, pp. 2400–2410 (2009)
30. Isa, D., Kallimani, V.P.: Using Self Organizing Map for Clustering of Text Documents. In: Proceeding of Expert System with Applications, pp. 44–50 (2008)
31. Darrudi, E., Hejazi, M.R., Oroumchian, F.: Assessment of a modern farsi corpus. In: The 2nd International Workshop on Information Technology and its Disciplines, Kish Island, Iran (February 2004)
32. Zhang, D., Lee, W.S.: Query-By-Multiple-Examples using Support Vector Machines. Journal of Digital Information Management 7(4), 202–210 (2009)
33. Makrehchi, M.: Taxonomy-based Document Clustering. Journal of Digital Information Management 9(2), 79–86 (2011)
34. Suzuki, T.: A Decision Tree-based Text Art Extraction Method without any Language-Dependent Text Attribute. International Journal of Computational Linguistics Research 1(1), 12–22 (2010)
35. Overbeek, S., van Bommel, P.: Elementary Patterns for Converting Textual and Visual Formalisms based on Set Theory and ORM. Journal of Digital Information Management 9(2), 64–71 (2011)
36. Jo, T.: NTSO (Neural Text Self Organizer): A New Neural Network for Text Clustering. Journal of Networking Technology 2(3), 144–156 (2010)
37. Thabtah, F., Hadi, W., Abdel-jaber, H., Aldiabat, M.: Rule Pruning Methods in Associative Classification Text Mining. Journal of Intelligent Computing 1(1), 1–12 (2010)
38. Yadav, N., Gupta, Y., Kumar, M., Sanyal, R.: Semantic Classification, Keyword Mining and Search Space Optimization for digital ecosystems. Journal of Multimedia Processing and Technologies 1(2), 131–140 (2010)

Recognition of Isolated Handwritten Persian Characterizing Hamming Network

Masoud Arabfard, Meisam Askari, Milad Asadi, and Hosein Ebrahimpour-Komleh

Department of Computer Engineering, Kashan University, Kashan, Iran
{Arabfard,Askari,Miladasadi}@grad.kashanu.ac.ir,
Ebrahimpour@kashanu.ac.ir

Abstract. In this paper we propose a system for recognition of isolated handwritten Persian characters. A novel method that uses derivation has been used for feature extraction. Hamming network has been used for classification in this system. Hamming network is a neural network fully connected from input layer to all neuron in output layer which calculate amount of resemblance between input patterns than training patterns. The training and test patterns were gathered from dataset over 47965 patterns. The 32 characters in Persian language were categorized into 9 different classes which characters of each class are very similar to each other's. The Classification rate with this approach is about 95 percent and Recognition rate in each class is about 90 percent. The results show an increment in recognition rates in comparison with our previous work.

Keywords: OCR, hamming network, derivative feature, Isolated Persian character.

1   Introduction

In the Isolated handwritten Characters recognition tasks, we try to detect and recognize isolated letters in an image. Handwritten Characters Recognition is the process of converting handwritten characters to intelligible codes for computer [1]. OCR has been a great interested subject to many computer scientists and others [2]. There has been an increasing interest among computer researchers to expand systems that can understand the written evidences. A computer with an ability to read human written document is more user friendly, because people learn to write at early age.

Many researchers have been done with the recognition of Latin, Chinese and other scripts. Many people at world live in Persian/Arabic countries that use similar character sets, but there are no many researches about recognition of Persian/Arabic characters. Also Persian/Arabic manuscript has not more changed during time, so Persian OCR is beneficial for reading ancient scripts [3].

The process of OCR has totally four steps: pre-process, feature extraction, classification and post-process. In pre-process step image must be prepare to be processed. In this step some work like noise removal, normalization, baseline detection and slope correction is done to get better results. In non-isolated Persian an additional preprocess must be done, letter in word must be separate, this step is named

P. Pichappan, H. Ahmadi, and E. Ariwa (Eds.): INCT 2011, CCIS 241, pp. 293–304, 2011.
© Springer-Verlag Berlin Heidelberg 2011

segmentation. But some systems like [4] and [5] have no segmentation and recognize in one step without partitioning. The next step is feature extraction. Feature extraction consists of extracting some information from the images. Useful feature make better results. Features divide into two types, statistical and structural. In the classification step system tries to determine the class of the instance from the features. The last step, post-process, is used in some system to correct the result, maybe by lexicon.

1.1 Related Works

There are many algorithms for separate and recognize the Persian/Arabic characters: In [6] recognition of typed Persian letters base on breaking the letters and authenticate broken character is proposed. In [7] the main feature is the number of horizontal and vertical black pixels on the character image. At the next step the feature of input character is compare with the trained character features by Bayes algorithm. Also there are some approaches that use a set of classifiers instead of one classifier to increase the performance. We can see the results of these methods in [8, 9].

In 2005, Mozaffari et al proposed a method for recognition of Arabic number which use both structural and statistical features [10]. After that a nearest neighborhood is used for classification. Their Dataset consist of 8 digits with 280 image of each for training set and 200 images for test set written by 200 people. The result rate 94.44% is reported for detection. In [11] Safabakhsh and Adibi are used continues HMM for recognition of handwritten Nastaaligh (a difficult type of Persian writing style) scripts. In this style many words overlap the others and make recognition difficult. First in pre-process step they removed ascenders and descenders to avoid mistake in order of letters. Their system used fifty words lexicon contain all kind of letters written by seven people. The test dataset consist of 100 words by two writers. This method was based on repeat. In each repeat step take away miss-detected words. The result rate was 69% by five repeat and 91% by 20 repeat. Our work is more practical than tow case that mentioned because it doesn't restricted to some Persian character or special style.

In [12] Zand has used Projection Profile to segment typed words. He used a horizontal projection profile histogram to separate lines and a vertical projection profile histogram to separate sub-words as we see in figure1. But in our work we have isolated handwritten characters and we have used derivative of three orientation projection profiles for main features as described in section 3.

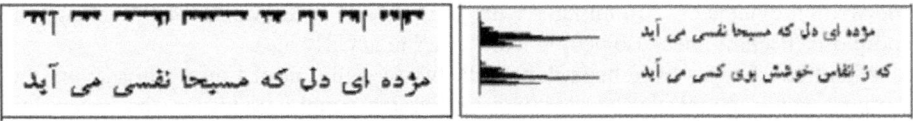

Fig. 1. Using horizontal and vertical histogram to separate lines and sub-words

In [13] Soltanzade and Rahmati have used profile of tow orientations features to recognize handwritten digits. These features aren't useful for all Persian handwritten characters because handwritten characters aren't in the same size (figure 2) so their projection histogram vectors haven't similar lengths and we can't recognize characters with this feature. To overcome on this problem we used the derivative of projection

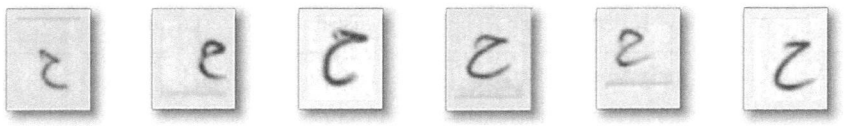

Fig. 2. A character with different sizes

profile on three orientations. By this way we only extract the variations of projection profile so it becomes independent of size of characters. We have explained these features in section 3.

1.2   Persian/Arabic Script

Persian script (also known as Farsi) is written from right to left and letter in sub-word are joined. Persian letter consist of 32 characters and Arabic letter is a subset of Persian letter. Persian characters in regard to their positions in words are divided in to four groups: separate, first, middle and end letters. These groups are shown in table 1. The choice of which group to use depends on the position of the letter in the word and neighbor letters. When letter join to each other sub-word is made. Each word consists of one or more sub-words and word never join to another word.

The lack of communication between researchers in Persian/Arabic OCR caused the repetition in this field. Also there is no standard database for Persian/Arabic OCR system to compare the systems. Some Competition like ICDAR tries to bring researcher together to fill this gap [14, 15].

In this paper letters are considered separately and focus is only on detecting isolated characters.

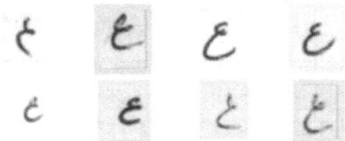

Fig. 3. Sample of character in popular dataset

Our approach has some profit over other works. For example some of them use a special typed font or a small database like a handwritten of one person but we use a huge and popular dataset which is one of its character samples shown in figure3. Some approach using a limited lexicon word and find pattern in them but in this method word pattern has no limit.

The dataset includes 47695 samples of Farsi/Arabic characters. 4216 images are used for training (8.8%) and the rest, 43479 images for test. The Persian alphabet and distortion of each character in dataset are shown below.

Table 1. Farsi/Arabic alphabet and distribution in test dataset

Name	Isolated	Initial	Medial	Final	Number of data in dataset
Alef	ا	-	-	ا	9192
Be	ب	بـ	ـبـ	ـب	1836
Pe	پ	پـ	ـپـ	ـپ	249
Te	ت	تـ	ـتـ	ـت	1233
Se	ث	ثـ	ـثـ	ـث	30
Jim	ج	جـ	ـجـ	ـج	282
Che	چ	چـ	ـچـ	ـچ	53
He	ح	حـ	ـحـ	ـح	1183
Khe	خ	خـ	ـخـ	ـخ	493
Dal	د	-	-	ـد	2344
Zal	ذ	-	-	ـذ	20
Re	ر	-	-	ـر	3562
Ze	ز	-	-	ـز	1955
Je	ژ	-	-	ـژ	61
Sin	س	سـ	ـسـ	ـس	3453
Shin	ش	شـ	ـشـ	ـش	369
Sad	ص	صـ	ـصـ	ـص	218
Zad	ض	ضـ	ـضـ	ـض	249
Ta	ط	ط	ـطـ	ـط	173
Za	ظ	ظ	ـظـ	ـظ	49
Ein	ع	عـ	ـمـ	ـع	1249

Table 2. (*Continued*)

Ghein	غ	غ	خ	غ	105
Fe	ف	ڣ	ڣ	ف	456
Ghaf	ق	ڤ	ڤ	ق	238
Kaf	ک	ک	ک	ک	315
Gaf	گ	گ	گ	گ	695
Lam	ل	ل	ل	ل	2369
Mim	م	م	م	م	4274
Nun	ن	ن	ن	ن	3572
Vav	و	-	-	و	1930
He	ه	ه	ه	ه	2305
Ya	ی	ﻴ	ﻳ	ی	3183

The rest of this paper is organized as follows: section 2 explain the pre-processing methods, section 3 presents the novel feature extraction method and classification data and section 4 describe applying hamming network on dataset. The proposed system is explained in section 5 and in section 6 the experimental results are reported. Finally the conclusions have followed in section 7.

2 Pre-processing

For existing images in our dataset which contain 95*77 pixels totally three operations applied as following:

2.1 Binarization

In binary operation an image pixels values is changed to 0 and 1 using step function. It means the pixels value higher than a threshold value converted to one and other values to zero. Threshold value is chosen according to the noises rate and background intensity in the dataset and is derived tentative. You can see an image before and after the binary operation in Figure 4.

2.2   Morphology Operator

Erosion is one of the morphological operations that are used for thinning object in the image [16].In this system a 4*4 Erosion operation are applied to removes noises from image. The noise must be smaller than 4*4 pixels to be removed. In Figure 4 you can see an image after morphological operation.

2.3   Centralization

In this operation, position of the characters in the image is achieved exactly, and then the character is transmitted to the center of image. Some dataset data was not written in the center of the image and by this operation if an object is on the corner of the image, the object shifted to the center of image. In Figure 4 you can see a centralized image.

2.4   Finding the Main Character Object

In this section the biggest part of the character is detected and other objects are eliminated by morphological operators [16]. This section is optionally and used only for clustering (described in proposed system section).

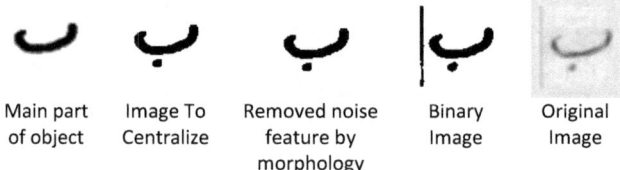

| Main part of object | Image To Centralize | Removed noise feature by morphology | Binary Image | Original Image |

Fig. 4. Preprocess Image

3   Feature Extraction

For extraction features of image Three-dimension (vertical, horizontal, diagonal)derivation is used. For this, assume all pre-processing operations are done on the image. If the image is Two Dimension matrix I(x, y) with L* M pixel, for calculate derivation of this image act as follows for each row and column:

$$\forall j = 1, 2, ..., L : D_1(j) = \sum_{i=1}^{M} I(j,i)$$

$$\forall i = 1, 2, ..., M : D_2(i) = \sum_{j=1}^{L} I(j,i)$$

(1)

In other words, calculate sum of the horizontal and vertical black pixel. Also, achieve the sum of the diagonal pixel with 45 degrees angle as follows:

$$k = (L + M), ..., 2, 1: \begin{cases} k \le M : D_3(k) = \sum_{\substack{i=k \\ j=1}}^{i=1} I(i,j) \\ k > M : D_3(k) = \sum_{\substack{i=M \\ j=K-M+1}}^{j=L} I(i,j) \end{cases} \tag{2}$$

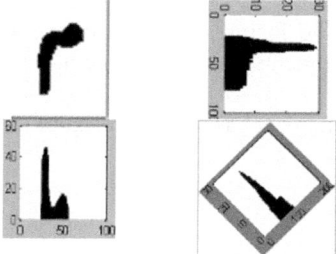

Fig. 5. Result of D1, D2 and D3

In the figure 5 the result of D1, D2 and D3 (vertical, horizontal, diagonal frequency) is shown. In calculus the first order derivative (measure of how a function changes as its input change) discrete function is shown below, equation is achieved [17]:

$$\frac{\partial f}{\partial x} = f(x+1) - f(x) \tag{3}$$

But as mentioned in [18] calculating the derivative on two adjacent points will have less sensitive to noise ratio as defined:

$$\frac{\partial f}{\partial x} = f(x+1) - f(x-1) \tag{4}$$

Now by applying derivative on the frequencies obtained of (3) the rate of changes on letter will be achieved. (figure6)

Then these patterns become the bipolar models by applying sign function.

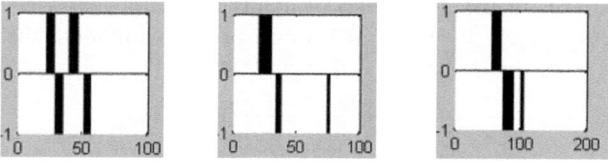

Fig. 6. Achieved rate of changes on letter

$$S_1 = Sign(\frac{\partial D_1}{\partial x}) \qquad S_2 = Sign(\frac{\partial D_2}{\partial y}) \qquad S_3 = Sign(\frac{\partial D_3}{\partial y}) \tag{5}$$

S1, S2 and S3 are one-dimensional matrixes of 0, 1 and -1values. Now we define a protocol to get the feature as follows:

1. For all adjacent with same values we consider only one of them.
2. To reduce the noise we consider threshold T. If the derivative value changed at less than T pixel and then re-takes the previous value of this change, this value is not considered.

By this protocol at most 60 features from an image will be achieved. So consider a vector features with 60 elements for each image and if feature is less than 60 put zero after features up to 60.

For example from the letter "ﻡ" is shown in figure (3) following feature is obtained.

F1= {0, 1,-1, 1,-1, 0}
F2= {0, 1,-1, 0,-1}
F3= {0, 1,-1, 0,-1, 0}

F1 and F2 are vertical and horizontal features and F3 is diagonal feature for letter "ﻡ".

4   Hamming Network

Hamming Network is a fully connected neural network which input layer neurons connect to all output layer neurons (figure 7). This network computes the hamming distance between inputs I and each of the P trained pattern [19].

$$x^T \cdot y = \sum_i x_i \cdot y_i = a - d$$
$$d = n - a$$
$$x^T \cdot y = 2a - n \tag{6}$$
$$a = 0.5(x^T \cdot y + n)$$
$$-d = a - n = 0.5(x^T \cdot y + n) - n$$
$$-d = 0.5(x^T \cdot y) - 0.5n$$

In formula (6), the matrix x is values of input data and matrix y is one of the network trained pattern. Finally by using WTA[1]network the minimum distance between the input and the most similar pattern will be selected [20].

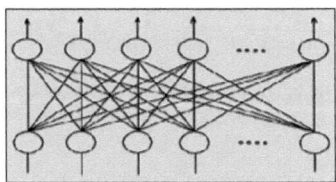

Fig. 7. Hamming Network

---

[1] Winner Take All.

5   Proposed System

After feature extraction we should classify characters in some groups. The proposed system has two steps to recognize the character. At the first step namely Classification, the system says that the target character belong to which group. After that in Recognition step the target character have been recognized exactly in the group.

5.1.1   Classification

Characters are clustered into 9 classes. These classes are shown in table 2. Each class contains a group of characters that have similar features and in each class the main part of character are the same.

In Persian we have many characters that their differences are only in dots, for example letter 'be' and 'pe'. For clustering we neglect these dots and consider characters in main form without dots. For eliminating these dots we hold only the main object (using preprocess section II.D) of the character.

After preprocessing and feature extraction (III) as said the features will give to the hamming network.

The hamming network output is the number of class that contains the input character.

In some uses this classification can help to solve the problems, for example in [21] similar classification used for number recognition on postal addresses.

5.1.2   Recognition

After the class of the characters is known, system must detect which character is given. For this purpose another hamming network is used by other input features than the first hamming network. In this stage it shouldn't remove dotes at pre-processing unit for searching in the class elements.

Input features in this stage are a one dimensional matrix by 7315 elements that contain all pixels of the input image. The output of this hamming network is the final result of recognition.

In some classes like class 1 there is only one element in the class, so Recognition stage is not needed. The handwritten recognition is well addressed in [22-23]

6   Experimental Result

The system is tested by 47695 samples of HDF-84 database. This database is a collection of about 10,000,000 isolated handwritten Persian characters.

4216 pattern is selected with minimum similarity to each other for training the hamming network. The detection rate for each class is shown in table 3. The average classification rate is 95 percent.

The recognition rate for each character in classes is shown in table 4. The average recognition rate is 91 percent.

As mentioned the recognition rate of "ا" and "ء" is %100 because their classes contain only one character.

Table 2. 9 classes for Farsi character's main body

1	2	3	4	5	6	7	8	9
١	ب	ج	د	س	ط	ک	ل	م
	پ	چ	ذ	ش	ظ	گ	ق	
	ت	ح	ر	ص			ن	
	ث	خ	ز	ض				
	ف	ع	ژ	ی				
		غ	و					
			ه					

Table 3. Percent Detection of Classes

Class	Percent detection
1	98.3
2	98.6
3	98.2
4	94.3
5	91.7
6	90.7
7	85.8
8	91.9
9	95.4

All experiments are performed on an Intel Core duo 1.6 GHZ personal computer with 1 GB of RAM. The average processing time of classification was about 1 millisecond and for full recognition were about 3 milli-seconds for each character.

This system first tested without classification which result showed that time for recognition being time consuming (each character detection take about 40 milliseconds) but when we use classification time reduced about 3 milliseconds by about the same results.

Table 4. Percent Detection OfCharacter in Class

Character	Percent detection	Character	Percent detection	Character	Percent detection	Character	Percent detection
ا	100	خ	97.1	ص	95.3	ک	63.8
ب	94.8	د	89.9	ض	86.9	گ	76.6
پ	97.4	ذ	100	ط	88.3	ل	93.4
ت	94.7	ر	94.1	ظ	85.7	م	100
ث	100	ز	92.3	ع	84.2	ن	84.2
ج	91.5	ژ	100	غ	95	و	89.1
چ	100	س	84.5	ف	93	ه	91.5
ح	95.1	ش	82.5	ق	74	ی	75.6

7   Conclusion

In this paper a novel feature extraction was proposed and used for recognition of isolated handwritten Persian character.

By classifying the input data into groups, our recognition time reduced, because system only should search the input character between characters in one class not all data in trained data.

This system is almost noise insensitive, because noise reduction methods are used in three stages, first morphological operators to remove most of noise, second in derivative by using threshold to remove unwanted intensity changes and at the last stage using the hamming network that gives good response by noisy inputs.

This system has another advantage over some other systems. Some of them use a limited word dictionary to verify the recognition and search in that dictionary. But this system has no dictionary and can find unlimited word from characters.

References

1. Rajavelu, A., Musavi, M., Shirvaikar, M.: A neural network approach to character recognition. Neural Networks 2, 387–393 (1989)
2. Young, T.Y., Fu, K.S.: Handbook of pattern recognition and image processing. Academic, Orlando (1986)
3. Lorigo, L.M., Govindaraju, V.: Off-line Arabic Handwriting Recognition: A Survey. IEEE Transactions on Pattern Analysis and Machine Intelligence 28, 712–724 (2006)

4. Alma'adeed, S., Higgins, C., Elliman, D.: Off-line recognition of handwritten Arabic words using multiple hidden Markov models. Knowledge-Based Systems 17, 75–79 (2004)
5. Khorsheed, M.S.: Recognizing handwritten Arabic manuscripts using a single hidden Markov model (2003)
6. Kabir, E., Bahari, K., Ahmadzade, M.R.: Recognition of Persian Typed Texts, MS. Dissertation, Electrical engineering Department, Tarbiat Modares University, Tehran, Iran (2005)
7. Safabakhsh, R., Dastpak, V.: Recognition of Persian typed Characters using projections. In: Third Annual CSI Computer CSICC 1997, Tehran, Iran (1997)
8. Huang, Y.S., Suen, C.Y.: A method of combining multiple experts for the recognition of unconstrained handwritten numerals. IEEE Trans. on Pattern Analysis and Machine Intelligence 17(1), 90–94 (1995)
9. Xu, L., Krzyzak, A., Suen, C.Y.: Methods of combining multiple classifiers and their applications to handwriting recognition. IEEE Transactions on Systems, Man and Cybernetics 22, 418–435 (1992)
10. Mozaffari, S., Faez, K., Ziaratban, M.: Structural decomposition and statistical description of Farsi/Arabic handwritten numeric characters (2005)
11. Safabaklish, R., Adibi, P.: Nastaaligh Handwritten Word Recognition Using a Continuous-Density Variable-Duration HMM, vol. 30 (2005)
12. Zand, M., Naghash, N., Monadjemi, S.A.: Recognition-based Segmentation in Persian Character Recognition. International Journal of Computer and Information Science and Engineering (2008)
13. Soltanzadeh, H., Rahmati, M.: Recognition of Persian handwritten digits using image profiles of multiple orientations. Pattern Recognition Letters 25(14), 1569–1576 (2004)
14. Mozaffari, S., Soltanizadeh, H.: ICDAR 2009 Handwritten Farsi/Arabic Character Recognition Competition, pp. 1413–1417 (2009)
15. Grosicki, E., Abed, H.E.: ICDAR 2009 handwriting recognition competition, pp. 1398–1402 (2009)
16. Gonzalez, R.C., Woods, R.E., Eddins, S.L.: Digital Image Processing using Matlab. Prentice Hall (2009)
17. Gonzalez, R.C., Woods, R.E.: Digital Image Processing, 3rd edn. Prentice Hall, Upper Saddle River (2008)
18. Nixon, M.S., Aguado, A.S.: Feature Extraction and Image Processing, 2nd edn. Academic Press (2008)
19. Mehrotra, K., Mohan, C.K., Ranka, S.: Elements of Artificial Neural Networks (2000)
20. Haykin, S.: Neural Networks A comprehensive Foundation, 2nd edn. Prentice Hall (1999)
21. Mowlaei, A., Faez, K.: Recognition of isolated handwritten Persian/Arabic Characters and Numerals Using Support Vector Machines, pp. 547–554 (2003)
22. Nasien, D., Haron, H., Hasan, H., Yuhaniz, S.S.: Chain Code Extraction of Handwritten Recognition using Particle Swarm Optimization. Journal of Intelligent Computing 1(4), 198–207 (2010)
23. Nebti, S., Boukerram, A.: Use of Nature-inspired Meta-heuristics for Handwritten Digits Recognition. International Journal of Computational Linguistics Research 1(1), 30–40 (2010)

Dual Particle-Number RBPF for Speech Enhancement

Seyed Farid Mousavipour and Saeed Seyedtabaii

Shahed University, Tehran, Iran
{Mousavipour,stabaii}@shahed.ac.ir

Abstract. In this paper, we propose a new single channel dual particle-number Rao-Blackwellized particle filter (RBPF). Additive noise i.e. white and color noises corrupt speech signal and degrade its intelligibility and quality. Quality measurement scores are ITU-T P.862.1 (PESQ), also computation cost in implementation are important. Particular emphasis is placed on the removal of colored noise, such as industrial noise. At first describe some of the similar method such as Kalman filter and particle filter. The simulation results show that the proposed method provides a significant gain in ITU-T P.862.1 score. Taking measure to reduce computational complexity by separating silent-speech and assign different particle number to each type of frames.

Keywords: Speech enhancement, Kalman filter, particle filter, PESQ.

1 Introduction

Processing of speech signal that has been degraded by additive background noise is of great interest in a variety of contexts. Speech enhancement aims at estimating clean speech, given noisy signal. Enhancement techniques are classified into single and multi channel categories. Single channel techniques are the most common real-time methods, since the second channel is not available in most of the applications, e.g. internet communication, speech recognition systems, and the case of speech-passing noise-cancelling headset.

Implementations of single channel systems are easy and less expensive than the multiple channel systems. However, because of the unavailability of the noise statistics, their algorithms are complicated and suffer from high computation cost and complexity.

Single channel speech enhancement algorithms can be roughly divided into three groups: spectral subtraction, sub-space analysis and filtering algorithms. The spectral subtraction approaches are straightforward and easy to implement [1]. However, they produce an audible distortion known as "ringing". Sub-space analysis operates in the autocorrelation domain, where the speech and noise components can be assumed to be orthogonal, whereby their contributions can be readily separated. Unfortunately, estimating the orthogonal components consumes high computation. Moreover, the orthogonality assumption is difficult to motivate.

Filtering algorithms may be implemented in time-domain, frequency domain or even jointed domains. Their main attempts are removing the noise component (Wiener) or estimate the noise and speech components (Kalman, Particle). The original

P. Pichappan, H. Ahmadi, and E. Ariwa (Eds.): INCT 2011, CCIS 241, pp. 305–318, 2011.

Kalman filter provides a minimum mean-squared error (MMSE) estimate of the clean speech if the assumed noise is Gaussian [2]. There have been numerous studies involving the enhancement of white noise corrupted speech [2, 3], however, in real world, colored noise assumption has been proved to be very effective for speech enhancement [4, 5]. In addition, filtering methods have been equipped with various Expectation Maximization (EM) parameter estimation algorithms. Iterative Kalman [5], Kalman-EM-iterative (KEMI) and Kalman-gradient descent-sequential (KGDS) algorithm [6] are among them.

In case of non Gaussian noise or nonlinear model assumption, the particle filters may be implemented for speech enhancement. PF requires very few assumptions about the noise Power Density Function (PDF) compared to what Kalman filter family requires.

Filtering type approaches generally require AR model parameters of the degraded speech signal. AR model exploits the local correlations in a time series by forming the prediction of the current sample as a linear combination of the immediately preceding samples. The readily available choice may be to draw the noise statistics from silent periods and speech model parameters from noisy speech periods. One of the EM parameter estimation algorithms have been accompanied with RBPF in [8]. In the algorithm presented in [7], speech and noise parameters are estimated by particle method and the state of the presumed linear Gaussian model is estimated by Kalman approach.

In this paper, dual particle-number RBPF is proposed that reduces the computation cost and complexity, impressively. The results are evaluated in comparison with the outcome of several well known Kalman and particle filter families of algorithms for speech enhancement such as: iterative Kalman filter, sequential and iterative Kalman filters, RBPF and constraint RBPF. White, colored and real industrial noise (drill) corrupted speech samples are adopted for assessment of the algorithm. Two indexes are considered: quality of the enhanced speech and computation time. The quality of the enhanced speech is exhibited by the PESQ score. The results show that in case of white and colored computer generated noise, the proposed method performance is similar to the original RBPF while the computation time has been dropped significantly. This is due to the provision embedded into the algorithm that assigns different particle number to the silent and the speech segments of the signal.

This paper is organized as follows. Speech and noise models are presented in section 2. Two variations of Kalman filter developed especially for speech enhancement are described in section 3. In section 4, PBRFs are detailed and in section 5 the proposed dual particle-number RBPF is elaborated. Section 6 evaluates the algorithm performance and finally conclusion comes in section 7.

2   Speech and Noise Model

The autoregressive (AR) model is popular for audio signals. This model exploits the local correlation in a time series by forming the prediction of the current sample as a linear combination of the immediately preceding samples. The speech AR model is as follows:

$$s(n) = \sum_{k=1}^{p} a_k \, s(n - k) + w(n) \tag{1}$$

Where s(n) is the clean speech signal, α is the AR parameters, p is the model order and $w(n)$ is a zero mean, white Gaussian excitation noise with variance σ_w. We may incorporate the more detailed voiced speech model in which the excitation process is composed of a weighted linear combination of an impulse train and a white noise sequence to represent voiced and unvoiced speech, respectively. However, this approach did not yield any significant performance improvements over the standard LPC modeling [6].

The source sequence is then contaminated by zero mean additive Gaussian noise $v(n)$, which is either white or colored but independent of $w(n)$.

$$y(n) = s(n) + v(n) \tag{2}$$

The canonical state-space model of $s(n)$ and $y(n)$ are as follows,

$$x_s(n) = [s(n-p+1)\, s(n-p+2) \dots s(n)]^T$$

$$x_s(n) = \begin{bmatrix} 0 & 1 & \dots & 0 \\ \vdots & \vdots & \ddots & \vdots \\ 0 & 0 & \dots & 1 \\ a_p & a_{p-1} & \dots & a_1 \end{bmatrix} x_s(n-1) + \begin{bmatrix} 0 \\ \vdots \\ 0 \\ 1 \end{bmatrix} w(n)$$

$$s(n) - [0 \quad \dots \quad 0 \quad 1]\, x_s(n) \tag{3}$$

We can rewrite it as:

$$x_s(n) = A_s\, x_s(n-1) + G_s\, w(n)$$

$$s(n) = C_s\, x_s(n)$$

$$y(n) = C_s\, x_s(n) + v(n) \tag{4}$$

Many of the actual noise sources may be closely approximated as low order, all-pole (AR) processes, in which case a significant improvement may be achieved by incorporating the noise model into the estimation process [5],

$$v(n) = \sum_{l=1}^{m} b_l\, n(n-l) + u(n) \tag{5}$$

Where m is noise AR order and $u(n)$ is a zero mean Gaussian noise not correlated with $w(n)$. It is assumed that the noise is wide sense stationary and is adequately described by the AR (q) model.

$$X_n(n) = A_n\, x_n(n-1) + G_n\, u(n)$$

$$v(n) = C_n\, x_n(n) \tag{6}$$

By adjoining states in (3) and (5) the augmented system has the form,

$$x_t(n) = A_t\, x_t(n-1) + G_t\, v(n)$$

$$y(n) = C_t\, x_t(n) \tag{7}$$

Where $x_t(n) = [\; x_s(n)\; x_n(n)]'$ and the augmented matrices are:

$$A_t = \begin{bmatrix} A_s & 0 \\ 0 & A_n \end{bmatrix}, G_t = \begin{bmatrix} G_s & 0 \\ 0 & G_n \end{bmatrix}$$

$$C_t = [C_s \quad C_n]\,, Q_t = \begin{bmatrix} \delta_w^2 & 0 \\ 0 & \delta_u^2 \end{bmatrix} \tag{8}$$

3 Kalman Filter Type

Kalman filtering belongs to the group of parametric methods of filtering. It is classified into two main categories: time domain and frequency domain. Most studies focused on the time domain Kalman filter. In the time domain Kalman filtering of speech signal, signal is segmented into 20-40 ms frames. Then, AR coefficients are extracted for each frame. In a single channel system, estimation of speech and noise model parameters is drawn from noisy speech frames. Kalman filter requires measurement noise variance that has to be *a priori* known.

3.1 Iterative Kalman Filter in Speech Enhancement

In [5], the main method of iterative Kalman filter referred to as scalar Kalman filter is described. Noise is wide sense stationary and it is assumed to be adequately described by the AR(q) model (5). Augmented state space is obtained as (6). This is the so-called, noise-free measurements problem in the estimation literature. In case that (6) is linear and noise PDF is Gaussian, the optimal estimate of the states is given by the Kalman solution. The Kalman state and time update equations are as follows:

$$x_t\; (n|n-1) = A_t\; x_t\; (n-1)$$

$$x_t(n) = x_t(n|n-1) - K(n)\,[y(n) - C_t^T x_t(n|n-1)]$$

$$P(n|n-1) = A_t\; P(n-1)A_t^T + G_t\; Q_t\; G_t^T$$

$$K(n) = P(n|n-1)\; C_t^T\, [C_t\; P(n|n-1)\; C_t^T]^{-1}$$

$$P(n) = [I - K(n)\; C_t]\, P(n|n-1) \tag{9}$$

Where $K(n)$ is a Kalman gain vector, $P(n/n-1)$ is *a priori* error covariance matrix and $P(n)$ is an error covariance matrix.

As equations show, knowledge of the noises statistics is required for acceptable performance of the algorithm. It must be noted here that Kalman filter offers an optimal estimate when the system parameters are known, so that it is important that the system matrices A_t, G_t and C_t and especially noise intensity, Q_t to be modeled as accurate as possible.

Iterative Kalman filter algorithm is initialized by segmenting the speech into (20-40 ms) frames, then, observation noise is estimated from the energy of silence frames within noisy speech signal. There are also other methods that may be used for the estimation of measurement noise required by Kalman approaches [15].

After first round of filtering, the enhanced speech obtained enters the second round of signal clean up. In each iteration observation and excitation noises STD's must be calculated. Output of the approach shows better SEG-SNR than what a single round filtering yields but the quality is unnatural. For improving naturalness, at the end of each iteration, low amplitude white noise is added to the enhanced speech signal. This improves the intelligibility. 3 or 2 iterations are shown to be adequate for attaining optimum quality.

In [4], a similar algorithm is proposed where extended Kalman filter algorithm is used for the estimation of the noise and clean speech statistics. The noise may also be non-stationary. In each frame, transition matrix (A_t) is calculated sample by sample as follows:

$$\hat{A}_t(n) = A_t(n-1) - K(n)C_t \qquad (10)$$

Where $K(n)$ is the Kalman gain. Simulation results show no more improvement regarding the previous method.

3.2   Iterative and Sequential Kalman Filter

This algorithm is proposed in [6] and is similar to [5]. In each frame augmented Kalman filtering is applied for the removal of noise from the degraded speech signal. Then, an EM method is followed to calculate more accurate parameters. Let r to be the vector of the all unknown parameters in the extended model,

$$r = [\alpha^T \quad g_s \quad \beta^T \quad g_v]$$

$$\alpha = [\alpha_p \quad \alpha_{p-1} \quad \cdots \quad \alpha_1]$$

$$\beta = [\beta_p \quad \beta_{p-1} \quad \cdots \quad \beta_1] \qquad (11)$$

The outcome of the EM is a new estimate, $\hat{r}$ for all of the parameters involved. The EM procedure has two main steps: state estimation and parameter estimation.

State Estimation

State estimation is conducted as follows,

$$\mu(t|N) = \widehat{x(t)}$$

$$P(t|N) = \widehat{x(t) x^T}(t) - \widehat{x(t)x(t)}^T$$

$$y = [y(1) \, y(2) \, \dots \, y(N)]^T \qquad (12)$$

Where y is the vector of the measured data in the current frame and $\mu(t|N)$ is the current state estimate based on $y(t)$, $t = 1, \dots, N$. State estimation procedure is the same as in Kalman filter as described by (9). Parameter estimation based on the EM method is guaranteed to converge to the ML estimate of all unknown parameters. By each iteration, the likelihood of the estimate of the parameters is increased.

Parameter Estimation

In the next step, 2 major parameters are estimated: AR coefficients of the clean speech and the observation noise variance as follows,

$$S(t-1) = P(t-1|t-1)F^T(P(t|t-1))^T$$

$$\hat{a}^{(l-1)} = -\left[\sum_{t=1}^{N} s_p(t-\widehat{1})s_p^T(t-1)\right]^{-1} \sum_{t=1}^{N} s_p(t-\widehat{1})s(t)$$

$$g_s^{(l-1)} = \frac{1}{N}\sum_{t=1}^{N}\left[\widehat{s^2(t)} + \left(\hat{a}^{(l+1)}\right)^T s_p(t-\widehat{1})s(t)\right] \tag{13}$$

Where $s_p(t-\widehat{1})s_p^T(t-1)$ is the upper left $p \times p$ sub-matrix of $\widehat{x(t) \, x^T}(t)$. Others such as $\widehat{s^2(t)}$ is similarly extracted from $\widehat{x(t) \, x^T}(t)$. In [6], AR coefficients of the colored noise is also obtained by similar equations. Since in this method the signal and noise parameter estimates are computed separately, the increase in computational complexity is unavoidable and quite moderate. The iterative-batch EM algorithm requires the use of an analysis window over which the signal and noise statistics are to be wide sense stationary.

4   Rao-Blackwellized Particle Filters

If linearity and Gaussian assumptions are not justified, alternative state estimation algorithm must be sought. Particle Filters (PF) constitute a family of solutions to the following general state estimation problem:

$$x_k = f(x_{k-1}, w_k)$$

$$z_k = g(x_k, v_k) \tag{14}$$

Where x_k represents the state vector at instant k, z_k is the vector of observations, w_k and v_k are the process and the observation noises, f is a signal transition function and g is a measurement function (both assumed to be known). The goal is to estimate the state based on all available observations data up to time k. The PFs introduce an approximate recursive solution for very weak assumptions: f and g may be non-linear, v and w may be non-Gaussian, at the cost of a more computationally expensive implementation [8]. Computation cost is depended on AR order and particle number and in some case lag smooth order. AR coefficients order increase matrix dimension. Each particle represented a KF procedure. If Particle number is increased, more computational is imposed. If the particle number exceeds its optimum quantity, it may cost divergence of the algorithm.

The sequential estimation method is based on Mounte-Carlo simulation, which can operate on the broadest range of state-space formulated problems [7, 9]. A general PF algorithm for speech enhancement has been presented in Table 1.

Table 1. A general PF algorithm for speech enhancement

- For every k (sample), do the following:
- For every $i \in \{1,2,\ldots,N\}$ (particle)
- Draw
  - $X_{k,i} \sim q(X_k|X_{k-1},Z_k)$
- And set
  - $X_{k,i} = \{X_{k,i}: X_{k-1,i}\}$
- Compute the unnormalized weights
  - $(\widetilde{W}_{k,i}) = W_{k-1,i} \dfrac{p(z_k|X_{k,i},Z_{k-1})\,p(X_{k,i}|X_{k-1,i},Z_{k-1})}{q(X_{k,i}|X_{k-1},Z_k)}$
- Compute the normalized factor $\sum_i \widetilde{\omega}_{k,i}$
- Obtain the normalized weights $\omega_{k,i}$
- resample particles

4.1   Low Cost RBPF Algorithm for Speech Enhancement

Some conditional dependencies between elements of the state vector can be analytically explicated and then there is no need to draw samples from the entire state space which leads to RBPF. RBPFs are in practice mostly used when part of the state is in a linear-Gaussian condition. RBPF algorithm for speech enhancement is detailed in Table 2.

Table 2. RBPF Algorithm For speech enhancement.

- For every k (sample), do the following:
- Run a PF on the sub-state x_k
- For every i (particle)
- update $p\big(x_k|X_{k-1,i},Z_k\big)$

The RBPF procedure reduces the variance of the error estimates [16], while, the dimension of the part of the state on which the PF is running is smaller. Its consequences are surely computation efficiency regarding the regular PF [5].

Figure 1 shows RBPF procedure in details. In the initialization step, RBPF assigns random numbers to some variables such as clean speech AR coefficients, observation noise STD, excitation noise STD. The observation noise variance can be determined in a plenty of ways, however, here it is estimated once, in the initialization step. To each particle, it is assigned AR coefficients that are produced by a Gaussian random number generator. Each random number is multiplied by random walk coefficient to reduce the risk of instability. Inappropriate AR coefficients may cause algorithms instability, therefore, if the AR coefficients of a particle is unstable, stability check discards the coefficient and generates new AR ones.

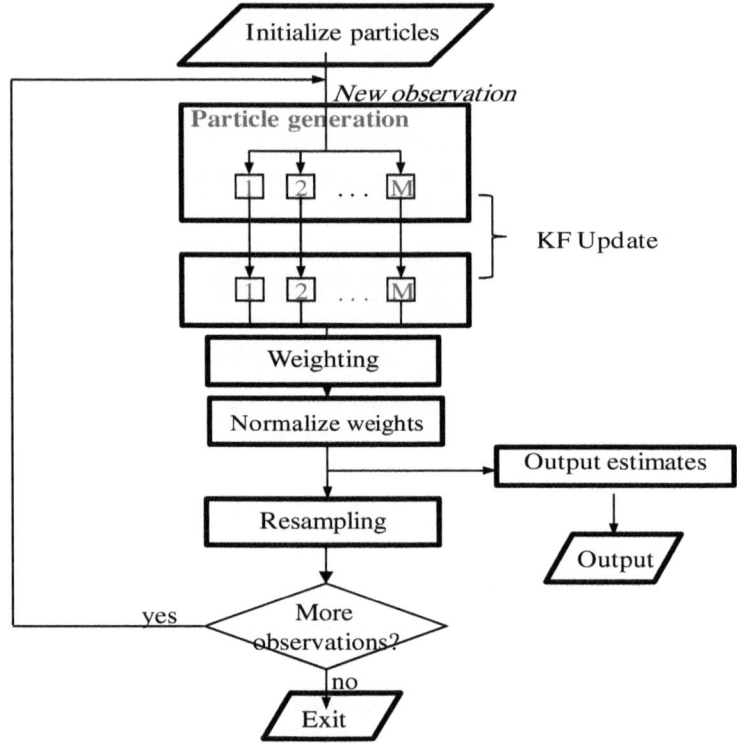

Fig. 1. RBPF procedure represented main steps

In the beginning of any speech signal, many frames can certainly be assumed to be silent frames. By estimating the additive noise signal statistics in this step, improving the performance of the speech enhancement method is substantially mounted. In some methods such as KEM, the noisy speech AR coefficients are used that impairs the estimation of the observation noise variance and clean speech characteristics.

The KF update step consists of the KF simple procedure that is applied to each particle. After updating the speech parameters such as transition matrix, A, and observation noise STD, The important weighting procedure is followed that evaluates the likelihood criteria. The criteria depends on the observation noise STD and Kalman filter gain $K(n)$,

$$w(n) = \sqrt{\frac{1}{Sp}} * e^{(-0.5*ep*ep/Sp)} \qquad (15)$$

Where Sp represents the observation noise variance and ep (error) is the difference between the observed and the estimated signal, $x(n) - \hat{x}(n)$. Then the normalization is imposed on each particle weight.

In the resampling step, particles with high value weight are kept and replicated and low weight particles are discarded.

Finally, the estimated results are stored. In case that a lag smooth scheme has been implemented, it is imposed on the results. The lag smooth scheme is useful for the reduction of unnatural variation in the processed speech.

4.2   A Constrained Sequential EM RBPF Algorithm

In [8], a Constrained Sequential EM (csEM) RBPF algorithm has been proposed to improve the accuracy of the speech enhancement algorithm. In the KEM method, an EM is applied to estimate the clean speech and colored noise parameters where there is not any constraint over the procedure. The csEM, on the other hand, estimates the model parameters recursively with constraints for some of the parameters. RBPF+csEM employs GAR model where the innovation sequence follows the generalized exponential distribution, which reflects the non-Gaussian characteristics. GAR model is a non-Gaussian extension of the AR model, where the same linear model (1) is used but the innovation v_t is assumed to be drawn from the generalized exponential distribution with mean zero.

$$p(v; R, \beta) = \frac{R\beta^{1/R}}{2\Gamma(^1/_R)} e^{-\beta|v|^R} \tag{16}$$

Where $\Gamma(.)$ is the gamma function, $^1/_\beta$ specify width of the density, and R is the shaping parameter of distribution.

RBPF+csEM is similar to [7] with some discrepancies. 1) the speech or noise can be non-Gaussian (GAR model), 2) a Constrained sequential EM step added after KF update to improve the accuracy of the estimation of the parameters, 3) Augmented state applied removes colored noise perfectly, 4) the EM algorithm is an iterative method which finds local maxima of the log-likelihood function, 5) the E-step involves calculating the expected log-likelihood and M-step updates parameters that maximize the expected complete data log-likelihood. The updating rules used in EM procedure are referred to as sequential Newton-Raphson EM. The outline of the sequential speech enhancement method is summarized in Table 3.

5   Dual Particle-Number RBPF in Speech Enhancement

To improve the performance and computation cost of the RBPF algorithms the following point should be especially regarded. In any speech signal, there are silent and spoken segments independent of language and accent. In standard speech database such as ITU dataset, 40% length of speech is silent. Silent frame model needs lower particles for accurate parameter estimation in case of RBPF. By assigning lower particles to the silent frames and higher particle number to the spoken frames, saving in the computation cost and consumed time is obtained. It also improves the convergence of the algorithm since discards the unemployed states and does not introduce more parameters than what is actually needed.

Table 3. A constrained sequential EM RBPF Algorithm for speech enhancement

---

Initialization step:

At $t = 1$,

- Draw particles for clean speech from noisy speech.
- Set the initial model parameters for clean speech and noise.
- Initialize EM step.

For $t = 2, \dots$

E step

- Particle generation.
- Weight update and normalize.
- Resample according to importance weights.
- KF update.
- Calculation of expected score.
- Estimation of clean speech.

M step

- Parameter updating for clean speech and noise.

However, when noise is added to speech signal, silent portion resembles so much to the spoken section. Spoken frames can be discriminated by checking frame power and zero crossing. There are several indexes that may be used in this respect as follows: 1) Spoken frames have high power and low zero crossing against low power-high zero crossing silent frames, 2) Sudden changes in signal energy indicates a beginning or an end to an impulsive noise, 3) The rate of change of the energy of the speech signal is limited by the inertia of human speech production system. It is widely accepted that the speech signal remains stationary within 5 to 10 ms segments, thus any quicker change in the speech signal can be attributed to noise, 4) Noise signal tends to be dominated by high frequency components and is much less autocorrelated than the speech signal.

Voice activity detectors employ such specifications to isolate voiced sections. Here, zeros-crossing and short time energy of signal is used for silent-spoken frames isolation.

After specifying silent-spoken frames, different particle number is assigned to each type of frames. If a spoken frame is processed and the next frame is silent, extra particles that are useless equalized to zero. For example, if for a spoken frame 1200 particles have been allocated and the number of particles for silent frames is 250, in this case 950 particles are nullified. This leads to decrease in computation cost and temporary memory.

6   Simulations and Results

For simulation purposes, ten noisy speech signals consist of 5 male and 5 female pieces of speeches are tested. The clean speech is from the NOIZEUS database sampled at 8 kHz. Noise types are white, computer generated colored noise and real industrial drill noise. The frame size is 200 samples, i.e. 25 ms frames and AR order p, is set to 12 for spoken frames.

Assessment of the quality of the processed speech signal is conducted by PESQ measure [13]. PESQ score is in a close match to the subjective tests score. Its minimum score is 0.5 and its highest point is 4.5, expressing the highest quality. In general case PESQ is sensitive to signal distortion and additive noise.

Algorithms that have been tried are:

1.   IKF where the number of iterations is set to 2.
2.   KEM
3.   RBPF: Mustiere algorithm
4.   csEM RBPF: Park algorithm

Where the estimation of the observation noise variance is conducted in silent frames.

The results have been depicted in Fig. 2. In Fig. 2(a), white Gaussian noise has been added to the signal for a wide range of SNR's from -5 to 10 db. The results indicate that the Mustiere algorithm supersedes the others.

In Fig. 2(b), the case of colored noise is investigated. Again under various SNR's speech enhancement are tested. What the results exhibit is that again the Mustiere algorithm is at the top while IKF is relatively close behind.

In the third test that the noise is a real drill device noise, RBPF of Mustiere leads the others in PESQ score following by the PARK algorithm.

What is worth of mentioning is that the RBPF based methods can perform well in speech enhancement, however, their computation cost is higher that their competitors. This is relieved by adopting dual particle-number strategy tested in this research. By incorporating the idea, the computation cost drops significantly as Table 4 vividly illustrates. The elapsed times are for a 25msec frames.

Table 4. Comparison between the proposed RBPF and Low cost RBPF[7]

mode	AR order	Particle Number	Time(sec)	PESQ
Normal	12	1200	110	1.65
1	6	600	14	1.62
2	3	200	0.7	1.60

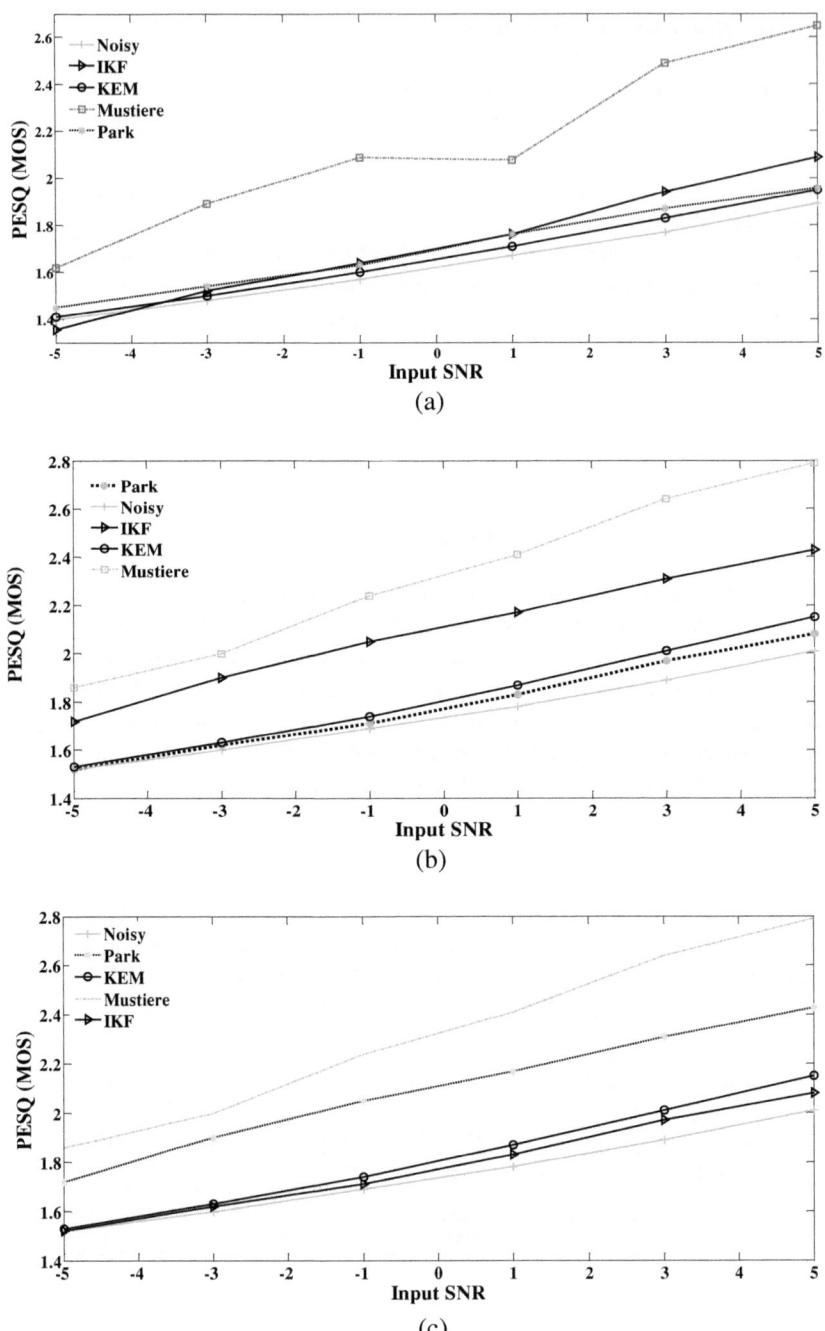

Fig. 2. PESQ value for various algorithms foe speech enhancement: (a) White noise, (b) colored noise, (c) drill noise

7   Conclusion

In this paper, the performance of several filtering algorithms for speech enhancement is evaluated. The algorithms either use 1) an approximate iterative and sequential EM or 2) RBPF for the model parameter estimation preceding the use of 1) Kalman filter or 2) RBPF for the state estimation and denoising of the speech signal. White, colored and real industrial noises are tested for evaluating the performance of the methods. The results show that RBPF methods render better quality than the IKF and KEM, while the RBPF computation cost exceeds IKF and KEM, substantially. Silent-spoken frames are treated differently in RBPF methods for the sake of computation saving in the proposed dual particle-number method. By the dual particle- number strategy for RBPF, its weakness is repaired while its performance is kept intact.

Acknowledgments. This work has been partially supported by the research department of Shahed University.

References

1. Martin, R.: Spectral subtraction based on minimum statistics. In: Proc. Eur. Signal Processing Conf., pp. 1182–1185 (1994)
2. Paliwal, K.K., Basu, A.: A speech enhancement method based on Kalman filtering. In: Proc. IEEE Int. Conf. Acoust., Speech, Signal Processing, Dallas, pp. 177–180 (1987)
3. Lim, J.S., Oppenheim, A.V.: All-pole modeling of degraded speech. IEEE Trans. Acoust., Speech, Signal Processing ASSP-26, 197–210 (1978)
4. Popescu, D.C., Zeljkovic, I.: Kalman Filtering of Colored Noise for Speech Enhancement. In: Proc. of IEEE CASSP, Seattle, USA, pp. 997–1000 (1998)
5. Gibson, J.D., Koo, B., Gray, S.D.: Filtering of colored noise for speech enhancement and coding. IEEE Trans. Acoust., Speech, Signal Processing 39, 1732–1742 (1991)
6. Gannot, S., Burshtein, D., Weinstein, E.: Iterative and sequential kalman filter-based speech enhancement algorithms. IEEE Transactions on Speech and Audio Processing 6(4), 373–385 (1998)
7. Mustière, F., Bouchard, M., Bolić, M.: Low-cost modifications of Rao-Blackwellized particle filters for improved speech denoising. Signal Processing 88, 2678–2692 (2008)
8. Park, S., Choi, S.: Rao-Blackwellized Particle Filter for Sequential Speech Enhancement. In: International Joint Conference on Neural Networks (IJCNN), pp. 1254–1259 (2006)
9. Ristic, B., Arulampalam, S., Gordon, N.: Beyond the Kalman filter: particle filters for tracking applications. Artech House, London (2004)
10. Mustière, F., Bolić, M., Bouchard, M.: Quality assessment of speech enhanced using particle filters. In: Proceedings of the IEEE International Conference on Acoustics, Speech and Signal Processing, pp. III-1197–III-1200 (2007)
11. Ephraim, Y., Malah, D.: Speech enhancement using a minimum mean square error log-spectral amplitude estimator. IEEE Trans. Acoust., Speech, Signal Processing 33, 443–445 (1985)
12. Ephraim, Y.: A Bayesian estimation approach for speech enhancement using hidden Markov models. IEEE Trans. Signal Processing 40, 725–735 (1992)

13. Hu, Y., Loizou, P.C.: Evaluation of objective measures for speech enhancement. in: International Conference on Spoken Language Processing, Philadelphia, USA, pp. 229–238 (2006)
14. Wei, Y., Yi, B.: Unscented Kalman Filtering Based on a Voiced-Unvoiced Speech enhancement. IEEE Transactions on Audio, Speech and Language Processing 15(4), 1193–1280 (2007)
15. Doblinger, G.: Computationally efficient speech enhancement by spectral minima tracking in subbands. In: Proc. Eurospeech, pp. 1513–1516 (1995)
16. Doucet, A., de Freitas, J.F.G., Gordon, N. (eds.): Sequential monte carlo methods in practice. Springer, New York (2001)

Exploring Congestion-Aware Methods
for Distributing Traffic in On-Chip Networks

Masoumeh Ebrahimi, Masoud Daneshtalab, Pasi Liljeberg,
Juha Plosila, and Hannu Tenhunen

{Masoumeh.Ebrahimi,Masoud.Daneshtalab,Pasi.Liljeberg,
Juha.Plosila,Hannu.Tenhunen}@utu.fi

Abstract. The performance of NoC is highly affected by the network congestion condition. Congestion in the network can increase the delay of packets to
be routed between sources and destinations, so it should be avoided. The
routing decision can be based on local or non-local congestion information. Methods based on local congestion condition are generally simple but they are unable to balance the traffic load efficiently. On the other hand, methods using
non-local congestion information are more complex while providing better distribution of traffic over the network. In this paper, we explored several proposed locally and non-locally congestion-aware methods. Then we discussed
about their advantages and disadvantages. Finally, we compared the methods
with each other regarding the latency metric.

Keywords: Networks-on-Chip, Congestion, Adaptive Routing Algorithms.

1   Introduction

As is predicted by the Moore's law, over a billion transistors could be integrated on a
single chip in the near future [1]. In these chips, hundreds of functional intellectual
property (IP) blocks and a large amount of embedded memory could be placed
together to form a multiprocessor systems-on-chip (MPSoCs) [1]. By increasing the
number of processing elements in a single chip, the traditional bus-based architectures
in MPSoCs are not useful anymore and new communication infrastructure is needed.
Network-on-Chip (NoC) has been addressed as a solution for the communication
requirement of MPSoCs [1][3][4][5]. The performance and efficiency of NoC largely
depend on the underlying routing technique which decides the direction a packet
should be sent [6].

   Routing algorithms are used in NoCs in order to determine the path of a packet
from a source to a destination. Routing algorithms are classified as deterministic and
adaptive algorithms. Implementations of deterministic routing algorithms are simple
but they are not able to balance the load across the links in a non-uniform or bursty
traffic [7][8]. The simplest deterministic routing method is dimension-order routing
which is known as XY or YX algorithm. The dimension-order routing algorithms
route packets by crossing dimensions in strictly increasing order, reducing to zero the

P. Pichappan, H. Ahmadi, and E. Ariwa (Eds.): INCT 2011, CCIS 241, pp. 319–327, 2011.
© Springer-Verlag Berlin Heidelberg 2011

offset in one direction before routing in the next one. Adaptive routing has been used in interconnection networks to improve network performance and to tolerate link or router failure. In adaptive routing algorithms, the path a packet travels from a source to a destination is determined by the network condition. So they can decrease the probability of routing packets through congested or faulty regions.

In this paper, we have investigated different well-known congestion-aware routing methods. The routing selections policies in some of them are based on local congestion information while for the rest of them are based on non-local congestion information. We discussed about the advantages and disadvantages of each method and their effect on routing decision and balancing the traffic load. In order to compare the efficiency of methods in term of latency, we have measured the packets delay in each method using uniform and hotspot traffic.

This paper is organized as follows. In Section II, different congestion-aware routing methods named DyXY, EDXY, NoP, and CAS are explained and discussed. The results are reported in Section III while the summary and conclusion are given in the last section.

2   Congestion-Aware Routing Algorithms

2D-mesh topology is a popular architecture for NoC design due to its simple structure, ease of implementation, and support for reuse [10]. The performance and efficiency of NoCs largely depend on the underlying routing methodology. Adaptive routing algorithms can be decomposed into routing and selection functions [9]. The routing function supplies a set of output channels based on the current and destination nodes. The selection function selects an output channel from the set of channels supplied by the routing function [10]. The selection function can be classified as either congestion-oblivious or congestion-aware schemes [9]. In congestion-oblivious algorithms, such as Zigzag [12] and random [13], routing decisions are independent of the congestion condition of the network. This policy may disrupt the load balance since the network status is not considered.

3   Dynamic XY (DyXY)

An adaptive deadlock free routing algorithm called Dynamic XY (DyXY) has been proposed in [14]. In this algorithm, which is based on the static XY algorithm, a packet is sent either to the X or Y direction depending on the congestion condition. It uses local information which is the current queue length of the corresponding input port in the neighboring routers to decide on the next hop. It is assumed that the collection of these local decisions should lead to a near-optimal path from the source to the destination. The main weakness of DyXY is that the use of the local information in making routing decision could forward the packet in a path which has congestion in the routers farther than the current neighbors. This situation could happen when the routing unit is one unit apart from the destination in X or Y dimension. Such non-optimal routing decisions increase the network latency in NoC.

Fig. 1 shows an example of DyXY method where the routing decision based on local congestion information leads to deliver a packet through congested area. In this example the nodes 0 and 15 are the source and destination of the packet, respectively. In the DyXY method, the source node 0 compares the occupied slots of the west buffer at node 1 and that of south buffer at node 4. Since the node 1 is less congested, the packet is sent to this node. When the packet arrives at node 1, it has to be delivered through nodes 2 or 5. According to the congestion condition shown in Fig. 1, the node 2 is less congested and thus the packet is delivered to node 2. At node 2, the packet has to pass through the most congested area (i.e. nodes 6, 7, 10, and 11) in the network to reach the destination node. As a result, the congested path is selected since the decision is made based on the local information; the packet could pass through less congested area (i.e. nodes 8, 9, 12, and 13) if non-local information is considered.

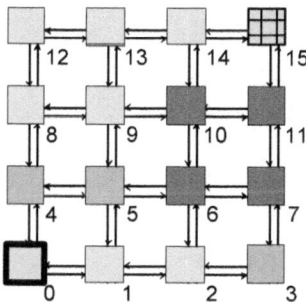

Fig. 1. An example of the DyXY method

4   Enhanced Dynamic XY (EDXY)

In EDXY [15], a wire is propagated along each row and column to carry the congestion information of the corresponding input buffers of the nodes. This information is propagated to the nodes in the adjacent row or column. In this way, each node in the network can be informed about the congestion condition of the nodes along the adjacent rows or columns.

In this method, every router first looks at the destination address of the packet. If the destination node is not located in the adjacent row or column, the packets are routed similar to DyXY method. However, if the destination address is just one hop apart from the router in either the X or Y direction, not only the queue length of the buffer in neighboring routers are considered, but also the congestion wire (based on the position of the destination) is used for routing.

An example is shown in Fig. 2 where a packet is delivered from the source node 0 to destination 15 and it is already at node 2. Based on DyXY method, since the node 3 is less congested than the node 6, the node 3 is selected as the next hop. However, by this decision the packet has to pass nodes 7 and 11 which are highly congested. In contrast, in EDXY method, in a similar situation (i.e. when a packet is located one hop away from the destination row or column and the neighboring nodes are not highly congested), the congestion conditions of the third and fourth columns are compared to each other; since the third column is not highly congested, the packet is sent through it and thus avoiding packets to be routed via highly congested nodes (i.e. nodes 7 and 11).

In a similar example as Fig. 1, when the nodes 6, 7, 10, and 11 are congested, at node 1, the EDXY method also sends packet to the X-direction and thus packets have to be routed through congested region due to the lack of global congestion information.

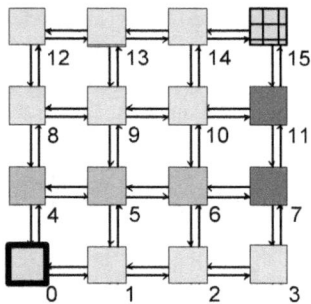

Fig. 2. An example of the EDXY method

5   Neighbor-on-Path (NoP)

In [16] the locality decision is extended to 2-hop neighbors. An example of the NoP method is shown in Fig. 3 where a packet is sent from source node 0 to destination 15. At source node 0, the packet can be sent either to node 1 or node 4. Based on NoP, the congestion value in the X direction is computed by considering the free buffer slots at the west input buffer of node 2 and south input buffer of node 5 (i.e. these nodes are located in the routing path to the destination). Similarly, the congestion value in the Y direction is measured by using the number of free buffer slots at the south input ports of node 8 and west input port of node 5. By comparing the obtained values in two directions, a packet is sent to node 1 or node 4. One of the shortcomings of this method is that the number of free buffer slots at the south and west input ports of node 5 is largely affected by the contention at north and east output ports. In other word, the congestion information of the corresponding input ports of node 5 is included in the congestion value of both X and Y directions. Since the congestion values at X and Y directions are compared with each other, the congestion status of node 5 cannot affect the routing decision. Moreover, NoP method suffers from the recursive nature of the routing algorithm, resulting in increased hardware overhead and router complexity. This method cannot be extended to look at the congestion of 3-hop neighbors due to the nonlinearly increased hardware overhead.

Following the example of Fig. 3, the packet is sent to the node 1 since the congestion status of node 2 is less than node 8. At node 1, the packet is sent to node 2 as the node 3 is less congested than node 9. As a result the packet has to pass through the highly congested area.

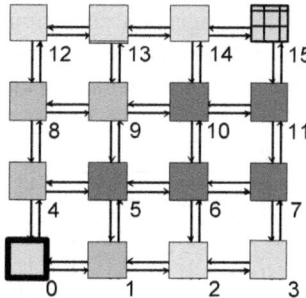

Fig. 3. An example of the NoP method

6   Agent-based Network-on-Chip (ANoC) along with Congestion-Aware Selection method (CAS)

In the Agent-based Network-on-Chip (ANoC) structure [17], the network is divided into several clusters in which a cluster includes a number of routers and a cluster agent. The design consists of two separate mesh networks: main data network and lightweight congestion network. The main data network connects the routers to each other to propagate packets over the network; while in the congestion network, cluster agents are communicated with each other to spread the congestion information. Each cluster agent performs two simple tasks. First, it collects the congestion information from the attached routers (local routers) and distributes the information to the neighboring cluster agents as well as the local routers; second, it forwards the received congestion information from the adjacent cluster agents to the local routers.

By distributing congestion information over the network, routing decision can be assisted by the local and non-local congestion information received from different regions of the network.

Depending on the relative position of the source and destination nodes, the Congestion-Aware Selection (CAS) method can be described in two parts as follow:

1)   The source and destination cluster agents are located in the same agent-row or agent-column

The congestion value for one output channel is calculated using the weighted sum of the 1-hop, 2-hop and 3-hop neighboring nodes. These nodes must be located in the minimal path and in the same network-row (network-column) as the source node.

Consider an example in Fig. 4 where the node 0 wants to communicate with the node 7. As can be seen in this figure, the nodes 0 and 7 are connected in the first row of the congestion network. The node 0 has to choose whether to send a packet to the node 1 or node 4. The congestion value at the X direction is computed by considering the congestion values of nodes 1, 2, and 3 while the congestion value at the Y direction is calculated by using the congestion statues of nodes 4, 5, and 6.

To put more emphasis on the congestion condition of nearby nodes, the higher weights are assigned to the closer nodes. In the CAS method, the weight of 3, 2 and 1 is given to the 1-hop, 2-hop and 3-hop neighbors, respectively.

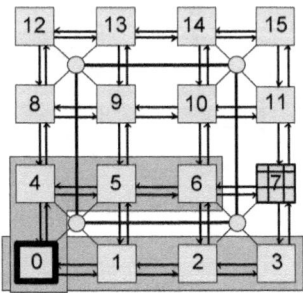

Fig. 4. An example of CAS method when source and destination are in the same row

2)   *Source and destination are not located in the same agent-row or agent-column*

In this case, the congestion value for each selected output channel is provided by the values of the adjacent node and the neighboring cluster. To place emphasize on the local congestion values more than non-local information, the neighboring nodes are assigned the weight of 3 while the congestion value of the adjacent clusters are given the weight of 2.

An example is shown in Fig. 5 where node 0 sends a message to the node 15. For the X direction, the congestion value is calculated by the weighting sum of the congestion values of the node 1 and the cluster 1, while for the other output channel, the congestion value of the node 4 is combined with the congestion value of the cluster 2.

The routing decision in this method is better than the other proposed methods. However, the structure of the congestion network is changed depending on whether the network dimensions are even or odd.

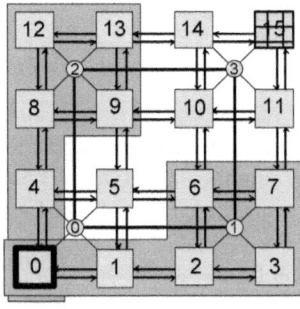

Fig. 5. An example of CAS method when source and destination are in different rows

7   Experimental Results

To compare the efficiency of the methods, a 2D-NoC simulator is implemented with VHDL to model all major components of the NoC. Simulations are carried out to determine the latency-throughput characteristics of each network. For all the routers, the data width was set to 32 bits. Each input virtual channel has a buffer (FIFO) with the size of 6 flits. The congestion threshold value is set to 4 meaning that the congestion condition is considered when 4 out of 6 buffer slots are occupied. In simulations, the latency is measured by averaging the latency of the packets when each local core generates 3000 packets. As a performance metric, we use latency defined as the number of cycles between the initiation of a message operation issued by a Processing Element (PE) and the time when the message is completely delivered to the destination PE. The request rate is defined as the ratio of the successful message injections into the network interface over the total number of injection attempts. For all routers, the frequency is set to 1GHz and the packet size is set to 5 flits.

8   Uniform Traffic Profile

In the uniform traffic profile, each processing element (PE) generates data packets and sends them to another PE using a uniform distribution [18][19][20]. The mesh sizes are considered to be 8×8 and 14×14. In Fig. 6, the average communication delay as a function of the average packet injection rate is plotted for both mesh sizes. As observed from the results, CAS leads to the lowest latency, and then DyXY, EDXY, and NoP. This was expected due to the distribution of traffic over less congested areas. Because of the ANoC structure (along with CAS method), each router can observe the congestion information of not only the neighboring routers, but also the routers residing beyond the neighboring routers.

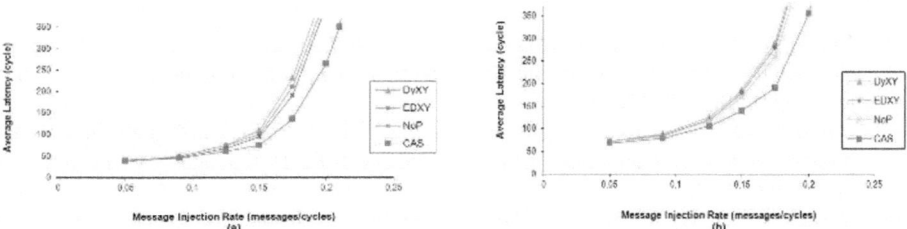

Fig. 6. Performance under different loads in (a) 8×8 2D-mesh and (b) 14×14 2D-mesh under uniform traffic model

9   Hotspot Traffic Profile

Under the hotspot traffic pattern, one or more nodes are chosen as hotspots receiving an extra portion of the traffic in addition to the regular uniform traffic. In simulations, given a hotspot percentage of H, a newly generated message is directed to each hotspot node with an additional H percent probability. We simulate the hotspot traffic with a single hotspot node at (4, 4) and (7, 7) in the 8×8 and 14×14 2D-meshes, respectively. The performance of each network with H = 10% is illustrated in Fig. 7. As observed from the figure, the CAS method achieves better performance compared to those of the other schemes.

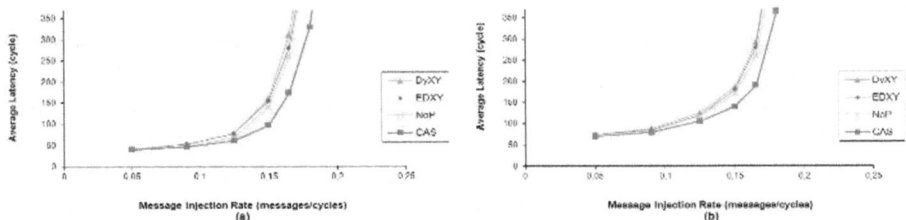

Fig. 7. Performance under different loads in (a) 8×8 2D-mesh and (b) 14×14 2D-mesh under hotspot traffic model with H=10%

10   Summary and Conclusion

In this paper, we have explained and investigated several congestion-aware routing methods in the realm of NoC. Among them, the decision making in the DyXY and EDXY methods are based on local congestion information; while the NoP and CAS methods consider not only the local information of the neighboring routers but also non-local congestion statuses of the nodes that are beyond the neighboring routers. We discussed about the advantages and disadvantages of each method and finally we compared the methods with each other in term of latency.

References

[1] Xu, J., Wolf, W., Hankel, J., Charkdhar, S.: A Methodology for design, modeling and analysis for networks-on-Chip. In: IEEE International Symposium on Circuits and Systems, pp. 1778–1781 (2005)

[2] Cesariow, O., Lyonnard, L., Nicolescu, G., et al.: Multiprocessor SoC platforms: a compo-nent-based design approach. In: Proc. Int. Conf. IEEE Design and Test of Computers, pp. 52–63 (2002)

[3] Towles, B., Dally, W.: Route packets, not wires: on-chip interconnection networks. In: Proc. DAC (2001)

[4] Benini, L., De Micheli, G.: Networks on chips: a new SoC paradigm. IEEE Computer (January 2002)

[5] Bertozzi, D., Benini, L.: Xpipes: A Network-on-Chip Architecture for Gigascale Systems-on-Chip. IEEE Circuits and Systems Magazine 2, 18–31 (2004)

[6] Wu, D., Al-Hashimi, B.M., Schmitz, M.T.: Improving Routing Efficiency for Network-on-Chip through Contention-Aware Input Selection. In: Proc. of ASP-DAC, pp. 36–41 (2006)

[7] Bertsekas, D., Gallager, R.: Data Networks. Prentice Hall (1992)

  [8] Dally, W.J., Towles, B.: Principles and Practices of Interconnection Networks. Morgan Kaufmann (2004)
  [9] Duato, J., Yalamanchili, S., Ni, L.: Interconnection Networks: An Engineering Approach. Morgan Kaufmann (2002)
 [10] Liang, J., Swaminathan, S., Tessier, R.: Asoc: a scalable, single-chip communication architectures. In: IEEE Int. Conf. on PACT, pp. 37–46 (October 2000)
 [11] Gratz, P., Grot, B., Keckler, S.W.: Regional Congestion Awareness for Load Balance in Networks-on-Chip. In: Proc. HPCA, pp. 203–214 (2008)
 [12] Badr, H.G., Podar, S.: An optimal shortest-path routing policy for network computers with regular mesh-connected topologies 38(10), 1362–1371 (1989)
 [13] Feng, W., Shin, K.G.: Impact of Selection Functions on Routing Algorithm Performance in Multicomputer Networks. In: International Conference on Supercomputing, pp. 132–139 (1997)
 [14] Li, M., Zeng, Q., Jone, W.: 'DyXY - a proximity congestion-aware deadlock-free dynamic routing method for network on chip. In: Proc. DAC, pp. 849–852 (2006)
 [15] Lotfi-Kamran, P., et al.: EDXY - A low cost congestion-aware routing algorithm for network-on-chips. Journal of Systems Architecture 56(7) (2010)
 [16] Ascia, G., Catania, V., Palesi, M.: Implementation and Analysis of a New Selection Strategy for Adaptive Routing in Networks-on-Chip. IEEE Transaction on Computers 57(6), 809–820 (2008)
 [17] Ebrahimi, M., Daneshtalab, M., Liljeberg, P., Plosila, J., Tenhunen, H.: Agent based On-Chip Network Using Efficient Selection Method. In: Proceedings of 19th IFIP/IEEE International Conference on Very Large Scale Integration (VLSI-SoC), pp. 110–115 (2011)
 [18] Boppana, R.V., Chalasani, S.: A Comparison of Adaptive Wormhole Routing Algorithms. In: Proc. Int. Symp. Computer Architecture, pp. 351–360 (May 1993)
 [19] Flugham, M.L., Snyder, L.: Performance of Chaos and Oblivious Routers under Non-Uniform Traffic., Technical Report UW-CSE-93-06-01 (July 1993)
 [20] Glass, C.J., Ni, L.M.: The Turn Model for Adaptive Routing. In: Proc. Symp. Computer Architecture, pp. 278–287 (May 1992)

A Model for Traffic Prediction
in Wireless Ad-Hoc Networks

Mahsa Torkamanian Afshar[1], M.T. Manzuri[2], and Nasim Latifi[3]

[1] International Campus of Sharif University of Technology,
Department of Science and Technology, Kish Island, Iran
`Mahsa_torkamanianafshar@yahoo.com`
[2] Sharif University of Technology, Department of Computer Engineering, Tehran, Iran
`Manzuri@sharif.edu`
[3] Zanjan Azad University, Department of Computer Engineering, Zanjan, Iran
`Nsm.latifi@gmail.com`

Abstract. In recent years, Wireless Ad-hoc networks have been considered as one of the most important technologies. The application domains of Wireless Ad-hoc Networks gain more and more importance in many areas. One of them is controlling and management the packet traffic. In this paper our goal is controlling the performance of every sections of pipeline of the factory by checking network periodically. Along the factory the traffic is modeled with a Poisson process. We present, with obtaining traffic packets at time (t) for each node in Wireless Ad-hoc Network, we can completely train a Neural Network and successfully predict the traffic at time (t+1) for each node. By this way we can recognize the inefficient sections in factory and try to fix it. The results of experiment have shown that proposed model has acceptable performance.

Keywords: Wireless Ad-Hoc Networks, Traffic Prediction, Neural Networks.

1   Introduction

Wireless Ad-hoc Networks including a set of wireless nodes that communicate with each other by direct communication links without the need for a central controller node [1].

Wireless system is not a desired option to the wired counterpart, because the wireless network will not ensure guaranteed QoS due to the unpredictable reaction of network traffic [2]. The different parameters such as user mobility, arrival pattern and diversified network requirement of user application are unpredictability.

In [3] presents various methods for traffic prediction. Some methods gather a large of historical traffic flow information data and analysis them to achieve useful traffic pattern. One of these methods is network traffic prediction based on Neural Network that several researches executed on kinds of network traffic modeling and prediction.

In [4] shows the traffic of ad-hoc networks can be estimated based on the number of routes that use the link (i, j). In this work they assumed that the traffic load on each route is equal.

P. Pichappan, H. Ahmadi, and E. Ariwa (Eds.): INCT 2011, CCIS 241, pp. 328–335, 2011.

In [5] proposed a new algorithm that called degree algorithm which uses node degree to allocate time slots based on the relative traffic estimation of a node. In this algorithm each node can specify its own degree by monitoring transmissions from neighbor nodes. The limitations of these two methods are they suppose equal traffic load distribution on each route.

In [6] authors present the improvement of accuracy in network traffic prediction with Seasonal Neural Network (SNN), a dynamic seasonal Time Serious Neural Network prediction model is proposed based on Artificial Neural Network (ANN) theory.

In [7] present the prediction of video stream with Neural Network for an efficient bandwidth allocation of the video signal. Since Neural Networks are the efficient methods to model, evaluate and predict the behavior of non-linear and non-stationary systems [8], and the network traffic is self-similar and non-linear, so we used Neural Networks for prediction. In this work the wireless ad-hoc network traffic is modeled according to a Poisson process. In [9-18], the packet traffic issue in wireless ad-hoc networks is extensively addressed and newer models in wireless ad-hoc networks are introduced and widely discussed.

2   Structure of Neural Network

One of the most functional Neural Networks is multilayer perceptron that is called MLP networks that has been trained by the help of back-propagation educational algorithm or BP.

This training method is known as back-propagation of error algorithm or in short form back-propagation or generalized delta rule. In a simple way we can consider BP algorithm as a reduced gradient for minimizing total square error from computed outputs by network. In fact BP training network belongs to gradient based training algorithm. In general the MLP network has an input layer, an output layer and also one or more hidden layers.

Here we prefer the situation in which this network has just one hidden layer with 30 neurons and we use the Levenberg–Marquardt algorithm (LMA) for analyzing the Neural Networks.

3   Proposed Model

Application of this project is for controlling the performance of every sections of pipeline of the factory. In this project we consider each part of the pipeline as a node and make a wireless ad-hoc network. We know that in each pipeline the ingredients should be added to each other sequentially to achieve our object finally.

When each pipeline does its task trustily, create one packet and send it to next pipeline which is as our next node. This packet contains number of the node, name of the material, time of passing and the IP address which has been created in physical layer.

Finally all of these packets are evaluated. So we can predict what will happen on our pipeline in the next time by using of Neural Networks. Sometimes in some of our pipeline we may face the increasing or decreasing of packets, therefore, we know that these data have a difference with data which Neural Network is learned and predicted. Then we notice the deficiency of pipeline.

4   Finding Traffic Packets of Each Node

When we are discussing network traffic packet prediction, we need to determine the traffic model. Considerable factors in our traffic model are the packet size and the arrival time of ingredients material.

We suppose that the sizes of packets are constant. On the other hand, the arrival time of ingredients and the packet sizes along the length of factory are modeled with a Poisson processes. The method for predicting traffic is depended to Back Propagation algorithm.

First of all, the distance between the nodes discussed as a primary test. It should be pointed out that these nodes are in a specific range and standard distance from each other, and they are in a direct line along the factory. Size of the sent packets recognize as follow: number of the node, name of the material, time of passing and the IP address which creates in physical layer. These primary values use in simulation and begin collecting dataset as follow. We consider two dimensional arrays of the nodes number (first node, second node, etc) and the materials number (first material, second material, etc). When each material reaches to the related node, the time determines (arrival time).

For creating the related packets, it is necessary to add the time of packet creating to the time of material arriving. By this way, we determine the packet in which nodes has been created and the time programming has completed.

Next step is creating packet traffic in nodes. For sending packets to the other nodes we assumed no packet is in the node; it means that primary value of the packets in each node is zero. Packet creating time is important, because we should understand algorithm will operate good or not. So we can train Neural Networks and predict traffic in wireless ad-hoc network.

Former dataset shows that which packet in any node and what time has been created. Then we can acquire traffic packets in the nodes at each moment. In the next section we present two dimensional arrays of nodes number and required time. The number of the sent packets in 1 second of a node is accounted by dividing bandwidth to packet size. This shows all the sent packets cannot be sent at once, because, node receives and sends a definite proportion of packets. We assumed in operation mood, traffic is smooth, so that traffic of some nodes would not be higher and lower. Therefore half of the operation is done in Packet create time (1s) related to receiving packets from former node and another half related to sending packets to the next node, then we can send a definite value of packets to next nodes.

Finally all the packets are sent and evaluated in destination. In the last step of gathering dataset, the time that the material passes from one node evaluates and packet creates. In arrival time, we search the times. If packet is created, it adds to packet traffic in nodes. By this method we can achieve the real value of traffic packets of each node at time (t+1).

Next section will show the predicted value of traffic packets at time (t+1) in wireless ad-hoc network.

Example 1: For using Neural Network in predicting wireless ad-hoc network traffic we should arrange the scenario in such a way that we can reach to the same range of traffic for different clocks in continual reputations. By using input data and the traffic which has been created out of it, we can train Neural Network. If we design the scenario in such a way that we can provide Neural Network's input, in contrast we should interfere in the factors that have effects on the process of the network. Some primary parameters of simulation, present in table 1.

Table 1. Simulation Parameters

Parameters	Value
Distance between Nodes	20 m
Factory length	2000 m
Number of nodes	Factory length/node distance
Packet size	10*8 bit
Packet create time	1s
Bandwidth	8000 bit per second
Number of hidden neuron	30

Typically, Fig. 1 show the real value of traffic packets in node 6 at time (t+1), and Fig. 2 show the predicted value of traffic packets at time (t+1) in wireless ad-hoc network. By comparing these two diagrams we consider that the prediction by Neural Networks is reasonable and observe that in node 6 the traffic packets are the same as the dataset.

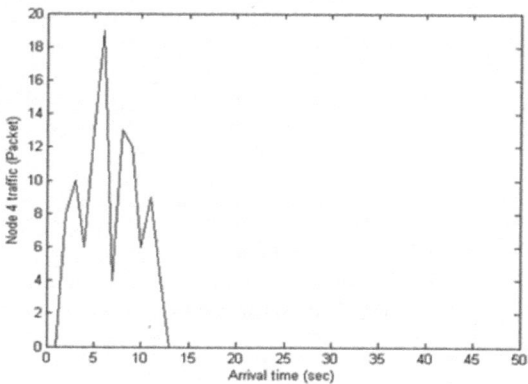

Fig. 1. Traffic packets for node 6 at time (t+1)

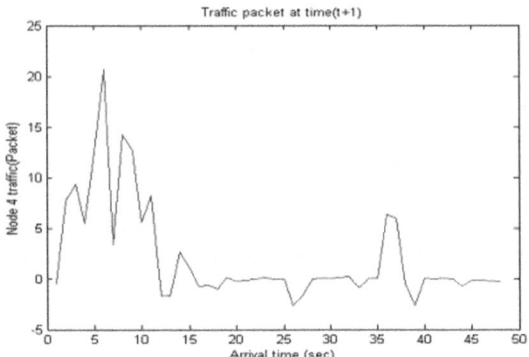

Fig. 2. Predicted value of traffic packets for node 6

5   Results

5.1   Performance Plot

The plot of the training errors, validation errors, and test errors appears, is shown in the Fig. 3. The result is reasonable no significant over fitting has occurred by iteration 12 (where the best validation performance occurs). As we see the error rate at epoch 1, 2, 3… 10 has a descending rate. In epoch 12 it shows the best situation.

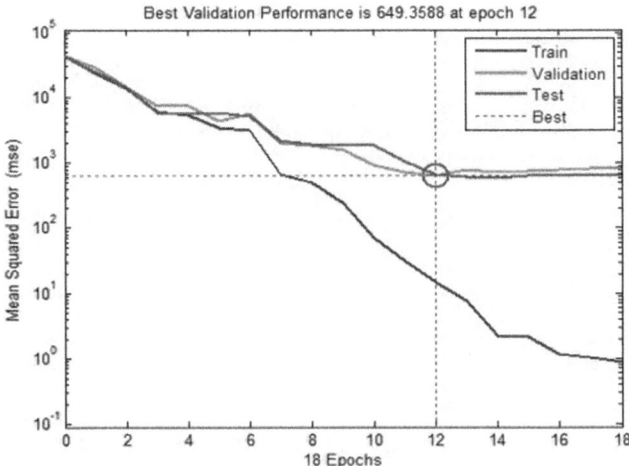

Fig. 3. Performance Plot

5.2   Regression Plot

If we click Regression in the training window, we can perform a linear regression between the network outputs and the corresponding targets. The output tracks the targets very well for training, testing, and validation, and the R-value is over 0.97 for the total response. Fig. 4 shows the results.

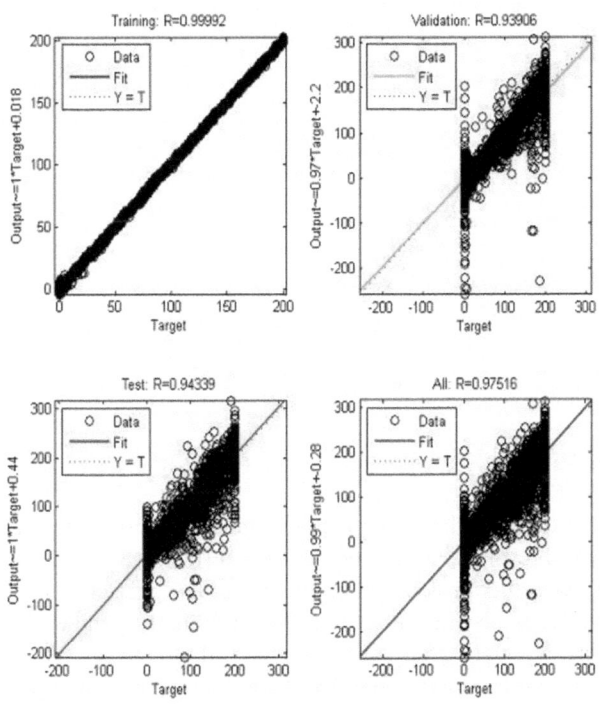

Fig. 4. Regression Plot

5.3   Training State Plot

As we see in this diagram, the gradient value has a descending path, which means error rate is decreasing by training. Validation section shows us the best situation that has been trained and it is at 12th epoch. If we deduce all the epochs that have been trained, from validation that is 6, it shows the best epoch rate. Fig. 5 shows the results.

The results of experiment have shown that proposed model have acceptable performance. Since the final mean-square error is small, the test set error and the validation set error has similar characteristics and no significant over fitting has occurred where the best validation performance occurs so the predictor reliability is reasonable.

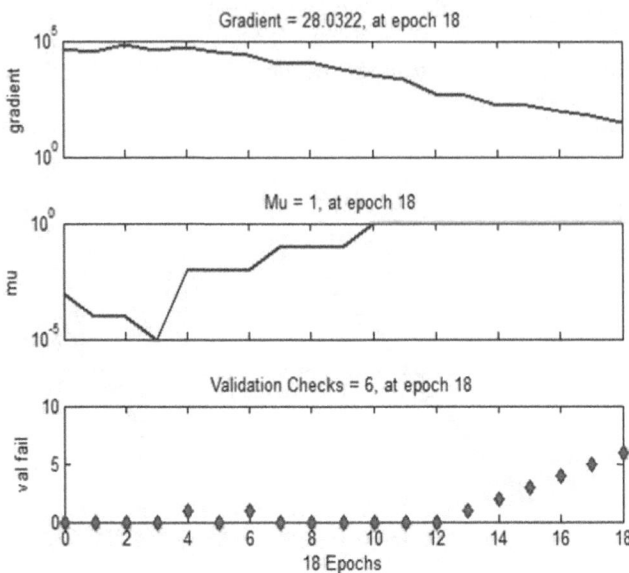

Fig. 5. Training state Plot

6   Conclusion

The obtained results show that our proposed model based on the MLP Neural Network is the acceptable model to recognize the inefficient sections in the factory that cause problems. Also this project has the management aspect besides the control aspect, because performance of each section from production line recognize by learning machine of Neural Network after time. However, the managers can recognize bottleneck in each section of production line by evaluating dataset and optimize that section of production line by changing the equipment and human resources. In this paper we assumed that our simulation environment is collision free and no packet loss can occur. The real world applicability of the proposed solution needs to be proven through hardware implementation.

References

1. Michail, A.E.: Algorithms for routing session traffic in wireless ad-hoc networks with energy and bandwidth limitations. In: Proceedings of 12th IEEE International Symposium on Personal, Indoor and Mobile Radio Communications (2001)
2. Gowrishankar, A., Satyanarayana, P.S.: Neural Network Based Traffic Prediction for Wireless Data Networks, pp. 379–389 (2008)
3. Gowrishankar, A., Satyanarayana, P.S.: Recurrent neural network based BER prediction for NLOS channels. In: 4th International Conference on Mobile Technology, Applications, and Systems and the 1st International Symposium on Computer Human Interaction in Mobile Technology, USA, pp. 410–416 (2007)

4. Mushabbar Sadiq, S.: Traffic estimation in mobile ad-hoc networks. M.S. thesis, Royal Institute of Technology, Stockholm, Sweden (2004)
5. Robertazzi, T., Shor: Traffic sensitive algorithms and performance measures for the generation of self- organizing radio network schedules. Proceedings of IEEE Trans. Commun. 41(1), 16–21 (1993)
6. Guang, C., Lianqing, X.: Nonlinear-periodical Network Traffic behavioral Forecast Based on Seasonal Neural Network Model. In: Proc. International Conference on Communications Circuits and Systems, pp. 683–687 (2004)
7. Oravec, M., Petráš, M., Pilka, F.: Video Traffic Prediction Using Neural Networks 5(4), 59–78 (2008)
8. Gowrishankar, S.: A time series modeling and prediction of wireless network traffic. Georgian Electronic Scientific Journal: Computer Science and Telecommunications 2 (2008)
9. Amine, K.M., Djamel, T.: A Novel transport protocol for wireless mesh networks. Journal of Networking Technology 2(2), 73–81 (2011)
10. Aslam, M.S., Rea, S., Pesch, D.: An innovative Hybrid Architecture and design for Wireless Sensor Networks. Journal of Networking Technology 2(1), 29–35 (2011)
11. Cihan, U.H., Efendioğlu, S., Toker, O., Gümüşkaya, H.: Delay Sensitive Wireless Protocols for Telerobotics Applications. Journal of Networking Technology 1(3), 118–125 (2010)
12. Hoeller, N., Reinke, C., Neumann, J., Groppe, S.: Dynamic Approximative Caching Scheme for energy conservation in WirelessSensor Networks. Journal of Networking Technology 2(1), 10–21 (2011)
13. Safar, M., Al-Hamadi, H., Ebrahimi, D.: PECA: Power Efficient Clustering Algorithm for Wireless Sensor Networks. Journal of Networking Technology 2(1), 1–9 (2011)
14. Khanfar, K., Al-Amawi, A.: The Impact of CSMA/CD and Token Ring on System Performance and Stability of Integrated Wired and Wireless Networks. International Journal of Web Applications 1(1), 14–23 (2009)
15. Ghazisaeedi, E., Zokaei, S.: Traffic Balancing with Dynamic Access Point Selection in WLANs. International Journal of Web Applications 1(3), 157–164 (2009)
16. Yaghi, K.A., Abu-Dawwas, W.A.: Forecasting Model for Long Life Cycle of Complex Recycling Technical Systems by Improving the Structure of the Neural Network. Journal of Networking Technology 1(4), 173–180 (2010)
17. Jo, T.: NTSO (Neural Text Self Organizer): A New Neural Network for Text Clustering. Journal of Networking Technology 2(3), 144–156 (2010)
18. Chen, C., Tan, J., Zhang, F., Yao, J.: Quality Prediction Model Based on Variable-Learning-Rate Neural Networks in Tobacco Redrying Process. Journal of Intelligent Computing 1(3), 157–164 (2010)

Predicating the Location of Nodes in Ad Hoc Network by Lazy Learning Method

Mohammad Jafari[1], Neda Abdollahi[1], and Hossein Mohammadi[2]

[1] Department of Electronic and Computer Engineering,
Zanjan Branch, Islamic Azad University, Zanjan, Iran
{jafari_m_2006,abdollahi_neda}@yahoo.com
[2] Computer Engineering Group, Zanjan University, Zanjan, Iran
hosm@znu.ac.ir

Abstract. Node position information is one of the important issues in many ad hoc network usages. In many ad hoc networks such as military or mobile sensor networks one or more central nodes need to know the location of all the nodes. In addition, in some routing protocols especially location aware protocols (LAR), the nodes should have the location of each others. Therefore, in some ad hoc network application, knowing the location of nodes is considered, but propagating the nodes position information in the network is the big challenge in ad hoc networks. Since, increasing the number of nodes lead to increase the traffic of the network exponentially. In this paper, we have applied special learning method to predict the node location. Thus, nodes don't need to propagate their location information regularly. By this method we can reduce the traffic overhead of network that increase the network's scalability.

Keywords: Mobile ad hoc network, Lazy Learning, Location Aware protocol, Greedy forwarding, Direct flooding.

1 Introduction

Mobile ad hoc networks (MANETs) represent complex distributed systems that comprise wireless mobile nodes that can freely and dynamically self-organize into arbitrary and temporary. Today, the growth of mobile devices usage make ad hoc networks a very challenging and considerable issue.

Node position information is one of the important subjects in many ad hoc network applications as mobile sensor networks, location aware routing (LAR) protocols and so on. The LAR protocols are powerful methods among the other routing protocols in ad hoc networks. In these protocols, routing algorithms rely on node's geographical coordinates [1]. Therefore, we need a system that can allocate nodes location for LAR algorithms. There are several mechanisms for specification the node's position [2, 3]. Global Positioning System (GPS) is one of the more accurate systems due to this purpose.

But propagating the nodes position information in the network is the big challenge in ad hoc networks. We need to propagate this information all over the network regularly. Since, increasing the number of nodes lead to increase the traffic of the network

P. Pichappan, H. Ahmadi, and E. Ariwa (Eds.): INCT 2011, CCIS 241, pp. 336–345, 2011.
© Springer-Verlag Berlin Heidelberg 2011

exponentially, which increase the traffic overhead of network that reduce the network's scalability.

On the other hand, if we reduce the times of propagating of node's geographical information, the LAR protocols wouldn't work properly anymore because the nodes' position may be changed. Therefore, some of the links may be lost and some other may be added to network.

In this paper, we have applied special learning method to predict the node location called Lazy Learning [4]. Thus, nodes don't need to propagate their location information regularly.

This paper is organized as follows. In the next section, ad hoc network routing by using geographical coordinates are briefly introduced. Section 3 introduces laze learning. Section 4 we proposed a new method for allocating the nodes location using lazy learning. Section 5 includes implementation and presents illustrative experiments. In Section 6 concludes this paper. Finally, section 7 suggests some future work.

2 Ad Hoc Network Routing by Using Geographical Coordinates

According to the introduction, one of the nodes' position information usages is in routing protocols. In routing protocols based on geographical coordinates, called location aware routing (LAR) protocols, routing algorithms find a path between source and destination nodes using nodes' position information. Therefore, LAR algorithms need a system to allocate nodes location. The node's position is provided by GPS [1] or other mechanisms [2, 3].

There are three main method In LAR protocols: greedy forwarding, direct flooding and hierarchical routing which is explained in A, B and C sub sections.

2.1 Greedy Forwarding

In this strategy a node forwards packets towards its neighbor that is the nearest to destination node. If there is not any nearest node to destination, the routing protocol use other methods to select the next steps[5].

In the case of there are more than one nearest node to destination, we have several choice to select the next hop such as NFP [6], MFR [7] or CR [8]. Figure 1 illustrates deferent choice for selecting the next hop using these algorithms.

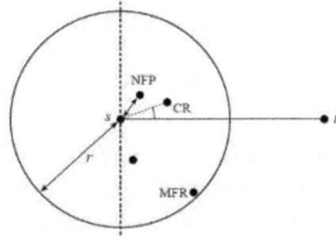

Fig. 1. Variants of greedy forwarding

2.2   Direct Flooding

With directed flooding nodes forward the packets to all neighbors those are located in the direction of the destination [5]. In this method, either the packet is forwarded to neighbors which are in the direction of destination node such as DREAM [9] algorithm or the method uses directed flooding only for route discovery like LAR [10] algorithm. Figure 2 shows which neighbors could be selected in DREAM algorithm for forwarding the packets towards the destination node.

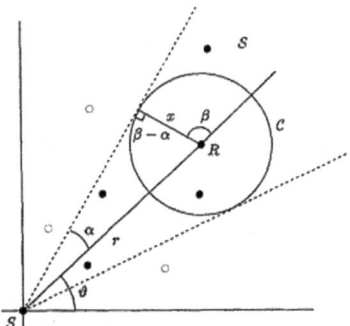

Fig. 2. Node selection for packet forwarding in DREAM algorithm

Figure 3 illustrates the nodes Cooperate to discover a route from the source to destination node in LAR algorithm.

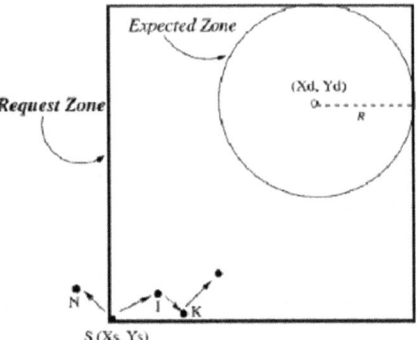

Fig. 3. Route discovery in LAR algorithm

2.3   Hierarchical Routing

Hierarchical routing is structured in two layers. This protocol uses the LAR algorithm for long distance forwarding and for short distance it applies proactive distance vector scheme. This protocol can use both algorithms together. It uses LAR when the packet forwarding starts from the source and uses proactive distance vector scheme when the packet become closer to destination node.

3   Lazy Learning

Lazy learning[4] is subfield of local learning, the target function located as locally in local learning and predication doing according to the distance measure of query point to surrounding examples (training data).

Lazy learning is a memory-based technique that postpones all the computation until an explicit request for a prediction is received.

3.1   Preliminary

Lazy learning approach use leave-one-out crass validation. Leave-one-out cross-validation (LOOCV) involves using a single observation from the original sample as the validation data, and the remaining observations as the training data. This is repeated such that each observation in the sample is used once as the validation data [11]. Leave-one-out cross-validation is often computationally expensive because of the large amount number of times the training process is repeated. However, using recursive method can reduce the amount of calculations.

One of the important tools for performs (LOOCV) is the PREES statistic method that can automatically and recursively calculate the predication of query point and obtain the error for each predication [12].

Then, according to the "winner takes all" theorem, final predication is calculated by one of constant, linear or quadrate methods [13].

For $x \in \mathbb{R}^m$ and $y \in \mathbb{R}$, Let us consider an unknown mapping $f: \mathbb{R}^m \to \mathbb{R}$ of which we are given a set of N samples $\{(x_i, y_i)\}_{i=1}^{n}$, where $\forall x_i: y_i = f(x_i)$. These examples can be collected in a matrix X of dimensionality $[N \times m]$, and in a vector y of dimensionality $[N \times 1]$.

Given a specific query point x_q, the prediction of the value $y_q = f(x_q)$ is computed as follows. First, for each sample (x_i, x_q) a weight w_i is computed as a function of the distance $d(x_i, x_q)$ from the query point x_q to the point x_i. Each row of X and y is then multiplied by the corresponding weight creating the variables $Z = WX$ and $v = Wy$, with W diagonal matrix having diagonal elements $W_{ii} = W_i$. Finally, a locally weighted regression model (LWR) is fitted solving the equation $(Z^T Z) = Z^T v$ and the prediction of the value $f(x_q)$ is obtained evaluating such a model in the query point:

$$y_q = x_q^T (Z^T Z)^{-1} Z^T v \qquad (1)$$

Lazy learning method is very accurate [12,13] and its error rate is calculated by equation 2.

$$e_j^{cv} = y_i - x_j^T \beta_j \qquad (2)$$

Where β_j is calculated from the distance between query point and its neighbors.

3.2   Lazy Learning Specification

In this section we declare some properties of lazy learning method. In this method if we use an appropriate training data set, the predicated value for query point would be very close to the real value. In other word, lazy learning method's error rate is very small that is one of the golden properties for this method.

Despite the method's high prediction accuracy, we need a small training data set and even by four training points, the method could predict the value of query point efficiently.

The third reason of choosing this method is that lazy learning postpones all the calculations till an explicit request receive. So, this can reduce node's energy consumption.

Therefore, lazy learning could be a suitable method for predicating node locations in ad hoc networks.

4   Predicating Node Position Using Lazy Learning

According to special specification of lazy learning method, we attempted to use this learning method to predicate the nodes location in ad hoc networks. We expect this learning method could predict next locations of a node from its previous locations. In other word, by using this learning method we try to follow nodes' movement in network. In this method each node can predicate the other nodes location until they change their velocity or movement direction. Therefore, a node needs to propagate their location information just in the case of changing its velocity or movement direction and other nodes can continue following the node by receiving this new location information. Thus, nodes don't need to propagate their location information regularly. So, this method can reduce the traffic overhead of network that increase the network's scalability.

4.1   One-Step Prediction

In one-step prediction method, an initial information form the various locations of a node are collected. Then, according to this information the next location of the node is predicted. For example, in last 10 seconds if a node's locations could be collected of every 2 second, the learning algorithm can predict the node's sixth location in 12th second. Then, the algorithm receives the seventh location in 14th second and predicts eighth location based on the five or six previous location information. Thus, the traffic of network reduced almost to the half. Figure 4 illustrate following of a node in ad hoc network.

In one-step learning method, by using a table of location information for whole nodes in a network or just a source and a destination node or one node's neighbors we can predicate node location.

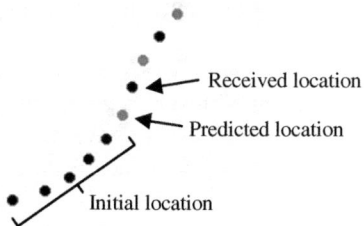

Fig. 4. Following of a node using learning method

4.2   Multi-Step Prediction

In multi-step prediction method, an initial information from some various locations of a node are collected as it is done in one-step prediction method. Then, till the velocity or movement direction of a node is not changed, we don't need to propagate the new location information and the learning algorithm can follow the node by its own pervious predicted location.

For example, the leaning algorithm receives various locations of a node in 10 seconds of every 2 second and predicts the sixth location. For the next step, the algorithm uses second to sixth location information as a primary information set and predicate the seventh location. Figure 5 illustrate following of a node in Multi-Step Prediction method.

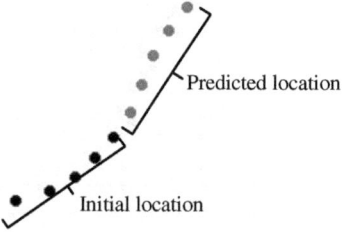

Fig. 5. Following of a node using Multi-Step Prediction

We can also use a table of the location information of whole nodes in a network or just a source and a destination node or one node's neighbors in this method.

5   Simulation Results

In this research, we used network simulator ns-2 software. We have generated random movements and also written various movement scenarios to sample deferent locations of a node. We have repeated the sampling of node's location in different time slice and various velocities then gives the initial location to three constant, linear and quadrate lazy learning methods based on multi-step prediction and compare the achieving result with the real values.

According to the results, we have shown in figure 6 to 9 the learning method can follow the node's movement with very high accuracy. In all figures, the horizontal axle shows the number of initial location we have used to predicating the next position of a node and the vertical axle shows coincidence Percentage between the predicted results and the real values.

In figure 6-a, we have sampled every 1 second and in figure 6-b we have sampled every 2 second.

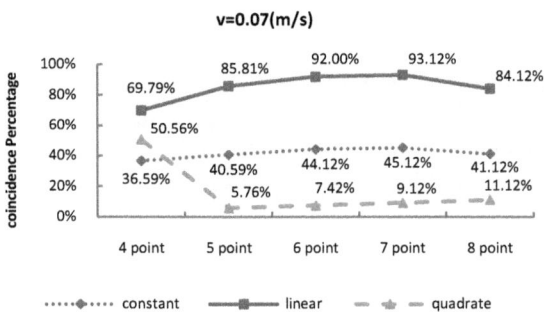

Fig. 6. a. Sampling the initial locations every 1 second

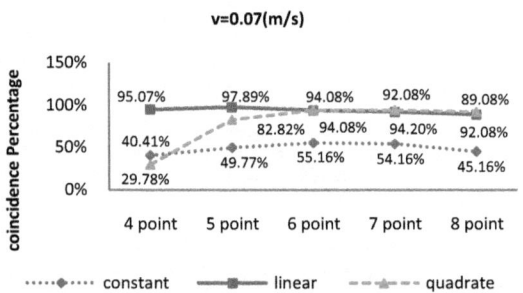

Fig. 6. b. Sampling the initial locations every 2 second

As it's shown in figure 6-a, in very low velocities such as $0.07^{m/s}$, if sampling is done every one second, the learning method cannot recognize the changes in movement. But figure 6-b shows that the predicted locations is closer to real location when we have sampled every 2 second in the same velocity, because lazy learning method is very sensitive to its neighbors. Therefore, choosing suitable initial data set plays an important role in the results of lazy learning method.

We have repeated the location sampling in $2.6^{m/s}$ and $4.6^{m/s}$ and show the results in figures 7 and 8.

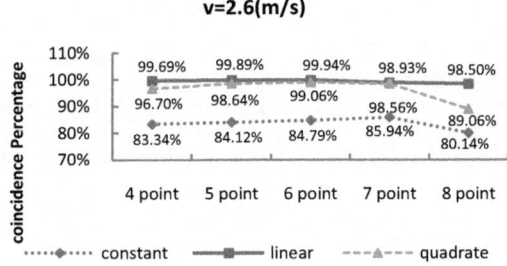

Fig. 7. a. Sampling the initial locations every 1 second

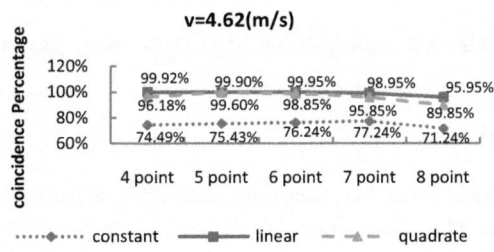

Fig. 7. b. Sampling the initial locations every 2 second

As you can see, figure 7 confirm the results of figure 6.   Since, the neighbors of query point don't surround it in initial data set, when we have increased the number of initial points the distance between the first initial point and the query point increased. Therefore, when we have used more than 5 or 6 initial points the accuracy of learning method would be reduced. We can easily see the effect of increasing the number of points in all figures.

Fig. 8. a. Sampling the initial locations every 1 second

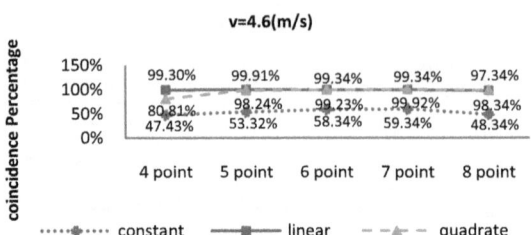

Fig. 8. b. Sampling the initial locations every 2 second

Quadrate lazy learning model is more accurate than the constant and linear models in lazy learning. Therefore, in one-step prediction the results of quadrate model are very close to the real positions. But, in multi-step prediction due to the Sensitivity of quadrate model to its neighbors, Occurrence of the small error in predicting the location cause the model could not follow the node. So, as you see in figure 6, 7 and 8 the results of linear model is the best and this model can follow the node better than other models.

To compare the linear and quadrate model, we have followed a node movement in long distance. Figure 9 confirm that linear model could follow the node better than quadrate model.

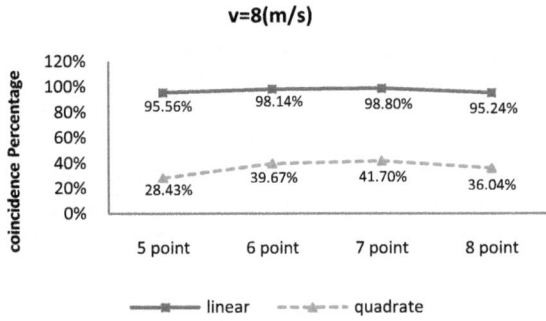

Fig. 9. Sampling the initial locations every 2 second

6   Conclusion

Simulation results show that lazy learning method can follow node movement with admissible accuracy. Therefore, nodes don't need to propagate their location information regularly which cause to reduce the traffic overhead of network and increase the network's scalability.

When we have used quadrate model we have increased the accuracy and sensitivity of lazy learning. In this case, the small error lead to increase the error rate and as the results show in figure 9, the quadrate model cannot follow the node movement efficiently. In spite of, in one-step prediction the coincidence percentage of quadrate model is the highest, but because of error aggregation, it does not follow the node movements efficiently in multi-step prediction.

Choosing suitable time slice for propagating node location information in ad hoc network is one of the important parameter in lazy learning method. In other word, we should choose large time slice for low speed movements and small time slice for high speed movements. Although, choosing large time slice for high speed movements don't have any problem for learning algorithm, but it may be not efficient for routing algorithms or other applications.

7 Future Work

Lazy learning method can predicate the nodes location with high accuracy. Therefore, using this method will reduce the ad hoc networks traffic overhead and increase the scalability. In our future work, we can study the effect of this method on the routing improvement, self organization and resource consumption in ad hoc networks.

References

1. Kaplan, E.D. (ed.): Understanding GPS: Principles and Applications, Artech House, Boston, MA (1996)
2. Wireless Communications & Mobile Computing (WCMC): Special issue on Mobile Ad Hoc Networking: Research. Trends and Applications 2(5), 483–502 (2002)
3. Savvides, A., Srivastava, M.: Location discovery. In: Basagni, S., Conti, M., Giordano, S., Stojmenovic, I. (eds.) Ad Hoc Networking. IEEE Press Wiley, New York (2003)
4. Aha, D.W. (ed.): Artificial Intelligence Review. Special Issue on Lazy Learning, pp. 1–6 (1997)
5. Chlamtac, I., Conti, M., Liu, J.N.: Mobile ad hoc networking: imperatives and challenges. Ad Hoc Networks 1(1), 13–64 (2003)
6. Takagi, H., Kleinrock, L.: Optimal transmission ranges for randomly distributed packet radio terminals. IEEE Transactions on Communications 32(3), 246–257 (1984)
7. Hou, T.C., Li, V.O.K.: Transmission range control in multi hop packet radio networks. IEEE Transactions on Communications 34(1), 38–44 (1986)
8. Kranakis, E., Singh, H., Urrutia, J.: Compass routing on geometric networks. In: 11th Canadian Conference on Computational Geometry (CCCG 1999), pp. 51–54 (1999)
9. Basagni, S., Chlamtac, I., Syrotiuk, V., Woodward, B.: A distance routing effect algorithm for mobility (DREAM). In: Proceedings of The Fourth Annual ACM/IEEE International Conference on Mobile Computing and Networking (MOBICOM 1998), Dallas, TX, USA, October 25–30 (1998)
10. Ko, Y.B., Vaidya, N.H.: Location-aided routing (LAR) in mobile ad hoc networks. ACM/Kluwer Wireless Networks 6(4), 307–321 (2000)
11. http://en.wikipedia.org/wiki/Cross-validation_(statistics)
12. Jafari, M., Khanteymoori, A.R.: Lazy Learning in Optimization Problems Using PRESS Statistics. In: Proceedings of the the Application of AI in industry, Bardsir (2010)
13. Birattari, M., Bontempi, G.: The lazy learning toolbox, for use with matlab, Technical Report TR/IRIDIA/99-7, IRIDIA-ULB, Brussels, Belgium (1999)

Advanced Dynamic Bayesian Network Optimization Model Applied in Decomposition Grid Task Scheduling

Leily Mohammad Khanli[1] and Sahar Namyar[2]

[1] University of Tabriz, Computer Science Department, Tabriz, Iran
[2] Islamic Azad University, Zanjan Branch, Department of Computer Engineering, Zanjan, Iran
Lmkhanli52@gmail.com, Sahar_namyar@yahoo.com

Abstract. This paper uses Bayesian optimization algorithm and decomposition approach for solving task scheduling problem in probabilistic grid computing systems to overcome the efficiency problem since it belongs to NP-complete problems. This paper introduces a Bayesian Optimization model that combines Dynamic Bayesian networks to manage uncertainty and evolutionary algorithms to solve the problem. Dynamic Bayesian networks use because the performance, reliability and cost of resources vary with time simultaneously and their availability is uncertain. This method decomposes the global problem to make the scheduling process simpler and achieve the QoS objectives efficiently. Instead of sending the jobs to the all resources, some local areas of resources with a controller consider and send the jobs to them. With the use of GridSim toolkit it will be proven that this model cause to achieve the QoS objectives such as minimizing the cost and time more efficiently.

Keywords: Grid computing, Task scheduling, Dynamic Bayesian Network, Decomposition approach, Genetic Algorithms.

1   Introduction

Grid computing and Grid technologies can now utilize idle computers all over the globe for satisfying the increasing demand of scientific computing community for more computing power. Geographically distributed computers, linked through internet in a grid-like manner as a type of distributed systems, are used to create virtual supercomputers of vast amount of computing capacity able to solve complex problems from e-science to overcome limitations on geographical location and hardware specification of computers in less time than known before [2].

"For a majority of grid systems, scheduling is a very important mechanism" [1]. In grid computing systems an application that could be software for solving a problem submitted by users. The computation split into jobs that require different processing capabilities and have different resource requirements (CPU, number of nodes, memory, software libraries, etc). In order to accomplish the job requirements, it is necessary to divide the jobs into several tasks and dispatch these tasks to computers which are currently idle [2]. The problem of scheduling in grid systems is much more complex

P. Pichappan, H. Ahmadi, and E. Ariwa (Eds.): INCT 2011, CCIS 241, pp. 346–361, 2011.

than its version on traditional distributed systems, (e.g. LAN environments) due to dynamic nature of grid systems and the high degree of heterogeneity and large number of resources and jobs submitted by different users, and due to the high heterogeneity of interconnection networks, existence of local schedulers and local policies on resources.   Job scheduling on computational grids is a large scale optimization problem. A large set of approaches have been delivered to find tradeoff between the complexity and performance [1]. Since grids are expected to be constructed by the contribution of computational resources across local areas of computers, most of these resources could eventually be running local applications and use their local schedulers. In order to the different ownership of resources, the full control over the grid resources cannot be considered. Other policies such as available storage, pay-per-use will consider [2]. So in the model that is used in this paper the best possible requirement is to assume a local scheduler in each local area.

The Grid and its related technologies will be used only if the users and the providers mutually trust each other. The system must be as reliable and robust. The reliability can be defined as the probability of any process to complete its task successfully as the way it was expected. In grid the reliability of any transaction can be improved by considering trust and reputation. Trust depends on one's own individual experiences and referrals from other entities. In [29] proposes a model which improves reliability in grid by considering reputation and trust.

Since mapping independent tasks onto a heterogeneous resource is NP-complete problem so the use of meta-heuristics is the defacto approach to cope with its difficulty. In population based meta-heuristics, such as Genetic Algorithms, the solution space is explored through a population of individuals that each individual represent a solution of problem and there are used methods for generating the initial population, computing the fitness of individuals as well genetic operators such as mutation and crossover to select the good individuals of population and replace the worst individuals of population by the newly generated descendent to transmit the genetic information from parents to offspring's [3,28].

The goal of optimal scheduling is to assign the task from task graph to m identical resources in grid environment in the way that is achieve the QoS objectives. This is a multi objective optimization problem; the two most important objectives are the minimization of makespan and the flow time of the system. It can be considered a lot of QoS objectives in grid environment. In this paper the aim is to achieve two QoS Objectives that are the showing the result in the minimum time and minimizing the cost.

Since in grid scheduling problem unpredictable computing and communication requirements may occur and also the available set of computing resources is shared among several users due to the dynamic nature of grid environment, It is considered as an uncertain problem. The information about the availability of resources is incomplete and imprecise under time. So the introduced model will use the dynamic Bayesian networks for handling the uncertainty.

In This paper The Bayesian optimization algorithm [4] [5], is used to combine Bayesian networks and evolutionary algorithms to solve task scheduling problem in grid environment. It evolves a population of candidate solutions to the given problem by statistically modeling the promising solutions found so far based on Bayesian networks [6] and sampling the build models to generate new candidate solutions of each iteration of the algorithm. The evolution process will repeat until the stop criteria are met. BOA searches the state space only in the neighborhood of previous best solution. For each evolution generation the BOA selects "good" solutions according to predefined criteria. That is very useful because the search will be occurring in promising regions of the search space [7].We combine the dynamic Bayesian networks and genetic algorithms as one of the evolutionary algorithms to find solutions with highest probability of achieving the QoS objectives as a criteria to find best solutions.

In the current study a new model will introduce, in this model the global problem decomposes into sub-problems to enhance the algorithm optimization performance. Some local areas of set of resources considered that each one has local schedule controllers. Each controller provides sub-chromosome as a sub-solution. Then a comparison mechanism will use to form a result chromosome as a solution of the problem. In this paper it is shown that this model will achieve the QoS objectives such as minimizing the cost and time.

The reminder of this paper is organized as following. Section 2 introduced the related work in scheduling approach, Bayesian optimization algorithm and scheduling under condition of uncertainty. In section 3, the proposed model for solving the problem of job scheduling is defined. The model is applied to the scheduler in section 4. The actual experimental results and analysis are illustrated with the use of GridSim toolkit in section 5. Finally the paper conclusion is defined in section 6.

2   Related Work

2.1   Scheduling Approach

There are meta-heuristic approaches, which explore the solution space and try to overcome local optimal solutions. Most of these approaches are based on a single heuristic method such as Local Search (Ritchie and Levine[8]), Genetic algorithms (GA)(Braun et.al [9], Zomaya and teh [10], Martino and Mililotti [11] , Abraham et.al [12], page and Naughton[13]) , Simulated annealing (Yarkhan and Dongara[14], Abraham et.al[12])or tabu search (Abraham et.al[12]).

2.2   Bayesian Optimization Algorithm

Unlike general evolutionary algorithm such as GA, BOA has no mutation operators. It explicitly models the statistic characters of optimized solutions, and uses the constructed model to guide the further search. Thus it can avoid the break of high order building blocks and behave more efficiently during optimization search [12].This model will use Bayesian optimization algorithm, that despite of genetic algorithms it doesn't have any mutation operator and it use the Bayesian network model to guide the search.

The original BOA firstly published in [15] that were able to solve single-criterion problems. Nowadays, BOA has been widely developed to solve different kinds of problems such as multi criterion optimization [16]. In the introduced model in this paper BOA can use as a multi criterion optimization in the way the allocation of resources can evaluate with multi QoS objectives.

2.3   Scheduling under Condition of Uncertainty

The multi criteria resource selection method implemented in the Grid Resource Management system([17]&[18]) has been used for the evaluation of knowledge obtained from the prediction system but because the available information was not enough, results of performance prediction methods may cause errors ([19]&[20]) . In [21] a normative model of stochastic grid resource environment, based on dynamic Bayesian network [22], to infer indirect influences and to track the time propagation of schedule actions in complex Grid environment is developed. Since the information for using the prediction methods was not enough ,and will determine over the time, this method will aid the dynamic Bayesian network in each local scheduler to infer indirect influences.

3   Defining a Model for Solving the Problem of Job Scheduling in Grid Environment

In the current study a model will introduce that simultaneously evaluate some scheduler controllers that has been considered in local areas. It has been a schema that decomposes the global problem into a set of sub problems, thus making the optimization process simpler. So it will be suitable for problem solving in grid computing systems. Local controllers produce a sub-solution. Then the local controllers cooperate with each other to produce the global solution that will be the main result of algorithm. It enhances the global optimization performance.

3.1   Using Dynamic Bayesian Networks

Dynamic Bayesian networks uses decision making mechanisms that deal explicitly with uncertainty since the information about the availability of resources is incomplete and imprecise over the time.

A Bayesian belief network is directed acyclic graph $G_k = G(t_k) = (V, E, p_k)$, which can be viewed as Bayesian network at time, whose nodes are the model variables and whose links represent local causal dependencies. For each node $v_i \in V$ a probability mass function (pmf) $p_k(v_i) = \{v_i(t_k)\}$ will define to characterize the environment uncertainty at time t_k [21]. The network topology as an abstract knowledge based hold independently of numerical assignments of conditional probabilities. A Bayesian network can be used as a probabilistic inference engine, which computes the posterior probability distribution for a set of query variables given the probability distribution for some evidence variables.

3.2   Constructing Dynamic Bayesian Network for the Proposed Model

This probabilistic model consists of a set of stochastic variables and joint distribution assigns probabilities to all possible states. The concept of conditional dependencies among variables is introduced by representing the local interactions. Each stochastic variable X_i is directly influenced by other variables, referred to as $parent(X_i)$. The probabilistic model constructed in terms of direct influences among the variables, quantified by conditional probability tables (CPT). The probability items in conditional probability table will define as $p(X_i|parent(X_i))$. In fig 1 the nodes in graph G represent the variables and the directed link from node $parent(X_i)$ to node X_i represent the probability relation between variable X_i and $parent(X_i)$.The probability dependency between these two nodes can be defined as equation 1:

$$p\{X_i|parentX_i\}= p\{X_i, parentX_i\}/\, p\{parentX_i\} \tag{1}$$

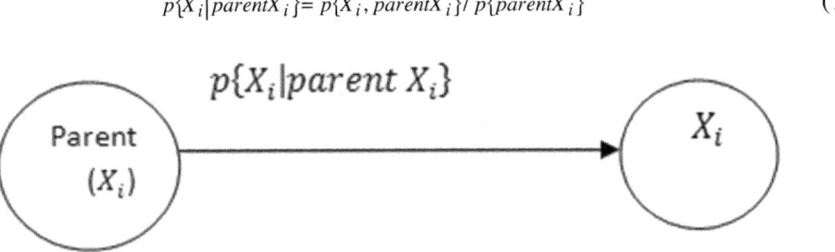

Fig. 1. The Bayesian network and probability dependency between nodes

In this model three set of variables will consider 1- actions 2- objectives 3- intermediate states. An action in this model is to allocate a time slot on a resource to a task Where A is the set of feasible actions. $p_k(A_q)$ Indicate the probability of allocating a certain resource to a task at time t_k . That considered as a prior probability that determine with system. Objectives are desired states of the model. O is the set of QoS objectives. These QoS objectives may be specified by users at eac h considered local areas. Some examples of QoS objectives in our model is showing the result in minimum time and minimizing the cost of using the resources at each considered area. Intermediate states are defined to differentiate those states that are not desired finishing states, but are useful in connecting the actions to the QoS objectives. All the intermediate states are forming a set S . For constructing the dynamic Bayesian network of the model the variables of the graph consist of actions, objectives and intermediate states will determine.

In this model the model variables will define as follow:

1. The actions: Actions illustrate the resource allocations to the tasks.
2. The intermediate system states: Two kinds of intermediate system states consider in this model:

    S1: achieving the minimum cost for each allocation
    S2: achieving the minimum time for each allocation

3. The objective states: Two objective states consider in this model:

O1: achieving the minimum cost for all allocations
O2: achieving the minimum time for all allocations

The directed links between variable nodes will determine according to QoS objectives policies in each local area. The probability parameters of the direct links and conditional probability tables (CPTs) identifying the conditional probability for each variable will set.

As shown in Fig2 in each controller for a defined task the probability of achieving the QoS objective of allocating a specific time slot on a resource will determine .The decision node evaluate the probability distribution of achieving the QoS objective for each action in a objective node. The utility node will apply a comparison mechanism to select the actions with the highest probability.

Decision networks [23-25], combine Dynamic Bayesian networks with two additional nodes: a decision node which represent the choices available and a utility node, which represent the utility function to be optimized [26]. In this model the decision node evaluate the probability distribution of achieving the QoS objective for each action. The utility node will use to be able to select among different actions with probabilities assign to the result states. The states will prefer with high probability of achieving the QoS objectives. For selecting the states with the highest probability the comparison mechanism will use. That is for each controller and for a certain objective a comparison will be done between the objective probabilities.

The model is shown in Fig 2.In each controller a dynamic evolution of the DBN-based scheduling through t_1 to t_k will be done.

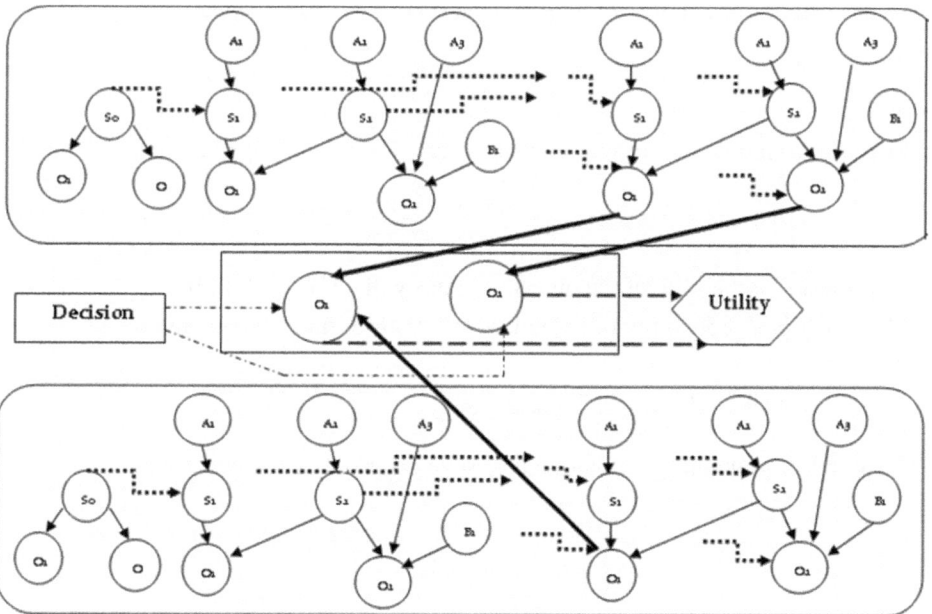

Fig. 2. The proposed model using decision network

Direct influence dependencies between all the objects of the system and their mechanisms are specified by conditional probability tables (CPTs) in Bayesian networks. Two kinds of probabilities will be in these tables: priori and posterior probabilities. In this model the priori probability is the probability of actions occurrence. That means it is the probability of allocating a certain resource to a task which can attained from the priori analysis of system; and the posterior probability is the probability of achieving the QoS objectives with the given actions and state of system.

The probability will propagate vertically from causal nodes to effect nodes and propagate horizontally from one time step to another.

In the proposed model the priori and posterior probabilities define as follow. Three priori probabilities will define in this model:

The probability of allocating a specific resource to a task. This probability is often 0 or 1. $p(a_i) = 0 or 1$

The probability of achieving the minimum cost of a resource. This probability is defined in equation 2.

$$p(\min\_\cos tR_i) = \frac{1}{\cos tR_i} \tag{2}$$

The probability of achieving the min time is defined in equation 3.

$$p(\min\_timeR_i) = \frac{1}{MIPSR_i} \tag{3}$$

The posterior probability of the intermediate states will define as follow:
The posterior probability of intermediate state is defined in equation 4:

$$p(\min\_alloc\_\cos tR_i) = p(\frac{1}{total\_\cos tRi}) = p(S_1 | a_i, \min\_\cos tR_i) \tag{4}$$

The posterior probability of intermediate state   is defined in equation 5:

$$p(\min\_alloc\_timeR_i) = p(\frac{1}{Finishtime - Starttime}) = p(S_2 | a_i, \min\_timeR_i) \tag{5}$$

The posterior probability of the objective states will define as follow:
The posterior probability of objective state O_1 is defined in equation 6:

$$p(\min\_total\_\cos tR_i) = p(\frac{1}{total\_\cos tR_i}) = p(O_1 | S_1, a_i, \min\_\cos tR_i) \tag{6}$$

The posterior probability of intermediate state O_2 is defined in equation 7:

$$p(\min\_total\_timeR_i) = p(\frac{1}{total\_timeR_i}) = p(O_2 | S_2, a_i, \min\_timeR_i) \tag{7}$$

These probabilities will use to form the chromosomes of each controller and the result chromosome.

4   Applying the Model to the Scheduler

For solving the scheduling optimization problem the concepts of genetic optimization algorithm combine with the proposed model.

4.1   The Encoding of the Problem

The individuals of population (also known as chromosome) refer to the solution of the problem. The encoding of these individuals is a key issue. For representing the encoding a vector is used that is called a *schedule*, two kinds of chromosomes are defined. One is sub-chromosome another one is global-chromosome. Sub-chromosome is a vector of size A (number of actions) , where $schedule[i]$ indicates the pair of the prior probability of allocating specific resource to a task and the probability of achieving the QoS objectives for each action .This will form a sub-chromosome for a task for a specific QoS objective. An example of a sub-chromosome with four actions for minimizing the cost illustrate in Table1.

Table 1. An example sub-chromosome

A1	A2	A3	A4
(0,0)	(0,0)	(1,0.73)	(0,0)

The global-chromosome is a vector of size T (number of task) where $schedule[i]$ indicate the pair of the resource ID allocate to the task and the QoS objective probability under the allocating strategy for the set of resources. This will form a global-chromosome for each controller for a specific QoS objective. An example of global-chromosome of a controller with four tasks for minimizing the cost illustrate in Table2.

Table 2. An example global-chromosome

1	2	3	4
(1,0.0001143)	(2,0.0001143)	(3,0.0001143)	(4,0.0001143)

The sub chromosomes and general chromosome will form in each controller. Then with the use of comparison mechanism the result chromosome will form.

4.2   Decision Making and Selecting Strategy with Considering Utility Function

Forming the chromosomes has two steps. Forming the sub-chromosomes and forming the global-chromosomes. For forming the sub-chromosomes two probability values should define, the probability of allocating a specific resource to a task and the probability of achieving the QoS objective. After forming the sub-chromosomes the allocating strategy for the set of resources will specify. For forming the global chromosomes for each controller two values should define. For each task resource ID that allocate according to the allocating strategy and the probability of achieving the QoS objective under the strategy should define. A comparison strategy will use to form the result chromosome that is the main result of the problem. The comparison strategy is choosing the chromosome with the highest probability of achieving the QoS objective. An example of three global chromosomes for each controller and the result chromosome illustrate in Table3.

Table 3. Created the result chromosome using global chromosomes

Global - chromosome 1

1	2	3	4
(1,0.0001143)	(2,0.0001143)	(3,0.0001143)	(4,0.0001143)

Global - chromosome 2

1	2	3	4
(1,0.000322)	(2,0.000322)	(3,0.000322)	(4,0.000322)

Global - chromosome 3

1	2	3	4
(1,0.0001285)	(2,0.0001285)	(3,0.0001285)	(4,0.0001285)

The result chromosome

1	2	3	4
(1, 0.000322)	(2, 0.000322)	(3, 0.000322)	(4, 0.000322)

As shown in this table, general chromosome2 is as result chromosome since the probability of achieving the QoS in this chromosome is higher than others. It is the main advantage of using chromosomes in controllers; that is the chromosome will select with the highest probability; it increase the probability of achieving the QoS objective in the whole system.

4.3   The Proposed Algorithm

The procedure of proposed algorithm for job scheduling in grid environment using the introduced model illustrate in FIG3.

As shown in this Fig in the first line the initial population as the initial chromosome will generate at random. The DBN in each controller for each time slice and for a QoS objective will create. The sub-chromosome will generate at lines 6-15 and the global-chromosome will generate at lines 16-23 and the result-chromosome will generate at lines 24-29.

```
 1 Generate initial population of assignment at random
 2 For each controller do
 3 For each time slice do
 4 For each QoS objective do
 5 For each task do
 6 /generating sub-chromosome
 7 Generate action nodes
 8 For each action do
 9 Generate prior conditional probability of allocating
10 special resource to the task
11 Generate prior conditional probability of achieving
12 the QoS objective with allocating the special resource
13 to the task
14   End For
15   End For
16 /generating global-chromosome
17 Generate task node
18 For each task do
19 Generate the resource ID allocate to the task
20 Generate posterior conditional probability of achieve
21 the QoS objective with allocating the special resource
22 to the task
23   End For
24 /generating result-chromosome
25 Compare the posterior conditional probability of
26 achieving the QoS objective item of global chromosome
27 Select the global chromosome with the highest prob
28 ability as the result chromosome
29 End For
30 End For
31 End For
```

Fig. 3. The procedure of proposed algorithm for job scheduling in grid environment using the introduced model

5   Experimental Result and Analysis

In this paper the simulation environment build on GridSim toolkit. GridSim toolkit supports modeling and simulation of heterogeneous Grid resources (both time and cost based) users and application models. This toolkit provides primitiveness for creation of application tasks, mapping of tasks to resources and their management [27].

To validate our work, we conducted experiments in a four resource grid. We simulate a simple workflow job including four tasks: t1: reading, t2: computing, t3: saving, t4: representing the result. The average length of these jobs is 2000 with deviate 20. Three controllers considered. The time zone of resources in each controller is different. The properties of resources in each controller are shown in table4. The action definition is shown in table5. S1 to S7 is the intermediate states. Two QoS objectives are considered. O1: Minimizing the cost.O2: Minimizing the time. The build DBN is shown in fig 4. The simulation result and the value of the posterior probabilities of intermediate states in controllers 1, 2, 3 are shown in tables 6, 10, 14. The simulation result and the value of the posterior probabilities of objective states in controllers 1, 2, 3 are shown in tables 7, 11, 15. The sub chromosomes for controllers 1, 2, 3 are shown in tables 8, 12, 16. The global chromosomes for controllers 1, 2, 3 are shown in tables 9, 13, 17. The result chromosome is shown in table 18. We compare our work with the approach that the result of the problem takes without considering local areas.

Table 4. The probabilities of resources

Controller1				Controller2				Controller3			
R	MIPS	cost	Time zone	R	MIPS	cost	Time Zone	R	MIPS	cost	Time Zone
R1	400	110	3:54	R1	350	120	7:08	R1	450	300	10:09
R2	100	220	3:54	R2	150	100	7:08	R2	100	250	10:09
R3	200	300	3:54	R3	500	50	7:08	R3	250	120	10:09
R4	500	50	3:54	R1	350	120	7:08	R4	300	100	10:09

Table 5. The action definition

Controller	action	Allocation
1	A1	Allocating R1 to t1
1	A2	Allocating R4to t4
1	A3	Allocating R3 to t3
1	A4	Allocating R2 to t2
2	A1	Allocating R5 to t1
2	A2	Allocating R7 to t3
2	A3	Allocating R8 to t4
2	A4	Allocating R6 to t2
3	A1	Allocating R9 to t1
3	A2	Allocating R12 to t4
3	A3	Allocating R11 to t3
3	A4	Allocating R10 to t2

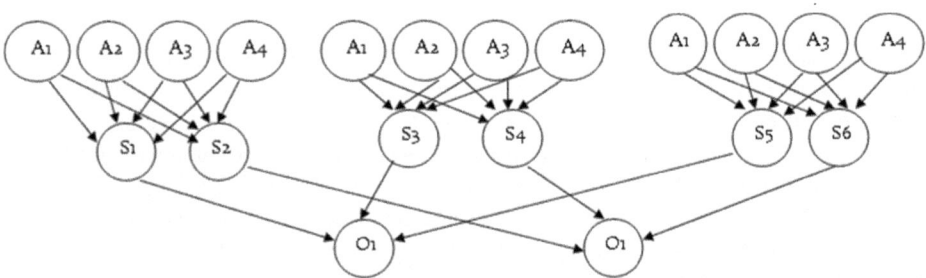

Fig. 4. Dynamic Bayesian Network used in the model

Table 6. The simulation result and the value of the posterior probabilities of intermediate states in controller 1

controller	task	resource	load	Cost	Start time	Finish Time	$p(min\_alloc\_cost\ R_i)$	$p(min\_alloc\_time\ R_i)$
1	1	1	1786. 19	491. 2	3. 2	7.6 6	0.002	0.2242
1	4	4	1875. 9	187. 59	0. 01	9.7 7	0.005	0.1024
1	3	3	2082. 34	312 3.51	5. 1	15. 52	0.0003	0.09596
1	2	2	2246. 65	494 2.62	4. 11	26. 58	0.0002	0.04450

Table 7. The simulation result and the value of the posterior probabilities of objective state in controller 1

controller	Total allocation cost	Total completion time	$p(min\_total\_costR_i)$	$p(min\_total\_timeR_i)$
1	8744.93	25.52	0.0001143	0.03918

Table 8. Sub-chromosomes for controller 1

A1	A2	A3	A4	A1	A2	A3	A4	A1	A2	A3	A4	A1	A2	A3	A4
(1,0.002)	(0,0)	(0,0)	(0,0)	(0,0)	(1,0.005)	(0,0)	(0,0)	(0,0)	(0,0)	(1,0.0003)	(0,0)	(0,0)	(0,0)	(0,0)	(1,0.0002)

Table 9. Global-chromosomes for controller 1

1	2	3	4
(1,0.0001143)	(2, 0.0001143)	(3, 0.0001143)	(4, 0.0001143)

Table 10. The simulation result and the value of the posterior probabilities of intermediate states in controller 2

controller	task	resource	load	cost	Start time	Finish Time	$p(min\_alloc\_cost\ R_i)$	$p(min\_alloc\_time\ R_i)$
2	1	5	1786.19	612.4	2.4	7.5	0.0016	0.196
2	3	7	2082.34	374.8	4.3	8.5	0.0026	0.2380
2	4	8	1875.9	2000.9	5.2	11.5	0.00049	0.1587
2	2	6	2246.65	1497.7	3.3	18.3	0.00066	0.066

Table 11. The simulation result and the value of the posterior probabilities of objective state in controllers 2

controller	Total allocation cost	Total completion time	$p(min\_total\_costR_i)$	$p(min\_total\_timeR_i)$
2	4485.95	18.03	0.000222	0.0554

Table 12. Sub-chromosomes for controller 2

A1	A2	A3	A4	A1	A2	A3	A4	A1	A2	A3	A4	A1	A2	A3	A4
(1,0.0016)	(0,0)	(0,0)	(0,0)	(0,0)	(1,0.0026)	(0,0)	(0,0)	(0,0)	(0,0)	(1,0.00049)	(0,0)	(0,0)	(0,0)	(0,0)	(1,0.00066)

Table 13. Global-chromosomes for controller 2

1	2	3	4
(5,0.000222)	(6, 0.000222)	(7, 0.000222)	(8, 0.000222)

Table 14. The simulation result and the value of the posterior probabilities of intermediate states in controller 3

controller	task	resource	load	cost	Start time	Finish Time	$p(\min\_alloc\_cost\ R_i)$	$p(\min\_alloc\_time\ R_i)$
3	1	9	1786.1	1190.7	2.45	6.42	0.00083	0.2518
3	4	12	1875.9	625.3	5.26	11.52	0.001599	0.1597
3	3	11	2082.3	999.5	4.35	12.68	0.001	0.12
3	2	10	2246.65	5616.6	3.36	25.83	0.00017	0.0445

Table 15. The simulation result and the value of the posterior probabilities of objective state in controllers 3

controller	Total allocation cost	Total completion time	$p(\min\_total\_cost R_i)$	$p(\min\_total\_time R_i)$
3	8432.24	25.52	0.0001185	0.03918

Table 16. Sub-chromosomes for controller 3

A1	A2	A3	A4	A1	A2	A3	A4	A1	A2	A3	A4	A1	A2	A3	A4
(1,0.00083)	(0,0)	(0,0)	(0,0)	(0,0)	(1,0.001599)	(0,0)	(0,0)	(0,0)	(0,0)	(1,0.001)	(0,0)	(0,0)	(0,0)	(0,0)	(1,0.00017)

Table 17. Global-chromosomes for controller 3

1	2	3	4
(9,0.0001185)	(10, 0.0001185)	(11, 0.0001185)	(12, 0.0001185)

Table 18. Result-chromosome

1	2	3	4
(5,0.000222)	(6, 0.000222)	(7, 0.000222)	(8, 0.000222)

With comparing the simulation result and in fig5 and fig6, it is clear that with considering local areas the two QoS probabilities of achieving the minimum time and cost is higher than the approach that is not consider the local areas.

As shown in fig5 and fig6 this approach increase 0.0001077 the probability of minimizing the cost and 0.0154 the probability of minimizing the time.

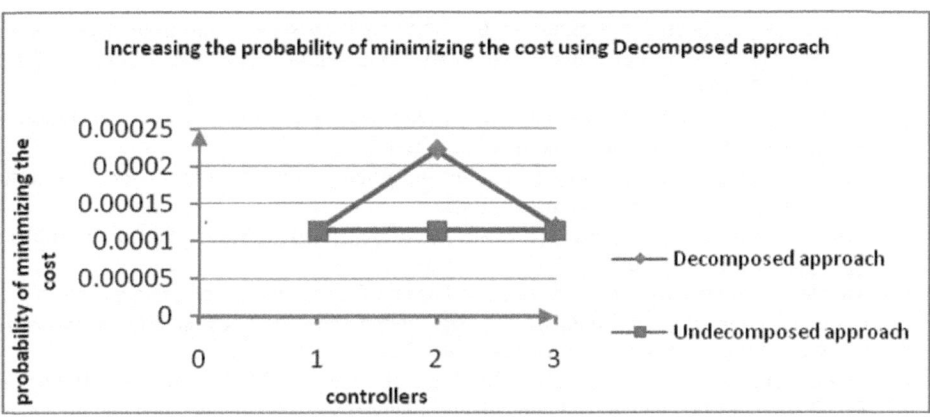

Fig. 5. Increasing the probability of minimizing the cost using decomposed approach

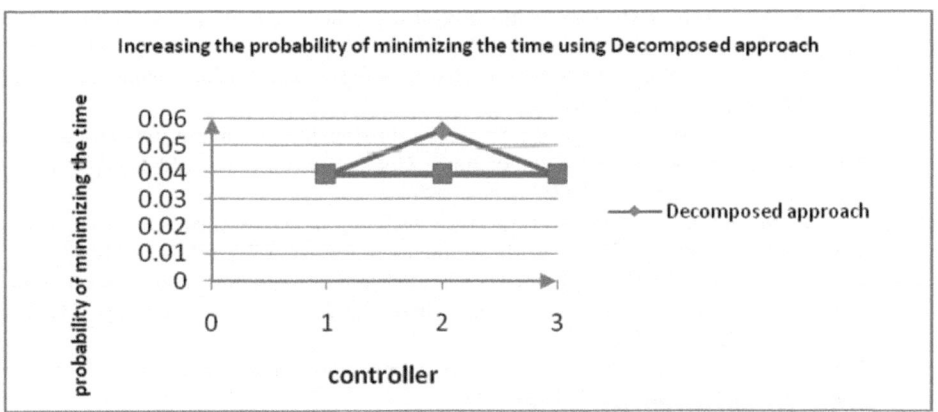

Fig. 6. Increasing the probability of minimizing the time using decomposed approach

6   Conclusion

In this paper it is proven that with considering local controllers and sending the tasks to them instead of sending the tasks to all the resources the probability of achieving the QoS objective such as minimizing the cost and time will increase.

References

[1] Xhafa, F.: A Hybrid evolutionary heuristic for job scheduling on computational grids, ch. 10. SCI. Springer, Heidelberg (2007)
[2] Xhafa, F., Abrahham: Computational models and heuristic methods for grid scheduling problems. Future Generation Computer Systems (2009), doi:10.1016/j.future2009.11.005
[3] Xhafa, F., Gonzalez, J.A., Dahul, K.P., Abraham, A.: A GA (TS) hybrid algorithm for scheduling in computational grids

[4] Pelikan, M., Goldberg, D., Cantu-Paz, E.: BOA: The Bayesian optimization algorithm. In: Proceedings of the Genetic and Evolutionary Computation Conference (GECCO 1999), pp. 525–532 (1999)

[5] Pelikan, M.: Hierarchical Bayesian optimization algorithm: Toward a new generation of evolutionary algorithms. Springer, New York (2005)

[6] Peal, J.: Probabilistic reasoning in intelligent systems. In: Networks of Plausible Inference. Morgan Kaufmann, San mateo (1988)

[7] Lei, Q., Yuan, X.T.: Cooperated Bayesian algorithm for distributed scheduling problem. Springer, Heidelberg (2006)

[8] Ritchie, G., Levin, J.: A fast effective local search for scheduling independent jobs in heteogeneos computing environment. In: 23rd Workshop of the UK Planning and Scheduling Special Interest Group PLANSIG (2004)

[9] Braun, H.J., Siegel, T.D., Beck, N., Blni, L.L., Maheswaran, M., Reuther, A.I., Roberson, J.P., Theyes, M.D., Yao, A.B: Comparison of eleven static heuristics for mapping a class of independent tasks onto heterogeneous distributed computing systems. Journal of Parallel and Distributed Systems (2001)

[10] Zomaya, A.Y., Teh, Y.H.: Observations on using genetic algorithms for dynamic load-balancing. IEEE Transactions on Parallel and Distributed Systems 12(9), 899–911 (2001)

[11] Di Martino, V., Mililotti, M.: Sub optimal scheduling in a grid using genetic algorithms. Parallel Computing 30, 553–565 (2004)

[12] Abraham, A., Buyya, R., Nath, B.: Nature's heuristics for scheduling jobs on computational grids. In: The 8th IEEE International Conference on Advanced Computing and Communications (ADCOM 2000), India (2000)

[13] Page, J., Naughton, J.: Framework for task scheduling in heterogeneous distributed computing using genetic algorithms. Artificial Intelligence Review 24, 415–429 (2005)

[14] YarKhan, A., Dongarra, J.: Experiments With Scheduling using Simulated Annealing in a Grid Environment. In: Parashar, M. (ed.) GRID 2002. LNCS, vol. 2536, pp. 232–242. Springer, Heidelberg (2002)

[15] Pelikan, M.: A Simple Implementation of Bayesian Optimization Algorithm in C++ (Version 1.0). Illigal Report 99011, 116 (1999)

[16] Oèenáŝek, J., Schwarz, J.: Estimation of distribution algorithm for mixed continuous-discrete optimization problems. In: 2nd Euro-International Symposium on Computational Intelligence, pp. 227–232. IOS Press, Kosice (2002)

[17] Kurowski, K., Nabrzki, J., Oleksiak, A., Weglarz: Multi criteria aspects of Grid resource management. Grid Resource Management State of Future Trends Table of Contents, 271–293 (2004)

[18] Domagalski, P., Kurowski, K., Oleksiak, A., Nabrzyski, J., Balaton: Sensor oriented Grid monitoring Infrastructures for Adaptive Multi criteria resource management systems (2005)

[19] Smith, W., Taylor, V., Foster, I.: Using Run-Time Predictions to Estimate Queue Wait Times and Improve Scheduler Performance. In: Proceedings of the IPPS/SPDP 1999 Workshop on Job Scheduling Strategies for Parallel Processing, pp. 202–219 (1999)

[20] Smith, W., Foster, I., Taylor, V.: Predicting Application Run Times Using Historical information (2004)

[21] Bin, Z., Zhaohui, L., Jun, W.: Grid Scheduling Optimization under Conditions of Uncertainty. IFIP International Federation for Information Processing (2007)

[22] Santos, L., Proenca, A.: Scheduling under conditions of uncertainty: a Bayesian approach. In: Proceedings of the 5th International Conference on Coordination Models and Languages, pp. 222–229 (2004)

[23] Horvitz, E., Breese, J., Henrion, M.: Decision theory in Expert systems and Artificial Intelligence. Technical report, Palo Alto Laboratory (1998)

[24] Pearl, J.: Probabilistic Reasoning in Intelligent systems, Networks of plausible inference. Morgan Kaufmann publishers (1998) ISBN: 1-55860-479-0

[25] Russell, S., Norvig, P.: Artificial Intelligence: A modern Approach. Prentice-Hall (1995) ISBN: 0-13-103805-2

[26] Santos, L.P., Proenca, A.: Scheduling under condition of uncertainty a Bayesian approach (1995)

[27] Murshed, M., Buyya, R., Abramson, D.: GridSim: A Toolkit for the modeling and simulation of distributed resource management and scheduling for grid computing. Concurrency and Computation: Practice and Experience, CCPE (2002)

[28] Gao., Y., Phillips., C., He, L.: GA and PSO-based Resource Scheduling for Orchestrated, Distributed Computing. Journal of Digital Information Management 7(6) (December 2009)

[29] Vivekananth, P.: Building reliability model in Grid Computing. Journal of Information Security Research 1(3/4) (September/December 2010)

An Efficient Live Process Migration Approach for High Performance Cluster Computing Systems

Ehsan Mousavi Khaneghah, Najmeh Osouli Nezhad, Seyedeh Leili Mirtaheri,
Mohsen Sharifi, and Ashakan Shirpour

School of Computer Engineering, Iran University of Science and Technology, Tehran, Iran
{msharifi,mirtaheri,emousavi}@iust.ac.ir,
{n_osuli,a_shirpour}@comp.iust.ac.ir

Abstract. High performance cluster computing systems have used process migration to balance the workload on their constituent computers and thus improve their overall throughput and performance. They however fail to migrate processes lively in the sense that moving processes are blocked (frozen) and are non-responsive to any requests sent to them while they are moving to their new destinations and have not reached and resumed their work on their new destinations. Previous efforts to prevent losing requests during process migration have been inefficient. We present a more efficient approach that keeps migrating processes live and responsive to requests during their journey to their new destinations. To achieve this, we have added a new state called the exile state to the traditional state model of processes in operating systems. A migratory process changes its status to the exile state before starting to migrate. All requests to the migratory process are executed locally on the old location of the process until the process reaches its destination computer and resumes its work anew. We show that our approach improves the performance of clusters supporting process migration by decreasing freeze time.

Keywords: High Performance Computing Clusters, Process Migration, Live Migration, Process Status, Distributed Systems.

1 Background

Process migration is the act of moving processes from one machine to other machines in distributed systems for load balancing, locality of resource usage, access to more processing power, and fault resilience. The context of a process (process state) to be migrated includes heap data, stack content, processor registers, address space, process running state, and process communication state (like open files or message channels) that all of them are essential for a process to continue its execution elsewhere [1],[2],[3]. The process running state is a part of process state that represents the running state of a process (Section 2).

Part of process state that has the most overhead in process migration mechanisms is the process address space that might have hundreds of megabyte of data [2],[3], so the transmission of address space in recent implementations has been mentioned more than other process state parts.

P. Pichappan, H. Ahmadi, and E. Ariwa (Eds.): INCT 2011, CCIS 241, pp. 362–373, 2011.
© Springer-Verlag Berlin Heidelberg 2011

In the following subsections, we will review process migration algorithms demonstrating how to transfer the process address space and how important are challenges of these algorithms.

In Section 2, we review the evolution of process models and explain the features of each state. In Section 3, we present our new efficient live process migration approach for high performance cluster computing systems. Section 4 reports an evaluation of the approach and Section 5 concludes the paper.

1.1   Total-Copy Algorithm

Total-Copy is the first and the most popular process migration algorithm [2] that is sometimes called eager (all) too [1]. Demos/MP [4], Amoeba [5], and Charlotte [6] are examples that use some versions of this algorithm in user level or kernel level. In this algorithm (Fig. 1) when a process is stopped executing in a source node upon migration, all of its state is transferred to the destination node and then resumes in the destination [4],[5],[6]. A modified version of this algorithm is eager (dirty) that is used in Mosix. This algorithm can be used only if the system has remote paging facilities. In this algorithm, just the modified pages are transferred at the migration start and then other pages are transferred on demand. The first cost of eager (dirty) is lower than Total-Copy [1] ,[7] ,[8],[9].

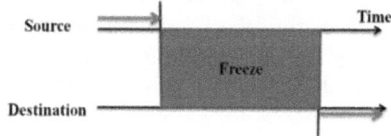

Fig. 1. Total-Copy algorithm

1.2   Pre-Copy Algorithm

The main goal of this algorithm when presented in System V [10] was to prevent failed communications in total copy algorithm [1]. In this algorithm, address space is transferred from source node to destination node while the process is executing on the source node (Fig. 2). When the number of modified migratory process's pages in source node becomes under some threshold, the process is frozen (blocked). Then all of the remaining process state is transferred and the process resumes in destination node [10]. The freeze time is lower than that in Total-Copy algorithm.

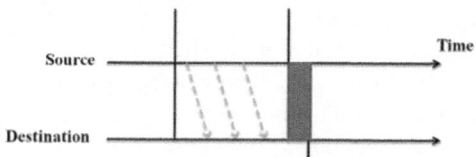

Fig. 2. Pre-Copy algorithm

1.3   Demand Paging Algorithm

This algorithm was first implemented in the Accent operating system by Zayas [2]. In this algorithm, the migratory process is frozen, the execution, the control data, and the address space metadata are transferred to destination node (Fig.3), but the address space remains in the source node. The destination node requests pages if it needs them. This algorithm is called Copy-On-Reference [11]. To improve this algorithm, some operating systems transfer one page of heap, stack, and code at migration time too [2].

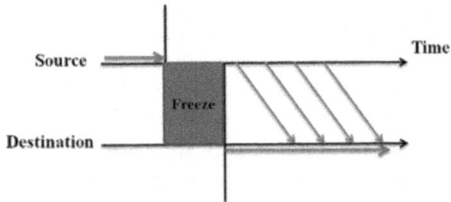

Fig. 3. Demand paging

1.4   File Server Algorithm

This algorithm was first developed by Douglis that uses an added machine as a file server in the Sprite operating system [12]. In the system the process is blocked, the modified pages and the modified file blocks are flushed to file server, and then the migratory process is resumed in the destination node and requests the pages from the file server if it needs them (Fig. 4). This algorithm is called Flushing [1].

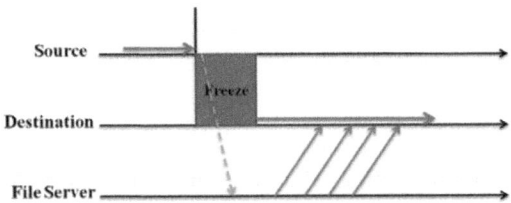

Fig. 4. File server

2   Evolution of Process State Models

In the early operating systems that were not multi-task, when a process execution was started, it used the processor until it was finished and so those systems did not need any process running state. In the recent operating systems that are multi-task and processes can execute interleaved, any process in its lifetime could have different running states (that are exclusive) [13]. The kernel should maintain the information of process running state in order to improve dispatcher's performance. For example,

LINUX operating system holds this information in *state* field in *task_struct* structure [14]. In the following subsections, we review process running state evolution.

2.1   Two-State Model

In this model, that is the primary model in operating systems, a process is in the RUNNING state or NOT RUNNING state (Fig. 5). The disadvantage of this model is that processes can be in the NOT RUNNING queue for two reasons: have finished their processor quantum or waiting for I/O. The dispatcher should search the entire list of processes to select a suitable process and spend unnecessary time resulting in lower performance [13].

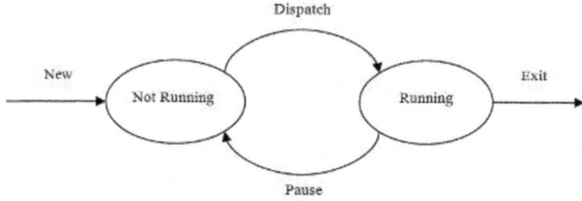

Fig. 5. Two state transition diagram

2.2   Three-State Model

MINIX uses a three-state process model (Fig. 6) [15].

— **RUNNING:** In this state, the process is executing its instructions.
— **READY:** The only resource that the process does not have in this state is the processor. The state of a process changes from RUNNING to READY when it finishes its processor quantum, or from BLOCKED to READY when its desired request for I/O has been satisfied.
— **BLOCKED:** When a process executes a system call for I/O and the I/O is not available in memory, the process is removed from the dispatcher queue, its register values are saved in the process table, and it is blocked until its I/O is brought to memory. A blocked process cannot continue executing even if the processor is idle.

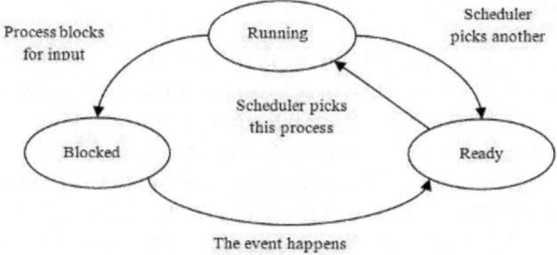

Fig. 6. Three-state transition diagram

2.3   Five-State Model

Another process state model contains five states (Fig. 7) [17]:

— **NEW:** This state denotes the case where a process is created in response to *fork()* or *exec()* system calls. Process structures and process identifier are allocated to the process, but the process is still not loaded into the memory possibly because of a restriction on the number of processes in the memory.

— **RUNNING:** This state is the same as in the three-state model.

— **READY:** In this state, the only resource that a process does not have is the processor. While the system is ready to execute a new process, one process can move from the NEW state to this state. On the other hand, a process can move from the RUNNING state to this state because of finishing the processor quantum or process pre-emption (because the event that a process with higher priority in BLOCKED state was waiting for has occurred).

— **WAITING:** The process is waiting for completion of I/O or the occurrence of a special event.

— **TERMINATED (exit):** In this state, the memory allocated to a process is released. In this state, the operating system releases the process. Only the accounting programs calculate process usages for billing purposes. A process may move to this state from the READY state because of termination of its parent process or from the BLOCK state because a parent process has killed his children.

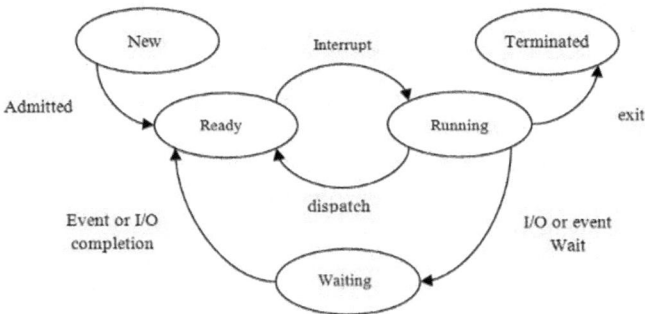

Fig. 7. Five-state transition diagram

2.4   Seven-State Model

Because the processor's speed is more than I/O speed, all processes in the memory may be in the WAITING state. In order to prevent busy waiting the processor time, a new state named SUSPEND has been introduced (Fig. 8) [17].

The NEW, TERMINATED, READY, RUNNING, and BLOCKED states are exactly similar to their counterparts in the five-state model. The states SUSPENDED & READY and SUSPENDED & BLOCKED are different. If all the processes in the main memory are blocked and the processor is idle, some blocked processes can be moved to secondary storage and theie state changed to BLOCK&SUSPEND. If the

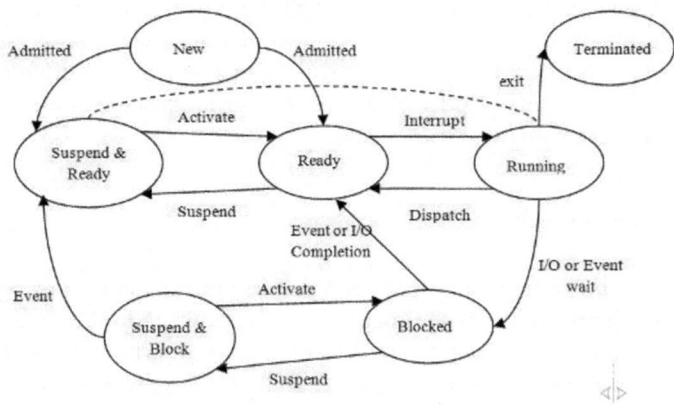

Fig. 8. Seven-state transition diagram

event that the process in the secondary storage was waiting for occurs, the process changes its state to this state and remains in secondary storage. If the event that the process in the secondary storage was waiting for occurs, the process changes its state to the READY&SUSPEND state and remains in the secondary storage.

2.5   Nine-State Model

In UNIX operating system [16], [17], the process state diagram has nine states (Fig. 9). In this model, the RUNNING state is split into USER RUNNING and KERNEL RUNNING, and the TERMINATED state is called ZOMBIE. The PRE-EMPTED state queue is the same as the READY IN MEMORY; their only difference

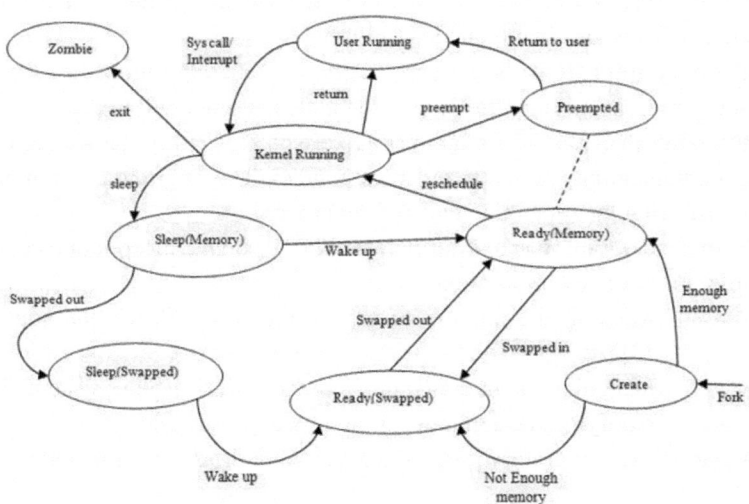

Fig. 9. Nine-state transition diagram

is how the process changes to this state. When the process is running in kernel mode and completes its execution in this mode, the kernel may decide to pre-empt the current process because of a ready process with higher priority. Therefore, the current process goes to this state. Notice that the process only could pre-empt when it is switching from kernel mode to user mode.

3   Our Approach

As we stated in previous sections, in the current implementations of process migration, there is a freeze time for the migratory process wherein the process cannot respond to any requests. For example, in the Total-Copy algorithm, the speed of address space transfer is too low even for processes with small address space sometimes taking several minutes. In the Pre-Copy algorithm, although we can have the small freeze time, but this time is dependent on the modified pages in the last step and may be more than the Total-Copy algorithm. In the Demand Paging algorithm, the freeze time is too small compared to other algorithms but its main disadvantage is that the source node should keep the address space until the completion of the process execution. This data dependency decreases the fault resilient.

The freeze time has overhead and decreases the performance, but it is important for the migratory process requiring to communicate with other processes. If the freeze time is too long, the migratory process is assumed to have failed and communications are terminated. This is important especially for HPC clusters because the number of critical requests with low waiting time is more than other distributed systems.

We can consider the following steps in process migration:

1) **Negotiation:** After negotiation between the source and destination nodes, if the destination accepts the migration request, an instance of a process is created in the destination node.

2) **Primary migration:** Some parts - based on the algorithm – of the process state are transferred to the destination node and imported to the new instance.

3) **Freezing process:** The migratory process is blocked in the source node and communications are temporarily suspended. The migration is completed by transferring the remaining parts of the process.

4) **Some means of forwarding references:** For ease of communication after migration we have 3 solutions:
    - Keeping the address of the destination node on the source node (Sprite)
    - Searching the migrated process with Multicasting (System V)
    - Notifying the communicating processes (Charlotte)

5) **Resume:** The migratory process is resumed in the destination node.

One challenge in process migration algorithm is to decrease the freeze time in step 3. Therefore, the number of the failed communications will be lower than the current implementations. As we noted in the previous section, there is no state that a process can migrate and respond to its requests. Therefore, if we define a new process running state that all the machines in the cluster could see, and move the process to this state while migrating, and enable the process to respond to the requests while it resides in this state, then the availability of the process is improved.

The new state (Exile) has been added to the seven-state process model (Fig.10). We describe this model in the following paragraphs.

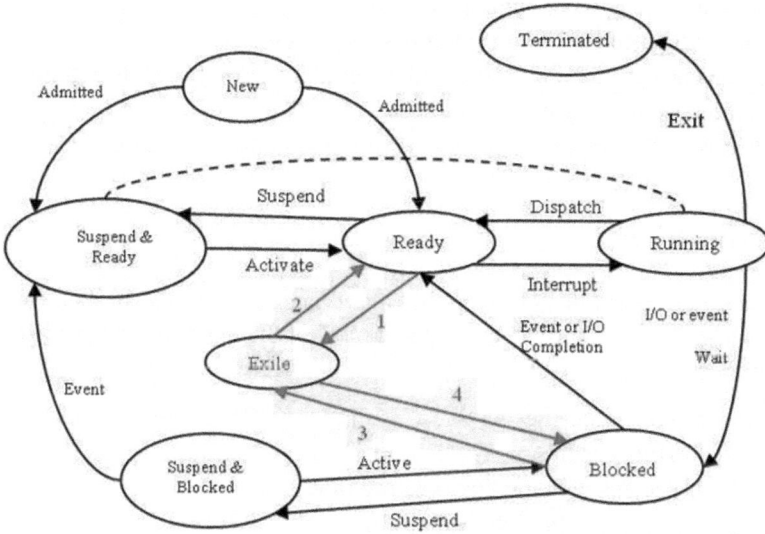

Fig. 10. Exile state in diagram.

If a process is in the NEW state and it is selected for migration, this migration means remote execution. In this paper, the migration does not mean remote execution. It means the process can migrate after starting its execution, but in the NEW state, only the kernel data structures have been allocated. Therefore, there is no transition between the NEW state and the Exile state.

If a process is in the RUNNING state and the load balancer selects it for migration, it moves the process to the READY state before migrating it.

If a suspended process (ready or blocked) is selected for migration, it is first moved to memory, its state is changed to READY or BLOCKED, and then to Exile state, and then it is migrated.

When the process is in READY queue and has been selected for migration, it will be better to change its state to Exile, because in the READY state there may be requests. On the other hand, after completing migration, the migratory process should move from Exile to READY state at destination node because the process state should be similar before and after migration.

In addition, if the process is waiting for an event in the BLOCKED state, it will be better to change its state to Exile because there may be signals from his parent and they should not be lost. Therefore, the new approach is like this:

1) **Negotiation:** After negotiation between the source and destination nodes, if the destination accepts it, an instance of a process will be created in the destination node.

2) **Primary migration:** Some parts - base on the algorithm – of the process state are transferred to the destination node and imported to the new instance.

3) **Go to Exile state:** The migratory process goes to this state and can responds to some requests that could not in BLOCKED state. The migration is completed by transferring the remaining parts of the process.

4) **Go to state that it was in it before migration.**

5) **Some means of forwarding references:** for easing communication after migration we have 3 solutions:

6) **Resume:** The migratory process is resumed in the destination node.

4   Evaluation

To evaluate our approach, we categorize the requests based on the "maximum time that the sender could wait for receiving respond" in three groups and carried out three experiments:

    a)   Critical processes with low waiting time. There are many such processes in HPC clusters.

    b)   Processes with medium waiting time.

    c)   Processes with high waiting time.

We have assumed the following waiting times in our experiments: a) 10 quantum, b) 30 quantum, and c) 50 quantum. In experiment 1 (Fig.11), we assumed the following numbers of processes a=20, b=30, c=40. That means 20 processes sent requests to a migratory process before the migratory process froze. Each one waited 10 quantum on average to receive response from the migratory process, 30 processes sent requests to the migratory process before the migratory process froze and each one waited 30 quantum on average to receive response, and 40 processes sent to the migratory process and each one waited 10 quantum on average to receive response. In experiment 2 (Fig.12), the numbers were (a=40, b=20, c=30), and in experiment 3 (Fig.13) are (a=30, b=40,c=20).

As Fig.11 shows, the minimum numbers of killed processes directly depend on the freeze time. When the freeze time decreases the number of killed processes decreases too. So in our approach because of the existence of a new state and because the migratory process can respond to requests in this state, the availability of the migratory process is increased. Fig.11 represents a distributed system with small number of critical requests.

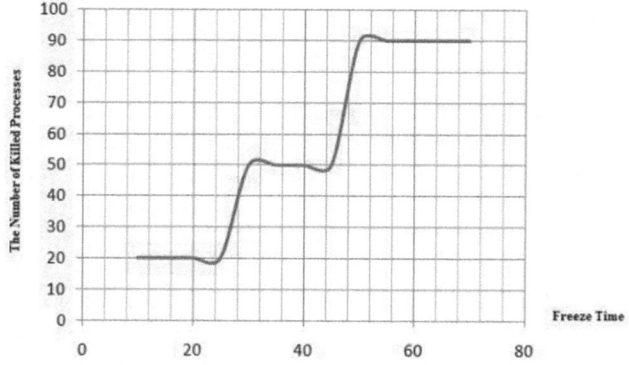

Fig. 11. Minimum number of killed processes
in experiment 1: a = 20, b=30, c=40

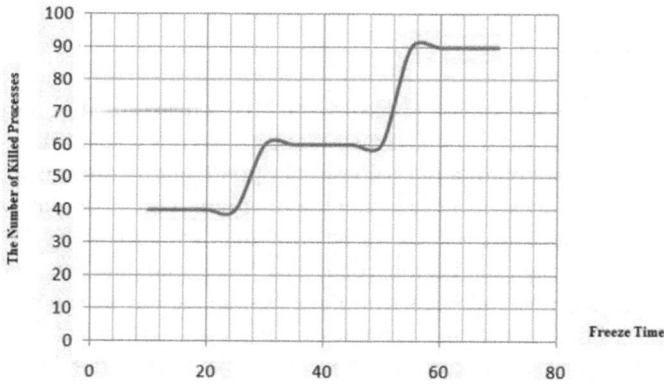

Fig. 12. Minimum number of killed processes
in experiment 2: a=40, b=20, c=30

In Fig.12, the number of processes in category (b) is more than in two other categories. This experiment is for HPC clusters, because in these systems the response time is very important in inter process communications. When the freeze time decreases, the migratory process can respond to more requests compared to current process migration mechanisms, and the performance is increased.

As Fig. 13 shows, when the freeze time of the migratory process is decreased the number of killed processes is decreased too. Therefore, in HPC clusters we need a process migration approach with small freeze time to improve the performance.

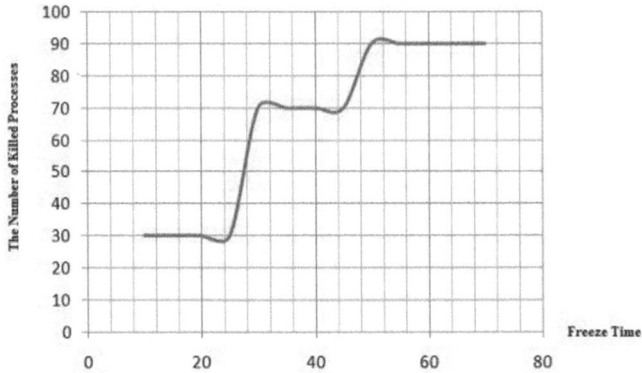

Fig. 13. Minimum number of killed processes
in experiment 3: a=30, b=40, c=20

5   Conclusion

One of the important challenges of processes in HPC clusters is the freeze time that
the migratory process cannot respond to any requests and the sender processes may be
killed because of not receiving any responses. In this paper, we propose to define a
new state, named exile, over the cluster that the migratory processes stay in that while
migrating. This state lets the process to be available and responsive to critical requests. Therefore, the communications does not break and the performance is increased. We evaluated this approach with the communications parameter. We considered three types of processes: critical processes, medium waiting time processes, and
high waiting time processes. The results showed that the proposed approach improves
the response time, and that it is especially essential for decreasing the killed rate of
critical processes. One of the future works can be evaluating this approach with computing parameter. The relationship between the quanta that we used in our experiments with three categories of requests can be nearer to real ones in HPC clusters.

References

1. Milojicic, F., Douglis, F., Paindaveine, Y., Wheeler, R., Zhou, S.: Process Migration.
   ACM Computing Surveys (CSUR) 32, 241–299 (2000)
2. Roush, E.T., Campbell, R.H.: Fast Dynamic Process Migration. Distributed Computing
   Systems, 637 (1996)
3. Ho, R.S.C., Wang, C., Lau, F.C.: Lightweight Process Migration and Memory Prefetching
   in openMosix. In: Parallel and Distributed Processing, Miami, pp. 1–12 (2008)
4. Michael, B.P.M., Powel, L.: Process Migration in Demos/MP. ACM SIGOPS Operating
   Systems Review 17, 110–119 (1983)

5. Steketee, C., Socko, P., Kiepuszewski, B.: Experiences with the Implementation of a Process Migration Mechanism for Amoeba. In: Computer Science, Melbourne, pp. 140–148 (1996)
6. Artsy, Y., Finkel, R.: Designing a process migration facility: The Charlotte experience. IEEE Computer, 47–56 (1989)
7. Barak, A., La'adan, O., Shiloh, A.: Scalable Cluster Computing with MOSIX for LINUX (1999)
8. Amnon Barak, O.L.: The Mosix Multicomputer Operating System for High Performance Cluster Computing. Future Generation Computer Systems 13, 361–372 (1998)
9. Barak, A., Shiloh, A.: The MOSIX Management System for Linux Clusters. Multi-Clusters and Clouds (2009)
10. Theimer, M., Lants, K., Cheriton, D.: Preemptable Remote Execution Facilities for the V System. In: Operating Systems Principles, Washington, pp. 2–12 (1985)
11. Paoli, D., Goscinski, A.: Copy on Reference Process Migration in Rhodos. In: Algorithms and Architectures for Parallel Processing, pp. 100–107 (1997)
12. Douglis, F.: Transparent Process Migration: Design Alternatives and The Sprite Implementation. Software—Practice & Experience 21, 757–785 (1991)
13. Tanenbaum, A.: Modern Oprating Systems, United States of America (2009)
14. Kumar, A.: TASK_KILLABLE: New process state in Linux. IBM (2008)
15. Tanenbaum, A.: Operating Systems Design and Implementation. Prentice Hall (2006)
16. Bach, M. J.: The design of the UNIX operating system. Prentice Hall (1986)
17. Stallings, W.: Operating Systems: Internals and Design Principles. Prentice Hall (2007)

Local Robustness: A Process Migration Criterion in HPC Clusters

Sina Mahmoodi Khorandi, Seyedeh Leili Mirtaheri, Ehsan Mousavi Khaneghah,
Mohsen Sharifi, and Siavash Ghiasvand

School of Computer Engineering, Iran University of Science and Technology, Tehran, Iran
{msharifi,mirtaheri,emousavi}@iust.ac.ir,
{sina_mahmoodi,ghiyasvand}@comp.iust.ac.ir

Abstract. Cluster computing systems require managing their resources and running processes dynamically in an efficient manner. Preemptive process migration is such a mechanism that tries to improve the overall performance of a cluster system running independent processes. In this paper, we show that blind migration of processes at runtime by such a mechanism does not lead to better performance. Instead, the preemptive process migration mechanism requires a criterion to determine if the migration of a process would enhance the cluster performance or not. We introduce a criterion called *local robustness* to guide the mechanism in this respect. The results of our experiments on a real implementation of a mechanism using this criterion have shown improvements to the overall performance of a Mosix cluster in terms of system response time compared to when processes were migrated blindly.

Keywords: Cluster Computing, Load Distribution, Process Migration, Local Robustness Criteria.

1 Introduction

Distribution of executive parts of a defined job among computing resources of a high performance computing (HPC) cluster system has been considered as a challenge [1, 2]. Modern clusters deploy mechanisms for process migration, load distribution, and resource discovery to execute wide range of jobs with higher rates of performance. Legacy mechanisms for balancing the loads on cluster nodes have proved inefficient because modern clusters may well contain heterogeneous nodes and that they must be scalable [2, 3, 4].

PBS-Maui and Condor are two traditional cluster management systems that use legacy mechanisms, while Mosix is considered as a manager for more modern clusters [1, 4]. Table 1 compares different features of these cluster managers. The Index column indicates the system feature that is measured by the load balancer for migration decisions. Each cluster manager in Table-1 has its own programming model for HPC. The legacy and commonly used model is the MPI-based programming model. BSP supports this model and uses a static job assignment mechanism without considering any system state changes at runtime. This model works well for cases there are no jobs to process locally. Condor does not use parallel programming models. It manages jobs that need numerous CPU cycles in a long period of time [1].

P. Pichappan, H. Ahmadi, and E. Ariwa (Eds.): INCT 2011, CCIS 241, pp. 374–382, 2011.

Table 1. Comparison of PBS-Maui, Condor, and Mosix [1, 4]

Cluster Manager Name	Migration Policy	Index	Dynamicity	Decentralized	Distribution Mechanism
PBS-Maui	Central RR	#Job	No	No	Remote Execution
Condor	Adaptive	CPU	Yes	No	Remote Execution and Migration
Mosix OpenMosix	Adaptive	CPU Memory	Yes	Yes	Remote Execution and Migration

Mosix uses a model that is closer to the MPI model but there are some major differences. Mosix does not provide a central daemon for splitting jobs into processes. There are no message queues either. In general, there is no superiority between the Mosix model and the MPI model. Each model works well in some cases. However, more specifically, Mosix is a more modern cluster manager because it allows the construction of MIMD clusters in addition to traditional SIMD clusters. The MPI model works well with I/O-bounded jobs because I/O-bounded jobs cannot migrate easily. If an I/O-bounded process migrates, destination machines make many remote system calls and increase communication costs. Mosix decides to migrate a process or not based on the cost the process must pay to run on remotely on the current machine when if it is migrated to a remote target machine. However, Mosix does not take proper decision when jobs contain a mixture of both CPU-bounded and I/O-bounded processes [4, 5].

In this paper, we present a new a criterion called *local robustness* to guide the migration mechanism in modern cluster managers to restrict it to migrate those processes that do not adversely affect the overall cluster performance.

The rest of paper is organized as follows. Section 2 discusses some efforts on achieving better performance based on selection policies. Section 3 presents our proposed local robustness concept and its goals Section 4 reports the results of our experiments on an OpenMosix platform. Section 5 summarizes and concludes our discussion about local robustness and the way forward.

2   Related Work

There are two sets of related works. One type of related works is presented in [10, 11]. In works like [10], there are two machines running some local or global jobs. A dynamic load distribution algorithm as well as remote execution mechanism is used for sending and receiving of jobs. In [10], a load distributor selects a pair of process and machine for remote execution operation. It chooses them based on their CPU requirement and the cost of migration. We will show in the next sections that it is not always possible to select the best pair due to the lack of global information about all cluster nodes. A similar work [11] has used process migration as a mechanism for the transfer of processes rather than careful migration of processes.

The second types of related works are reported in [3, 6]. Mosix was amongst the pioneered modern cluster managers anxious about the large number of process migrations resulting in lowering the overall cluster performance and process starvation. That is why Mosix has limited the number of process migrations [3] using a pre-migration processing we call local robust policy to prevent process starvation. The same policy has been used in [6] to determine transferring mechanism. Load balancing algorithm presented in [6] uses administrative parameters. Therefore, each machine makes decision based on its own administrative parameters. When load balancer fails to assign a process to a suitable machine, the robustness parameter degrades. To prevent performance degradation, the load balancer migrates a process to another node. In [6], robustness is defined as a function of administrative parameters. Administrators must trace system performance to tune this parameter.

3   Local Robustness

Every load balancer has to decide when to migrate a process and to where. Blind migration may adversely affect the cluster performance rather than improving it. Given the lack of information on the process lifetime and future behavior, the load balancer must use heuristics and set policies to guide its decision [3, 6, 7]. Robustness is such a policy that is used in the distribution of processes. The proposed method in [8] uses robustness as the measure of satisfying the goals' of a process against some perturbation. This definition is also used in [6]. This definition is flawed because it contradicts with scalability and robustness that are critically required by modern distributed systems including modern HPC cluster systems. In modern systems, cluster nodes are independent, may well be heterogeneous, and distributed in large scales. A more advanced definition and criterion, we call it *Local Robustness* in this paper, is required.

Generally, a system is robust when it can withstand or overcome adverse conditions [9]. We use this definition for local robustness. A load balancer decides to decide which processes to select to migrate to which remote hosts; it uses some local robustness policies based on system goals. In this paper, we introduce a procedural way to help in making correct decisions leading to improved overall cluster performance.

Considering a goal of system to have as few process migrations as possible, all migration decisions on a local node is a parameter for evaluation of perturbation and migration policy. The need to migrate is a local perturbation. A policy might be to defer some migrations until next decision phase. This policy may result in reducing future migrations. It is imperative that any policy might result in probabilistic improvement. Local robustness policies must improve robustness parameter. In the next section, a system is simulated to show the improvements due to local robustness satisfying system distribution goals. There are four steps for applying local robustness policy to load distribution [8].

To deal with the problem of selecting suitable target machines to migrate processes, we use a four-step robust measurement as a standard way of handling this problem [8]. Each local robustness policy has a set of goals, which defines the system performance features. They must satisfy their proposed conditions. For example, all jobs submitted to the cluster must complete running in two hours, or the number of migrations of each process must be less than four per hour. These constraints are affected by factors such as process requirements and machine heterogeneity. If a process is sought as the best candidate for migration, it could be a good candidate in it migrated machine too, resulting in its multiple migrations.. After defining these conditions and goals, the load distributor must be configured to reduce the migrating-enabled process set with respect to local robustness policy. The four steps of local robustness are:

1. *Performance Feature*: In this step, a set of parameters and their acceptable conditions are defined. In load distribution, four parameters are important, namely the average response time, the average number of migrations for processes initiated on a local machine, the first response time, and the total duration. One may consider one or more of these parameters.
2. *Perturbation Parameter*: Perturbation of processes and machines.
3. *Impact of Perturbation on Performance Features*: Determining a pair of <process, machine> affects the performance features. These effects must be analyzed using probabilistic methods due to dynamic nature of processes.
4. *Robustness Metric*: This metric helps the load balancer to decide what pair is better for migrating.

4 Mosix Case Study

The Mosix load balancer uses a vendor-customer model for deciding on migrations [4, 5]. Processes buy resources such as CPU, memory, and I/O with time units [12]. It works based on the allocation of the next quantum of scheduler (Eq. 1).

$$diff=RemoteMachineCost-ProcessMigCost-ProcessIODependency- \qquad (1)$$
$$LocalMachineCost .$$

The Mosix load balancer migrates a process with maximum *diff*. Fig. 1 shows the results of running our first experiment on an OpenMosix cluster with 4 nodes each containing an Intel 2.5 GHz CPU and 512 MB of memory.

The horizontal axis in Fig. 1 contains three numbers showing the need of each process. The first one is the I/O dependency, the second one is the memory need, and the last one is the CPU need. The red line shows the real running time of each process. The blue line shows the real CPU time used, and the green line shows the difference between these two.

The difference between reality and goal is due to multitasking and process migrations. In this experiment, all processes were created at the same time on one node and then distributed to other machines in the cluster. Since processes may contain some I/O operations, some time is wasted due to I/O operations on non-home machines. In the next experiment, we use a local robust policy to show this point.

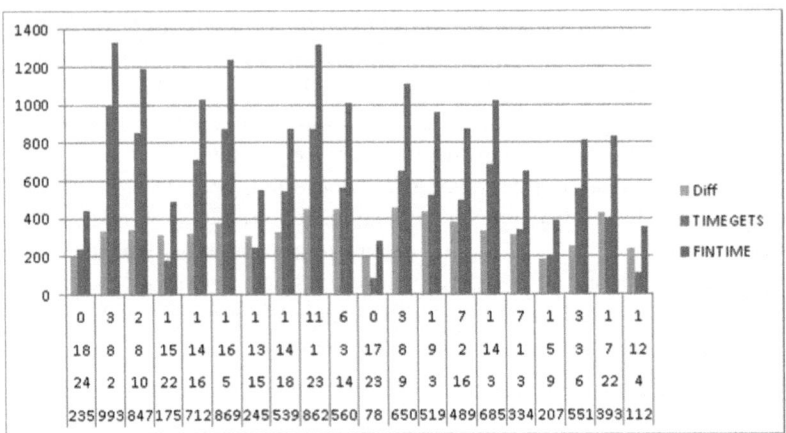

Fig. 1. Differences between CPU Get and Time spent for each process exp-1

As we noted before, there is no rule to classify process types in this experiment. Therefore, a local robustness' goal could be to reduce the number of process migrations to reduce starvation. To do this, the load balancer can use the number of migrations of a process as its perturbation and then limit the number of migrations by a tuned threshold. Fig. 2 shows the result of this experiment on previous set of processes.

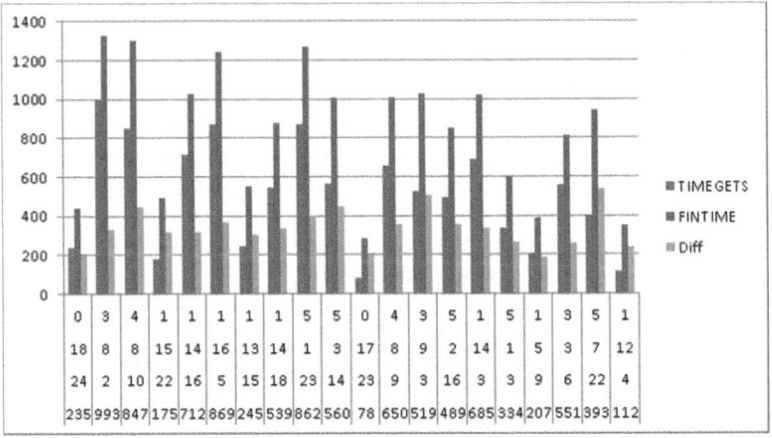

Fig. 2. Differences between CPU Get and Time spent for each process exp-2

In the second experiment, some differences have decreased and some others have increased. The result shows that the average response time and turnaround time have been decreased (Fig. 4). In fact, the local robust policy has limited the migrant processes. Eq. 2 shows this policy model.

$$\Phi = max(diff(p)) \text{ where } p \text{ is in } \{p | \ mig(p) < threshold\} \qquad (2)$$

This model has a major disadvantage. Defining a suitable threshold is a problem. In our experiments, the average number of migrations has been set as a threshold for the load balancer. In order to overcome this challenge, we define a process to be migration-enabled if it spends some defined time on its host. This time can be a function of previous migration time of the process. Fig. 3 shows the result of third experiment.

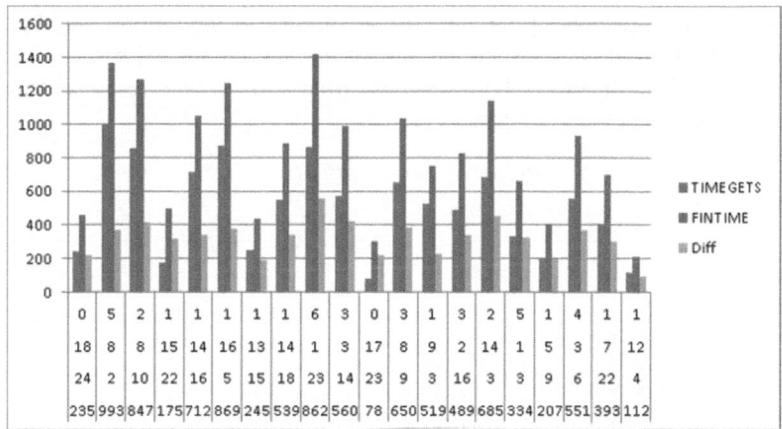

Fig. 3. Differences between CPU Get and Time spent for each process exp-3

Again, in some cases, difference has decreased and in some others has increased. In this scenario, the average number of migrations, average response time, and the first response times have decreased but the total execution time has increased. For situations like this, the load balancer can use some heuristic methods to estimate process lifetime and improve the result. Prediction of process lifetime may well be inaccurate and a menace to load balancing decisions. Eq. 3 shows this local robustness model.

$$\Phi = max(diff(p)) \text{ where } p \text{ is in } \{p| \text{ onemigtime}(p)*c < hosttime, c \text{ is a constant}\} \quad (3)$$

Fig. 4 demonstrates a comparison between these three experiments. Note that the value of c as a constant depends on the application at hand and varies from one application to another; it has to be given a value by experience on the application in mind.

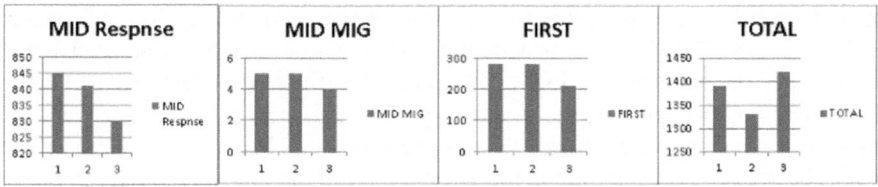

Fig. 4. Comparison between three methods

We carried out another experiment with a selection mechanism that chose the second process from the list containing a pair of <machine, process>. The mentioned list was sorted based on diff value. If there was no second process, the best process was considered as a candidate for migration. Fig. 5 shows the results of this experiment

This method has lead to better results than when no local robustness policy was used. The average response time, the average number of migrations, and the total time have decreased whereas the execution time of the first completed process is increased. Indeed, in HPC applications, both response time and average response time are important. Eq. 4 shows local robustness model.

$$\Phi = second\text{-}max(diff(p))$$ (4)

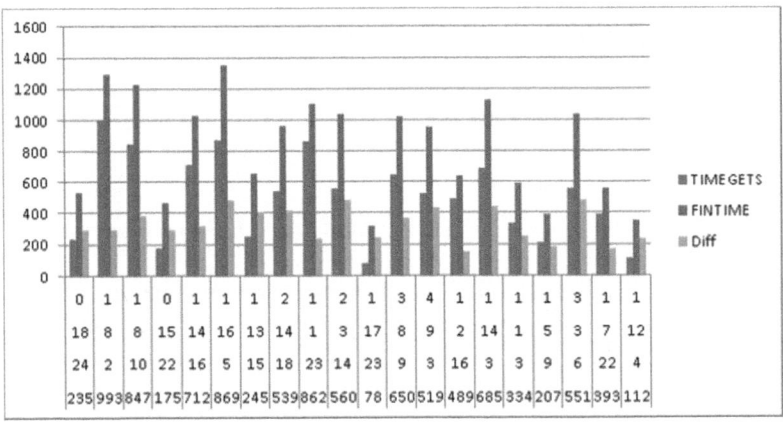

Fig. 5. Differences between CPU Get and Time spent for each process semi-second-best

When a process is selected as the best candidate for migration once, it may be selected again as a candidate in future. The second best process is a pair of <process, machine>. Indeed, there is less probability for the second best process to be selected as the second best process again in future on another machine. Usually a combination of heuristic methods and analyzed probabilistic policies can lead to more promising results in line with the goals of local robustness. Analyzing the probability of what will happen in future is very difficult due to unforeseen nature of processes form the operating system view. By using the application type and tuning cluster for such an application type, MIMD goal is violated. Fig. 6 shows a comparison between response times of each process. Fig. 6 illustrates that if a process has many I/O dependencies and has occupied memory and used few CPU cycles, it may be better stopping the local robust policy. It also demonstrates that it is better to use the second-best local robustness policy, as there are processes with completely different resource requirements.

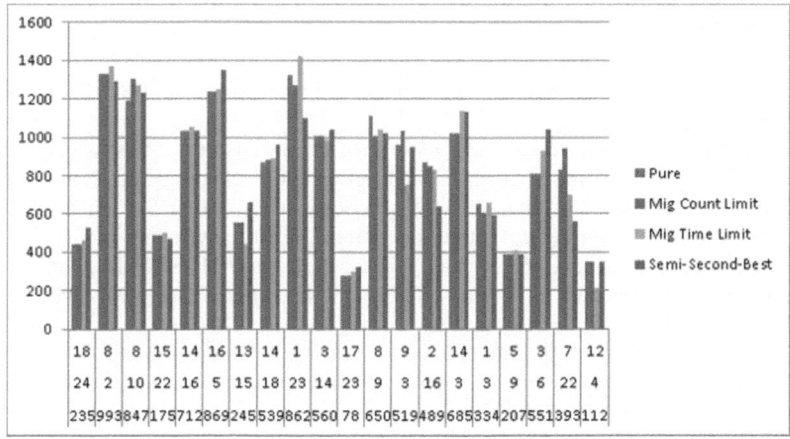

Fig. 6. Comparison between four local policies

5   Conclusion and Future Work

Load distribution has been brought forth for discussion since the beginning of computer clusters. A reason for this is the wide range of processes that need computational power of clusters. Due to unpredictable nature of processes, load distribution mechanism must be developed to adapt to process requirements. On the other hand, modern clusters have MIMD architecture that must be able to run processes with different resource requirements. Therefore, a dynamic and online load distribution mechanism must satisfy user requirements and support administrators' decisions.

One of the popular solutions to distribute load among cluster resources is preemptive process migration. We have shown that a blind preemptive process migration mechanism does not suit high performance cluster (HPC) systems as it reduces their performance. Therefore, load distributor needs some policy to make better decisions on selecting the best pair of <process, target-machine> at decision making times that cannot be detrimental to cluster performance. We have called these policies *local robustness policies*. The local robustness policy we proposed had a set of goals, some perturbation against those goals, and a probabilistic solution.

The work on local robustness concept can be further studied in several ways. The introduction of a new parameter to show local robustness as a numerical value can lead to better migration decisions leading to higher system performance. This parameter should denote a probabilistic value stating the probability of being better in the future with respect to defined goals. Determining local robustness policy based on the nature and requirements of each application is another opportunity to apply local robust concept. Our experiments showed that the selection of a second-best pair of <process, machine> in deciding which process to migrate leads to better results than selecting the best pair.

References

1. Sterling, T.: Beowulf Cluster Computing with Linux, 2nd edn. The MIT Press, London (2002)
2. Sharma, S., Singh, S., Sharma, M.: Performance Analysis of Load Balancing Algorithms. In: 38th World Academy of Science, Engineering and Technology, pp. 269–273 (2008)
3. Barak, A., La'adan, O.: The Mosix Multicomputer Operating System for High Performance Cluster Computing. J. Future Generation Computer Systems 13, 361–372 (1998)
4. Barak, A., Braverman, A., Gilderman, I., Laadan, O.: The MOSIX Multicomputer Operating System for Scalable NOW and its Dynamic Resource Sharing Algorithms. Technical report, The Hebrew University (1996)
5. Keren, A., Barak, A.: Opportunity Cost Algorithms for Reduction of I/O and Interprocess Communication Overhead in a Computing Cluster. IEEE Transactions on Parallel and Distributed Systems 14, 39–50 (2003)
6. Beltran, M., Guzman, A.: How to Balance the Load on Heterogeneous Clusters. International Journal of High Performance Computing Applications 23, 99–118 (2009)
7. Harchol-Balter, M., Downey, A.B.: Exploiting Process Lifetime Distributions for Dynamic Load Balancing. ACM Transactions on Computer Systems 15, 253–285 (1997)
8. Ali, S., Maciejewski, A.A., Siegel, H.J., Kim, J.K.: Measuring the Robustness of a Resource Allocation. IEEE Transaction on Parallel and Distributed System 15, 630–641 (2004)
9. Online Oxford Dictionary, http://oxforddictionaries.com (last access 2011)
10. Lau, S.M., Lu, Q., Leung, K.S.: Adaptive Load Distribution Algorithms for Heterogeneous Distributed Systems with Multiple Task Classes. Journal of Parallel and Distributed Computing 66, 163–180 (2006)
11. Khan, Z., Singh, R., Alam, J., Kumar, R.: Performance analysis of Dynamic load Balancing Techniques for Parallel and Distributed Systems. International Journal of Computer and Network Security 2, 123–127 (2010)
12. Ghiasvand, S., Khaneghah, E.M., Khorandi, S.M., Mirtaheri, S.L., Nezhad, N.O., Mohammadkhani, M., Sharifi, M.: An Analysis of MOSIX Load Balancing Capabilities. In: International Conference on Advanced Engineering Computing and Applications in Sciences, Lisbon, Portugal, November 20-25 (2011)

Data Clustering Using Big Bang–Big Crunch Algorithm

Abdolreza Hatamlou[1], Salwani Abdullah[2], and Masumeh Hatamlou[3]

[1] Islamic Azad University, Khoy Branch, Iran
hatamlou@iaukhoy.ac.ir
[2] Data Mining and Optimization Research Group, Center for Artificial Intelligence Technology,
Universiti Kebangsaan Malaysia, 43600 Bangi, Selangor, Malaysia
{hatamlou,salwani}@ftsm.ukm.my
[3] Tarbiat Moallem University, Tehran, Iran

Abstract. The Big Bang–Big Crunch (BB–BC) algorithm is a new optimization method that is based on one of the theories of the evolution of the universe namely the Big Bang and Big Crunch theory. According to this method, in the Big Bang phase some candidate solutions to the optimization problem are randomly generated and spread all over the search space. In the Big Crunch phase, randomly distributed candidate solutions are drawn into a single representative point via a center of population or minimal cost approach. This paper presents BB-BC based novel approach for data clustering. The simulation results indicate the applicability and potential of this algorithm on data clustering.

Keywords: Big Bang-Big Crunch algorithm, Cluster analysis.

1 Introduction

Based on the Big Bang and Big Crunch theories a new evolutionary algorithm was recently developed and is called as BB-BC algorithm where BB stands for Big Bang and BC stands for Big Crunch [1]. The main feature of the Big Bang phase is the production of disorder and randomness by energy dissipation or consumption; whereas, placing the randomly distributed particles in order is the characteristic of the Big Crunch phase. In the Big Bang phase, the BB-BC algorithm randomly generates points which will be shrunk into a single representative point through the center of mass in the Big Crunch phase. Eventually after the series of Big Bangs and Big Crunches the randomness distribution in the search space during the Big Bang gets smaller about the average point computed during the Big Crunch, and then the algorithm converges to a solution. Recently, the BB-BC algorithm has been successfully applied in some applications [2-5].

This paper intends to demonstrate the applicability and effectiveness of the BB-BC algorithm in cluster analysis. Clustering is the act of partitioning a set of objects into groups in such a way objects within the same group are similar between themselves and dissimilar to objects belonging to other groups [6]. It is an important data analysis technique that is used in a large variety of applications such as marketing and costumer analysis, document clustering, computer vision, anomaly detection, biology, and medicine [7-12].

P. Pichappan, H. Ahmadi, and E. Ariwa (Eds.): INCT 2011, CCIS 241, pp. 383–388, 2011.

The remaining of this paper is organized as follows. In Section 2, we have explained briefly the clustering problem. Review of BB-BC and its application on cluster analysis is described in Section 3. Experiments and results is presented and discussed in Section 4. Finally, the conclusion of this work is given in Section 5.

2   Cluster Analysis

Cluster analysis is the procedure of dividing a given set of n objects $O = \{O_1, O_2,..., O_n\}$, each of them explained by d attributes into a finite number of k partitions, also called clusters $C = \{C_1, C_2,..., C_k\}$, so that the objects in the same cluster will be similar to one other and different from the objects in other clusters based on some similarity or dissimilarity functions. To find centers of clusters, the problem can be defined as an optimization problem.

A famous objective function for measuring goodness of a clustering solution is the total mean-square quantisation error (MSE) [6]:

$$f(O,C) = \sum_{l=1}^{k} \sum_{O_i \in C_l} d(O_i, Z_l)^2 \tag{1}$$

where $d(O_i, Z_l)$ specifies the dissimilarity between object O_i and cluster center Z_l.

There are different functions for calculating the distance between objects in clustering problem. One of the popular and widely used distance functions is the Euclidean distance, where between any two objects O_i and O_j is defined by [6]:

$$d(O_i, O_j) = \sqrt{\sum_{p=1}^{d} (o_i^p - o_j^p)^2} \tag{2}$$

In this paper, we have used the Euclidean distance for calculating the distance between data objects.

3   Big Bang–Big Crunch (BB–BC) Method for Data Clustering

The BB–BC method is composed of two phases [1]: a Big Bang phase, and a Big Crunch phase. In the Big Bang phase, some candidate solutions to the optimization problem are randomly generated and distributed in the search space. As in the case of other evolutionary algorithms in the first Big Bang the initial solutions are uniformly distributed throughout the search space. The Big Crunch phase begins after the Big Bang phase by calculating the center of all candidate solutions called as "center of mass", where 'mass' refers to the inverse of objective function value.

Actually, the Big Crunch phase is a convergence operator that has many inputs (candidate solutions) but only one output (center of mass). The formula below is used to calculate the point representing the center of mass (x^c):

$$x^c = \frac{\sum_{i=1}^{N} \frac{1}{f^i} x^i}{\sum_{i=1}^{N} \frac{1}{f^i}} \tag{3}$$

where x^i is a solution within an n-dimensional search space generated, f^i is the fitness value of this solution, N is the number of candidate solutions in the Big Bang phase.

After the Big Crunch phase, the Big Bang phase is repeated again and the new solutions are generated by utilizing the previous knowledge (center of mass) by distributing the new off-springs around the center of mass via a normal distribution process in all the directions. When the number of algorithm iterations increases, the standard deviation of the normal distribution function decreases. New solutions are created based on the following formula:

$$x_{new}^i = x^c + \frac{lr}{k} \qquad i = 1, 2, ..., N \tag{4}$$

where r is a random number from a standard normal distribution which changes for each candidate, l is a parameter for limiting the size of the search space, and k is the iteration step.

These successive explosion (Big Bang phase) and contraction (Big Crunch phase) steps are carried out repeatedly until a termination criterion has been met. Here, a maximum number of iterations is used as the termination criterion.

The search capability of BB-BC algorithm used in this article for the purpose of data clustering. In order to apply BB-BC algorithm for data clustering a 1-dimension array is used to represent a candidate solution to the clustering problem. Each candidate solution is regarded as a set of k initial cluster centers where each cell in array is a cluster center dimension. Fig. 1 shows an example of a candidate solution for a problem with k clusters, where each data object has d attributes.

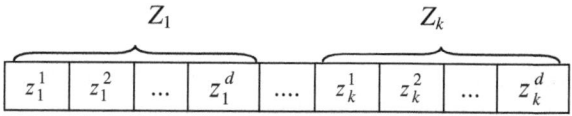

Fig. 1. Example of a candidate solution

Based on the above description, in our proposed algorithm the following steps should be done and repeat:

Step 1: Random generation of initial population

In this step, a set of initial solutions are randomly generated from the input dataset. Each solution represents k cluster centers.

Step 2: Evaluation

Calculate the fitness values of all the candidate solutions according to Eq. (1).

Step 3: Big Crunch pahese

Calculate the center of mass using Eq. (3). Best fit candidate can be chosen as the center of mass instead of using Eq. (3).

Step 4: Big Bang phase

Generate new solutions around the center of mass by adding or subtracting a normal random number to the center of mass (x^c). The value of the random number decreases as the iterations elapse.

Step 5: Check the termination criteria

The algorithm will be stopped if the termination criterion is met, else it will go back to step 2.

4   Experimental Results

In this section, we show the applicability of the BB-BC algorithm on data clustering using four benchmark datasets. The datasets are all well-known Iris, Wine, Contraceptive Method Choice and Wisconsin breast cancer datasets taken from Machine Learning Laboratory which are described as follows [13]:

Iris (n=150, d=4, k=3): This dataset was collected by Anderson (1935). It contains three classes of 50 objects each, where each class refers to a type of iris flower. There are 150 random samples of iris flowers with four numeric attributes in this dataset. These attributes are sepal length and width in cm, petal length and width in cm. There is no missing value for attributes.

Wine (n=178, d=13, k=3): This dataset contains the results of a chemical analysis of wines grown in the same region in Italy but derived from three different cultivars. This dataset contains 178 instances with 13 continuous numeric attributes. There is no missing attribute value.

Contraceptive Method Choice also denoted as *CMC* (n = 1473, d = 10, k = 3): This dataset is a subset of the 1987 National Indonesia Contraceptive Prevalence Survey. The samples are married women who either were not pregnant or did not know if they were at the time of interview. The problem is to predict the choice of current contraceptive method (no use has 629 objects, long-term methods have 334 objects, and short-term methods have 510 objects) of a woman based on her demographic and socioeconomic characteristics.

Wisconsin breast cancer (n = 683, d = 9, k = 2): This dataset contains 683 objects each of which described by nine features: clump thickness, cell size uniformity, cell shape uniformity, marginal adhesion, single epithelial cell size, bare nuclei, bland chromatin, normal nucleoli, and mitoses. There are two clusters in the dataset: malignant (444 objects) and benign (239 objects).

We have compared the performance of the BB-BC algorithm with three well known clustering algorithms including k-means [14], genetic algorithm [15] and particle swarm optimization algorithm [16]. The quality of the solutions is given in terms of the best, average and worst values of the clustering metric (Eq. 1) after 10 independent runs for each of the four datasets. This metric known as sum of intra-cluster distances. The standard deviation of solutions (Std) for each algorithm is given to check the viability and stability of algorithms. It is clear that the small value for the sum of intra-cluster distances and Std is desirable. Table 1 shows these results.

For the iris dataset, the average of solutions found by BB-BC is 96.67718, while this value for the k-means, GA and PSO is 106.05, 125.19 and 97.23 respectively. It means that, BB-BC can find high quality solutions compared to other methods. Moreover, the standard deviation of the BB-BC algorithm is smaller than other algorithms. In other words, it is reliable than other approaches. Based on the results for the wine and CMC datasets, we can see the effectiveness of the BB-BC algorithm. For the cancer dataset, the best, average and worst solutions and standard deviation of the BB-BC algorithm are 2964.38764, 2964.38813, 2964.38894 and 0.00050 which are much better than those of other algorithms.

Table 1. Simulation results of intra cluster distances for clustering algorithms

Data set	Criteria	K-means	GA	PSO	BB-BC
Iris	Best	97.33	113.98	96.89	96.67718
	Average	106.05	125.19	97.23	96.77319
	Worst	120.45	139.77	97.89	97.40443
	Std	14.63	14.56	0.347	0.22260
Wine	Best	16555.68	16530.53	16345.96	16299.53193
	Average	18061.00	16530.53	16417.47	16304.29787
	Worst	18563.12	16530.53	16562.31	16309.50918
	Std	793.21	0	85.49	2.87718
CMC	Best	5842.20	5705.63	5700.98	5700.63051
	Average	5893.60	5756.59	5820.96	5744.03239
	Worst	5934.43	5812.64	5923.24	5780.27270
	Std	47.16	50.36	46.95	26.63582
Cancer	Best	2999.19	2999.32	2973.50	2964.38764
	Average	3251.21	3249.46	3050.04	2964.38813
	Worst	3521.59	3427.43	3318.88	2964.38894
	Std	251.14	229.73	110.80	0.00050

In general, the results given in Table 1 show that the BB-BC optimization approach can be considered as a viable and an efficient algorithm to find optimal or near optimal solutions of the clustering problems.

5   Conclusion

The BB-BC is a novel heuristic algorithm that can be used for solving search and optimization problems. The applicability and potential of BB-BC in cluster analysis is shown via the simulation results. The simulation results confirm that the BB-BC algorithm is a suitable and reliable technique for data clustering. It has a simple structure and provides high quality clusters in term of sum of intra-cluster distances. For future research, we believe that the BB-BC algorithm can be applied to other applications successfully. Moreover, its performance can be improved via combining with some other meta-heuristic algorithms properly.

References

1. Erol, O.K., Eksin, I.: A new optimization method: Big Bang-Big Crunch. Advances in Engineering Software 37, 106–111 (2006)
2. Kaveh, A., Talatahari, S.: Optimal design of Schwedler and ribbed domes via hybrid Big Bang-Big Crunch algorithm. Journal of Constructional Steel Research 66, 412–419
3. Kaveh, A., Talatahari, S.: Size optimization of space trusses using Big Bang-Big Crunch algorithm. Computers & Structures 87, 1129–1140 (2009)
4. Kumbasar, T., Eksin, I., Guzelkaya, M., Yesil, E.: Adaptive fuzzy model based inverse controller design using BB-BC optimization algorithm. Expert Systems with Applications (2011)
5. Tang, H., Zhou, J., Xue, S., Xie, L.: Big Bang-Big Crunch optimization for parameter estimation in structural systems. Mechanical Systems and Signal Processing 24, 2888–2897
6. Han, J.: Data Mining: Concepts and Techniques. Academic Press (2001)
7. Fan, J., Han, M., Wang, J.: Single point iterative weighted fuzzy C-means clustering algorithm for remote sensing image segmentation. Pattern Recognition 42, 2527–2540 (2009)
8. Kerr, G., Ruskin, H.J., Crane, M., Doolan, P.: Techniques for clustering gene expression data. Computers in Biology and Medicine 38, 283–293 (2008)
9. Kim, K.-J., Ahn, H.: A recommender system using GA K-means clustering in an online shopping market. Expert Systems with Applications 34, 1200–1209 (2008)
10. Liao, L., Lin, T., Li, B.: MRI brain image segmentation and bias field correction based on fast spatially constrained kernel clustering approach. Pattern Recognition Letters 29, 1580–1588 (2008)
11. Mahdavi, M., Chehreghani, M.H., Abolhassani, H., Forsati, R.: Novel meta-heuristic algorithms for clustering web documents. Applied Mathematics and Computation 201, 441–451 (2008)
12. Moshtaghi, M., Havens, T.C., Bezdek, J.C., Park, L., Leckie, C., Rajasegarar, S., Keller, J.M., Palaniswami, M.: Clustering ellipses for anomaly detection. Pattern Recognition 44, 55–69 (2011)
13. Blake, C.L.: UCI repository of machine learning databases, http://www.ics.uci.edu/-mlearn/MLRepository.html
14. Forgy, E.W.: Cluster analysis of multivariate data: efficiency versus interpretability of classifications. Biometrics 21, 2 (1965)
15. Cowgill, M.C., Harvey, R.J., Watson, L.T.: A genetic algorithm approach to cluster analysis. Computers & Mathematics with Applications 37, 99–108 (1999)
16. Ching-Yi, C., Fun, Y.: Particle swarm optimization algorithm and its application to clustering analysis. In: 2004 IEEE International Conference on Networking, Sensing and Control, vol. 2, 782 pp. 789–794 (2004)

Improvement of the Performance of QEA Using the History of Search Process and Backbone Structure of Landscape

M.H. Tayarani N., M. Beheshti, J. Sabet,
M. Mobasher, and H. Joneid

University of Southampton,
Khayyam Institute of Higher Educations
mhtn1g09@ece.soton.ac.uk

Abstract. In order to improve the exploration ability of Quantum Evolutionary Algorithm (QEA) and helping the algorithm to escape from local optima, this paper proposes a novel operator which uses the history of search process during the previous iterations to lead the q-individuals toward better parts of the search space. In the proposed method, in each iteration the history of the solutions is stored in a set called the history set. The history of solutions contains some information about the fitness landscape and the structure of better and worse solutions. This paper proposes a new operator which exploits this information to make a figure about the backbone structure of the fitness landscape and lead the q-individuals to search better parts of the search space. The proposed algorithm is tested on Knapsack Problem, Trap Problem, Max-3-Sat Problem and 13 Numerical Benchmark functions. Experimental results show better performance for the proposed algorithm than the original version of QEA.

Keywords: Optimization Algorithms, Quantum Evolutionary Algorithms, Landscape Analysis.

1 Introduction

The concept of fitness landscape, introduced by Wright[1] demonstrates the dynamics of biological evolutionary optimization. This concept has been useful for the analysis and understanding of evolutionary algorithm's behavior. Fitness landscape analysis techniques are used to better understand the influence of variation operators when solving a combinatorial optimization problem[2]. The result of fitness landscape analysis can be used in designing a memetic [3,4] and evolutionary algorithms[5].

Quantum Evolutionary Algorithms are new optimization algorithms proposed for class of combinatorial optimization problems [6]. QEA uses probabilistic representation for possible solutions and this characteristic helps the q-individuals to represent all the search space simultaneously. Several works try to improve the performance of QEA. Combining the concepts of Immune systems and QEA, [7] proposes an immune quantum evolutionary algorithm. In another work [8] proposes a novel particle swarm quantum evolutionary algorithm. A new adaptive rotation gate is proposed in [9] which uses the probability amplitude ratio of the corresponding states of quantum bits. Inspired by the idea of hybrid

P. Pichappan, H. Ahmadi, and E. Ariwa (Eds.): INCT 2011, CCIS 241, pp. 389–400, 2011.
© Springer-Verlag Berlin Heidelberg 2011

optimization algorithms, [10] proposes two hybrid-QEA based on combining QEA with PSO. In [11] a novel Multi-universe Parallel Immune QEA is proposed. In the algorithm all the q-individuals are divided into some independent sub-colonies, called universes. Since QEA is proposed for the class of combinatorial optimization problems, [12] proposes a new version of QEA for numerical function optimization problems. A novel quantum coding mechanism for QEA is proposed in [13] to solve the travelling salesman problem. In another work [14] points out some weaknesses of QEA and explains how hitching phenomena can slow down the discovery of optimal solutions. In this algorithm, the attractors moving the population through the search space are replaced at every generation. A new approach based on Evolution Strategies is proposed in [15] to evolve quantum unitary operators which represents the computational algorithm a quantum computer would perform to solve an arbitrary problem. In order to preserve the diversity in population and empower the search ability of QEA, [16] proposes a novel diversity preservation operator for QEA. Reference [17] proposes a sinusoid sized population QEA that makes a tradeoff between exploration and exploitation. While QEA is suitable for combinatorial problems and is relatively weak for real coded problems like numerical function optimization problems, several works have focused on this foible. Reference [18] proposes a probabilistic optimization algorithm, which similar to QEA uses a probabilistic representation for possible solutions.

How an evolutionary algorithm can use the information about the fitness landscape which it has visited during the search process? Many researchers have tried to study the landscape of optimization problems. During the search process, evolutionary algorithms search through the search space and visit many solutions and local optima. The visited solutions and their fitness represent the backbone structure of the fitness landscape. Using this information, evolutionary algorithms can be informed to search better parts of the search space for better solutions. This paper proposes a new operator for QEA which uses the information gathered from the fitness landscape and uses it to lead the q-individuals toward better parts of the search space. In the proposed method, the best, worst and median solutions during each iteration are stored in a set called history of solutions. After the population converged, the history of solutions is used to reinitialize the population with the values representing better parts of the search space with higher probability.

This paper is organized as follows. Section 2 introduces Quantum Evolutionary Algorithm and its representation. In section 3 the proposed algorithm is proposed and its parameter is investigated. Experimental results are performed in section 4 and finally section 5 concludes the paper.

2   QEA

QEA is inspired from the principles of quantum computation, and its superposition of states is based on qubits, the smallest unit of information stored in a two-state quantum computer. A qubit could be either in state "0" or "1", or in any superposition of the two as described below:

$$|\psi\rangle = \alpha |0\rangle + \beta |1\rangle \tag{1}$$

Where α and β are complex numbers, which denote the corresponding state appearance probability, following below constraint:

$$|\alpha|^2 + |\beta|^2 = 1 \tag{2}$$

This probabilistic representation implies that if there is a system of m qubits, the system can represent 2^m states simultaneously. At each observation, a qubits quantum state collapses to a single state as determined by its corresponding probabilities.

Consider $i - th$ individual in $t - th$ generation defined as an m-qubit as below:

$$\begin{bmatrix} \alpha_{i1}^t & \alpha_{i2}^t & \cdots & \alpha_{ij}^t & \cdots & \alpha_{im}^t \\ \beta_{i1}^t & \beta_{i2}^t & \cdots & \beta_{ij}^t & \cdots & \beta_{im}^t \end{bmatrix} \tag{3}$$

Where $\left|\alpha_{ij}^t\right|^2 + \left|\beta_{ij}^t\right|^2 = 1$, $j = 1, 2, ..., m$, m is the number of qubits, i.e., the string length of the qubit individual, $i = 1, 2, ..., n$, n is the number of possible solution in population and t is generation number of the evolution.

2.1   QEA Structure

In the initialization step of QEA, $[\alpha_{ij}^t \ \beta_{ij}^t]^T$ of all q_i^0 are initialized with $\frac{1}{\sqrt{2}}$. This implies that each qubit individual q_i^0 represents the linear superposition of all possible states with equal probability. The next step makes a set of binary instants, x_i^t by observing $Q(t) = \{q_1^t, q_2^t, ..., q_n^t\}$ states, where $X(t) = /x_1^t, x_2^t, ..., x_n^t/$ at generation t is a random instant of qubit population. Each binary instant, x_i^t of length m, is formed by selecting each bit using the probability of qubit, either $|\alpha_{ij}^t|$ or $|\beta_{ij}^t|$ of q_i^t. Each instant x_i^t is evaluated to give some measure of its fitness. The initial best solution $b = max_{i=1}^n \{f(x_i^t)\}$ is then selected and stored from among the binary instants of $X(t)$. Then, in 'update' $Q(t)$, quantum gates U update this set of qubit individuals $Q(t)$ as discussed below. This process is repeated in a while loop until convergence is achieved. The appropriate quantum gate is usually designed in accordance with problems under consideration.

2.2   Quantum Gates Assignment

The common mutation is a random disturbance of each individual, promoting exploration while also slowing convergence. Here, the quantum bit representation can be simply interpreted as a biased mutation operator. Therefore, the current best individual can be used to steer the direction of this mutation operator, which will speed up the convergence. The evolutionary process of quantum individual is completed through the step of "update $Q(t)$". A crossover operator, quantum rotation gate, is described below. Specifically, a qubit individual q_i^t is updated by using the rotation gate $U(\theta)$ in this algorithm. The $j - th$ qubit value of $i - th$ quantum individual in generation t, $[\alpha_{ij}^t \ \beta_{ij}^t]^T$ is updated as:

$$\begin{bmatrix} \alpha_{ij}^t \\ \beta_{ij}^t \end{bmatrix} = \begin{bmatrix} cos(\Delta\theta) & -sin(\Delta\theta) \\ sin(\Delta\theta) & cos(\Delta\theta) \end{bmatrix} \begin{bmatrix} \alpha_{ij}^{t-1} \\ \beta_{ij}^{t-1} \end{bmatrix} \tag{4}$$

Where $\Delta\theta$ is rotation angle and controls the speed of convergence and determined from Table 1. Reference [19] shows that these values for $\Delta\theta$ have better performance.

Table 1. Lookup Table of $\Delta\theta$, the rotation gate. x_i is the $i-th$ bit of the observed binary solution and b_i is the $i-th$ bit of the best found binary solution.

x_i	b_i	$f(x) \geq f(b)$	$\Delta\theta$
0	0	false	0
0	0	true	0
0	1	false	0.01π
0	1	true	0
1	0	false	-0.01π
1	0	true	0
1	1	false	0
1	1	true	0

3   The Proposed Algorithm

In QEA by converging the algorithm the quantum bits converge to the true values of $[\alpha\ \beta]^T = [0\ 1]^T$ or $[\alpha\ \beta]^T = [1\ 0]^T$. In this condition the algorithm is trapped in a local optimum and has little chance to escape from the local optimum. The proposed method in this paper is a novel reinitialization operator for the population of QEA which improves the diversity of the population and helps the algorithm to escape from the local optima. In the proposed algorithm in each generation, the convergence of the population is calculated and when the population converged, it is reinitialized based on the information it has gathered about the fitness landscape during its previous search steps. The convergence of the population is calculated as [23]:

$$C = \frac{1}{n \times m} \sum_{i=1}^{m} \sum_{j=1}^{n} \left| 1 - 2 \left| \alpha_{ij} \right|^2 \right|$$

Where C is the convergence of the population, m is the size of population (the number of the q-individuals in the population) and n is the number of q-bits in the q-individuals (the dimension of the problem). Initializing the population when it converges, gives the q-individuals a new chance to search the search space and find new solutions. Instead of giving the values to the q-individuals to represent the whole search space with the same probability, this paper proposes a new method which uses the history of search process during the past generations to make better q-individuals, representing the better parts of the search space with higher probability. There are many researches trying to understand the fitness landscape behavior of optimization problems [1,2,3,4]. Some of them try to exploit that in making new algorithms with better performance [5]. In this paper we propose a new method which during its search process gathers some information about the fitness landscape of the problem. Once the q-individuals are trapped in a local optimum, using the gathered information the proposed method reinitializes the q-individuals. Having some ideas about the fitness landscape, the proposed algorithm reinitializes the q-individuals to represent the better parts of the search space with higher probability. The pseudo code of the proposed algorithm is as follows:

Proposed Algorithm
begin
   $t = 0$
1. initialize Q^0
2. make X^0 by observing the states of Q^0.
3. evaluate X^0
4. Store X^0 into B^0. Store the best solutions among X^0 into b.
5. while not termination condition do
   begin
      $t = t + 1$
6.   make X^t by observing the states of Q^{t-1}
7.   evaluate X^t
8.   Update Q^t using Q-gate
9.   store the best solutions among B^{t-1} and X^t into B^t
10. update $\mathcal{H}^b$, $\mathcal{H}^m$ and $\mathcal{H}^w$.
11. if the population has converged, reinitialize q-individuals based on $\mathcal{H}^b$, $\mathcal{H}^m$ and
     $\mathcal{H}^w$. Then eliminate the members of $\mathcal{H}^b$, $\mathcal{H}^m$ and $\mathcal{H}^w$.
12. if migration-condition then do the global or local migration.
   end
end

QEA has a population of quantum individuals $Q^t = \{q_1^t, q_2^t, ..., q_n^t,\}$ where t is generation step and n is the size of population. A comprehensive description of QEA can be found in [6]. The QEA procedure is described as:

1. In the initialization step all qubits α_{ij}^0 and β_{ij}^0, $i = 1, 2, ..., n$ and $j = 1, 2, ..., m$ are initialized with $1/\sqrt{2}$. It means the probability of observing 0 and 1 for all qubits is equal.
2. In this step the binary solutions $X^0 = \{x_1^0, x_2^0, ..., x_n^0\}$ at generation $t = 0$ are created by observing Q^0. Observing x_{ij}^t from qubit $\begin{bmatrix} \alpha_{ij}^t & \beta_{ij}^t \end{bmatrix}$ is performed as below:

$$x_{ij}^t = \begin{cases} 0 & if \ U(0,1) < |\alpha_{ij}^t|^2 \\ 1 & otherwise \end{cases} \tag{5}$$

   Where $U(.,.)$, is a uniform random number generator.
3. All solutions in X^t are evaluated with fitness function.
4. Store X^0 into B^0. Select best solution among X^0 and store it to b.
5. The while loop runs until termination condition is satisfied. Termination condition can be considered as maximum generation condition or convergence condition.
6. Observe X^t from Q^{t-1}.
7. Evaluate X^t by fitness function
8. Update Q^t
9. Store the best solutions among B^{t-1} and X^t to B^t. If the fittest solution among B^t is fitter than b then store the best solution into b.

10. The best, median and worst possible solutions among the binary solutions X^t are added to $\mathcal{H}^b$, $\mathcal{H}^m$ and $\mathcal{H}^w$, where $\mathcal{H}$ is the history of X, containing the best, median and the worst possible solutions found in previous searches, since the last time the population has been reinitialized until current iteration t.

11. Here the convergence status of the population is checked. If the population has converged, the population is reinitialized based on $\mathcal{H}$. The new q-individuals are reinitialized as follows:

$$\mathcal{B}_i = \frac{1}{\sum_{j=1}^{t-t'} e^{-\frac{j}{\lambda}}} \sum_{j=1}^{t-t'} e^{-\frac{j}{\lambda}} \mathcal{H}_{ij}^b \tag{6}$$

$$\mathcal{M}_i = \frac{1}{\sum_{j=1}^{t-t'} e^{-\frac{j}{\lambda}}} \sum_{j=1}^{t-t'} e^{-\frac{j}{\lambda}} \mathcal{H}_{ij}^m \tag{7}$$

$$\mathcal{W}_i = \frac{1}{\sum_{j=1}^{t-t'} e^{-\frac{j}{\lambda}}} \sum_{j=1}^{t-t'} e^{-\frac{j}{\lambda}} \mathcal{H}_{ij}^w \tag{8}$$

Where $\mathcal{H}^b$, $\mathcal{H}^m$ and $\mathcal{H}^w$ are the history of best, median and worst possible solutions respectively, $\mathcal{H}_{ij}^b$ is the $i-th$ bit of $j-th$ possible solution in $\mathcal{H}^b$, t is current iteration, t' is the last iteration which the population has been reinitialized (i.e. $\mathcal{H}^b$ has $t-t'$ members). Here $j=1$ represents the most recently added solution to the history set and $j=t-t'$ represents the first solution added to the history set after the reinitialization step. $\mathcal{B}_i$ is the weighted average of $i-th$ bit among all the possible solutions in $\mathcal{H}^b$. As it is seen in 6 the solutions in the more recent iterations have more weight and so more influence on $\mathcal{B}_i$, $\mathcal{M}_i$ and $\mathcal{W}_i$. If $\mathcal{B}_i$ is near 1, it means that in most of better possible solutions, this bit has the value of 1, and it is better to give a value to this q-bit which represents 1 with higher probability. Analogously, if $\mathcal{W}_i$ is near 1, it means that in most of worse possible solutions, this bit is 1, therefore it is better to give a value to this q-bit which represents 0 with higher probability. Accordingly, this paper proposes the following method for reinitialization step:

$$q_{ij}^t = \frac{\pi}{4} + [2\mathcal{B}_i + \mathcal{M}_i - 3\mathcal{W}_i] \times \frac{\pi}{16} \tag{9}$$

Where $j = 1, 2, ..., n$, n is the number of q-individuals in the population, $i = 1, 2, ..., m$, m is the number of q-bits in the q-individuals, i. e. the dimension of the problem.

The proposed reinitialization operator gathers information from its previous searches and reinitializes the q-individuals with the values representing better parts of search space.

3.1 Parameter Tuning

As it is seen in step 11 of the proposed algorithm, the proposed algorithm has a parameter of λ. This section tries to find the best parameter for the proposed algorithm for several benchmark functions. The size of population for all the experiments is set to

25, and the parameter is set to λ=(1,10,20,30,40,50,60,70,80,90,100). Figure 1 shows the parameter setting for the proposed algorithm on Knapsack problem and Schwefel problem. The results are averaged over 30 runs. This paper finds the best parameter for the proposed operator for several benchmark functions and the results are summarized in Table 2. The average of the best parameter over all the benchmark functions is λ=30.

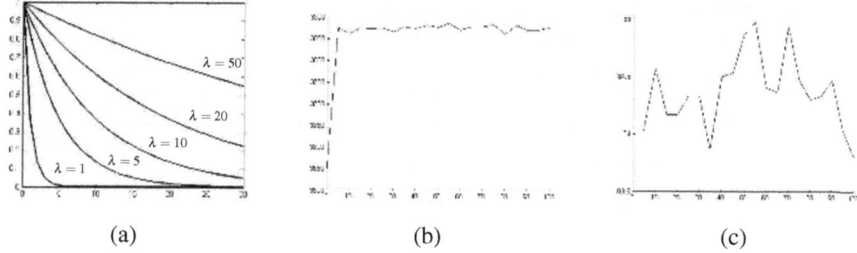

(a)   (b)   (c)

Fig. 1. a) The weight of the solutions as a function of iterations. The vertical axis is the weight and the horizontal axis is time difference from the solution in history set and current iteration. The effect of the parameter λ on the performance of the proposed algorithm: b) on Generalized Schwefel's Function 2.26, c) Knapsack problem Penalty Type.

Table 2. Best parameter for the proposed Update operator. The results are averaged over 30 runs.

Problem	λ	Problem	λ	Problem	λ	Problem	λ
Kpck Rep 1	15	Kpck Rep 2	20	Kpck Pen 1	20	Kpck Pen 2	45
Trap	10	Schwefel	10	Rastrigin	35	Ackley	40
Griawank	25	Penalized1	35	Penalized2	40	Schwefel 2.22	25
Michalewicz	45	Goldberg	35	Sphere	30	Rosenbrock	40
Schwefel 2.21	25	Dejong	50	Max-Sat $\alpha = 6$	5		

4   Experimental Results

The proposed algorithm is compared with the original version of QEA to show the improvement on QEA. The best parameters as found in previous sections are used in order to provide fair comparison between the proposed algorithm and the original version of QEA. The parameters of QEA is set to the best parameters found in [6]. The experimental results are performed on Knapsack problem Penalty type 1 and 2, Knapsack problem Repair types 1 and 2, Trap problem, Max-3-Sat and 13 numerical function optimization problems, for the dimension of 100 and 250. The population size of all algorithms for all of the experiments is set to 25; termination condition is set for a maximum of 1000 iterations. The parameter of QEA is set to Table 1. The parameter of the proposed algorithm is set to the values found in previous section. Due to statistical nature of the optimization algorithms, all results are averaged over 30 runs.

Table 3 shows the experimental results on the proposed algorithm and the original version of QEA. According to Table 3, the algorithm improves the performance of QEA significantly, and in all the experimental results, the proposed algorithm reaches better results.

Table 3. Experimental results on Knapsack problem, Trap Problem, Max-3-Sat and 13 numerical function optimization problems. The number of runs is 30. Mean and STD represent the mean of best answers and standard deviation of best answers for 30 runs respectively. m is the dimension of problem.

| | $m=100$ | | | | $m=250$ | | | |
| | QEA | | Proposed Algorithm | | QEA | | Proposed Algorithm | |
Problem	Mean	STD	Mean	STD	Mean	STD	Mean	STD
Kpck Pen 1	4964.5	337.9	5057	368.3	11562	828	12602	1151
Kpck Pen 2	3616.1	154.9	3869	221.8	8668	321	9551	576
Kpck Rep 1	3785.2	173	3919	208	9091	404	9784	592
Kpck Rep 2	3966.8	46.13	3967	46.03	10414	242	10420	237
Trap	68.32	4.04	85.13	8.66	144	8.29	118.986	18.9
Max-Sat $\alpha=2$	0.989	0.010	0.999	0.012	0.976	0.013	0.983	0.015
Max-Sat $\alpha=4$	0.967	0.009	0.981	0.013	0.949	0.009	0.957	0.012
Max-Sat $\alpha=6$	0.955	0.008	0.965	0.012	0.941	0.009	0.948	0.011
Max-Sat $\alpha=8$	0.945	0.007	0.954	0.010	0.932	0.008	0.937	0.0009
Max-Sat $\alpha=10$	0.938	0.007	0.953	0.010	0.927	0.007	0.935	0.0093
Schwefel	-2.5×10^4	2523	-2.2×10^4	3490	-7.6×10^4	4490	-7.2×10^4	5891
Rastrigin	-149.4	159.2	26.26	212.1	-1182	292	-878	398
Ackley	-19.83	0.05	-19.98	0.003	-19.99	5×10^-4	-20	1×10^-5
Griewank	-1006.6	271.7	-656.5	386.8	-3870	556	-3208	768
Penalized 1	-5.4×10^4	1.5×10^4	-3.4×10^4	2.2×10^4	-2.1×10^5	2.8×10^4	-1.7×10^5	4.0×10^4
Penalized 2	-1.6×10^5	9.0×10^4	-1.5×10^5	8.3×10^4	-6.2×10^5	2.2×10^5	-7.2×10^5	1.7×10^5
Michalewicz	174.28	30.87	208.85	40.75	286	54	357	74
Goldberg	-15.26	3.2	-12.29	4.1	-54.20	6.0	-50.60	7.4
Sphere Model	-3.7×10^8	1.9×10^8	-1.7×10^8	2.5×10^8	-1.8×10^9	4.6×10^8	-1.3×10^9	6.2×10^8
Schwefel 2.22	-251.79	38.15	-199.77	54.07	-828	67.5	-734	95.7
Schwefel 2.21	-86.53	1.55	-80.49	3.48	-95.59	0.39	-92.58	1.3
Dejong	-1.6×10^6	9.2×10^5	-7.4×10^5	1.1×10^6	-1.9×10^7	5.8×10^6	-1.4×10^7	7.7×10^6
Rosenbrock	-2.8×10^8	1.5×10^8	-1.4×10^8	2.0×10^8	-1.5×10^9	3.4×10^8	-1.0×10^9	4.9×10^8

5   Conclusion

Using the history of the search process this paper proposes a novel operator to improve the performance of QEA. In the proposed method in each iteration the history of solutions during the search process are stored. This history contains useful information about the backbone structure of the landscape, and helps to find the better and worse parts of the search space. In the proposed method, after the population converges, the history of the solutions is used to reinitialize the solutions to represent better parts of the search space with higher and worse parts of the search space with lower probability. The proposed algorithm is tested on Knapsack, Trap, Max-3-Sat and 13 Numerical benchmark functions and experimental results show better performance for the proposed algorithm than the original version of QEA.

The proposed averaging method used in this research is not the only way of exploiting the information in previous steps. Another way of using this information could be the clustering algorithm proposed in [5] or other aggregation methods. In our future works we will work on other methods of using this information.

References

1. Wright, S.: The roles of mutation, inbreeding, crossbreeding, and selection in evolution. In: Proc. 6th Congr. Genetics, vol. 1, p. 365 (1932)
2. Tavares, J., Pereira, F.B., Costa, E.: Multidimensional Knapsack Problem: A Fitness Landscape Analysis. IEEE Trans. on Sys., Man, and Cyb. Part B 38(3)
3. Moscato, P.: On evolution, search, optimization, genetic algorithms and martial arts: Toward memetic algorithms, Caltech Concurrent Computation Program, California Institute of Technology, Pasadena, Tech. Rep. 790 (1989)
4. Moscato, P., Norman, M.G.: A memetic approach for the traveling salesman problem implementation of a computational ecology for combinatorial optimization on message-passing systems. In: Valero, M., Onate, E., Jane, M., Larriba, J.L., Suarez, B. (eds.) Parallel Computing and Transputer Applications, pp. 177–186. IOS Press, Amsterdam (1992)
5. Qasem, M., Prugel-Bennett, A.: Learning the Large-Scale Structure of the MAX-SAT Landscape Using Populations. IEEE Trans. on Evol. Comp. 14(4) (August 2010)
6. Han, K., Kim, J.: Quantum-inspired evolutionary algorithm for a class of combinatorial optimization. IEEE Transactions on Evolutionary Computing 6(6) (2002)
7. Li, Y., Zhang, Y., Zhao, R., Jiao, L.: The immune quantum-inspired evolutionary algorithm. In: IEEE International Conference on Systems, Man and Cybernetics (2004)
8. Wang, Y., Feng, X.-Y., Huang, Y.-X., Zhou, W.-G., Liang, Y.-C., Zhou, C.-G.: A Novel Quantum Swarm Evolutionary Algorithm for Solving 0-1 Knapsack Problem. In: Wang, L., Chen, K., S. Ong, Y. (eds.) ICNC 2005. LNCS, vol. 3611, pp. 698–704. Springer, Heidelberg (2005)
9. Gao, H., Xu, G., Wang, Z.: A Novel Quantum Evolutionary Algorithm and Its Application. In: The Sixth IEEE World Congress on Intelligent Control and Automation (2006)
10. Yu, Y., Tian, Y., Yin, Z.: Hybrid Quantum Evolutionary Algorithms Based on Particle Swarm Theory. In: 1st IEEE Conference on Industrial Electronics and Applications (2006)
11. You, X., Liu, S., Shuai, D.: On Parallel Immune Quantum Evolutionary Algorithm Based on Learning Mechanism and Its Convergence. In: Jiao, L., Wang, L., Gao, X.-b., Liu, J., Wu, F. (eds.) ICNC 2006. LNCS, vol. 4221, pp. 903–912. Springer, Heidelberg (2006)
12. Cruz, D., Vellasco, A.V.A., Pacheco, M.M.B.: Quantum-Inspired Evolutionary Algorithm for Numerical Optimization. In: IEEE Congress on Evolutionary Computation (2006)
13. Feng, X.Y., Wang, Y., Ge, H.W., Zhou, C.G., Liang, Y.C.: Quantum-Inspired Evolutionary Algorithm for Travelling Salesman Problem. Computational Methods, 1363–1367 (2007)
14. Platelt, M.D., Schliebs, S., Kasabov, N.: A versatile quantum-inspired evolutionary algorithm. In: IEEE Congress on Evolutionary Computation (2007)
15. Hutsell, S.R., Greenwood, G.W.: Applying evolutionary techniques to quantum computing problems. In: IEEE Congress on Evolutionary Computation (2007)
16. Tayarani- N, M.-H., Akbarzadeh-T, M.-R.: A Cellular Structure and Diversity Preserving operator in Quantum Evolutionary Algorithms. In: IEEE World Conference on Computational Intelligence (2008)
17. Tayarani- N, M.-H., Akbarzadeh-T, M.-R.: A Sinusoid Size Ring Structure Quantum Evolutionary Algorithm. In: IEEE International Conference on Cybernetics and Intelligent Systems Robotics, Automation and Mechanics (2008)
18. Tayarani- N, M.-H., Akbarzadeh-T, M.-R.: Probabilistic Optimization Algorithms for Numerical Function Optimization Problems. In: IEEE International Conference on Cybernetics and Intelligent Systems Robotics, Automation and Mechanics (2008)
19. Tayarani- N, M.-H., Akbarzadeh-T, M.-R.: Magnetic Optimization Algorithm, A New Synthesis. In: IEEE World Conference on Computational Intelligence (2008)
20. Khorsand, A.-R., Akbarzadeh-T, M.-R.: Quantum Gate Optimization in a Meta-Level Genetic Quantum Algorithm. In: IEEE International Conference on Systems, Man and Cybernetics (2005)

21. Zhong, W., Liu, J., Xue, M., Jiao, L.: A Multi-agent Genetic Algorithm for Global Numerical Optimization. IEEE Trans. Sys., Man and Cyber. 34, 1128–1141 (2004)
22. Koumousis, V.K., Katsaras, C.P.: A Saw-Tooth Genetic Algorithm Combining the Effects of Variable Population Size and Reinitialization to Enhance Performance. IEEE Trans. Evol. Comput. 10, 19–28 (2006)
23. Han, K., Kim, J.: Quantum-Inspired Evolutionary Algorithms with a New Termination Criterion, H_ε Gate, and Two-Phase Scheme. IEEE Trans. on Evolutionary Computation 8(2) (2004)
24. Zhong, W., Liu, J., Xue, M., Jiao, L.: A Multi-agent Genetic Algorithm for Global Numerical Optimization. IEEE Trans. Sys., Man and Cyber. 34, 1128–1141 (2004)

Appendix: Benchmark Optimization Problems

In this section, two combinatorial optimization problems, Trap problem and Knapsack problem and 13 numerical function optimization problems are discussed to evaluate the proposed algorithms.

Trap problem is defined as:

$$f(x) = \sum_{i=0}^{N-1} \left(x_{5i+1}, x_{5i+2}, x_{5i+3}, x_{5i+4}, x_{5i+5} \right)$$

Where N is the number of traps and

$$Trap(x) = \begin{cases} 4 - ones(x) & if \ ones(x) \leq 4 \\ 5 & if \ ones(x) = 5 \end{cases}$$

Where the function *ones* returns the number of ones in the binary string x. Trap problem has a local optimum in $(0,0,0,0,0)$ and a global optimum in $(1,1,1,1,1)$.

Knapsack problem is a well-known combinatorial optimization problem which is in class of NP-hard problems. Knapsack problem can be described as selecting various items x_i $(i = 1, 2, ..., m)$ with profits p_i and weights w_i for a knapsack with capacity C. Given a set of m items and a knapsack with capacity of C, select a subset of the items to maximize the profit $f(x)$:

$$f(x) = \sum_{i=1}^{m} p_i x_i$$

subject to

$$\sum_{i=1}^{m} w_i x_i \leq C$$

Where $C = \frac{1}{2} \sum_{i=1}^{m} w_i$, $w_i, p_i = R(1, v)$, and $R(1, v)$ is a uniform random number generator and $v = 10$.

In solving Knapsack problem with QEA here we describe two methods: QEA based on penalty functions and QEA based on repair method. In QEA based on penalty functions, a binary string of m length represents an individual x. The fitness function is defined as:

$$f(x) = \sum_{i=1}^{m} p_i x_i - Pen(x)$$

Where $x = (x_1, x_2, ..., x_m)$, x_i is 0 or 1, p_i is the profit of item i, w_i is the weight of item i, and C is the capacity of the knapsack. If $x_i = 1$, the $i - th$ item is selected for the knapsack and $Pen(x)$ is the penalty function which is defined as:

$$Pen_1(x) = log_2 \left(1 + \rho \left(\sum_{i=1}^{m} w_i x_i - C \right) \right)$$
$$Pen_2(x) = \rho \left(\sum_{i=1}^{m} w_i x_i - C \right)$$

Where ρ is $max_{i=1}^{m} p_i / w_i$

In GA based on repair method each individual x is evaluated as:

$$f(x) = \sum_{i=1}^{m} p_i x_i'$$

Where x' is the repaired vector of the original vector x. For repairing the vector x, we select item i from x which $x_i = 1$ and remove it from knapsack (reset $x_i = 0$) until the following constraint is satisfied:

$\sum_{i=1}^{m} w_i x_i \leq C$

Here we consider two types of repair function:

1- Random repair: select item i randomly.

2- Greedy repair: sort all items in the knapsack in the decreasing order of their profit to weight ratio and then select item i with lowest ratio.

Global numeric optimization problems arise in many fields of science, engineering, and business [24]. Here we use 13 benchmark maximization functions for testing our proposed algorithm. The $f_1 - f_8$ are multimodal functions where the number of local optima increases with the problem dimension. For example f_1 has about 6^n local optima in $[-500, 500]^n$ and f_2 has about 10^n local optima in the search space of $[-5.12, 5.12]^n$.

Generalized Schwefel's Function 2.26:

$f_1(x) = \sum_{i=1}^{n} \left(-x_i \sin \sqrt{|x_i|} \right), U = [-500, 500]^n$

Generalized Rastrigin's Function:

$f_2(x) = \sum_{i=1}^{n} x_i^2 - 10\cos(2\pi x_i) + 10, U = [-5.12, 5.12]^n$

Ackley's function:

$f_3(x) = -20 \exp\left(-0.2\sqrt{\frac{1}{n}\sum_{i=1}^{n} x_i^2} \right) - \exp\left(\frac{1}{n}\sum_{i=1}^{n} \cos(2\pi x_i) \right) + 20 + e, U = [-32, 32]^n$

Generalized Griewank Function:

$f_4(x) = \frac{1}{4000}\sum_{i=1}^{n} x_i^2 - \prod_{i=1}^{n} \cos\left(\frac{x_i}{\sqrt{i}} \right) + 1, U = [-600, 600]^n$

Generalized Penalized Function 1:

$f_5(x) = \frac{\pi}{n}\left\{ 10\sin^2(\pi y_1) + \sum_{i=1}^{n-1}(y_i - 1)^2 \times [1 + 10\sin^2(\pi y_{i+1})] + (y_n - 1)^2 \right\} + \sum_{i=1}^{n} u(x_i, 10, 100, 1),$

Where

$u(x_i, a, k, p) = \begin{cases} k(x_i - a)^p & x_i > a \\ 0 & -a \leq x_i \leq a \\ k(-x_i - a)^p & x_i < -a \end{cases}$

and

$y_i = 1 + \frac{1}{4}(x_i + 1), U = [-50, 50]^n$

Generalized Penalized Function 2:

$f_6(x) = \frac{1}{10}\left\{ \sin^2(3\pi x_1) + \sum_{i=1}^{n-1}(x_i - 1)^2 [1 + \sin^2(3\pi x_{i+1})] + (x_n - 1)^2 [1 + \sin^2(2\pi x_n)] \right\} + \sum_{i=1}^{n} u(x_i, 5, 100, 1), U = [-50, 50]^n$

Michalewicz Function:

$f_7(x) = -\sum_{i=1}^{n} \left(\sin(x_i) \times \left(\sin\left(\frac{i x_i^2}{\pi} \right) \right)^{2n} \right), U = [-\pi, \pi]$

Goldberg & Richardson Function:

$f_8(x) = \sum_{i=1}^{n} g_i h_i$

$g_i = [\sin(5\pi x_i + 0.5)]^2$

$h_i = \exp\left(-2.0\log(2.0)\frac{(x_i - 0.1)^2}{0.64} \right), S = [-1, 1]^n$

Sphere Model:
$$f_9(x) = \sum_{i=1}^{n} x_i^2, U[-100, 100]^n$$
Schwefel's Function 2.22:
$$f_{10}(x) = \sum_{i=1}^{n} |x_i| + \prod_{i=1}^{n} |x_i|, U = [-10, 10]^n$$
Schwefel's Function 2.21:
$$f_{11}(x) = max_i \{|x_i|, 1 \le i \le n\}, U = [-100, 100]^n$$
Dejong Function 4:
$$f_{12}(x) = \sum_{i=1}^{n} ix_i^4 + Gauss(0, 1), U = [-10, 10]^n$$
Rosenbrock Function:
$$f_{13}(x) = \sum_{i=1}^{n-1} 100 \left(x_{i+1} - x_i^2\right)^2 + (1 - x_i)^2, U = [-2, 2]^n$$

Where U is the search space and n is the problem dimension. These functions have several local minima and one global minimum. Since they are used for maximization process, we use it with a negative sign change $f(x)$ for fitness function.

A New Initialization Method and a New Update Operator for Quantum Evolutionary Algorithms in Solving Fractal Image Compression

M.H. Tayarani N., M. Beheshti, J. Sabet,
M. Mobasher, and H. Joneid

University of Southampton,
Khayyam Institute of Higher Educations
mhtn1g09@ece.soton.ac.uk

Abstract. Fractal Image Compression (FIC) problem is a combinatorial problem which has recently become one of the most promising encoding technologies in the generation of image compression. While Quantum Evolutionary Algorithm (QEA) is a novel optimization algorithm proposed for class of combinatorial optimization problems, it is not widely used in Fractal Image Compression problem yet. Using statistical information of range and domain blocks, and a novel magnetic update operator, this paper proposes a new algorithm in solving FIC. The statistical information of domain and range blocks is used in the initialization step of QEA. In the proposed update operator the q-individuals are some magnetic particles applying attractive force to each other. The force two particles apply to each other depends on their fitness and their distance. The proposed algorithm is tested on several images and the experimental results show better performance for the proposed algorithm than QEA and GA. In comparison with the full search algorithm, the proposed algorithm reaches comparable results with much less computational complexity.

Keywords: Optimization Algorithms, Quantum Evolutionary Algorithms, Fractal Image Compression.

1 Introduction

Fractal Image Compression, proposed by Barnsley has recently become one of the most promising encoding technologies in the generation of image compression [1]. The high compression ratio and the quality of the retrieved images attract many of researchers, but the high computational complexity of the algorithm is its main drawback. One way of decreasing the time complexity is to move from full search method to some optimization algorithms like Genetic Algorithms. From this point of view, several works try to improve the performance of fractal image compression algorithms using Genetic algorithm. In [2] a new method for finding the IFS code of fractal image is developed and the influence of mutation and the crossover is discussed. The low speed of fractal image compression blocks its way to practical applications. In [3] a genetic algorithm approach is used to improve the speed of searching process in fractal image compression. A new method for genetic fractal image compression based on an elitist model is

P. Pichappan, H. Ahmadi, and E. Ariwa (Eds.): INCT 2011, CCIS 241, pp. 401–413, 2011.

proposed in [4]. In the proposed approach the search space for finding the best self similarity is greatly decreased. Reference [5] makes an improvement on the fractal image coding algorithm by applying genetic algorithm. Many researches increase the speed of fractal image compression but the quality of the image will decrease. In [6] the speed of fractal image compression is improved without significant loss of image quality. Reference [7] proposes a genetic algorithm approach which increases the speed of the fractal image compression without decreasing of the quality of the image. In the proposed approach a standard Barnsley algorithm, the Y. Fisher based on classification and the genetic compression algorithm with quad-tree partitioning are compared. In GA based algorithm a population of transformations is evolved for each range block. In order to prevent the premature convergence of GA in fractal image compression a new approach is proposed in [8], which controls the parameters of GA adaptively. A spatial correlation genetic algorithm is proposed in [9], which speeds up the fractal image compression algorithm. In the proposed algorithm there are two stages, first the spatial correlations in image for both the domain pool and the range pool is performed to exploit local optima. In the second stage if the local optima were not satisfying, the whole image is searched to find the best self similarity. A schema genetic algorithm for fractal image compression is proposed in [10] to find the best self similarity in fractal image compression.

Using statistical information of the image, this paper proposes a novel initialization method for QEA. The proposed algorithm has two steps. At the first step the statistical information of the image is extracted. The information consists of the variance of every domain and range block in the image. Then the best region for each range block is found. In the second step, for each range block, QEA searches among domain pool and finds the best domain block and transformation. Here the information gathered in the first step is used to find the best initialization for quantum bits. This paper also proposes a new update operator for QEA, inspiring magnetic field theory which offers more interaction among q-individuals and binary solutions. In the proposed algorithm, the binary solutions with higher fitness apply stronger force to the q-individuals. Performing this new method, the q-individuals have more chance to find better solutions in less time. The proposed algorithm is tested on several images and experimental results show better performance for the proposed algorithm than GA and original version of QEA.

The rest of the paper is organized as follows. Section 2 introduces QEA, in section 3 the new algorithm is proposed and in section 4 is experimented on several images and finally section 5 concludes the paper.

2   Quantum Evolutionary Algorithm

QEA is inspired from the principles of quantum computation, and its superposition of states is based on qubits, the smallest unit of information stored in a two-state quantum computer. A qubit could be either in state "0" or "1", or in any superposition of the two as described below:

$$|\psi\rangle = \alpha|0\rangle + \beta|1\rangle \tag{1}$$

Where α and β are complex numbers, which denote the corresponding state appearance probability, following below constraint:

$$|\alpha|^2 + |\beta|^2 = 1 \qquad (2)$$

This probabilistic representation implies that if there is a system of m qubits, the system can represent 2^m states simultaneously. At each observation, a qubits quantum state collapses to a single state as determined by its corresponding probabilities.

Consider $i-th$ individual in $t-th$ generation defined as an m-qubit as below:

$$\begin{bmatrix} \alpha_{i1}^t & \alpha_{i2}^t & \cdots & \alpha_{ij}^t & \cdots & \alpha_{im}^t \\ \beta_{i1}^t & \beta_{i2}^t & \cdots & \beta_{ij}^t & \cdots & \beta_{im}^t \end{bmatrix} \qquad (3)$$

Where $\left|\alpha_{ij}^t\right|^2 + \left|\beta_{ij}^t\right|^2 = 1$, $j = 1,2,,m, m$ is the number of qubits, i.e., the string length of the qubit individual, $i = 1,2,,n, n$ is the number of possible solution in population and t is generation number of the evolution. If there is, for instance, a three-qubits ($m = 3$) individual such as 4:

$$q_i^t = \begin{bmatrix} \frac{1}{\sqrt{2}} & \frac{1}{\sqrt{3}} & \frac{1}{2} \\ \frac{1}{\sqrt{2}} & \frac{\sqrt{2}}{\sqrt{3}} & \frac{\sqrt{3}}{2} \end{bmatrix} \qquad (4)$$

Or alternatively, the possible states of the individual can be represented as:

$$q_i^t = \frac{1}{2\sqrt{6}}|000\rangle + \frac{1}{2\sqrt{2}}|001\rangle + \frac{1}{2\sqrt{3}}|010\rangle + \frac{1}{2}|011\rangle +$$

$$\frac{1}{2\sqrt{6}}|100\rangle + \frac{1}{2\sqrt{2}}|101\rangle + \frac{1}{2\sqrt{3}}|110\rangle + \frac{1}{2}|111\rangle \qquad (5)$$

In QEA, only one qubit individual such as 4 is enough to represent eight states, whereas in classical representation eight individuals are needed. Additionally, along with the convergence of the quantum individuals, the diversity will gradually fade away and the algorithm converges.

2.1 QEA Structure

In the initialization step of QEA, $[\alpha_{ij}^t \ \beta_{ij}^t]^T$ of all q_i^0 are initialized with $\frac{1}{\sqrt{2}}$. This implies that each qubit individual q_i^0 represents the linear superposition of all possible states with equal probability. The next step makes a set of binary instants; x_i^t by observing $Q(t) = \{q_1^t, q_2^t, ..., q_n^t\}$ states, where $X(t) = \{x_1^t, x_2^t, ..., x_n^t\}$ at generation t is a random instant of qubit population. Each binary instant, x_i^t of length m, is formed by selecting each bit using the probability of qubit, either $|\alpha_{ij}^t|$ or $|\beta_{ij}^t|$ of q_i^t. Each instant x_i^t is evaluated to give some measure of its fitness. The initial best solution $b = max_{i=1}^n \{f(x_i^t)\}$ is then selected and stored from among the binary instants of $X(t)$. Then, in 'update' $Q(t)$, quantum gates U update this set of qubit individuals $Q(t)$ as discussed below. This process is repeated in a while loop until convergence is achieved. The appropriate quantum gate is usually designed in accordance with problems under consideration.

Table 1. Lookup Table of $\Delta\theta$, the rotation gate. x_i is the $i-th$ bit of the observed binary solution and b_i is the $i-th$ bit of the best found binary solution.

x_i	b_i	$f(x) \geq f(b)$	$\Delta\theta$
0	0	false	0
0	0	true	0
0	1	false	0.01π
0	1	true	0
1	0	false	-0.01π
1	0	true	0
1	1	false	0
1	1	true	0

In QEA, the quantum bit representation can be simply interpreted as a biased mutation operator. Therefore, the current best individual can be used to steer the direction of this mutation operator, which will speed up the convergence. The evolutionary process of quantum individual is completed through the step of "update $Q(t)$". A crossover operator, quantum rotation gate, is described below. Specifically, a qubit individual q_i^t is updated by using the rotation gate $U(\theta)$ in this algorithm. The $j-th$ qubit value of $i-th$ quantum individual in generation t, $[\alpha_{ij}^t \ \beta_{ij}^t]^T$ is updated as:

$$\begin{bmatrix} \alpha_{ij}^t \\ \beta_{ij}^t \end{bmatrix} = \begin{bmatrix} cos(\Delta\theta) & -sin(\Delta\theta) \\ sin(\Delta\theta) & cos(\Delta\theta) \end{bmatrix} \begin{bmatrix} \alpha_{ij}^{t-1} \\ \beta_{ij}^{t-1} \end{bmatrix} \tag{6}$$

Where $\Delta\theta$ is rotation angle and controls the speed of convergence and determined from Table 1. Reference [11] shows that these values for $\Delta\theta$ have better performance.

3   The Proposed Method

Fractal Image Compression algorithms search all the domain pool for each range block and find the best domain block with best transform which matches the range block. Conventional fractal image compression algorithms use a full search algorithm in domain pool which is a time consuming procedure. Evolutionary algorithms are suitable for this problem because they can find an appropriate domain block with a transform without performing a full search in domain pool. Since Quantum Evolutionary Algorithms are proposed for combinatorial problems like knapsack problem [14] and fractal image compression is in the class of NP-Hard problems, QEA is highly suitable for FIC.

Initialization is an important part of Evolutionary Algorithms. By initializing possible solutions with appropriate values, we can lead the algorithm to search better parts of the search space and help it to reach better solutions with less computation time. Since QEA is a new method, a small number of works have focused on initialization step in this algorithm and no research has worked on the initialization step in fractal image compression. This paper proposes a novel initialization method for QEA in fractal image compression which uses statistical information of the domain pool to find the best region for each range block.

Searching among all the domain pool for each range block is time consuming and there is a need to some new methods to help the Evolutionary Algorithms finding better solution with higher speed. There are several works in the fractal image compression field that use the variance of domain blocks and range blocks to speed up the search process. Here the statistical information of domain pool is used in the initialization step.

The domain blocks are coded by their horizontal and vertical address in the image. Therefore a solution is a binary string having 3 parts, p_x, p_y, p_T, representing the horizontal and vertical location of domain blocks in the image and the transformations respectively. The length of the possible solution for a $M \times N$ image is:

$$m = \lceil log_2(M) \rceil + \lceil log_2(N) \rceil + 3 \qquad (7)$$

Where m is the size of the possible solutions. Here 8 ordinary transformation are considered: rotate $0°, 90°, 180°, 270°$, flip vertically, horizontally, flip relative to $45°$, and relative to $135°$. The procedure of the proposed method is as follows:

Proposed Algorithm
1. Find the variance of all the domain and range blocks.
2. For each range block do
    begin
3.   Find the n nearest domain blocks to the range block. Code the n domain blocks.
4.   Initialize the n q-individuals in Q^0, based on the coded domain blocks.
      $t = 0$
5.   while not termination condition do
      begin
        $t = t + 1$
6.   make X^t by observing the states of Q^{t-1}
7.   evaluate the particles in X^t and store their performance in magnetic fields B^t
8.   normalize B^t according to 13
9.   evaluate the mass M^t for all particles according to 14
10.   for all q-individuals q_i^t in Q^t do
        begin
11. $F_i = 0$
12.   find N_i
13.   for all x_u^t in N_i do
14. $F_{ij} = F_{ij} + \frac{(x_{uj}^t - (\beta_{ij}^t)^2) \times B_u^t}{D(x_i^t, x_u^t)}$
          end
15.   for all q-individuals q_i^t in Q^t do
          begin
16. $v_{ij}^{t+1} = \frac{F_{ij}}{\eta \times M_i}$
17. $q_{ij}^{t+1} = q_{ij}^t + v_{ij}^{t+1}$
          end
      end
    end
end

QEA has a population of quantum individuals $Q(t) = \{q_1^t, q_2^t, ..., q_n^t\}$, where t is generation step and n is the size of population.

The description of the proposed algorithm is as follows:

1. In this step the variance of all the domain and range blocks is calculated.
2. This step performs a search on domain pool for each range block.
3. Here the variance of the blocks is used to find the similarity between range and domain blocks. If the domain pool is D and D_k is the $k-th$ domain block in domain pool, then the most similar domain block to the range block R_i is:

$$S_1 = \{D_j | D_j \in D, \forall k \neq j, D_k \in D \Rightarrow |v(R_i) - v(D_j)| \leq |v(R_i) - v(D_k)|\} \qquad (8)$$

The second most similar domain block to the range block R_i is:

$$S_2 = \{D_j | D_j \in D - S_1, \forall k \neq j, D_k \in D - S_1 \Rightarrow |v(R_i) - v(D_j)| \leq |v(R_i) - v(D_k)|\} \qquad (9)$$

And the $n-th$ most similar domain block to the range block R_i is:

$$S_n = \left\{ D_j | D_j \in D - \bigcup_{i=1}^{n-1} S_i, \forall k \neq j, D_k \in D - \bigcup_{i=1}^{n-1} S_i \Rightarrow |v(R_i) - v(D_j)| \leq |v(R_i) - v(D_k)| \right\} \qquad (10)$$

Where n is the size of the population in QEA and S_n contains the $n-th$ most similar domain blocks to the range block R_i. After finding the n most similar domain blocks, these domain blocks, $S_1, S_2, ..., S_n$ are coded as binary solutions and stored to $Y_1, Y_2, ..., Y_n$ to be used for the initialization step.

4. This step is the initialization step of QEA. In this step the n q-individuals in the population are initialized based on the n most similar domain blocks found in the previous step. In the proposed algorithm the address part of q-individuals $Q(0)$, p_x, p_y are found as follows:

$$q_{ij}^0 = \begin{cases} \left[\sqrt{1 - \frac{i-1}{2(n-1)}} \quad \sqrt{\frac{i-1}{2(n-1)}} \right]^T & if \ Y_{ij} = 0 \\ \\ \left[\sqrt{\frac{i-1}{2(n-1)}} \quad \sqrt{1 - \frac{i-1}{2(n-1)}} \right]^T & if \ Y_{ij} = 1 \end{cases} \qquad (11)$$

Where Y_{ij} is the $j-th$ bit of the code of $i-th$ most similar domain block to the range block, $i = 1, 2, ..., n$, n is the size of the population in QEA, m is the size of q-individuals, $j = 1, 2, ..., m - 3$. The bits in p_t part of q_{ij}^0 are set to:

$$q_{ij}^0 = \left[\frac{\sqrt{2}}{2} \quad \frac{\sqrt{2}}{2} \right]^T$$

For $i = 1, 2, ..., n$, and $j = m - 2, m - 1, m$.

5. This step makes a set of binary instants $X^t = \{x_i^t | i = 1, 2, ..., n\}$ at generation t by observing $Q^{t-1} = \{q_i^{t-1} | i = 1, 2, ..., n\}$ states, where X^t at generation t is a random

instant of qubit population and n is the size of population. Each binary instant, x_i^t of length m, is formed by selecting each bit using the probability of qubit, either $|\alpha_{ij}^{t-1}|^2$ or $|\beta_{ij}^{t-1}|^2$ of q_i^{t-1}. Observing the binary bit x_{ij}^t from qubit $[\alpha_{ij}^t\ \beta_{ij}^t]^T$ performs as:

$$x_{ij}^t = \begin{cases} 0 & if\ R(0,1) < |\alpha_{ij}^t|^2 \\ 1 & otherwise \end{cases} \tag{12}$$

Where $R(.,.)$ is a uniform random number generator.

6. Each binary instant x_i^t is evaluated to give some measure of its objective. In this step, the fitness of all binary solutions of X^0 are evaluated and stored in B^t.

7. Next the normalization is performed on B^t. The normalization is performed as:

$$B_i = \frac{B_i - Min}{Max - Min} \tag{13}$$

Where: $Min = minimum_{i=1}^n(B_i^t), \qquad Max = maximum_{i=1}^n(B_i^t)$

The magnetic field of each particle is normalized in the range of [0-1]. This is because the fitness values of possible solutions are problem dependent. The range of the fitness of the possible solutions can be in any range, since the amount of the magnetic field controls the movement of the particles, we normalize the amount of magnetic field.

8. In this step the mass of all particles is calculated and stored in M^t:

$$M_i^t = 1 + B_i^t \tag{14}$$

9. In this step in the "for" loop, the resultant force of all forces on each particle is calculated.

10. At first the resultant force F_i to particle x_i^t is initialized to zero.

11. In the proposed algorithm, each particle interacts only with its neighbors i.e. each particle applies its force only to its neighbors. In this step the neighbors of x_i^t are determined randomly. Each possible solution has 4 neighbors.

12. In this step, the applied force to particle x_i^t by its neighbor's x_u^t, $\forall x_u^t \in N_i$ is calculated.

13. The force which is applied by x_u^t to x_i^t relates to the distance between two particles and the magnetic field of x_u^t. It is calculated as:

$$F_{ij} = \frac{\left(x_{uj}^t - (\beta_{ij}^t)^2\right) \times B_u^t}{D(x_i^t, x_u^t)} \tag{15}$$

Here F_i shows the force applied to q-individual q_i^t. The part "$x_{uj}^t - (\beta_{ij}^t)^2$" shows the direction which the q-individual moves and $(\beta_{ij}^t)^2$ is the probability of q_i^t representing state "1". Where $D(.,.)$ is the distance between each pair of neighboring particles and is calculated as:

$$D(x_i^t, x_u^t) = \frac{1}{m} \sum_{j=1}^m |x_{ij}^t - x_{uj}^t| \tag{16}$$

Where x_i^t and x_u^t are $i-th$ and $u-th$ binary solutions of the population in iteration t respectively and x_{ij}^t is the $j-th$ bit of $i-th$ binary solution in iteration t. This step is the main step in the proposed algorithm.

14, 15, 16. In these steps the location of q-individuals are updated. The proposed update operator has two advantages. First according to 15 the observed binary solutions with higher fitness have bigger magnetic field B and apply stronger force to the q-individual, therefore the better binary solutions exert stronger attraction force. Here unlike Q-Gate the movement of q-individuals is not constant throughout the search process and varies for various q-individuals and even various dimensions. Second in the proposed update operator even the inferior binary solutions have effect on the q-individuals but with smaller amplitude. Accordingly the interaction among possible solutions is much more than Q-Gate and the inferior binary solutions participate in the search process.

3.1 Parameter Tuning

As it is seen in step 16 of the algorithm, the proposed algorithm has a parameter of η. This section tries to find the best parameter for the proposed update operator. Since fractal image compression is a time consuming algorithm and finding the best parameter needs several experiments for several values of the parameter, this section finds the best parameter for some benchmark functions which are much faster. The size of population for all the experiments is set to 25, and the parameter is set to η=(1,2,3,4,5,10,15,20,25,30,35,40,45,50). Figure 1 shows the parameter setting for the proposed algorithm on Knapsack problem and Generalized Schwefel's Function 2.26. The results are averaged over 30 runs. According to Figure 1, the best parameter for Knapsack problem repair type 1, the best parameter is η=5, the best parameter for Knapsack penalty type 2 is η=20 and the best parameter for Generalized Schwefel is 10. This paper finds the best parameter for the proposed update operator for several benchmark functions and the results are summarized in Table 2. As it is clear in Table 2, for all the numerical function problems the best parameter for the proposed update operator is 10.

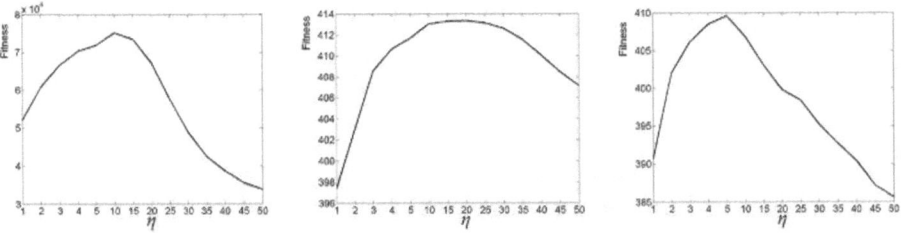

Fig. 1. The effect of the parameter η on the performance of the proposed algorithm on Generalized Schwefel's Function 2.26, Knapsack problem Penalty Type 2 and Trap problem

Table 2. Best parameter for the proposed Update operator. The results are averaged over 30 runs

Problem	η	Problem	η	Problem	η	Problem	η
Kpck Rep 1	5	Kpck Rep 2	35	Kpck Pen 1	5	Kpck Pen 2	20
Trap	2	Schwefel	10	Rastrigin	10	Ackley	10
Griawank	10	Penalized1	10	Penalized2	10	Kennedy	10
Michalewicz	10	Goldberg	10	Sphere	10	Rosenbrock	10
Schwefel 2.21	10	Dejong	10	Schwefel 2.22	10		

Table 3. Experimental results on Lena, Pepper, and Baboon. The results are an average over 10 runs.

Picture	Method	Pop Size	MSE Computations	PSNR
Lena	Full Search	-	59,474,944	28.85
	QEA	30	6,144,000	28.49
		25	5,120,000	28.28
		20	4,096,000	28.95
		15	3,072,000	27.43
	Proposed Method	30	6,144,000	28.59
		25	5,120,000	28.42
		20	4,096,000	29.04
		15	3,072,000	27.57
	GA	30	6,144,000	28.11
		25	5,120,000	28.04
		20	4,096,000	27.55
		15	3,072,000	27.27
Pepper	Full Search	-	59,474,944	29.85
	QEA	30	6,144,000	29.55
		25	5,120,000	29.09
		20	4,096,000	28.87
		15	3,072,000	28.12
	Proposed Method	30	6,144,000	29.65
		25	5,120,000	29.29
		20	4,096,000	28.92
		15	3,072,000	28.52
	GA	30	6,144,000	29.14
		25	5,120,000	28.92
		20	4,096,000	28.64
		15	3,072,000	28.11
Baboon	Full Search	-	59,474,944	20.04
	QEA	30	6,144,000	19.28
		25	5,120,000	19.18
		20	4,096,000	18.95
		15	3,072,000	18.62
	Proposed Method	30	6,144,000	19.65
		25	5,120,000	19.33
		20	4,096,000	19.07
		15	3,072,000	18.73
	GA	30	6,144,000	19.17
		25	5,120,000	19.02
		20	4,096,000	18.65
		15	3,072,000	18.41

4   Experimental Results

This section experiments the proposed algorithm and compares the proposed algorithm with the performance of GA and original version of QEA in fractal image compression. The proposed algorithm is examined on images Lena, Pepper and Baboon with the size of 256×256 and gray scale. The size of range blocks is considered as 8×8 and the size of domain blocks is considered as 16×16. In order to compare the quality of results, the PSNR test is performed:

$$PSNR = 10 \times log \left(\frac{255^2}{\frac{1}{M \times N} \sum_{i=1}^{N} \sum_{j=1}^{M} (f(i,j) - g(i,j))^2} \right) \tag{17}$$

Where $M \times N$ is the size of image. The crossover rate in GA is 0.8 and the probability of mutation is 0.003 for each allele. Table 3 shows the experimental results using proposed algorithm and GA. The number of iterations for GA, QEA and the proposed algorithm for all the experiments is 200. The parameter η is considered as $\eta = 10$. According to Table 3 the proposed algorithm improves the performance of fractal image compression for all the experimental results.

5   Conclusion

In order to improve the performance of QEA in solving Fractal Image Compression problem, this paper proposes a novel magnetic update operator which works better than conventional q-gate update operator. This paper also uses the statistical information of range and domain blocks to lead the possible solutions toward better parts of the search space to help them finding better solutions. Finally experiments on Lena, Pepper, and Baboon pictures show an improvement on evolutionary algorithms solving fractal image compression.

References

1. Xing-yuan, W., Fan-ping, L., Shu-guo, W.: Fractal image compression based on spatial correlation and hybrid genetic algorithm. Journal of Vis. Commun. Image R, 505–510 (2009)
2. Xuan, Y., Dequn, L.: An improved genetic algorithm of solving IFS code of fractal image. In: IEEE 3rd International Conference on Signal Processing (1996)
3. Chen, X., Zhu, G., Zhu, Y.: Fractal image coding method based on genetic algorithms. In: International Symposium on Multispectral Image Processing (1998)
4. Mitra, S.K., Murthy, C.A., Kundu, M.K.: Technique for fractal image compression using genetic algorithm. IEEE Trans. on Image Processing 7(4), 586–593 (1998)
5. Xun, L., Zhongqiu, Y.: The application of GA in fractal image compression. In: 3rd IEEE World Congress on Intelligent Control and Automation (2000)
6. Gafour, A., Faraoun, K., Lehireche, A.: Genetic fractal image compression. In: ACS/IEEE International Conference on Computer Systems and Applications (2003)
7. Mohamed, F.K., Aoued, B.: Speeding Up Fractal Image Compression by Genetic Algorithms. Journal of Multidimention Systems and Signal Processing 16(2) (2005)
8. Xi, L., Zhang, L.: A Study of Fractal Image Compression Based on an Improved Genetic Algorithm. International Journal of Nonlinear Science 3(2), 116m–124m (2007)

9. Wu, M., Teng, W., Jeng, J., Hsieh, J.: Spatial correlation genetic algorithm for fractal image compression. Journal of Chaos, Solitons and Fractals 28(2), 497–510 (2006)
10. Wu, M., Jeng, J., Hsieh, J.: Schema genetic algorithm for fractal image compression. Journal of Engineering Applications of Artificial Intelligence 20(4), 531–538 (2007)
11. Han, K., Kim, J.: Quantum-inspired evolutionary algorithm for a class of combinatorial optimization. IEEE Transactions on Evolutionary Computing 6(6) (2002)
12. Han, K., Kim, J.: Quantum-Inspired Evolutionary Algorithms with a New Termination Criterion, H_ε Gate, and Two-Phase Scheme. IEEE Trans. on Evolutionary Computation 8(2) (2004)
13. Zhong, W., Liu, J., Xue, M., Jiao, L.: A Multi-agent Genetic Algorithm for Global Numerical Optimization. IEEE Trans. Sys., Man and Cyber. 34, 1128–1141 (2004)

Appendix: Benchmark Optimization Problems

In this section, two combinatorial optimization problems, Trap problem and Knapsack problem and 13 numerical function optimization problems are discussed to evaluate the proposed algorithms.

Trap problem is defined as:

$$f(x) = \sum_{i=0}^{N-1} (x_{5i+1}, x_{5i+2}, x_{5i+3}, x_{5i+4}, x_{5i+5})$$

Where N is the number of traps and

$$Trap(x) = \begin{cases} 4 - ones(x) & if\ ones(x) \leq 4 \\ 5 & if\ ones(x) = 5 \end{cases}$$

Where the function $ones$ returns the number of ones in the binary string x. Trap problem has a local optimum in $(0,0,0,0,0)$ and a global optimum in $(1,1,1,1,1)$.

Knapsack problem is a well-known combinatorial optimization problem which is in class of NP-hard problems. Knapsack problem can be described as selecting various items x_i $(i = 1, 2, ..., m)$ with profits p_i and weights w_i for a knapsack with capacity C. Given a set of m items and a knapsack with capacity of C, select a subset of the items to maximize the profit $f(x)$:

$$f(x) = \sum_{i=1}^{m} p_i x_i$$

subject to

$$\sum_{i=1}^{m} w_i x_i \leq C$$

Where $C = \frac{1}{2} \sum_{i=1}^{m} w_i$, $w_i, p_i = R(1, v)$, and $R(1, v)$ is a uniform random number generator and $v = 10$.

In solving Knapsack problem with QEA here we describe two methods: QEA based on penalty functions and QEA based on repair method. In QEA based on penalty functions, a binary string of m length represents an individual x. The fitness function is defined as:

$$f(x) = \sum_{i=1}^{m} p_i x_i - Pen(x)$$

Where $x = (x_1, x_2, ..., x_m)$, x_i is 0 or 1, p_i is the profit of item i, w_i is the weight of item i, and C is the capacity of the knapsack. If $x_i = 1$, the $i - th$ item is selected for the knapsack and $Pen(x)$ is the penalty function which is defined as:

$$Pen_1(x) = log_2 (1 + \rho (\sum_{i=1}^{m} w_i x_i - C))$$
$$Pen_2(x) = \rho (\sum_{i=1}^{m} w_i x_i - C)$$

Where ρ is $max_{i=1}^{m} p_i / w_i$

In GA based on repair method each individual x is evaluated as:

$$f(x) = \sum_{i=1}^{m} p_i x_i'$$

Where x' is the repaired vector of the original vector x. For repairing the vector x, we select item i from x which $x_i = 1$ and remove it from knapsack (reset $x_i = 0$) until the following constraint is satisfied:

$\sum_{i=1}^{m} w_i x_i \leq C$

Here we consider two types of repair function:

1- Random repair: select item i randomly.

2- Greedy repair: sort all items in the knapsack in the decreasing order of their profit to weight ratio and then select item i with lowest ratio.

Global numeric optimization problems arise in many fields of science, engineering, and business [13]. Here we use 13 benchmark maximization functions for testing our proposed algorithm. The $f_1 - f_8$ are multimodal functions where the number of local optima increases with the problem dimension. For example f_1 has about 6^n local optima in $[-500, 500]^n$ and f_2 has about 10^n local optima in the search space of $[-5.12, 5.12]^n$.

Generalized Schwefel's Function 2.26:

$f_1(x) = \sum_{i=1}^{n} \left(-x_i \sin \sqrt{|x_i|} \right), U = [-500, 500]^n$

Generalized Rastrigin's Function:

$f_2(x) = \sum_{i=1}^{n} x_i^2 - 10\cos(2\pi x_i) + 10, U = [-5.12, 5.12]^n$

Ackley's function:

$f_3(x) = -20\exp\left(-0.2\sqrt{\frac{1}{n}\sum_{i=1}^{n} x_i^2} \right) - \exp\left(\frac{1}{n}\sum_{i=1}^{n} \cos(2\pi x_i)\right) + 20 + e, U = [-32, 32]^n$

Generalized Griewank Function:

$f_4(x) = \frac{1}{4000}\sum_{i=1}^{n} x_i^2 - \prod_{i=1}^{n} \cos\left(\frac{x_i}{\sqrt{i}}\right) + 1, U = [-600, 600]^n$

Generalized Penalized Function 1:

$f_5(x) = \frac{\pi}{n}\left\{ 10\sin^2(\pi y_1) + \sum_{i=1}^{n-1}(y_i - 1)^2 \times [1 + 10\sin^2(\pi y_{i+1})] + (y_n - 1)^2 \right\} + \sum_{i=1}^{n} u(x_i, 10, 100, 1),$

Where

$u(x_i, 10, 100, 1) = \begin{cases} k(x_i - a)^p & x_i > a \\ 0 & -a \leq x_i \leq a \\ k(-x_i - a)^p & x_i < -a \end{cases}$

and

$y_i = 1 + \frac{1}{4}(x_i + 1), U = [-50, 50]^n$

Generalized Penalized Function 2:

$f_6(x) = \frac{1}{10}\left\{ \sin^2(3\pi x_1) + \sum_{i=1}^{n-1}(x_i - 1)^2 [1 + \sin^2(3\pi x_{i+1})] + (x_n - 1)^2 [1 + \sin^2(2\pi x_n)] \right\} + \sum_{i=1}^{n} u(x_i, 5, 100, 1), U = [-50, 50]^n$

Michalewicz Function:

$f_7(x) = -\sum_{i=1}^{n} \left(\sin(x_i) \times \left(\sin\left(\frac{ix_i^2}{\pi}\right) \right)^{2n} \right), U = [-\pi, \pi]$

Goldberg & Richardson Function:

$f_8(x) = \sum_{i=1}^{n} g_i h_i$

$g_i = [\sin(5\pi x_i + 0.5)]^2$

$$h_i = exp\left(-2.0log(2.0)\frac{(x_i-0.1)^2}{0.64}\right), S = [-1,1]^n$$

Sphere Model:

$$f_9(x) = \sum_{i=1}^{n} x_i^2, U[-100, 100]^n$$

Schwefel's Function 2.22:

$$f_{10}(x) = \sum_{i=1}^{n} |x_i| + \prod_{i=1}^{n} |x_i|, U = [-10, 10]^n$$

Schwefel's Function 2.21:

$$f_{11}(x) = max_i\{|x_i|, 1 \leq i \leq n\}, U = [-100, 100]^n$$

Dejong Function 4:

$$f_{12}(x) = \sum_{i=1}^{n} i x_i^4 + Gauss(0,1), U = [-10, 10]^n$$

Rosenbrock Function:

$$f_{13}(x) = \sum_{i=1}^{n-1} 100\left(x_{i+1} - x_i^2\right)^2 + (1 - x_i)^2, U = [-2, 2]^n$$

Kennedy multimodal function generator:

$$f_{14}(x) = min_{j=1}^{n}\left(\sum_{i=1}^{n}\left[\frac{1}{1+exp(-x_i)}\right]^2 + \frac{(j-1)^{0.15}}{15}\right), U = [-4, 4]^n$$

Where U is the search space and n is the problem dimension. These functions have several local minima and one global minimum. Since they are used for maximization process, we use it with a negative sign change $f(x)$ for fitness function.

Partial and Random Updating Weights in Error Back Propagation Algorithm

Nasim Latifi and Ali Amiri

Islamic Azad University, Zanjan Branch, Department of Computer Engineering, Zanjan, Iran
Nsm.latifi@gmail.com, A_amiri@iust.ac.ir

Abstract. One of the introduce discussions in the field of using MLPNN, as a tools for data classification is related to the error back propagation algorithm which use to train the network. It has challenges for large-scale and heterogeneous data such as, lack of memory and low–speed convergence, besides, computational load is high. In this paper proposed method with partial and random updating some of weights instead of all of them in each iteration, cause to decrease computational rate, improve lack of memory's problem and somewhat increase convergence speed. Result of experiments on two standard dataset, demonstrate efficiency of algorithm.

Keywords: MLP, EBP, Neural Networks.

1   Introduction

Today Multilayer Perceptron Neural Network (MLPNN) is one of the most important machine learning tools that is used in the various fields such as, solve complex classifying problems including non-linear separable samples, estimate function and perform many of calculation tasks that require to prediction. MLPNN is the feed forward multilayer network with non-linear activation function that learning in this type of networks is supervised and use gradient-based algorithms and specially error back propagation (EBP) algorithm to train network.

Error back propagation algorithm or generalized delta rule is a reduction gradient method to minimize all of computed output error squares by network [3]. Generally, the learning process in the EBP algorithm describes as a step-by-step and iterative weight correction, in the negative gradient of Mean Squared Errors (MSE) function [1]. The error calculates from the difference between the desired value and the output value from the last layer. This error is back propagated to the neurons of the previous layers [1]. Some parameters have high effect in performance of MLPNN including: initializations, the learning rates selection, topology of the network, the number of hidden layers, the number of neurons, the amount of training data, convergence speed, type of activation function, etc [1].

When we use MLPNN in some of scope such as video data classification with so high data volumes and dimensions and heterogeneous training samples, there are two basic problems: 1) low convergence speed 2) high network size in large-scale data as

P. Pichappan, H. Ahmadi, and E. Ariwa (Eds.): INCT 2011, CCIS 241, pp. 414–421, 2011.

video and another problem is in lack of memory to maintain and update weights. Therefore, time/space order of algorithm may be so high and sometimes implementation of network is impossible [2]. The propagation algorithms were effectively implemented in [9, 10, 11].

In this paper we try to decrease the number of computational operations, the amount of consumption memory and the number of weights that evaluate in each step by random selection and updating some of weights instead of all them. Also in compared to standard EBP algorithm, proposed algorithm has high convergence speed.

Construction of this paper is following: in section 2 we will have review on structure of MLP NN and EBP algorithm. In section 3, the proposed method that uses partial and random updating is evaluated. The result of experiments describe in the section 4 and general conclusion in section 5.

2   MLPNN and EBP Algorithm

Fig. 1 shows a MLPNN with 3 layers (an input layer, a hidden layer and an output layer); each layer includes set of neurons which the entry of a neuron is being from external sources or other outputs neurons. Neuron sets divide to several discrete subset and all neurons in a subset is attributed to same layer. In this network each neuron in a layer connects to next layer neurons, through adjustable weighted links. MLPNN uses the EBP algorithm for training network, hence, learning algorithm adjust weights, by back propagating the computed error from output to previous layers, as, by iterating this operation decrease error gradually.

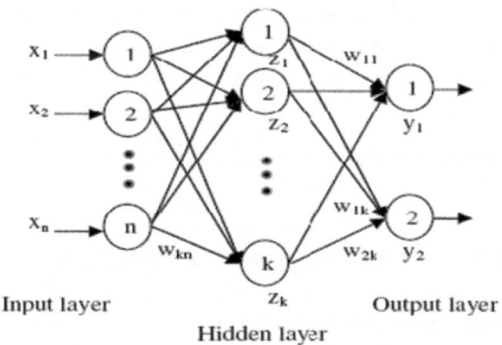

Input layer   Hidden layer   Output layer

Fig. 1. 3 layer MLPNN

If $\{X^i, D_i\}_{i=1}^h$ be the training set of network ($X^i = [x_{i1}, x_{i2}, \ldots, x_{in}]^T$ input pattern and d_i desired output), so in the EBP algorithm, for output layer neurons, error is computed as [1], [2]:

$$e_c^i(n) = D_i(n) - Y_c(n) \tag{1}$$

Where Y_c is output of neuron c in output layer. The weights initialize randomly and adjust during the learning step. The EBP algorithm uses the following equation for adjusting the weights between neurons of output layer (Y_c, c=1, ..., m) and neurons of hidden layer (Z_b, b=1, ..., k) in iteration nth:

$$w_{bc}(n + 1) = w_{bc}(n) + \mu Y_b(n)\delta_c(n) \tag{2}$$

Where μ is learning rate and δ is the back propagated error that computes as below:
For output layer

$$\delta_c(n) = e_c(n)f'(y_c(n)) \tag{3}$$

For hidden layer

$$\delta_b(n) = f'(y_b(n)) \sum_{c=1}^{m} \delta_c(n)w_{bc}(n) \tag{4}$$

Where m is the number of neurons in the output layer. If MLP NN includes more than one hidden layer, therefore in the next step this equation should be compute for other hidden layer.

Whereas in the EBP algorithm with momentum parameter, variation of weight is combining of present gradient and previous gradient, in fact, this method is a sample of a change in decrease gradient method. Sometimes by adding momentum parameter to updating weight equation, convergence is been faster and it allow to network perform weights adjustment by large step when variation of weights be in same direct for some training pattern, at the same time, network able to use smaller learning rate until don't show large reaction to probable errors in training patterns. So we have

$$W_{bc}(n + 1) = w_{bc}(n) + \mu Y_b(n)\delta_c(n) + \eta[w_{bc}(n) - w_{bc}(n - 1)] \tag{5}$$

Or

$$\Delta W_{bc}(n + 1) = \mu Y_b(n)\delta_c(n) + \eta \Delta w_{bc}(n) \tag{6}$$

Where η is momentum parameter and $0 < \eta < 1$.

In this paper our means of standard EBP are the EBP algorithm with momentum parameter. Learning process complete when; e (n) <= Emax (Emax: predefined error).

3   Proposed Method

In standard MLPNN When learning process performs, all of the weights in network update on each iteration of learning algorithm, so, convergence speed for large-scale data is low, besides, computational load rate, the amount of consumption memory and the number of weights that evaluate in each step is high. We know that one of the most significant parameter in evaluation performance and improvement artificial neural networks is convergence speed that in this filed different research is done [1], [3], [6], [7], etc. But in this paper our main goal are that the computational load rate can decrease and the lack of memory's problem improve. In proposed method we only select and update some of weights instead of all them in each iteration of algorithm.

We assume that MLPNN has K layers and the number of nodes in i^{th} layer is:

$$N_i, \text{ for } i = 1, \dots, K \tag{7}$$

And M_i the number of weights between i^{th} and $i+1^{th}$ layers is:

$$M_i = N_i \times N_{i+1} \text{ for } i = 1, \dots, K-1 \tag{8}$$

We define a parameter as S. The amount of it is one of values of set R= {1,2,3,4,5}, (S∈R), every time an experiment performs.

In each step of updating weights, the number of weights which randomly select and update in each layer is:

$$p_i = {}^1/_S \times M_i \tag{9}$$

So, in n^{th} iteration of algorithm the number of selected weights is

$$P(n) = \sum_{i=1}^{K-1} p_i(n) \tag{10}$$

Fig. 2 shows a sample of proposed method performance.

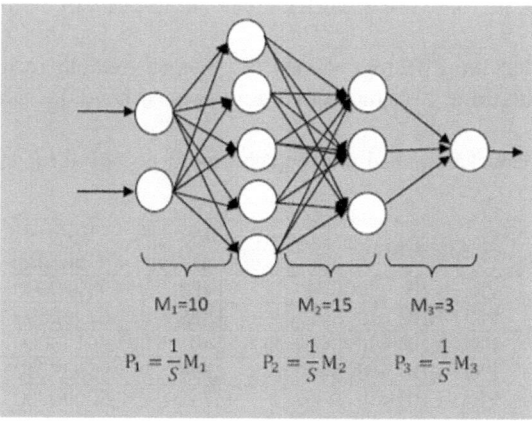

Fig. 2. A sample of proposed method performance

The following semi code indicate the implementation of this process using MATLAB:

```
For i=K-1:-1:1
        M = num of nodes (k)*number of nodes (k+1);
        P =ceil (1/S*M);
    For f=1:P
        m=randint (1, 1, [1, number of nodes (k)]);
        n=randint (1, 1, [1, number of nodes (k+1)]);
       Δw(m,n,k)=μ*δ(n,k+1)*Y(m,k)+η*Δw(m,n,k);
        W(m,n,k)=W(m,n,k)+Δw(m,n,k);
    End
End
```

In this paper we assume μ =0.04 and η=0.4.

4   Experimental Results

The experiments are performed over Vehicle and Iris datasets. the features and assumptions related to datasets and structures of MLP NN used for everyone explain as below:

- Vehicle dataset: this dataset including about 250 samples and 2 classes. Each sample has 18 properties. We have 4-layers MLPNN, the input layer has 18 neurons and there are 2 hidden layers, first layer including 10 neurons and second layer 8 neurons. We assume dataset is noisy with SNR= 10 db.
- Iris dataset: this dataset including about 150 samples and 1 class. Each sample has 4 properties. We have 4-layers MLPNN, the input layer has 4 neurons and there are 2 hidden layers, both of them including 5 neurons.

Table 1 shows that the different values of S have evident influence in the rate of performed computations, also the convergence speed have the same efficiency.

Table 1. Rate of calculations and convergence speed of *PRU-EBP* algorithms over *Vehicle dataset (10-8)*

Algorithm	Number of Iteration	Rate of Calculation
PRU-EBP with S=1	1422	98049000
PRU-EBP with S=2	1826	62962500
PRU-EBP with S=3	3405	79143000
PRU-EBP with S=4	2258	38933250
PRU-EBP with S=5	3765	52696000

The results in fig. 3 demonstrate that different values of S have effect to convergence speed of algorithm.

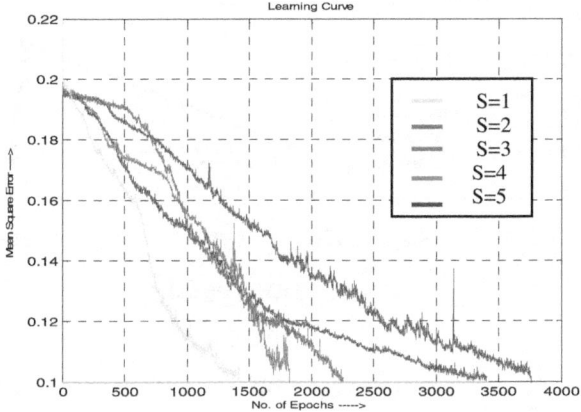

Fig. 3. Convergence comparison for *PRU-EBP* algorithms over *Vehicle dataset (10-8)*, *Emax=0.1*

The result of experiments on Iris dataset are in Table 2, as shown in all cases (S=2, 3, 4, 5) rate of calculations are decreased except in S=1. In S=2, 5 convergence speed is increased in addition to rate of calculations decreased. As for Table 2, it is better to select a PRU-EBP algorithm increase convergence speed as is possible and too decrease computational load. Of course we can prefer one to another among the two efficiency parameters, depending to algorithms application in various fields. For example in large-scale data classification as video data, it is suitable to select an algorithm which have both high convergence speed and low memory usage rate.

Table 2. rate of calculations and convergence speed of *PRU-EBP* algorithms, *Standard-EBP* and *SPU-EBP* algorithms over *Iris dataset(5-5)*

Algorithm	Number of Iteration	Rate of Calculation
Standard-EBP	415	3112500
PRU-EBP with S=1	525	3937500
PRU-EBP with S=2	247	963300
PRU-EBP with S=3	980	2646000
PRU-EBP with S=4	892	1873200
PRU-EBP with S=5	277	415500
SPU-EBP	947	1775082

In Fig. 4 and Table 2, we compare convergence speed and computational load of three algorithms; standard-EBP, SPU-EBP algorithms and PRU-EBP algorithm. In [2], SPU-EBP algorithm using the sequential and partial updating of weights. The results present our proposed algorithm has appropriate performance in similar condition and the result is acceptable.

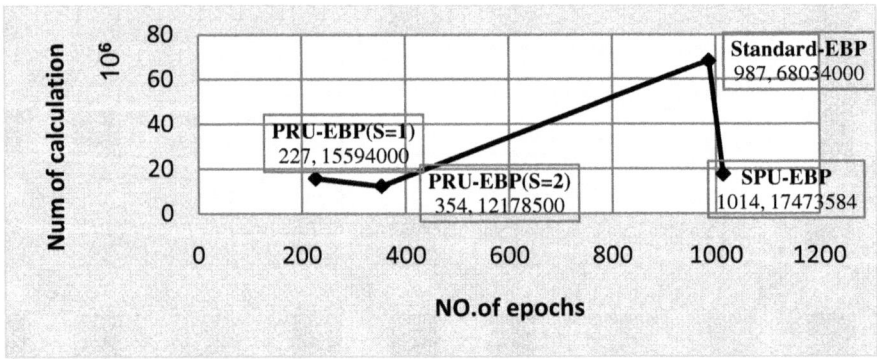

Fig. 4. Comparison of 3 algorithms (Standard-EBP, SPU-EBP and PRU-EBP for S=1, 2) and SNR=10db, Emax=0.18

The gained result from Table 2 and also Fig.4 show that the convergence speed and computational load of PRU-EBP algorithm is faster than standard-EBP and SPU_EBP algorithms. And also the results of Table 1 and 2 describe that type of data and structure of neural network has direct effect on convergence speed and computational load of algorithms. in Table 1 we saw that had least rate of calculations for S=2,4 while in Table 2 we have least rate of calculations to S=2, 5.

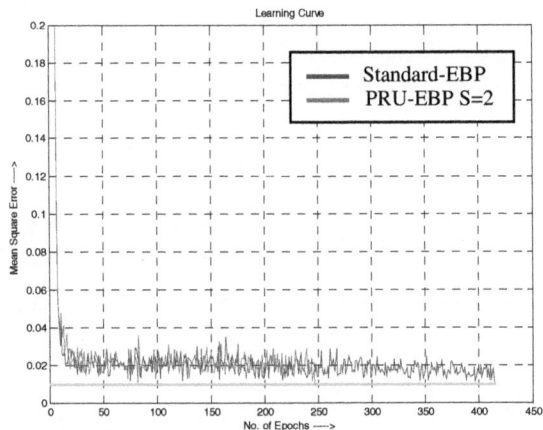

Fig. 5. Convergence comparison of two algorithms *(Standard-EBP, PRU-EBP S=2), Iris (5-5)*

5   Conclusion

In this paper we evaluated partial and random updating weights in error back propagation algorithm. The results of experiment have shown that proposed algorithm have acceptable performance in compared to other two algorithms. We can use the proposed algorithm for working on large-scale data because the calculations rate and memory consumption have decreased. In the compared of standard-EBP although the convergence speed in some cases is improved but it is rather low and is not more significant. Our next target is significantly increasing the convergence speed of the proposed algorithm by using adaptive filtering.

References

1. Didandeh, A., Mirbakhsh, N., Amiri, A., Fathy, M.: AVLR-EBP, A Variable Step Size Approach to Speed-up the Convergence of Error Back-Propagation Algorithm. Neural Processing Letters 3(2), 201–214 (2011)
2. Rahmani, N.M., Amiri, A., Fathy, M.: Partial Update Error Back Propagation Algorithm. In: Proceedings of the 15th Iranian Conference on Electrical Engineering, Tehran, Iran (2010)
3. Sarkar, D.: Methods to Speed Up Error Back-Propagation Learning Algorithm. ACM Computing Surveys 27(4), 545–644 (1995)
4. Wilamowski, M.B.: Advanced Learning Algorithms, February 17. IEEE (2010)
5. Rojas, R.: The Back propagation Algorithm. Neural Networks (1996)
6. Abid, S., Faniech, F., Jervis, B.W., Cheriet, M.: Fast training of multilayer perceptrons with a mixed norm algorithm. In: The IEEE Intl. Joint Conference on Neural Networks (IJCNN 2005), Canada, vol. 2, pp. 1018–1022 (August 2005)
7. Mulawka, J.J., Verma, B.K.: Improving the Training Time of the Backpropagation Algorithm. International Journal of Microcomputer Applications 13(2), 85–89 (1994)
8. Verma, B.: Fast training of multilayer perceptrons (MLPs). IEEE Trans. Neural Netw. 8(6), 1314–1321 (1997)
9. Haykin, S.: Neural Networks, a comprehensive foundation, 2nd edn. Prentice Hall International Inc., McMaster University, Hamilton, Ontario, Canada (1998)
10. Gamal-Eldin, A., Descombes, X., Charpiat, G., Zerubia, J.: Multiple Birth and Cut Algorithm for Multiple Object Detection. Journal of Multimedia Processing and Technologies 1(4), 261–277 (2010)
11. Chen, C., Tan, J., Zhang, F., Yao, J.: Quality Prediction Model Based on Variable-Learning-Rate Neural Networks in Tobacco Redrying Process. Journal of Intelligent Computing 1(3), 157–164 (2010)

A Distributed Algorithm for γ-Quasi-Clique Extractions in Massive Graphs

Arash Khosraviani and Mohsen Sharifi

Iran University of Science and Technology, Iran
akhosraviani@comp.iust.ac.ir,
msharifi@iust.ac.ir

Abstract. In this paper, we investigate the challenge of increasing the size of graphs for finding γ-quasi-cliques. We propose an algorithm based on MapReduce programming model. In the proposed solution, we use some known techniques to prune unnecessary and inefficient parts of search space and divides the massive input graph into smaller parts. Then the data for processing each part is sent to a single computer. The evaluation shows that we can substantially reduce the time for large graphs and besides there is no limit for graph size in our algorithm.

Keywords: Distributed Quasi-Clique Extraction, MapReduce Graph Algorithm, Distributed Graph Processing.

1   Introduction

In recent years, the amount of existing data has been drastically increased in the world. The International Data Corporation [1] has anticipated that the amount of global information reaches more than 1.8 zettabytes by the end of 2011. Considering the fast growth of information amount, data processing methods have also been changed.

One way of processing these amounts of data is to model them in massive graphs. The core of social networks like Facebook is a graph, which keeps people, relations and all their interests [2]. The Facebook graph has more than 750 million nodes that each is connected to 130 other nodes on average [2]. Internet pages and their connections also would create a graph that is used for page ranking. The amount of internet pages archive is over two petabytes and grows at rate of 20 terabytes every month [1]. Processing massive graphs is also applicable in bioinformatics in order to process the relationship between proteins and genes. GenBank [3] is a good example that its amounts of data is doubling every 9 to 12 months.

In current applications, we model complicated networks as large graphs with more parameters. This huge data causes storage problems and extremely increases the processing time. On the other hand, there are graph algorithms with high time complexity that have been left unsolved or solved just with few vertices.

P. Pichappan, H. Ahmadi, and E. Ariwa (Eds.): INCT 2011, CCIS 241, pp. 422–431, 2011.
© Springer-Verlag Berlin Heidelberg 2011

One of the very important algorithms in social networks and Web is finding the very dense spots of a graph. A dense subgraph indicates more interactions between web pages, the higher popularity of a community or sensitive spots in a network. From theoretical point of view, these subgraphs are more powerful and because of having tight connections, disconnection of a link does not matter. In addition, broadcasting of data takes place at high speed [4].

Finding dense subgraphs is an NP-complete problem [5]. The main algorithms operate based on complete enumeration of subgraphs and pruning search spaces. Because of high time complexity, these algorithms are just capable of processing small amounts of data. Other algorithms are heuristic. Heuristic algorithms do not extract all available result but according to the type of application, they try to get optimized results.

In this paper, we investigate the challenge of increasing the size of graphs for finding γ-quasi-cliques. The amount of existing data is extremely large that it is not possible to store and analyze them in a single system. We propose a solution based on distributed graph processing. Distributed systems are appropriate choice for data-intensive computing because of their low costs and high scalability. Nevertheless, because of close relation between nodes and edges, distributed graph processing is difficult. In recent years and after the development of technologies related to distributed systems, new models of distributed data processing have been presented including BSP and MapReduce. We use MapReduce programming model to propose our algorithm. In addition, common algorithms use some known techniques to prune unnecessary and inefficient parts of search space. In the proposed solution, these rules are applied for dividing the input graph to make distributed processing possible.

The rest of the paper is organized as follows. In section 2, we discuss some preliminaries and define the problem. In section 3, we briefly review previous works. In section 4, we propose our algorithm. An evaluation study is reported in section 5 and Section 6 concludes the paper.

2   Preliminaries

In this section, we get through the basic notations and provide the necessary background for problem statement and MapReduce model

2.1   The γ-Quasi-Clique Extraction Problem

A graph is defined as $G(V, E)$ in which V indicates the vertices of the graph and E denotes its edges. Considering the vertex set $S \subseteq V$, G_S is called an induced subgraph of G and includes all edges $\{v, u\}$ in $E(S)$ with both vertices included in S. $|S|$ refers to the number of vertices of the subgraph and $\deg_S(v)$ specifies the degree of vertex v within S. The other important criterion is the diameter of graph, indicates with $\text{diam}(G)$. The diameter of a graph is the maximum distance between two vertices and is defined as $\text{diam}(G) = \max\{\text{dist}(v, u) \mid v, u \in G\}$. In the rest of this paper, the term "graph" refers to a simple, undirected and acyclic graph.

Among different definitions of dense graphs, we chose the γ-quasi-cliques. Having the graph G (V, E) and the parameter $0 \leq \gamma \leq 1$, sugraph $G_S \subseteq G$ is denoted as a γ-quasi-clique if $\forall v \in S$: $\deg_S(v) \geq \gamma.(|S|-1)$. In fact, the parameter γ indicates the density rate of the graph. As we see in the definition, γ-quasi-clique is a subgraph that its minimum vertex degree would not be less than what has been defined.

We are looking to find subgraphs with $\gamma \geq 0.5$ with a MapReduce based algorithm. We are more interested in mining tightly connected subgraphs, so γ is selected more than 0.5. Because of applying the algorithm on massive graphs, it is preferred to implement it in a distributed form. Distributed systems are an appropriate option for data-intensive computing because of their low costs and high scalability. In addition, the assumption of $\gamma \geq 0.5$ helps us simply distribute the data among different computers. For future programming, we propose the algorithm based on MapReduce programming model. In this model, the algorithm must be defined as Map and Reduce functions. Next, we describe MapReduce model.

2.2   The MapReduce Programming Model

MapReduce is a distributed programming model originally introduce by Dean and Ghemawat [6], which is highly scalable and well suited for commodity machines. The programming concept of MapReduce is simple and based on a set of Map and Reduce functions. Map function takes an input pair and produces a set of key/value pairs. After the computation, it groups data with similar keys and passes the values as an input to Reduce. The Reduce function merges data with the same key together and produces a smaller output. The MapReduce underlying automatically hides the details of parallelization, fault tolerance, data distribution and load balancing.

Considering the point that open source tools related to BSP model are less than MapReduce and at the same time have not been much developed, we have chosen MapReduce model to simplify the implements. Cohen [7] argues that the hard part of graph programming with MapReduce is the need to change the programmer's way of thinking.

3   Related Works

The dense subgraphs extraction algorithms are divided into several categories based on different density definition and methods used: Clique, Quasi-Clique, K-Core, K-Plex, and K-Club are some examples of these categorizations based on density measurement. Most related works are focused on mining cliques and quasi-cliques because these problems cannot be solved in polynomial time.

Considering the method used, the algorithms are divided into two categories. Exact enumeration algorithms that extract all existing subgraphs are placed in the first group. Since these algorithms are time consuming, they have not been practiced on massive graphs. In this group, an enumerating tree is created as the search space and pruned by rules of graph theory. One of the most important research done is referred to Zeng et al. [8] that introduced an efficient algorithm called Cocain. The same authors extended their work for out-of-core mining of quasi-cliques [9]. These two articles include many pruning techniques of search space that is practiced on γ-quasi-cliques with γ≥0.5. Liu and Wong [10] in their proposed algorithm called Quick have used novel techniques to prune the search. Quick algorithm finds quasi-cliques with size at least min_size. Pei et al. [11] suggested another algorithm called Crochet to mine cross quasi-cliques among a set of several input graphs and return quasi-cliques that are in all graphs. Uno [12] uses reverse searching method for searching through the tree to reach at polynomial delay. Of course, according to Uno's definition, the subgraph that has higher density among subgraphs with same number of vertices is dense.

For real applications like social networking that have very large graphs, extracting all dense subgraphs is impractical. To this, there are heuristic algorithms that can discover dense graphs quickly and with relative accuracy. Certainly, these algorithms do not guarantee to identify all exiting subgraphs. The most important study that has been done for massive graphs is referred to Gibson et al. [13]. They used Shingling technique to propose a recursive algorithm for discovering large dense bipartite graphs. Abello et al. [14] have introduced an algorithm called GRASP that extracts γ-quasi-cliques in massive graphs using greedy randomized adaptive search algorithm. In this method, possible answers are detected and then some vertices are added to initial set to expand the result. In addition, there is no need that all vertices are included in the memory. Graph Clustering is one of traditional problems of graph theory in which each vertex is placed in a cluster. High similarity between graph clustering and dense subgraph extraction has caused common clustering algorithms such as spectral clustering are considered as heuristic methods for discovering quasi-cliques. You can find some examples of clustering-based algorithms in [15-17]. Also because quasi-cliques are very applicable in bioinformatics, many heuristic methods have been introduced in this era [16, 18, 19].

All of the algorithms discussed are executed sequentially on a single computer system, but there are also parallel and distributed algorithms. Jonathan Cohen [7] provided some of graph-processing algorithms in the form of MapReduce model and mining quasi-cliques is also included. However, Cohen has given a different definition of quasi-cliques. According to his definition, a quasi-clique or Truss is a subgraph in which each vertex would be at least part of k triangle. His proposed algorithm is based on counting the number of triangles connected to a vertex. Tsourakakis et al. [20] proposed an algorithm called DOULION for counting the number of triangles. This algorithm has been implemented on Hadoop parallel platform. Gargi et al. [17] introduced a three-stage algorithm for finding cliques in a graph. The main stage implementation is done using MapReduce model. Zhang et al. [21] are clustering graphs using graph topology and topological similarity of vertices. Their method is based on BSP model. There is a parallel algorithm in [22] that is in massive graph processing domain. Nevertheless, the algorithm uses a set of computers with shared memory. The main idea is to use stack instead of tree for keeping search space. It helps several processes keep working simultaneously on data.

4   Proposed Method

Due to graph data structure that is continuous, no distributed algorithm has yet been provided for mining γ-quasi-cliques. In this part, we introduce an algorithm based on MapReduce model. Our suggested algorithm divides the massive input graph into smaller parts, based on common pruning techniques. After breaking down the input graph, the required data for processing each part is sent to a single computer and is processed by one of the common methods.

Assume that G (V, E) is a graph with at least one γ-quasi-clique called S. To extract S we can create an enumerating tree of vertices and prune it using rules related to gamma quasi-cliques. Finally, to find the best possible answer, the tree is traversed using the depth-first search algorithm.

First, we have to extract some basic information from the input graph. These include the degree of each vertex and its adjacent neighbors. The information is extracted by one MapReduce job. The input is in the form of undirected edges that have been stored as "vertex 1/ vertex 2" tuples in the distributed file system. In the Map function for each input tuple, two tuples are written in output, which in each, one of the vertices is the key and the other is the value. Thus in the Reduce function for each input key, the value includes all adjacent neighbors of the vertex and the degree. This information would be written in the output. At this stage and before writing the output, we can apply some pruning techniques.

Pruning based on canonical form: If the string representing graph G is the smallest possible string, it is called canonical form G and is demonstrated with CF(G) = a1a2...an. In other words, the string representing graph G should be sorted alphabetically. Later we would use the canonical form as MapReduce key to avoid repetition in the search space.

Pruning based on the minimum size of graph: in some applications, small graphs are not appropriate and it is necessary to have a graph with number of vertices more than min_size. According to the γ-quasi-clique definition, in such a circumstance, vertices with degree lower than γ.(|min_size|-1) can be omitted. Thus, we just write down the vertices with degree more than γ.(|min_size|-1) in the output. This will reduce the amount of intermediate data. The Pseudocode of the first job is given below:

```
map(String key, String value):
    // key: unused
    // value: edge list <head, tail>
    ParseVertices(value);
    EmitIntermediate(head, tail);
    EmitIntermediate(tail, head);

reduce(String key, Iterator values):
    // key: a vertex
    // values: a list of adjacent vertices
    int degree = 0;
    for each v in values:
            degree ++;
    if (degree > min_size)
            Emit( key, degree+"/"+CF(values) );
```

Next, we split the graph into subgraphs and send each subgraph to a computer for mining γ-quasi-cliques. The main problems here are how to split the graph and how to collect all the data related to vertices and edges of each subgraph. We divide the graph according to the pruning rule based on the diameter of graph.

Pruning based on the diameter of graph: Pei et al. [11] have proved that the diameter of subgraph S has an upper bound based on the value of parameter γ. The diameter of the subgraph, which is indicated by diam (G), is defined in form of diam(G) = max{dist(v, u) | v, u ∈ G}. In other words, from every vertex in the graph we can reach other vertices using diam(G) edges. They use this rule to reduce the number of candidate vertices in the search space. You can see the upper bounds below:

$$
diam(G) \begin{cases} = 1 & if\ 1 \geq \gamma > \frac{n-2}{n-1} \\ \leq 2 & if\ \frac{n-2}{n-1} \geq \gamma \geq \frac{1}{2} \\ \leq 3\lfloor \frac{n}{\gamma(n-1)+1} \rfloor - 3 & if\ \frac{1}{2} > \gamma \geq \frac{2}{n-1}\ and \\ & n \bmod\ (\gamma(n-1)+1) = 0 \\ \leq 3\lfloor \frac{n}{\gamma(n-1)+1} \rfloor - 2 & if\ \frac{1}{2} > \gamma \geq \frac{2}{n-1}\ and \\ & n \bmod\ (\gamma(n-1)+1) = 1 \\ \leq 3\lfloor \frac{n}{\gamma(n-1)+1} \rfloor - 1 & if\ \frac{1}{2} > \gamma \geq \frac{2}{n-1}\ and \\ & n \bmod\ (\gamma(n-1)+1) \geq 2 \\ \leq n-1 & if\ \gamma = \frac{1}{n-1} \end{cases}
$$

We are looking for γ-quasi-cliques with γ > 0.5 and considering the above results the diameter must be less than two. Accordingly, we split the graphs to subgraphs with maximum diameter two and then send each subgraph to a single computer for processing. In order to do this, for each vertex the adjacent neighbours and their neighbours are collected and sent to a computer.

What we do is that first assume a vertex for instance, 'a', as input in the Map function along with its degree and the list of the adjacent neighbours. Then for vertex 'b' existing in the list, we make a new record with 'b' as key and vertex 'a' with all input data related to it as value. This way, all data related to 'a' is copied for all its adjacent neighbours. Putting 'b' as the key causes the data related to neighbours and neighbours of neighbours of 'b' would be gathered in one Reduce function. Adding source vertex at the beginning of value helps us to indicate which vertex the data is related to.

Therefore, all data related to adjacent neighbours of a vertex and their neighbours can be collected in the Reduce function. In the previous example, all adjacent vertices of 'b' and their neighbours are retrieved in the Reduce function. Considering the point that each Reduce is executed on one computer, a semi-dense subgraph can be retrieved and analyzed separately. To this end, the two MapReduce jobs are enough to find γ-quasi-cliques but we need to do some optimizations to reduce the data size and computing time. First we should omit the vertices with deg(v)≤γ.(|min_size|-1), based on Pruning technique based on the minimum size of graph. Then we use a technique introduced in [10].

Pruning based on the upper bound of the number of vertices: lets $deg_{min}(g)=\min\{indeg_g(v) + exdeg_g(v): v \in g\}$ and g be the final γ-quasi-clique. Then the upper bound of the number of vertices in g will be $|g|\leq deg_{min}(g)/\gamma+1$. Based on this pruning technique, if the subgraph has more vertices than $|\deg_{min}(g)/\gamma|+1$ it would not be written in the output. Thus, the list of vertices that have the necessary features are written in the output as the key.

You can see the proposed algorithm in the following:

```
map(String key, String value):
      // key: unused
      // value: degree/adjacent vertices
      adjacentVertices[] = ParseVertices(value.adjacentVertices);
      for each v in adjacentVertices:
            EmitIntermediate(v, key+"/"+value);

reduce(String key, Iterator values):
      // key: a vertex
      // values: list of adjacent vertices and their neighbors
      for each v in values
            relatedData[] = ParseData(values);
      quasiClique = UpperBoundPruning(relatedData[]);
      //Do Upper Bound Pruning
      if (quasiClique ≠ NULL)
            Emit(quasiClique, NULL);
```

In the third and final MapReduce job, shared keys, which are also shared subgraphs are detected and omitted. Like known word count example, this is done using Reduce function features. Intermediate data with same key are sent to one Reduce function. In the Reduce function, each subgraph is analyzed separately based on a common γ-quasi-clique algorithm and the result would be written in disk as final output.

5   Evaluation

In order to evaluate our proposed algorithm, we will calculate its computational complexity based on Afrati and Ullman computational model [23]. In this model, algorithms are networks of interconnected processes that have data stored as files. MapReduce algorithms are a special case of these algorithms. We can evaluate these kinds of algorithms by the amount of data that must be moved among the processes. They assume a lower bound b and an upper bound s on the data movement cost. A process can have O(s) communication cost if s is the upper bound.

We need to measure the communication cost and processing cost of the algorithm. Based on Afrati and Ullman model definition [23], the total communication cost (total processing cost, respectively) is the sum of the communication (processing, respectively) costs of all processes. The maximum sum, over all paths, is defined as the elapsed communication (processing, respectively) cost.

To begin, we will calculate each MapReduce job costs separately. In first job, we want to find vertices neighbours and degrees. Suppose that the number of vertices is $|V|=n$. The algorithm input is a list of edges and based on number of vertices, the number of edges would be $\gamma.\frac{n(n-1)}{2} < |E| \le \frac{n(n-1)}{2}$. Thus, each Map process takes input of maximum size n^2, which is the total number of edges and minimum size b. So the total communication cost is $O(n^2)$ and the elapsed communication cost is $O(b)$. In the processing step, the Map process just reads each edge and generates two edges.

Therefore, total and elapsed processing cost in this step is like the previous costs. Because of data duplication in Map phase, total communication cost of intermediate data becomes $O(2n^2)$. Each vertex is analyzed separately so due to maximum parallelization we can achieve, elapsed cost changes to $O(n)$. In Reduce function, all computation costs are the same as intermediate data communication costs.

Second job begins with communication and processing costs as before, $O(2n^2)$ and $O(n)$. Map function generates new intermediate data as the number of adjacent neighbours for each vertex. Considering each vertex is in average connected to 130 other vertices, total communication cost and total Reduce processing cost increase to $O((130n)^2)$. Considering that for Reduce phase, we have n computers, elapsed cost is $O(130^2n)$.

Since in the suggested algorithm each vertex is analyzed separately and is produced for the data, two main problems occur. First, the amount of middle data produced is a lot. For example, in a social network, each vertex is in average connected to 130 other vertices [2]. In such a circumstance, the amount of middle data would be at least 130 times more than input data. We are forced to produce large amount of data in order to analyze large-scale graphs. In addition, in data intensive computing, it is not strange to have and generate more and more data. However, the point is that the size of the input graph is extremely reduced, using pruning techniques and the processing is done in parallel. Therefore, we can substantially reduce the time for large graphs. Besides there is no limit for graph size as MapReduce model is very scalable.

Data redundancy is another problem too, i.e. it is possible for a subgraph with 100 vertices to be analyzed 100 times. We have tried to reduce the amount of redundancy also. The algorithm detects semi-cliques in second job and writes them as keys. Then in final step, we have used MapReduce programming model feature to remove duplicated keys.

Finally, processing costs in depends on the γ-quasi-clique extraction algorithm used. We can divided the massive graph into smaller subgraphs in $O(130^2n)$, which each subgraph is capable of being γ-quasi-clique. The size of the input graph is extremely reduced but final analysis of subgraphs determines the time complexity.

6   Conclusion and Future Works

In this paper, we have presented a distributed algorithm for γ-quasi-clique extraction. In proposed algorithms, we divide the massive input graph into smaller parts, based on pruning techniques. After breaking down the input graph, the required data for processing each part is sent to a single computer and is processed by one of the common methods. The algorithm is based on MapReduce model and has the ability to scale well. We also evaluate our algorithm using Afrati and Ullman computation model and it was determined that due to graph size reduction, the processing time extremely reduces.

As a future work, we are going to implement the algorithm using Hadoop framework. After the implementation we can see the experimental results. Much development in the algorithm optimization can be done as future works. In addition, we can focus on other distributed programming models like BSP to compare the two algorithms too.

References

1. Gantz, J., Chute, C., Manfrediz, A., Minton, S., Reinsel, D., Schlichting, W., Toncheva, A.: The diverse and exploding digital universe. IDC White Paper 2 (2008)
2. http://www.facebook.com/press/info.php?statistics
3. http://www.psc.edu/general/software/packages/genbank
4. Grimmett, G.: Percolation. Springer, Heidelberg (1999)
5. Feige, U., Peleg, D., Kortsarz, G.: The dense k-subgraph problem. Algorithmica 29, 410–421 (2001)
6. Dean, J., Ghemawat, S.: MapReduce: simplified data processing on large clusters. In: The 6th Conference on Opearting Systems Design & Implementation, vol. 6, p. 10. USENIX Association, San Francisco (2004)
7. Cohen, J.: Graph Twiddling in a MapReduce World. Computing in Science and Engineering 11, 29–41 (2009)
8. Zeng, Z., Wang, J., Zhou, L., Karypis, G.: Coherent closed quasi-clique discovery from large dense graph databases. In: Proceedings of the 12th ACM SIGKDD International Conference on Knowledge Discovery and Data Mining, pp. 797–802. ACM, Philadelphia (2006)
9. Zeng, Z., Wang, J., Zhou, L., Karypis, G.: Out-of-Core Coherent Closed Quasi-Clique Mining from Large Dense Graph Databases. ACM Transactions on Database Systems 32 (2007)
10. Liu, G., Wong, L.: Effective Pruning Techniques for Mining Quasi-Cliques. In: Daelemans, W., Goethals, B., Morik, K. (eds.) ECML PKDD 2008, Part II. LNCS (LNAI), vol. 5212, pp. 33–49. Springer, Heidelberg (2008)
11. Pei, J., Jiang, D., Zhang, A.: On Mining Cross-Graph Quasi-Cliques. In: KDD 2005. ACM, Chicago (2005)
12. Uno, T.: An Efficient Algorithm for Solving Pseudo Clique Enumeration Problem. Algorithmica 56, 3–16 (2010)
13. Gibson, D., Kumar, R., Tomkins, A.: Discovering large dense subgraphs in massive graphs. In: Proceedings of the 31st International Conference on Very Large Data Bases, pp. 721–732. VLDB Endowment, Trondheim (2005)
14. Abello, J., Resende, M., Sudarsky, S.: Massive Quasi-Clique Detection. In: Rajsbaum, S. (ed.) LATIN 2002. LNCS, vol. 2286, pp. 598–612. Springer, Heidelberg (2002)
15. Agarwal, G., Kempe, D.: Modularity-maximizing graph communities via mathematical programming. The European Physical Journal B - Condensed Matter and Complex Systems 66, 409–418 (2008)
16. Bader, G., Hogue, C.: An automated method for finding molecular complexes in large protein interaction networks. BMC Bioinformatics 4, 2 (2003)
17. Gargi, U., Lu, W., Mirrokni, V., Yoon, S.: Large-Scale Community Detection on YouTube for Topic Discovery and Exploration (2011)
18. Ucar, D., Asur, S., Catalyurek, U., Parthasarathy, S.: Improving Functional Modularity in Protein-Protein Interactions Graphs Using Hub-Induced Subgraphs. In: Fürnkranz, J., Scheffer, T., Spiliopoulou, M. (eds.) PKDD 2006. LNCS (LNAI), vol. 4213, pp. 371–382. Springer, Heidelberg (2006)

19. Hu, H., Yan, X., Huang, Y., Han, J., Zhou, X.J.: Mining coherent dense subgraphs across massive biological networks for functional discovery. Bioinformatics 21, i1213 (2005)
20. Tsourakakis, C.E., Kang, U., Miller, G.L., Faloutsos, C.: DOULION: counting triangles in massive graphs with a coin. In: Proceedings of the 15th ACM SIGKDD International Conference on Knowledge Discovery and Data Mining, pp. 837–846. ACM, Paris (2009)
21. Zhang, Y., Wang, J., Wang, Y., Zhou, L.: Parallel community detection on large networks with propinquity dynamics. In: Proceedings of the 15th ACM SIGKDD International Conference on Knowledge Discovery and Data Mining, pp. 997–1006. ACM, Paris (2009)
22. Zhang, Y., Wang, J., Zeng, Z., Zhou, L.: Parallel mining of closed quasi-cliques, pp. 1–10. IEEE (2008)
23. Afrati, F.N., Ullman, J.D.: A New Computation Model for Cluster Computing (2009)

Author Index

Batch number: 09473985

Printed by Printforce, the Netherlands